W9-CHE-965

The Concise Encyclopedia of Antiques

VOLUME TWO

The Concise Encyclopedia of Antiques

VOLUME TWO

COMPILED BY THE CONNOISSEUR
EDITOR: L. G. G. RAMSEY, F.S.A.

Publishers
HAWTHORN BOOKS, Inc.
New York

 This book was designed and produced for *The Connoisseur* by Rainbird, McLean Ltd, London, and printed in England by W. S. Cowell Ltd, Ipswich and London. It is published simultaneously in England.

LIBRARY OF CONGRESS CARD NUMBER 55-5162

THE CONTENTS

FOREWORD

In any country the art produced by its painters and the works of art fashioned by its craftsmen are a perpetual mirror of the society for which they were originally produced. Whether made for kings or cardinals, merchants or simple villagers, we have in these objects of art a fascinating record which not only reflects much of the social history of the time but also serves to indicate the uses to which particular pieces were put, and for what reason they were thought to have been created. At the same time, just as many contemporary English words have their derivations from the Roman, so very many terms used in describing antiques today derive originally from French usage and nomenclature. Thus we now find such terms incorporated and accepted into the English language of antiques as secretaire, bonheur-du-jour, mille-fleur, grisaille, chaise-longue, credence, chinoiserie, commode, jardinière, ormolu, dinanderie, and so on.

It is therefore natural that one of the most important sections to this second volume of the already successfully established *Connoisseur Concise Encyclopedia of Antiques* should deal with the furniture of France: and in the space available it has been covered from 1500 to The Revolution. We deal with French furniture not only because it is an important side of the acquisition and study of antiques which was not included in the first volume, but also for another reason. It is not generally realized that England is extraordinarily rich in important French eighteenth-century furniture, especially in pieces coming from the former *Mobilier de la Couronne de France*. There are many who have noted the masterpieces of French furniture at the Wallace Collection and at the Victoria and Albert Museum. But it is less well known that these collections are rivalled both numerically and qualitatively by the Royal Collections at Windsor Castle and at Buckingham Palace. Some of these pieces – among them J. H. Riesener's celebrated jewel-casket at Windsor made for the Comte and Comtesse de Provence, his superb roll-top desk at Buckingham Palace and, again, the 'Artois' cylinder-top desk, stamped three times beneath the top with the marks of François Gaspard Teuné, at Windsor – were treated in great detail in *The Connoisseur Coronation Book* in 1953.

As will be clearly and immediately apparent, much that is important in the collection of antiques, and which owes its origin or influence to France, or its development to French craftsmen, can be seen on the dust-cover to this book. It is appropriate that the backcloth to this significant array should be a Mortlake tapestry; for, until its activities were checked by the Civil Wars in England in the 1640's, the products of the Mortlake factory enjoyed a very high reputation in Europe. At an important period of its foundation we also find, among fifty weavers from the Netherlands, the name of Philippe de Maecht (lured somehow from Paris) as being the most notable.

The light-hearted elegance that is characteristic of rococo art under Louis XV and Louis XVI found expression in the new fashion for small, intimate decorations. Notable amongst these were the delicate porcelain pieces already dealt with in the first of these volumes. But of the same period we find small bronzes, their form often closely related to the productions of the Sèvres factory. If the reddish colour of the bronze provided a particularly well-suited base for gilding, and obtained a rich effect, more remarkable still at this period of the second half of the eighteenth century were the furniture mounts and ornamental articles made by the Parisian *ciseleurs-doreurs*. The quality of the finish on the finest Louis XVI mounts are without parallel in the whole history of metal-working. It is also only during recent years that the superior quality of the ormolu work produced by Matthew Boulton in Birmingham in the late eighteenth century has been generally appreciated.

It is in the section Objects of Vertu, which suggest a state of mild mystery intermixed with fantastically, expensively and exquisitely constructed objects in precious metals, that we find the mass of French terms which appear in every museum and auction-room catalogue. We are, in fact, in the century of the *bonbonnière*, the *drageoire* and the sweetmeat- or comfit-box. Louis XIV's hearty dislike of snuff is well known, but, even when campaigning, he carried gold and silver boxes containing small pastilles of aniseed with which to sweeten his breath, of which Madame de Montespan had complained. Consider, too, the English dandy Lord Petersham, who, when congratulated on a particularly fine blue Sèvres snuff-box from his collection, replied that 'it was a nice summer box but would never do for winter wear'. Later we become submerged in *piqué*, *repoussé* and *cloisonné* work. We read of English, Russian, Swiss and Scandinavian snuff-boxes and of the activities of the great reviver of the four-colour gold process of the eighteenth century, as well as the forgotten art of translucent enamelling on a prepared *guilloché*-field, Peter Carl Fabergé.

In the following nineteenth century we find two more subjects which have many adherents today: the remarkable French glass paperweights, produced in the St Louis, Baccarat and Clichy factories, and the beautifully modelled bone and ivory ship models, many of which were made in England by French prisoners captured during the Napoleonic Wars.

Those who already study the history of music, or who acquire collectable musical instruments, will appreciate that here is a wide, complex and highly interesting subject. There may be today as many as a set of a dozen volumes dealing with the study of one instrument. We can regard them in a number of ways: their evolution and construction, how they have been played, the most suitable music to which to harness their performance, as social documents and as antiques.

Although the heraldry is frequently confusing, it is the special interest of armorial china and glass that the coats of arms which it displays can reveal not only the identity of the original possessor but, particularly when the arms show a marriage, the date when the service was made. If these were all, until about 1755, made in China, at Ching-te-chen, a service of a different kind, the Imperial Russian, or 'Frog', Wedgwood service was made in the same period of the eighteenth century by Mr Josiah Wedgwood for the Empress Catherine of Russia. The Empress is believed to have paid £3,000 for it, and Wedgwood wrote: '. . . there will not be near the profit upon this service that we have upon our commonest painted goods'. At the same time we have other typically English subjects in Toby Jugs, Sheffield Plate, Cottage Pottery and Popular Art, Victoriana and Modern Watercolours.

To complete the international flavour of this second guide for the beginner collector (and 'ready reference' for the established collector) are Netsuki and Inro, American Silver, and Japanese Prints. All three, particularly the former, are subjects which are continually attracting the collector's attention and which at the same time never fail to provide a wide field of academic interest.

L. G. G. RAMSEY

Editor, *The Connoisseur*

The Concise Encyclopedia of Antiques

VOLUME TWO

FRENCH FURNITURE

FROM 1500 TO THE REVOLUTION

By R. A. CECIL

To collectors and connoisseurs in England French furniture, and particularly that of the late seventeenth and eighteenth centuries, presents certain problems. Firstly, the range of materials employed on the embellishment of certain pieces extends far beyond wood; secondly, the wealth and admixture of motifs, veneers, inlays, and the profusion of metal ornament are often alien to English taste; and thirdly, the number of craftsmen to be found in Great Britain who are competent to appreciate and repair French furniture is still so small that valuable pieces are in constant danger of being badly treated with the wrong substances.

From the historical point of view, the various periods and styles have become so bound up with the reigns of the three Kings of France, Louis XIV, XV and XVI, that it is frequently difficult to realize that these styles and fashions in designing and decorating furniture often began long before, and ended long after, the rather arbitrary dates connected with them.

Nevertheless, the regnal divisions into which the subject has been conventionally split up have their uses in indicating the approximate style and period in which a piece of furniture may have been produced, and they have therefore been retained for the purposes of this study.

THE RENAISSANCE AND SEVENTEENTH CENTURY

In spite of the large amount of furniture which was made in France in the sixteenth century, not very much has come down to us, and what has is almost completely undocumented. We are thus very seldom in a position to say when a given piece of furniture was made, for whom it was made, or by whom. A great deal of research has at one time or another been devoted to distinguishing between the various provincial centres where furniture was produced in the sixteenth century – whether, for instance, at Lyons or in the *Ile de France* – but the theories put forward are not very convincing, and it is safer to assume that most of the best furniture was made in Paris and probably for the Court, and that such known provincial pieces are variations on a style existing at the central point.

By far the largest number of such pieces to have survived are made of walnut, usually elaborately carved. The most common piece is the dresser (q.v.), but tables, chairs, beds, cabinets and cupboards are also found. These take various forms and are often covered with carving, the dressers particularly receiving the most elaborate treatment in this respect.

The carving is usually in the Italian style, imported into France by the wars of Francis I, and the engravings of Du Cerceau and others were important in distributing knowledge of the motifs which were employed at Court. The absence of any local inspiration for design meant that the Court style became predominantly Italian in character, as did the architecture of the period also. Often a decorative motif on a piece of French Renaissance furniture is taken direct from a known Italian engraving or plaquette. It is also important to remember that furniture at this date was intended easily to be taken to pieces and moved about (hence the word *mobilier*), and this can almost always be done with the pieces which we are considering.

With the more secure ways of life which came in with the seventeenth century, furniture began to become more stable, and thus the opportunities for decoration more appropriate. But France sadly lacked the craftsmen to carry out the elaborate inlays which were the fashion in Italy and which were favoured at Court after the arrival of Marie de Médicis as Queen of Henri IV. Up to the foundation of the Gobelins factory in 1663, therefore, the period is one of constant infiltration of foreign craftsmen, from whom, of course, Frenchmen in the next generation were to learn much.

The engravings of Adam Bosse, however, show how sparsely furnished the rooms of the prosperous members of society were, and do not show the elaborate cabinets and *bureaux* which have come down to us, and which must have been not only rare luxury products but almost entirely made by foreign craftsmen. These often incorporate elaborate carving, marquetry, and also intricate mirror arrangements in the interiors. They are usually designated as French in the absence of knowledge as to who actually made them, but it seems likely that Italian and Flemish craftsmen must have been largely involved. The taste for the Italian style was further extended by the rise to power of Cardinal Mazarin, himself an Italian, whose personality dominated the French scene through the minority of Louis XIV.

THE LOUIS XIV PERIOD

Le Roi Soleil came to the throne in 1643 at the age of five. It can be well imagined therefore that the artistic characteristics which have become associated with his name did not come into existence at once. Indeed, the changes of style in furniture did not begin to appear until the King's majority and the establishment under Colbert of that great organization for the production of objects of art, the *Manufacture Royale des Meubles de la Couronne* at Gobelins in 1662. This foundation, as much an act of policy as everything else, was intended to co-ordinate control of all the applied arts in France to the glorification of the Crown and the State, and under its brilliant first director, Charles Le Brun, achieved its aim at least for a generation. The establishment of the *Manufacture* is, in fact, the cardinal event in the history of French decoration and furnishing, for it was under its aegis that all the foreign and native talent and experience which had been employed for two generations previously was incorporated and made to serve as a foundation for the establishment of new standards of taste and craftsmanship, this time wholly French in style and intended to serve a national aim.

As is well known, the first great task awaiting the *Manufacture* soon after its foundation was the decoration and furnishing of the new palace at Versailles, which was to become the cradle of French decorative taste for the centuries to come, and to demand an output of lavish expenditure unparalleled in history. It is only the more unfortunate that almost all the furniture produced during the first years of the *Manufacture*'s existence has disappeared, and even the celebrated silver furnishings of Versailles were later all melted down to provide bullion to support the various wars of the later years of the reign.

What remains, then, must be regarded as only a fraction of what once existed, and by far the most important series of furnishings which have come down to us are the productions of the workshop of André Charles Boulle (1642–1732), the most celebrated cabinet-maker of the whole period, and the great exponent of the marquetry which bears his name. Boulle was trained under foreign influences, and his achievement lies in his adaptation of foreign techniques to his own original ideas, and to the combination of a new monumentality and elegance of design with a perfection of craftsmanship in a very complicated and elaborate technique.

In his early years he almost certainly worked in wood marquetry, following designs similar to those produced in Italy and Flanders, and to this was sometimes added the use of small amounts of metal for decorative purposes; but the intricate marquetry of tortoiseshell and brass with which we associate his name is, to all intents and purposes, an individual creation.

The principal innovations in furniture design during the period were first of all the chest of drawers, or *commode*. It can be said to date from about 1700, though it probably did not come into general use until rather later. The other main type to be evolved was that of the writing-table, or *bureau*. This first begins to appear before the turn of the century in the form of a table-top with two sets of drawers beneath, flanking a knee-hole, and later took on its more usual form of a flat table with shallow drawers under the top.

The demand for Boulle furniture diminished in the middle years of Louis XV's reign but returned in full force in the last quarter of the eighteenth century, when the neo-classical style came into its own. Often the same designs, motifs and techniques were used, and it is sometimes extremely difficult to be certain in which period a piece was made when the quality of marquetry and bronze are the same.

It must be remembered that all furniture at this time, and indeed later, was made in order to harmonize with the rich carving and painted decoration of the setting for which it was intended, and designs which may appear over-elaborate when isolated would often seem at home in their original positions.

THE LOUIS XV PERIOD

When considering the characteristics of anything connected with what has become known as the Louis XV or rococo styles in France, it is important to remember that their evolution was gradual, and indeed began some years before the date when the *Grande Monarque* actually died. The genesis of rococo design can, in fact, be traced back to the last years of the seventeenth century, and the engraved compositions of an artist such as Jean Berain provide ample evidence of the new feeling which finally usurped the classicism, formality and monumentality exemplified by the creation of Versailles.

It was, however, the removal in 1715 of the central personality in the formal and centralized Court and Government, and the succession of a small boy, with the consequent reign of a pleasure-loving Regent, which provided the circumstances for the change in taste which can be so readily observed in the years which immediately followed. It is, however, a mistake to isolate the style of the Regency with what followed and to try to identify objects as belonging to the *Style Régence* unless they can be proved to have been created within the years 1715 to 1725. It is much more sensible to regard the products of these years as the first-fruits of what was to become the *Style Louis Quinze* proper, and the absence of documentary evidence providing the necessary dating makes this course more prudent.

The new style inevitably, however, received its first impetus from the Court of the Regent Orléans at the Palais Royal, and almost at once there is a lightness to be observed in interior decoration and furniture. The relaxation of the rigid etiquette of the Louis XIV's court, caused apartments, and therefore furnishings, to be smaller and less formal, and gave opportunities for lightness, fantasy and colour impossible twenty years before. Gradually, therefore, the heavy monumental furnishings made for Versailles at the Gobelins gave place to smaller, more elegantly contrived pieces suited to the lighter and more informal atmosphere of the new type of interior decoration.

More and more, furniture was adapted and decorated to harmonize with wall decoration, which, being also almost exclusively of wood, created a harmony of design and craftsmanship never equalled outside France. The Boulle technique passed temporarily out of fashion, though the *atelier* continued to produce furniture throughout the eighteenth century and Boulle himself did not die until 1732. The new taste favoured elaborate wood marquetry overlaid with delicate gilt-bronze mounts, and during the period the combination of these types of decoration reached a perfection of design and execution only surpassed by the subsequent period. The opening up of trade routes with the Far East brought a large number of oriental goods on to the home market, with the result that a taste for lacquer was created, both applied in the original from China or Japan, or imitated in France and applied locally. A number of oriental woods useful for marquetry were also imported, notably kingwood and, later, purple-wood, which was used very widely. Other woods used for veneering and inlaying were tulip-wood, hazelwood, satin-wood, casuarina and sycamore, often mixed in elaborate floral, pictorial or geometrical designs, framed with fillets of box and holly. The range of design was very wide and soon began to be used with remarkable skill.

Apart from relaxation in formality, the earlier part of the reign did not witness any very startling change in the actual types of furniture used, and the forms prevalent under Louis XIV still lingered on, particularly the wardrobe, or *armoire*, and the chest of drawers. The former, however, while keeping its monumental proportions, was often constructed of plain wood undecorated except for carving; while the latter underwent a number of changes in design. The main tendency was for straight lines and flat surfaces to become curved and *bombé*, and for the functional purposes of the piece to be concealed beneath the general scheme of decoration. The two commodes on Plate 2 show these characteristics well, the divisions between the drawers being invisible beneath the designs of the marquetry and mounts. There is, however, not one straight line to be found on either piece. The extreme rococo tendency towards asymmetry did affect mounts and *bronzes d'ameublement*, though not for very long.

The latter part of the reign, with its increase of luxury expenditure, saw the creation of a large number of new types of furniture, mainly small, and nearly always intended for female use. The *secrétaire à abattant* began to appear in the fifties, also the *bonheur du jour*, the *bureau-toilette*, work-tables and other pieces, while commodes, chairs, sofas and *bronzes d'ameublement* of all kinds were produced in large quantities. This is the period also of the greatest *ébénistes*, including Oeben, Riesener, Leleu, Dubois and others, and it is in the sixties that foreign craftsmen, particularly Germans, began to arrive in Paris to seek their fortunes, usually finding them, in the profusion of demands for furniture. Madame de Pompadour played a large part in forming the taste of her time by her constant purchases of objects of all kinds and the *Livre-Journal* of Lazare Duvaux, from whom she bought so much, gives a very clear picture of how much money was spent. She was not responsible for the introduction of the neoclassic Louis XVI style, however, as she died in 1764, and many of the portraits of her, even just before her death, show her surrounded by furniture, particularly in the advanced Louis XV style.

A word should be said here about the actual creation of a piece of eighteenth-century French furniture. First of all a designer, sometimes the *ébéniste* himself, though sometimes equally a decorator, produced a drawing of the piece. This was then made by an *ébéniste* in wood, veneered and inlayed if necessary. Mounts and fittings were then produced by a sculptor and a *fondeur*, and if required were gilded by a *doreur*, thus often involving members of three craft guilds and two artist designers. Occasionally painters were also involved, thus bringing in yet another guild. When one considers the number of different craftsmen employed on a single piece of furniture, the harmony and perfection so often achieved are the more remarkable.

THE LOUIS XVI PERIOD

As is well known, the main characteristic of the Louis XVI style is the return to classical forms and motifs after the exuberance and fantasy of the rococo. This tendency begins to make itself felt at least twenty years before Louis XV died, and it is indeed this particular regnal division which is so misleading. Between 1750 and 1774 a very large amount of furniture was made incorporating classical tendencies, and it is most important to realize this when attempting in any way to date a given piece of furniture from stylistic evidence. The change of taste was very gradual, as the artistic writings of the time show, and, as elsewhere in Europe, was motivated very largely by the discovery of the Roman remains in the old Kingdom at Naples, at Pompeii and Herculaneum. The subsequent interest in classical subjects aroused by such writers as de Caylus and the contempt poured on the rococo also played its part. From a purely stylistic point of view it can be said that the Louis XV style proper had worked itself out and the return to classicism came therefore as a necessary reaction, and antidote. In spite of the enormous expenditure on furniture in the seventies, both by the Court and private patrons, no very striking innovations took place in actual furniture design. The main feature of the reign was, however, the perfecting of processes used hitherto to an unprecedented degree. This is particularly the case with ormolu, which has never attained before or since such refinement as it did at the hands of Gouthière, Thomire, Forestier (q.v.), and others. Apart from the elaboration and refinement of marquetry, plain woods, and particularly mahogany, begin to be used as veneers, and the rather controversial embellishment of furniture with porcelain begins to make its appearance (*see* Porcelain). The large number of German *ébénistes* increased, of which Weisweiler and Beneman (q.v.) were the most celebrated. The work of Jacob in making chairs also reached its highest peak, and Boulle furniture became fashionable again and was produced in large quantities.

The influence of Queen Marie Antoinette on the taste and craftsmanship of her time, with particular reference to furniture, has often been stressed. It is true that she employed extensively and lavishly the incomparable craftsmen whom she found in Paris on her arrival as Dauphine, but, apart from this expenditure and a liking for beautiful objects, it is doubtful if she possessed any real understanding of the visual arts, and she certainly was no rival of Madame de Pompadour in this respect. It has also been suggested that her nationality attracted many German-born craftsmen to Paris but, in fact, the influx of foreign workmen had started and become an established fact long before there was any question of her being Queen of France. She undoubtedly did employ Riesener, Weisweiler and Beneman very extensively, but chiefly because of their qualities as craftsmen, and only then on the advice of the *Garde Meuble*.

GLOSSARY

Appliques: *see under* Wall-lights.

Armoires: *see under* Wardrobes.

Artisans Libres: the name given to craftsmen who chose to work outside the guild jurisdiction and who sought refuge in what were known as *lieux privilégiés* in Paris. Being exempt from guild charges and regulations, they were a continual source of irritation to the guilds, particularly as they included a large number of foreign *ébénistes* who came to Paris in the mid-eighteenth century. These included some of the finest craftsmen of the time, a number of whom later became *maître-ébénistes*.

Athénienne: a form of candelabrum consisting of an urn supported on a classical tripod, invented in 1773 by J. H. Eberts, editor of the famous *Monument de Costume*. The name derives from a painting by J. B. Vien entitled '*La Vertueuse Athénienne*', which shows a priestess burning incense at a tripod of this type. They were made of patinated bronze with ormolu mounts, but not many survive. They are, however, typical of the classicizing tendencies of the last quarter of the eighteenth century.

Bibliothèque-Basse: a low cupboard fitted with shelves for books, and doors often of glass but sometimes fitted with grilles.

Bombé: lit. 'inflated, blown out', i.e. of convex form generally on more than one axis.

Bonheur-du-Jour: a small writing-table usually on tall legs, and sometimes fitted to hold toilet accessories and bibelots. It first appeared *c.* 1760, but remained in fashion for a comparatively short time.

Boulle marquetry: the name given to the type of inlay evolved for use on furniture in the late seventeenth century by André Charles Boulle (1642–1732) (q.v.).

The process involves the glueing of one or more thin layers of tortoiseshell to a similar number of brass. The design of the marquetry is then set out on paper, and this is pasted on to the surface. The pattern is then cut out by means of a saw. After this, the layers of brass and tortoiseshell are separated and can be made to form two distinct marquetries by combining the materials in opposite ways: either with the design formed by the brass on a ground of shell, known as *première partie* or first part, or the exact opposite, known as *contre-partie*, or counter-part, with the design in shell on a ground of brass. These two types of inlay can then be glued on to a carcase in the form of a veneer. Often the two types are found side by side as part of the same design, in order to give contrast. Again, when pieces are made in pairs one is often veneered with *première partie* and the other with *contre-partie* marquetry.

The brass in the *première-partie* marquetry was often engraved naturalistically, frequently very finely, and was sometimes combined with other substances, such as pewter, copper, mother-of-pearl and stained horn, again usually to give contrasts and naturalistic effects to the design. Additional colour was also give occasionally by veneering the shell over coloured foil, usually red or green.

The carcases on to which Boulle marquetry is veneered are usually found to be of oak or deal, and the parts which are not covered by the inlay are veneered with ebony, coromandel-wood or purple-wood, in order to tone with the shell of the inlay.

Finally, Boulle furniture is usually lavishly mounted with ormolu, so as to protect the corners and the more vulnerable parts of the inlay, but the mounts are frequently also adapted in a decorative manner to form hinges, lock-plates and handles. It will be noticed that the ormolu is sometimes fully gilt, which provides a strong decorative contrast with the inlaid brass; equally, the bronze is sometimes left ungilt, and therefore harmonizes with the metal inlay to a greater extent.

Boulle furniture, so much in demand in the reign of Louis XIV, went out of fashion during most of that of his successor, but it did not cease to be made, and the Boulle *atelier* continued to turn out pieces from time to time. They were therefore ready when, under Louis XVI and the classical revival, the taste for this type of furniture returned, and at this period a very large number of pieces were made, often using the original designs, mounts and processes as in the former period. It is thus often extremely difficult to tell whether a piece was made in one period or another, and it is better not to be too dogmatic about this, as there are very few distinguishing characteristics. Two may perhaps be mentioned: the engraving of the brass inlay is less common in the Louis XVI period and, when it does appear, of inferior quality; secondly, the use of other metals than brass and freer designs are slightly more common.

In the earlier period a large number of designs for Boulle marquetry are derived from the engravings of Jean Berain, who was, like Boulle, also employed by the Crown.

Boulle marquetry is sometimes erroneously referred to as Buhl. This is a Teutonic adaptation of Boulle's name for which there is no justification.

Boxwood (*Buis*): a very closely-grained wood of a yellow colour found frequently in Europe and elsewhere. Extensively used in France for fillets to frame panels of marquetry.

Bras de Lumière: *see under* Wall-lights.

Bronzes d'Ameublement: a term with no exact English equivalent covering all furniture, practical or decorative, made of bronze, patinated or gilt. It embraces such items as candelabra, candlesticks, wall-lights, chandeliers, fire-dogs, clock-cases, mounts for furniture and porcelain, etc. Their manufacture was the particular province of the *fondeurs*, *ciseleurs* and *doreurs*.

Bureau-plat: a writing-table supported on tall legs with a flat top with drawers beneath. Began to appear towards the end of the seventeenth century.

Bureau-toilette: a piece of furniture for female use combining the functions of a toilet- and writing-table.

Canapé: the ordinary French word for a sofa. Evolved in many forms during the Louis XV period.

Canapés: *see under* Sofas.

Candelabrum (*candelabre*): a lighting appliance with branches supporting sockets for more than one light. They took many forms, but are usually made of ormolu, sometimes with figures in patinated bronze. They were often made in pairs or sets of four.

Candlesticks (*flambeaux*): a portable lighting appliance with one socket for a single light or candle. Large numbers were made almost exclusively of ormolu in the late seventeenth and eighteenth centuries, usually in pairs or sets of four, but sometimes in larger quantities.

Cartonnier: a piece of furniture which took various forms. Usually it stood at one end of a writing-table (*bureau-plat*) and was intended to hold papers. It was sometimes surmounted by a clock. Also sometimes called a *serre-papier*.

Causeuse: a large chair or small sofa to accommodate two persons. Roughly corresponds to the small English settee. Sometimes referred to colloquially as a love-seat.

Chairs (*sièges*, *chaises*): in the Renaissance period those made in France were on the whole very simple, constructed of plain wood, usually walnut, and carved with conventional motifs in the Italian style. Often they are of the ecclesiastical type with high backs carved in relief. Others have carved arms and stretchers. These types continued into the early seventeenth century, usually accompanied by some upholstery.

Such chairs of the Louis XIV period as have come down to us are also almost always of plain wood, carved in the classical manner. The backs are high, often with elaborately carved cornices. The legs are also elaborately carved and are often joined with stretchers. The chairs are upholstered on seats and back, either with embroidery, velvet, or with cane. Tapestry does not appear until later in the eighteenth century.

In the Louis XV period the design of chairs became less formal and the carving soon began to be carried out in the rococo manner. The outlines of the upholstered backs and seats, and the legs, gradually became curved and bowed until there is not a straight line in the whole design. Often chairs of the Louis XV period are of considerable size and of rather a heavy appearance. They are upholstered usually with silk, velvet or brocade, but sometimes with tapestry, which begins to make its appearance at this time.

In the Louis XVI period chairs, in particular, take up the prevailing neo-classical style, the change being noticeable soon after 1755. Legs gradually become straighter, as do the outlines of backs, seats and arms, and the motifs employed in the carving derive from classical sources, the most commonly found being the acanthus leaf in various forms, the wave-like band and the Ionic capital, as well as symmetrical garlands of flowers. It was at this time that the carving of chairs, particularly those produced by G. Jacob, reached the very greatest refinement, both of design and detail.

The frames of chairs of the Louis XV and Louis XVI periods are usually made of beech, birch or walnut, and they are often gilt. It is important to remember, however, that they may not originally have been so. Sometimes the wood forming the frames was left plain and unadorned, more often they were painted white, or white and partly gilt. Equally, a chair may have been originally plain or painted, and then gilt before the end of the eighteenth century. More often gilding or regilding was carried out in the nineteenth century, and often very coarsely. Collectors should bear this in mind when judging both the style and condition of French chairs.

Chandeliers (*lustres*): a branched lighting appliance consisting usually of several lights which can be suspended from a ceiling. Large quantities were made in France in the seventeenth and eighteenth centuries, but not many have survived. They were made of various materials: ormolu, wood, crystal, glass, and occasionally porcelain.

Chenets: *see* Fire-dogs.

Clock-cases: elaborate clock-cases made their appearance in the Louis XIV period and were often treated in the most monumental manner. They became a special product of the Boulle *atelier*, as they did of the workshop of Cressent later. In the Louis XV and Louis XVI periods they took almost any form which appealed to their creators, and a great deal of the ingenuity both of design and craftsmanship went into their production. Roughly, they divide themselves into five main types: wall or cartel clocks, mantel clocks, pedestal clocks, *régulateurs* and bracket clocks, the names of which are self-explanatory.

If the movement or make of a clock is

known and the date is established, the collector should remember that it may have originally been placed in another case. This is not uncommon.

Commode: the normal French word for a chest of drawers, which seems to date from the early eighteenth century.

Corner-cupboard (*encoignure*): this type of furniture consists of a triangular cupboard containing shelves and closed by a door, which is sometimes curved. It is made to fit into the right-angled corner of a room. *Encoignures* begin to appear in France during the Louis XV period, and are usually made in pairs, often *en suite* with a secretaire or chest of drawers. They continued to be made right up to the Revolution.

Coromandel or **zebra-wood:** a form of ebony with light-coloured striped markings found on the Coromandel coast (*see also under* Ebony).

Cylinder-top desk (*bureau à cylindre*): a writing-table, incorporating drawers and writing accessories, the functional part of which is closed by means of a curved panel fastened with a lock. It is usually supported on tall legs and differs from a roll-top desk (q.v.) in that the curved panel is in one piece and not slatted.

Doreurs, Corporation des: the craft guild responsible for gilding in all its forms. The organization was similar to that of the *menuisiers-ébénistes*, except that the apprenticeship lasted five instead of six years. There were three hundred and seventy *Maîtres-doreurs* at the end of the eighteenth century (*see also* Ormolu).

Dresser (*dressoir*): a piece of furniture on which plates, eating materials, etc., were placed before serving at table. It was very widely used in the Renaissance period and appeared in a number of forms, but always including a cupboard closed by doors above and below shelves. They are usually made of walnut and are often very elaborately carved with classical motives. The dresser seems to have dropped out of use in the seventeenth century.

Ébéniste: the ordinary French term for a cabinet-maker concerned in making veneered furniture as distinct from a *menuisier* (q.v.). The word derives from the ebony (*ébène*) to be found on the earliest veneered furniture in France. It is not found, nor are *ébénistes* associated by name with the *menuisiers*' guild, until 1743, by which time the use of ebony was more or less confined to pieces in the Boulle technique. Although permitted by guild regulations to work in plain wood like the *menuisiers*, an *ébéniste* usually confined his activities to techniques requiring veneer or inlay (*see also under* Menuisiers-Ébénistes).

Ebony (*ébène*): a hard wood, black and finely grained, sometimes found with brown or purple streaks. Found commonly in tropical climates in Asia, Africa and America. Extensively used in France for veneering furniture, particularly in combination with Boulle marquetry (*see also under* Coromandel or Zebra-wood and Boulle marquetry).

En arbelette: an expression used for shapes and forms which have a double curve similar to that of a cross-bow.

Encoignures: *see under* Corner-cupboards.

Espagnolette: a decorative motif popularized by the engravings of Gillot and Watteau and consisting of a female head surrounded by a large stiff collar of a type worn in Spain in the seventeenth century. It was used frequently in the early eighteenth century as a mounted decoration for furniture.

Etagère: a small work-table consisting usually of shelves or trays sets one above the other. The word is of nineteenth-century origin, the ordinary term used earlier being *table à ouvrage*.

Fire-dogs (*chenets*): an appliance for use in a fireplace to support the logs of a fire. These were usually made in pairs of iron with bronze ends or finals, sometimes patinated and sometimes gilt. They took various forms during the Louis XV and XVI periods, when the ornamental parts are usually made of ormolu and are often of the finest quality.

Flambeaux: *see under* Candlesticks.

Fondeurs, Corporation des: the craft guild responsible for casting and chasing metal, either for sculpture, furniture or *bronzes d'ameublement*. It was organized similarly to those of the *menuisiers-ébénistes* and *doreurs*.

Garde Meuble de la Couronne: the

department which dealt with all matters connected with the furnishing of the Royal palaces in France. It was established by Louis XIV in 1663, and survived until the end of the monarchy. Very fortunately, its records survive more or less intact.

The first inventory of furniture belonging to the Crown was completed in 1673 and has been published in full by M. Emile Molinier (*see* Bibliography), but the most important item among the records is the *Journal*, instituted in 1685 and continuing until 1784. In it every piece acquired for the Crown was scrupulously entered and given a number, with dates of delivery, the name of the maker, costs and measurements, its eventual destination in the Royal palaces, and a full description. The numbers often correspond with those painted on the backs of existing pieces (*see* Inventory numbers), and these can be thus identified fairly closely from the descriptions and measurements.

The *Journal* consists in all of eighteen volumes and 3,600 pages, of which only a small proportion are missing, and is preserved in the *Archives Nationales* in Paris. After 1784 a new system of recording was introduced, but the same numbers were preserved, and these, in fact, continued to be used until well into the nineteenth century.

Gobelins, Manufacture Royale des: the State-supported organization founded by Letters Patent at Gobelins in 1667 through the inspiration of Colbert, Louis XIV's finance minister. It was designed to provide, apart from tapestry, all products of the luxury arts, including furniture, and its first great task was the equipment of the interior of the Palaces of Versailles. It owed its success and great reputation to the energies of its first director, Charles Le Brun, who made it into the foundation stone of the organized applied arts in France.

Guéridon or **Guéridon table:** a small piece of furniture, usually circular, intended to support some form of light. In the seventeenth century it sometimes took the form of a negro figure holding a tray, and the name derives from that of a well-known Moorish galley-slave called Guéridon. Subsequently the term was extended to cover almost any form of small table on which candelabra, etc., might be placed.

Holly (*houx*): a hard wood with a fine, close grain. White or greenish white in colour. Found commonly in Europe and Western Asia. Used extensively for fillets to frame marquetry (*see also* Boxwood).

Inventory numbers: these are often found usually painted or branded on furniture made for the Crown or Royal Family of France. They often refer to the *Journal du Garde Meuble de la Couronne*, which has survived intact for some periods between the late seventeenth century and the Revolution. When accompanied by a Palace letter (q.v.), the numbers may refer to the inventories made of that particular Royal residence which may or may not be still extant. Considering everything, the documents of furniture made for the French Crown have survived in an extraordinary number of cases.

The discovery of an inventory number of any kind on a piece of French furniture of whatever date, is always worth the closest investigation, as it may be able to be identified.

Kingwood (*palissandre*): *see under* Rosewood.

Lacquer: a form of resinous varnish capable of taking a high polish. Its chief application to furniture in France dates from the early eighteenth century, when it was imported for this purpose from China and Japan. The Oriental lacquer was also often imitated in France and then applied to furniture locally (*see also under* Vernis Martin).

Lambrequin: a short piece of hanging drapery, often imitated in metal or wood for decorative purposes.

Lustres: *see under* Chandeliers.

Marquetry (*marqueterie*): the ordinary word for a design formed of substances inlaid on a carcase in the form of a veneer. It can consist of various types of wood, combined with such materials as tortoiseshell, brass, pewter, copper, mother-of-pearl, etc. It is found in Italy in the sixteenth century and in Flanders in the seventeenth century. It was from these sources that it came to be imported into France mainly by the foreign craftsmen working at the courts of Henri IV and Louis XIII. After the majority of Louis

XIV, Boulle marquetry (q.v.) came to be used extensively. In the eighteenth century, the possibilities of wood marquetry were developed until they reached their ultimate perfection in the works of J. H. Riesener (q.v.).

Menuisier: the term corresponds roughly to the English 'carpenter' or 'joiner'. In France, as far as furniture was concerned, the menuisiers were responsible for making chairs, beds and other furniture made from plain or carved woods, as distinct from veneered pieces which were the province of the *ébénistes* (q.v.). Although permitted by guild regulations to work in both techniques, they seldom did so (*see also* Corporation des Menuisiers-Ebénistes).

Menuisiers-Ébénistes, Corporation des: the craft guild which embraced all craftsmen engaged in making wood furniture.

An apprentice began his training with a *maître-ébéniste* or *maître-menuisier* at the age of fourteen, and it lasted for six years, after which he entered on his next stage, known as *compagnonage*. This lasted for three to six years, according to whether the craftsman had served his apprenticeship in Paris or elsewhere. During this time the *compagnon* was paid for the work he did. After his *compagnonage* the craftsman was ready to become a *maître* of the guild, but often the period was extended because of lack of vacancies or because of his inability to pay the fees required. These were fairly large and were devoted to the running expenses of the guild. The number of *maîtres* was limited. In 1723 there were nine hundred and eighty-five and in 1790 this figure had not increased. The King, moreover, had the right to create *maîtres* on his own authority.

A *compagnon* had to submit a specimen of his work before receiving the *maîtrise*, but once a *maître*, he was permitted to open a shop in his own name, in which he could employ some *compagnons*, and was required to take in one apprentice at least. At his death his widow could continue to direct his business, provided that she had qualified *compagnons* to assist her.

After 1751 a *maître* was also required to stamp the furniture he put on sale (*see* Stamps).

In addition to the apprentices, *compagnons* and *maîtres*, there were two other types of craftsmen involved in the guild organization. Firstly, the maintenance of standards was in the hands of a *syndic* and six *jurés*, elected once a year from among the *maîtres*, whose duty it was to examine the specimens submitted by aspiring *maîtres* and also to inspect all workshops in Paris four times a year and examine work in hand. All pieces of furniture approved by the *jurés* were stamped with the monogram J.M.E. (*juré*, or *jurande des menuisiers-ébénistes*) (*see also* Stamps).

Meuble à hauteur d'appui: a term used extensively at all periods for any low bookcase or cupboard, usually between three and four feet high.

Meuble d'entre deux: a term used in the eighteenth century for a type of furniture which usually consists of a cupboard or chest of drawers flanked at each side by a set of shelves. Often these are open but sometimes are enclosed by a curved door forming a small cupboard with shelves.

Ormolu: an English word in use from about the middle of the eighteenth century, derived from the French term '*bronze dorée d'or moulu*'. Its most accurate equivalents are '*bronze dorée*' or gilt bronze. Ormolu is the substance from which all objects covered by the term *bronzes d'ameublement* are made, e.g. lighting fixtures, including candelabra and candlesticks, clock-cases, appliances for doors and fireplaces, as well as mounts for furniture. Its manufacture was the function of two craft guilds; the *Fondeurs* (q.v.) and the *Doreurs* (q.v.). Its preparation consisted of a model in wood or wax being produced by a sculptor, often of some note; this was then cast in bronze by a *fondeur*, usually by the *cire perdue* method, but sometimes from a mould of clay or sand (*see* article on Bronzes). The casting was then tooled and chased until the required degree of finish had been achieved. This last process (known as *ciselure*) was carried to an extraordinary degree of refinement in France in the eighteenth century, and the tools which the *ciseleurs* used are illustrated in the *Encyclopédie*, showing the precision which could be obtained. The bronzes when finished were

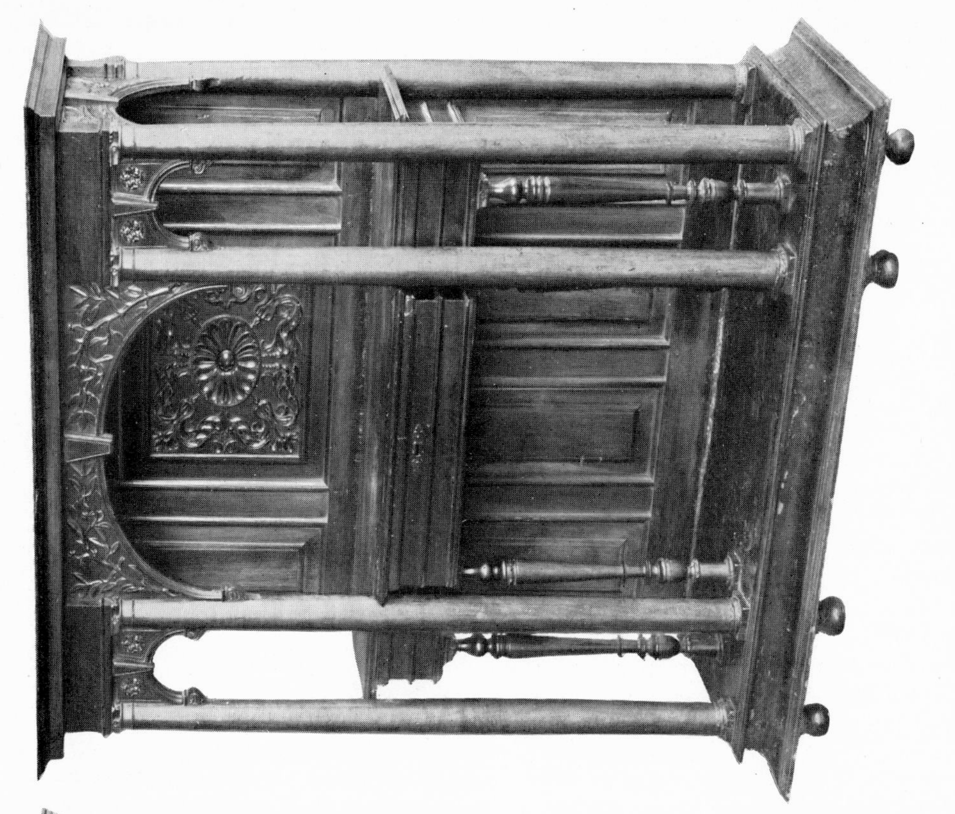

(B) Walnut Cabinet, second half of the sixteenth century.
Victoria & Albert Museum.

(A) Carved Walnut Dresser, second half of the sixteenth century.
Victoria & Albert Museum.

PLATE I

To face page 24

(A) Chest of Drawers (*commode*), made by A. Gaudreau and J. Caffiéri in 1739, for the bedroom of King Louis XV at Versailles. A perfect example of the Louis XV style on a monumental scale. *Wallace Collection.*

(B) Chest of Drawers (*commode*), by Charles Cressent. It seems probable that Cressent himself also executed the mounts. *Wallace Collection.*

(A) Writing table (*bureau-plat*) of deal veneered with ebony and Boulle marquetry of a general type, showing the Louis XIV development of this type of furniture. *Wallace Collection.*

(B) Chest of Drawers (*commode*), veneered on oak with mahogany, and stamped by J. H. Riesener. *Wallace Collection.*

PLATE 3

Toilet Mirror of oak veneered with ebony and Boulle marquetry of brass on tortoiseshell. A good example showing marquetry of a design in the manner of Jean Berain. *Wallace Collection.*

PLATE 4

To face page 25

often merely dipped in acid and then lacquered, and this often needed to be done more than once, when the surface became dirty.

If they were required to be gilt, this was usually done by the mercury process, of which detailed particulars are also given in the *Encyclopédie*. It consisted of coating the bronze with a paste formed by dissolving gold in heated mercury. The bronze thus coated was then itself heated, and the mercury driven off, when the gold was left adhering to the surface of the metal. The fumes of the mercury vapour produced at this stage were very dangerous and the heating had to be carried out in a furnace with a strong draught. Finally, when the process was completed the gold was either burnished or given a matt finish, according to requirements, but sometimes both types of finish were used on the same piece for purposes of contrast.

During the Louis XIV period the leaf-gilding of bronzes was sometimes employed, and occasionally bronzes were silvered, although this is rare at any time.

It is important to remember that only the finest bronzes were gilt in the manners described, the remainder being merely dipped and lacquered. The owners of furniture and *bronzes d'ameublement* in the eighteenth century were also not averse from having their ormolu regilt by the mercury process in order to keep it in a bright condition. So far as one can judge from contemporary accounts, ormolu was never allowed to become as dull or dirty as it often is today, and there seems to have been no taste for patina for its own sake.

The craft of making ormolu reached its height towards the middle of Louis XVI's reign, the chief exponents being Pierre Philippe Thomire, E. Forestier and others. During the Napoleonic period the quality of ormolu declined, mainly owing to the cost of gilding by the mercury process. Later in the nineteenth century, however, with the advent of machinery and mass-production methods, fine ormolu was produced, and although it often lacks the personal perfection which the earlier craftsmen gave it, it is sometimes very difficult to distinguish between a piece produced in 1770 and another made in the same style in 1860. Connoisseurs and collectors should always keep an open mind about this.

Palace letters: these, with inventory numbers (q.v.), are often painted or branded on furniture and occasionally stamped on *bronzes d'ameublement*, made for the French Crown. On veneered furniture they are usually to be found on the carcase at the back or under marble slabs, but in the case of chairs and *menuiserie* generally, they are often in the under parts and sometimes on the bottom of the upholstered seats. They almost always take the form of the initial letter or letters of the palace concerned beneath a crown. Thus F=Fontainebleau; C.T.=Château de Trianon; W (two Vs)=Versailles; S.C.=Saint Cloud, etc. Like inventory numbers, their existence on furniture of any date is worth careful investigation.

Parquetry (*parquetage*): a word connected, as its French equivalent implies, with the laying of floors. It is sometimes used in connection with furniture inlaid with geometrical designs in the manner of a parquet floor. It should be used with caution and is not really applicable to furniture at all.

Porcelain: in the Louis XV and Louis XVI periods there were two important uses of porcelain in connection with furniture. Firstly, for purely decorative purposes, actual pieces of porcelain were mounted with ormolu, often of very high quality. This is what became known as 'mounted porcelain', and the pieces so embellished came not only from the French factories of Vincennes and Sèvres but also from Meissen, and particularly from the Far East, *celadon* and *famille rose* being specially favoured. The ormolu decoration is usually confined to ornamental bases and bands for the necks of vases, but is sometimes extended to form handles, knobs for lids, etc. It is screwed on to the porcelain by means of a hole bored in the latter. The types of porcelain chosen are usually vases of various shapes, shallow bowls, ewers, and particularly the famous bunches of flowers from the Meissen factory, which were imitated at Vincennes. Sometimes groups of *biscuit de Sèvres* were similarly mounted. The demand for all these types was very high and extended right up to the Revolution, the usual changes in style being noticeable.

The other principal use to which porcelain was put did not come into fashion until the latter part of Louis XVI's reign. This consisted of the inlaying of plaques of porcelain into the veneered surfaces of pieces of furniture. This method of decoration, although it sometimes produces an extremely sumptuous effect, is often criticized on the grounds that it lies outside the scope of practical cabinet-making, and it has always been foreign to English taste. The covering of parts of furniture with porcelain does certainly make the pieces much more fragile, and there is evidence to show that a number of the plaques adorning extant pieces are not in fact the originals.

The porcelain so used almost always came from the Sèvres manufactory and often, therefore, has the Royal monogram with or without date letters or painters' marks. If a date letter is found and is genuine, it may help to date the piece of furniture fairly exactly, but it is always possible that the plaque is not the original, and may have replaced another, in which case the date letter may bear no relation to the year in which the furniture was made.

The porcelain is let into cavities in the carcase and kept in position originally by means of ormolu fillets. Martin Carlin and Adam Weisweiler were two *ébénistes* who appear to have specialized to some extent in making furniture of this kind, and the custom of mounting porcelain of any date on furniture was particularly prevalent in the nineteenth century, during the Restoration and reign of Louis Philippe. Collectors should always bear in mind that the porcelain on furniture may be a later addition or replacement, and this is particularly to be suspected if there is any lack of harmony between the furniture and the plaques, or any confusion of dating.

Purple-wood (*amaranthe, bois violet*): a wood with an open grain which is fairly hard. It is brown in its natural state but turns purple on exposure to the air. Found chiefly in Brazil and French Guinea. Very extensively used for marquetry in France in the eighteenth century.

Roll-top desk (*bureau à cylindre*): similar to a cylinder-top desk (q.v.) but the writing-table and fittings are enclosed by a curved slatted panel. The French term is the same for both types of desk.

Rosewood or **Kingwood** (*palissandre*): a course-grained wood, dark purplish brown or black in colour, varying considerably in hardness. Found in India, Brazil and the West Indies.

Satinwood (*bois de citron, bois satiné*): a fairly hard wood, with a very close grain. It is yellow or light brown in colour and has a lustrous surface somewhat like that of satin, It is found in Central and Southern India, Coromandel, Ceylon, and in the West Indies.

Secretaire (*secrétaire, secrétaire à abattant, écritoire*): a piece of furniture which came into use about 1748–60. Normally consists of a desk closed by a drop-front which falls down to form a writing-table revealing small drawers in the interior. The drop-front is usually supported in its horizontal position by counterweights within the carcase, but occasionally by struts. Beneath are doors sometimes concealing drawers, or a cupboard with shelves or a strong box. Another form is found supported on tall legs joined by a stretcher.

This type of furniture was very popular in the later Louis XV and Louis XVI periods and very often fitted with a number of secret drawers for concealing papers.

Serre-Papier: *see under* Cartonnier.

Settee: *see under* Causeuse.

Siegès: *see under* Chairs.

Sofas (*canapés*): the sofa as we know it developed in the Louis XIV period out of the day-bed (or *lit de repos*). It became established more or less in its present form in the Louis XV period as a regular part of a *mobilier de salon*, and was often made to match a set of chairs and *causeuses*, in which case it was upholstered similarly.

Stamps: various names and letters are often found stamped on furniture made in the eighteenth century or later. The principal and most important of these is the stamp (*estampille*), giving the name and often the initials of the *ébéniste* who made the piece of furniture concerned, which, after 1751, he was compelled by guild regulations to strike on all his work, unless he happened to be a privileged craftsman working for the Crown. Before 1751 *estampilles* are very rarely found.

These stamps are a most important means of identifying the makers of individual pieces of furniture, but it must be borne in mind that sometimes they only refer to the repairer of a piece as distinct from its original maker. Thus some pieces bear more than one *estampille*, and it is often doubtful which *ébéniste* was the actual maker. The importance of the stamps, however, was only rediscovered in 1882, as a result of an exhibition held in Paris under the auspices of the *Union Centrale de Arts Décoratifs*, and as an unfortunate consequence, a number of false signatures have been applied to furniture since that date by unscrupulous dealers. Connoisseurs and collectors should be on their guard against this and also against the attribution of unstamped pieces to individual *ébénistes* on grounds of style alone.

The *estampille* is of roughly uniform size and format, usually incorporating the *ébéniste*'s name and initials, but sometimes the surname only (*see pp.* 28–30). They are usually found in an inconspicuous place on the carcase of the piece, often on the bottom or top rails, front or back, under marble tops, etc. Very occasionally they appear on the surface of the veneer itself, and sometimes panels of marquetry are signed in full by their makers.

Another important stamp to be found on furniture after 1751 is that of the *jurés*. It consists of a monogram incorporating the letters JME (*juré* or *jurande des menuisiers-ébénistes*), and its presence implies that the piece concerned has passed the standard required by the *jurés* of the guild (*see* Menuisiers-Ébénistes, Corporation des).

In addition to the *estampille* and the *juré*'s stamp, furniture made for the Crown sometimes, though by no means always, bears the stamp of the *Garde Meuble de la Couronne* (q.v.). Inventory numbers and palace letters (q.v.) are usually painted or branded, but seldom stamped, on furniture.

In the eighteenth century *bronzes d'ameublement* are very rarely stamped, but sometimes they do bear signatures. Jacques Caffiéri frequently signed his work with his surname. Inventory numbers and palace letters are even rarer, but they do occasionally occur on bronzes, and where they can be checked with existing documents they are found to be of eighteenth-century origin.

Tricoteuse: a term probably of nineteenth-century origin, applied to a small work-table surrounded by a gallery, part of which can be lowered to contain sewing materials.

Vernis Martin: a term applied generically to all varnishes and lacquers used for furniture and interior decoration in France during the eighteenth century. It derives from the brothers Martin, who in 1730 were granted a monopoly to copy Chinese and Japanese lacquer. They also evolved a special kind of coloured varnish, which was applied in a large number of coats and then rubbed down to give it lustre. It was available in a number of colours, including grey, lilac, yellow and blue, but the most famous was the green, which was often applied to furniture. Vernis Martin was also used to decorate *boiseries*, carriages, fans and small boxes. The Martin family were much patronized by the Court and by Madame de Pompadour (*see also under* Lacquer).

Wall-lights (*bras de lumière, appliques*): a lighting appliance usually of more than one light which can be fixed flat to the surface of a wall. They were very popular in the Louis XV and Louis XVI periods and large numbers were made, usually of ormolu and often in pairs or sets of four or six. The *ciselure* and gilding on many of them are often of very high quality.

Wardrobes (*armoires*): the wardrobe developed out of the cupboard and the cabinet in the late seventeenth century and was treated monumentally by Boulle and his *atelier*, many being made for the Crown and very sumptuously decorated (*see* Plate 5). From the constructional point of view it consists of a straight, upright cupboard closed by two doors and with one or more shelves on the undecorated interior. It survived into the early Regency, sometimes of plain carved wood, but as rooms became smaller it seems to have disappeared. A number, however, were made in the Boulle technique in the Louis XVI period from earlier designs. Some also were made of plain wood under the Empire.

AUTHOR'S NOTE

I would like to acknowledge with gratitude the assistance I have received from the writings and advice of Mr F. J. B. Watson in compiling this article.

LIST OF CABINET-MAKERS AND CRAFTSMEN

BENEMAN, Jean Guillaume

German by birth. Came to Paris *c.* 1784 but seems to have been trained prior to this date, when he is first mentioned as being employed by the *Garde Meuble de la Couronne*. In 1785 he became a *maître-ébéniste* but without going through the normal formalities. His employment by the Crown coincides with the disfavour into which Riesener fell owing to his high charges. Beneman made a large amount of furniture for Queen Marie Antoinette and the Court, and was employed also to repair earlier furniture in the possession of the Crown. He collaborated with all the leading craftsmen of the time, including Boizot and Thomire, but his furniture retains usually a rather heavy Teutonic appearance. He seems to have specialized in making commodes and *meubles d'entre deux*. He was officially employed under the Directoire and Consulate, but his name disappears about 1804. He used the stamp:

G • BENEMAN

BOULLE, André Charles

Born in Paris in 1642, the son of a carpenter, and died there in 1732. His training was very various, and he appears to have worked at different times as a painter, architect, engraver and bronze worker, as well as an *ébéniste* of importance. He worked as an *artisan libre* from 1664 onwards, but in 1672 he was appointed *ébéniste du Roi* through the intervention of Colbert. From this time he worked continually for the Crown and established a workshop in which he employed about twenty assistants, who were constantly at work providing furniture for the new palace at Versailles.

Boulle did not invent the marquetry which has become associated with his name, the combination of metal and tortoiseshell in the form of an inlay being used since the sixteenth century in Italy and Flanders; but he did evolve a particular type which he adapted to the taste and requirements of the time.

He possessed a large collection of old master drawings from which he may easily have drawn inspiration for his mounts. His ingenuity as a designer was very great, as can be seen from a series of engravings which he published, and from a number of his drawings which exist. But throughout his career his actual style changed very little. He never signed his work and his authenticated productions are very rare. The only pieces which can be said definitely to be by him are two commodes originally made for the Grand Trianon and now in the palace at Versailles.

CAFFIÉRI, Jacques

Born 1678, son of Philippe Caffiéri, and came from a large family of sculptors. Became one of the chief exponents of the rococo style in France and was employed extensively by the Crown at Versailles, Fontainebleau and elsewhere. He also occasionally worked as a portrait sculptor. He often signed his bronzes with his surname only, and his chief works are to be found at Versailles, the Louvre, Paris, the Wallace Collection, and elsewhere. Died 1755.

His son, Philippe Caffiéri, was also a sculptor of note, and occasionally collaborated with his father in bronze work.

CARLIN, Martin

Very little is known about the life of Carlin. His place and date of birth are unknown. He died in Paris in 1785. He is first mentioned in 1763 and became a *maître-ébéniste* in 1766. He worked for Queen Marie Antoinette and the Royal Family, but it is uncertain whether he received an official appointment with the *Garde Meuble*. He supplied a large amount of furniture through the dealer Darnault.

Carlin was a most refined and delicate craftsman. He worked particularly in lacquer and with plaques of Sèvres porcelain.

CRESSENT, Charles

Born at Amiens in 1685, the son of François Cressent, a sculptor, and grandson of a cabinet-maker. He was apprenticed to his father, but probably learned cabinet-making from his grandfather. He became a member of the *Académie de Saint Luc* in Paris in 1714, and in 1719 married the daughter of Joseph Poitou, an *ébéniste* working for the Duc d'Orleans, and he also at this time was given commissions by the Regent. After this he seems officially to have abandoned sculpture for *ébénisterie*, but he was several times prosecuted by the *Corporations des Fondeurs* and *Doreurs* for casting and gilding his own mounts. In 1723 he was actually forbidden by law to produce mounts not made by a qualified *fondeur*. This type of litigation was repeated from time to time throughout his life.

The Regent died in 1723 but Cressent continued service with his son Louis, Duc d'Orleans, as late as 1743, on the Duc's retirement from public life. He also worked for important private patrons in France, and carried out important commissions for King John V of Portugal and the Elector Karl Albert of Bavaria. With the profits from the sale of his furniture Cressent formed an impressive collection of works of art, which he three times tried unsuccessfully to sell owing to financial difficulties. The first sale in 1748 was, in fact, withdrawn owing to fresh orders received for work. Cressent died in 1768.

His best work is never stamped. Towards the end of his life he did use the stamp: C. CRESSENT, but it never appears on pieces of very great quality and should always be treated with suspicion in view of his fame in his lifetime and later. The identification of his work therefore depends almost entirely on documents and tradition.

DUBOIS, Jacques and Réné

Jacques Dubois was born in Paris *c.* 1693. He became a *maître-ébéniste* in 1742, and was elected a *juré* of the guild in 1752. He specialized in the use of lacquer both Oriental and European, and died in 1763, the same year as Oeben, whose stock he helped to value. He used the stamp:

IDUBOIS

After his death his widow carried on the business with the help of her sons, the most celebrated of which was Réné (born 1757), who always used his father's stamp. He became a *maître* in 1754, was much patronized by Marie Antoinette, both before and after she became Queen, and also by the Court and nobility. He worked mainly in the Louis XVI style and eventually abandoned cabinet-making for selling furniture. He died in 1799.

FORESTIER, Étienne Jean and Pierre Auguste (1755–1838)

Two brothers, the sons of Étienne Forestier (*c.* 1712–68). All three were *fondeurs-ciseleurs*, and after the father's death his widow carried on the business with her two sons. Their names constantly occur in the Royal accounts, and they are known to have worked at Versailles and Compiègne, and for the Prince de Condé. After the Revolution, Pierre Auguste established a successful workshop, supplying furniture, *bronzes d'ameublement*, etc.

GAUDREAU, Antoine Robert

One of the most celebrated of the known *ébénistes* of the Louis XV period. He was born *c.* 1680, and was in the Royal service from 1726. He became a *syndic* of the *ébénistes* guild in 1744, and worked for the Crown and also later for Madame de Pompadour. Among his most important works are a medal cabinet and a commode, which were made for the King's private apartments at Versailles. On the latter he collaborated with J. Caffiéri, who signed the bronzes. It is now in the Wallace Collection (Plate 2A). He died in 1751.

GOUTHIÈRE, Pierre

The most celebrated of the late eighteenth-century *fondeurs-ciseleurs-doreurs*. Born at Bar-sur-Aube in 1732, the son of a saddler. He is known to have been in Paris by 1758, where he became a *maître-doreur*. He was employed by the Crown between 1769 and 1777, but after the latter date his name disappears from the Royal accounts. He had, however, a large number of private patrons, including the Duc d'Aumont and the Duchesse de Mazarin. He also worked for Madame du Barry at Louveciennes. He was constantly in difficulties financially, and his patrons were almost always behind with their payments. In 1788 he was declared bankrupt, and he never completely recovered, although he lived on until 1813 and died in poverty. Gouthière's signed works are exceedingly rare and can be supplemented by a few which are able to be identified by documents. Almost all bronzes of any quality of the Louis XVI period have been attributed to him, and it is only recently that the increased study of the Royal accounts have revealed the names of other *ciseleurs-doreurs*, who seem to have been his equals in many cases, even though we know little more than their names.

The attributions of bronzes to Gouthière on grounds of style alone should be made with great caution.

JACOB, Georges

Was born in Burgundy in 1739 and died in Paris in 1814. Little is known of his early life, but he was the founder of a long line of makers of furniture who specialized in the production of chairs. He is thus usually thought of as *menuisier*, although he did carry out some works in the *ébéniste*'s technique. He was made a *maître-ébéniste* in 1765 and carried on his business in his own name until 1796, when he sold it to his two sons, Georges II and François Honoré. On the former's death in 1803 the latter took the name of Jacob-Desmalter and joined with his father until the latter's death in 1814. He then carried on the business himself until 1824, and his son continued it up to 1847. The first Jacob was a craftsman with an extraordinary wealth of invention, and his designs for chairs are of the utmost elegance, but are also pleasantly varied so that they do not often repeat themselves. He also made a number of beds, which show the same qualities. He worked extensively for the Crown and in consequence was denounced at the Revolution, in spite of his friendship with the painter Jacques Louis David. His own work is usually stamped:

G ♦ IACOB

LELEU, Jean François

Born in Paris in 1729, and died there in 1807. Trained under J. F. Oeben (q.v.), after whose death in 1763 he hoped to be chosen to take over the direction of the workshop. Oeben's widow's choice, however, fell on Riesener, whom she married, and Leleu never became reconciled to this. He became a *maître-ébéniste* in 1764, and worked both for the Court and for private patrons. He was also employed by Queen Marie Antoinette, Madame du Barry, and the Prince de Condé. He became successively *juré* and *deputé* of the *ébénistes*' guild, and in 1780 went into partnership with his son-in-law, C. A. Stadler, who succeeded to the business in 1792.

Leleu was a very versatile craftsman and worked in a number of styles; he seems to have been as equally at home in the advanced rococo as with the most severe neo-classic, and he also used Boulle marquetry and Sèvres porcelain to decorate his furniture. He used the stamp:

J·F·LELEU

OEBEN, Jean François

Born *c.* 1720, the son of a postmaster at Ebern in Franconia. He married in Paris in 1749, but we do not know the date of his arrival there from Germany. He entered the workshop of C. J. Boulle in 1751, and on the latter's death in 1754 Oeben succeeded him as *ébéniste du Roi* and was granted lodgings at the Gobelins, whence he moved in 1756 to the Arsenal. While working for Boulle, he was also employed by Madame de Pompadour and others, and after his move to the Gobelins he began in 1760 his most celebrated work – the monumental *Bureau du Roi Louis XV*, which, however, was not completed until after his death.

Riesener, who was one of his assistants, succeeding him at the Arsenal, together with Leleu. Oeben also collaborated with Carlin and with P. Caffieri. He died bankrupt in Paris in 1763, when his widow carried on the business until 1767, when she married Riesener, who then carried on the business in his own name.

Oeben only became a *maître-ébéniste* in 1761 under special circumstances, having worked for the Crown for so long. His stamp on furniture is therefore rare, and when found it is more probable that the piece was made by Riesener before he took over the business, as Madame Oeben continued to use her husband's stamp while running the workshop herself.

After Cressent and Gaudreau, Oeben is the most celebrated *ébéniste* of Louis XV's reign. He specialized in elaborately-planned pieces, fitted with secret drawers and complicated locking devices, but, owing to the amount of furniture which must necessarily have left his workshop unstamped, his work cannot easily be identified.

RIESENER, Jean Henri

The most famous *ébéniste* of the eighteenth century in France. Born at Gladbeck, near Essen, in 1734, but it is not known when he came to Paris. He entered Oeben's workshop at the Gobelins about 1754, and moved with him to the Arsenal. At Oeben's death he was selected by the widow to take over the workshop, and he married her in 1768, the year when he became a *maître-ébéniste*. In 1769 Riesener completed the great *Bureau du Roi Louis XV*, which his predecessor had left unfinished (*see under* Oeben). In 1774 he succeeded Joubert as *ébéniste du Roi*, and for ten years enjoyed the patronage of the Crown to a hitherto unprecedented degree, as expenditure during that decade was higher than it had ever been. His wife died in 1776, and seven years later he remarried, but unhappily.

After 1784 his prosperity began to decline and he was made drastically to reduce his prices by the Treasury. It was at this time that Beneman to a certain extent succeeded him in the favour of the Court. Queen Marie Antoinette, however, seems to have remained faithful to Riesener throughout, for she continued to order furniture from him right up to the Revolution.

He continued in business during and after the Revolution but never actually reinstated himself. He seems to have retired in 1801 and died in Paris in 1806.

Riesener's stamp appears frequently on furniture of all kinds in the Louis XVI period, but it is probable that works bearing Oeben's stamp may also be by him, and made while he was working for Madame Oeben before their marriage (*see* Oeben).

J•H•RIESENER

He was the most versatile, and became the most accomplished *ébéniste* of the time, and certainly deserved the success he obtained. His work covers nearly all types of furniture in use, and he specialized in highly elaborate marquetry, mostly in geometrical designs.

THOMIRE, Pierre Philippe

Born 1751, the son of a *ciseleur*. Worked under the sculptors Pajou and Houdon. In 1783 entered the service of the Sèvres porcelain factory. From 1784 onwards he was frequently employed by the Crown to make mounts for furniture, and often collaborated with G. Beneman. In 1785 he was commissioned by the City of Paris to make a candelabra celebrating the American Declaration of Independance for presentation to General Lafayette (now in the Louvre).

He built up a large workshop, which is said to have employed as many as eight hundred workmen. He worked extensively under the Empire and received a number of important commissions from the Emperor himself. The firm was known as *Thomire-Dutherne et cie*, and Thomire himself retired from business in 1823 but did not die until 1843. It by no means always follows that bronzes stamped with the name Thomire are by Pierre Philippe himself. More probably they are products of the workshop.

ROENTGEN, David

Born near Frankfurt in 1743, the son of the cabinet-maker Abraham Roentgen, whose workshop at Neuwied on the Rhine he took over in 1772 and developed considerably. He first came to Paris in 1774 and received patronage from Queen Marie Antoinette. This established his reputation which, by the time of his second visit in 1779, had increased considerably, and he established a depot in Paris for selling furniture, as he did also in Berlin and Vienna. He travelled widely and visited Italy, Flanders and Russia, where he sold a great deal of furniture to the Empress Catherine II.

In 1780 he was compelled to become a *maître-ébéniste* in Paris, using the stamp: DAVID, and in 1791 was made Court furnisher to King Frederick William II at Berlin. He was ruined by the Revolution and his depot in Paris was confiscated. His workshop at Neuwied was also overrun by Republican troops. He returned there in 1802, however, and died in 1807.

Roentgen specialized in furniture veneered with extremely elaborate pictorial marquetry and fitted with complicated mechanical devices, concealing secret drawers and multiple locks. His furniture was mostly made outside France and is seldom stamped.

WEISWEILER, Adam

Born *c.* 1750 at Neuweid and trained in the workshop of Roentgen (q.v.). Established in Paris before 1777. Became a *maître-ébéniste* in 1778. He worked for the dealer Daguerre and, through him, supplied a large amount of furniture for the Royal palaces, and particularly for Queen Marie Antoinette at Saint Cloud. He was a good business man, and in consequence survived the Revolution safely, and was employed under the Empire, during which time he executed commissions for Queen Hortense. He was still in business in 1810. He used the stamp:

A·WEISWEILER

BOOKS FOR FURTHER READING

G. H. BAILLIE, *Watchmakers and Clockmakers of the World*, 2nd ed., N.A.G. Press Ltd (London, 1947).

MARIE JULIETTE BALLOT, *Charles Cressent, Sculpteur, Ébéniste, Collectionneur*, published in 'Archives de l'Art Français', nouvelle période, tome X (Edouard Champion, Paris, 1919).

Le Décor Intérieur au XVIIIe siècle à Paris et dans la Région Parisienne. Boiseries sculptées et Panneaux peints. (G. Van Oest, Paris, 1930.)

ALFRED DE CHAMPEAUX, *Le Meuble*. Tome I: 'Antiquité, Moyen Age et Renaissance'. Tome II: 'XVIIe, XVIIIe et XIXe Siècles. 2 vols., 1885. (Paris, n.d.)

Dictionnaire des Fondeurs, Ciseleurs, Modeleurs en Bronze et Doreurs depuis le moyen-âge jusqu'à l'époque actuelle. 1st vol., A–C. (J. Rouam, Paris, 1886.)

HENRI CLOUZOT, *Le Style Louis-Phillipe-Napoléon III*. 'Arts, Styles et Techniques.' (Collection publiée sous la direction de Norbert Dufourcq.) (Larousse, Paris, 1939.)

PIERRE DU COLOMBIER, *Le Style Henri IV–Louis XIII*. (Arts, Styles et Techniques.) (Collection publiée sous la Direction de Norbert Dufourcq.) (Larousse, Paris, 1941.)

ÉMILE DACIER, *Le Style Louis XVI*. 'Arts, Styles et Techniques.' (Collection publiée sous la direction de Norbert Dufourcq.) (Larousse, Paris, 1939.)

DENIS DIDEROT AND J. LE R. D'ALEMBERT, *Encyclopédie, ou Dictionnaire raisonné des Sciences des Arts et des Métiers, par une Société de gens de lettres*. A–Z. 17 vols.; Supplément, 4 vols.; Planches, 11 vols.; Supplément aux planches, 1 vol. (Paris and Amsterdam, 1751–77.) Table, 2 vols.

LADY DILKE, *French Furniture and Decoration in the Eighteenth Century*. 4to. (George Bell & Sons, London, 1901.)

JULES GUIFFREY, *Les Caffiéri. Sculpteurs et fondeurs-ciseleurs. Étude sur la Statuaire et sur l'art de bronze en France au XVIIe et au XVIIIe siècles*. (Paris, 1877.)

Inventaire Général du Mobilier de la Couronne sous Louis XIV (1663–1715). 2 vols. (Paris, 1885.)

HENRY HAVARD, *Dictionnaire de l'Ameublement et de la Décoration depuis le XIIIe siècle jusqu'à nos jours*. 4 vols. (1887–90.) (Quanton, Paris, n.d.)

Les Boulle. 'Les Artistes Célèbres.' (L. Allison et Cie, Paris, 1892.)

GUILLAUME JANNEAU, PIERRE DEVINOY, and MADELEINE JARRY, *Le Siège en France du Moyen Age à nos jours*. (P. Hartmann, Paris, 1948.)

GUILLAUME JANNEAU and PIERRE DEVINOY, *Le Meuble Léger en France*. (P. Hartmann, Paris, 1952.)

ALBERT KEIM, *La Décoration et le Mobilier à l'Époque Romantique et sous le Second Empire*. (Nilsson, Paris, n.d.)

FISKE KIMBALL, *Le Style Louis XV. Origine et Évolution du Rococo*. Translated from English by Mlle. Jeanne Marie. (A. et J. Picard, Paris, 1949.

DENISE LEDOUX-LEBARD, *Les Ébénistes Parisiens* (1795–1830), *leurs œuvres et leurs marques*. (Gründ, Paris, 1951).

HECTOR LEFUEL, *Georges Jacob, Ébéniste du XVIIIe siècle*. Paris (Archives de l'Amateur, 1923).

ÉMILE MOLINIER, *Histoire Générale des Arts appliqués à l'Industrie*. Tome II: 'Les Meubles du Moyen Âge et de la Renaissance'. Tome III: 'Le Mobilier au XVIIe et au XVIIIe siècle'. (?1898.) (Paris, n.d.)

Le Mobilier Royal Français aux XVIIe et XVIIIe siècles. Histoire et description. 5 vols. (E. Lévy, Paris, 1902.)

JULIETTE NICLAUSSE, *Thomire, Fondeur-Ciseleur* (1751–1843). *Sa Vie-Son Œuvre. Préface de Louis Réau*. (Gründ, Paris, 1947.)

SEYMOUR DE RICCI, *Louis XIV and Regency Furniture and Decoration*. (Batsford, London, 1929.)

Louis XVI Furniture. (Heinemann, London, n.d.)

JACQUES ROBIQUET, *Gouthière, Sa Vie-Son Œuvre*. Essaie de Catalogue Raisonné. (Renouard, Paris, 1912.)

COMTE FRANÇOIS DE SALVERTE, *Les Ébénistes du XVIIIe siècle, leurs œuvres et leurs marques*. 4th edition. (G. Vanoest, Paris-Bruxelles, 1953.)

Le Meuble Français d'après les Ornemanistes de 1660 à 1789. (G. Van Oest, Paris, 1930.)

THOMAS ARTHUR STRANGE, *An Historical Guide to French Interiors, Furniture Decoration, Woodwork and Allied Arts during the last half of the Seventeenth Century, the whole of the Eighteenth Century, and the early part of the Nineteenth*. 3rd impression. (McCorquodale & Co. Ltd, London, 1950.)

ANDRÉ THEUNISSEN, *Meubles et sièges du XVIIIe siècle*. Menuisiers, Ébénistes, Marques, Plans et ornamentation de leurs œuvres. (Éditions 'Le Document', Paris, n.d.)

PIERRE VERLET, *Le Style Louis XV*. 'Arts, Styles et Techniques.' (Collection publiée sous la direction de Norbert Dufourcq.) (Larousse, Paris, 1942.)

Le Mobilier Royal Français: Meubles de la Couronne conservés en France. I. (Éditions d'Art et d'Histoire, Paris, 1945.)

HENRI VIAL, ADRIEN MARCEL and ANDRÉ GIRODIE, *Les Artistes Décorateurs du Bois* (*Répertoire alphabétique des Ebénistes, Menuisiers, Sculpteurs, Doreurs sur bois, etc, ayant travaillé en France aux XVIIe et XVIIIe siècles*). 2 vols. 4to. (I: A–L; II: M–Z.) Paris. Vol. I: Bibliothèque d'Art et d'Archéologie, 1912. Vol. II: Libraire de la Bibliothèque d'Art de l'Université de. (J. Schemit, Paris, 1922.)

VICTORIA AND ALBERT MUSEUM, LONDON. *A Guide to the Salting Collection*. (Board of Education, London, 1926.)

The Panelled Rooms: III—The Boudoir of Madame de Sérilly. (H.M.S.O., London, 1915.)

Catalogue of the Jones Collection. Part I: Furniture, by Oliver Brackett. 4to. (H.M.S.O., London, 1922.) Part II: Ceramics, Ormolu, Goldsmiths' Work, Enamels, Sculpture, Tapestry, Books and Prints. (Board of Education, London, 1924.)

ROGER-ARMAND WEIGERT, *Jean I. Bérain, Dessinateur de la Chambre et du Cabinet du Roi* (1640–1711). 2 vols. Première Partie: Sa Vie-Sa Famille-Son Style. Deuxième Partie: L'Œuvre Gravé. (Editions d'Art et d'Histoire, Paris, 1937.)

Le Style Louis XIV. 'Arts, Styles et Techniques.' (Collection publiée sous la direction de Norbert Dufourcq.) (Larousse, Paris, 1941.)

E. WILLIAMSON, *Les Meubles d'Art du Mobilier National* (Choix des plus belles pièces conservées au Garde-Meuble et dans les Palais nationaux de l'Elysée, du Louvre, de Versailles, de Trianon, de Fontainebleau, de Compiègne et de Pau). 2 vols. (1883–5.) (Baudry et Cie, Paris, n.d.)

EUROPEAN TAPESTRIES AND CARPETS

By GEORGE WINGFIELD DIGBY

(*A*) EUROPEAN TAPESTRIES

WOVEN TAPESTRY must be distinguished from embroidery in tent or cross stitch on canvas. The latter is not true tapestry, although it has been used to serve some of the same purposes, such as upholstery and wall hangings. Correctly, it should be called needlework. Needlework is not capable of the subtler effects of tapestry, neither is it so strong and durable, nor can it be made into such large hangings. Single tapestries sixteen to eighteen feet high and twenty-five to thirty feet long were not uncommon in the Middle Ages. Tapestry is woven on a loom, the coloured weft threads covering the warp and forming a pattern as well as building a close-knit texture.

Tapestry can be woven either on an upright loom or on a horizontal loom. The former is known as high-warp (*haute-lisse*), the latter as low-warp (*basse-lisse*) tapestry. In the Middle Ages high-warp tapestry was considered superior. It is slower to make, but the work can be more exact and allows for subtler effects of texture, which are the hall-mark of good tapestry; although this can only be recognized by the connoisseur. The weaver sits at his upright loom, divides his warp with

FIG. 1. High-warp loom at the Gobelins. (From *Diderot's Encyclopedie*, 1760–80.)

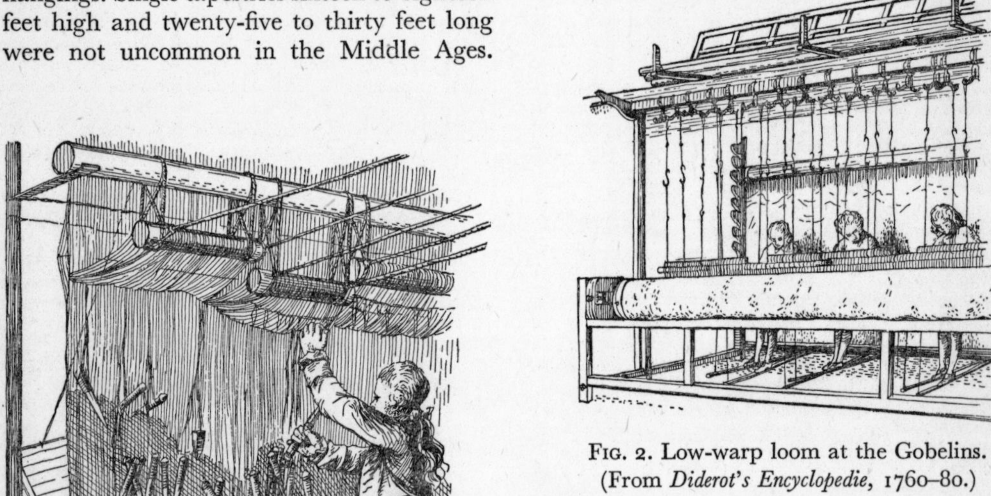

FIG. 2. Low-warp loom at the Gobelins. (From *Diderot's Encyclopedie*, 1760–80.)

Wardrobe (*armoire*) veneered on oak with ebony and Boulle marquetry of brass and tortoiseshell. Attributed to André Charles Boulle and perhaps made for a member of the Royal Family. A perfect specimen of the monumental style of the Boulle *atelier*. *Wallace Collection.*

PLATE 5

To face page 32

(A) *Secrétaire à abattant* made by J. H. Riesener in 1780 for the use of Queen Marie Antoinette at Versailles. Repaired by G. Beneman in 1788 and moved to Saint Cloud. A particularly fine example of this type of piece. *Wallace Collection.*

(B) *Secrétaire* veneered with tulip-wood and king-wood, and mounted with ormolu. A typical Louis XV design. *Victoria & Albert Museum* (*Jones Collection*)

(A) Combined work-, writing- and reading-table veneered on oak with tulip-wood and mounted with plaques of Sèvres porcelain. By M. Carlin. *Wallace Collection.*

(B) Arm-chair of birch carved, gilt, and upholstered with Beauvais tapestry. Stamped by G. Jacob. A typical product of the Jacob *atelier*. *Wallace Collection.*

PLATE 7

(A) Cartel Clock. The case made by C. Cressent, *c.* 1747. A particularly fine example of a Louis XV clock-case. *Wallace Collection.*

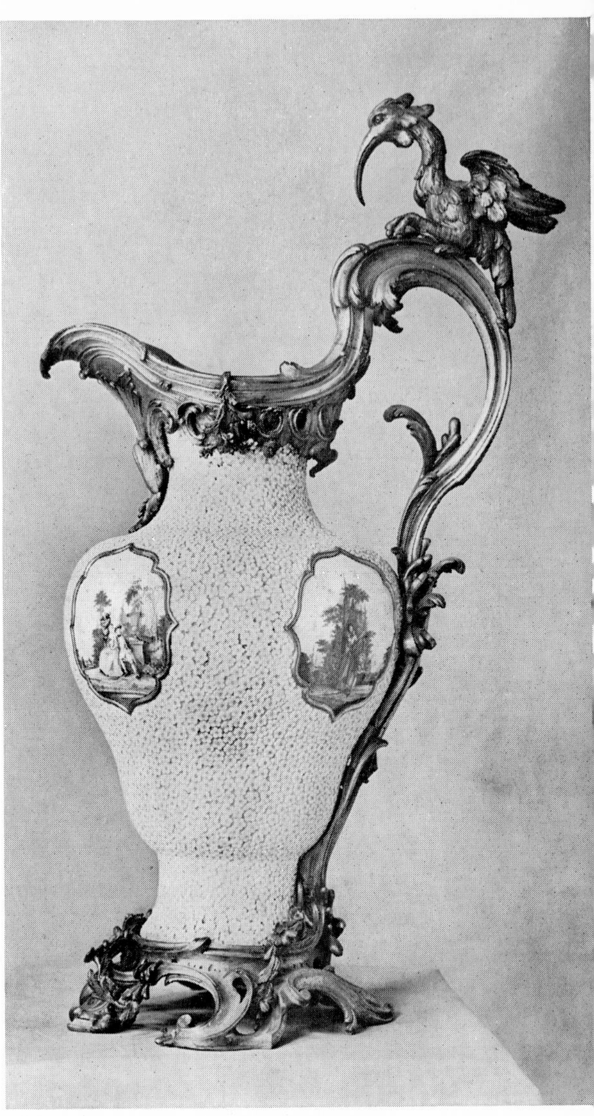

(B) Ewer of Meissen porcelain mounted with ormolu, and made between 1745 and 1749. *Wallace Collection.*

PLATE 8

Mantel Clock of ormolu, perhaps by P. P. Thomire. *Wallace Collection.*

PLATE 9

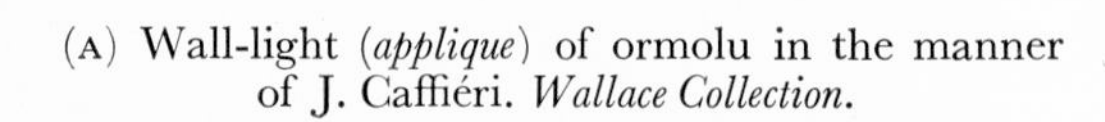

(A) Wall-light (*applique*) of ormolu in the manner of J. Caffiéri. *Wallace Collection.*

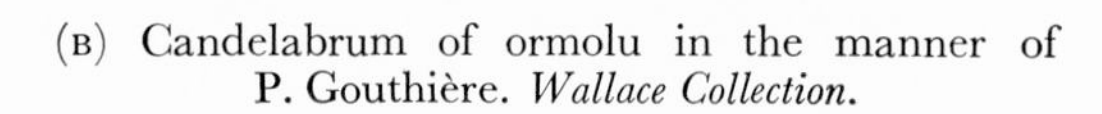

(B) Candelabrum of ormolu in the manner of P. Gouthière. *Wallace Collection.*

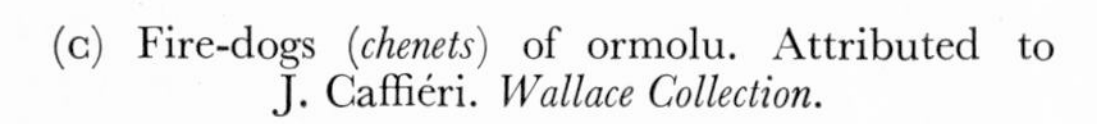

(C) Fire-dogs (*chenets*) of ormolu. Attributed to J. Caffiéri. *Wallace Collection.*

PLATE 10

To face page 33

his left hand with the aid of leashes, and inserts his coloured wefts in accordance with his cartoon (or actual-size model), which is placed behind him. He works with the back side of the tapestry towards him, and he can see the face by means of a mirror. For closer inspection he need only move round to the front of his loom.

The low-warp weaver has advantages of speed, because he controls his warp with treadles, which leave both his hands free. But his cartoon is placed under the horizontal warp and is relatively less visible. Nor can he see the face of the cloth until weaving is completed (Vaucanson's eighteenth-century metal loom could be moved into a vertical position for inspection). Also, the cartoon has to be drawn in reverse (*see* Cartoon). At the Gobelins, where both methods were employed, it was reckoned that at least a third more low-warp tapestry could be woven in a given time. None the less, it is very difficult, if not impossible, to tell low-warp tapestry of *best quality* from high-warp.

Wool is always used for the warp except in German medieval tapestry, where linen took its place. The weft, which is always a much finer thread than the warp, is principally wool. But in finer tapestries silk is also used, sometimes in great quantity. Gold and silver thread adds to the sumptuous effect of a tapestry, and has been employed lavishly for the richest hangings.

Medieval tapestry depended more on texture and the use of few, but contrasting dyes, than later tapestry. The use of colour contrasts and silk for high-lights and tonal variations, as well as the artificial creation of minute holes to show (for example) muscular articulation in the 'flesh' parts, should be studied. Fifteen to twenty-five different dye-tones in a medieval tapestry are rarely exceeded. Because they depended on these simple, structural means, they have tended to last better than later tapestries, which lose more with fading, tarnish and surface wear.

When the low-warp tapestry of Brussels first assumed the primacy about 1500–10, there was still much emphasis on texture. This was the great period for tapestries rich in gold and silver, and although metal thread had certainly been much used in precious fifteenth-century tapestries, a rather new effect was achieved. But from this date on there tended to be a marked increase in the number of dyes employed for a given tapestry. Forty or fifty different dye-tones can be counted in certain typical Flemish tapestries of the period 1510–25, and the *Hunts of Maximilian* (Brussels, *c.* 1530) contain eighty-three dyes, arranged in twenty-seven scales of two to five tones each (computed at the Gobelins). Weavers were obviously relying more on tonal variety (as in painting) than on the simpler effects of textural structure. During Le Brun's regime at the Gobelins 140 tones would commonly be expected in one tapestry. But under Oudry (*c.* 1730) the count had risen to 400–500. Neilson is said to have used 580 for one tapestry in the *Nouvelles Indes* set. Finally, in the nineteenth century the chemist Chevreul obtained 14,420 different dye-tones for the Gobelins weavers; this (paradoxically) spelt the ruin of tapestry weaving; for fifteen really bright and vivid dyes are better than fifteen thousand dull and lifeless ones.

The tendency towards increased colour tints noted above must not, of course, be condemned out of hand. As long as dyes and designs were good and weavers skilful, this made different types of effect possible in tapestry, with the proviso that these effects were more easily lost with fading (which to some extent can never be avoided). To condemn pictorial effects in tapestry is also a somewhat superficial point of view. The best artists have always designed for tapestry, or had their pictures copied; there are different ways of putting to advantage the textural beauties of wool, silk and metal thread; it is only when this is disregarded or abused by weaver or designer that tapestry ceases to be beautiful.

The different tapestry styles will be found briefly noted in the Glossary under Countries and Factories. Familiarity with these, and particularly a study of borders, will make the attribution of a tapestry to a particular school relatively easy. Factory or city marks are conclusive when found, provided the border or galloon (*see* Glossary) has not been re-applied from another piece. Also, there was some pirating of the Brussels mark. A law of 1528 first introduced the use of a mark for the city of Brussels. This was re-enforced and applied to other Flemish cities in 1544. Later factories in other countries always adopted a city mark. The different marks can be studied in Thomson's or Goebel's books on Tapestry (*see* Bibliography). Weavers' and workshop marks are often difficult to identify. Apart from a few well-established cyphers the majority are not certainly known, and few city archives have survived or been sufficiently scrutinized to identify them. An inverted figure 4 (often found) is thought to be a merchant's mark. One other class of signature should be mentioned, that is names woven usually on the borders of costume worn by figures in the tapestries rich in gold and silver of the early Brussels period. Some of these names undoubtedly refer to designers and occasionally to weavers, but some rather exaggerated attempts to interpret obscure and fragmentary names have been made (*see* articles by Mme Crick-Kuntziger, Brussels Cinquantenaire publications and Societé Royale d'Archeologie de Bruxelles).

The subjects used for tapestry are extremely varied. The Bible, classical history and mythology, medieval romance lore and history have all been freely drawn on, as well as such subjects as months and seasons, planets, allegorical themes, and purely formal designs such as grotesques and verdures. Many subjects are very difficult to identify without study of the literary sources available to the designer and popular at the time. The literature of tapestry contains a great number of these identifications.

GLOSSARY

(*Note.*—Only the most important factories are treated separately. For others see under the country. Examples: Beauvais is treated separately, Sheldon appears under England.)

Alentours: *see* Borders.

Arras: under the Dukes of Burgundy in the fourteenth to fifteenth centuries Arras became a synonym for tapestry (as did Gobelins later) and 'thread of Arras' denoted the highest quality. Only one hanging has survived which can with absolute certainty be attributed to Arras: this is the story of SS. Piat and Eleuthère in Tournai Cathedral, dated 1404. Throughout the fourteenth and fifteenth centuries Arras, with its great rival Tournai, produced enormous quantities of tapestry besides famous pieces of special quality. The city was razed in 1477, never recovered its position, and was a Habsburg possession from 1493–1640. (*See also* Franco-Burgundian.)

Aubusson and Felletin: it is rare to see tapestries from these workshops in La Marche on the road between Bordeaux and Lyon, which date from earlier than the eighteenth century. But they also flourished in the sixteenth and seventeenth centuries; although they lost many workmen abroad in 1685 (Revocation of the Edict of Nantes). Aubusson tapestry is generally less fine than that of Beauvais and was made for the less pretentious houses of the aristocracy and bourgeoisie. Felletin tapestries tend to be coarser, and at Bellegarde, nearby, where the weavers only worked in the winter months, the most rustic of French hangings were produced. Aubusson copied the Verdure, animal, and *Fable* designs of Oudry, Boucher's *Chinoiseries*, and Huet's pastorals, interpreting them very effectively in their somewhat coarser texture. In the late eighteenth and nineteenth centuries much tapestry for upholstery was woven.

Beauvais: founded in 1664 as a private enterprise supported by the State (Colbert), it was to Beauvais that foreign princes and lords had recourse to obtain tapestry in the French taste and by the best designers of the Courts of Louis XIV, XV and XVI (*see* Gobelins). Béhagle (who came from Tournai) created the first successful Beauvais period (1684–1705). Particularly popular were the *Grotesques* after Bérain's designs, which are still frequently met with; also the first *Tenture Chinoise*, after Bernansal. An even more prosperous period followed under Oudry, painter at Beauvais from 1726 and inspector from 1734. His own designs included, besides landscape & animal scenes, the famous *Fables de la Fontaine* series, which were particularly popular as an ensemble of hangings and upholstery. Tapestry covers for suites of chairs and *canapés* (settees) remained a special feature of

Beauvais throughout the eighteenth and nineteenth centuries. In the 1730s and '40s Boucher's designs attained a pre-eminence which they have never lost, i.e. the *Italian Comedy*, the *Amours des Dieux*, the *Chinese set* (Second Tenture Chinoise). The weaving at Beauvais achieved a very fine texture at this time; much silk and finely-tinted dyes were used. But it should be remembered that not all Beauvais tapestry is of this excessively fine quality; good but less expensive furnishing tapestry was always produced there. Also, many eighteenth-century designs were reproduced throughout the nineteenth century, but as the dyes had been over-refined and an excessive number of tones were used, they easily fade to a rather dull and lifeless uniformity, lacking life and brilliance. The last triumph at Beauvais were the *Pastorals* designed by Huet and woven in the decade before the Revolution.

Borders: except in German tapestries, borders are rarely seen on tapestries until the beginning of the sixteenth century. They then began to play a very important part in the general effect, and the best artists of the day were called in to design them. Very beautiful and varied effects were produced, especially in the sixteenth and seventeenth centuries. In the eighteenth frame-borders became general, but the *alentours* which surround a subject inset in the main field, and enliven it with rococo displays of drapery and flowers, create an effect which is really that of an enlarged border. The style of a tapestry border is very important in determining questions of date and workshop and is sometimes a certain indication of this. Normally, borders were woven in one piece with the main field, and it is important to see whether a border has been re-applied. (*See also* Galloons.)

Boutique d'Or: a name given to the Paris seventeenth-century factory of De La Planche and Comans (q.v. under France).

Brussels: capital of Brabant and the Netherlands since 1483, Brussels became Europe's leading centre of tapestry weaving from about 1500, and retained its reputation throughout the seventeenth and eighteenth centuries, though eclipsed by Louis XIV's Gobelins factory since 1670–80. It is probable that Brussels's rise to fame was connected with the low-warp weaving method (*see* Introduction), which was always practised there (but which was not considered the equal of high-warp tapestry in the Middle Ages). Brussels's reputation was definitely sealed by Pope Leo X's order for the weaving of tapestries for the Sistine Chapel from Raphael's cartoons (q.v.) (about 1515). But as a tapestry designer Bernard van Orley and his school exercised a far greater influence at Brussels in the first half of the sixteenth century. The *History of Jacob*, newly acquired at Brussels, and the *Hunts of Maximilian* at the Louvre are superb examples of his style. Francis I of France, England's Henry VIII, and the Emperor Charles V all had recourse to Brussels for specially fine sets (the *Great Scipio*, *Story of Abraham*, now at Hampton Court, the *Conquest of Tunis*), and it was there also that the Duke of Marlborough ordered his set of *Victories* (*c.* 1712). Throughout the sixteenth, seventeenth and eighteenth centuries the Habsburgs were Brussels's chief patrons, and the finest sets can still be seen at Vienna (the earlier pieces, before about 1515, are in Spain). Brussels also has a good collection.

Among the many outstanding workshops that of Van Aelst, de Pannemaker and Geubels should be mentioned for the sixteenth century. Jan Raes, Martin Reymbouts and the Leyniers family excelled in the seventeenth. The large and extravagantly designed baroque tapestries of that century were probably less popular in England than sets with subjects taken from Roman or Biblical history. Mythological subjects were also in great favour, especially those set in wooded landscapes and surrounded with rich floral borders. So, too, were *genre* and peasant subjects taken from paintings and designs after the second David Teniers. These so-called 'Teniers tapestries' were in vogue from the late seventeenth and all through the eighteenth century. J. van der Borcht (senior, who also signed himself in the latinized form 'A. Castro'), J. de Vos, and various members of the Leyniers and van den Hecke families are names frequently met with on Brussels tapestries of this period.

The mark, a red shield between two B's (for Brussels, Brabant) is normally seen in the border of a Brussels tapestry since the Edict of 1528 (*see* Introduction). Needless to say, Brussels tapestries vary tremendously in quality. Many seventeenth and eighteenth-century pieces are poor in colour (the reds often fading to brown) and show signs of hurried execution. But the best of all periods can hold their own anywhere, and a good commercial standard for sound but unpretentious tapestry was maintained throughout this long period.

B B

FIG. 3. Brussels mark.

Cartoon: the full-scale painted design according to which the tapestry is woven. The high-warp weaver works with the cartoon on wall or easel behind him. For low-warp tapestry it is cut into sections and placed below the horizontal warp. It is therefore designed left-handed, as it is like a mirror image which will be reproduced in reverse. For this reason a cartoon for low-warp tapestry can always be recognized (*see* Raphael Cartoons). The original sketches from which the cartoons are enlarged are known as *Petits Patrons*.

Chamber: a chamber (or chambre) of tapestries refers to a set meant to cover the walls of a living-room. The expression is often met with in medieval and later inventories.

Denmark: Frederick II engaged Hans Knieper of Antwerp and other weavers to make tapestries for Kronborg Castle in 1577. Much of the set representing his 111 ancestors, himself and son, Christian IV, are still preserved. In the late seventeenth century the Skania Wars were woven in tapestry for Rosenborg Castle. Small workshops have also worked in Denmark, and cushion covers of Danish origin are sometimes encountered.

Ell: the ell (French *aune*) is the measure used for tapestry. The English ell is 45 inches, the Flemish 27 inches, the French $46\frac{3}{4}$ inches. Thus 12 Flemish ells are approximately 7 French, or a square French ell equals 3 square Flemish ells.

England: tapestry-weaving was undoubtedly practised in England in medieval times, but mostly on a small scale for armorial pieces or coarse verdures. Finer pieces may have been worked but cannot now be identified. The weavers' main occupation was certainly repairing the innumerable tapestries which were in constant use, and need of cleaning and restoration. There was a London corporation of Tapissers in 1331. Edward III ordered an enquiry in 1344 and issued a decree relative to this corporation in 1364. Tapestries were also woven in monasteries. There was a 'Tapicer' (as well as a 'webster') among Chaucer's Canterbury pilgrims.

Flemish and Dutch, as well as French, weavers fleeing from religious persecution, settled in England in the sixteenth century. William Sheldon claimed his factory, set up under Richard Hyckes in about 1560, as the first in England. This cannot be strictly accurate, but Sheldon's workshops at Barcheston in Warwickshire and Bordesley in Worcestershire are certainly the first about which anything definite is known and whose productions can be identified. The tapestry maps of local counties are known from fragments bought from his house at Weston by Horace Walpole in 1781; they bear a date 1588. These and another set woven at least a generation later and in good condition, can be seen at the Victoria and Albert Museum. Other hangings from Chastleton House, Gloucestershire (verdures with scenes inset and dated 1595) are known, as well as a considerable number of cushion-covers, which were much used in the days of hard oak benches; also small cushions, book-bindings, and glove gauntlets. Sheldon tapestry is rather coarse and shows analogies in style with the carved wooden fire-places of Elizabethan and Jacobean country houses. To furnish these it was singularly appropriate, and this little weaving enterprise flourished successfully at least till the founding of Mortlake.

The Mortlake factory (q.v.), which began work in 1620, was under royal patronage and vied not unsuccessfully with Europe's other leading centres. It was the only first-rate weaving establishment England has ever had, and it flourished until the Civil War. At the restoration it resumed a more limited activity.

From about 1670 the weavers gradually drifted away to set up independently in Soho and elsewhere. Under Queen Mary, Anne and the first two Georges, English tapestries were made once again in smaller workshops, and though the work was modest it was not unoriginal (*see* Mortlake, Soho). Peter Parisot (a naturalized Frenchman) wove tapestry in Fulham in the mid-eighteenth century, chiefly for upholstery and fire-screens. In Chelsea, Le Blon wove a portrait *Head of Christ* by a patent process; about a dozen examples are known. In the nineteenth century William Morris revived tapestry-weaving at Merton Abbey (1881), and the firm of Morris & Company continued until the Second World War.

Flemish (or Netherlands): the term Flemish tapestry, as distinct from French, is only applicable after the fall of the Burgundian dukes in 1477 (for earlier tapestry *see* Franco-Burgundian). Flanders, Brabant and Hainault, which included the famous tapestry cities of Tournai, the ruined Arras, and the rising Brussels, were then ruled for the Habsburgs by Mary, Governess of the Netherlands, and in 1515 came under Charles V's empire. The Netherlands and France grew further and further apart, and Flemish tapestry became distinct in style and workmanship from French.

Brussels (q.v.) was already in the first decade of the sixteenth century the leading tapestry city, but there was also Bruges, Antwerp, Tournai, Oudenarde and Enghien.

Fig. 4. Oudenarde mark.

The late medieval period was famous for its religious tapestries, finely woven with much silk and lavish use of gold and silver thread; many were made on a very large scale. Brussels was certainly the principal centre for these, but some were probably made at Bruges. The kind of tapestry which Cardinal Wolsey and Henry VIII bought for church and palace can still be seen at Hampton Court and the Victoria and Albert Museum. At this time it was a common diplomatic ruse to be in Flanders 'under cover of buying Arras'. Antwerp, a great seaport, was also a principal market, but tapestries were made there, and the 1544 laws prohibited its use of the Brussels mark (though not wholly successfully). Antwerp catered especially for foreign markets in the seventeenth and eighteenth centuries, England included (*see* Wauters family). Tournai, with high-warp looms, continued to produce pastoral and other subjects in Late Gothic style, which are often mistaken for French weaving. Its decline in the sixteenth century was rapid, and indeed the terrible religious wars severely affected the Flemish looms. The revival inaugurated by the Archduke Albert and Isabella in 1606 was furthered by the renown of Rubens and Jordaens, who both designed celebrated tapestries, and by the Exhibition Gallery established at Brussels in 1655.

Meanwhile at Oudenarde and Enghien a steady stream of less pretentious tapestries were woven and the former remained famous for its verdures (q.v.), adapting its style in the latter part of the seventeenth century to landscape verdures, which were popular throughout the eighteenth century. During the sixteenth, seventeenth and eighteenth centuries the most widely commercialized tapestry was Flemish. It included many different qualities and never ceased to produce masterpieces under special patronage. From Flemish cities weavers were recruited for the several dozen factories which rose and fell in almost every European country.

France: the Hundred Years War reduced French tapestry in the fifteenth century to a secondary position (*see* Franco-Burgundian). But the tapestries woven in the Touraine in the wake of the Court, although not sumptuous, attain the highest level of craftsmanship and artistic effect. Almost all survivors date from the early years of the sixteenth century, although they are completely medieval in feeling. They have always been particular favourites. The *Dame à la Licorne* (Cluny, Paris) has the typical *mille fleurs* field on a red ground. It is the *chef d'œuvre* of this group, which includes the *Vie Seigneuriale* with the more typical blue ground. Touraine weaving is high-warp, the colours are brilliant but restricted in number (15 to 25), the glamorous effects are produced by simple means. It is probable that the weavers were migratory. They worked for the Church as well as the nobility, and the long hangings to go above choir stalls depicting the story of local saints are typical of the school (examples at Cluny Museum, Angers, Beaune). The masterpiece among these religious tapestries is the set of huge hangings of the *Life of the Virgin* at Rheims.

In the mid-sixteenth century a workshop was started at Fontainebleau. Other high-warp workshops were active in France when Henri IV set up an important factory in Paris in 1607. For this he summoned Marc de Comans from Brussels and François de la Planche from Antwerp with a team of Flemish workers with low-warp looms. There was resistance to this, but the factory installed in

FIG. 5. Paris mark.

the Faubourg St Marcel proved a resounding success. Particularly noted for the fine quality of its silken texture and the imposing formality of its borders, its designers included Simon Vouet and Rubens. *Artemisia*, *Constantine*, *Gombaut et Macée* and landscape verdures were among its most famous subjects. The factory was combined with the Gobelins (q.v.) in 1662. (*See also* Beauvais, Aubusson and Felletin.)

Franco-Burgundian: the great development of medieval tapestry seems to have taken place in the fourteenth century, principally in France at Paris and Arras. But the Hundred Years War drove the French Court from Paris to the Loire, and it was the Dukes of Burgundy who patronized the fifteenth-century florescence of tapestry. Apart from the *Apocalypse* tapestries at Angers, woven by Nicolas Bataille of Paris (*c.* 1375–80), and the *Nine Worthies* at the Cloisters, New York, scarcely a fourteenth-century piece is known. Even fifteenth-century tapestries are rare, but the *Clovis* set at Rheims, the *Caesar* set at Berne, and *Alexander* in the Palazzo Doria, Rome, are eloquent remains of famous hangings which figured in inventories and chroniclers' accounts of marriages or court festivities. The Burgundian dukes fostered the arts and raised tapestry to the level of diplomatic gifts as highly prized as gold. Philip the Good inherited Flanders, Artois and Hainault (1384), which included Arras and Tournai, the two great tapestry cities of the fifteenth century. At Tournai were woven the Golden Fleece tapestries (Story of Gideon); Henry VII of England acquired there his *Trojan War* tapestries (at Westminster till 1800) from the renowned Pasquier Grenier; and the *Hunts of the Unicorn* (the Cloisters, New York), than which no finer set exists, shows the extraordinary quality of the Franco-Burgundian school. With Charles the Bold's defeat and death in 1477, French and Flemish tapestries diverged as different schools (q.v.).

Galloons: the plain, ribbon-like outer border of a tapestry. The factory and weaver's mark, when used, are woven into the galloon.

German and Swiss: there are three twelfth-century German tapestries preserved at Halberstadt Cathedral, the earliest known. In the Middle Ages tapestries were chiefly woven in monasteries and convents as altar frontals, or to hang above choir-stalls. But they were also woven with lay subjects, especially as long bands to hang above wainscoting. Romantic love scenes (*Minneteppich*), illustrations of popular romances, wild men and women with mythical beasts, virtues and vices and other allegorical subjects were the commonest. The chief centres of production were in Alsace, in the Middle Rhine, the Upper Rhine (including Switzerland and Lake Constance) and Franconia. The best examples can be seen at Basel, Zürich, Munich and Nuremberg. After the fifteenth century there was a rapid decline in quality.

In the seventeenth and eighteenth centuries the larger German courts each sought to create its own tapestry establishment. The most important of these were at Munich, where Hans von Biest wove *The Months* and other ambitious tapestries for the Wittelsbachs (early seventeenth century), and where Santigny and de Chedeville worked in the eighteenth century. P. Mercier left Aubusson for Berlin in the late seventeenth century; in

1714 he went to Dresden and was replaced by Jean Barraband, whose Bérainesque *Grotesques* are often mistaken for Beauvais weavings. Charles Vigne succeeded him, and his *Chinoiseries* correspond with, but do not closely resemble, the contemporary Soho chinoiseries. In the 1780s Pirot worked at Wurzburg, but his *Italian Comedy* set was a doubtful success.

Gobelins: at the Gobelins (Paris) a royal factory was set up in 1662. Le Brun was placed at its head; there were ateliers of both high- and low-warp weavers; no expense was spared; and all the tapestry was the property of the King. Within twenty years Le Brun and his designers had created several new styles of tapestry and made the Gobelins renowned for sumptuous quality and originality. The different series of *Portières*, the *Seasons and Elements*, the *Months or Maison Royales* and the *History of the King* were novel and wonderful achievements. By 1694 one hundred sets (880 pieces) had been woven, mostly with gold. After Louis XIV's declining later years the Regency and Louis XV styles were reflected at the Gobelins. In 1730 Oudry became director, and though he overemphasized pictorial effects, his *Chasses de Louis XV* was a masterpiece. As at Beauvais, his style gave place to that of Boucher. In the latter part of the eighteenth century Neilson, who was Scotch by birth, was the most influential weaver. Until then no Gobelins tapestry could be bought from the factory, being reserved exclusively for kingly and diplomatic use. France's financial embarrassments led to Neilson's taking special orders from abroad, and the sets of tapestry with furniture to match, as at Osterley, were the result. The classicism of the late eighteenth century did not interpret well in tapestry, and it is difficult to see the nineteenth century as anything but a steady decline.

Gobelins tapestries are always of the highest quality, though many of the eighteenth-century picture-like sets are far from pleasing. Since the Revolution they have always been expensive on the market, if in tolerable condition, and rightly so. Some rather less good tapestries are met with which were made as private orders by the heads of ateliers. They are not marked with the fleur-de-lis and factory name, and can be identified by reference to Fenaille's inventory of the manufacture (*see* Bibliography).

Holland: during the sixteenth-century religious wars many weavers migrated to Holland, notably Francis Spierincx (1592, from Antwerp). He did much work for Protestant English patrons, including *The Armada* set (burnt in the Houses of Parliament, 1834) and the lovely *Story of Diana*, at Knole. Spierincx and Karl van Mander worked at Delft, Coppens at The Hague, and Alexander Baert at Amsterdam, the last two in the latter part of the seventeenth century. Landscape verdures bearing their signatures are sometimes seen.

Ireland: under Charles II tapestry as well as linen was woven at Chapelizod (Dublin). In 1689 John Lovett, its director, fled to England with thirty-eight pieces, but none of these has ever been identified. Under Robert Baillie and the weaver J. van Beaver tapestries were woven for the Irish House of Lords in 1728–9. Two of these, *Defence of Londonderry* and *Battle of the Boyne*, are in the Bank of Ireland, Dublin.

Italy: the Estes set up a notable factory at Ferrara in the fifteenth century under Nicholas and John Karcher. *Playing Boys in Vines* and *Grotesques* can be attributed to this workshop, but it was eclipsed in the sixteenth century by the Medici factory in Florence under John Rost (from Brussels) and Karcher (from Ferrara). At Florence during the sixteenth century many beautiful and unusual tapestries were made. They excelled in the originality of their designs, a lavish use of silk, and certain dyes not met with in other tapestries. Bronzino's *Story of Joseph* and Bacchiacca's *Grotesques* were special triumphs. The workshops were active on a reduced scale throughout the seventeenth century. Outside Florence, where there is a fine collection, these tapestries are very rare. Cardinal Barberini inaugurated tapestry-weaving in Rome in 1633. An important set from there is in New York Cathedral. From 1737 tapestries were woven at Naples.

Looms, High- and Low-warp: *see* Introduction.

Marks and Signatures: *see* Introduction.

Marlborough wars: the Duke of Marlborough ordered tapestries to commemorate his *Victories* (*c.* 1712), which now hang at Blenheim Palace. Woven by Judocus de Vos, they were (probably) designed by De Hondt (and school), who had previously designed the *Art of War*, Series I (1696). The *Art of War* set (woven by Le Clerc and van der Borcht) was popular with the German princes who fought in the War of the League of Augsburg. After the Spanish Succession War a second *Art of War* set, based on the first series and, ironically, on *Marlborough's Victories*, was woven for German princes and English generals (Lords Cobham, Orkney and General Lumley, etc.). For practical purposes it is only necessary to distinguish the *Victories* from the two Art of War series, which often appear on the market and are notable weavings.

Minneteppich: German or Swiss fifteenth-century tapestries depicting scenes of romantic love. The best examples are at Basel (Historisches Museum).

Mortlake: Charles I, as Prince of Wales and later King, took an active interest in this establishment, which worked for the Court and rivalled the Paris factory set up by Henry IV and on whose charter it was modelled. Already active in 1620, Mortlake enjoyed a very high reputation in Europe until checked by the Civil Wars in the 1640s, which also caused the sale abroad of most of its finest works (now in Paris and Sweden). Prince Charles' purchase in 1623 at Genoa for £300 of the seven extant cartoons of the *Acts of the Apostles* by Raphael undoubtedly did much to enhance Mortlake's name. Other notable subjects woven were *The Months* and *Vulcan and Venus* (based on sixteenth-century originals), *Playing Boys* and *Hero and Leander*, designed by Francis Clein, who was brought from Rostock as chief designer. Sir Francis Crane was in charge until 1636, and was succeeded by Sir Sackville Crowe at the Restoration. Rather later Verrio succeeded Cleyn. Among the fifty weavers from the Netherlands, Philippe de Maecht (lured somehow from Paris) was the most notable.

A few good sets were woven under Charles II from the old cartoons, but the more elaborate and beautiful borders were abandoned and a decline rapidly set in. Lord Ralph Montague became Master of the Great Wardrobe and acquired Mortlake in the 1670s. Soon the former, established at Hatton Garden in 1679, incorporated the best weavers from Mortlake. Francis Poyntz, last technical director of Mortlake, who wove the *Battle of Sole Bay* (Hampton Court), worked there as manager (1667–85), as did Stephan Demay and Thomas Poyntz. The Mortlake mark, red cross on white shield, continued to be used, as it resembles the Arms of the City of London.

Fig. 6. Mortlake and Soho mark.

Some weavers left Mortlake to set up independently, as William Benood in Lambeth (*c.* 1670), who signed a *Horses* set at the Victoria and Albert Museum. In 1685 the Great Wardrobe was moved to Soho (q.v.), and Mortlake was finally wound up about the year 1700.

Moth: when infected with moth, tapestry should be sprayed with a solution based on DDT, pyrethrum, or lauryl pentachlorphenate. Silverfish and cockroaches should also be watched for. When stored in a cupboard or chest paradichlorobenzine crystals are an excellent preventative. But they need renewing, as they evaporate.

Norway: tapestry, often medieval in character, continued to be woven as a peasant industry in the seventeenth and even eighteenth centuries, chiefly at Vaage in Gudbrandsdalen.

Petits Patrons: *see* Cartoons.

Raphael's cartoons: Pope Leo X ordered a set of ten tapestries of the *Acts of the Apostles* from Raphael's designs for the Sistine Chapel (*c.* 1513). The cartoons prepared by Raphael were sent to Peter van Aelst's workshop in Brussels for weaving, and seven were in place by Christmas, 1519. The original tapestries are still at the Vatican. The weavers, as was customary, kept the cartoons and many later sets of tapestries were woven from them, or from duplicated cartoons. In 1623 seven of the original cartoons were bought for Mortlake and are now in the Victoria and Albert

Part of a Tapestry from 'The Virtues and Vices': Cupid and Hymen. Tournai, *c.* 1500.
Arditti and Mayorcas.

PLATE II

To face page 40

(B) Teniers Tapestry: The Fish Quay. Brussels, first half of the eighteenth century. *Perez Ltd.*

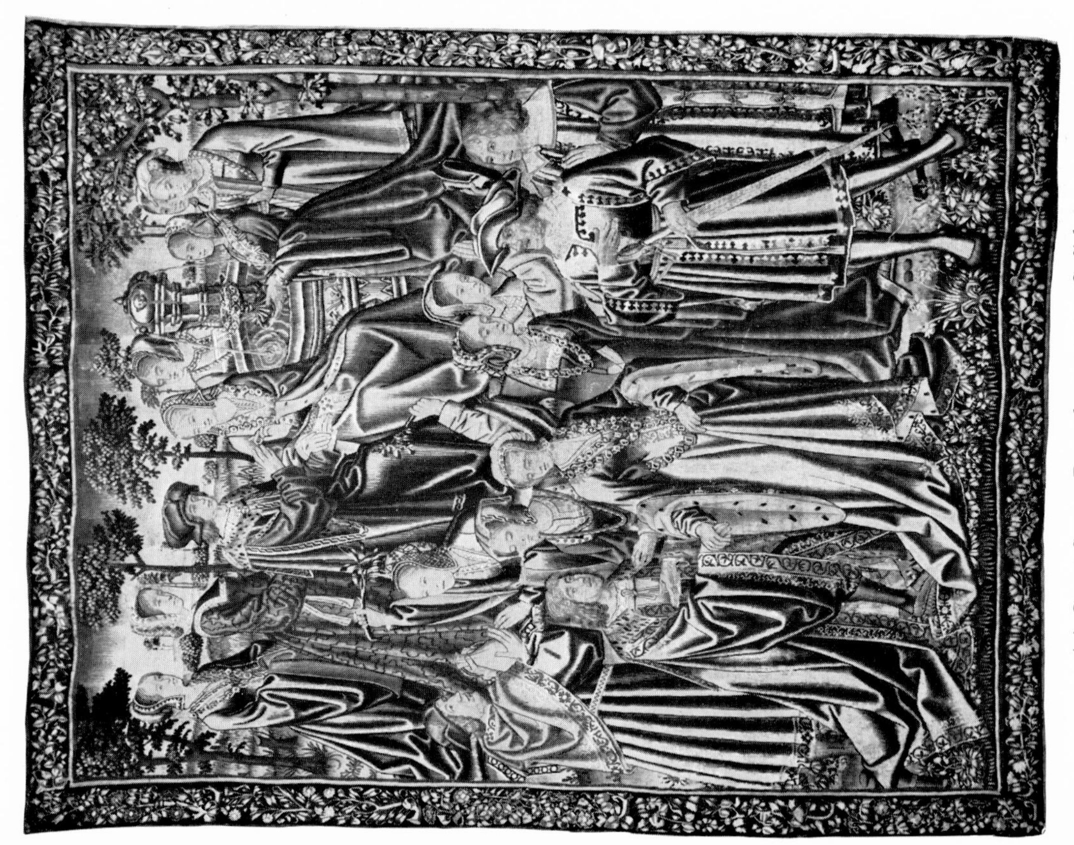

(A) Court Scene. Brussels, 1510–25. *C. John.*

(A) Landscape – Verdure. Brussels, c. 1700. *Perez Ltd.*

(B) Tapestry Screen. Soho or Fulham, mid-eighteenth century. *Perez Ltd.*

Arabesque. Soho (Joshua Morris), *c.* 1725. *The Pelham Galleries.*

PLATE 14

Pile Carpet by Passavant of Exeter, dated 1757. *Victoria and Albert Museum.*

Pile Carpet. Beauvais or Aubusson, late eighteenth century. *The Vigo Art Galleries.*

PLATE 16

Looped Pile Carpet. Spanish, 1797. *Victoria & Albert Museum.*

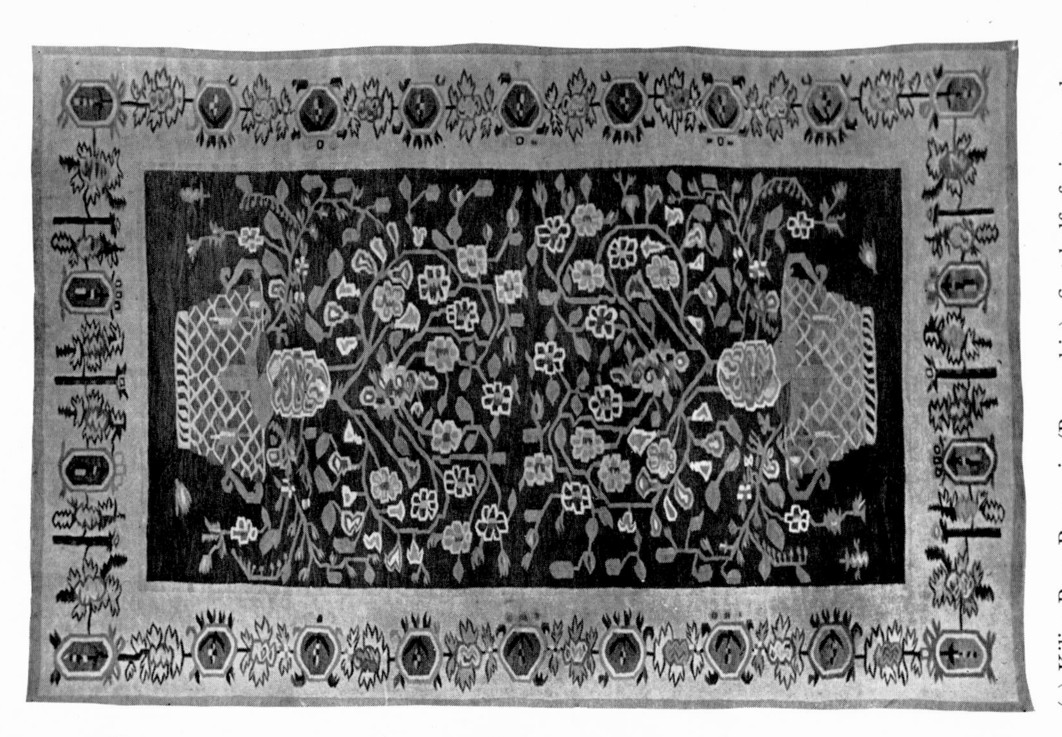

(B) Kilim Rug. Rumania (Bessarabia), first half of nineteenth century. *Perez Ltd.*

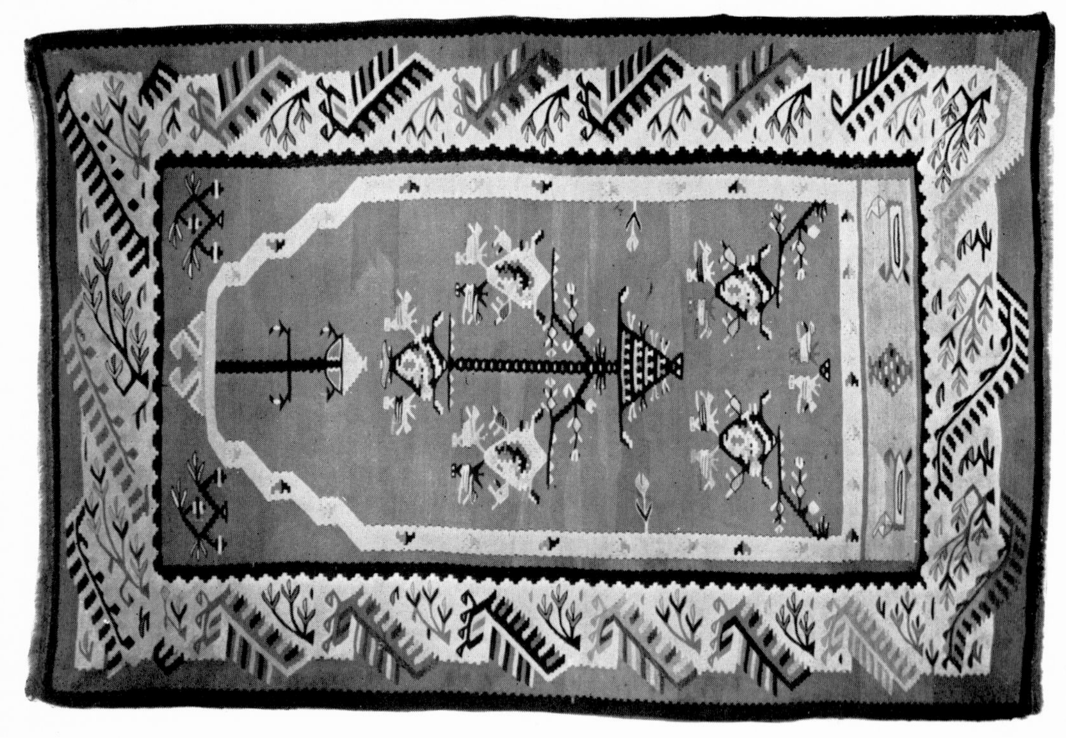

(A) Kilim Prayer-rug. Yugoslavia, first half of nineteenth century. *The Vigo Art Galleries.*

PLATE 18

To face page

Museum. They were repeatedly woven as tapestry at Mortlake, as well as at Brussels and Paris in the seventeenth and eighteenth centuries. The cartoons were drawn in reverse for low-warp weaving.

Repair and Preservation: the old method of repair was re-weaving the worn weft threads, inserting new warps where necessary. Darning the worn parts on to a backing is much cheaper, but when subsequently washed the backing tends to shrink. A stout backing well applied to a tapestry helps to support its weight and can be removed for washing. Washing is generally the only satisfactory method of cleaning, but needs expert handling. Apart from insects (*see* Moth), the chief danger to tapestry is dampness, which causes mildew. Atmospheric humidity is also an important condition in fading, the harm caused by light intensity being relative to humidity. The drier the atmosphere the less harm is done by light.

Russia: Peter the Great set up a factory at St Petersburg in 1716 under Béhagle's son from Beauvais. It remained active, particularly in the mid-eighteenth century, until 1858, copying pictures in the Hermitage Collections, especially by Raphael and Guido Reni. Portraits were also favourite subjects.

Sheldon: *see* England.

Soho: when the Great Wardrobe moved to Great Queen Street, Soho, in 1685, Mortlake was virtually abandoned and Soho became the centre of production, most workshops apparently having some connection with the Wardrobe. From 1689–1727 the leading figure was John Vanderbank. *Chinoiserie* tapestries 'in the Indian manner' on brown grounds were very much in vogue (signed pieces in the Victoria and Albert Museum and Yale University). He was succeeded by Paul Saunders (active as late as 1758), known for his romantic landscapes (*Pilgrimage to Mecca* at Petworth). Joshua Morris wove *Arabesques* (or grotesque) sets designed by Adrian de Clermont, a French immigrant. These tapestries, entirely in keeping with early eighteenth-century taste, are perhaps the most distinguished contribution of the period. Bradshaw, who was connected with Morris at Soho, wove tapestries after pictures by Watteau and Pater in rather questionable taste (set at Ham House). In general, a great deal of tapestry seems to have been woven under William and Mary, Queen Anne, and George I and II. It is simple and unpretentious, small in scale and restrained in design, and the borders are reduced to a minimum. It was designed for the smaller country and town houses and admirably suitable for its purpose. Scenes from Ovid's *Metamorphoses* were the most popular subjects of all. The Mortlake mark was still used. More costly tapestry was, of course, still imported, and also tapestry made at Antwerp especially for the English market by the Wauters family (q.v.).

Spain: an early seventeenth-century workshop in Madrid (St Isabel) was succeeded in 1720 by the St Barbara factory under the van der Goten family, which lasted till 1808. *Genre* and other rustic and everyday subjects were popular, as well as Procaccini's *Don Quixote* set. Goya designed about forty-five tapestries for the factory.

Switzerland: *see* German and Swiss.

Terniers: *see* Brussels.

Verdure: tapestry with a design based principally on floral and plant forms. Sixteenth-century verdures with wonderful scrolling foliage are especially noteworthy. In the second half of the seventeenth century formal verdure patterns changed into landscape-verdures. The many styles of verdure have always been favourite furnishing tapestries. Oudenarde, Enghien, Lille, Aubusson and Felletin specialized in verdures.

Wauters family: Michael and Philip Wauters of Antwerp worked specially for the export trade in the latter part of the seventeenth century. Apart from connections in Vienna, Paris, Lisbon and Rome, they studied the English market carefully and produced for it *pièces de petits dimensions à la mode d'Angleterre*. They imitated popular English sets such as *Hero and Leander*, *Playing Boys*, *Metamorphoses*, and the Duke of Newcastle's *Horsemanship* series. Their mark, however (now established by Mme Crick-Kuntziger of Brussels), is distinctive and their work can nearly always be distinguished from English weaving (*see* Fig. 7). Peter Wauters was also connected with them.

FIG. 7. Mark of Philip Wauters of Antwerp.

(*B*) EUROPEAN CARPETS

When carpets first came to Europe from the Near East in the fifteenth and sixteenth centuries they were used as covers for tables, cupboards and chests, or were placed before the altar in church or chapel. Only kings and the higher nobility used foot-carpets, and they were a mark of rank. A small number of knotted pile carpets in imitation of Oriental ones were made in Europe. English examples date from the sixteenth and early seventeenth centuries. Some of the patterns follow Turkish models, others are like contemporary English embroideries. It was in France, at the Savonnerie, that a Western style of carpet was created which was taken up by different countries when the use of floor carpets became more general in the eighteenth century. But Oriental carpets were also imitated with the needle working in tent and cross-stitch on canvas. In the eighteenth century this was developed into a purely European type of needlework carpet, especially in England. Besides these, cheaper forms of carpeting were used in the sixteenth, seventeenth and increasingly in the eighteenth, centuries. Apart from tapestry, woollen cloth with a nap, patterned ply-weaving, and moquette (woven as a velvet or plush) were used, the narrow woven strips being sewn together.

GLOSSARY

Abruzzi: *see* Italy.

Alpujarras: *see* Spain.

Aubusson: knotted pile carpets were made at Aubusson from 1742 and at nearby Felletin from 1786. An upright loom was used as at the Savonnerie, but the carpets were considerably cheaper. Women, who were not allowed to work at the *basse-lisse*, and children were employed for low wages. Eighteenth-century Aubusson carpets were designed by the Court painters and were of excellent quality. Tapestry or smooth-faced carpets were also made, especially in the nineteenth century. With the Revolution the production of moquette carpets (q.v.) was introduced.

Axminster: Thomas Whitty began the weaving of knotted pile carpets, at first inspired by Turkish models and then learning from Parisot at Fulham (q.v.) (1750–5). In 1757–9 he won three awards from the Royal Society of Arts, submitting six carpets for the 1759 competition. His prices were more moderate than Moore or Passavant (q.v.), and his industry thrived and was continued by his son. The large carpet made for Carlton House (*c.* 1790, at Buckingham Palace) and a fine carpet at Ramsbury Manor, Wiltshire, are surviving examples of his work. A little later Axminster carried out important orders for Brighton Pavilion (1810–20). Parts of these still exist. The Victoria and Albert Museum has a carpet of this period, or slightly later. Before the Axminster workshops closed down in 1835 two important carpets were made for the Goldsmiths's Hall and the Sultan of Turkey. The looms were taken over by Wilton (q.v.).

Beauvais: knotted pile carpets in the Savonnerie manner were made between 1780–92 and again for a few years under Napoleon.

Bessarabia: *see* Rumania.

Brussels carpets: *see* Moquette.

Donegal: Alexander Morton organized the weaving of coarse knotted carpets in Donegal at the request of the Congested Districts Board in 1898. Pile carpets are still woven there.

Exeter: Claude Passavant, a native of Basel, and successful wool merchant and manufacturer at Exeter, started the subsidiary enterprise of making expensive hand-knotted carpets. He bought up Parisot's equipment in 1755 (q.v.) and took many of his men to Exeter. In 1758 he was a competitor for the Royal Society of Arts prize and gained an award. A beautifully made and excellently designed carpet by him in the Victoria and Albert Museum is marked 'Exon 1757' and may be the prize-winning piece. Another dated 1758 is at Petworth. Giuseppe Baretti, secretary of the Royal Academy, wrote a favourable account of his factory in 1760 and reported on his success; but his carpets, which were more expensive than Thomas Moore's of Moorfields (q.v.), are extremely rare.

Finland: the Ryijy (pronounce R-üi-y-ü) rugs of Finland are in the old Norse tradition of knotted pile technique, which may go back to the Danish Bronze Age quite independently of Near Eastern influence, as Sirelius states (*see* Bibliography). Although derived from Norway and Sweden, in the sixteenth century Finnish pile-weaving already enjoyed a special reputation. Made primarily for bed-coverings, sleigh-rugs, or horse-cloths, they have a very long knotted pile, but the ground texture of wool or linen is not thick and there are usually ten to twenty shoots of weft between the rows of knots. The knotting technique is also curious and varied. Made on a narrow

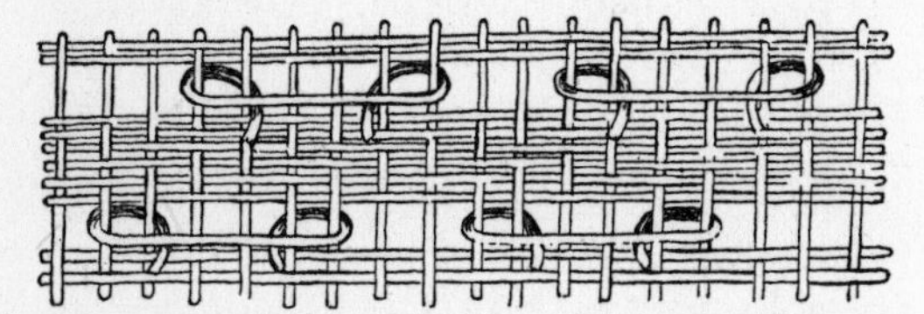

FIG. 10. A variety of Finnish carpet knot. (From U. T. Sirelius, *Handwoven Carpets of Finland*, 1925.)

loom, two widths were joined together, but a wide loom was also used. Patterns vary from plain-colour weavings and geometric motives to simple floral patterns. It was customary for a girl to make a rug for her dowry, and many such pieces are dated, though few after 1860. The making of these exceptionally attractive rugs has been revived in the present century.

Frome: William Jesser, of Frome, entered (unsuccessfully) for the Royal Society of Arts prize for hand-knotted carpets in 1759, but nothing further is known about his manufacture.

Fulham: Peter Parisot, an ex-Capuchin monk from Lorraine, procured the patronage of the Duke of Cumberland for a carpet-knotting factory in Fulham. He is supposed to have employed as many as a hundred workmen, many from the Savonnerie, but owing to extravagances he was forced to sell up within five years (1755). A portrait of the Duke, dated 1755, is probably his work, and pile fire-screens are occasionally found.

Hispano-Moresque: *see* Spain.

Italy: Pope Clement XI founded a carpet-weaving establishment at San Michele, Rome, in the Savonnerie manner (early eighteenth century). Peasant weavers in the Abruzzi highlands and in Sardinia have continued to weave rugs which are really stout coverings for beds, marriage coffers, or carts, although knotted pile pieces and kilims are very occasionally found. Generally they are ply or double-cloth weaves (called *Karamania*) or woven with a floated weft pattern. The patterns have a marked geometric tendency, but derive from traditional Late Medieval and Renaissance designs, just as the better-known Perugia linen and cotton frabrics do.

Jacquard loom: *see* Moquette.

Jugoslavia: kilim or tapestry-woven rugs were woven in Bosnia, Serbia and the Banat throughout the nineteenth century; looped or knotted pile examples are occasionally found. Typical Slav geometric patterns of lozenges and zig-zags are general, with floral and tree motives also treated geometrically. Prayer carpets with a niche are not uncommon. These rugs have many points of similarity with Rumanian rugs.

Kidderminster: probably the oldest centre of rug production in England, the early pieces were smooth-faced and without a true pile—that is to say, a cheap form of carpeting. Kidderminster carpets were often mentioned in inventories: for example, '4 carpetts of Kidderminster stuff', in the Countess of Leicester's inventory, 1634. Two-ply or double-cloth carpets were made there from 1735, when Pearsall & Brown built their factory. But in 1753 Brussels carpets or moquette (q.v.) was introduced by Brown in rivalry with Wilton. A thousand looms were at work in 1807, rising to two thousand and twenty in 1838. Jacquard looms were introduced about 1825, and the use of jute rather earlier.

Kilmarnock: double-cloth carpeting was made from 1778 and three-ply was perfected in 1824.

Moorfields: Thomas Moore, of Moorfields, successfully competed for a Royal Society of Arts award in 1757. An account of his workshop, where hand-knotted carpets of the highest quality were produced, was given by Lady Mary Coke in 1768. A carpet was then being woven for Lord Coventry, to cost 140 gns. Moore was extensively used by the architect Robert Adam, and a number of his carpets have survived in beautiful condition, as well as Adam's designs for them at the Soane Museum. The carpet at Syon House is inscribed 'by Thos. Moore 1769'. There are two at Osterley, made about 1775 and 1778; and Chippendale recommended him to Sir Edward Knatchbull in 1778, who paid him £57 for a carpet for Mersham le Hatch. Moore's carpets in neo-classical design were sumptuous additions to the houses they furnished.

Moquette: woven on the principle of velvet, but in coarser wool and linen materials, moquette is allied with plushes and Utrecht velvet as an upholstery or carpeting material. Tournai seems to have been its chief centre in the Middle Ages. It was much used in the sixteenth to eighteenth centuries. Abbeville was the chief centre of production in France from 1667. Antwerp, Amsterdam, Utrecht and Leyden and Thuringia, in Germany, were other centres of production. Known as 'Brussels carpet' in England, it was made at Norwich and Bradford besides Kidderminster and Wilton in England. The use of the Jacquard loom greatly increased and cheapened production in the early nineteenth century.

William Morris: his first carpets were made about 1878 at Hammersmith (mark: hammer, river and letter M); from 1881 at Merton Abbey. The later two- and three-ply carpets were woven for Morris & Co. at Heckmondwike (Yorks).

Needlework carpets: in the sixteenth and early seventeenth centuries Oriental carpets were much copied in Europe in cross- and tent-stitch on canvas. This was quite suitable for use on tables and cupboards, for which they were intended. There is a good collection in the National Museum, Zürich, and some superb English examples in the Victoria and Albert Museum. In the eighteenth century they were again in favour, but the designs were now purely European, with lavish floral patterns for the floor of boudoir or drawing-room. Many of these carpets have survived in England, but they are rarely found in good condition, as they wear easily. Their beauty depends as much on the brilliant dyes used as on the design. The fashion continued into the nineteenth century, but these pieces can be recognized by design and colour. Italian carpets embroidered entirely in silk are occasionally seen.

Norway: double-cloth rugs for covers and cushions were made in the eighteenth and nineteenth centuries; a looped-pile technique is rarer.

Norwich: Norwich carpets are mentioned in seventeenth-century inventories. Possibly Turkey-work (q.v.) was made there as well as cloth carpeting and moquette (q.v.).

Poland: peasant kilim rugs, like those of the Ukraine and Rumania, were woven in the eighteenth to nineteenth centuries. Some knotted pile rugs of the seventeenth century are also known. They are West European in style and the quality excellent.

Rumania: tapestry-woven rugs were woven in every village as covers and wall-hangings, and many pieces are dated (eighteenth to nineteenth centuries). Lozenge and geometric patterns prevail in Wallachia and Moldavia, floral designs in Oltenia and Bessarabia. The floral patterns tend to be large and sprawling and the field and border are scarcely differentiated. Oltenian rugs are reputed to have the best dyes, and Turkish influence is evident in their more regular and compact designs and their firmer borders. The main tradition of Oltenian designs is supposed to derive from the period of Constantine Brancovan (late seventeenth century). Floral, tree and bird patterns are common in Bukovina. Although apt to be garish and loud, the best Rumanian weavings are a very attractive form of peasant art. Knotted pile rugs are occasionally found in Bessarabia.

San Michele: *see* Italy.

Sardinia: *see* Italy.

Savonnerie: knotted pile carpets in the Turkish manner were first successfully made in France by Pierre Dupont, whom Henry IV installed in the Louvre in 1606. In 1627 the old soap works on the Quai de Chaillot, called the Savonnerie, were acquired and Dupont's partner, Simon Lourdet, began work there with orphan children as apprentices. The Louvre and Savonnerie workshops flourished, particularly under Louis XIV. Large carpets were made for the Grande Gallerie du Louvre and the Salle d'Apollon (pieces still preserved in the Louvre), whilst others were given as diplomatic presents, including one to the King of Siam, which was restored at the Gobelins in 1910. A suite of carpet and upholstery for chairs and settees was made for Mazarin. Pierre Dupont died in 1644 (he wrote a treatise on carpet-making, *La Stromatourgie*) and was succeeded by his son, who removed to the Savonnerie in 1672. During the eighteenth century work continued steadily at the Savonnerie, although many of the workmen emigrated. Not till 1768 were Savonnerie carpets available to private individuals, but prices were very high and few pieces sold. Under Napoleon the looms were kept busy. The Savonnerie was amalgamated with the Gobelins in 1825, where some looms are still at work. It was the Savonnerie which set the standard for European hand-knotted carpets and created a style

FIG. 8. Savonnerie carpet knotting. Note the gadget for forming the knotted loops, which are subsequently cut. (From *Diderot's Encyclopedie*, 1760–80.)

which was copied far afield. Fig. 8 shows the method of knotting used for a line of knots of the same colour; the Turkish knot was used (*see* article 'Oriental Carpets' in *The Concise Encyclopædia of Antiques*, page 224).

Scotch carpets: double-cloth or ply weavings for the floor, also known as Kidderminster or Ingrain.

Spain: Hispano-Moresque carpets were woven in Spain in the early Middle Ages. Unlike Near Eastern carpets, they were generally woven with the single-warp knot.

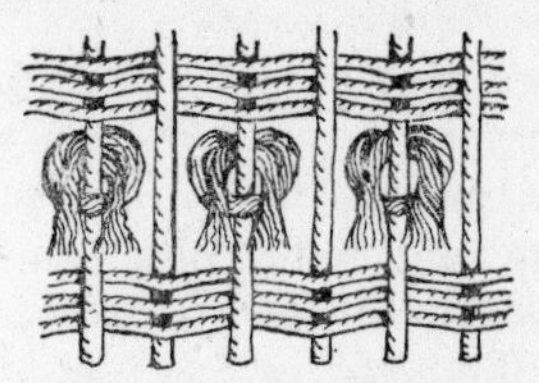

FIG. 9. Single-warp Spanish knot.

Murcia was still the centre of production in the fifteenth century, when many carpets were woven with the arms of leading Spanish families. After the defeat of the Moors, the 'Mudéjar' style, based largely on Renaissance silk patterns, developed in the sixteenth and seventeenth centuries, with important centres at Cuenca and Alcaraz. There is a fine collection of all these types at the Victoria and Albert Museum. There was a royal factory at Madrid in the eighteenth century.

The looped pile peasant weavings, chiefly from the Alpujarras Mountains in South Spain, are the best of all European peasant rugs, and until recently were plentiful and cheap. They were made as bed-covers and rugs for out-of-doors use in a great variety of patterns, often in black and white, but also in red and green and mixed colours. Cross-stitch needlework carpets in similar style were also plentifully made. Cloth rugs or covers with floated weft pattern in wool, like the Italian Abruzzi weavings, were also made in Spain.

Sweden: knotted pile rugs as in Finland (q.v.) were made throughout the eighteenth and nineteenth centuries as well as double-cloth weavings.

Turkey work: this was the name generally given to carpets, cushions and upholstery knotted in the manner of Near Eastern rugs in sixteenth- and seventeenth-century inventories. Apart from larger carpets and rugs, Turkey-work cushions appear to have been made in not inconsiderable numbers in England, though they are now rare. Examples can be dated throughout the seventeenth century, and armorial cushions are noteworthy: for example, a set at Norwich Cathedral (1651); at Pembroke College, Cambridge (1666–7); at Brasenose College, Oxford (1666). In the eighteenth-century cross-stitch embroidery took the place of knotted pile for upholstery.

Ukraine: tapestry-woven rugs, akin to those of Rumania and Yugoslavia, were made as a peasant craft. The Turkish influence in some is clear; others have the sprawling floral patterns akin to those of Bessarabia. West European influence appears in the middle and latter nineteenth century.

Wilton: although a charter for clothiers was granted in 1701, it is doubtful whether carpets were then made there. Lord Pembroke introduced Brussels carpet or moquette (q.v.) looms in 1740. From that date Wilton was in keen rivalry with Kidderminster. The cutting of the looped velvet pile was probably an early speciality of Wilton, a type of carpeting subsequently called by its name. Wilton carpets, made on velvet or moquette looms in narrow strips with simple geometrical patterns, were certainly much used in eighteenth-century houses, as well as the costlier knotted pile carpets. The Brighton Pavilion accounts, for example, record orders for both. It is unlikely that knotted pile carpets were made at Wilton until the acquisition of the Axminster looms in 1835, since when they have continued to work.

BOOKS FOR FURTHER READING

EUROPEAN TAPESTRIES

General

G. L. Hunter, *The Practical Book of Tapestries* (Lippincott, 1925).

Betty Kurth, *Gotische Bildteppiche aus Frankreich und Flandern* (Munich, 1923).

André Lejard, *French Tapestry* (Paul Elek, 1946).

W. G. Thomson, *A History of Tapestry* (Hodder & Stoughton, revised 1930).

Reference

J. Badin, *La Manufacture de tapisseries de Beauvais* (Paris, 1909).

L. Baldass, *Die Wiener Gobelins – Sammlung* (Vienna, 1920–21).

E. A. B. Barnard and A. J. B. Wace, *The Sheldon Tapestry Weavers and Their Work* (Oxford, 1928).

Marthe Crick-Kuntziger, *Maitre Knoest et les tapisseries 'signées'* (Liege, Georges Thone, 1927).

J. Destrée, *Tapisseries des Musées royaux du Cinquantenaire à Bruxelles* (Brussels, 1910).

M. Fenaille, *L'Etat general des Tapisseries de la Manufacture des Gobelins*, 6 vols. (Paris, 1903–23).

H. Goebel, *Wandteppiche*, 6 vols. (Leipzig, 1923–34).

H. C. Marillier, *English Tapestries of the Eighteenth Century* (Medici Society, 1930).

EUROPEAN CARPETS

General

A. F. Kendrick and C. E. C. Tattersall, *Hand-woven Carpets, Oriental and European*, 2 vols. (Benn Bros., 1922).

C. E. C. Tattersall, *A History of British Carpets* (F. Lewis, 1934).

Ciba Review, No. 23, *The European Carpet* (Basel, 1939).

Reference

L. Bracquenié and J. Magnac, *La Manufacture de la Savonnerie* (1924).

E. Dumonthier, *Le Mobilier National. Etoffes et Tapis d'ameublement des 17 et 18 siècles* (Paris, 1910) (*see* plates 6, 22 to 32).

Henri Ernst (edition), *Les Tapis Roumains* (Paris, 1928).

Hispanic Society Handbook (Hispanic Society of America, 1938).

Albert Santier, *Tappeti Rustici Italiani* (1922).

U. T. Sirelius, *Handwoven Rugs of Finland* (1925).

S. Szuman, *Anciens Kilims en Pologne et en Ukraine* (Poznán, 1929).

Zagreb Ethnological Museum, *Peasant Carpets of Yugoslavia* (Zagreb, 1929).

OBJECTS OF VERTU

By A. KENNETH SNOWMAN

The phrase 'objects of vertu' has about it an agreeable air of archaism which is in keeping with the rarified atmosphere in which works of art made by our elders and, in this instance, betters are constantly changing hands. Originally the 'vertu' suggested some magic quality efficacious in the cure and even prevention of diseases of the mind and body, but later this particular aspect was rather forgotten, and the emphasis transferred to the worth of the craftsmanship and the beauty of the materials.

Mallory, in his *Morte d'Arthur* describing the prizes to be awarded to a victorious knight, specifies:

> 'and if so be that he be a wedded man, that his wife shall have the degree, and a coronal of gold beset with stones of virtue to the value of a thousand pound, and a white gerfalcon.'

In the *Aedes Walpolianae* virtu has already about it an unmistakable flavour of rare and curious antiquity.

'Objects of Vertu' as a category nowadays includes most small articles, generally in precious materials, upon which the loving patience of a diligent craftsman has been exercised, such as boxes of all types, card-cases, *étuis*, *nécessaires*, *châtelaines*, and so on. No catalogue of such objects can ever claim to be in any way complete, and the glossary that follows is merely a necessarily simplified introduction to a fascinating subject. I have not included in it such articles as scent-bottles, seals or bodkin-cases, which require no explanation.

Having regard to this limited scope in relation to the immensity of the field, I have thought it wiser to devote the major part of the space available to an examination of fine boxes, in the belief that what is true of these is usually true of all the other articles embraced by the title. The materials and practical methods used in the making of snuff-boxes are discussed in some detail because it is as a result of an exact appreciation of the technical quality of a box that a collector can learn to discriminate for himself between a genuine or spurious article. If a piece is authentic, the period is not difficult to trace. What is not so easy, but far more interesting, is to find the exact town of origin, or even the specific craftsman who made it.

The miniature in art has held a special appeal throughout history, and it is therefore easy to understand why small objects, exquisitely fashioned in precious metals, and sometimes enamelled and set with jewels, should have exerted, and still do exert, an almost hypnotic appeal upon collectors. Originally, of course, most of these objects purported at least to have a practical use. Too much emphasis should not, however, be placed on this, the most humdrum of their qualities. Let us rather frankly declare: 'Give us the luxuries of life and we will dispense with its necessities'.

GLOSSARY

Boxes: apart from those used for snuff, so many different types of boxes appear in museum and auction-room catalogues that

I have thought it useful to include a brief list of those most frequently encountered:

BONBONNIÈRE, DRAGEOIRE, SWEETMEAT OR COMFIT-BOX: boxes containing sweets and cachous for sweetening the breath were normally carried about the person in the seventeenth and eighteenth centuries.

BOITE-À-MOUCHE OR PATCH-BOX: taffeta patches, which were applied to the faces of both men and women, were far more varied and original than is generally supposed. Patterns were by no means confined to a mere modest spot, star or half-moon. We hear of one design, particularly enterprising if a shade overstated, taking the form of a complete coach and horses which covered almost half the wearer's face.

ROUGE-BOX: many round boxes without hinges were designed for rouge. It is incorrect to describe them as snuff-boxes, as these were invariably hinged.

Breloque: a small ornament attached to a watch-chain or *châtelaine*.

Bygones: any large objects no longer in use, such as obsolete agricultural implements, old-fashioned spits, fenders, bellows, and so on.

Callot figures: miniature figures, usually amusing or grotesque, in silver or gold, enamelled or gem-set, are known as Callot figures. This is a reference to the French engraver Jacques Callot (1592–1635), who specialized in vivid drawings of beggars and cut-throats and the swaggering characters of the *Commedia dell'Arte*. Craftsmen of Augsburg and Nürnberg made many figures of this sort, often with a baroque pearl serving as head or body. Italian and French examples are generally more difficult to find.

Camaïeu: a style of monochrome painting.

Carnet: note-book.

Chase: to make grooves or indentations in metal, thus, in effect, to carve in relief.

Châtelaine: a clasp from which various small objects are suspended by means of a chain. Fastened at the waist, the *châtelaine* was originally worn by the mistress of the house, and keys, seals, watches, nutmeg-graters, quizzing-glasses and countless other articles are to be found attached to the ends of their chains.

Giselé: chiselled.

Cochins: the small cartouches or vignettes, named after their inventor, depicting contemporary events. *Cochins* were used decoratively on boxes and many other objects of vertu.

Couvercle à charnière: hinged lid.

Damascene: to inlay one metal with a design in another of contrasting colour such as gold or silver. The name derives from the fine work on the blades of Damascus swords.

Directoire: the style prevalent in France during the period of the Directory, which was in control from 1795 to 1799. Less elaborate than the Empire style.

Emboss: to carve in relief. Literally to cause protuberances or bosses. Chasing and embossing are merely two different ways of describing the same operation.

Enamel: a form of glass which, when heated, may be applied by fusion to a metallic surface. When colourless this is known as flux. Enamel may be *Translucent* or *Opaque*; *Opalescent Enamel* is the term most frequently used to describe the milky semi-transparency which is obtainable by a careful mixture of both.

PAINTED ENAMELS: this process is really self-explanatory. Some of the earliest pieces were enamelled in the very attractive style shown in the Louis XIII comfit-box on Plate 20. Later the Swiss perfected the technique of painting extremely highly-finished scenes and pictures in enamel on a prepared *fondant* ground. Very often a coating of counter-enamel is applied on the reverse side of the painted surface to counteract any stress which may be brought about in the firing.

EN PLEIN ENAMELLING: the enamelling most typical of the Louis XV and Louis XVI periods is known as *en plein*, which indicates that the colour has been applied directly on the body of the object and not on *plaquettes* introduced at a later stage. The gold ground or field is prepared by being carved into and engraved to form a sunken bed, sometimes on several levels, to receive the enamel, the top layer of which should be flush with the gold surrounding surface. This operation is also known as *basse-taille* or *sur fond reservé* enamelling.

(A) Silver and oak Jacobite snuff-box with head of Charles II in the Boscobel Oak with a *putto* supporting three crowns, and two mounted Roundheads. *Hakim.*

(B) Queen Ann engraved silver snuff-box. *Selby Wilkinson.*

(C) George I engraved silver tobacco-box by Edward Cornock, 1714. *Hancock.*

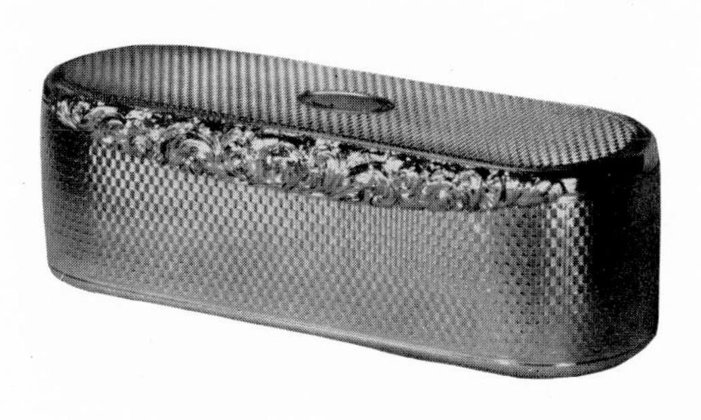

(D) Gold engine-turned snuff-box. London, 1822–3. *Private Collection.*

(E) George III engine-turned gold snuff-box. London, 1807. *David Black.*

(F) Shaped and embossed silver gilt 'Castle' snuff-box. London, 1812. *Hancock.*

PLATE 19

(A) Louis XIII enamelled gold comfit-box, *c.* 1630. *Hakim.*

(B) Engraved gold and polychrome enamelled Louis XV bodkin case. *Hakim.*

(C) & (D) Engraved gold and polychrome enamelled Louis XV snuff-box, by Jean George, 1755–6. Reproduced from *Tabatières des Collections du Musée du Louvre*, by Nocq and Dreyfus.

(A) Three examples of Louis XV craftsmanship: rock-crystal snuff-box gold mounted *en cage*, with a diamond floral thumb-piece; bloodstone and gold cagework *bonbonnière* containing a watch, the key of which is shown below: red and green chiselled gold needle case. *Wartski.* (B) French eighteenth-century tortoiseshell and gold *piqué* box. *Hakim.* (C) Georgian embossed gold quizzing glass. *Private Collection.* (D) Georgian *repoussé* gold pocket telescope set with pearls. *Private Collection.* (E) Georgian topaz quartz and chased gold vinaigrette showing pierced and engraved grille through transparent top panel. Set with turquoise thumb-piece. *Hakim.* (F) Georgian engine-turned gold nutmeg grater. *Private Collection.*

(A) Louis XV *chinoiserie* gold and mother-of-pearl snuff-box decorated in gold relief with astronomers. Sides ornamented with *singeries* playing with mathematical instruments and birds within finely-chiselled wavy gold borders, interior lined with gold. Paris, 1756. Farmer General Julien Berthe. Maker, Jean Frémin. *Spink & Son Ltd.*

(B) Louis XVI gold 'Winter' snuff-box with sepia *grisaille* and green enamelled snow scenes and red, green and white enamelled borders. By Jean Joseph Barrière with mark of Farmer General Jean Batiste Fouache and date letter for Paris, 1779. *Wartski.*

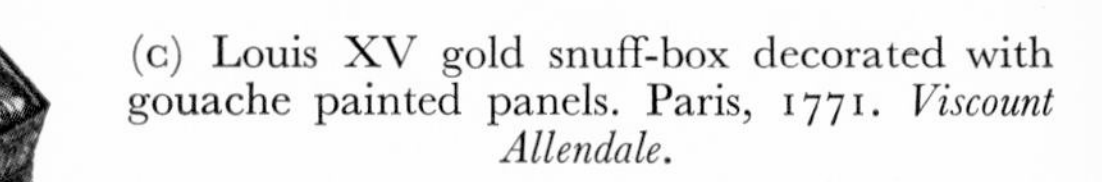

(C) Louis XV gold snuff-box decorated with gouache painted panels. Paris, 1771. *Viscount Allendale.*

(D) Louis XVI gold snuff-box, the lid with a panel enriched with rose diamonds set singly on a background of blue and white enamels, the sidepillars with split 'pearls' in white enamel on a blue field, the base similarly decorated. The royal blue translucent enamel takes on a bright greenish hue when the box is moved. By Joseph-Etienne Blerzy, date letter Paris, 1789. *Wartski.*

(A) French eighteenth-century enamelled gold Callot figure of a monkey in gold as a Chinese Market Gardener, the head and chest in baroque pearls, bearing gem-set fruit in a mother-of-pearl basket and standing on a pearl and lapis-lazuli base. *Wartski.*

(B) Georgian enamelled gold scent *flacon. Wartski.*

(C) Pale blue agate and gold *nécessaire* with gold implements and a diamond push-piece. *Sestieri.*

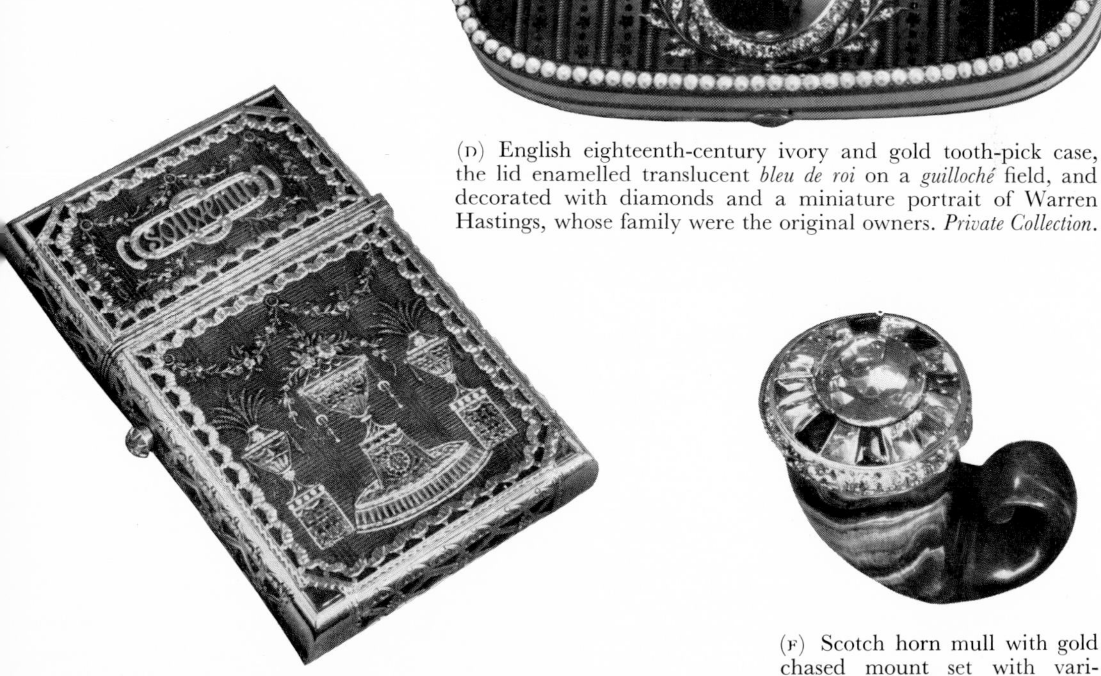

(D) English eighteenth-century ivory and gold tooth-pick case, the lid enamelled translucent *bleu de roi* on a *guilloché* field, and decorated with diamonds and a miniature portrait of Warren Hastings, whose family were the original owners. *Private Collection.*

(E) Early nineteenth-century Swiss gold souvenir case enamelled royal blue with red, green and gold *paillons. Wartski.*

(F) Scotch horn mull with gold chased mount set with vari-coloured semi-precious stones. *Wartski.*

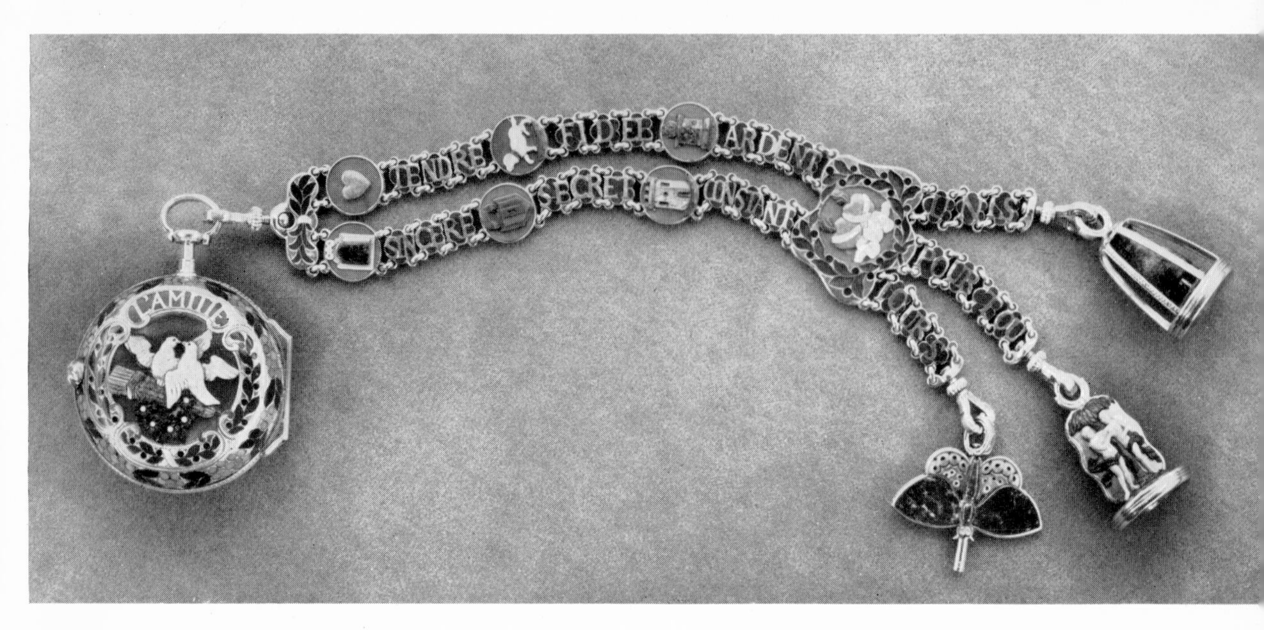

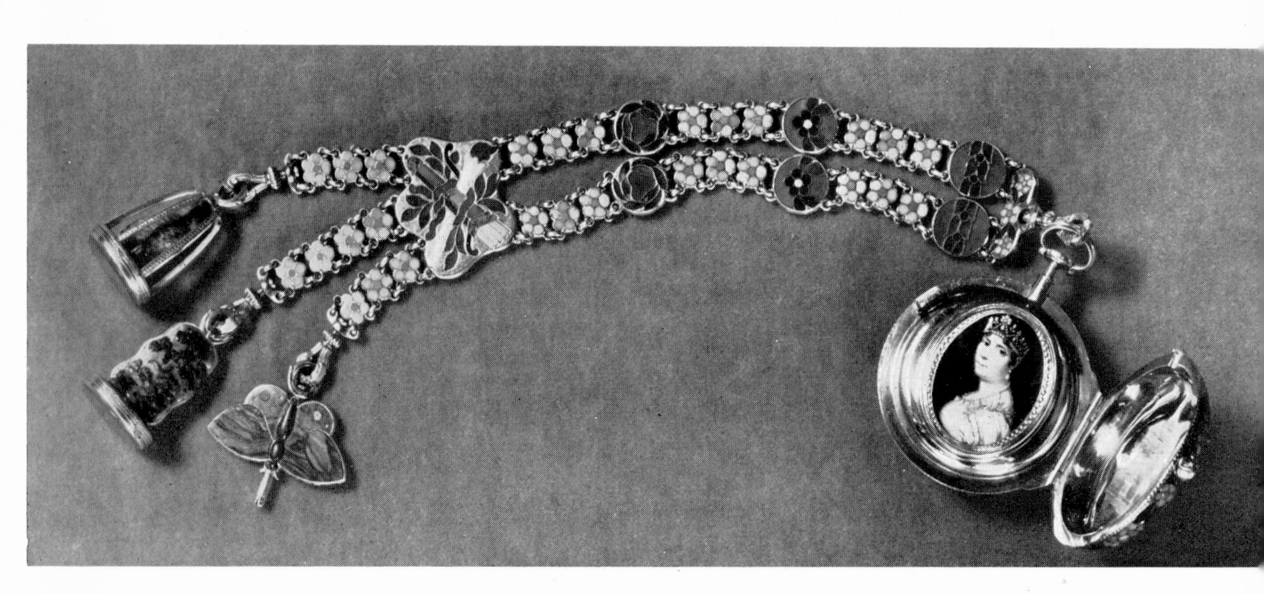

Royal watch and *châtelaine* by Neuber, the watch case decorated in hardstones with two billing doves in relief, inscribed on gold and with lapis inlay *Tendre*, *Fidel*, *Ardent*, *Sincère*, *Secret*, *Constant*, *Unis pour toujours*, each quality set with its appropriate symbol. The reverse of the chain, inlaid on a gold ground with flower heads, hearts, a torch and quiver in hardstones including turquoise, with moth key and two seals in similar technique, one depicting Adam and Eve and the Tree of Knowledge with the serpent and the inlaid word *prudent*, the other an owl in a cage with the word *veillant*. Concealed in the back of the watch by L'Epine is a miniature of the Empress Josephine attributed to Isabey. A gift from Josephine to Napoleon, it was made *c.* 1804. *Wartski.*

PLATE 24

CLOISONNÉ: one of the most ancient forms of enamelling involving the use of a network of raised metal enclosures, or *cloisons*, which is applied to the object chosen. The enamel is poured into these *cloisons*, the metal tops of which remain exposed, allowing the different colours in each one to be distinctly shown.

CHAMPLEVÉ ENAMELLING: grooves, often in very graceful linear designs, are carved in the metal which is to be treated, and these are filled with enamel, which is polished down so that the top surface is exactly level with the surrounding metal. This inlaid enamel is thus, as the name of this technique implies, a raised field.

PLIQUE À JOUR ENAMELLING is the name given to the vivid stained-glass effects obtained when an object consists of an unbacked honeycomb of cells, each filled with translucent enamel through which the light passes freely.

EN RONDE BOSSE ENAMELLING is the term applied to the opaque enamel, generally white, covering subjects carved in the round.

COTEAU ENAMELLING: a complicated process invented by Jean Coteau, the eighteenth-century Geneva craftsman, for which he used different coloured *motifs*, including red and green *paillons* as well as the more conventional gold variety against *bleu de Roi* translucent backgrounds, giving a vivid effect of relief.

Engine-turning: mechanically engraving decorative patterns on a metal.

Engraving: the incising of a pattern on metal with a burin or graver.

Étui: a small case, designed to contain sewing implements, penknives, etc. Formerly also a case for surgical instruments. Although both terms are used rather loosely, the principal difference between an *étui* and a *nécessaire* appears to lie in the fact that the former is to be carried in the pocket, whereas the latter is built to be set down on a table.

Fabergé: born in 1846, Peter Carl Fabergé, a Russian descended from a Huguenot family in Picardy, brought about an extraordinary revolution in taste in the final decade of the century. In brief, he declared that valuable materials were of little importance where the craftsmanship was wanting. He delighted in overcoming technical problems and revived the four-colour gold processes of the eighteenth century as well as the forgotten art of translucent enamelling on a prepared *guilloché* field. He often designed, and always scrutinized at every stage, each piece made by his five hundred or so highly-skilled craftsmen working in St Petersburg and Moscow. These pieces were of great variety and ranged from boxes, clocks and miniature frames to automatic toys and bell-pushes.

His work in every type of semi-precious stone remains unsurpassed, and his lively animal studies and miniature flowers, usually in rock crystal pots which are carved to appear as though they are half filled with water, are eagerly collected. His feeling for the right material was unerring, and his objects, as a result, are invariably informed with an unmistakable vitality. Gold and silver cigarette-cases by Fabergé display a seemliness of style and a precision of hinging rarely attained before or since. Apart from his completely original work, he enjoyed designing *pastiches* of earlier manners, and these exercises today often fetch higher prices than the originals themselves: they are rarer.

Fabergé is perhaps most celebrated for his fantastic procession of Easter Eggs, each with its own concealed surprise, made annually for the Tzar, his greatest patron, to present to the Tzarina. The House of Fabergé had an elaborate but easily understood system of signing the objects it produced. It is therefore absurd and inaccurate, as well as unjust to his many talented contemporaries, to suggest, as does a recent publication on Gold Boxes, that 'the name "Fabergé" denotes not only the works from his own hands and those which he designed but also any beautiful *bibelots*, *objets d'art*, and gold boxes of pre-revolution days'. The firm ceased operating with the Revolution, and in 1920 Carl Fabergé himself died an exile in Switzerland.

Georgette: popular name for a snuff-box made in the style of Jean George, the Paris goldsmith (*see* Plate 20).

Grisaille: a method of painting in grey monochrome.

Guilloché: engine-turned.

Gypcière: an antique purse generally suspended from the girdle and often bearing pious mottoes or texts.

Hand-coolers: semi-precious stones carved in the form of eggs, and of a similar size, for the purpose expressed in their name. Highly polished agates, marbles, and interesting pieces of blue-john were favourite materials chosen for these attractive objects.

Lacquer: a resinous varnish composed of pale shellac in alcohol and various colouring agents. Japanese work in this material reached an extremely high standard, and decorative panels were quite often imported into Europe to be incorporated in the work of goldsmiths here.

Monté à cage: a description of the elegant framework or cage, usually gold or silver, holding together the panels of an object such as a box, *étui* or *flacon*.

Meander: an ornamental labyrinthine pattern of lines winding in and out, or crossing one another.

Mulls: Scottish snuff mulls (the Highland pronunciation of 'mill') vary a great deal within the limits imposed by their form. They are natural horns, sometimes twisted at the tapering end. The open aperture is surmounted by a decorative hinged lid often set with semi-precious stones. The local cairngorm, a pale topaz, is the most usually found. Dr Mott observes in his edition of *Dekker's Gull's Hornbook* that 'The Scotch mull, or sneeshing mull, was often accompanied by a spoon and hare's foot attached by chain, the one for applying the snuff to the nose, the other for wiping the upper lip' (*see* Plate 23).

Nécessaire: a container for miscellaneous small tools and instruments designed for various purposes. Our ancestors entered with gusto into every aspect of living in an embarrassingly complete and thorough manner, and included among the paraphernalia of toilet and household equipment, usually referred to in sales' catalogues as 'implements', we find such engaging items as toothpicks, tweezers, ear-picks and tongue-scrapers. Queen Elizabeth was reputedly never without her ruby- and diamond-studded ear-pick on state occasions.

The more conventional implements to be found in *nécessaires* and *étuis* include snuffing-spoons, pencils, funnels for powders, scent-bottles, scissors and other sewing and manicure instruments, and very often ivory tablets for notes and prescriptions.

The *nécessaires* themselves are made in the same variety of materials as snuff-boxes.

Neuber: Johann Christian Neuber (1736–1808) was the maker of extremely beautiful and original boxes in hardstones. Usually round or oval, these boxes would consist entirely of small-shaped panels of different stones selected for their colour and translucence or opacity, held by a finely wrought gold webbing. The inlay work is of a uniformally high order, the whole surface being absolutely smooth, and the gentle harmonies of tone and colour combine happily with the different patterns, which almost invariably radiate boldly from the centre. Many boxes were composed of stones specially chosen for their local interest; numbers would be engraved on the slender gold skeleton mount, each referring to a particular little stone panel. Inside these boxes, which are known as *Stein Kabinetts Tabatieren*, a book serving as a key should be found listing in full the names of the various specimens numbered on the box.

Sometimes these numbered lists would be hidden within a secret compartment or drawer, which springs open when a particular part of the box is pressed. Miniatures or carved or engraved gem stones are usually set in the centre of the lids. He by no means restricted his expression to boxes alone, and the laborious technique, which was his life work, was used very successfully in the designing of *carnets*, *étuis*, *châtelaines* and centre-pieces, as well as a table and even an elaborate fireplace. **Christian Gottfried Stiehl** (1708–92) was Neuber's most celebrated contemporary working in the same manner, and examples from his hand are equally prized.

Niello: a black alloy containing lead inlaid decoratively on metal surfaces.

Paillons: small decorative spangles in

gold, silver or colours cut into formal shapes and set between layers of translucent enamel.

Papier-mâché: paper pulp mixed with gum arabic or lacquer and china clay is pressed into the form desired, varnished, decorated and given a final glaze.

Piqué: it would be difficult to better Major Dent's classic definition of this charming form of decoration. Accordingly, I set it down in full: 'Gold or silver in point or strip, on either shell or ivory; and if mother-of-pearl be included as a very frequent added decoration, it would, with but few exceptions, cover all *piqué* work from the time of Louis XIII to the present day'.

The gold points or *clous d'or*, as they are called, are known as *piqué point*, and the inlaid strips *piqué posé*. Tiny points of gold tracing the design are described as *foules point d'or*. Early French *piqué* objects often incorporate gnats, flies, vine leaves, birds, clusters of grapes and peacocks, the sunbirds emblematic of Louis XIV, *le Roi Soleil*. Apart from boxes of all descriptions, fans, bodkin-cases, games counters, *étuis*, shuttles, *flacons* and *carnets* are found, to enumerate only a few of the articles chosen for decoration in this manner. The technique was practised principally in France, England, Holland, Spain, Germany and Italy.

Plaquette: ornamental tablet applied to enamelled boxes, *étuis*, and so on.

Pomander: globular receptacle for perfume or aromatic disinfectants, very often divided into hinged cells or *loculi*. Usually in silver or gold, 'musk-balls' were an essential item of equipment when appearances in public were contemplated in medieval and Renaissance times.

Poudre d'écaille: a composition of powdered tortoise-shell coloured to the required tint by a dye.

Quatre-couleur: the art of combining various colours of carved gold in a decorative scheme. The colour of gold is determined by the nature of the alloy. If copper is added to the pure gold, the result will be a red gold, if silver is added a green gold is obtained, and so on. Many subtle effects are possible as the balance of the alloy is varied.

Ramponneau: *Tabatière à la Ramponneau* indicates a box designed in the form of a barrel.

Rasp: a grater. Ivory tobacco-rasps are quite common.

Regence: Philippe d'Orleans was Regent during the minority of Louis XV from 1715 to 1723. This period is not distinguished by any specific style whatever.

Repoussé: metal hammered into relief, the pattern being, as the name suggests, pushed up from the back. A cheap method of treating metal to give an impression of embossing. Many lovely and simply-designed early silver articles have been shamefully ruined by the nineteenth-century craftsman's unholy passion for this technique, which, when employed with a decent control, can yield charming results.

Rocaille: term referring to the liberal use of rococo scrolls and arabesques in the decorative arts.

Samorodok: a technique used by the nineteenth-century Russian goldsmiths for obtaining a 'rough-cast' surface on silver and gold, giving the effect of a nugget.

Sand-blast: a method of obtaining a matt finish on a metal by directing a jet of sand by means of compressed air or steam.

Shagreen: shark-skin often dyed green.

Snuff-boxes: the full significance of the snuff-box is not always appreciated. It was, in small, an elegant epitome of an age of elegance. The gentleman in an eighteenth-century *salon* who brought out his latest box with an elaborate armoury of appropriate gestures and finger movements, did so secure in the cosy assurance of his own superb and unerring connoisseurship, and quietly watchful of the splendid effect his performance of the snuffing ceremony was producing on his rapturous friends.

Anyone with the leisure and inclination to cultivate his taste was far more concerned about the harmonious colouring, and the graceful proportions of his new snuff-box than he was about its success as a receptacle for snuff. It must also be remembered that the standard of taste was a good deal higher two hundred years ago than it is today: and, after all, 'one had as good be out of the world, as out of the fashion'.

Mere serviceability became less and less important as the boxes became more and more elaborate. Miniature paintings were mounted at first under the lid, then, when it was seen that the snuff destroyed their surface, on the lid of many snuff-boxes. Watches were sometimes set inside, and occasionally even tiny musical movements.

There were special boxes for every season and every occasion, boxes for use during the winter months were sometimes decorated with painted panels of snow scenes (*see* Plate 22), those with flowers or romantic *fêtes champêtres*, and so on, would be more suitable for summer wear. A military man, or one interested in music or hunting could have his favourite pursuit depicted graphically on his boxes. The colour schemes and patterns of enamelling chosen were sometimes designed to match a particularly attractive brocade, silk or velvet. The greatest painters in miniature devoted their energies to the decoration of boxes, and such names as Blarenberghe and De Savignac grace the catalogues of the finest collections the world over. Frederick the Great is supposed to have owned a collection of over fifteen hundred boxes.

Many shapes and amusing forms were adopted. One of the prettiest little boxes in the great Wallace Collection at Hertford House, London, is really a tiny golden foot-bath exquisitely enamelled (*see* Plate 27), and there is a particularly enchanting example in the form of a carriage in the Louvre.

Such little conceits known as *fantaisies* do not turn up very often, however, and the collector who finds some comparable treasure can certainly congratulate himself.

Snuff itself was not always popular or even accepted. In 1634 the Tzar Michael of Russia issued a decree to the effect that second-offence snuff-takers should have their noses amputated. Louis XIV was somewhat less drastic in his own treatment of the problem, which he felt was getting out of hand. He is traditionally believed to have ordered his Royal Physician Fagon to deliver a public address setting out in detail the evils of snuff, so that the habit, which was rapidly gaining ground at Court, might be stamped out once and for all. Much of the effect of his eloquence was lost on his audience, however, owing to this gentleman's absent-minded but recurring pinches of snuff. When it became obvious that nothing could be done to stop this pleasurable occupation, the State and the Church, as might have been expected, turned it to their advantage by charging revenues.

The *boite à portrait* was really a snuff-box masquerading under a designedly ambiguous name, the painted likeness mounted on the lid serving as a passport into a court where snuffing was frowned upon. It should be emphasized at this point that women of fashion, no less than men, were great snuffers.

French snuff-boxes: very occasionally a Louis XIII or XIV box makes a brief appearance on the market, but fine examples are extremely rare and very quickly acquired by collectors. The great *Siècle de la Tabatière* is the eighteenth century; and the boxes made in Paris during the reigns of Louis XV and Louis XVI are justifiably prized as vivid and elegant records of an age far removed from our own.

The vicious 'sumptuary laws' in France, which were framed in order to prevent fashionable jewellery being worn by anyone whose blood was not of a sufficiently pellucid azure, were considerably relaxed in the face of mounting indignation soon after the last of them was promulgated in 1701. The stage was now clear for the goldsmiths and allied craftsmen to play their parts freely. Every possible material was used and every conceivable technique employed to produce boxes of startling beauty. Many of these materials and techniques are briefly described under their own headings in this glossary.

In an artistic society the emphasis is always placed on the craftsmanship lavished on an object rather than on the intrinsic worth of the material used, and we find some of the most aesthetically satisfying boxes in wood, steel, *papier-mâché* and horn. Tortoise-shell, mother-of-pearl and natural stone contribute their own particular qualities in endless variations, in addition to the precious metals silver and gold.

Louis XV gold boxes are usually recognizable by their all-over rococo flamboyance – when they are enamelled, the coloured design generally covers the panels of the box in a continuous pattern, often involving the most complicated system of scrolls and arabesques, undisturbed even by the division where the opening occurs. This would never be the case in a typical Louis XVI box, where each panel, whether above or below the division, would have its own completely independent design. It is difficult to avoid describing the majority of the boxes of the Louis XV period as Romantic, especially in view of the aesthetic revolution towards classicism that took place half-way through the century. The wavy line, so characteristic of the flanges, decorations, *plaquettes*, and actual forms of these boxes was superseded by the ordered straight lines, which became fashionable as a result of the concerted efforts of Madame de Pompadour, her talented younger brother, the Marquis de Marigny, in his official capacity as *Ordonnateur-Général des Bâtiments du Roi*, and François Boucher, *Premier Peintre du Roi*.

The crusade towards a sober simplicity became known at the time as *Le style à la Reine*. Nowadays it is described with more constitutional but less historical accuracy as *Le style Louis Seize*. Charles Nicholas Cochin, the engraver and archaeologist, published his famous attack on the *Rocaille* in the *Mercure de France* in 1754, in which he pleaded 'may we not at least hope that when a thing is square without offence, they will leave it so, and not torment it into an absurd design!' Trenchard Cox reminds us that the *Style Louis Seize* 'was crystallized about the year 1760, fourteen years before the accession of the sovereign from whom it takes its name'.

It should not be concluded from the foregoing paragraphs that any eighteenth-century French box will immediately be seen with ease to fall into one or other of these two main classes. Exceptions abound, and examples bearing all the outward characteristics of one reign may be found, on examination, to be stamped with the hall-marks of the other. This is inevitable and understandable, as, after all, each box was made as an individual article by a highly-skilled master-craftsman and not as a mere cypher in a programme of mass production.

Panels and *plaquettes* painted in miniature very often reproduced paintings or details from paintings by artists in vogue or Renaissance masters. Those represented most frequently and with the most consistent success were the French painters of *fêtes champêtres* and *scènes galants* such as Watteau, Boucher, Fragonard, Lancret, and so on. Teniers *genre* subjects were a favourite choice as well as still-life groups and scenes from French and Dutch *paysagistes*.

The amateur who has had the opportunity of handling and examining fine boxes for a number of years often develops for himself a surprisingly sure flair for their period and provenance. The broad distinction between the romanticism of Louis XV and the classicism of Louis XVI work, however, remains valid. The authors of the superb catalogue of the snuff-boxes in the Louvre have observed that the makers of boxes most often represented in collections, and therefore the most prolific, are Drais, Ducrollay, George, de Beaulieu, Sageret, Hardivilliers, Moynat, le Bastier, Tiron and Vachette. They formed a very close society with family as well as artistic ties, just as the Swiss watch manufacturing community is related in our own day. Their particular marks are illustrated below in the section dealing with this fascinating subject.

The French Revolution points the gulf between the works we have been discussing and those that followed. The feeling against the aristocracy and everything that went with their apparatus of gentle living was not as strong as might have been expected. Luckily for the craft which concerns us here, Napoleon was pleased to approve of snuff-boxes, both as containers for the dust he so enjoyed and as carefully calculated gifts when these were required as tangible gestures to help along some diplomatic campaign upon which he was engaged.

The more extravagant forms and designs were, however, generally abandoned and a certain discipline descended upon the Paris workshops. A miniature painting of the Emperor within a frame of diamonds or

'FARMER-GENERAL' MARKS ON SOLD OBJECTS		
Charles Cordier 1722–1727	 	*Charge:* Hand *Discharge:* Holy Spirit
Jacques Cottin 1727–1732		*Charge:* Crowned Dolphin's Head *Discharge:* Crowned Mace
Hubert Louvet 1732–1738		*Charge:* Griffon's Head *Discharge:* Dog's Head
Louis Robin 1738–1744		*Charge:* Foot *Discharge:* Fox Head
Antoine Léchaudel 1744–1750		*Charge:* Arm *Discharge:* Salmon's Head
Julien Berthe 1750–1756		*Charge:* Bull's Head *Discharge:* Hen's Head
Eloi Brichard 1756–1762		*Charge:* Portcullis *Discharge:* Shell
Jean-Jacques Prévost 1762–1768		*Charge:* Interlaced Laurels *Discharge:* Hound's Head
Julien Alaterre 1768–1775		*Charge:* Flower Pattern *Discharge:* Helmeted Head
Jean-Baptiste Fouache 1775–1781		*Charge:* PARIS as monogram *Discharge:* Monkey's Head
Henri Clavel 1781–1783		*Charge:* Two entwined floral 'L's *Discharge:* Alexander's Head or Cherub's Head
Henri Clavel 1783–1789		*Charge:* Two entwined 'L's *Discharge:* Peasant's Head, replaced in 1786 by Parrot's Head
Jean-François Kalendrin 1789–	 	*Charge:* Encircled 'A' *Discharge:* Vine Leaf or Eye

MARKS OF SOME OF THE MOST PROMINENT PARIS EIGHTEENTH-CENTURY GOLDSMITHS	
Noël Hardivilliers Master-goldsmith in 1729	
Barnabé Sageret Appointed to Duke of Orleans 1731	 
Jean Ducrollay Master-goldsmith in 1734	
Jean Moynat Master-goldsmith in 1745	
Jean-Marie Tiron Master-goldsmith in 1748	
Jean George Master-goldsmith in 1752	
Charles le Bastier Master-goldsmith in 1754	
Pierre-François Drais Master-goldsmith in 1763	
Pierre-François-Mathis de Beaulieu Master-goldsmith in 1768	
Adrien-Jean-Maximilien Vachette Master-goldsmith in 1779	
Vachette's mark in the form used during the Revolutionary period	

carved laurel leaves surmounting the lid of a box was a favourite decorative device, and another was quite simply a large initial N. Previous to Napoleon's complete assumption of power the initials R.F., for *Republique Française*, were frequently used.

With the exception of enamel painting on miniatures, which achieved great naturalism, enamel work on the actual body of the Empire box tended to become more formal and monochromatic (*bleu de Roi* was the colour most often employed) as the treatment of the gold areas became more elaborate and new techniques were discovered by the indefatigable *ciseleurs* at the bench.

After Napoleon, the Bourbons saw the decline of this national craft, owing in part to the new commercialism among manufacturers and in part to the increasing rarity of snuff addicts.

The *poinçons* on French gold objects of the eighteenth century are not readily available to the collector, and it is for this reason that the following notes are included here.

Marks on French boxes: the marking of gold articles in eighteenth-century France was strictly enforced by the Guilds, and a complete set of *poinçons*, or punch-marks, comprises the following:

The personal mark of the maker, who was required to show his initials encased in a cartouche beneath a crowned *fleur-de-lis*.

This last emblem was understandably replaced after the Revolution, and in 1797 a new mark, consisting of the maker's initials within a diamond or lozenge-shaped outline, had to be adopted by law.

Together with the maker's mark his personal symbol or '*différent*' is usually punched within two dots (*grains de remède*), a reference to the margin of two grains by which he was allowed to vary the 20¼ carats gold standard.

The crowned date letter D indicates the year 1720, when the *Ferme Générale* was established, and from then on a new letter of the old French alphabet was allocated to every year by the *Maison Commune* (Fig. 1).

The style of lettering altered when a series was completed, to avoid confusion when the alphabet was restarted. From 1784 to 1789 (the year of the Revolution) the letter P was used with the last two figures of the date added, P84 for 1784 and so on, thus: (*right*)

Fig. 1

Fig. 2

The Farmer-General was in effect a collector of taxes, and every goldsmith was required to submit his gold for assay and to pay the tax applicable. His receipt took the form of the charge (*en charge*) mark, stamped when the box was first presented in its unfinished state, and the discharge (*décharge*) mark added when the box was completed and the money actually paid. Each *fermier-général* remained in office for six or seven years and had his own distinctive mark. They were men of substance who paid for their sinecure. A common error, common even in certain allegedly authoritative works, is to regard the gentlemen listed on the left of the opposite page as the makers of the boxes which bear their marks, and not merely government tax-collectors.

English snuff-boxes: the English snuff-box up to the end of the reign of George I exemplifies exactly the famous restraint of the island race about which so much has been written. In silver or gold, the decoration, if any, was generally confined to an emblazoned coat of arms, or an elegantly engraved monogram (*see* Plate 19). The work, proportions, and over-all solidity left nothing to be desired; the designs were always well-bred and stylish without seeming to strain for effect. In form they were inclined to the conventional, rectangular, oval or lozenge shapes being preferred.

The British Isles were characteristically impervious to the various changes of fashion which went on across the dividing strip of Channel, and as the years went by the only real development – there was no departure – took the form of more elaborate and substantial embossed mounts and a tendency towards larger boxes. The typical George III box was composed of gold panels, engine-turned with one of the favourite patterns, barley, fox-head, honeycomb, waves, lines or basket, bounded by raised carved foliate or floral borders. Engraved stone and enamelled panels, miniature portraits and jewelled cyphers, all had their place in the well-disciplined schemes of the British hammermen in their workshops.

Works destined for sale abroad had, of course, to be designed rather differently, and snuff-boxes intended for the French, or the English with French taste, are easily recognizable *pastiches*. The French Huguenots who settled in England in the early part of the eighteenth century undoubtedly brought with them many ideas from their own country. The most celebrated of the goldsmiths who carried out designs in the Continental manner in Britain was George Michael Moser. Born in Schaffhausen in 1706, his boxes were usually oval and brightly enamelled on a *guilloché* field, their lids surmounted by oval portrait miniatures or enamel-painted classical subjects. He was one of the founders of the Royal Academy and its first Keeper.

The German taste for boxes carved in natural stones, such as agate and jasper, is occasionally to be seen in English eighteenth-century examples.

Among the most interesting of these works for export were the imaginative confections of James Cox and his followers for the Chinese court. Often encrusted with carved moss agates, cornelians and other semi-precious stones – even brightly-coloured pastes were not scorned – the boxes and other objects of his manufacture, such as clocks, bottles and *étuis*, usually concealed some surprise in the form of a tiny musical movement, articulated mechanical automata or *scènes galants*.

When a prominent citizen was granted the freedom of the city, it was customary for a box decorated with the suitable insignia to be presented at the same time. These Freedom Boxes were not always rectangular, very often a round form was adopted in which cases there would be no hinge.

With the nineteenth century, and its increased industrialism, the decline in taste so painfully evident in other art forms was not able to disturb the institution of the traditional English snuff-box, beyond a slight coarsening in the carving, an occasional habit of employing several different and clashing patterns of engine-turning on one box and a too frequent deterioration in the matter of proportion and line.

In England 22-carat gold marked with the lion passant was insisted upon by law until 1798, when 18-carat gold was authorized. Instead of the lion passant, a crown and the figure 18 was now the official mark, and the lion passant only struck on 22-carat gold. In 1844 this mark was also replaced by the crown and the figure 22. The lion was not stamped on gold after this date.

Russian boxes: to compare barbaric St Petersburg in the eighteenth century with the sophisticated European capitals is to hold up for comparison a virago with a lady of quality. A wealthy ruling class desperately bent on acquiring the latest luxuries at all cost, quite naturally became a centre, albeit a remote centre, of the goldsmith's art.

Catherine the Great, a lavish patroness of the arts as well as a tremendously vivid personality, assured all craftsmen and tradesmen willing to embark on the long and difficult journey from Europe of a warm and profitable welcome. Thus it was that so many magnificent French, German and English boxes found their way to the best collections in Russia.

Many of these foreign goldsmiths decided to settle in this new country, where their efforts were so richly rewarded. Their work often took on a certain quality native to Russia, owing partly, no doubt, to the influence of the local craftsmen, who were imbued with the old Byzantine spirit. French *pastiches* made in St Petersburg have about them a distinct character which is not recognizably Parisian. Russian Empire boxes are many and various. Alexander I, whose reign opened the nineteenth century, emulated Napoleon's custom of immortalizing himself by having his likeness applied to the centre of the lids of snuff-boxes, more often than not encircled by a frame of diamonds or a wreath of carved laurels.

The boxes of this epoch were very like those in France, with occasional irrepressible

A

B

C

(A) Late eighteenth-century gold and hardstone box, one of the celebrated *Stein Kabinetts Tabatièren*, by Neuber; numbered and containing the original booklet listing 77 stones of Saxony from which the box is composed. Simulated pearls surround a bouquet of flowers in hardstone relief set in the centre of the lid. *Wartski.*

(B) An eighteenth-century Berlin bloodstone and gold snuff-box decorated with *relief mosaik* in stained ivory, mother-of-pearl and lapislazuli. *Wartski.*

(C & D) Moss-agate and chased gold presentation snuff-box from the collection of Frederick the Great, the lid with a wide border of large brilliant-cut diamonds, some with pink and yellow foil, and closely encrusted with smaller diamonds, in the centre a spray of lotus, tulips and other flowers tied with a ribbon band, and similar floral sprays on the sides divided by vertical bands in coloured golds, the base with a narrow foliate border in coloured gold enclosing a hunting scene after Oudry in hardstones and coloured golds in low relief. *Bulgari.*

D

PLATE 25

To face page 56

PLATE 26

(A) & (C) Rock-crystal and gold French Empire rouge box set with a cornelian intaglio within an enamelled border. A fine example of chiselled gold work. *Wartski.*

(B) Eighteenth-century French mother-of-pearl and gold manicure set comprising ivory writing panels, two pencils, and a mirror. *Wartski.*

Reverse of A

(D) Louis XV tortoiseshell and gold *piqué* note-book with a gold pencil.

(E) Eighteenth-century French agate and gold scent *flacon* with an applied floral *motif* in dia-

(F) Eighteenth-century English Shagreen and gold mounted *nécessaire*, with gold implements and two scent bottles with Chelsea

FANTAISIE BOXES

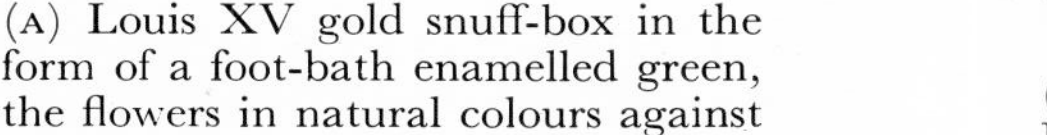

(A) Louis XV gold snuff-box in the form of a foot-bath enamelled green, the flowers in natural colours against brown backgrounds. *Wallace Collection.*

(B) Eighteenth-century silver gilt Dresden box in the form of a shoe, enamelled pale blue with landscapes in natural colours. *Sestieri.*

(C) Late eighteenth-century Swiss gold snuff-box shaped as a tulip, enamelled red and yellow and decorated with split pearls. *Sestieri.*

(D) French Empire chased gold snuff-box designed as a book 1810. *Selby Wilkinson.*

(E) Two Fabergé *bonbonnières*, a slice of crystallized fruit in smoky quartz, and a pale golden quartz crab apple, both set with rose diamonds. *Wartski.*

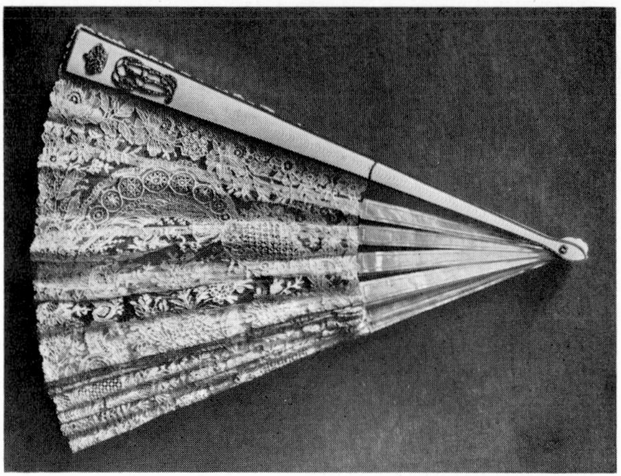

(A) Opalescent white enamelled gold, mother-of-pearl and Brussels lace fan, bearing the crowned monogram of Princess Sofia Demidoff in rose diamonds. *Wartski*.

(B) Rock-crystal heart-shaped cachou box set with rubies and diamonds. *Private Collection*.

(D) Tube of tooth-paste *flacon* in silver and gold enamelled pale blue. *Duchess of Devonshire*.

(E) Raspberries in a rock-crystal jar in rhodenite, nephrite and gold. *Royal Collection at Sandringham*. By gracious permission of Her Majesty The Queen.

(C) Working model roulette wheel in two-colour gold, enamelled translucent grey-blue on a white onyx base. *Private Collection*.

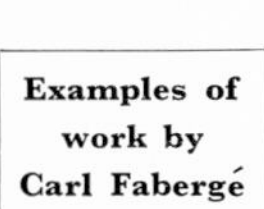

(F) Gold cigarette case enamelled opalescent white, and decorated with floral reliefs in carved golds of colour, with a rose diamond thumbpiece. *Wartski*.

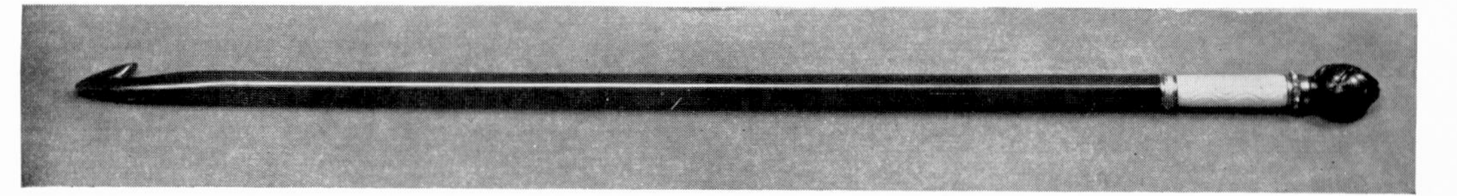

(G) Nephrite crochet-hook with a red and green gold-carved collar, enamelled opalescent white and set with rose diamonds. *Wartski*.

PLATE 28

Russian exuberances in design to disturb the measured discipline of the Empire style. The most notable craftsman of that period was Keibel, whose boxes have now become rare. With the subsequent lowering of standards of execution and taste, the history of the snuff-box in Russia would finish were it not for the name of Fabergé. His achievement is briefly outlined under his name earlier in this glossary. His was not the only firm to make fine boxes, but it was his example and boundless imagination that encouraged such excellent goldsmiths as Morozov, Hahn, Khlebnikov, Ovtchinnikov and Bolin.

The continuous activity in the workshops of St Petersburg and Moscow in the nineteenth century turned out to be a brief Indian summer warming the years before the Revolution which put an immediate and icy stop to all purely creative endeavour in Russia.

German boxes: the rich natural mineral deposits in and around Saxony no doubt account for the tradition, established as far back as the sixteenth century, of using elaborately carved semi-precious stones for decorative purposes. Dresden was the ancient Saxon capital, and it is there that many of the finest German snuff-boxes were designed and made. The sheer delight in selecting a suitable piece of mocca-stone or amethyst-quartz and hollowing out the centre and carving the exterior is easy to understand. Very often these stone boxes were mounted *en cage* so that the beauty of the material is shown to the best possible advantage.

Neuber was the most celebrated of the Dresden craftsmen who employed a mosaic technique reminiscent of Italian *pietra-dura* work, and in many respects deriving from it. It has been very properly pointed out that a similar technique was practised by the Egyptians in the Eighteenth Dynasty. Neuber's work, consisting mainly but not exclusively of boxes, is examined in detail under his own name in this glossary.

Frederick the Great established an industry for the making of snuff-boxes in Berlin with a shrewd eye on the prospects of lucrative results from sales abroad. These boxes were generally encrusted, in direct contrast to the inlay work in Dresden. The use of diamonds set *en masse* and backed with subtly-coloured foil is well illustrated in the splendid agate box on Plate 25.

An effective technique, known as *Relief-mosaik*, involved the cementing of various decorative *motifs* carved in materials such as ivory, sometimes stained, mother-of-pearl or coral, on to the stone body of the box itself. The results of this method were sometimes florid in the extreme, but it is nevertheless true that the world has inherited numerous brilliantly successful examples of this work: 18-carat gold was invariably used, although no marks were insisted upon.

Frederick the Great's craftsmen had been largely influenced by French work, apart from those stone techniques which were peculiarly their own, and, with the closing of the eighteenth century, the Germans relapsed into the ungainly tastelessness that seems to be their birthright.

Austrian boxes: the Vienna of the Hapsburgs in the eighteenth century saw many splendid boxes made under the understandably powerful influence of the French style. The most brilliant artist-designer of the period was Philipp Ernst Schindler. During the latter end of the century the mosaic technique of Neuber spread to Vienna, and, always receptive to ideas from abroad, the French 'Empire' box made its appearance in due course. The four-colour gold work on these boxes was carried out in a particularly lavish and exaggerated form, not always pleasant to behold, and it is this excess, frequently coupled with the unhappy idea of giving their boxes *bombé* sides as though they had been squashed, that distinguishes them from their superior French models.

Alsatian boxes: towards the end of the eighteenth century the family Kirstenstein of Strasbourg were working in a native style which centred round their immense talent for high relief carving in gold. Minutely-carved hunting scenes in realistically expressed forests, markedly German in feeling, seen through protective crystal panels, form the sides, top and bottom of these boxes.

Swiss boxes: the importance of the tourist trade in Switzerland has never been overlooked by its inhabitants, and travellers have invariably been encouraged to acquire souvenirs of their visit to the land of lakes and high mountains. The enamelling industry in the early nineteenth century flourished in Geneva, and gold boxes were produced in prodigious quantities: some for this passing business and others for sale in the Orient. The 'souvenir' boxes usually featured extremely banal glimpses in enamel of local scenic splendour or else selected details from popular paintings by approved old masters.

The artistic cliché, in fact, saw its apotheosis on the banks of Lac Léman at this period. The boxes intended for Eastern markets are, on the whole, far more acceptable, although the exactly opposite view is generally held by museums and collectors in Europe today. They often resemble gay, multicoloured cushions with their fancy shapes and scalloped edges. Cartouches containing trophies, fruit, flowers or groups of musical instruments depicted in brightly-coloured enamels would be set against equally vivid backgrounds. The 'chocolate box' results were not always unpleasing, and there is about them, at any rate, nothing either glum or pretentious.

Fantaisie boxes were produced in great numbers in the form of animals, flowers, books and so on. The tulip box seen in Plate 27 illustrates the style most usually adopted very clearly. The silhouette of the particular subject chosen would form the basis of the box, which was usually shallow. Half pearls (sometimes termed split pearls) set close together often bordered Swiss boxes, and parts of the gold surfaces were frequently reserved and treated in one of a number of traditional ways. A favourite model was the rectangular triptych – the central portions to be filled with snuff and the sections flanking it fitted with a watch movement and sometimes a mechanical scene.

Trefoil and Butterfly boxes were also designed with separate-shaped compartments, each one intended for a different purpose. Swiss enamelling generally is characterized by its bright and brittle appearance. Set an eighteenth-century enamelled French box beside a Swiss example of the eighteen-thirties and the difference is as abundantly obvious as that between champagne and lemonade. The most well-known maker in Switzerland was Jean-Louis Richter (1766–1841), and his best boxes fetch very high prices. The main achievements of the industrious Swiss craftsmen undoubtedly lie in the realm of automata, musical- and bird-boxes, form-watches and complicated mechanisms generally, all of which are outside the province of this section.

Scandinavian boxes: gold boxes of Swedish provenance are frequently thought to be French; their refinement of execution and similarity in design make a close examination absolutely necessary. Franz Bergs (1725–77), the King's own goldsmith, made boxes in Stockholm that yield nothing in delicacy and quality to the finest and most *racé* examples from Paris. Scandinavian 'Empire' boxes are also extremely distinguished.

Vernis-Martin: About 1740 Robert Martin discovered his celebrated formula while searching for the secret of Oriental lacquer. His glazed varnishes, with their decorative paintings on *papier-mâché*, wood, ivory and metal were often mounted as boxes, *carnets* and *nécessaires*.

Verre eglomisé: a method of soldering gold leaf or a painted surface between two thin glass panels.

Vinaigrette: small box fitted with a hinged inner lid or grille, sometimes simply perforated or, more often, pierced in elaborate and attractive designs. A perfumed sponge is secreted underneath this grille and the aroma escapes through it when the box is opened. Usually in silver or gold, vinaigrettes are often beautifully engraved or chased.

BOOKS FOR FURTHER READING

Antique Gold Boxes, by Henry and Sidney Berry Hill. (Abelard Press, New York, 1953.)

Antique Jewellery and Trinkets, by Fred W. Burgess. (London. George Routledge & Sons Ltd, 1919.)

Livre Journal de Lazare Duvaux. (Paris, 1881.)

Piqué – A beautiful Minor Art, by Herbert C. Dent. (*The Connoisseur*, 1923.)

Tabatières des collections du Musée du Louvre, par Henry Nocq et Carle Dreyfus. (Paris. Les Editions G. Van Oest, 1930.)

The Book of Snuff and Snuff Boxes, by Mattoon M. Curtis. (Liveright Publishing Corporation, New York, 1935.)

NETSUKE AND INRO

By M. T. HINDSON

THE conventional dress of Japan had no pockets, so it was convenient to carry necessities attached to a cord, at the end of which was a toggle to be pushed through the belt to hold the objects secure. This toggle was called a 'netsuke' (=end attachment) and was carved to represent various subjects. One of the necessities carried at the other end of the cord was an 'inro' (=seal case), which was a small box of one or more sections fitted together and lacquered or carved with pictures of sundry subjects. The cords were threaded through an 'ojime' (=a cord-holder), which could be slid down the cord to hold the inro shut (Plate 29A). Other objects thus carried included brush-and ink, flint-and-steel, wallet, pipe-case and tobacco pouch. The heavier the weight to be carried the larger the netsuke had to be.

The Japanese were fond of art in miniature, as is illustrated by their tiny gardens of dwarfed trees and their *haiku* poems, which condensed into seventeen syllables the whole of the poet's thought. This national genius for condensation was brought to a high pitch in netsuke and inro, not only by their small size but by the subject's symbolical and reticent treatment. As they were commonplace things of everyday use, however, they were never expected to portray the sublime thought of a religious painting but rather to represent in a homely or even jocular way the charms of daily life. For this reason they are sometimes made light of, but for this very reason they, even so, have a general appeal.

(*A*) NETSUKE

The early history of netsuke is very obscure, for they were then considered to be of no value and would be thrown away when chipped or worn, like an old glove. The earliest book that discusses them seriously was the *Soken Kisho*, published in 1781 (hereinafter referred to as *S.K.*). This book (in Vol. 7) mentions about fifty carvers' names and discusses their work, with illustrations, so that we know the types of netsuke prevalent at that time. Some had evidently been brought from China (known as *Tobori*= Chinese carving), where indeed the netsuke may have originated, as the dress was similar. These early netsuke were generally made of ivory and not signed by the maker. They were chiefly made in the capital cities of Tokyo, Kyoto, and Osaka, where ivory was more readily obtainable, or the smaller town of Nagoya, where wood was the medium chosen. By the end of the eighteenth century more artists took up the profession of netsuke carving and then began the great era of this art, when artists became better known and took to signing their work. At first the netsuke were simple and bold in design, but towards the middle of the nineteenth century the designs became more naturalistic and intricate, while at the end of the century the simple rotundity of the piece was sometimes sacrificed to the fashion for detail. After the revolution of 1868 European dress gradually came into favour and the need for netsuke declined; they were then made for export as European collecting then began. Under this stimulus the art degenerated into commercialism and great numbers of spurious pieces were turned out, though many fine netsuke were still made, and indeed still are.

The commonest form of netsuke is one with two holes at the back for the cord to pass through, often one hole being larger than the other, to take the knot of the cord. When there is some natural aperture in the design, these holes (called *himotoshi*=cord passage) are unnecessary, though they are sometimes added. Some netsuke of a long shape were intended to be stuck between the belt and the dress, the cord-hole being at the top – these were called *Sashi* (=stuck-in) or *Obi-hasami* (=held between belt) (Plate 29B). Another form was solid and rounded with a spindle through the middle, pierced to receive the cord; these were called manju (=cake) and were generally incised with a design in *intaglio rilevato*, though sometimes carved in openwork (Plate 30A). Mask netsuke are not much different from the ordinary form, and represent the masks used in the national drama, etc. The holes are at the back, usually on a bar across the hollowed mask which strengthens it (Plate 30B). A frequent form consisted of a metal disc inserted in the top of a round ivory or wood casing; these were called *Kagami-buta* (=mirror-lid) (Plate 30C). Less common forms were box netsuke (*hako*), ash-tray (*sui-gara-ake*), compass, sun-dial, etc.

Various sorts of ivory were used, including marine tooth, which is hard and takes a fine polish. Almost all hard woods were used and even the softer ones, which, however, were generally lacquered over in colours, except by the Hida school, who used Korean pine unlacquered for their cubist carvings (called *ittobori*=one cut), where the sap-wood, being of a lighter colour, was utilized in the design (Plate 30D). Stagshorn was popular, being hard and cheap. Bullock horn was plentiful, but liable to split and rarely used. Antelope horn is harder (Plate 30E). Bone is common in early netsuke, but fell out of favour as ivory became more readily procurable. Tortoise-shell was used as the different colours showed up attractively on a polished surface (Plate 30F). *Umimatsu*, or brown coral, is a hard substance found in coastal districts and was often employed effectively. *Umoregi*, or jet, takes a beautiful polish but is rare (Plate 31A). Jade, amber, crystal, porcelain, and many other materials were used. Sometimes a combination of substances was used, notably by the *Shibayama* family, who gave their name to the method of introducing coloured inlays of shell, etc., into their ivory carvings. Later artists developed this inlay work to include many materials such as metal, and when restrained this can be very beautiful, but if exaggerated it becomes too showy (Plate 31B).

The subjects represented in netsuke are countless. In early days the immortals and mythical creatures were largely in vogue. The twelve animals of the Zodiac had special significance, being allocated to the hours of the day and night and also to the years. All natural history has a favoured place in Japanese art which occurs nowhere else to the same extent, hence plants, fruits, insects, birds, reptiles, fishes, etc., were frequent subjects. There were also all the legends, myths, and historical figures; also symbols of luck and emblems of long life; there is no space here to particularize these, as this has been adequately done elsewhere. Saints, lucky gods and religious characters were also portrayed, and often in a humorous or irreverent manner. Japanese national customs were also illustrated, such as the Tea Ceremony, Noh Drama, Festivals, Games and Toys, Artisans' Tools, Domestic Utensils, etc., all found a place in netsuke and, in fact, quite an ethnographical collection has already been made of the wide range of subjects of this kind.

There have been well over two thousand makers who have signed their works besides a host of others who worked before it became the fashion to sign or who worked for private patrons and were too modest to sign (Plates 31C and D). When a piece is not signed one must judge its date and value by its appearance alone and assess that elusive quality which may entitle it to be called a work of art. When it is signed, however, one should know something about the man who made it, the sort of work he did and the way his work is appreciated. The signature, of course, does not make a work of art, for many could imitate a signature who could not create a masterpiece, and indeed the signatures of well-known masters were often enough forged. A forger, however, is not often a great artist, or he would sign his own name, so with care a forged signature can generally be detected. Of the two thousand odd artists, about a hundred of the most important are listed below.

GLOSSARY

Anraku: End eighteenth century. A great master who had talented pupils with similar names.

Bazan: 1833–97. Wood. Noted for his rotten pears. Signed in relief. (Plate 31E.)

Chohei: Eighteenth–nineteenth century. Lacquered work with inlays. (Plate 31A.)

Chokusai (b. 1877): A late craftsman who did superlative work in ivory, carefully finished and beautifully stained. Most expressive. (Plate 29A.)

Deme: Family of early mask carvers. Their signatures on mask netsuke usually indicate them to be copies of their original large masks.

Doraku: Early nineteenth century. Excelled in delicate ivory carvings of animals, shells, etc.

Dosho: Pupil of above: similar work, beautifully done.

Gambun: Eighteenth–nineteenth century. Celebrated for representations of mushrooms, etc., overrun by metal ants, snails, etc.

Garaku: Mentioned in *S.K.* Great talent in ivory animals. Also wood.

Genkosai (b. 1806): Original and clever. Ivory shells, etc., which often were carefully carved in the interior.

Goho: Early nineteenth century. Subtle carver of shell groups, etc. All his work possesses great distinction and finesse. Close observer of nature. (Plate 31F.)

Gyokkosai: Eighteenth–nineteenth century. Ivory figure groups with fine facial expression.

Gyokuhosai Ryuchin: Mid-nineteenth century. Ivory groups of fishes, etc. etc.

Gyokuyosai: Eighteenth–nineteenth century. Chiefly ivory. Master of above.

Gyokuzan, Asahi: 1842–1923. A famous modern whose work is rare. Was a priest and carved skulls to perfection.

Hakuryo: Mid-nineteenth century. Tiger groups, etc., in ivory. Plentiful.

Hakuunsai (b. 1853): Prolific carver of ivory mask groups. Good work. Father also.

Harumitsu: Mid-nineteenth century. Wood animals; inventive yet realistic.

Hideharu: Early nineteenth century. Delicate compositions in wood, sometimes erotic.

Hidemasa: Early nineteenth century. First-class artist, especially of ivory figures with decorated dress. A signature which is often forged.

Hikaku: Early nineteenth century. Small ivory netsuke, well carved.

Hironobu, Kakuyusai: Early nineteenth century. Tasteful carver; some inlay work.

Hojitsu: Early nineteenth century. Variety of subjects in wood with consummate skill and inventiveness. A later artist with this name made ivory manju, etc.

Hokei: End nineteenth century. Specialist in red lacquer (over wood). Professor at the Tokyo Art School. Justly renowned. Rare.

Horaku: Early nineteenth century. Rare artist in wood. Sometimes worked in *umoregi*.

Hosai, Oishi: 1828–1900. Skilled artist, chiefly in wood.

Hoshin: Mentioned in *S.K.* Versatile artist in wood and ivory.

Hoshu: Late artist in wood with inlays in the Tokoku manner.

Houn (b. 1824): Renowned artist in wood. Granted the title of '*Hogen*'.

Hozan: Mid-nineteenth century. Genius in wood. Given the title '*Hokyo*' for his Buddhist figures.

Ikko: Early nineteenth century. A great master in ivory animals, etc. More than one artist of this name, whose signatures are different (*see* signature below). (Plate 32A.)

Ikkosai: Mid-nineteenth century. Ivory groups of figures, etc. More than one artist.

Ikkwan: Mid-nineteenth century. Most illustrious artist, who made wood animals with fine hair work, beautifully finished; his rats were especially famous. Chiefly used plum wood of a mellow colour. Inconspicuous masterpieces.

Ippo: Early nineteenth century. Shell groups in ivory.

Issai, Ogasawara: Illustrations of his work given in *S.K.*

Issan, Sa: Early nineteenth century. Animals in wood. Most skilful treatment. (Plate 32B.)

Itsumin, Hokyudo: Mid-nineteenth century. A cunning artist in wood animals.

Ittan: Mid-nineteenth century. Animals and gods in wood.

Jobun: Eighteenth century. Wood figures. Master of Joryu.

Joryu, Shounsai: Eighteenth–nineteenth century. Pupil of above. Legendary subjects in ivory.

Joso, Miyasaki: Late nineteenth century. Founder of a school of craftsmen in wood at Tokyo, who mostly took the character '*so*' into their names. Faultless work.

Jugyoku, Ryukosai (b. 1816): An artist of first rank who used all materials with equal mastery. In portrayal of human physiognomy he was unequalled. Some of the work bearing this famous signature seems to be counterfeit. (Plate 32C.)

Kagetoshi: Eighteenth–nineteenth century. One of the great masters of this early period. Excelled at finely hollowed-out work in ivory of scenes with animals and figures under trees. An exceptional craftsman whose work was badly copied and forged.

Kikugawa: A family of ivory carvers who chiefly made *manju*.

Kisui: End eighteenth century. Carved figures, demons, mermaids, etc., with great distinction.

Kiyokatsu: Mid-nineteenth century. Ivory groups of fruits and vegetables of exquisite beauty.

Kohosai, Ueda: Early nineteenth century. Various subjects in ivory always with great originality and skill. Especially fond of botanical studies. (Plate 32D.)

Kokei: Early nineteenth century. Excelled at small netsuke of wood animals, especially tigers (the '*ko*' in his name means tiger). Belonged to the *Minko* school.

Kokusai (b. 1835): A most individual artist who chiefly used stagshorn. He was an 'entertainer' in the Yoshiwara quarter of Tokyo and made netsuke as a side-line, full of witty inventiveness. He usually signed '*Koku*' only. A man of genius who could not be forged (*see* Rensai).

Komin: Although several artists bore this name, they wrote it in different ways. This late artist had an unmistakable signature followed by his *kakihan* (=seal), and worked in tortoise-shell and wood, often lacquered. His range was unlimited and his work is characterized by exquisite delicacy and refinement. Once his work is known it is easily recognized again. (Plate 30F.)

Koseki, Naito: Late nineteenth century. A shrine carver in wood who made some netsuke to special order. Two of his netsuke are illustrated in the famous collection of W. L. Behrens, which consisted of nearly six thousand netsuke and were sold at Glendinings in 1913–14. A modern genius.

Koun, Takamura (b. 1851): Late ivory carver of great talent. Rare.

Kusai: Intricately detailed work in wood. Rare.

Kwaigyokusai Masatsugu (1812–92): Front-rank artist whose works are in great demand. He used ivory and often made netsuke which opened to reveal the most intricate work inside. His minute care is noticeable in the way the eyes of animals are inlaid like jewels. In his long life his style varied and he used different variations of his name. (Plate 32E.)

Kwanman: Early nineteenth century. A rare artist who showed fastidious taste. He worked with relish and never repeated a model. He usually signed as 'living at Iwami' in beautifully firm characters. (Plate 30E.)

Kyokusai: Late nineteenth century. Beautiful wooden figures with ivory additions.

Kyokuzan: Late nineteenth century. Naturalistic carver in wood and ivory. Rare.

Masachika: Early nineteenth century. Noted for his monkeys in wood.

Masaka (b. 1868): A most realistic late artist in ivory rats, etc., who became famous. His work was bought by the Emperor.

Masakatsu (b. 1839): Son of Masanao I of Yamada. His work was in his father's style but even more beautiful and skilful. Because of his poor health his work is rather scarce. He died in 1899. (Plate 33C.)

Masakazu: There were at least eight artists with this name. One took his name from Masanao of Kyoto and another from Masanao of Yamada and yet another from Tomokazu of Gifu. Their respective works resembled those of their masters.

Masanao: Two great masters bore this name besides about ten others. One was Masanao of Kyoto, mentioned in the *S.K.*, a most fertile genius in ivory and the founder of a famous school. He usually signed in an oval cartouche. (Plate 33A.) The other was Masanao of Yamada, who lived later (1815–90) and worked in wood, especially making naturalistic animals. (Plate 33B.) His pupils, Masanao II and Masanao III, did similar work from the same models, and indeed it is difficult to separate their products.

Masanobu, Adachi (b. 1839): Obtained the title of '*Hogen*' for his sensitive work in carving minute interior landscapes in ivory which are remarkable *tours de force*. His works are scarce.

Masayoshi (1819–65): Master of above. Wood animals with distinction of design and exceptional workmanship, easily recognizable by the pointed paws of the animals.

Masayuki, Hoshunsai: Eighteenth–nineteenth century. A most accomplished and original artist in stagshorn. A pupil of the same name worked in wood and used his master's *kakihan* (=seal).

Minko (1735–1816): Mentioned in the *S.K.* One of the great masters in wood whose works have special character. The weaker examples bearing this signature may have been by pupils in his studio. (Plate 33D.)

Minkoku, Genriosai: Eighteenth–nineteenth century. Two early masters of this name, one of whom sometimes signed '*Genriosai*' only. Chiefly wood figures. Later men with this name did less distinguished work.

Mitsuaki (b. 1848): Most accomplished in ivory and wood, often beautifully inlaid. Was a court artist and a professor of the Tokyo Fine Arts College.

Mitsuharu: Mentioned in *S.K.* School of Masanao of Kyoto.

Mitsuhide: Eighteenth–nineteenth century. Excelled at monkeys in ivory and wood. (Plate 33E.)

Mitsuhiro, Ohara (1810–75): A genius in the cunning imitation of nature with delicacy of finish and tasteful staining of ivory. Fond of botanical subjects, but very versatile. The peculiar charm of his work is difficult to analyse; it always has an elusive 'quality' which is affecting. Unfortunately, one often sees coarser pieces signed with his beautiful signature and rather rawly stained, which look very like forgeries. (Plate 33F.)

Miwa: The earliest artist of this name is mentioned in the *S.K.* and flourished at that time (1781). He made small netsuke in heavy wood of figures with masterly facial expressions. Later pupils bore the same name and did similar work but had slightly different seals – not always used, so the detection of forgeries, if any, is difficult.

Natsuki: Eighteenth–nineteenth century. Distinguished work in wood and ivory. Rare.

Natsuo (1828–1898): A metal craftsman of undoubted genius, who occasionally made discs for Kagami-buta. Very rare.

Okatomo: Mentioned in the *S.K.* and justly famous for animals and birds (especially quails) in ivory. His fame has, however, attracted forgers more than any other name except Tomotada, and most horrible stained netsuke are seen bearing this distinguished signature (generally quails). Happily, the other members of his school who did similar work have escaped this indignity. Okatori, Okakoto and Tomokoto made beautiful netsuke which were never counterfeited.

Otoman: Early nineteenth century. A famous carver of ivory animals, especially tigers. Rare.

Rakumin, Ho (1804–77): Granted the title of '*Hogen*'. Celebrated for wood figures, etc. Often added sobriquets to his signature.

Rantei: Mid-nineteenth century. Ivory animals. Granted the title of '*Hogen*', which he signed on his best work, which was truly inspired, but much was turned out of his studio of a commercial nature, perhaps made by pupils, of whom there were many – Ranko, Ranichi, Ransen, etc. His signature is given below and an example of his work in Plate 33G.

Rensai (b. 1832, retired in 1876): His work shows great individuality, somewhat resembling Kokusai (q.v.) in style, in his preference for stagshorn and in his habit of omitting the '*sai*' (meaning 'studio') from his signature.

Ritsuo (1663–1747): Celebrated lacquer artist. Netsuke rare.

Ryo: Modern ivory artist who did work similar to Saneo, skilful but often too fragile for true netsuke. Appreciated in Japan.

Ryomin (b. 1833): Belonged to a large school where several artists had this name. Manju and dainty figure groups. They chose the inside of the tusk, which is denser, whiter, and takes a fine polish. (Plate 30A.)

Ryukei: Worked 1804–30. Awarded the title of '*Hogen*'. Founded a school in Tokyo, of which some later members bore the same name. Wood figures of superb design, sometimes with ivory additions.

Saneo: Modern ivory artist who made intricate figure groups which generally require such careful handling that they are 'false netsuke'.

Sanko: Mentioned in *S.K.* Ivory figures. His tiny signature is often hidden in a corner or the folds of the dress, and has to be searched for.

Sansho, Kokeisai (d. 1936): Most original artist in wood of figures treated humorously or even fancifully. Sometimes inspired.

Sari: End eighteenth century. A truly creative artist in wood animals. Rare.

Seimin: Several well-known artists of this name. One did fine work with walnut shells and another humorous groups of ivory frogs.

Seiyodo: A renowned family of carvers living at Iwami at the end of the eighteenth century. The founder was Tomiharu (born 1733). Their work has an intimate character and each piece is unique, usually bearing an inscription in tiny calligraphy. The daughter, Bunshojo, who died in 1838, also made fine netsuke, beautifully signed in raised lettering, as also did the grandson, Gansui. This distinguished group, which included Toshiharu, Kwanman, and Goho, carried the art of netsuke-making to a high level.

Sekishu: Mid-nineteenth century. Carved wooden tortoises up to a great age which, according to the inscriptions, exceeded one hundred years.

Sessai (1821–1880): Granted the title of '*Hokyo*'. Used wood and *umimatsu*.

Shibayama: A family who gave their name to their characteristic inlay work.

Shoko: Mid-nineteenth century. Excelled at wood animals, especially frogs.

Shugetsu, Higuchi: Mentioned in *S.K.* Granted the title of '*Hogen*'. Founded a school of wood-carvers in Tokyo and left several pupils and descendants. Principally wood figures (gods, demons, ghosts, etc.) of a decided character. Many of his pupils were almost equally distinguished.

Shuzan, Yoshimura: An outstanding artist described by the *S.K.*, where illustrations of his original genius are given. He was granted the title of '*Hogen*' and exercised great influence on the netsuke-carving of his time. He is said not to have signed his work and, as much of it was copied, the collector must decide for himself its authenticity. They were large figures in soft wood, lacquered over. The signature found on some smaller pieces of the same type, but newer, is probably intended to mean that they were copies of his work though they were done by a man who took that name.

Soko (1868–1935): One of the most brilliant carvers of the Joso school. Chiefly wood figures crisply cut showing remarkable vitality. (Plate 30B.)

Sukenaga: Early nineteenth century. Leader of a school at Hida who had two completely different styles of work: (1) cubist animals in soft wood (Plate 30D) and (2) highly naturalistic carvings of reptiles, etc., in hard wood. There were many members of this school who all took their master's initial syllable '*suke*' into their names. All their work is very fine of its kind and can hardly be distinguished from that of their master.

Tadakazu: End nineteenth century. Famous for wood tortoises. His work was copied by pupils, and much of that is of a commercial character.

Tadatoshi: End eighteenth century. Pupil of Tametaka. Wood animals well composed and carved. Many of his pupils took the '*Tada*' into their names. They all did beautiful work – Tadakuni, Tadayuki, and Yukitada – but the greatest of them all was Tadayoshi.

Tadayoshi: Worked 1830–60, and was

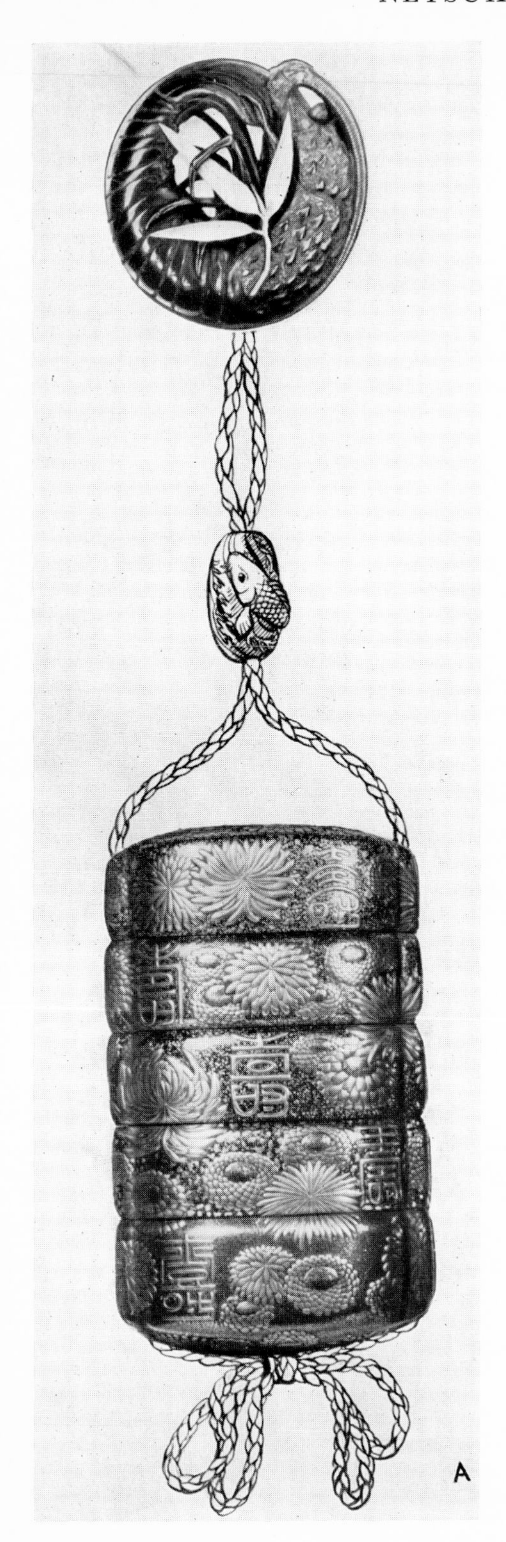

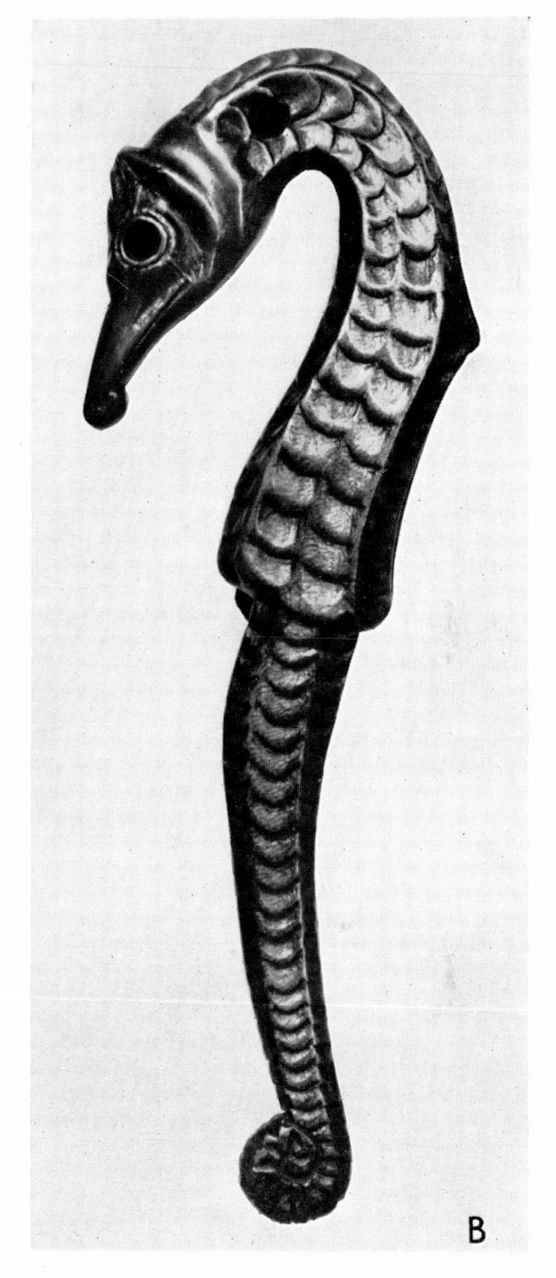

(B) Sashi netsuke.

(A) Inro by Kajikawa of Chrysanthemums and the JU character (=long life) in gold takamakiye on different grounds in each section. Netsuke of Crayfish (=long life) by Chokusai. Ojime of Carp and Waterfall (=pertinacity).

PLATE 29

To face page 64

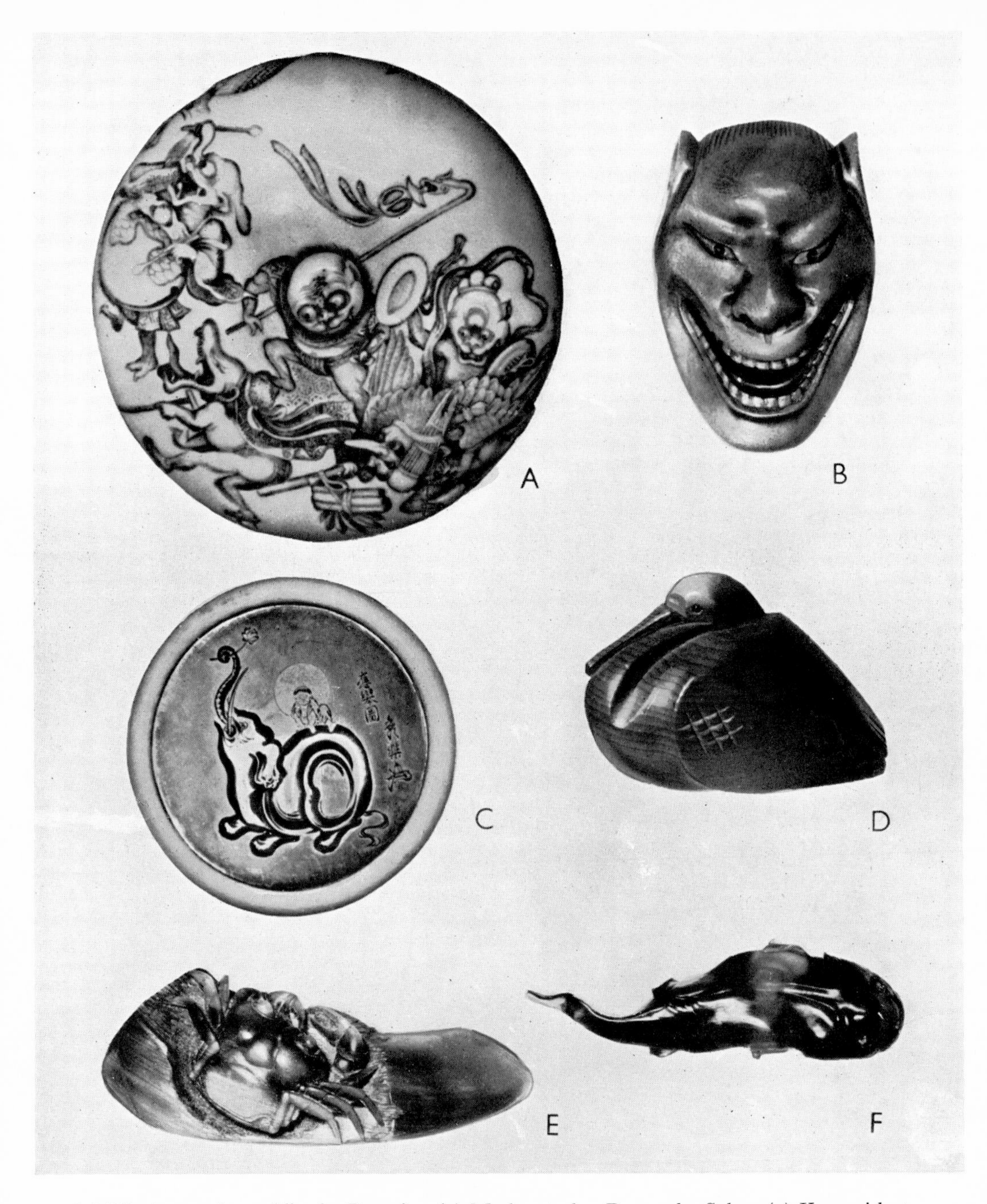

(A) Manju netsuke: goblins by Ryomin. (B) Mask netsuke: Demon by Soko. (C) Kagami buta: Fugen on elephant by Shuraku. (D) Made of Korean pine. Ittobori work. Crane by Suketoshi. (E) Made of antelope horn: Crab on seaweed by Kwanman of Iwami. (F) Made of tortoiseshell: Catfish by Komin.

PLATE 30

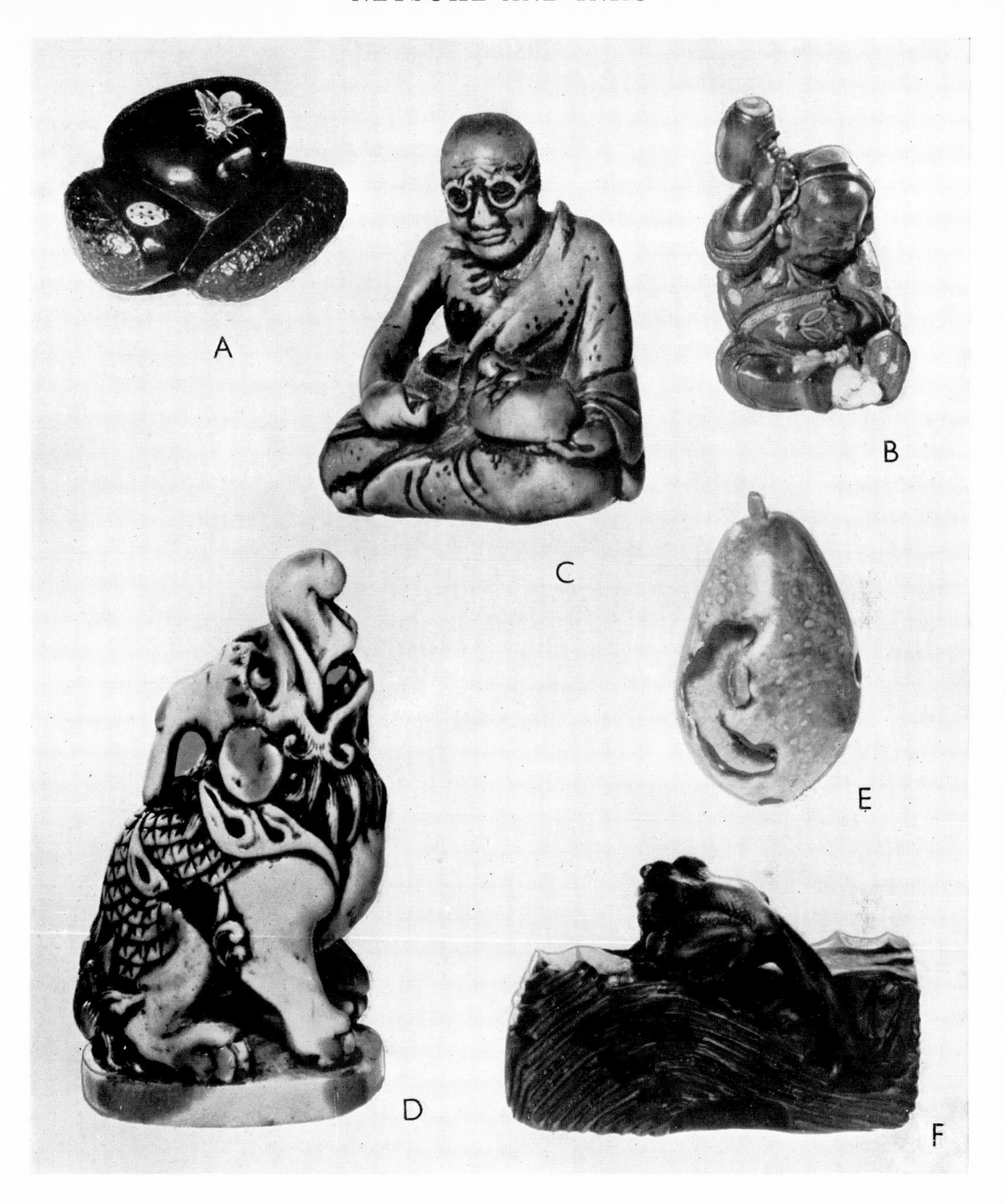

(A) Made of Umoregi: Chestnuts and insects by Chohei. (B) Made with various inlays: Daikoku, god of wealth, by Tokoku. (C) Early unsigned netsuke of a maskmaker. (D) Early unsigned netsuke of a Baku, the devourer of bad dreams. (E) Rotten pear by Bazan. (F) Frog on rotten log by Goho.

PLATE 31

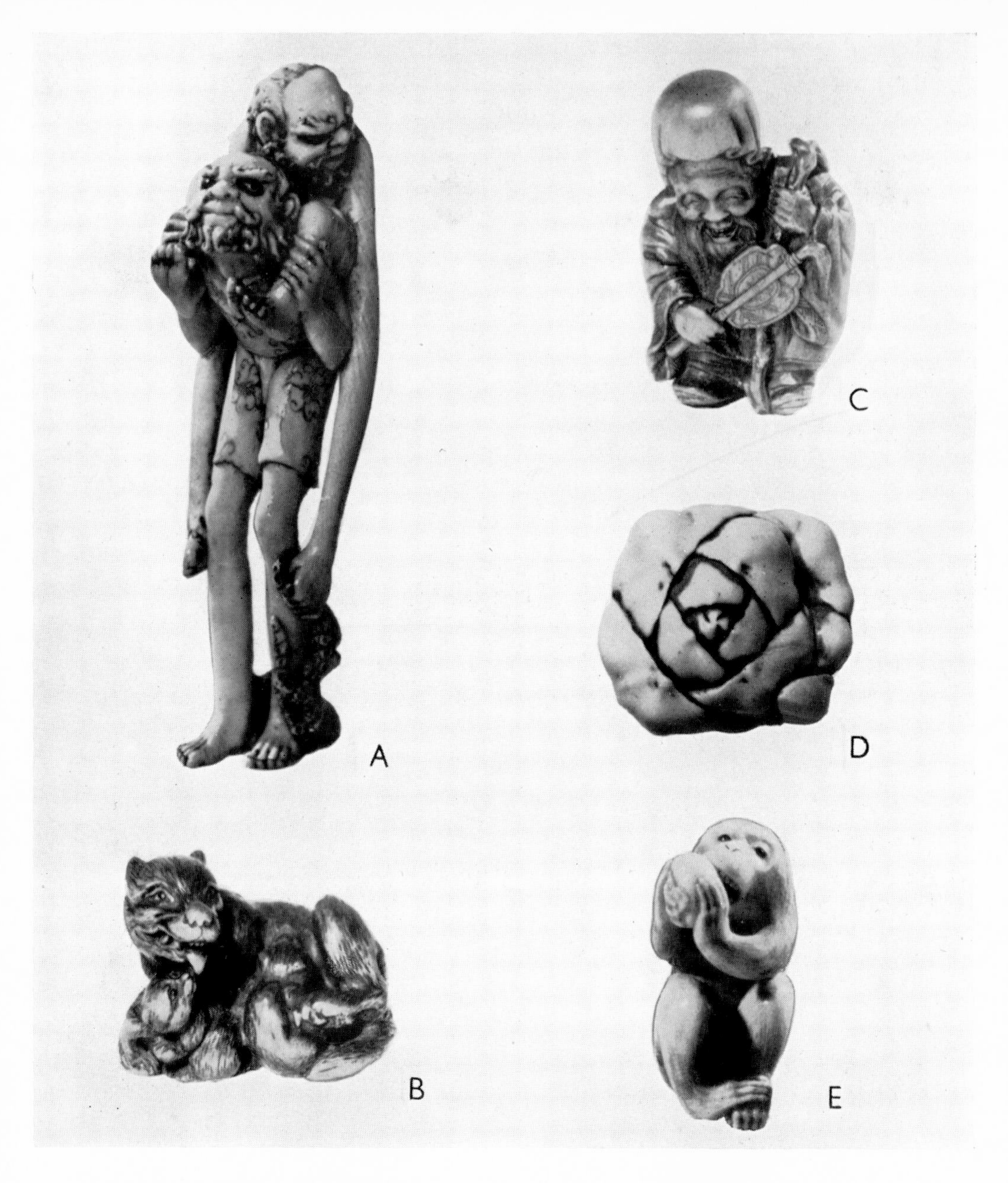

(A) Ashinaga and Tenaga by Ikko. (B) Bitch and pups by Issan. (C) Fukurokuju, god of longevity, by Jugyoku. (D) Lily bulb by Kohosai. (E) Monkey and persimmon by Kwaigyoku.

PLATE 32

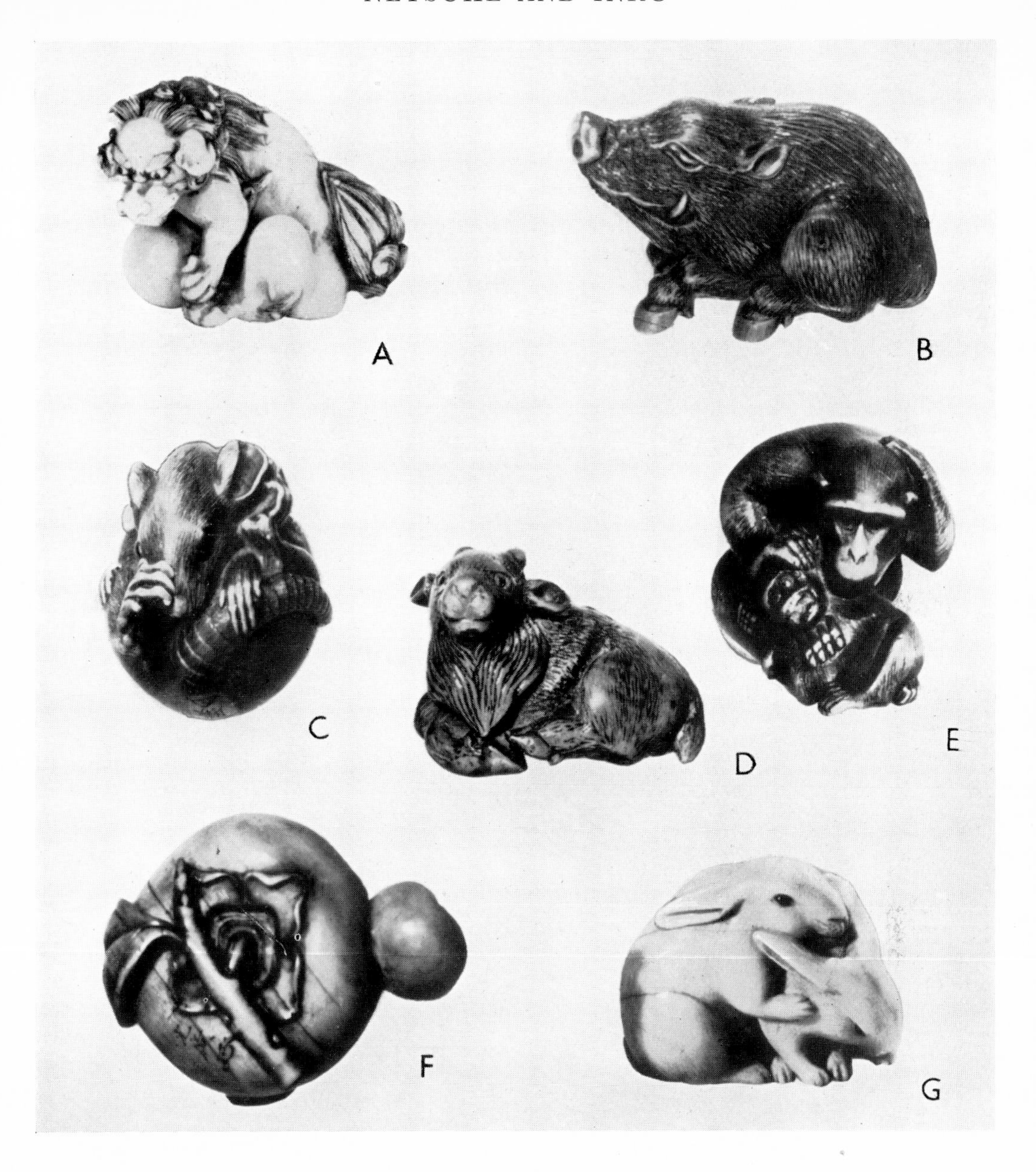

(A) Shishi by Masanao of Kyoto. (B) Boar by Masanao of Yamada. (C) Rat by Masakatsu. (D) Goat by Minko. (E) Monkeys by Mitsuhide. (F) Persimmons by Mitsuhiro. (G) Rabbits by Hogen Rantei.

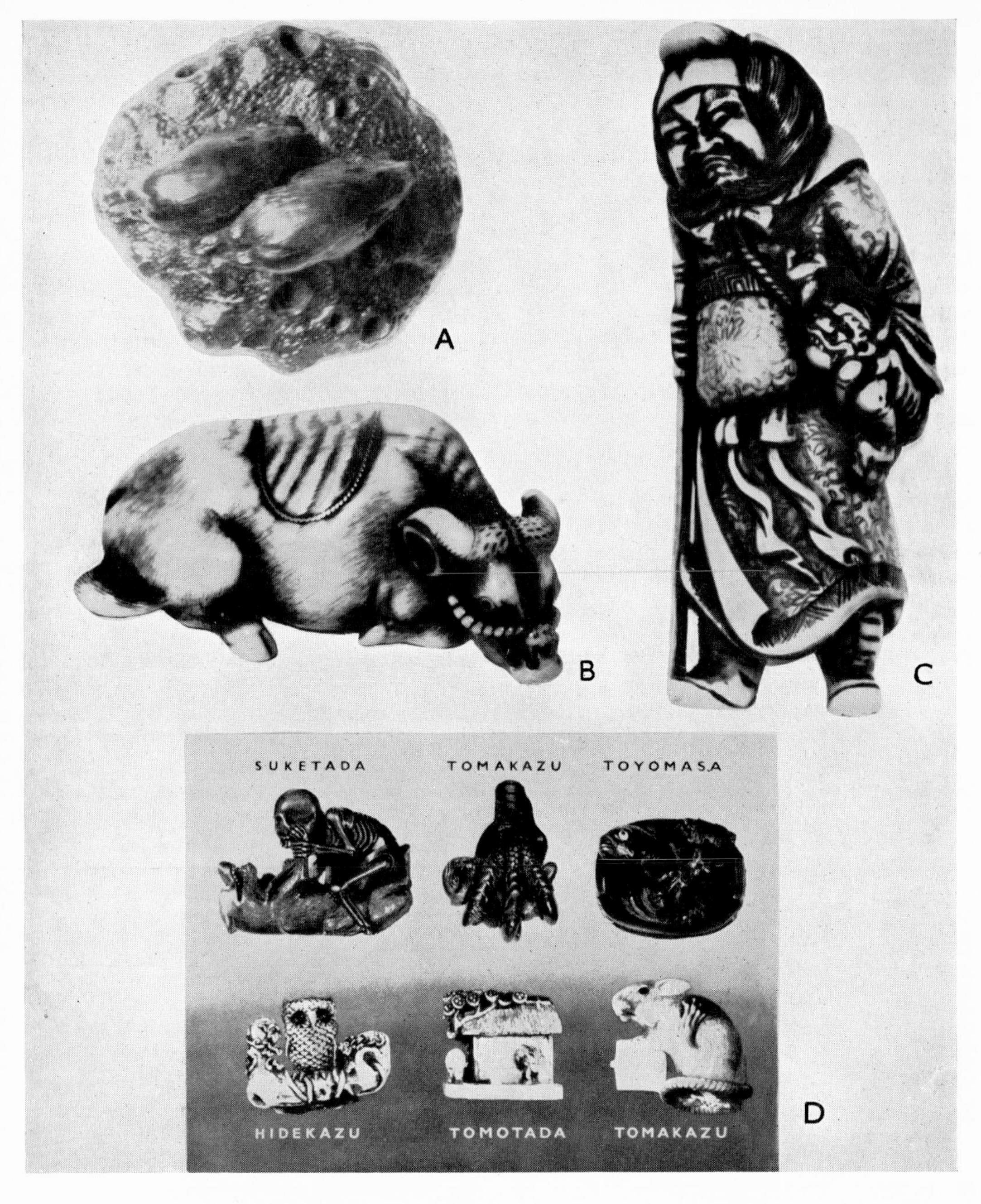

(A) Boars on a rock by Tametaka. (B) Ox by Tomotada. (C) Shoki, the demon-queller, with captured demon, by Yoshinaga. (D) Six masterpieces. These are about half natural size.
Sidney L. Moss.

PLATE 34

To face page 65

granted the title of '*Hogen*', which he often introduced into his signature. His works are unspectacular creations, full of subtlety and beauty and distinguished by their faultless finish. He used the raised signature common to that school and often added 'living at Nagoya'.

Tametaka: Last half of eighteenth century. Mentioned in the *S.K.* A renowned artist, full of eccentricities and versatile. His name is especially associated with boars in wood, brimming with vitality. He invented the raised signature which was perfected by his school, as above. (Plate 34A.)

Tokoku (1846–1913): A superb modern technician who introduced various inlays into his wood figures. He had a famous school in Tokyo with pupils who bore the same and similar names (Kokoku, Ryukoku, etc.). His work is in great demand. (Plate 31B.)

Tomochika (1800–73): Founded a school of carvers of ivory figure groups. They were very prolific and continued so until modern times. Their work was distinguished in early days but became commercialized.

Tomokazu: Early nineteenth century. Renowned for wood-carvings of animals, especially monkeys and tortoises, which are sensitively treated and deserve close examination for full appreciation. He generally signed in an oval cartouche. There are forgeries, but there also were other Tomokazus.

Tomotada: Recorded by the *S.K.* as a great artist and especially famous for his oxen, delicately carved and full of spirit. This is a name which was greatly forged even in his own lifetime, and one can safely say that most of the oxen bearing this signature are spurious. The ox was a talisman for good calligraphy and great was the demand for them. He signed in a rectangular cartouche. (Plate 34B.)

Tomotane: Mentioned in *S.K.* Rare. Another of this name was of the Tomochika group.

Toun, Takamura (1846–1910): Pupil of Houn. Was created a '*Hogen*'. Ivory figures with fine inlay work.

Toyen, Morikawa (1820–94): A celebrated late artist who imitated the ancient carvings of Nara with fidelity. Rare.

Toyomasa (1773–1856): Well known for his wood animals with yellow horn eyes carved with originality and verve. Leader of a large school at Tamba. His pupils, Toyokazu, Toyoyasu, etc., did similar work.

Yasuaki: A gifted modern who worked in the style of Toun.

Yoshinaga: End eighteenth century. Distinguished for his vigorous ivory carvings of figures and animals. Founded a school at Kyoto, which included Yoshimasa, Yoshitomo, Yoshitada, who did similar work. (Plate 34C.) Mentioned in the *S.K.*

Zeshin (d. 1891): A sublime artist in lacquer who made a few netsuke.

SIGNATURES. Artists chose their own art-names (called '*Go*') of two syllables sometimes followed by '*sai*' (=studio). They often adopted as one of the syllables a part of their master's name. From a study of these names it is often possible to guess roughly to which school an artist belonged, especially if the repeated syllable is an uncommon one. Another help in deciding to which school an artist belonged is the shape of the cartouche, if any, in which the artist carved his signature. These surrounds were oval, rectangular, etc., and may be regarded as an integral part of the signature. There are at least two distinct ways of reading the Japanese characters: (1) by translating them into the Chinese sound (called the '*on*') and (2) by translating them into the Japanese equivalent (called the '*kun*'). In translating from a dictionary either one or the other of these two forms must be employed throughout. There are also at least two ways of writing the characters themselves: (1) the block letter (called '*Kaisho*') and (2) the cursory script (called '*Sosho*'). If artists had always used the Kaisho form, it would be a fairly easy matter to look up the characters in a dictionary, but they often used the Sosho form, which is so different from Kaisho, that only a person acquainted with the conventional abbreviations can read it unless he learns each signature by its appearance alone. For this reason, in the list of artists above, no characters have been given, as it might merely mislead, but a few artists are listed below, showing their names in Kaisho and their actual signatures in Sosho in order to illustrate the difference. It may be mentioned that artists were often honoured by a title such as '*Hogen*' or '*Hokyo*', and these titles were sometimes introduced into their signatures.

COLLECTING. The chief points to be looked for in a netsuke are:

(1) Aesthetic quality: this is a matter for personal judgment.
(2) Workmanship, skill, thoroughness.
(3) Functional suitability: rounded edges without projections which catch the dress or break off; hard substance which takes a good polish.
(4) The subject should be expressed in the simplest form without finical details which clash and destroy each other.
(5) Age, coloration, patina, freedom from blemishes and breaks.
(6) Signature, especially those above-named if reasonably authentic.

It is important that Netsuke should be kept in drawers and not exposed *en masse* when they clash and are injured by a strong light or undue heat. They should be cleaned or polished by a soft brush or the hand (over a carpet, in case they fall). A catalogue should be kept which should record source, history, signature, etc., as such details are so easily forgotten. Photographs or drawings give life to the catalogue, and these must be of exactly natural size. Associations should be sought with other collectors, as these can be mutually helpful. Netsuke should be handled often and re-examined appreciatively or critically. Tastes change.

	KAISHO	SOSHO
GYOKUZAN	玉山	
IKKWAN	一貫	
IKKO	一虎	
JUGYOKU	壽玉	
RANTEI	蘭亮	
TADATOSHI	忠利	
TAMETAKA	爲隆	

(*B*) INRO

As inro were used jointly with netsuke, they have a similar history, but they were more regarded than netsuke in early times, and hence there are more of the earliest types. They are generally of lacquered wood, sometimes with additions of ivory, shell, etc. The shape is always roughly the same but the number of compartments varies from one to five. Though intended at first for seals, these compartments came to be used for medicines and sundry needs. Slight variations of form and arrangement occur as, for example, when the cases are enclosed in a surrounding sheath.

Like netsuke, this art was described in the *Soken Kisho* of 1781 (Vol. 6) and illustrations given, with artists' names, but it was not so fully treated. Like netsuke, inro were sparsely signed in the eighteenth century and increasingly so in the nineteenth. The subjects introduced into the decoration were also similar, save that the artist painted them on a surface and hence could work freely at landscapes, etc., where the netsuke carver was more restricted. Such scenes are characterized by graceful charm and the reticent elimination of unessentials for which Japanese art was notorious.

Japanese lacquer-work was a very skilled profession and only the highly-trained could attempt it, in contrast to netsuke, which any peasant or artisan could make for himself.

LACQUER TECHNIQUE. The lacquer used in this process is the natural gum of a sumach tree (*Rhus vernicifera*) mixed with various pigments and with gold and silver. Raised designs were produced by building up with gesso and other compositions. Some of the terms used in this art are:

Aogai: Mother-of-pearl inlay; made from Haliotis shell.

Chinkinbori (=sunk gold engraving): Incised design with gold rubbed in.

Fundame: Powdered gold worked to a matt surface.

Giobu: Irregular pieces of foil mixed with lacquer, giving a mottled effect.

Hiramakiyé (=flat-sown picture): Flat decoration.

Hiramé (=flat aspect): Small pieces of gold or silver leaf placed on the lacquered surface, fairly wide apart but evenly spread.

Jidai (=ancient): Period piece, say seventeenth century.

Kinji (=gold ground): Like *fundame*, but burnished to look like leaf.

Kirikane (=cut gold): Cut squares of gold leaf embedded on the lacquer.

Mokumé (=wood aspect): Imitation of wood graining.

Nashiji (=pear ground): Gold dust sprinkled on the lacquer and then polished like aventurine. Various forms, e.g. *Muranashiji* indicates that the gold is spread in irregular patches.

Rogin: Like *kinji*, but of silver.

Roiro: Black with a high polish. Also called 'mirror black'.

Sabeji (=rust ground): Imitation of old iron, etc.

Samenuri: Fish-skin applied after staining. Shagreen.

Takamakiyé (=raised sown picture): Design in high relief, modelled in composition, and then lacquered in the desired colours.

Togidashi (=polishing out): Design made in colours and then rubbed down to an absolutely even surface, which gives a water-colour effect.

Tsuishu (=heap red): A deep surface of solid red lacquer is made, of several layers, and the design is carved *in the lacquer*.

Tsuikoku (=heap black): Similar to above, but black.

Yasuriko (=file powder): Metal filings sprinkled on surface, often graduated, not deeply laid like *nashiji*.

INRO-MAKERS. Whereas well over two thousand netsuke-makers signed their works, less than a quarter of that number signed inro. The chief names were:

Chikanao: Mentioned in *S.K. Fundame* with inlay of *aogai*.

Chinyei: Specialist in *chinkinbori*.

Chohei: Eighteenth–nineteenth century. Inlay work. Also made netsuke (q.v.).

Doho, Igarashi (d. 1678): *Takamakiyé*. Good, but rare.

Gyokuzan, Jitokusai: Early nineteenth century. Various. Beautiful quality, exquisitely finished.

Hanzan (1743–90): Pupil of Ritsuo; porcelain incrustations.

Hokei: Late nineteenth century. Great specialist in *Tsuishu*. Also made netsuke (q.v.).

Inagawa: Family of some generations who generally signed the family name only. Especially beautiful work in *Togidashi*.

Jokasai: First of this name was seventeenth century. His son followed, and perhaps others. Various styles.

Kajikawa: Family of several generations. Often signed family name only, but over twenty members signed individually, sometimes giving their seals as well. (Plate 29A.)

Kakosai: Prolific late artist of various potentialities.

Kenzan: Brother of Korin. A potter. Made porcelain inro.

Koami: A family of nineteen generations. Despite their number, signed work is not common.

Koma: Another long family. Well over fifty members, who generally signed in full and not merely with the family name. Their inro were generally flattish without a fluted edge to the cord-holes. Noted for rich red and stately gold sheen.

Korin, Ogata (1658–1716): Noted for incrustations of *aogai* and pewter on a ground of matt gold. Was created a '*Hokyo*'. Small-sized inro.

Koyetsu (1557–1637): Similar style to Korin; bold and easily forged.

Moyei: Early nineteenth century. Famous for beautiful *Togidashi*.

Ritsuo (1663–1747): Memorable artist noted for bold designs with inlays like Korin, which some think too big for inro, but suited to larger works.

Shibayama family. Characteristic inlay work in ivory. Also made netsuke.

Shigeyoshi, Hasegawa: *Togidashi* and *Hiramakiyé*. Rather rare.

Shiomi Masanari: Early eighteenth century. Versatile artist renowned for fine-coloured *Togidashi*. Signature is in tiny characters at the side and easily missed. Probably more than one man of this name up to nineteenth century.

Shokwasai: Prolific late artist who did *Takamakiyé* figures with ivory hands and feet. Slightly commercial but quite effective.

Shunsho: Family of tasteful artists noted for exquisite *Togidashi*.

Somada: Family who invented the style of designs made almost entirely of greenish *aogai* inlay, to which their name was given. Their work is rarely signed.

Soyetsu: Seventeenth century. Pupil of Koyetsu. Similar style. Not always genuine.

Tatsuki: Family noted for large inro of bold design in *Takamakiyé*, etc.

Toshihide: Consummate artist in *Togidashi* of birds, plants, etc.

Toyu: A versatile master, probably more than one. One called Kwanshosai and sometimes signed this name only, which may mean work turned out by his *atelier*. Highly-finished and beautiful work, especially in fine *Togidashi*. Several members of his school began their names with *To* (=peach).

Yosei: Large family of several generations noted for *Tsuishu* carving.

Yoyusai: Early nineteenth century. Fine work but not of the finest. *Hiramakiyé* in gold, etc.

Zeshin (1807–91): The most renowned lacquer artist of modern times. His imitations in lacquer of other materials is astounding. Nothing was beyond him and everything he did had refinement and beauty. He had sons and pupils who carried on his stylish work.

BOOKS FOR FURTHER READING

A. Brockhaus, *Netsuke* (Leipzig, 1905). In German. A thorough treatise, well illustrated, and giving a long list of artists with many facsimile signatures.

O. Daniels, *Dictionary of Japanese Sosho Writing Forms*. Contains all likely characters in their Kaisho form with the Sosho rendering of it. Indexed in roman type according to the 'ON' sound, but not the 'KUN' equivalent.

W. H. Edmunds, *Pointers and Clues to the Subjects of Japanese and Chinese Art* (London, 1934).

H. L. Joly, *Legend in Japanese Art* (London, 1908).

F. W. Jonas, *Netsuke* (Kegan, Paul, 1928). With illustrations and a long list of artists' names and list of Inro makers.

Koop and Inada, *Japanese Names and How to Read Them* (London, 1923). Characters are in dictionary form according to the number of brush strokes used in forming them.

Yusuru Okada *Netsuke* (Japan, 1951). In English, giving a brief summary of the subject and a small account of some 300 artists.

Ueda Reikichi, *Netsuke* (Japan, 1934). In Japanese. A second edition, 1943. Not translated.

V. F. Weber, *Koji Hoten* (Paris, 1923). Two vols. in French. A colossal work covering all Japanese art in dictionary form and an exhaustive index.

The various auctioneers' catalogues of sales of Netsuke and Inro are a useful guide to collectors, especially if well illustrated, as were those of the Behrens and the Trower, Tomkinson, Joly, Gilbertson, Reiss Collections.

METALWORK

By J. F. HAYWARD

This section deals with a miscellaneous selection of articles which have not been covered in other parts of this and the preceding volume concerned with the metal crafts. It excludes, therefore, jewellery, gold and silver, Sheffield plate, pewter, arms and armour. Few of the subjects discussed below concern articles that are collected on their own, but they are often sought by the collector to form a background for a collection of conventional type. Many of them, such as andirons, brass candlesticks, caskets, locks and keys, form an essential feature of the 'period' interior. The number of small objects made of metal and used about the house that were treated in a sufficiently attractive or imaginative way to interest the collector is enormous, and it has not been practicable to deal with more than a few. For this reason methods of decoration, as well as actual objects, are included in the glossary which follows. With the exception of such 'big game' as medieval aquamaniles or Limoges enamels, which are out of reach of the average collector, all the articles referred to are to be found, if not in the more modest antique shops, at least in those specializing in the base metals.

The term 'base metal' is an unfortunate one, since it inevitably suggests a certain inferiority of quality. In fact, many of the articles described in this section were treated with no less exquisiteness of detail and delicacy of touch than the precious metals. Most suitable for the rendering of delicate ornament is steel, which, by reason of its hardness, could be sawn, filed, or chiselled to a lacelike fineness, such as can be found in the snuff-boxes, étuis, scissors and chains made at Brescia in the seventeenth century or in Paris in the eighteenth century. By reason of the enormous labour involved, steel was not used where high relief was required. In this case bronze was the most suitable material, cast, chased and finally gilt. The reddish colour of the bronze provided a particularly well-suited base for gilding, and a very rich effect was obtained. Amongst the finest work achieved in this medium are the caskets and clock-cases produced in South Germany in the second half of the sixteenth century. But more remarkable still are the furniture mounts and ornamental articles made by the Parisian Ciseleurs-doreurs in the second half of the eighteenth century. The quality of the finish on the finest Louis XVI mounts is unsurpassed in the whole history of metal-working. On the Continent these mounts have long been collected for their own sake, but in England it is only within the last twenty-five years that even the excellent work in ormolu produced at Matthew Boulton's Birmingham factory in the late eighteenth century has been recognized.

Not only did the workers in the base metals achieve an excellence of quality which rivalled that of the contemporary goldsmiths, they frequently made use of the precious metals in order to enrich their own productions. The various techniques of inlaying and encrusting the surface of base metal with gold, silver, or another base metal were extensively used by the metal craftsmen throughout the history of the craft. The most ambitious and imaginative use of damascening was made by Italian craftsmen in the sixteenth century, probably inspired by the examples they saw from the Near East. The most elaborate damascened ornament was applied to armour and weapons, but the same craftsmen who decorated Milanese armour also executed the damascened enrichment on caskets and furniture mounts, and these latter can be obtained at a price far below that commanded by armour. The Milanese technique of enriching iron with gold and silver was paralleled by the Venetian technique of damascening brass with precious metal. Their manner was strongly influenced by the Orient, and the earlier brass vessels decorated in Venice are not easily distinguishable from those of Near Eastern origin.

The text of this section is only concerned with those pieces which have some pretensions to artistic merit. But alongside them, in the limitless field of folk art, innumerable unassuming objects, well designed for their simple domestic function, await the collector.

Andirons: the iron fire-dog or andiron dates back to Roman times, but the earliest known examples date from the fifteenth century. As long as the fireplace occupied the central position in the hall, the fire-dog was of purely utilitarian design, but when the former was transferred to a side wall, becoming an important decorative feature, the fire-dog also received ornamental treatment. The earliest surviving fire-dogs conform to a standard type, whether of English, French, German, or Flemish origin, namely an arched base enriched with Gothic cusping, supporting a pilaster, the front of which is decorated with running scrolls (Fig. 1). Sixteenth- and seventeenth-century fire-dogs were made to the same design but with Renaissance instead of Gothic ornament (Fig. 2). Fire-dogs of this type were made of cast iron, the English ones being produced by the Sussex iron-masters. There seems from an early date to have been a distinction between andirons and fire-dogs. The former term was used for the large dogs, standing three feet or more high, which were intended to decorate the fire-place (Plate 35C). Though these andirons could also be used, they were usually accompanied by a smaller pair of fire-dogs proper, which stood closer into the hearth and supported the burning logs.

The earlier andirons were of wrought iron, but as early as the sixteenth century they were garnished with silver. In the seventeenth century andirons entirely of silver were produced and there was a fashion for them in England after the Restoration. Numbers have survived from this date, not only in the royal palaces but also in many country houses, and are not out of reach of the wealthy collector. The Restoration andiron had a particularly handsome baroque form, consisting of a pedestal on volute or claw

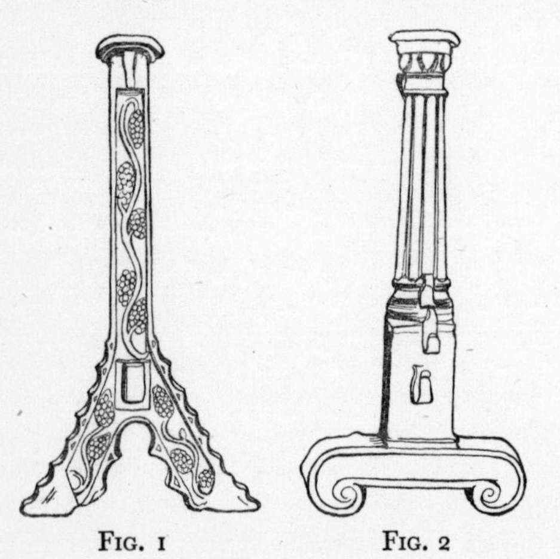

Fig. 1 Fig. 2

Fig. 3

feet supporting either a flaming vase or a figure. The finest examples are of great magnificence and weight of silver. Similar designs were also produced for the less wealthy in gilt brass (Fig. 3). The introduction of the grate in the eighteenth century rendered the fire-dog superfluous.

Of the Continental andirons by far the most handsome type are the North Italian ones of the sixteenth and seventeenth centuries. These were cast in bronze and take the form of an elaborately-worked pedestal supporting a figure of a warrior or a goddess.

Aquamanile: this term is used to describe the bronze ewers used in the Middle Ages for pouring water over the hands of guests after each course of a meal. As forks were not normally employed for conveying food to the mouth, frequent washing of the hands was indispensable. Though originally referring to all kinds of ewer, the term is now confined to a particular type of medieval ewer of naturalistic form, the most popular being a lion on whose back crouched a dragon, serving as a handle. Other forms include a monster, a knight on horseback wearing a great helm, etc. Medieval aquamaniles of this type were cast by the *cire-perdu* process and no two were exactly alike; many reproductions have, however, been cast from moulds in recent times. The earliest examples date from the thirteenth century, but they continued in use until the sixteenth century, when they were replaced by the more convenient ewer of helmet shape. They are now objects of extreme rarity, and few authentic examples are to be found in private ownership (Plate 35B).

Brass candlesticks: European candlesticks as early as the twelfth century are known but are not likely to be seen outside museums or cathedral treasuries. The earliest examples obtainable by the collector are the pricket candlesticks of enamelled copper made at Limoges in the thirteenth century. These are exceedingly rare and are pieces of high price. The only medieval candlesticks within the reach of the ordinary collector are the various fifteenth-century types produced in the Low Countries in one or other of the towns in the valley of the Meuse.

The earliest form of candlestick was the pricket, in which the candle was stuck on a metal, usually iron, spike projecting from the wax-pan (Plate 36A). The socket type, in which the candle was held in a cup or socket, did not become usual until the fourteenth century, though it was certainly known much earlier (Plate 35A).

The Mosan candlesticks were, until 1466, mostly produced in the town of Dinant (*see* Dinanderie), and from there they were exported all over western Europe. Though the brass-workers became dispersed during the latter part of the fifteenth century, they continued to work in just the same style that they had developed at Dinant. This is indicated by the remarkable uniformity of design of sixteenth-century, and earlier, candlesticks found in different European countries. From the thirteenth century onwards a large range of types were made, beginning with the rare figures of animals or monsters supporting a pricket, continuing with the fourteenth-century tripod prickets decorated with octagonal mouldings, and evolving in the fifteenth century into two main types: firstly, the pricket with tall, domed base, moulded stem and large grease-pan immediately below the pricket (Plate 36A). The second type, which probably reached western Europe from the Near East, has a tall base of trumpet form to the top of which is attached a wide rim or flange serving as a grease-pan. The stem is decorated with lenticular mouldings and the socket is provided with a vertical opening resembling in shape a Gothic window, through which a spike could be inserted to eject the candle stub. As the sixteenth century advances the mouldings applied to the stem became more numerous, some four or five in number (Plate 36B).

In the course of the late sixteenth and early seventeenth century the grease-pan, instead of being formed from the upper surface of the base, became independent and was set on the stem just above the base. About the middle of the century it moved up farther, reaching a position half-way up the stem, as in the typical English candlesticks of this epoch (Plate 36D). They are very simply constructed of a hollow tube of trumpet form decorated with a series of grooves running horizontally around the stem at regular intervals. The contemporary Continental candlestick is usually of more sophisticated form with finely-proportioned baluster stem (Plate 36C). Towards the end of the seventeenth century the grease-pan completed its upwards move and reached a position just under the socket. Finally, at the end of the century the lip of the socket was turned over to give a small grease-pan, the grease-pan proper abandoned, and instead a depression cut in the top of the base.

The eighteenth-century candlestick (Plate 36F) went through the variations of style familiar in the evolution of silver, that is, octagonal baluster in the first quarter, shell-base and vase-shaped baluster in the middle of the century and, finally, the square-base and section of the neo-classical style in the latter years of the century.

Some idea of date can often be gained from the method of construction of brass candlesticks. Until the late seventeenth century the stem and socket were cast solid in one piece and attached to the base by means of a screw thread or a tenon which projected through a hole in the centre of the base and was then burred over to hold it in place. About 1670 a new method was introduced by which stem and socket were hollow cast in two pieces and then brazed together, thus saving much metal. In the nineteenth century there was a return to solid casting in one piece.

Caskets: the earliest caskets likely to come the way of the collector are those made in Sicily during the thirteenth to fourteenth

FIG. 4. FRENCH CASKET, blued iron damascened with grotesques in gold

century. They are constructed of ivory with brass mounts, and are believed to have been the work of Arabic craftsmen. The Near Eastern element in them can be seen, not in any constructional detail but in the painted ornament with which the finer examples were enriched. This ornament often introduces Cufic characters or amorphous scrollwork of Saracenic origin. Caskets or small coffers of the fifteenth century are far less rare than the earlier examples; there were two main types, those constructed entirely of iron and those of wood, sometimes covered with leather and always furnished with more or less elaborate bands of iron. Such caskets were made in France (Plates 37A and 37B), the Low Countries, Germany (Plate 37C), and Spain, and it

FIG. 5. SOUTH GERMAN CASKET, iron with mounts of gilt brass; late sixteenth century

is often difficult to be certain of the country of origin, especially of the earlier types (Plate 37A). Subsequently, recognized national types emerge. One French type is entirely of iron with arched lid. The earlier examples have applied Gothic tracery ornamentation, the later ones have a plain surface with either etched or damascened ornament (Fig. 4). The Spanish type is of almost rectangular section with only slightly curved walls. It is of wood covered with one or more layers of tinned sheet iron, pierced with reticulated ornament. This type is provided with stout bands and an elaborate lock decorated with Gothic pinnacles.

FIG. 6. MINIATURE CASKET, South German, *c.* 1600

(A) Socket candlestick cast in the form of Samson overcoming the Lion. Latten. Mosan; thirteenth century. *Victoria & Albert Museum.*

(B) Aquamanile, latten, Mosan; twelfth century. *Victoria & Albert Museum.*

(C) Pair of andirons, iron, the crowns (of later date) of bronze. Arms of Henry VIII and crest of the Boleyn family. *Knole.*

(D) Ewer. Flemish; fifteenth century, decorated by a Saracenic craftsman in Venice. *Victoria & Albert Museum.*

PLATE 35

Face page 72

(A) Pricket candlestick, brass. Flemish; sixteenth century. *Messrs S. W. Wolsey*

(B) Candlestick, latten English; early sixteenth century. Dug up in Cornhill, London. *Messrs S. W. Wolsey.*

(C) Pricket candlestick, brass. Flemish; seventeenth century. *Messrs S. W. Wolsey.*

(D) Candlestick, brass. English; mid-seventeenth century. *Victoria & Albert Museum.*

(E) Candlestick, brass enriched with polychrome enamel. English; seventeenth century. *V. & A. Museum*

(F) 'Church Wardens' candlestick from Gresford Church, dated 1748; inscribed with church wardens' names. *Messrs S. W. Wolsey.*

(A) Casket, wood, covered with cuir-bouilli, brass mounts. French; fifteenth century. *Collection of Mrs I. G. Wolsey.*

(B) Casket, leather bound with iron straps. French; sixteenth century. *Private Collection.*

(C) Painted wood casket with iron mounts. German; first half of sixteenth century. *Mrs I. G. Wolsey.*

(D) Casket, etched copper with mounts of gilt brass. South German; late sixteenth century. *Victoria & Albert Museum.*

(E) Casket, iron damascened with gold and silver. Milanese; second half of the sixteenth century. *Victoria & Albert Museum.*

(F) Casket, chiselled steel. German or Austrian, early eighteenth century. *Victoria & Albert Museum.*

(A) Perfume-burner, ormolu. English (Birmingham) *c.* 1770. *Victoria & Albert Museum.*

(B) Candelabrum. Ormolu with marble base, probably executed by Gouthière. French, *c.* 1770–80. *Victoria & Albert Museum.*

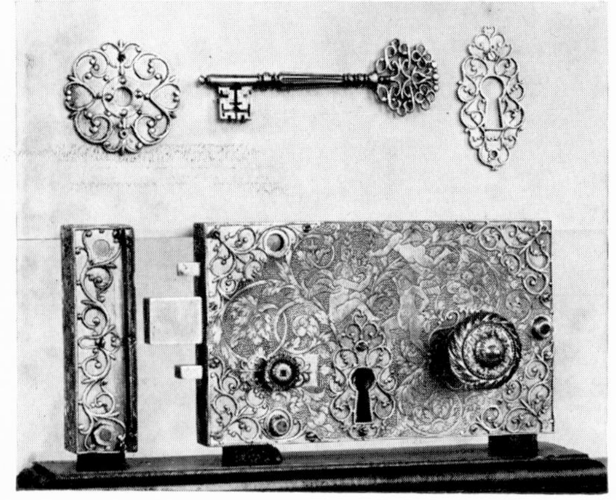

(C) Brass lock and key. English; late seventeenth century. *Victoria & Albert Museum.*

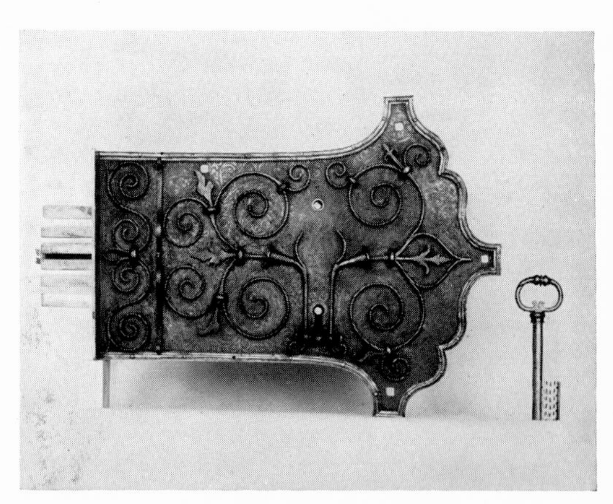

(D) Lock, the lock-plate etched with foliage. German, dated 1610. *Victoria & Albert Museum.*

PLATE 38

The most common German type dates from the second half of the sixteenth century and shows no trace of the Gothic ornament which persisted so long into the sixteenth century in the locksmiths' workshops. It is rectangular in plan and is constructed of iron sheet sometimes enriched with mounts of gilt brass. The whole of the exterior surface is etched with floral scrolls or with hunting or allegorical subjects. The lock, which is accommodated on the underside of the lid, is of great elaboration, shooting as many as a dozen bolts. These coffers were made in Nürnberg and Augsburg but are never signed (Fig. 5 and Plate 37D). On the other hand, the miniature caskets of gilt brass, sometimes enriched with silver and even enamel, and engraved instead of etched, are usually known as Michael Mann boxes because so many of them bear the signature of a Nürnberg locksmith of that name (Fig. 6).

Fine coffers of English manufacture do not appear before the second half of the seventeenth century, when we find the very rare but incomparable works of the Bickfords (e.g. the jewel casket of Queen Mary II in the Victoria and Albert Museum) and the fairly common but extremely attractive caskets with fall fronts veneered with oyster marquetry and furnished with elaborate gilt brass hingework.

Chiselled and cut steel: the art of steel chiselling is a by-product of the locksmith's and gunsmith's trade. Small articles have been chiselled from iron or steel since the

7 8

Fig. 7. Snuff-box, Brescian; late seventeenth century

Fig. 8. Snuff-box, Brescian; dated 1694

Middle Ages, but from the collector's point of view, four main groups can be recognized. Firstly, the articles made in the northern Italian city of Brescia in the seventeenth and eighteenth centuries. These include snuff-boxes, scissors, tweezers and thimbles, usually chiselled and pierced with floral scrollwork interspersed with monsters, similar in design to the ornament familiar on Brescian-made firearms (Fig. 7). The most distinguished Brescian artist, who usually signed his works, was Matteo Acqua Fresca (Fig. 8). The second group was produced in Paris by the same chisellers who decorated sword and gun furniture of the period of Louis XIV and Louis XV. Characteristic of their work are the chatelaines, étuis, shuttles and, more rarely, snuff-boxes, usually chiselled with classical figure subjects against a gilt stippled ground. Similar but somewhat coarser work was also produced in Germany (Plate 37F). The third group was produced by the artists of the Imperial Russian small arms factory at Tula. The factory was founded by Peter the Great, and their work dates from the eighteenth century. The artisans mastered not only the art of chiselling iron but also of encrusting it with various softer metals and of faceting it (cut-steel). Besides smaller objects, such as candlesticks and caskets, the Tula factory also turned out large pieces of furniture and even mantelpieces entirely constructed of cut and faceted steel. The last group is English and flourished at first about the middle of the eighteenth century in Woodstock in Oxfordshire and subsequently at Birmingham in the Soho works set up by Matthew Boulton. The Woodstock cottage industry produced both chiselled and faceted steel but the Birmingham factory, which eventually put Woodstock out of business, concentrated on cut steel. They made sword hilts, buttons, chatelaines, buckles and cheap jewellery. Cut steel was used as a more durable alternative to marcasite in the late eighteenth and early nineteenth century.

Copper-work: owing to the difficulty of working copper in its pure form, it has not been extensively used by the metal-worker. In the sixteenth and early seventeenth century caskets, clock-cases, and scientific instruments were frequently made of copper, which was subsequently engraved and gilt (Plate 37D). Those parts of the case or instrument which were cast were, however, made of brass or bronze. Owing to its suitability for engraving, it was much used for flat surfaces which were to be decorated in this way. The only other significant European use of copper was by the Italian coppersmiths, who made ewers, basins, and other vessels. The earlier examples were decorated with fine engraving, and in the seventeenth century embossed with bold floral ornament of baroque character, but vessels in this last group do not as a rule rise above the level of peasant art.

Cutlery: the history of eating knives goes back to remote antiquity, but for the collector it may be said to commence in the fifteenth century. Knives dating from the Romano-British period have been excavated in considerable numbers, but the condition of these is usually such that they are more likely to attract the archaeologist than the collector. Until well into the sixteenth century the history of cutlery is that of the knife only. Forks were known in the Middle Ages but were normally used only for carving the joint of meat. An extremely rare type of fork was also used in noble households for eating certain kinds of fruit, the juice of which might stain the fingers, but examples of these are not likely to be met by the collector.

The ordinary eating knife of the fifteenth century was of too simple a character to be considered worth preserving, and the only examples which have come to light have been discovered in the course of excavations. On the other hand, knives with handles of precious materials, either hardstone, gold or silver, have been valued on account of their beauty, and a few have survived through the ages (Figs. 9 and 10). The most beautiful medieval knives are those made for members of the Burgundian court; a number of these exist, all in museums. Their handles are of silver-gilt enriched with the heraldic bearings of the original owner in translucent enamel.

The inventories of the property of the Tudor monarchs show that they possessed many sets of fine cutlery contained in cases of leather or wood, and mounted in handles of hardstone or ivory. None of these pieces can now be identified, if indeed they still exist, but there are a number of sixteenth-century types of cutlery that may still be found. These include the Flemish type with handle of brass or latten furnished with wooden scales. The finials of the handles are often formed as horses' hooves, and the rivets holding the scales as horse-bells, but the finest examples are engraved with minute religious subjects. These Flemish knives were exported to England in quantity and many have been dug up in London.

The French sixteenth-century type has a handle of gilt iron, the finial chiselled in the form of an animal or monster, the scales being of ivory or mother-of-pearl (Fig. 11). The most beautiful is undoubtedly the Italian form, which has a flat pilaster-like handle of silver, sometimes enriched with niello, surmounted by a gilt bronze finial in the form of a capital (Fig. 12).

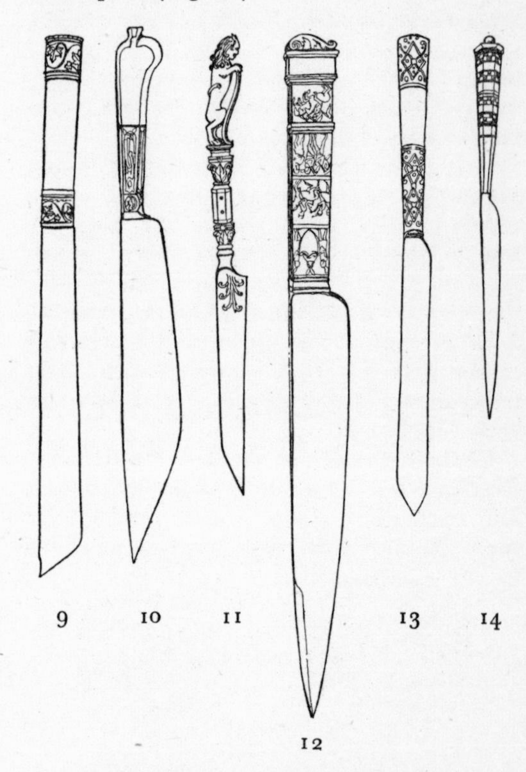

Fig. 9. Carving-knife, ivory handle with silver-gilt mounts; fourteenth century

Fig. 10. Carving-knife, ivory handle with enamelled silver shoulder; Italian; late fifteenth century

Fig. 11. French; sixteenth century

Fig. 12. Italian; late fifteenth century

Figs. 13 and 14. London-made Knives of the early seventeenth century

Although forks had not yet entered into general use in northern Europe, a single fork is usually found along with a set of knives by the latter part of the sixteenth century. It was probably intended for carving and for serving. The true serving knife, sometimes known as a Présentoir, which appears in the fifteenth century, has a thin broad blade, with the edges either parallel or widening slightly towards the point, which was either cut off square or slightly rounded.

Little is known of English knives made before the seventeenth century, and it is difficult to distinguish them from imported Flemish knives. No sixteenth-century English knives of fine quality are known to exist. By the early seventeenth century, however, the English cutlers were making cutlery as fine as that of any other country. The work of the London cutlers can be recognized by the dagger-mark which was struck on all blades made by members of the Cutlers' Company, in addition to the maker's mark. A characteristic feature of London knives of the first half of the seventeenth century was the decorative treatment of the shoulders, which were either damascened with gold or encrusted with silver (Figs. 13 and 14).

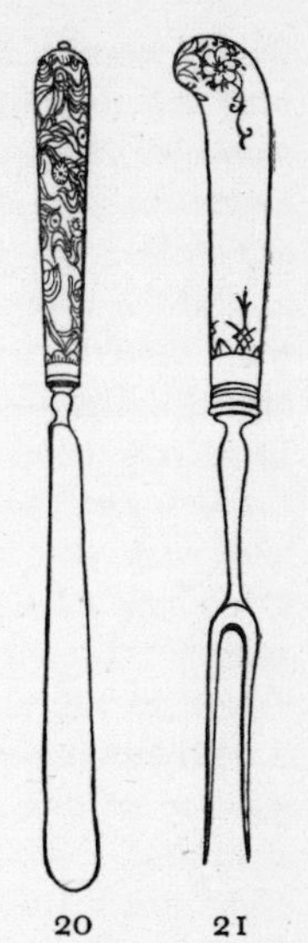

The main source of knife blades in western Europe was the German town of Solingen, whence blades were exported all over Europe, being fitted with handles in the locality to which they had been sent. A Solingen stamp on a blade does not necessarily signify that the handle was also made there.

In the seventeenth century the usual materials for handles were ivory, silver, and various kinds of hardstone, especially agate. Of the great variety of types of handle made, the most attractive are the Dutch wedding knives, made in pairs with handles entirely of silver finely engraved with Biblical subjects and grotesques, often after the designs of the Liége-born engraver Johann Theodor de Bry (Fig. 19).

In the eighteenth century ivory and agate gave way to porcelain or stoneware as a fashionable material for handles (Figs. 20, 21), but silver remained usual for all except the cheaper grades made of horn or wood. The characteristic eighteenth-century knife has a handle of pistol shape in which is mounted a curved blade of so-called 'scimitar' form. Since the late seventeenth century the fork had become a normal feature of the dining table in northern as well as southern Europe. Though forks had been familiar objects since early in the seventeenth century, they were long used by preference for holding the meat while it was being cut, not for conveying it to the mouth. The extreme sharpness

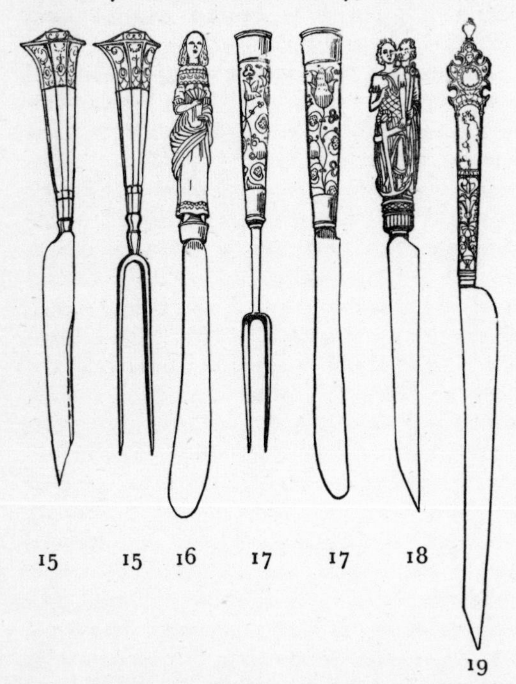

FIG. 15. IVORY HANDLES, gilt brass terminals; German; early seventeenth century

FIG. 16. CARVED IVORY HANDLE; English, *c.* 1680

FIG. 17. IVORY HANDLES, piqué with silver; English, *c.* 1690

FIG. 18. CARVED IVORY; Dutch; end of seventeenth century

FIG. 19. Dutch; first half of the seventeenth century

FIG. 20. HANDLE OF VENETIAN MILLEFIORE GLASS; late seventeenth century

FIG. 21. HANDLE OF BOW PORCELAIN; mid-eighteenth century

of the prongs of the early two-pronged forks may account for this delay in their exploitation. In Italy, where forks were in use in the sixteenth century, they were made of silver, which did not take so sharp a point.

Cutlery ceases to be of interest to the collector by the early nineteenth century. The last sets of cutlery worthy of notice are the travelling sets composed of knife, fork, spoon, beaker, etc., which were still produced until well into the nineteenth century, and were often mounted in gold or silver. Otherwise nineteenth-century cutlery was machine produced to more or less standardized patterns.

Damascening: the art of encrusting the surface of iron, steel, brass, or copper with gold or/and silver has been known and practised since antiquity, especially in the Near East, but at no time in Europe has it flourished more than in Milan during the middle and second half of the sixteenth century, where it was a by-product of the thriving armourers' trade. Thin iron sheets were embossed, often in a rather summary manner, with subjects from Roman history or mythology against landscape backgrounds and damascened with gold and silver. The Milanese damascening of this period is of fine quality and bears comparison with the best Saracenic work. Damascened plaques were made in quantity to more or less standard shapes and were sold to cabinet-makers, who mounted them on ebony caskets, chest of drawers, and even large pieces such as tables and mirrors. Though the majority of the damascened ironwork encountered by the collector is likely to be of Milanese origin, there were highly competent damasceners at work elsewhere in Europe, in Augsburg and Nürnberg, in Paris and in other Italian cities. In the seventeenth century some fine damascening was done on English sword and knife handles, probably by immigrant Italian artists. The detailed ornament that could be achieved by damascening was not appreciated in the age of baroque, when a rather more vigorous spirit was admired, and the art did not survive the sixteenth century in Italy (Plate 37E).

Dinanderie: small brassware made in or around the Flemish town of Dinant, near Liége. Whereas elsewhere bronze was mostly employed for the manufacture of domestic vessels, the presence of zinc deposits around Liége led the founders of the valley of the Meuse to adopt brass in preference. The town of Dinant became by the late Middle Ages so famous for its brassware that the name Dinanderie was used to describe the production of the whole region. Typical articles made were aquamaniles, basins, jugs, cooking vessels and candlesticks, many of them quite simple objects for domestic purposes. Amongst the more splendid achievements of the Mosan craftsmen may be mentioned lecterns and fonts. In 1466 the town of Dinant was sacked by Philippe le Bon, and as a result the brass-founders emigrated, partly to other towns in the valley of the Meuse but partly to France and England (Plates 35A, B and D).

Enamelled brassware: copper was used for preference rather than brass for enamelling in the Middle Ages, and apart from a few harness ornaments and the Garter stall-plates preserved in St George's Chapel, Windsor Castle, medieval enamelled brassware does not exist. During the seventeenth century a cheap form of enamelling was introduced in England and on the Continent in which brass was used as a base. The enamel was of the *champlève* type, but instead of the depressions for the enamel being cut out by hand they were cast in one with the object. Such a method was unsuited for the production of small or fine objects, but it was applied to quite a variety of brassware, including andirons, candlesticks (Plate 2E), stirrups and horse harness, and sword hilts. English enamelled brassware of this type usually goes by the name of 'Surrey' enamel, but there are no grounds for thinking that such articles were produced in the county of Surrey. Similar objects were made on the Continent; amongst the Continental items not made in England are small caskets and knife handles. The place of manufacture is not known, but it may have been in the Meuse region.

Enamelled brass objects of particularly crude quality were produced in Russia until comparatively recent times; coarsely-enamelled brass ikons, mostly dating from the nineteenth century, survive in such large numbers that one suspects they must have been made for export. The colour range of all this enamelled brass is restricted; blue, red, green, yellow, and white are most usual.

Etched metalwork: the art of etching is believed to have originated in the process of ornamenting armour with acid etching first introduced in the second half of the fifteenth century. In the sixteenth century small objects of iron, brass, copper, and even silver, were commonly decorated with etched ornament. This technique of ornament was particularly popular in Germany in the second half of the sixteenth century, and was applied to a great variety of objects. In the case of small articles, such as cutlery, tools, watch-cases, locks and scientific instruments, panels of mauresque ornament (Plate 37D) were used, the larger surfaces available on caskets or clock-cases were decorated with figure subjects. The finest etched ornament is to be found on the various tools, instruments and articles of military equipment made for the Saxon Court. Whether these were produced in Dresden or obtained from Nürnberg or Augsburg, is uncertain. The etched ironwork of Nürnberg and Augsburg had an importance comparable with that of the damascened panels made in Milan. Etched ornament is also found on French and Italian locksmiths' work but it does not approach the quality achieved by the German craftsmen (Plate 38D).

Gemellion: this term describes a basin provided with a spout at the base and used for the liturgical washing of the hands at the Mass. Though the ornament found on them is in most cases of secular character, their use seems to have been mainly ecclesiastical. The spout at the side indicates that they were intended to serve as ewers for pouring water rather than as basins for receiving it. The gemellion was one of the standard productions of the enamelling shops at Limoges, and the majority of those known are decorated with Limoges enamel. They date from the thirteenth and fourteenth centuries.

Keys: the key collector can hope to include not only medieval but even Roman keys in his collection, for these have survived, though almost invariably in excavated state, in considerable numbers. With a very few exceptions that are hardly likely to come within the reach of the collector, the medieval key was devoid of ornament. It had, nevertheless, qualities beyond those of mere function, since the form of the bow and the proportion between bow, shank, and bit shows the sense of design that is natural to the craftsman. The bow usually took some simple Gothic form, such as a trefoil or quatrefoil, the shank was plain and the bit was thin with parallel sides. Gothic keys showing great elaboration of ornament should be regarded with suspicion (Figs. 22, 23).

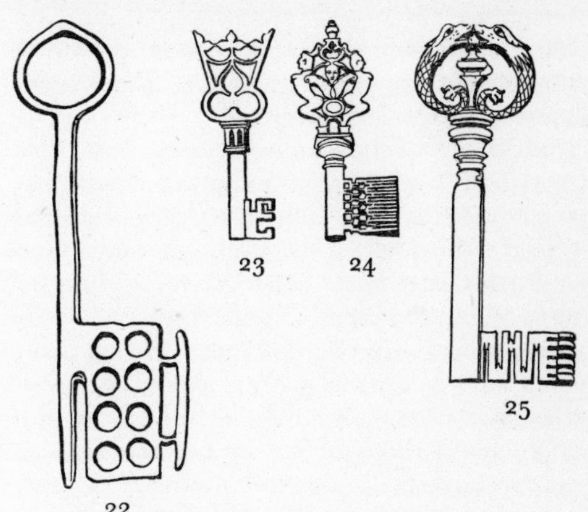

FIG. 22. Fourteenth century
FIG. 23. French; fifteenth century
FIG. 24. French; sixteenth century
FIG. 25. French; second half of the sixteenth century
FIG. 26. FRENCH 'MASTERPIECE' KEY; seventeenth century

It was not till the mid-sixteenth century that keys became the object of elaborate decorative treatment. The hundred years from about 1550 to 1650 were dominated by the French locksmiths, and in no other country was the beauty of their fine steelwork even approached. The finest French keys of the Renaissance were elaborate creations; the bow was composed of addorsed winged figures supported by an Ionic or Corinthian capital

(Figs. 24, 25). The shank was hollow and of complex section, triangular with incurved sides, square-, heart-, or cloverleaf-shaped. Instead of the thin bit of the fifteenth century, the bit was stoutly built, splaying outwards from the shank. These finely-wrought French Renaissance keys were much sought after by collectors during the latter years of the nineteenth century, and numbers of them were faked to meet this demand.

With the French masterpiece lock (*see* article on 'Locks') went a characteristic form of key with a very large bow of pyramidal design. The sides of the pyramid were filled with pierced tracery, and it was supported by a ring, the axis of which was at right angles to the axis of the shank. The ring was filled with tracery of Gothic design. Keys of this type continued to be made according to the regulations of the French locksmiths' guilds right up till the Revolution (Fig. 26).

At the same time as English locks began to achieve a high standard, so also did English keys. Amongst the most attractive English keys are those with the bows pierced with the royal cypher or with the arms of some noble

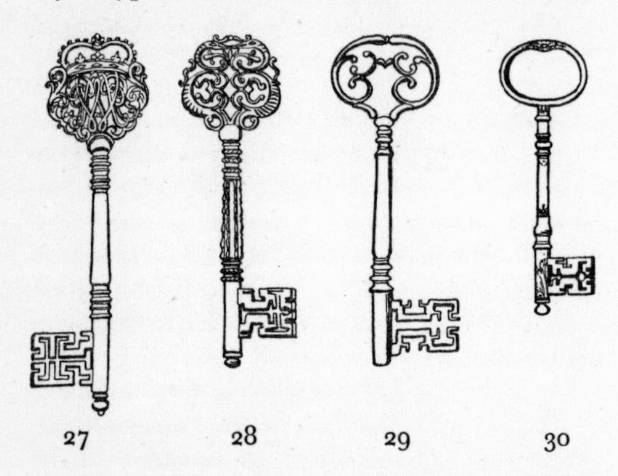

27 28 29 30

FIG. 27. English; crowned cypher of William III

FIG. 28. English, *c.* 1700

FIG. 29. English; early eighteenth century

FIG. 30. English; early nineteenth century

FIG. 31. CHAMBERLAIN'S KEY; French; eighteenth century

FIG. 32. Italian; seventeenth century

family (Figs. 27–30). Characteristic of the eighteenth century, both in England and on the Continent, are the Chamberlains' keys, made of gilt brass and worn attached to a silk rosette as a badge of office (Fig. 31). Numbers of these survive, especially those of the smaller German princedoms. Neither German nor Italian keys achieved great artistic quality; the latter conformed to one type with a circular bow filled with roughly-executed debased Gothic tracery (Fig. 32).

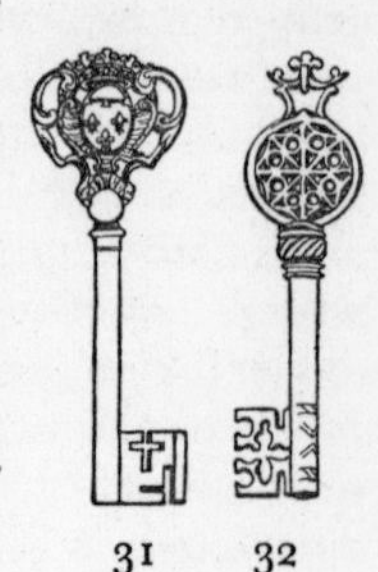

31 32

Locks: though locks of a simple kind go back to the Romans, it was not till the late fourteenth and fifteenth century that locksmiths began to produce articles that could be recognized as works of applied art. The fifteenth century was the great age of French locksmithing, and both door and chest locks of the greatest elaboration of workmanship were made in large numbers. These fifteenth-century locks are of interest, not on account of their mechanism but exclusively on account of the chiselled and applied ornament. The face of the lock was divided into compartments by buttresses surmounted by pinnacles; each of the compartments was filled with pierced tracery like a Gothic window; and all these ornamental details were chiselled, cut or sawn out of iron. The skill developed by the locksmiths of the time in dealing with their intractable material has never been surpassed. A feature of these French Gothic locks is the high relief in which their ornament was worked. Layers of tracery of varying design were set one on top of another, and the ground was covered with scarlet cloth known as 'marouflage' (Fig. 33).

The more elaborate Gothic locks are usually identified as French, but fine work

FIG. 33

was also done by the German and Spanish locksmiths, the style of the latter being derived from German sources. Medieval locks were not signed, and nationality can only be determined by stylistic comparison. German locks can be recognized by their shape; whereas the French lock was of rectangular shape, the sides of the German lock splayed outwards. The Germans made less use of the sawn tracery which is so prominent a feature of French locks, using conventional foliate forms in embossed and pierced iron.

As a whole the European locksmiths were strongly conservative, and it was not till about the middle of the sixteenth century that Gothic was finally displaced by Renaissance ornament. An important development in the history of the lock was the practice introduced in the late sixteenth century of placing the chest or coffer lock on the inside instead of the outside. This change diverted attention to the mechanism, which from now on became more complex, and at the same time put an end to the elaborately-ornamented locks of medieval type. The German smiths showed particular ingenuity in devising complicated locks and padlocks; their speciality was the locks fixed on the underside of the lids of iron coffers. These often shot as many as twelve bolts, all actuated by turning a single key.

In addition to locks, the medieval and Renaissance smiths produced handsome door furniture. Of particular interest are the finely-chiselled bolts made about the middle of the sixteenth century for the French royal palaces and decorated with the royal devices or those of Diane de Poitiers. These French pieces are not always comparable in quality with late Gothic door furniture but their historic associations make them interesting.

The predominance of the French locksmith remained unchallenged during the first half of the seventeenth century. Towards the close of the sixteenth century the French locksmiths' guilds required apprentices to submit an extremely elaborate lock as their masterpiece, and the finest French locks of this period are these masterpieces, not intended for use but to display the proficiency of the maker. They were of rectangular shape and the keyhole was invariably covered by a hinged flap of metal, the catch for which was concealed in the ornament of the lock-face. In addition to making the lock and key, the latter with thin comb-like wards, the apprentice was expected to be able to chisel and engrave as well. The engraving often betrays a rather inexperienced hand, though the more difficult chiselling is usually masterly. The production of these apprentice locks went on according to much the same formula, until the French Revolution put an end to the Guild system.

German and northern locks generally of the seventeenth and early eighteenth century have the characteristic shape shown in Plate 38D. A feature of most German locks is the dome, a cylindrical housing in which were fitted the drill pin and the wards. German locks were sometimes of very large size; they were either etched or somewhat coarsely ornamented with foliate ornament either cut with a chisel in the surface of the lock or applied in cut sheet-iron.

It was not until the second half of the seventeenth century that the work of English locksmiths achieved great importance. Outstanding amongst English locksmiths were the various members of the Bickford family, whose names appear on a group of locks which combine complexity of technical design with superb decorative quality. The Bickfords probably worked in London, but comparably fine work was done by locksmiths in the provinces, such as Richard Hewse of Wootton Bassett and John Wilkes of Birmingham. The manner of the Bickfords can be identified by the tracery of brass alternating with blued steel, with which they covered the lock face. Amongst their patrons were Queen Mary II (jewel casket in the Victoria and Albert Museum) and the Grand Duke Cosimo III of Tuscany (lock also in the Victoria and Albert Museum). The typical English lock of the late seventeenth and eighteenth century had a brass case, which was either engraved or decorated with applied cast ornament. Some magnificent locks of this period are still to be seen on the doors of the State Apartments at Hampton Court Palace and in some of the great country houses (Plate 38C).

While the Continental locksmiths fitted their locks with ormolu cases in the fashionable rococo style, in England the plain brass case remained usual until the Adams Brothers introduced, with their designs, a new refinement into English door furniture. The finely-finished Adam locks and door-plates achieved a very handsome effect when set on the figured mahogany doors of the period.

Nineteenth-century locks have little appeal to the collector, the only exception being the door-locks made in France in the Empire style, but few of these are likely to come the way of the collector in England.

Ormolu: the term 'ormolu' (from the French *or moulu*) is used to describe decorative objects and furniture mounts of the eighteenth and nineteenth centuries, cast in bronze or brass and gilt. Though cast and gilt bronze was by no means an innovation in the eighteenth century, it was used in France to an extent that could not be paralleled in previous epochs. Ormolu was not by any means an exclusively French production, similar work was done in Germany, England, and elsewhere, but the fineness of design and perfection of finish of the French artists was never equalled. While the main volume of production was of furniture mounts, vases, candlesticks, chandeliers, andirons, ink-stands and clock-cases were also made.

These objects were cast, chiselled, and finally fire-gilt. True ormolu should be distinguished from cheaper objects cast in the same moulds and from the same metal, which were roughly finished and lacquered instead of being chiselled and fire-gilt. Ormolu of the Régence and Louis XV periods was never so finely finished as that of the Louis XVI and Empire periods (Plate 38B). During the first half of the century French furniture was very lavishly decorated with ormolu, and the effect was achieved by mass of ornament rather than by detail. Later, when marquetry and parquetry were going out of fashion, we find less florid mounts against a background of figured mahogany, a setting which showed them off to the maximum advantage. In the Empire period the ormolu mounts played, if possible, an even more important role, and furniture was constructed as a vehicle for the display of fine ormolu. Such was the detail of the chiselling put into good work, that it was hardly less expensive than similar articles made of silver-gilt.

After the Restoration in France we find a deterioration in standards of production, and the large-scale reproduction of earlier styles, but throughout the nineteenth century there were still craftsmen who could turn out very fine work in this medium, and it is extremely difficult to distinguish between eighteenth-century ormolu and the best of the nineteenth-century reproductions.

In England the Birmingham firm of Boulton & Fothergill produced ormolu vases, candlesticks and perfume-burners during the 1760s and '70s. The finish was never up to the highest French standards but the designs, furnished by the Adam Brothers, were of great elegance and fitness for purpose (Plate 38A). There was no great demand for furniture mounts in England, but many houses of the second half of the eighteenth century still retain their ormolu door furniture made by Boulton after Adam designs.

Paktong: an alloy of copper, nickel and zinc, of whitish colour, resembling silver when polished. Grates, candlesticks and other domestic appliances were made of this metal in the last third of the eighteenth century. The name is derived from the Chinese, who used the metal for hinges and furniture mounts. It is also known as Tutenag, which, properly speaking, is zinc without admixture of other metals.

Pilgrims' signs: cast from lead, these badges were distributed at the shrines of medieval Europe to pilgrims, and were worn in the hat or on the person as evidence that the pilgrimage had been completed. These little objects, worthless in themselves, usually bore some allusion to the saint at whose shrine they were received. The best-known pilgrims' sign is the shell of St John of Compostella in Spain. The most popular English shrine was that of St Thomas at Canterbury. Pilgrims' signs, being made of lead, bear a superficial resemblance to the notorious class of fake lead medallions and amulets of the Middle Ages, made in London about the end of the nineteenth century, and commonly

(B) HISHIKAWA MORONOBU. A page from the picture-book *Ukiyo Hyakunin Onna-ye* ('One Hundred Pictures of Earthly Women'). *Sumi-ye, 1681. British Museum.*

(A) TORII KIYONOBU I. The actor Nakajima Kanzayemon I in character. *Tan-ye, c.* 1705.

PLATE 39

(A) Okumura Masanobu. Geisha girls going to a play. *Beni-ye, c.* 1755. *British Museum.*

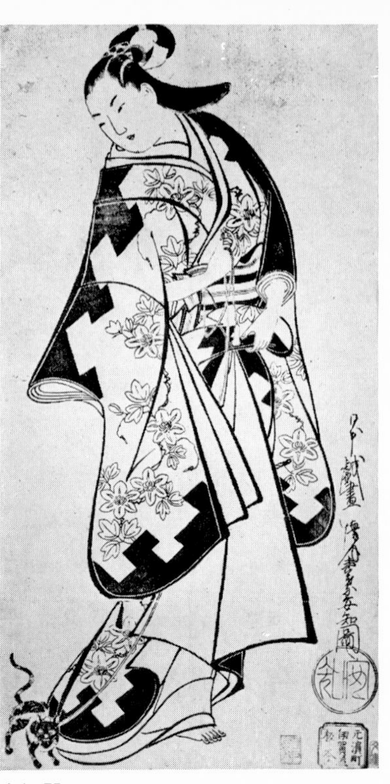

(B) Kwaigetsudo. A beauty with a cat on a lead. *Sumi-ye. Guimet Museum.*

(C) Torii Kiyonaga. A young lady with two attendants behind holding an umbrella. Polychrome, *c.* 1783. *Museum of Fine Arts, Boston.*

(D) Suzuki Harunobu. O-Sen, a noted tea-house beauty, serving a customer. Polychrome, *c.* 1768. *British Museum.*

(A) KORUSAI. Pillar print. *Honolulu Academy of Arts.*

(B) KATSUKAWA SHUNSHŌ. The actor Bandō Mitsugorō as a Daimyō. Polychrome, *c.* 1775–80. *British Museum.*

(C) ISHIKAWA TOYONOBU. Girl closing her umbrella. Three-colour print. *Hashirakake, c.* 1760. *British Museum.*

(A) Nishikawa Sukenobu. A page from the picture-book of woman's occupations, *Yehon Tokiwa Gusa.* Published 1731. *British Museum.*

(B) Chōbunsai Yeishi. 'Evening under the murmuring pines.' Triptych, part of a series called a 'Popular Version of the Romance of Genji'. Polychrome, *c.* 1793–4. *British Museum.*

PLATE 42

(A) Katsushika Hokusai. Travellers crossing the sand at low tide to the island of Enoshima. One of the 'Thirty-six Views of Fuji'. Polychrome, 1823–8. *British Museum.*

(B) Utagawa Kuniyoshi. The Soga Brothers' Revenge. The fight of the two brothers against the retainers of Suketsune during a rainstorm. Triptych, *c.* 1845. *British Museum.*

(C) Ando Hiroshige. Beggars importuning travellers at Takasaki. One of the 'Sixty-nine Stations on the Kisakaido'. Polychrome *c.* 1840. *British Museum.*

PLATE 43

(A) ISODA KORYŪSAI (attributed to). Pheasants and Peach Blossom. Polychrome, *c.* 1775. *British Museum.*

(B) KATSUSHIKA HOKUSAI. Wagtail and Wisteria. One of a set of Flowers and Birds. Polychrome, *c.* 1828. *British Museum.*

(A) KITAO SHIGEMASA. Two geisha girls and a maidservant. Unsigned. *c.* 1778. *British Museum.*

(B) TŌSHŪSAI SHARAKU. The actor Matsumoto Kōshirō IV in rôle. Polychrome, with mica background, 1794. *British Museum.*

PLATE 45

(A) KITAGAWA UTAMARO. Mother and Daughter. Polychrome, *c.* 1795. *Honolulu Academy of Fine Arts.*

(B) UTAGAWA TOYOKUNI. Two actors as a man and a woman in a scene from a play. Polychrome, *c.* 1795–6. *British Museum.*

PLATE 46

To face page 8

known after their inventors as 'Billies and Charlies'. The lettering of any inscription on a putative pilgrims' sign should therefore be examined with care, as it is in this feature that the fakers betrayed themselves.

Venetian-Saracenic brassware: amongst the numerous craftsmen from the Near East who settled in Venice during the later Middle Ages were metalworkers and damasceners. The earlier productions of the Arabic craftsmen in Venice are hardly to be distinguished from those they had made in their native countries, but towards the end of the fifteenth century and in the sixteenth century European elements became more apparent. The brasswares made by these immigrant Saracenic smiths included ewers, dishes, bowls, candlesticks and perfume-burners or hand-warmers. The earliest examples were engraved with pure, that is completely abstract, arabesques, and damascened with gold and silver, but their Western origin is often shown by the presence of an Italian coat of arms introduced into the ornament. By the mid-sixteenth century Italian-born craftsmen using Renaissance ornament had replaced the Saracenic smiths. On these later pieces not only is the ornament derived from contemporary pattern books but it introduces figure subjects. At the same time the damascening, which on the earlier pieces had been of exquisite quality and refinement, was restricted to a few summary details. The craft survived the sixteenth century only in a degenerate form (Plates 35D).

BOOKS FOR FURTHER READING

C. T. Bailey, *Knives and Forks*, Medici Society (London, 1927).

A. Bonnin, *Tutenag and Paktong* (Oxford, 1924).

British Museum, *Guide to the Medieval Room*, 1st ed. (1907).

A. Byne and M. Stapley, *Spanish Ironwork*, The Hispanic Society of America (1915).

H. R. de l'Allemagne, *Histoire du Luminaire* (Paris, 1891).

H. R. de l'Allemagne, *Les Accessoires du Costume et du Mobilier*, 3 vols. (Paris, 1928).

E. B. Frank, *Old French Ironwork*, Harvard University Press (1950).

J. Starkie Gardner, *Handbook on Ironwork*, 3 vols., Victoria & Albert Museum (various editions).

A. H. Hayward, *Colonial Lighting* (Boston, 1923).

I. H. Hefner-Alteneck, *Serrurerie du Moyen Age et de la Renaissance* (Paris, 1870).

J. B. Himsworth, *The Story of Cutlery*, Benn (London, 1953).

A. Kippengerger, *Die deutschen Meister des Eisengusses im 16 Jahrhundert* (Marburg, 1931).

Seymour Lindsay, *Iron and Brass Implements of the English House*, Medici Society (London, 1927).

J. Tavenor-Perry, *Dinanderie* (London, 1910).

W. Twopeny, *English Metalwork*, Constable (London, 1904).

JAPANESE PRINTS

By J. HILLIER

THE Japanese print was 'discovered' soon after the opening up of the country to foreign visitors in 1854, and considerable impetus was given to the formation of collections later in the century by the enthusiasm of the French Impressionists and their protagonists, who found much that appealed to their aesthetic senses, ever tuned to receive the new, the adventurous, the unacademic, in the calculated design and arbitrary use of form and colour, of the Japanese print designers. The most immediately attractive of these exotic engravings were the colour-prints of the late eighteenth century, but in the methodical way of the European art-historian it was not long before the origin of these gay pictures were traced back to black outline prints of the seventeenth century.

Indeed, the earliest wood-engravings made in Japan belong to a very remote period. Some can reliably be given to the eighth century and, as wood-engravings are still being published in Japan, the term 'Japanese print' might conceivably embrace everything from the crude Buddhistic cuts of an almost legendary antiquity to the pseudo-Picasso abstractions of post-war Tokyo artists. Specifically, however, the term is usually held to apply to the productions of a certain school of mainly Yedo artists, the Ukiyo-ye, which arose in the mid-seventeenth century and whose work was virtually ended by the time of the Restoration in 1868.

The collector may not wish to limit himself strictly to this school: book illustrations of great beauty and originality were designed during the Tokugawa or Yedo period (1615–1868) by painters of various other schools whose styles differ vastly from the Ukiyo-ye. Nor need strict regard be given to the limits of the period: one needs to study the illustrated books of the early seventeenth century for the light they throw on the development of the designer's art; and though it is convenient to consider 1868 as a date closing a particular chapter of Japanese art, specimens of the work of artists who flourished thereafter may well be included in a collection, if for no other purpose than to exhibit the changes the 'Western invasion' brought about. But here it will only be possible to deal with the Japanese print in the usually accepted sense.

At the outset it should be remarked that Japanese prints are all wood-block prints and were issued as much in bound or book form as in the form of separate broadsheets. Folding albums (*gwajō*) and picture books (*yehon*) must come within a collector's purview, for no study of the art of the Japanese print as a whole can be complete unless the prints in books are considered side by side with those published as separate sheets. Moreover, whereas practically all the broadsheets were produced by the Ukiyo-ye School, artists of the classical, naturalistic and impressionistic schools were responsible for some of the loveliest and most remarkable picture books ever printed, East or West.

Technique: Wood-engraving is the traditional, and almost exclusive, means of reproduction in Japan, as in the East generally. By the inheritance of the centuries-old lore of the craft, and by a rigorous apprenticeship, engravers were capable of almost incredible feats in making a facsimile of an artist's brush-drawing. The painter-engraver was unknown: the engraver was a skilled craftsman whose sole task was to make a faithful reproduction of the artists' designs, just as the German engravers made facsimiles of Dürer's designs.

The wood used was normally cherry-wood 'on the plank', in contrast to 'on the end grain' as in Europe since Bewick's day. The drawing, made on thin paper, was usually pasted face down on to the block, and the paper then scraped to render the drawing perfectly visible. The engraver or, more properly, cutter, for he used a cutting knife not an engraving tool, made incisions along both sides of the lines, afterwards removing the wood between, leaving the lines in relief.

The printer was, in his way, as much artist-craftsman as the engraver. The ink was brushed on to the block, pigments being mixed with a little rice paste to give them consistency, and the impression taken by placing paper over the face of the block and burnishing the back with a rubbing implement called a *baren*. When colour-printing from blocks was introduced, a great deal devolved upon the printer. Black ink proofs were taken from the 'key-block' prepared from the artist's drawing, and the proofs then pasted down on to additional blocks, a separate one for each colour to be printed, the artist indicating on each proof, for the engraver's guidance, the area to be printed in the chosen colour.

In making a colour-print, the same sheet of proofing paper had to pass first over the 'key-block' and then over each colour-block in turn. Accurate 'register' was achieved by a simple arrangement of a right-angle cut in the blocks at one side with a corresponding guide-line cut at the opposite side.

In addition to the increase in the number of colour-blocks used, various refinements were introduced to embellish the prints, mentioned in the account that follows:

The 'Ukiyo-ye' or 'Passing world' school: To explain the genesis of the Japanese print it would be necessary to go far beyond the limits I have been set, but the greatest single impetus to its development came from HISHIKAWA MORONOBU (1626–94). Though not the titular founder of the Ukiyo-ye school (which came to be the Popular school identified with the common people, notwithstanding the fact that its founder was an aristocrat named Matabei), Moronobu came at a time when there was a rapidly expanding demand for illustrated literature of every kind – classical poetry, legend, novel, everyday happenings, descriptions of the well-known landmarks of the country, and especially of the capital, Yedo. Owing to his tutelage in several different schools of Japanese painting, he was capable of drawing in a number of styles, but his most justifiably admired prints and book illustrations show the early Ukiyo-ye style at its best. The bold line and undulating swing in the drawing, coupled with a compact and rhythmic pattern in the design, are characteristics that mark the work of all succeeding Ukiyo-ye artists, and in his treatment of his subject-matter we discern already the sophistication, the raciness and the vulgarity that, in greater or lesser degree, are in the make-up of all subsequent prints of the school. Apart from his development of book illustration as an art, Moronobu is also accredited with the production of the first separately printed sheets, called *ichimai-ye*.

Contemporaries of Moronobu, responsible for much fine work in book illustration, were HINAYA RYŪHO, YOSHIDA HANBEI, ISHIKAWA RYUSEN, and SUGIMURA JIHEI, all more or less independent of Moronobu. A little later there were Moronobu's direct pupils, MOROSHIGE and MOROFUSA.

Towards the end of the seventeenth century prints began to be issued to record the *Kabuki* drama, the popular plays that were filling the Yedo theatres with devotees whose fanaticism was not only equal to the strain of day-long performances but also gave rise to a demand for pictures of favourite actors in their rôles in the latest 'thriller'. Women were debarred from the stage and female parts were played by men, some actor families specializing in women's rôles. It was natural that the People's Theatre should have been recorded by the Ukiyo-ye artists, and actor-prints are as numerous in their output as portraits of the reigning courtesans, the other principal subject.

Among the earliest to make these prints was TORII KIYONOBU (1664–1729), a great artist who had much influence on the development of the actor-print, and whose own gift of expressive draughtsmanship and swirling design was never equalled. His pupils and followers include many of the best designers of the early eighteenth century – KIYOMASU I (1696?–1716?); KIYOMASU II (1706–1765); KIYONOBU II (1702–52?); KIYOSHIGE, KIYOTADA, KIYOTOMO, and TERUSHIGE.

Most of these early prints were hand-coloured, at first with *tan*, a strong red-lead pigment, later with more elaboration. *Printing* of colours by wood blocks did not occur until many years later.

Other powerful 'Primitives', as artists up to the introduction of colour-printing in 1764 are called, are a group of four or five artists bearing the name KWAIGETSUDŌ, whose superb *kakemono-ye* are among the rarest and the most coveted of all Japanese prints; and NISHIKAWA SUKENOBU (1674–1754), whose work is almost confined to book illustrations, in which the rough boldness of his contemporaries is tempered with a grace and gentleness that was to have an immense effect upon aftercomers. Another great artist, a publisher, too, with a flair for technical devices, was OKUMURA MASANOBU (1686–1764). Owing something to Moronobu, Kwaigetsudō and Sukenobu, and passing through phases when the influence of each of these masters predominated in turn, Masanobu's fusion of strength and grace produced some of the loveliest prints of the first half of the seventeenth century. To him is probably attributable the introduction of *urushi-ye*, the 'lacquer-prints' with applied metal dusts, whose glint still catches the eye, as it was meant to catch the eye of the Yedo purchaser over two hundred years ago. His pupil TOSHINOBU (active 1725–50) also made some very attractive prints of this type.

About 1740, or soon after, occurred the momentous substitution of block-printing of the colours for the hand application that had prevailed hitherto. It is a matter of wonder that colour-printing had not been introduced before, since it had been practised in China a century earlier and the Chinese colour-prints must have been known to the Japanese. Possibly the expense involved in making multiple blocks had been a deterrent, for the prints were, after all, purveyed to the less affluent members of the community. As it was, for many years the colour-blocks were limited to two, most often *beni* (red) and green, hence the name *beni-ye*.

Okumura Masanobu has been credited with the introduction of the two-colour process, but by 1740 a number of gifted artists were working in the medium, any one of whom was capable of making the innovation. The most prominent were the Torii masters, KIYONOBU II, KIYOHIRO (active 1737–68), and KIYOMITSU (1735–85), all carrying on in the family tradition of actor-print designing, and NISHIMURA SHIGENAGA (1697–1756), whose later work shows the trend towards a new ideal of womanhood that was to lead to the exquisite fragility of Harunobu's child-women. The prints of the Ukiyo-ye school were not only a mirror of the life of the time, the daily events, the customs and festivals, but also the glass of fashion. In them one follows the changing predilection of the Yedo male for women of Junoesque amplitude of form in the early years of the eighteenth century, garbed in clothes decorated with patterns that have large pictorial motifs, to the diminutive *musume* of the 'sixties, disporting herself in silks that have the most intricate of pretty designs worked upon them. With this change, quite a gradual one, but speeded up after the introduction of the *beni-ye* prints, came another, no less significant, in the subjects portrayed, an introduction of a more domestic setting, of scenes from play or legend or even daily life, that are in some way made to seem idyllic, to belong to a never-never land of the Japanese artists' imagination.

This magical world is perhaps most the creation of Shigenaga's pupils – ISHIKAWA TOYONOBU (1711–85), SUZUKI HARUNOBU (1730?–70), ISODA KORYŪSAI (active 1764–80), and KITAO SHIGEMASA (1739–1819).

Toyonobu was the earliest, and, under the name of Shigenobu, designed hand-coloured prints before 1737. His later work, contemporary with that of Kiyomitsu and Kiyohiro, has an individual charm that has caused one Japanese enthusiast to call him the 'lyric poet of Ukiyo-ye'. Harunobu has been accredited – rightly or wrongly, it hardly matters – with the introduction of the full colour-print which made its appearance about 1764. The innovation coincided with the issue of a flood of calendar prints for the year 1765, a number of which are known to have been designed by Harunobu. Between 1765 and his premature death in 1770 Harunobu designed hundreds of prints that design, colouring and an exquisite fancy combine to render among the most charming of all the prints of this school.

The introduction of polychrome printing was more the culmination of a gradual development than a sudden innovation, for three and four blocks had been used with entrancing effect by Toyonobu, Kiyomitsu and Kiyotsune between 1760 and 1765, but the year 1765 is used as an arbitrary line between the 'Primitives' and their successors. Thereafter, whilst there is little new technically in the production of the print once Harunobu and others had introduced a whole range of lovely colours hitherto untried, and the printers had perfected relief-printing, blind-printing or *gauffrage*, and the use of gold and silver dusts and mica backgrounds, many great artists arose to make the fullest use of the perfected medium.

Koryūsai was not only a master of that most typically Japanese, and most exacting, format the *hashirakake*, the long panel print designed to hang on pillars, but he also popularized the large *ōban* sheet with pictures that are really 'fashion-plates' showing the reigning beauties in the latest creations of the *haut-couturiers*. KATSUKAWA SHUNSHŌ (1726-92) brought to the narrow *hoso-ye* actor-print wonderful powers of dramatic design, and tutored a whole school of artists, most of whom, like SHUNKŌ, SHUNJŌ, SHUNDŌ, SHUNYEN and SHUNSEN, repeated almost exactly the style of their master, whilst SHUNYEI, though associated with the theatre, developed on more individual lines. IPPITSUSAI BUNCHŌ (active 1760–79) is sharply distinguishable from all his contemporaries, however similar his subject-matter, for qualities that spring more, we feel, from an unusual personality than from any especial adroitness of hand. He was equally at home in the theatrical print as in the idyllic composition in Harunobu's vein.

After Harunobu's death in 1770 and Koryūsai's retirement about 1780, TORII KIYONAGA (1752–1815) came to the fore, and in the 'eighties was responsible for a vogue for tall women of regal mien, who now ousted the diminutive *musume* from favour. The diptych and triptych forms, in which the design is carried over two or three sheets, had an especial appeal to Kiyonaga, and through his magnificent example became popular formats with all succeeding Ukiyo-ye artists. As the creator of the currently fashionable feminine 'type', Kiyonaga influenced practically all his contemporary print designers, except perhaps the conservative, Shunshō. SHUNCHŌ and SHUNZAN, originally pupils of Shunshō, and SHUNMAN, who had studied under Shigemasa, were perhaps the most successful followers of the Kiyonaga model, the work of each having certain distinguishing traits, the recognition and identification of which is one of the subtler pleasures of connoisseurship. KITAO MASANOBU (1761–1816), another pupil of Shigemasa's, designed some splendid prints in the early 'eighties and seemed to vie for a time with Kiyonaga as the arbiter of fashion in Ukiyo-ye, but deserted painting for literature when quite a young man.

Throughout its history the Ukiyo-ye school received the stimulus from a new genius in its midst just when the influence of the last was beginning to wane. So now, as Kiyonaga went into retirement about 1790, KITAGAWA UTAMARO (1753–1806) became this new and revitalizing force. Beginning as a devotee to the Kiyonaga manner, and producing many lovely prints before 1790 rather in his style, Utamaro was afterwards responsible for a number of innovations – three-quarter-length 'portraits' with mica backgrounds; large portrait heads in which the design relies on the outlined features of the face and the decoratively coiffured hair; and, for a time, affectedly elongated girls whose extravagant height he used both to show to best advantage the glorious clothes they wear, and to create sweeping and decorative compositions.

CHŌBUNSAI YEISHI (active 1780–1800) was another artist who came to his maturity under the benign influence of Kiyonaga. He brought to his designs a refinement that makes his courtesan of the hour and his princess of olden times indistinguishable. His pupils, YEISHŌ, YEIRI and YEISUI, were also responsible for prints of unusual refinement.

Two artists stand somewhat apart from their fellow print-designers of the last decade of the eighteenth century: TOSHŪSAI SHARAKU (active 1794–5) and YEISHŌSAI CHŌKI (active 1782–95). The actor-prints of Sharaku are phenomenal, even in company with the most powerful productions of such gifted contemporaries as Shunshō, outstanding in this field, or Shunyei, whose large 'portrait heads' preceded those of Sharaku by several years. His sudden emergence as a print-designer, his short career, and his *faire brutale*, constitute the great mystery of the Ukiyo-ye. Chōki, much influenced by Kiyonaga, Utamaro and Sharaku, designed a small number of prints of beauties, mostly printed on mica backgrounds, that are as distinctive among the *bijin-ye*, from subtleties of design and vague distortion of forms, as Sharaku's are among the theatrical prints.

The last years of the eighteenth century saw the beginning of a deterioration in the standard of print- and picture-book production, which seems to have been a reflection of changing social conditions in Yedo, the growth of the demand for prints, a consequent increase in the output of the artists, and a coarsening of the fibre both of those that purchased and those that made the prints. In a fuller study than is possible here of the social *milieu* in which this thoroughly native art thrived, account would have to be taken of the political background of Yedo under the Tokugawa dictators, of the successive eras of prosperity and misrule, of wild extravagance among the rulers' favourites and the wealthy merchants, of famine and destitution among the common people, of police-state totalitarianism and sumptuary edicts, of underground movements among the oppressed, of natural calamities of earthquake and conflagration. Superficially, little or nothing of this is reflected in the prints, which we date more by changes in a courtesan's coiffure than by the laws affecting her existence, but the apparently inconsequential veering of fashion from Moronobu's time until the Revolution of 1868 was often the result of factors below the surface. Certain it is that stronger causes than a simple failure of powers in the artists have to be found for the degeneration which set in at the end of the century. It infected the later work of Utamaro and of his pupils HIDEMARO, TSUKIMARO and KIKUMARO, and of his followers like YEIZAN, BUNRŌ and RYŌKOKU, but it is most glaring in the prints of UTAGAWA TOYOKUNI (1769–1825) and his pupils.

Toyokuni (a pupil of TOYOHARU (1733–1814), founder of the Utagawa sub-school and himself principally remembered for *Uki-ye*, or 'perspective pictures'), was an accomplished artist who, in the 'nineties, designed many fine prints, though one thinks of him more as a plagiarist of Utamaro, Sharaku and Shunshō than as an artist of originality. Some of his early actor-prints, however, are superb, and it is in comparison with these that his later work, almost entirely theatrical, seems so slipshod and vulgar.

Of the vast number of pupils of Toyokuni, it is possible to mention only a few. Apart from KUNIMASA, whose 'large heads' are as rare and as much sought after as Sharaku's, most of the pupils were prolific and their prints are common. KUNISADA (1786–1864), who later took over the name of Toyokuni (being the third of the name, since Toyoshige, another pupil, had already used it from the death of Toyokuni I in 1825 until his own death in 1835), produced enough fine prints to prove he was capable of great things, but his enormous output of actor-prints succeeds only in overpowering us with a welter of riotous pattern and colour.

KUNIYOSHI (1797–1861) is more interesting, and is justifiably renowned for his great battle-pieces founded on the events of the clash between warring clans in medieval Japan. His landscapes are also noteworthy.

But the first half of the nineteenth century produced its own great masters – KATSUSHIKA HOKUSAI (1760–1849) and ANDŌ HIROSHIGE (1797–1858). Hokusai's life spans a vast number of changes in the art of the Ukiyo-ye school, and his own early work, contemporary with that of Kiyonaga and Shunshō, has something of the style and much of the charm that was in the air they breathed in that halcyon period. But his finest work was in landscape, a new development in Ukiyo-ye art, and in prints of birds and flowers that take something from the *kwachō* of the aristocratic masters of China and Japan. These prints are probably the best known of all Japanese prints and maintain their hold upon us whatever fashions in collecting may decree; 'others abide our question . . .'

Hiroshige is another artist whose work of most account is in landscape and whose lovely renderings of the Japanese scenery, his capture of transient atmospheric effects by the skilful use of the utmost art at the colour-printer's command, has endeared him to most Western collectors. KEISAI YEISEN (1790–1848) was also capable of fine things in landscape, but his *bijin-ye* suffer from the faults of vulgarization that vitiate so many of these late artists' gifts.

Most of Hokusai's pupils developed a talent, which Hokusai had had in large measure, for designing *surimono*, and collections can be formed of these enchantingly conceived and exquisitely printed little sheets of greeting, invitation or commemoration. SHINSAI, TAITŌ, HOKKEI, GAKUTEI and SHIGENOBU excelled in this miniature art.

Disparagement of the prints of the 'decadence' has become what has been called the 'correct' view of Japanese prints, and this is no place to dispute the generally adopted attitude. On the other hand, the wholesale condemnation of everything produced after 1800 is manifestly wrong, and many things of real merit can be collected from the vast mass of prints surviving from the period by artists whose names I have not had space to mention. Picture-books, for reasons hard to find, were often much better printed during this period than the prints, and offer a rich mine of material to the collector.

Collecting: 'Orthodox lines' would probably be a matter for dispute, for collecting today is conditioned largely by what remains to collect. Even a great fortune, and a long period of patient collecting, would not be able to bring together collections on the scale and of the scope of those of, say, Hayashi or Happer. One tendency nowadays is for small but select collections to be formed of a hundred or two outstandingly lovely prints, with no particular deference to chronology or completeness, or even to artists' traditional reputations – the supreme example of this type is the famous Ledoux Collection. Another method is for specialization, with a focus either on one period or one artist, or even on a particular type of print, for instance, *surimono*, or illustrated novels, or landscape prints.

Condition and 'state' are naturally of the utmost importance. Much reprinting from the original blocks was done contemporaneously, and many of the best prints have been copied, with intent to deceive or otherwise. Expertise in distinguishing the genuine first impression from reprints and facsimiles only comes through seeing and handling multitudes of specimens of all kinds, so that one learns the tell-tale variations in colour and in the texture of the paper, the surest guides where it is not possible to compare the actual woodcut lines with those of a known authentic impression.

The collector's ideal should, of course, always be a first impression in immaculate, unfaded condition, but very few prints, and even fewer *yehon*, have survived in that state. Remember, originally they were sold to the commoners of Yedo, the prints to be exposed to the light and to the discolouring fumes of charcoal fires, the picture-books to be thumbed through, often without the care we pay to them as 'works of art'.

Value of prints and books, therefore, turns on three things: the stature of the artist; the comparative rarity of his work; and condition. A few artists' prints could only be secured – if ever the chance occurred – at something over £500; any print by Kwaigetsudō and certain rare masterpieces of Toyonobu, Kiyonaga and Utamaro are of this order. Fine prints by most important artists of early period vary from, say, £25 up to several hundreds of pounds, but hosts of good prints can be obtained for far less than £25. The finest *yehon* may well fetch £25 to £150, but those who collect with an eye to acquiring representative examples of an artist's work (and are not too concerned about the charge of 'heresy' that some will make against them), can pick up odd volumes and detached sheets for a modest outlay. Every collector will find his own level of outlay and his own particular sphere for specialization.

GLOSSARY

Ban: size (*see* Chūban, Kōban and Ōban).

Baren: the burnisher used in hand-printing from blocks.

Beni: a pink or red pigment obtained from saffron flowers.

Beni-ye: pink picture: generally applied to two-colour prints, in which the *beni* was used with one other colour, usually green.

Beni-zuri-ye: pink-printed pictures, a more correct term for the two-colour prints.

Bijin-ye: pictures of beautiful girls.

Chūban: a vertical print about 11×8 in.; medium-sized.

Fude (or **Hitsu**)**:** a brush; also painted with a brush.

Gauffrage: blind-printing, producing an embossed effect without colour.

Gwa: picture or drawing; drew (at the end of an artist's signature).

Gwafu: book of sketches.

Gwajō: album of folding pictures.

Harimaze: sheets printed with two or more irregularly-shaped subjects, to be divided up by the purchaser.

Hon: a book.

Hoso-ye: small vertical narrow picture, about 12×6 in.

Ichimai-ye: single-sheet pictures.

Ishi-zuri: stone-print.

Kabuki: dramatic performances.

Kakemono: hanging picture, rolled up when stored.

Kakemono-ye: prints in the form of hanging pictures, usually about 26–28×10–12 in.

Key-block: the engraved block from which the outline of the picture was printed.

Kōban: a size smaller than the chūban, about 8×7 in.

Kwachō: bird and flower pictures.

Meisho-ki: guide-books to famous places.

Mon: badge or device serving as a sort of heraldic emblem for actors, courtesans, and others.

Naga-ye: Kakemono-ye.

Nishiki-ye: brocade pictures, colour-prints.

Ōban: full-size, 15×10 in.

Sumi-ye: ink-pictures, i.e. printed in black only.

Surimono: literally 'printed things', especially prints used for greetings or to mark special occasions.

Tan-ye: pictures coloured by hand with *tan*, a red-lead pigment.

Tanzaku: narrow vertical prints, inscribed with verses, about 14×6 in.

Tate-ye: upright pictures.

Uchiwa-ye: fan-shaped pictures.

Uki-ye: 'perspective' prints.

Urushi-ye: lacquer prints.

Ye-goyomi: pictorial calendars.

Yehon: picture book.

Yoko-ye: horizontal pictures.

BOOKS FOR FURTHER READING

L. Binyon, *A Catalogue of Japanese and Chinese Woodcuts in the British Museum* (London, 1916).

L. Binyon, and O'Brien Sexton, J. J., *Japanese Colour Prints* (London, 1923).

L. N. Brown, *Block Printing and Book Illustration in Japan* (London, 1924).

J. Hillier, *Japanese Masters of the Colour Print* (London, 1954).

A. W. Ruffy, *Japanese Colour Prints* (Victoria and Albert Picture Book, London, 1952).

E. F. Strange, *Japanese Colour Prints* (Victoria and Albert Museum Handbook, London, 1910).

(A) Landscape Study at Hungerford by Paul Nash. *Collection: Mrs Dudley Tooth.*

(B) The Medway above Rochester by Rowland Hilder. *Artist's Collection.*

PLATE 47

To face page 88

(A) Edinburgh by Henry Rushbury, R.A. *Royal Academy.*

(B) The Fountain by A. S. Hartrick, R.W.S. *Private Collection.*

PLATE 48

(A) River Garden, Bridgnorth, by Frances Hodgkins. *Tate Gallery.*

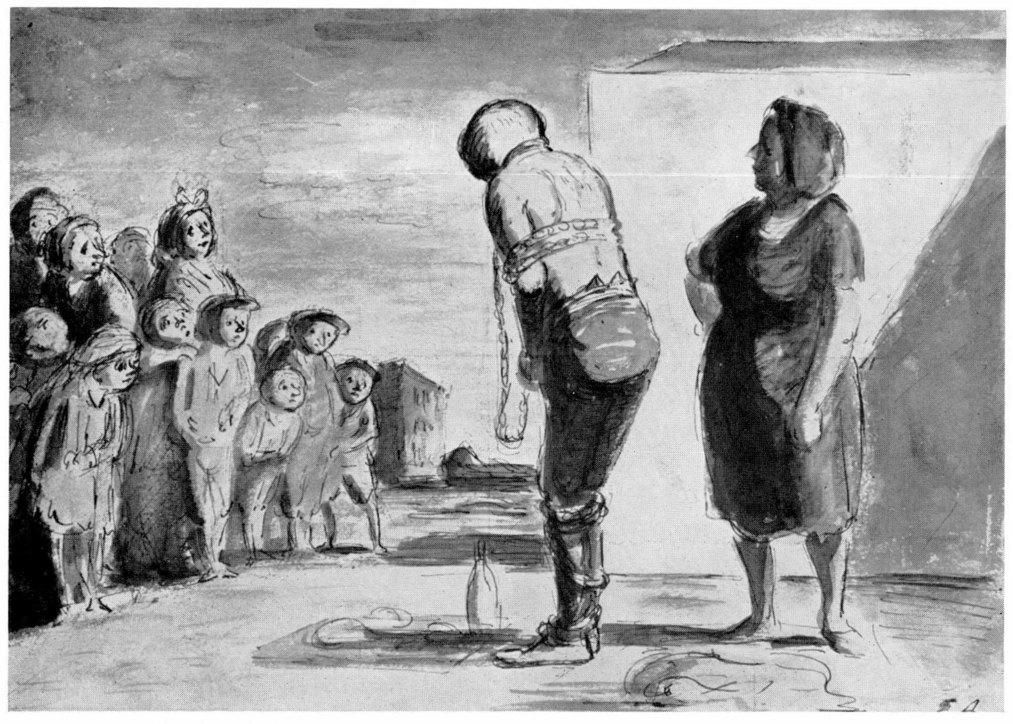

(B) The Chained Man by Edward Ardizzone, A.R.W.S. *Artist's Collection.*

PLATE 49

(B) Loch Earn by Sir D. Y. Cameron, R.A. *Collection: Ian MacNicol.*

(A) Stillingfleet All Saints by John Piper. *Collection: Mrs Hughes.*

PLATE 50

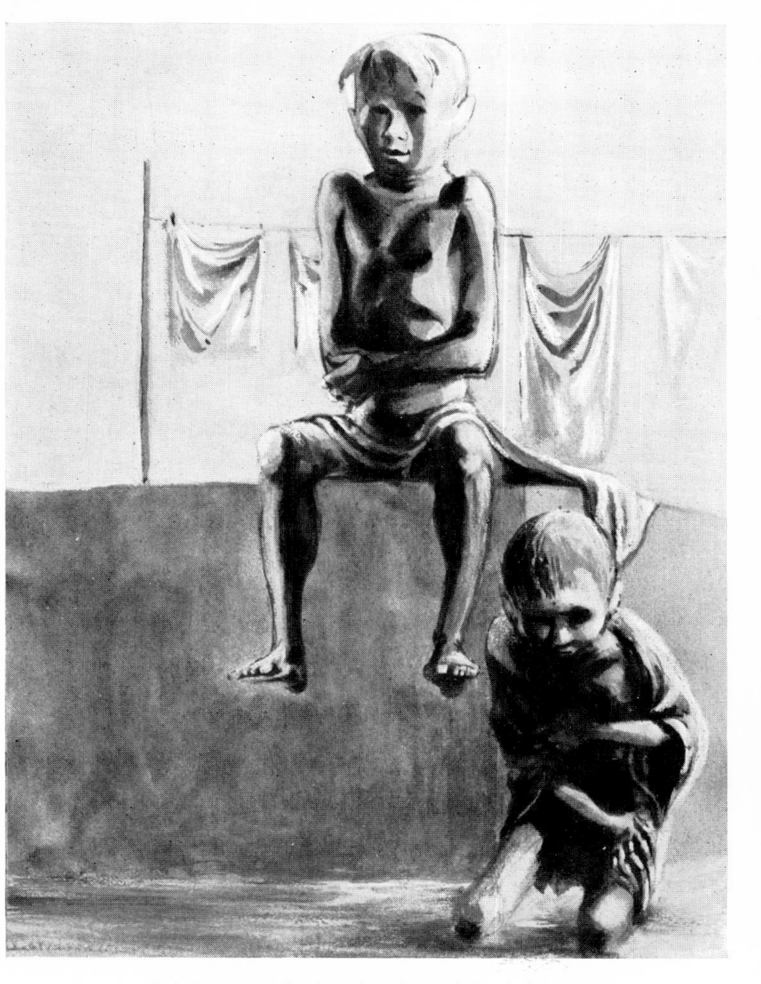

(A) The Cold Morning by Michael Ayrton.
Collection: The Contessa Roberti, Rome.

(B) Nomads in an Abandoned Château by Sir W. Russell Flint, R.A.
Artist's Collection.

(A) Bucklebury Oaks by Thomas Hennell, R.W.S. *Victoria & Albert Museum.*

(B) A Bright Winter Day by S. R. Badmin, R.W.S. *Artist's Collection.*

PLATE 52

(A) The River, Ironbridge by P. Wilson Steer, O.M. *Collection: Tate Gallery.*

(B) Harvest at Fairlight by P. H. Jowett, C.B.E. *Private Collection.*

PLATE 53

(A) Back view of a girl in a pinafore, seated, by Gwen John.
Collection: Mrs V. White.

(B) Petra by David Jones. *Collection: Miss H. Sutherland.*

PLATE 54

To face pag

MODERN WATERCOLOURS

By ARNOLD PALMER

In the preceding volume Mr Adrian Bury, writing of the *Old English Watercolours*, brought his survey down to Evelyn Cheston, who died in 1929. For the starting-point of the observations which now follow, the year 1939 has been chosen: that is to say, the field includes all artists working at the outbreak of the last war. But whereas Mr Bury was able to give a list of ten exponents who, generally after the passage of a century or a century and a half, had settled themselves firmly into a position of leadership, no such expression of finality is possible or even desirable in the case of artists still, or till yesterday, in our midst. Mr Bury was Posterity; he knew where he was, and that his readers would know where they were, and that there was authoritative support ready, in the event of need, for quotation. We cannot tell how Posterity will judge our day; of Posterity, indeed, it is usually safe to make only one assumption, that it will disagree with us. But our inability to attempt precision or rely on acceptance should, so far from depressing, encourage the new, intending collector. The words of counsel added, for his benefit, to the end of this survey will be few and tentative only.

Two other points call for brief comment before we embark on our main business. The extreme, or at least extraordinary, growth of nationalist sentiment has produced a state of affairs where, though Mr Bury could with propriety entitle his article *Old English Watercolours*, its sequel cannot, without causing offence, be called *Contemporary English Watercolours*. Secondly, it must be realised that all British painters, with hardly an exception, experiment from time to time in watercolour and other light media, with the result that many coloured drawings, some of them very beautiful, are every year produced by men and women whose reputation rests on oil painting. Such works can be collectors' gems; but, with regret, such artists, however famous, have been omitted from consideration here. The choice from the regular and recognized practitioners is sufficiently difficult without them.

In 1939, when our period opens, there were perhaps three British painters in watercolour whose work enjoyed something like worldwide repute, and it is an indication of the persistently national quality of this branch of art that, of the three, the one most esteemed at home met with the least general acceptance abroad. **P. Wilson Steer**, O.M. (1860–1942), was a notably quiet and retiring man; he confessed to membership of no societies save the New English Art Club, was content with one or two intimate friends, and asked nothing of the world save to be left alone with his paint-box. (When advised that he could charge certain expenses in relief of income-tax, he expressed doubt whether a man whose work gave him such happiness was justified in making the claim.) The subdued lights of morning and evening on the water of harbours, rivers, estuaries and seashores were what he particularly loved to render; they accorded with his own gentle nature, and all his long life he never wearied of them. Returning from one of his expeditions, he would walk round, it is said, to his frame-maker and, placing on the counter a portfolio of drawings, ask anxiously which, if any, that stern judge considered worthy of framing (Plate 53A). Towards the end his sight slowly faded, but his late work, if more and more tenuous, never dwindled into nothingness or lost its memories. His influence has been considerable, but his secrets, being far more than merely technical, are not to be had for the asking. His would-be imitators do not concern us, but in the charming paintings of **Philip Connard**, R.A., anyone may see how an influence can nourish a genuine and serious artist.

Earlier in his long life the name of **Sir Frank Brangwyn** was more widely known on the Continent than that of any other living English artist; and a retrospective exhibition of his work shown at Burlington House in 1952 revealed to younger generations the stature of a man hardly known to some of them save by repute. Fashions change in fifty years; the passage of time seemed to have dealt a little less kindly, perhaps, with his watercolours than with his pencil drawings and etchings; but no one who saw that exhibition can have doubted that he was in the presence of an artist of marked personality, skill and versatility. The last and much the youngest of the trio, **Sir William Russell Flint**, R.A., may suitably be left until we come to the Royal Society of Painters in Water Colours (R.W.S.), over which he presides. It is time we turned back to our starting point of 1939, and to artists who were then but are no longer living.

Of these, many people would agree that **Walter Richard Sickert** (1860–1942, the exact contemporary of Steer) and **Paul Nash** (1889–1946) are the most significant. Sickert, one of the giants of his age, was not primarily a painter in watercolour but (unlike Augustus John) he employed the medium sufficiently often for our purposes. Echoes of Degas, a fondness for the French scene and the French view of life – all these are to be found in his work, giving it a flavour not provided by any other English painter. Although he lived to an advanced age, although his work had for long been greatly admired, the usual readjustment which follows an artist's death has not made its appearance and it seems certain that his high reputation is safe from all but slight and passing recessions. The much younger Paul Nash had, by contrast with Sickert, little of the cosmopolitan about him. As far as anyone can be free of echoes, he was free; he was perhaps the first watercolour painter of importance to sound the modern note. He has suffered from a crowd of imitators quick to seize on his manner though rarely sufficiently serious or endowed to penetrate more deeply; and in this way his wide influence has so far advantaged the public, rather than professional, education (Plate 47A).

Outside their painting, both Sickert and Paul Nash were active and articulate members of the world of art. The war was only a day or two old when there died in France (in Sickert's beloved Dieppe) an artist of a very different kind, a Welshwoman who hid herself from the world, whose voice was never heard, whose known pictures, even, were few and scattered. It is true that **Gwen John** (1876–1939) was already represented in the Tate by one or two small pictures, but they, declining to make the faintest effort to be heard amid the clamour of a national collection, were generally overlooked by the casual visitor who, if he identified her at all, thought of her as the sister of a famous brother. A posthumous exhibition of her work, held in Bond Street a few years later, focused attention on her and brought her a reputation that, though it might not have astonished, would have embarrassed her; a subsequent show at the Tate, shared between her, Frances Hodgkins and Ethel Walker, strengthened the conviction that one more artist of the greatest fastidiousness, devotion and accomplishment had lived and died unappreciated (Plate 54A).

Of her two co-exhibitors on that occasion **Ethel Walker** (1867–1951) – long admired in both lay and professional circles as a colourist at once rapturous and subtle, a woman who found eighty-four years all too brief a span for recording the excitements of the visual world – had recently died full of honours, Dame Ethel Walker, R.A.; while **Frances Hodgkins** (1869–1947), after a curious career, late in which she had completely changed her approach to life and painting, turning from the representational to highly imaginative 'arrangements', claimed a loyal and enthusiastic following among the more intellectual art lovers (Plate 49A). Possibly the testing time has still to come, yet the reputations of these two fine painters seem firm enough to resist the normal buffets of fashion.

On the theme of the careers and fortunes of artists, **A. S. Hartrick** (1864–1950) provides yet another variation. At one time well known as an illustrator, and then as a lithographer, he presently, for a number of reasons, dropped from the public eye while continuing to rise in the esteem of his fellow professionals. His watercolours, absurdly cheap for many years and still cheap today, seem a sound investment for the collector of modest means since, at the worst, he will acquire small paintings of enduring charm, whose company he will never regret (Plate 48B). Several of the younger men, to whom reference will shortly be made, held him in almost boundless regard and chose him as their guide. The most devoted, perhaps, of all, **Thomas Hennell** (1903–45), an artist of high achievement and infinite promise, was killed when serving as an official War Artist; he is represented in the Tate Gallery as well as in the Imperial War Museum at Lambeth. But splendid as his war-recordings are, thrilling as he found the new, strange surroundings, wide as his interests had always been, he (like Hartrick) had gone and would surely have returned, for his chief inspiration, to the English countryside and its multiple vocations (Plate 52A).

Eric Ravilious (1903–42) was, similarly, killed on service as a War Artist. Everybody knows his designs on Wedgwood plates and mugs; some people consider that his influence on industrial art is likely to prove his main legacy. Such a belief, if true, possibly increases rather than diminishes the interest of his paintings, but it does not concern us here. He was a gay, original, and engaging painter rather than an important one; it is impossible not to enjoy his pictures, and it is part of their attraction that they make no portentous demands. He knew just what he could do, he never embarrasses us with pretentious talk or long words, and even his little mannerisms avoid affectation. Another casualty among the War Artists, **Albert Richards** was a young man of brilliant promise, so young, indeed, that he can have left very little work behind him save that which, at Lambeth, shows what he did, and what he might have done.

There remain four more of these obituary notices. **Sir W. W. Russell**, R.A. (1867–1949) never achieved the public recognition that was his due, and part, at least, of the explanation for this is not hard to find. He was a good teacher and a good committee man, who knew his own mind, seldom talked off the point, and was open to reason. Thus both in and out of the Royal Academy his services as an administrator were in demand, his hours in his studio correspondingly curtailed. Not only, then, was his output limited, but in addition his pictures are apt to be small and reticent; he was small and reticent in person, with a rather forbidding air utterly at variance with the lively sympathies which lay beneath it. He shunned publicity, though it was hardly necessary for him to do so, since the newspapers would have been hard put to capturing their readers' imagination with so correct, so unbohemian, so prim a figure. What he really was like can be seen in his pictures. He was a beautiful painter, whose work may be enjoyed, if you make a point of looking for it, at the Tate and other public galleries at home and in the Commonwealth. In the particularly choice collection of diploma works of the R.W.S., a little watercolour by Walter Russell more than holds its own with the best.

Neither **Sir David Cameron**, R.A. (1866–1945) nor **Sir Muirhead Bone** (1876–1953), two eminent Scotsmen, can need introducing to even the newest of collectors. D.Y. Cameron's Scottish landscapes are marked by a peculiar airy stillness, very pleasant to live with; it is a sign of their genuineness that when, as with some of the earliest examples, they are beginning to date a little, that process seems to be turning to their advantage (Plate 50B). Bone's astonishing powers of draughtsmanship, his impeccable proportion, perspective, scale, were usually devoted to black-and-white, but his watercolours, if sometimes more open to criticism, were sufficiently numerous to warrant the inclusion here of one of the most accomplished artists of the century.

Last in these obituary notes, **Charles Ginner**, A.R.A. (1878–1952), resembles no other painter in, or indeed, out of, the company here assembled. In watercolour or in oil he sought precision and fidelity, and achieved a realism so absolute that it became slightly unreal. Though often attracted by landscape, especially at that moment when there were no leaves unopened, no leaves fallen, no leaves missing from his portraits of the trees, the urban scene became him best; his houses, his walls were so meticulously rendered that his friends used to urge him to join the Bricklayers' Union. Such work, if not to everyone's taste, will always have its fascinated admirers. It is hard to see how, along the lines he laid down, any artist could have progressed farther; it is no less hard to think that his work is not, at the lowest estimate, assured of its position among the curiosities of painting.

The reader must be prepared for a slight change in approach as we turn to living artists – men and women who, if ageing, have the best part of a life's work to speak for them and, if young, may exceed or never fulfil the predictions of the critics. Comparison and discrimination become out of place and stupid, and little more will be attempted here than to mention painters admired by one section or another of the instructed public and (hardly less important) to indicate when possible where their work can be seen.

The two largest of the annual exhibitions of watercolours are those held by the Royal Institute (R.I.) and in the Royal Academy (South Room): in the opinion of many people, both are too large and run the risk of killing the eagerness they have aroused. Let us begin with something smaller lying at the heart of the affair. The Royal Society of Painters in Water Colours (R.W.S.), founded in 1804, is the oldest watercolour society in our island, if not in the world, and it has never lost the prestige of its seniority. With its forty members and twenty-five or thirty associates, it holds two shows, in spring and autumn, and since works by outside artists are not admitted, the exhibitions are of convenient size; they possess, too, other characteristics worthy of note. Election, eagerly sought and hard to gain, comes only to men and women sufficiently accomplished to satisfy the critical standards of the members; and in case any reader dismisses that statement as mere phrase-making, it may be revealed that one of the most famous of its senators applied seven times before being admitted. The prices his pictures fetch, the attention or inattention of art editors, wide repute or comparative obscurity – these factors are apt to play little or no part in deciding the fate of a candidate. It happens, then, that many of the members cannot afford to devote their lives to painting and are compelled to spend time in teaching. It follows, too, that at the Society's gallery in Conduit Street there is always to be had a true indication of the state of the British school, of the endless varieties which may be played on a traditional theme.

The President, **Sir William Russell Flint**, R.A., may be described, without fear of contradiction, as the best-known watercolour painter in the country. His wonderful technique, and the eager outlook on life which finds expression in his pictures, have combined to secure him this enviable position, and not only at home, indeed, but throughout the English-speaking world. His industry, while responsible for a flow of large or medium-sized works of hardly varying quality, sustains a brisk market from which he is far from being the sole beneficiary. There can be few people, and certainly no readers of these pages, who are unfamiliar with his work, if only in reproduction (Plate 51B).

The diversity of manners to be found within the Society's walls is much wider than is often supposed. The miniature, almost stereoscopic views of **S. R. Badmin** (Plate 52B), the light and vigour of a **Dame Laura Knight**, R.A., the quiet greys and brown of an **Oliver Hall**, R.A. or a **Mildred Eldridge**, the vivid glow of a **Margaret Fisher Prout**, A.R.A. or a **Gerald Moira**, the Gallic wit of a **Walter Bayes**, the Cockney bustle of an

Edward Ardizzone (Plate 49B), or the romantic strangeness of an **Edward Bawden** – there is scarcely an exhibition, from January to December, from extreme Right to extreme Left, in which some or others of these would not be welcomed and acclaimed. If anyone finds them all equally attractive, it can only be that all leave him lukewarm; if anyone loses his heart to none of them, he must be a born bachelor of art.

Several of the most important painters in the Society have still to be mentioned. **P. H. Jowett** achieves his individual harmonies by use of an exceptionally wide range of colour; his melodious pictures hold a wealth of orchestration which repays study (Plate 53B). **R. T. Cowern** is not a very prolific exhibitor, but his pictures, usually rather small, usually country scenes, are wonders of grace and delicacy. Again, the drawings of **Henry Rushbury**, R.A., whether in colour or monochrome, are worth all the attention that anyone cares to bestow on them. His favourite topics are urban scenes, city streets or sea-ports, and he has many competitors in that sort of thing. Some of them are not far behind him in training and assiduity, very few are comparable in perfection. A young collector, no matter in what direction his tastes may lie, can teach himself much by seeking to analyse the peculiar quality of a Rushbury drawing (Plate 48A).

With his friend Thomas Hennell, **Vincent Lines** used to devote himself to the English countryside. Lately the fields and harbours of northern France have attracted him; the skies are as pale, the airs as restless on one shore of the Channel as on the other, and these are the tints and temperatures he loves to render. Very different in intention and method, **Kenneth Rowntree's** pictures are easier to identify than to anticipate. He is still, and may well remain, an experimentalist, whose successes more than compensate for his failures, who will always have a future, if an unpredictable one. Lastly, there is **Charles Cundall**, R.A., today better known for his oil-paintings, but when at his best with few superiors in watercolour. If we must now leave the old Society with many admirable painters still not mentioned, we like to think that our readers, turning to the Conduit Street Gallery in spring and autumn, will enjoy the satisfaction of discovering them for themselves.

The Royal Institute of Painters in Water Colours (R.I.) is only some twenty-five years younger than the R.W.S., but there are notable differences between the two. Besides having a larger membership the R.I., like the Royal Academy, admits pictures from non-members. In its large exhibitions, therefore, one may see the work not only of the members but also of sundry promising young artists who cannot yet put magical initials after their names. One may see, too, the uncommissioned paintings of some of the leaders of commercial or industrial art, of men like the President, **Norman Wilkinson**, whose posters one looks for when changing trains at junctions, or **Rowland Hilder**, whose botanical plates are often the most beautiful and delightful of all the features of the best magazines (Plate 47B). There was a time when such references, to such people and such artists, would have been thought out of place in a serious estimate of the watercolour. Today there are many good judges who believe that if Posterity decides, as well it may, that we are in, or beginning, a minor renaissance, it will pay close attention to the influence of men like Wilkinson and Hilder, of Ravilious, Ronald Searle, John Ward, and others who have sallied out and sought the adversary, and won him over. Indeed, among the famous names of the past, there are more precedents for the industrial artist than is commonly supposed, and anyone starting to make a collection today might take a novel and profitable line by acquiring the spontaneous work of the best designers of posters and advertisements.

Two more happy hunting grounds for the collector must not be overlooked – the New English Art Club, where the watercolour section, if small, is invariably choice, and (in some ways the most important, since it is the best attended of all) the Royal Academy which, at its summer exhibitions, offers the second largest of the annual displays of watercolours. Ten years ago it was persuaded, by Sir William Russell Flint, to open not merely its doors but also its membership to artists who confine themselves to watercolour – a belated but significant gesture – and already there is one Associate whose election seems attributable to this innovation; among the full members there are always men, like that good painter **R. V. Pitchforth**, who show a fondness, if not a preference, for the South Room.

Moreover the pictures, like all pictures at Burlington House, are magnificently shown. How ironic, how cruel then, is the fate of some of them, the best of them, presented or bequeathed to the nation and housed at the Tate Gallery! There, while a happy world of Ambassadors and Peeresses, of foreign languages and silvery laughter, fills and overfills, in receptions as frequent as they are brilliant, the central hall and the splendid rooms beside it, what happens to the contemporary watercolour, 'notre art national'? Like an unwanted child, illegitimate or deformed, it is thrust out of sight, below stairs, where not even the echoing step of the occasional explorer can bring life to its pinched features, gleaming wanly in the semi-darkness and old before their time.

Unlike their elders, few of the younger men have studied abroad, in Paris or elsewhere, or been able to travel so frequently; the Aristocratic-Romantic age of Mrs Radcliffe and Byron, Scott and Turner, has gone. So, if landscape still predominates in the pictures we have been looking at, we hunt in vain for sunsets in the Pyrenees, storms in the Alps or eruptions in Sicily; instead, we find smaller heights and more restrained weather, a wet afternoon on the Quantocks or, at the most, snow on the Grampians. The gorgeous palaces ('Warwick Castle from the Avon'), the solemn temples ('Lincoln Cathedral, west front') have fared worse still, being largely supplanted by the flower-piece, the nature study, the interior, and the unidentified portrait. There is no cause for regret, we may even rejoice that our artists, more than any preceding generation of artists, have taught us to find beauty in our everyday homes and surroundings. In the extraordinary awakening, during the last decades, of interest in our own island, an interest revealed by the endless volumes of local history and topographical records pouring from the presses, by the growth of societies jealous of our heritage and active in preserving its outward features, by the public resentment, if often vain, of the self-satisfied ignorance of local authorities – in this wide movement our artists have played, consciously or unconsciously, a leading part.

There are still five or six painters left to the last not from their importance, still less from their lack of it, but simply because, through age or disposition, they do not lend themselves to classification. One or two of them exhibit, it is true, with the London Group, but that association is likewise difficult to classify, having no easily ascertainable H.C.F. In any case, its watercolour room is apt to be its weakest, only rescued from negligibility by the work of a few of the steadier hands, such as the happy, graceful landscapes of **H. E. du Plessis**. Our more revolutionary painters seem not to favour the watercolour, 'they cannot paint a watercolour', as one of their leaders has observed, 'without doing so as if it were a religious rite'. Perhaps (like those other outmoded forms, the berceuse and triolet) it is too gentle for their often violent moods, perhaps it does not offer a suitable outlet for scorn and irritability. But the most important of them are not, of course, susceptible to generalisations of this kind. **Graham Sutherland**, for instance, sometimes employs watercolour in preliminary designs for work carried out, or at least contemplated, in oil; whatever their purpose, they have their own independent existence and value, and their own eager collectors.

John Piper, a careful student of Turner and the other masters of the craft, has successfully evolved a technique suited to all media. Unlike Steer, whose effects in oil and watercolour differed widely, a Piper picture seen across a room can be reticent about the composition of the colour into which the artist has dipped his brush. He was trained as an architect and, insubstantial as his buildings may appear, he shares his old masters' fondness for the great church and the imposing mansion and never fails to appreciate and comment on the essential features. His outlook, even in his early work, has always been dramatic; it has led to, and is not the result of, designs for the theatre. He is one of the few living artists who already has his imitators on both easel and backcloth (Plate 50A). The theatre, indeed, attracts many of the younger men, such as **Michael Ayrton**, whose paintings are seldom seen in mixed exhibitions; one has to await his one-man shows. He is exceptional, too, in his generation for having studied abroad, as distinct from acquiring Continental traits from imported (and selected) best-sellers (Plate 51A).

A reference to Lady **Edna Clarke-Hall** might possibly have been inserted in the earlier, brief allusion to the New English Art Club, but nowadays it is rarely indeed that we experience the delight afforded by her pictures. They are as scarce in the auction room as in the gallery; the fortunate owners, it is clear, do not willingly part with them, Her name was never a household name, save in the homes of connoisseurs; her work, like the voice of an old lady, is easily drowned, but in any attentive company commands immediate respect by its tone of quiet authority and the perfection of its elocution.

Our survey began with Wilson Steer, a man who loved friends but was shy of colleagues. It may appropriately end with another resolute independent. Few painters can have experimented so little with oil, have made so early a choice in favour of watercolour, as **David Jones**, and few have retained so personal a view of the world about them. His pictures, often rather large, are pervaded by an airy and iridescent lightness all their own – they create a world of their own; and if, in a one-man show, they occasionally echo one another, in a mixed exhibition one of his pale watercolours is capable of making all the rest seem commonplace. The estimation of so original an artist must always be the reverse of automatic, the impact unpredictable; but for some people he has long been one of the most interesting as well as one of the most beautiful of living painters in watercolour (Plate 54B).

The experienced collector will have decided, without our help, where his tastes lie and who are the men he means to pursue. These notes are for the young, or at least the new, collector. Although some forty artists have been mentioned the choice, as was remarked earlier, has not been easy, and for several of those named there might have been substituted other artists with claims hardly or no less strong. Let not, therefore, the shy beginner pay excessive attention to this, or to anyone else's, selection. His first object should be to train and educate his eye, to form his own tastes. This he can do only by looking and looking and looking, and it is for that reason that we have stressed the local arrangements of the art, its principal foci outside the dealers. Though his instinctive preferences will quickly announce themselves, he should be slow to trust them or to assume from the start that painters whose work does not immediately appeal to him are necessarily men of sensitiveness inferior to his own. The eye, if it is to learn, must work, and the work, though anything but dull, is often hard. It calls for application and persistence, and it is unending.

Yet when all is said and done, pictures are like faces; other people may be right, one's own opinion may be wrong, but one has to come back to it, to a personal reaction independent of glamour and publicity, to something impossible to pin down. That is why it is important not to be deceived by calf-love, not to be in a hurry but, when one is sure of oneself, to respond and, if means permit, to acquire. To buy as an investment is unwise, to buy as an investment on the strength of someone else's views is particularly unwise, however instructed and honest they may be. Anyone who buys for snobbish reasons, because he has been told that an artist is 'the coming man', is apt to find himself doomed, and with justice, to live with pictures he does not like and cannot sell. On the other hand anyone who, having taken pains to form and formulate tastes of his own, chooses a picture as he chooses a friend will be warmed and ennobled by an act of sympathy, cheered by congenial company, and just possibly rewarded, some years later, by the discovery that he has carried off a prize. The chance is slight, but it is the best available.

CHINESE 'LOWESTOFT' AND EXPORT PORCELAIN

By GEOFFREY WILLS

THE first Chinese porcelain to leave the country where it had been made were pieces that had been manufactured for use in China itself. They had been brought home to the West by those few travellers who had penetrated the then unknown Orient. It was not until the seventeenth century that porcelain began to be made and decorated in China, especially to the order of European buyers.

The Jesuit Fathers: the Europeans who were concerned in the first place with the production of porcelain in China were the French Jesuit Fathers. These men, of whom the most famous in this connexion was Père D'Entrecolles, began to establish themselves in the country in about A.D. 1600. It was not until some fifty years after this date that a tangible result of their presence became apparent. This was the making of pieces of porcelain bearing representations of the crucifix accompanied, in many cases, by the letters *I.H.S.* It is uncertain whether they were made for export to Japan for the use of Christian converts in that country or for export to Europe. Whatever their intended destination, a few examples of these early wares, decorated in blue on a white ground, exist today, and their designs have an unquestionably European inspiration. However, in some instances, with a typically Chinese tolerance, Buddhist symbols have been incorporated in the patterns!

About half a century later there was a further output of religious designs. On this occasion there is no doubt that the products were made for export. Large quantities of porcelain were manufactured on which were painted copies of the Crucifixion and other Biblical scenes from both the Old and the New Testaments. Some were in full colours, but mostly they were in Schwarzlot.* While the majority were in the form of plates and dishes, there are in existence also a number of secular articles, such as tea-sets, which were doubtless for display rather than for use, painted quite inappropriately with such designs.

Armorial decoration: most popular form of decoration that was called for from China by patrons in England, and in Europe generally, was heraldic. Just as it was then the fashion that silver plate should bear the arms or crest of the owner, so it was the same with porcelain. This may be accounted for by the fact that the shapes of the majority of the articles were copied from pieces of silver, which it was intended that the porcelain should replace, and it was not unnatural that such decoration as the originals bore should be copied in addition.

The making of porcelain in European forms commenced at the beginning of the eighteenth century. Such pieces can be dated by a combination of factors: the shape of the article; the style of decoration and the colours used in painting it; the type of porcelain used in the manufacture; and, in some cases, by the armorial bearings. With the aid of the latter it is possible sometimes to date a piece of china to within a few years. It may so happen that a marriage or a death caused a change to have taken place in the emblazoning of a coat of arms, and from this it can be found during which years the particular bearing was current.

(A) Bowl decorated in blue with a scene of the Crucifixion. Early eighteenth century. Diameter $5\frac{7}{8}$ in.
Victoria & Albert Museum.

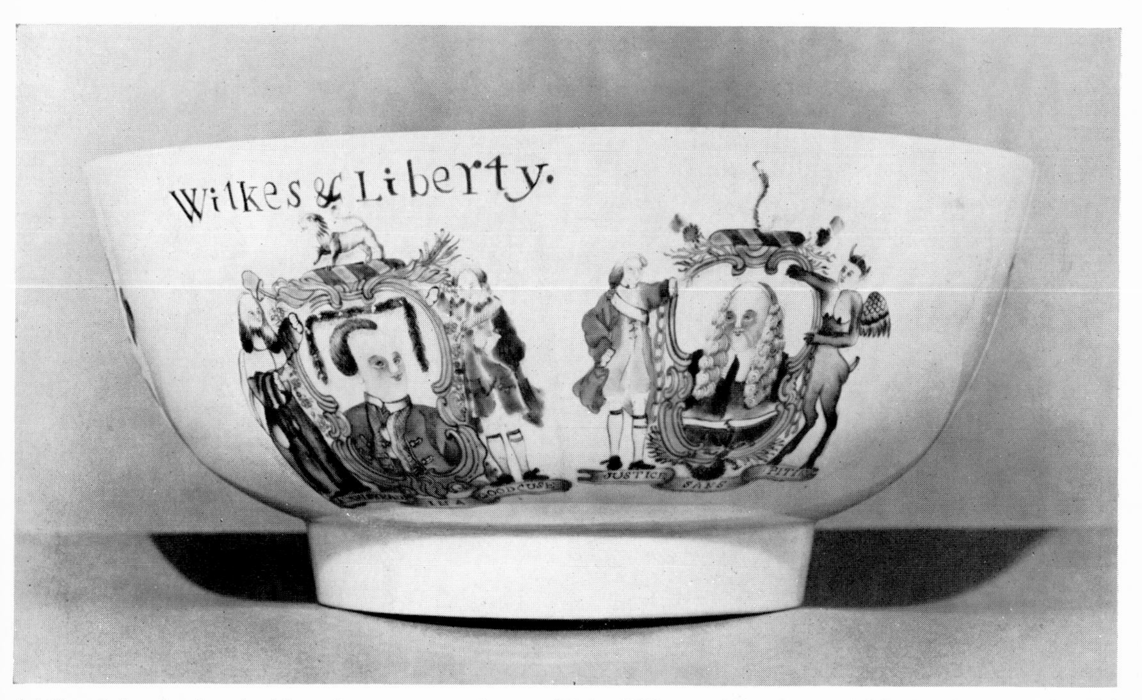

(B) Punch-bowl painted with caricature coats of arms of John Wilkes and Lord Mansfield. The former with Lord Camden and Lord Temple as supporters, and the latter with King George III and the Devil. About 1770. Diameter $10\frac{1}{2}$ in. *Private Collection.*

PLATE 55

(A) Fukien group of Europeans with a dog. Height $6\frac{1}{2}$ in. *Victoria & Albert Museum.*

(B) Candlestick in the form of a European lady. First half of eighteenth century. Height $7\frac{3}{4}$ in. *Victoria & Albert Museum.*

(C) Candlestick, about 1770. Height $6\frac{5}{8}$ in. *Private Collection.*

(D) Man and woman dancing, after a Meissen model of about 1735. This was made also at Chelsea and Bow. Mid-eighteenth century. Height $5\frac{1}{2}$ in. *Victoria & Albert Museum.*

(A) Dish with the Royal arms of England and inscription in Dutch. Early eighteenth century. Diameter $15\frac{1}{8}$ in. *Victoria & Albert Museum.*

(B) Dish decorated in blue with figures of European musicians; the border with Chinese landscapes. Early eighteenth century. Diameter $13\frac{3}{8}$ in. *Victoria & Albert Museum.*

(C) Plate painted with two figures of Scotsmen; the border with vignettes of birds and landscapes. Mid-eighteenth century. Diameter 9 in. *Victoria & Albert Museum.*

(D) Pattern plate. The back inscribed with the name of a dealer in Canton: SYNGCHONG. About 1790. Diameter $9\frac{3}{4}$ in. *Victoria & Albert Museum.*

(A) Part of a tea-set painted with a scene of the Crucifixion in schwarzlot. First half of eighteenth century. *Boston Museum of Fine Arts.*

(B) Covered vase of European form. About 1800. Height about 13 in. *Boston Museum of Fine Arts.*

(C) Part of a dinner service painted with the coat of arms of Newman. About 1790. *Boston Museum of Fine Arts.*

PLATE 58

To face page

In a few cases the original accounts have been preserved in a family, together with the china to which they relate. One such example is the bill, now preserved in the British Museum, referring to the service shipped from Canton in 1731 for a member of the Peers family. Two pieces of the actual china are in the same museum. Such careful and fortunate preservation of the original documents is, of course, very exceptional, and goes far to help in dating many other similar pieces.

Variety of articles: the output of porcelain for export was not confined by any means to articles solely for use at the table. Any attempt to provide a complete list of the many different things that were made would be doomed to failure. In this type of porcelain it is not untrue to suggest that there is nothing new under the sun, and frequently it is surprising to find what the Chinese potters and painters attempted to copy in a medium that was often completely unsuitable. However, although the result was usually a technical success, it must be agreed that it was far from being also an artistic one.

Next in popularity to table-services were punch-bowls. These were made in many sizes and decorated in an infinite variety of styles. Many bear the scene of an English fox-hunt round the outside, and some of these are completed by having the fox painted on the inside of the bowl. Others have accurate copies of European paintings and engravings, such as Hogarth's *Calais Gate*, of which a fine example in full colours is in the Victoria and Albert Museum, London. Others refer to political events, of which the bowl with caricature portraits of John Wilkes and the Lord Chief Justice Lord Mansfield (Plate 55B) is typical. Others bear externally, say, a group of flowers, but beneath the base is a well-painted amorous scene, best kept concealed from the general gaze.

A list of other utilitarian articles could be a lengthy one, and would include: candlesticks, cache-pots (in which a flower-pot stands), water-cisterns, shaving-bowls, chamber-pots, wall brackets, salt-cellars, pepper- and sugar-casters, knife-handles, snuff-boxes, tea-caddies and beer tankards.

Figures: apart from such articles intended for daily use in the home, pieces that could serve none other than a decorative purpose were also made. Figures with attempted European features and in Western clothing, such as the lady in Plate 56B, are typical. There are also figures of animals copied from Dutch Delft pottery, and from other originals. An interesting group is that of a man and woman dancing, illustrated in Plate 56D. This is known to have been first modelled at the Meissen (Dresden) factory about the year 1735 and, besides the Chinese copies, it was also imitated in England at both Chelsea and Bow. Few other groups can have been made at so many different factories in so many countries within the space of about twenty-five years. In the category of figures may be included jugs. Copies of jugs of the Toby type also exist in Chinese eighteenth-century porcelain.

The factories: the articles enumerated above were all made in one or other of the great factories grouped at Ching-Tê-Chên and decorated, with the exception of blue-and-white pieces, mostly at the port of Canton. Figures, groups and other pieces were made also at the factories of Tê-Hua in the Province of Fukien. The porcelain made there was of a distinctive creamy-white colour, and was not usually decorated in the East. Much of it was imported into Holland and Germany and coloured in those countries. Small groups composed of figures wearing recognizably European costume are found in this ware, also tankards with rounded bodies and reeded necks taken from a model known in German stoneware. This type of porcelain, which dates from the mid-seventeenth century, is known as Blanc de Chine.

One further group of eighteenth-century export porcelains was decorated in underglaze blue, together with touches of red and some slight gilding. It was based on that exported from Japan, and is known by the name of the port whence the original was sent to the West, Imari.

Late in the eighteenth century exportations from China included a large proportion of so-called Mandarin wares. These were painted with panels of figures within minutely patterned borders. In the next century came the Canton style, which features butterflies and flowers on a celadon-green ground.

Apart from a knowledge of the rôle played by the various East India Companies in trading with the Orient, little is known of the details of how this large trade was handled. The pattern plate illustrated in Plate 57D provides evidence that the business was not conducted in any haphazard fashion.

The Lowestoft myth: it must be admitted that the word *Lowestoft* applied to this section is something of a misnomer. In actual fact there is no real connexion whatsoever between Lowestoft, a fishing port in Suffolk on the east coast of England and the porcelain produced in the factories of China. Certainly a type of porcelain was made for some years in a factory established at Lowestoft. The decoration applied to many of the productions of these minor works comprised bouquets of pink roses and groups of figures and was, by a coincidence, very similar to the decoration then current on porcelain from the Far East. This English porcelain itself does not compare at all with the hard Oriental product, and the two are not likely to be confused.

The widespread misapprehension over the origin of the Chinese pieces arose towards the end of the nineteenth century through a mistake in a book,* and, in spite of repeated corrections over the past seventy-five years, collectors and dealers in both England and the United States continually refer to Chinese porcelain made to European order as *Lowestoft*. From being applied, in the first place, to pieces with a particular type of floral decoration, the term has been extended to cover the whole group of export porcelains, and today almost any piece of Chinese porcelain which displays in shape and decoration any obvious sign of European influence is designated by this inappropriate term.

* See Glossary.

GLOSSARY

Allen, Robert (1744–1835): an artist at the Lowestoft, Suffolk, porcelain factory from 1757, and manager there from about 1780. On the closing of the works in 1802 Allen set up as an enameller of white porcelain on his own account. A Chinese tea-pot and cover in the Schreiber Collection at the Victoria and Albert Museum, London, has the body painted with a Crucifixion scene, the cover bears some flowers, and the base is signed: *Allen, Lowestoft*. The religious scene was painted in China, and the flowers probably in Lowestoft by Allen, who added his name to the whole.

Batavia: a trading station of the Dutch East India Company in Java; after which is named a type of decoration that was popular during the mid-eighteenth century. It comprised shaped panels (often in the form of leaves), which are painted with flowers, reserved on a caramel-brown ground.

Blanc de Chine: the porcelain known as *blanc de Chine* was made at Tê-Hua in the Province of Fukien. This china, in which the white varies in colour from a deep ivory to the starkest bluish white, was first manufactured some time during the Ming dynasty (1368–1644). The factory specialized in figures of the numerous deities and sages of the Buddhist faith, and there must be few persons interested in Oriental china who have not seen one of the typical graceful statuettes of Kuan-yin (Goddess of Mercy) that were made in great quantities.

From about 1650 this factory began to make pieces that show European influence. A soldier, perhaps Dutch, dates from this time; another well-known figure of a man wearing a tricorn hat is probably rather later. It has been pointed out that the inhabitants of Fukien Province are extremely superstitious, and it has been suggested that this may explain why there exist *blanc de Chine* groups and figures of Europeans placed in typically Chinese settings and attitudes. For example, there is a group in which a European is seen standing on the head of a dragon, which symbolizes the attainment of the highest literary honours. The small mugs of stoneware form are thought generally to be of Western origin, and to have been copied from a German specimen.

Tê-Hua porcelain was occasionally painted in China, but when coloured is found to have been decorated more often in Holland or Germany during the eighteenth century than in its country of origin. The ware was exported principally from the port of Amoy.

Calligraphy: Chinese copying of European handwriting was purely mechanical and, as may be expected, many mistakes occurred in the transcription of verses, mottoes and inscriptions sent from the West. Letters were omitted, or formed into unpronounceable digraphs, and the letter *N* was rendered frequently as И. A typical mistake of another type was the careful copying of a coat of arms on each piece of a service, with the addition of the words *These are the Arms of myself and my wife*, which had been written on the pattern sent from England.

Canton: the principal port on the coast of China for trade with Europe in the eighteenth and nineteenth centuries (*see* East India Company). Porcelain was brought to Canton by river from Ching-Tê-Chên. From the middle years of the eighteenth century increasing quantities of the porcelain were sent unpainted, and decoration was applied to order by artists in enamelling shops at the port. *Canton* is the familiar name for a nineteenth-century Chinese porcelain exported to Europe. It bears a decoration of butterflies, flowers, etc., on a celadon-green ground.

Chaffers, William: editor of the famous work *Marks and Monograms on Pottery and Porcelain*, first published in 1863. He was responsible for the error by which a great quantity of Chinese porcelain was ascribed to the English Lowestoft factory. At this distance of time it seems strange that such a mistake ever should have occurred, and even stranger that some of the greatest ceramic experts of the period should have joined the argument, and produced complicated theories that were no less remote from the truth.

Ch'ien Lung: during the reign of this emperor, who was on the throne from 1736 to 1795 and who abdicated at the advanced age of eighty-six, was produced much of the porcelain decorated to the order of Europeans. The Emperor Ch'ien Lung was a noted patron of the arts, and encouraged the making of porcelain in his country. He was interested in Western culture, and there is no doubt that he encouraged the making of many pieces of china based on the design of French articles sent as presents to Peking from the King of France, or ordered from Paris by the Jesuits at the command of the Emperor.

Ching-Tê-Chên: the town situated on the south bank of the River Ch'ang, where pottery and porcelain has been made, almost without cessation, for many centuries. In the early years of the eighteenth century the population ran to a million persons, all of whom were employed, it was stated, in the production of porcelain that was fired in some three thousand kilns.

Compagnie Dessin (French: Company pattern): the French name for porcelain made to European order in the Far East, and imported by the *Compagnie des Indes*, the French East India Company.

Decoration:

1650 The earliest designs on Chinese export porcelain were of a religious character. The blue-and-white pieces, dating from this time, painted with religious scenes and emblems, are the subject of some argument as to whether they were made for use by Christian converts in China and Japan rather than for export to the West (*see* Plate 55A).

1700 Still with decoration in blue are cups, saucers, etc., painted with European figures, and inscriptions in French. Coloured figures were made (Plate 56B).

1725 At about this time the first pieces painted with English and other coats of arms in colours began to be made in quantities. In these early importations the coat of arms is usually of a large size with elaborate mantling (Mantling: the scrollwork, etc., surrounding the actual coat of arms).

Schwarzlot decoration, especially of religious subjects, was also exported.

1750 The coat of arms grew smaller and the mantling was simplified.

1770 The coat of arms was usually in a simple shield.

1790 The coat of arms was in a spade-shaped shield, and the rest of the piece is plainly decorated with the Gold Star, or some similar bordering. The surface of the china is often of the texture of an orange skin. The pattern-plate (Plate 57D) is of this date. In contrast, the complicated Mandarin patterns were also being made.

1825 Butterflies and flowers painted on a celadon-green ground were becoming popular, the so-called Canton style (*see* Blanc de Chine).

D'Entrecolles, Père François Xavier: a Jesuit missionary who went out to China in the year 1698. At a time when all the nations of Europe were trying actively to discover the secrets of porcelain manufacture he informed his compatriots of the methods of the Chinese potters. Two long letters, detailing with accuracy all that he had seen and heard, were written by him in 1712 and 1722, and published later in Paris. These documents are still the basis of much of our knowledge of porcelain-making in China. Père D'Entrecolles died in Peking in 1741.

The letters have been translated into English, and are most accessible in *Porcelain: its Nature, Art and Manufacture* by William Burton, London, 1906.

East India Company: the Honourable East India Company was incorporated in 1600, and had a monopoly of trade between England and the East. *Factories* (warehouses) were established for trading with China during the second half of the seventeenth century at Tongking, Amoy, Tainan (on Formosa), and at Gombron in the Persian Gulf. None lasted for more than a few years. In 1715 Canton became the principal port, and the Chinese side of all business came under the regulation of the *Co-hong*, a closed corporation of the local merchants. The Company formed a Council of Supercargoes to deal with them.

In addition to the ships belonging to the East India Company, licences were granted to the vessels of other traders, and there were in addition numerous unlicenced and unprincipled interlopers. Before long the vessels of the licensees and the unlicensed outnumbered those of the Company and, in turn, the total number of British vessels outnumbered those of all the other trading companies of the European nations. The *factories* of the various trading nations fronted the Pearl river, and contemporary views of them are found on porcelain and in paintings on canvas and glass. The East India Company was dissolved in 1858.

Fakes: modern imitations of eighteenth-century Chinese porcelain, painted with coats of arms, have been made in large quantities. Those made at Herend, in Hungary, are not so plentiful as those of Samson of Paris.

Fukien: *see* Blanc de Chine.

Gold Star: a pattern commonly used as a border for tea and dinner services, etc., towards the end of the eighteenth century, and in the early years of the century following. It is in the form of a band of dark blue overglaze enamel, with small gold stars set on it at equal intervals. It was, and is, very popular in America.

Gombron: in the early part of the seventeenth century the English East India Company established a *factory* at the port of Gombron, in the Persian Gulf. As a result of this, native Persian ware and Chinese porcelain imported into England from this source were referred to indiscriminately as *Gombron ware*. As late as the 1770s Horace Walpole wrote of *two basins of most ancient Gombron china*, which may have been either Persian or Chinese. The modern name of the port is Bandar Abbas.

Imari: a port in Japan which gave its name to a porcelain made in that country and decorated in a distinctive style in underglaze blue, iron red, and gold. Similar patterns in these colours on Chinese porcelain are known also as *Imari*, or *Chinese Imari*.

India ware: the term in general use in England during the eighteenth century for imported Chinese porcelain. It gained currency owing to the fact that the East India Company held a monopoly of trade with the East. It sold the goods it imported by auction at India House, London. This building in the City was demolished in 1861.

Iron red: a red pigment made from an oxide of iron; used to decorate ceramics.

Jesuit: the first Western influence brought to bear on the Chinese potters and painters was through the Jesuit missionaries. The first of these came to reside in the country towards the end of the sixteenth century. The life of these men was an arduous one, and they did all they could to promote good relations between East and West. One of them, Père Le Comte, wrote: *'Tis computed that since the year 1580 about 630 Jesuits and 200 Priests of other Orders have been sent out of several parts of Christendom to* CHINA; *half of which never landed in that Kingdom, and but very few of them ever return'd, being taken off either by Diseases, or intercepted by the* DUTCH *in the Straits of* SUNDY, *and* MALACA, *or else executed by the Civil Powers for disturbing the Publick Peace. . . .*

Le Compte, Père Louis: a Jesuit missionary who published in Amsterdam in 1697 *Memoirs and Observations made in a late Journey through China*. The book was issued in translation in London in the same year. Le Compte devotes several pages to porcelain and mentions that blue-and-white was the principal product. He adds that the European merchants foolishly bought anything that the Chinese were willing to sell.

Lowestoft: a factory for the making of soft-paste porcelain was established at Lowestoft, Suffolk, England, in 1757. During the forty-five years of its existence it turned out coloured and blue-and-white wares that are pleasant but not outstanding in either painting or potting. A proportion of the decoration was in the form of bouquets of flowers and groups of Oriental figures. Both are not dissimilar from the patterns that were then being imported on porcelain from China.

Mandarin: late eighteenth-century decoration of groups of figures wearing official dress, painted in panels within borders of elaborate diaper and other patterns.

Marks: marks are not generally to be found on Chinese porcelain made for export. Two pieces of blue-and-white in the Victoria and Albert Museum are marked; a bottle bears a capital 'G' and beneath a plate is the word 'BEVERE'. The plate illustrated in Plate 57D bears the name *Syngchong* on the back. There is a plate, also in the same museum, inscribed *Canton in China 24th Jany. 1791* (*see* Syngchong).

Nankin: port in China from which were shipped large quantities of porcelain with decoration in underglaze blue. This was known as *Nankin china* in the eighteenth century. The name is still current.

Samson: this Paris porcelain factory is well known for clever copies of old armorial Chinese porcelain, which have been made there for more than half a century. The coats of arms are often those of Great Britain or of France, or of some famous person, as Lord Nelson. Examined closely, these copies should not deceive the collector, but in an ill-lighted room a costly mistake might easily be made. Samson's productions sometimes bear a simulated Chinese 'seal' mark or a disguised 'S' beneath the base in red.

Schwarzlot (German: black lead): decoration in black monochrome usually in imitation of engraving. Frequently found with the addition of slight gilding and with the flesh tones rendered in iron red.

Syngchong: a dealer in Canton *circa* 1800. A large bowl belonging to the Corporation of the City of New York, bearing a view of the city and the arms of the corporation, and dated 1802, is inscribed on the outside of the rim of the base: *This bowl was made by Syngchong in Canton, Fungmanhe Pinxt.*

Underglaze blue: the blue painting is applied directly upon the ware before it is glazed. The surface of the finished article is smooth and shiny and the painting is *under* the glaze.

BOOKS FOR FURTHER READING

J. A. LLOYD HYDE, *Oriental Lowestoft* (New York, 1936 and Newport, Monmouthshire, 1954).

MARGARET JOURDAIN and SOAME JENYNS, *Chinese Export Art in the Eighteenth Century* (London, 1950).

Most of the standard works on Chinese porcelain contain a chapter devoted to export porcelain and, usually, typical specimens are illustrated.

COTTAGE POTTERY AND POPULAR ART

By REGINALD G. HAGGAR, R.I.

This study includes country pottery produced for cottage, farm or ale-house use, as well as 'wares of common stamp; copper lustre jugs, and tea things of tawdry colouring and coarse quality, and painted in flaring tints; painted pot marbles, and drinking mugs with names in letters of pink or purple' which *Chambers' Edinburgh Journal*, 23rd November 1839, said were manufactured in quantity at the smaller Staffordshire potworks for use of the poor. These constituted the indigenous popular art of the people.

Slipware: apart from medieval pottery, English slipware reached its finest flowering at the end of the seventeenth century, and shares, with the contemporary Jacobean style, robustness of expression, lavish and sometimes unrestrained use of ornament and, more important, a certain crude vitality. While these characteristics are fairly constant, each district developed a well-defined local style.

The normal products of all country potworks were lead-glazed utility articles, undecorated, or, at most, given a simple slip finish; and they often satisfy hand and eye because of functional honesty and simplicity.

DERBYSHIRE: the earliest clay-decorated pottery (apart from medieval and Tudor wares) appears to have been made at Tickenhall. Narrow dark tygs with applied pads of white clay shaped roughly into the form of flowers or stags' heads are characteristic, but many of the notched dishes decorated with 'trailed' slip formerly attributed to Derbyshire are now generally accepted as Staffordshire wares. The Derbyshire slipware factories (Tickenhall and Bolsover) continued in operation until the end of the eighteenth century.

KENT: between 1612 and 1721 (possibly longer), bowls, candlesticks, cisterns, dishes, mugs, porringers, posset-pots, puzzle-jugs, tygs, and useful crockery decorated with various forms of slip were made at Wrotham. These have distinctive features: (1) applied pads inscribed with initials and dates surrounded by effects of 'stitchery', perhaps in imitation of appliqué embroidery; (2) use of rosettes, stars, and masks; and (3) the occasional inclusion of the place-name (Wrotham) in the decoration.

Early products of this factory were simple in shape and ornament; later wares were generally over-elaborated in a rather tasteless manner. Two potters have been identified with certainty: George Richardson (1620–87) and Nicholas Hubble (d. 1689).

Something of the Wrotham flavour may be perceived in the red slipwares made at Brabourne, Deal, Dunkirk, High Halden and Pembury in the nineteenth century; there may have been some continuity.

NORTH STAFFORDSHIRE: the best English slipwares were made in the Potteries from about 1660 onwards, and those associated with the name Toft represent the high-water mark of technical accomplishment. Of the three Tofts – Thomas, Ralph and James – the former died a pauper in 1689. There is no certainty that the wares marked Toft were made by them, although the balance of evidence supports this tradition. Hearth Tax returns for Shelton and Stoke parish registers prove that the family was living in Shelton at this period. Tiny fragments of a signed Toft dish have recently been excavated in Hanley.

Surviving signed pieces fall into two classes: (1) large circular dishes, (2) jugs, posset-pots and loving-cups. The latter are extremely rare. Analogous unmarked pieces include divided baking dishes, bleeding-bowls, cradles, egg-stands, honey-pots, owl jugs, Dutch ovens and posset-pots.

Toft dishes are usually encircled with trellis borders with a rim panel enclosing the name. Heraldic or figure motifs, usually Royalist in character, formed the centre decoration – the Royal arms, rampant lions, the Boscobel oak, the pelican in her piety, fleur-de-lis, cavaliers and mermaids.

A Toft Circular Dish

Other names which occur on wares of similar type include Glass, Meir, Osland, Simpson, Taylor, Wright, Chatterly, Heath, Ward, Wood and Ley. Women's names, such as MARGERE NASH and MARY PERKINS, occur individually or as part of inscriptions. The style continued well into the eighteenth century.

Posset-pots, bell-shaped or straight-sided, were attractively decorated by dividing the surface into zones of ornament and lettering, and counterchanging the colours; or by tiers of floral and conventional designs with suitable inscriptions, such as THE.BEST.IS.NOT. TOO.GOOD.FOR.YOV. The tulip is a frequent feature of decoration. Not uncommonly the lower portion was enriched with feathered or combed slip to contrast with the trailed or painted slip above. Dog-Latin inscriptions, names, initials and dates are frequent. Sometimes the name indicates ownership (MARY OUMFARIS YOUR CUP 1678), at others the maker. The initials I.B. and R.F. commonly occurring in association with others may stand for Isaac Ball and Robert Fletcher. Such wares were made as indications of loyalty or to celebrate birthdays, betrothals or weddings.

Dishes with notched edges, decorated in relief with conventional or figure subjects picked out with painted slip and roulette impressions, form a distinctive category. They were made by pressing a bat of clay upon a 'pitcher' mould in which the design had been incised before firing. The outline relief ornaments were filled in with patches and spots of various coloured slips.

Certain wares of this kind have been ascribed to a period before the Civil War on the strength of the costume of figures depicted upon them. But they are more likely of late seventeenth- or early eighteenth-century date. Such archaisms are not uncommon. The initials R.S. (Ralph Simpson, 1651–1724) and I.S. (John Simpson of Rotten Row, Burslem) are to be found on dishes ornamented in this manner with fleur-de-lis and pomegranates. Samuel Malkin (1668–1741), parish clerk of Burslem, made similar wares decorated with sun-faced flowers or religious and proverbial subjects ('Burd in Hand', Adam and Eve, 'Wee three logerheads', etc.). His usual mark was S.M. Wares akin in treatment but of later date have been identified by means of a mould inscribed and dated 1751, made by William Bird.

Pottery decorated in the *sgraffiato* technique by scratching through a dark-brown coating of slip to expose the light-coloured clay beneath were made about 1725–30. Hares, rabbits, dogs, birds and flowers vigorously incised through the slip coating are typical. The tool-marks of the potter, usually much in evidence, give a pleasant sense of surface texture. Another *sgraffiato* type of later date – *c.* 1745–80 – shows less vigorous and rather neater workmanship. The chief decorations comprise checks, stripes, wavy bands, and lines cut through a white slip over a deep-brown clay. The type is associated, erroneously, with Ralph Shaw.

These pottery styles were continued throughout the eighteenth and into the nineteenth century. Finely-feathered slip-dishes of the second half of the eighteenth century, with the letter 'H' inscribed upon them, have been excavated in Hanley recently. Other wares with individual but unidentified initials have been found upon other sites. These initials may be early factory or workmen's marks. Redware factories were still working in North Staffordshire as late as 1834 at Goldenhill, Red Street, and in Shelton. A country pottery making bottles, pitchers, vinegar kegs and settling-pans also existed at Ipstones.

South Staffordshire: there is clear evidence of an early and extensive manufacture of slipwares in this area. Robert Plot (writing in 1677) refers to 'divers sorts of *Vessels*' made at Wednesbury 'which they paint with Slip, made of a *reddish* sort of *Earth* gotten at Tipton'. These wares have never been identified, but probably resembled the slipwares of North Staffordshire in character. The industry lasted until the end of the eighteenth century, when the workers migrated to the north of the county.

Coarse earthenwares were made by a number of firms at Bilston (where the Myott family worked for several generations) and Kingswinford from the beginning of the nineteenth century.

Herefordshire: wares similar in character to those made in Staffordshire, comprising tygs, posset-pots (sometimes with pads of clay impressed with coats of arms), jugs, costrels, cooking stoves, skillets, steens, piggins, candlesticks and dishes were made at Boresford, Whitney-on-Wye, and Upton Bishop; and at Dickendale, Deerfold Farm, and Shirley Farm in Deerfold Forest. A crude kind of *sgraffiato* consisting of scratchy zig-zag lines was usual on the plates. The glaze varied from pale straw to copper green. These farmer potters flourished from about 1610 to 1750.

Worcestershire: country crockery, including slipware, was made also at Gorsty Hill, near Halesowen, until comparatively recently, and at Polesworth in Warwickshire.

Buckinghamshire: the brownish black manganese-glazed red earthenwares made at Aylesbury from *c.* 1701–93 (Thomas Brackley, potter) contrasts with the crockery made at Brill, ten miles east of Oxford from late eighteenth century until about 1900. Money-boxes, bottles and lampstands as well as ordinary kitchen crocks were made. The ware has a speckled dirty appearance. In the Ashmolean Museum there is a covered steen, incised 'Thomas Hullocks Brill 1791' of rather finer quality. Late nineteenth-century redwares were made also at Leafield near Oxford by George and Alec Franklin.

Yorkshire: pottery of a distinctly medieval character was made by John Wedgwood and his descendents at Yearsley near Easingfold. It included great pancheons and jars with names and dates inscribed under a strong green glaze. But in general the later products of the peasant craftsman have been overshadowed by the productions of the Yorkshire industrial potters. In all districts where suitable clay existed, coarse red, yellow, and black wares were made. The old saying 'Like Falsgrave pottery, rough and ugly' indicates the popular estimate of these wares. There were numerous little workshops in the Leeds and Castleford districts. Combed and mottled wares were made at Norton, near Stockton, from about 1850 onwards. Pot Howcans, near Halifax, run by the Halliday family, made good trailed slipware, including salt kits, from about 1850 to 1890. Similar wares were made by the Catheralls at Swill Hill and Bradshaw Head; and by a factory at Midhope, near Sheffield.

Cumberland: slipwares, marked by dexterous use of the trailed slip technique, were made until late in the nineteenth century at Weatherigg's Pottery, Penrith. These included salt kits decorated with cleverly disposed white wavy lines and dots upon a dark ground.

Lancashire: at Blackburton simple slipwares were also made about the same time. These late slipwares are usually a little hard and mechanical in treatment. The old freedoms, which rendered the early slipwares so exciting, disappeared.

(A) Spring and Autumn. Earthenware decorated with enamel colours. Height, $5\frac{1}{2}$ in. Marked WALTON impressed. Staffordshire, *c.* 1820. *Mrs Frank Nagington.*

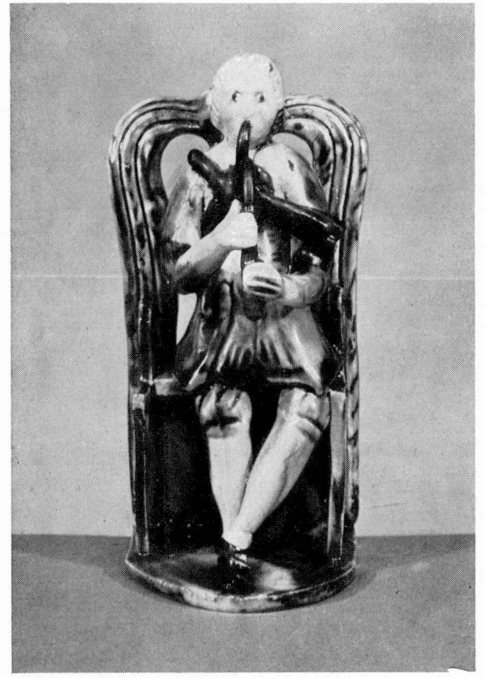

(B) Seated piper. Earthenware. Height, $5\frac{1}{2}$ in. Astbury, Staffordshire, *c.* 1740. *Frank Partridge & Sons Ltd.*

(C) Figure hold-all. Cream earthenware underglaze sparingly stained with oxides. Height, $9\frac{3}{4}$ in. Whieldon or early Ralph Wood, Staffordshire, *c.* 1750. *Mrs Frank Nagington.*

PLATE 59

To face page 104

(A) Posset-pot. White earthenware with dark-brown slip, decorated in the *sgraffiato* style. Height, 7¾ in. Diameter, 10 in. Staffordshire, dated 1730. *Frank Partridge & Sons Ltd.*

(B) Dutch Oven. Red earthenware with trailed slip. Height, 10 in. Staffordshire, *c.* 1700. *Hanley Museum and Art Gallery.*

(C) Egg-stand. Brown earthenware with white trailed slip. Diameter, 6 in. Staffordshire, *c.* 1690. *Hanley Museum and Art Gallery.*

(D) Posset-pot. Light earthenware with decoration in buff, dark brown, and white slip. Diameter, 8½ in. Initials I B (Isaac Ball?) and R F (Robert Fletcher?) dated 1696. Staffordshire. *Hanley Museum and Art Gallery.*

(A) Coronation mug. Earthenware with black transfer engraved by James Kennedy of Burslem, 1831. *Hanley Museum and Art Gallery.*

(B) Mug. Earthenware with 'mocha' decoration. Height, 3 in. Lettered underneath 'M. Clark 1799'. Staffordshire. *Christchurch Mansion Museum, Ipswich.*

(C) Jug. Earthenware with silver 'resist' on canary ground. Height, $4\frac{3}{4}$ in. Staffordshire, *c.* 1805. *Mrs Frank Nagington.*

(D) Jug. Buff earthenware with enamel colouring. Height, $9\frac{1}{2}$ in. Garrison Pottery, Sunderland, *c.* 1840. *Hanley Museum and Art Gallery.*

(A) Jar. Red earthenware inlaid with white slip. Height, $8\frac{7}{8}$ in. Inscribed M R E AVERY 1811. Chailey, Sussex. *Hanley Museum and Art Gallery.*

(B) Salt kit. Dark brown earthenware with white trailed slip. Height, $11\frac{1}{2}$ in. Inscribed 'R. Parker, Clifton 1887'. Weatherigg's Pottery, Penrith. *Hanley Museum and Art Gallery.*

(C) Tyg. Red earthenware with applied pads of white clay. Height, $6\frac{1}{2}$ in. Initials T P E and I L, date 1636. Wrotham, Kent. *Hanley Museum and Art Gallery.*

(D) Harvest jug. Red earthenware covered with white slip and decorated in the *sgraffiato* style. Height, 9 in. Edwin Fishley, Fremington, North Devon. 1851. *Hanley Museum and Art Gallery.*

SUSSEX: numerous potworks were working in Sussex from the end of the eighteenth century, notably at Chailey, Brede, Rye, East Grinstead, Dicker, and Burgess Hill. The wares produced are usually sunny orange lead-glazed earthenwares; darker pieces are not uncommon, and sometimes the glaze was flecked with minute iron spots.

Agate wares were made at Burgess Hill. Inlaid decorations, consisting of formal arrangements of sprays, leaves, rosettes and stars, formed with printers' types and punches, are typical of the productions of the Norman family at Chailey: similar wares were made at Brede, Rye, and Dicker, and at Bethersden in Kent. Tea canisters, milk churns, flasks, tobacco-jars, fir-cone money-boxes, bird-callers and hedgehogs were made, as well as the usual farmhouse crockery. Cadborough specialized in 'Sussex Pigs'.

HAMPSHIRE AND SURREY: extensive potteries existed at Frimley, Farnborough, and Cove at the beginning of the nineteenth century. Little is known of them. Pipkins, venisons, money-boxes, pitchers, bowls, bed-pans and stool-pans for sale to Whitechapel Jews were made by William Smith (1790–1858) at Farnborough. A family named Harris potted at Wrecklesham, Surrey, about the same time. Similar factories existed at Fareham, Hants., at Verwood, Dorset, and in Gloucestershire.

WILTSHIRE: ferruginous earthenwares with an iridescent brownish black glaze were made over a long period (*c.* 1600–*c.* 1800) near Salisbury. Incised decorations and inscriptions occur. The most distinctive products were the footed loving cups or christening goblets.

SOMERSET: the rough, vigorous pottery of Donyatt and Crock Street forms an important class in which fantastic forms were combined with a free vernacular *sgraffiato* style. Tygs with bird-whistle lids, fuddling-cups with intertwined handles, puzzle jugs, vases with several apertures, and money-boxes, as well as useful wares were made. They were lead-glazed and stained with patches of copper green. Dates from 1677 have been recorded, but the bulk of the pottery produced was made in the eighteenth and nineteenth centuries. Other Somerset potworks existed at Pill and Bridgwater.

DEVONSHIRE: a group of potteries flourished at Barnstaple, Bideford, and Fremington, making redwares for the West Country and South Wales markets from the seventeenth to the nineteenth centuries. In fact, some factories still operate in this district, although the character of the product has changed. Pilchard pots and harvest jugs were made as well as ugly elaborate watch-stands, honey-jars and other vessels. The harvest jugs may be identified by the coil at the lower attachment of the handle and the bold chevron which often adorns the neck. The principal potters were the Fishley family. Similar *sgraffiato* wares were manufactured at Honiton, where there are extensive clay beds.

CORNWALL: Truro alone survives of the dozen or so potworks which formerly made pancheons and pitchers in the Duchy.

CAMBRIDGESHIRE: at Ely Jabez Lucas produced redwares at the end of the eighteenth century, inlaid with white clay. This unusual technique was otherwise almost entirely confined to Sussex.

SUFFOLK: at Wattisfield a redware factory has existed from the seventeenth century and is still flourishing. Brown-glazed gotches, breadpans, milk steens, washbowls and frying-pans were the staple products. Some slipwares were probably made. The pottery was worked by the Death family, 1734–1808, and by the Watsons subsequently. A nineteenth-century potworks making slipwares existed in the Rope Walk, Ipswich: W. Balaam was the potter.

ESSEX: incised pottery with a purple-brown glaze was made at Gestingthorpe, near Halstead (dates recorded range from 1685 to 1770). Jugs with cylindrical necks, narrow tubular spouts and three handles have survived.

WALES: slipware potteries existed in Flintshire at Buckley Mountain (Joseph Hayes, 1756–1842, potter) and at Bagilt, near Flint, in the first half of the nineteenth century. In South Wales potworks flourished at Bridgend, Pencoed, and Ewenny, where useful crockery was extensively made, as well as puzzle jugs and many-handled wassail bowls decorated with name of owner and maker in *sgraffiato* slip, for use in the Welsh custom of Mari Lwyd.

Peasant Styles: a considerable quantity of industrial cream-coloured earthenware in the closing decades of the eighteenth century was decorated in on-glaze enamels with stylized rustic and floral motifs in red and black. This restricted palette, occasionally diversified with other colours, particularly green and a striking but rather dissonant puce, was combined with spiky foliage and feathery scrolls. Leeds and Staffordshire were centres of this production. The motto 'God Speed the Plough' indicates the class for whom it was made.

In the nineteenth century a peasant style based upon the type of painting used in the 'resist' lustre technique was developed by Staffordshire craftsmen. Three palettes of colour were employed: (1) monochrome blue; (2) black, sage green, dirty pink, and blue; and (3) yellow, orange, blue, and green. Floral arabesques, completely covering the wares, and built up by skilful brushwork, are characteristic decorations. Hearts, initials, and dates occur with sufficient frequency to suggest that many of the pieces were intended as love tokens. Dates from 1814 to 1835 have been noted. Copelands, Rogers, and Adams are among the known makers, but quite a few pieces were probably bought in the white and decorated by outside enamellers.

Lustre pottery: lustre decoration on pottery became popular in the first half of the nineteenth century. Who invented it is not known with certainty. Josiah Wedgwood certainly experimented with lustre decorations from about 1790, and his successors made use commercially of silver, pink (gold), and 'moonlight' lustre from about 1805. John Hancock claimed to be the first to produce lustre in Staffordshire, while John Gardner has been credited with the earliest commercial use of silver lustre at Wolfe's factory in Stoke. The early history of lustre decoration is therefore obscure. At least three other craftsmen made early contributions in this field: Richard Horrobin (1765–1830), of Tunstall, joiner, mechanic, organ-builder, whose obituary stated 'he may be considered the reviver of gold lustre on china and earthenware'; John Aynsley (1752–1829), 'the first lusterer' at Lane-End; and Peter Warburton (1773–1813), who took out a patent in 1810 for 'printing landscapes and other designs from copper plates in gold and platinum'.

The English potters, once the secret of applying metallic solutions to china and earthenware became known, made extensive, and often non-ceramic, use of the material. The earliest wares are undoubtedly the best, but vast quantities were produced in the 1850s for export through the firm of Burgess, Dale, and Goddard to the United States. Later wares were produced for the fairground and the pot hawker.

The popular appeal of the material accounts for the allusive nature of the subjects chosen for decoration, which cover the whole field of contemporary life—politics, sport, religion, travel, domestic experience. Pious quatrains may be matched by crude licentious doggerel. The lustre decorator was certainly all things to all men. He smothered his wares with metal to provide the poor with imitation 'plate'. For the religious he offered patterns of eminent respectability, but when the market demanded it he could descend to the earthy coarseness of a Bewick or a Rowlandson.

There are six classes of lustre: (1) plain (gold, silver or copper), evidently intended to imitate more precious materials; (2) painted; (3) decorated in 'resist', usually in silver but occasionally in purple or other lustre; (4) lustre in conjunction with transfer-prints or enamel decoration; (5) lustre on moulded relief decoration; and (6) on pottery figures, used to pick out armour, or all over to make them resemble precious metal. 'Resist' decoration was sometimes effectively combined with a coloured ground, yellow or buff.

The centres of manufacture were Longton, Burslem, Swansea (where good silver lustre was made), and Sunderland. Splashed and crudely mottled pink lustre was extensively used in the North East in conjunction with prints of the 'Wear' Bridge or 'The Sailor's Farewell'. Surprise mugs were ornamented in like manner. At these North Country factories the folk element was completely dominant.

'Dipped' pottery: a class of pottery which had a long vogue – from about 1750, when it was introduced by Thomas Heath of Fenton, until the death of King Edward VII – and which was made in Glasgow, Newcastle-on-Tyne, and Swansea as well as Staffordshire, consisted of slip decorated pottery produced under industrial conditions for the dairy, tavern, and the farmhouse. Shrimp, nut and beer measures have survived in quantity, but 'tea things', toilet sets, tobacco jars, jugs and ornamental pieces were also made in it.

The earliest wares made in this category were marbled slipwares, dating from about 1760, and often surprisingly beautiful in colour; but other styles were quickly developed. Clean hygienic-looking band treatments in blue, ochre and dark brown, sometimes plain, occasionally with deftly-executed slip motifs superimposed, were popular. An attractive decoration comprised coloured bands with added dendritic effects in brown, blue, or (much later) pink. This was known as mocha. Wavy bands of two or more coloured slips, worked together with the fingers (finger-trailing), or with a brush, were made in the 1830s. An imitation mocha, known as 'Moco', was made for export.

Dipped pottery was rarely marked, although the makers were numerous – Adams of Tunstall, J. and R. Riley of Burslem, Copeland and Garrett of Stoke, Broadhurst of Fenton, Tams of Longton, Green of Church Gresley, and Malings of Newcastle-on-Tyne among others. Few pieces can be dated with certainty. A small mug in the Christchurch Mansion Museum, Ipswich, lettered 'M Clark 1799' is believed to be the earliest surviving dated example of mocha ware.

Salt-glazed stoneware: most early salt-glazed stonewares do not concern us, they were made for the upper classes. The popular will to form, however, is evidenced by the owl and bear jugs, the streaky blue-and-white agate animals, the bell figures and 'pew' groups, and the scratch blue loving cups, mugs and punch-bowls which confirm the traditional conception of the Englishman as hard drinking, hard living. While the inscriptions might be crude, even obscene, the forms were generally refined and the potting of the highest quality. What is said here of the white salt-glaze of Staffordshire is equally applicable to the nut-brown stonewares of Nottingham (Morley family, potters) and Derbyshire. It is, however, to the later products of these factories that we must turn for popular imagery. Spirit flasks in all sorts of quaint and unusual forms, mask mugs and pitchers, and Toby jugs were made by Bournes of Denby, Joseph Thompson of Hartshorne, Oldfield of Chesterfield, and by the London factories – Stephen Green, and Doulton & Watts of Lambeth. Reform flasks and greyhound jugs enjoyed enormous popularity in the 1830s and later.

Transfer-printed pottery: this class of industrial pottery is of great importance because it made possible greater production, and so widened the potters' market to include even the poorest cottager. The earliest transfer-prints (the process was introduced before 1765) were done overglaze in black, more rarely in colour. Subjects were often crude popular moralities, pleasantries concerning marriage, caricature prints after Rowlandson or Gillray, and decorations commemorating national events or heroes, as well as floral and other more conventional styles of ornament. The work of the 'black-printer' had a considerable vogue which lasted well into the nineteenth century.

Underglaze printed decorations began to make their appearance towards the end of the eighteenth century. Blue, black, and brown were the first colours used, but blue soon ousted the less attractive tints, and between 1800 and 1830 vast quantities of blueprints were produced for home and overseas markets. All sorts of subjects were used for decoration, some taken from books of travel others from historical prints, portraits of celebrities, illustrated Bibles, or the works of famous painters. As the vogue for blue passed other colours were introduced – orange, mulberry, chrome-green, and rose-pink. The most popular pattern was the almost ubiquitous 'Willow'. Nearly every early nineteenth-century industrial factory in

Staffordshire and the Out-Potteries made blue-printed earthenware.

Figures: the image toys labelled 'Astbury' or 'Astbury-Whieldon' are the most direct expression of pure clay technique in English pottery. They owe nothing to foreign influence, and are conceived in simple terms and worked out in a broad manipulative technique which died out about 1750.

The potters who made them knew little about the fashionable world and rarely attempted anything outside the range of their own experiences. Their best-known works are mounted hussars, grenadiers, topers, dancers, bands of musicians, or women seated upon high-backed chairs fondling pet dogs; and only occasionally do echoes of the fashionable world, in the form of opera singers or orators, occur. They were made, in fact, not for the big house but for the cottage or farm, and were evidently sold in the cheapest markets.

'Astbury' or 'Astbury-Whieldon' are convenient labels covering many potters making similar wares, including John Astbury of Shelton, Thomas Astbury of Lane Delph, Samuel Bell of Newcastle-under-Lyme, Edward and William Warburton of Fenton Low, and Thomas Whieldon. It was probably Whieldon who was responsible for the more developed specimens. And with Whieldon we begin to notice the impact of the outside world in clumsy attempts to emulate classical sculpture (the 'Spinario') or Chinese porcelain figures.

The 'pew' and 'arbour' groups, made in salt-glazed stoneware and tortoiseshell-glazed earthenware, are extremely rare, and were evidently the work of potters of uncommon sensibility and skill. The names of those who made them are not known.

In addition to figures, cats, dogs, rabbits, cows and other animals were made. There is little to choose in quality between images made in stoneware and those made in common earthenware. The harder material was used expressively for depicting character and detail: the coarser body was perfectly suited to 'pinching out' droll characters to which life and colour were added by splashes of metallic oxides in the lead glaze.

Ralph Wood of Burslem lifted this ceramic sideline from its humble origin and developed it into a specialized craft – the craft of the figure-maker – and something was lost in the process. The humour of the Wood figures is quieter than that of the earlier pieces: a vein of sentiment creeps in, particularly with figures believed to have been modelled by John Voyez (*c.* 1735–1800), and in place of expressive manipulation we have careful character modelling and a closer regard for anatomical truth. Ralph Wood catered for more specialized markets, hence the changes in style and treatment. The best of the Wood figures are not those inspired by literary sources, such as 'Hudibras' (adapted from engravings by Hogarth) or the 'Sweep' which Voyez copied from a Lunéville model by

FIG. 1. 'HUDIBRAS'

Cyfflé, but those which satirize contemporary events and personalities. The 'Vicar and Moses' and the original 'Toby' jug deserved their widespread and long-lived popularity. They were original works of popular art. The chief characteristic of the early Wood figures is the clever tooling of the models to set off the lovely washes of translucent coloured glazes.

The younger Ralph Wood was responsible for a further development – the use of bright on-glaze enamels – which made previous figures seem dowdy and old-fashioned. The itch for novelty resulted in the multiplication of models and colour effects. Lustre and cheap gilding were introduced. By the end of the century dozens of factories turned to this lucrative trade, many backstreet potters turning out gaudy images for street hawkers, whose cry 'Buy my images!' became familiar in town and village.

The late eighteenth-century and early nineteenth-century figure-makers developed distinctive types. The makers of 'Pratt' figures used a palette of high-temperature colours dominated by yellow and blue. Enoch Wood made large lifeless statues of classical or literary subjects and competent busts of Wesley; tree background groups in gay enamels were made by Walton, Salt, Tittensor, Dale, and Selman; powerful but crude representations of popular sports were made by Obadiah Sherratt; the ubiquitous 'china' dogs and flatbacks of political, criminal, or military celebrities were turned out by the thousand from the factories of Sampson Smith, William Kent, and William Machin from 1850 down to the Edwardian era. The trade did not die out until the First World War.

These were characteristic types: what Staffordshire did one day, Liverpool and Leeds, Sunderland, Swansea and Scotland did with variations the next.

This Victorian flowering of the craft of the image-maker gave rise to vast quantities of cheerful crudities which mirror perfectly the tastes and interests of common people. They were, in fact, the last expression of the folk will to form and colour.

GLOSSARY

Agate: salt-glazed stoneware or lead-glazed earthenware made in imitation of semi-precious stones by wedging together different coloured clays.

'Astbury' type: classification of Staffordshire pottery in which red and white clays are combined under a transparent lead glaze. Similar wares covered by a glaze splashed with metallic oxides are generally styled 'Astbury-Whieldon'.

Ballot box: a common name for a Salt Kit.

Barm pot: pot for storing barm or yeast (*see also* Salt Kit).

'Battle for the Breeches': theme of popular imagery concerning marriage occurring on seventeenth-century slipware and as a subject for nineteenth-century spill vases. Possibly made by Obadiah Sherratt.

Bear jug: model in the form of a bear hugging a dog, illustrating the sport of bear-baiting. The detachable head serves as a cup. Made in Staffordshire and Nottingham, eighteenth century.

Bellarmine: big-bellied stoneware bottle with a bearded mask in relief, named after Cardinal Bellarmine (1542–1621). Frequently cited in contemporary literature and used in magic and witchcraft.

Bellringers' jugs: jugs for serving ale to bellringers, kept in the church tower, as at Macclesfield, or in the home of a ringer.

Bird call: pottery whistle in the form of a bird. Sometimes built into old chimneys as a charm against evil spirits.

Bird fountain: wall bracket with a projecting socket for water, made in blue-printed, lustred, or enamelled earthenware, eighteenth and nineteenth centuries.

Black-printing: 'A term for applying impressions to glazed vessels, whether the color be black, red, or gold' (William Evans, 1846).

'Bocage': foliage or tree background to pottery figures.

Body: mixture of clay from which pottery is made.

Bull-baiting: pottery groups showing a bull goring or tossing a dog, often upon table bases supported by six legs, popular

FIG. 2. BULL-BAITING

c. 1830–35. Said to have been made by Obadiah Sherratt. (Fig. 2.)

Bussa: large earthenware pot commonly kept in old Cornish cottages for salting down pilchards.

Butter-pot: cylindrical earthenware vessel made to hold fourteen pounds of butter, made at Burslem in the seventeenth century for use at Uttoxeter market. An Act of 1661 regulated abuses in the manner of making and packing the pots.

Capacity mug: cylindrical measure made in stoneware, earthenware, mocha ware, etc., from the seventeenth century. The presence of a Royal Cypher or an Excise Stamp provides a clue as to date.

Carpet balls: used in the Victorian game of carpet bowls, made in brown stoneware or white earthenware coloured with starry, ringed, or flowery patterns. A set comprised six patterned and one white or self-coloured balls. Made in Scotland and Staffordshire. The Parr family of Burslem specialized in them.

Castle Hedingham: pseudo-medieval and Tudor pottery was made here by Edward Bingham (b. 1829). Sometimes mistaken for authentic, fifteenth-, sixteenth-, and seventeenth-century wares.

Cats: popular ornaments made in delftware, slipware, and salt-glaze, *c.* 1670–1750.

Chill: earthenware oil lamp shaped like a large candlestick with a lipped cup large enough to hold two cups of 'train' (pilchard oil), used in Cornwall before candles. Sometimes rendered STONEN CHILL.

'China' dogs: mantelpiece ornaments in the form of spaniels, Welsh sheep dogs, French poodles, greyhounds, etc., made in earthenware, and sold extensively in Wales and the West Country. Made by Sampson Smith, James Dudson, William Kent, and many others in Staffordshire and Scotland; rarely marked.

Christening goblets: footed four-handled loving cups with whistles attached for calling for replenishment, specially associated with Wiltshire, and used for christenings, harvest homes, etc. A favourite inscription is HERE IS THE GEST OF THE BARLY KORNE GLAD HAM I THE CILD IS BORN. Dates from 1603 until 1799 recorded. (Fig. 3.)

FIG. 3. CHRISTENING GOBLET

Combed slip: a technique in which a marbled or feathered effect is achieved by brushing together, while wet, two or more different-coloured slips.

Costrel: flat, circular bottle with loop handles for suspension from the shoulder, used by field workers.

Cottages: used as night-light shields, pastille burners, and mantelpiece ornaments. The latter frequently represent the scenes of sensational crimes, such as the Red Barn at Polstead (Maria Marten) or Stanfield Hall (the Rush murders).

Cow-milk jug: model of cow with mouth and tail forming spout and handle. Filled from an aperture in the back. Based upon a Dutch model introduced into England about 1755. Made in Staffordshire, South Wales, Yorkshire, and Scotland.

Cradle: presentation piece for a newly-married couple, having the same significance as the 'La Fécondité' dish. Slipware specimens recorded from 1673 until 1839. Used as a hold-all or pipe-tray.

Crazing: fine network of cracks in the glaze caused by unequal shrinkage of body and glaze.

Cuckoo: bird call in the form of a large spotted bird perched upon a fence, with four smaller birds. Commonly made in slipware, nineteenth century. (Fig. 4.)

FIG. 4. CUCKOO

FIG. 5. FUDDLING-CUPS

Delftware: earthenware coated with a glaze made opaque by the addition of tin ashes, named after Delft in Holland, which became an important centre of manufacture in the seventeenth century.

Dendritic: having tree-like markings.

'Doctor Syntax': fine underglaze blue transfer-prints representing the adventures of Doctor Syntax, used as tableware decorations by James and Ralph Clews, Cobridge, *c.* 1821. Pottery figures were also popular. *The Tours of Dr. Syntax in Search of the Picturesque* by Dr Combe, with illustrations by Thomas Rowlandson, published 1815–21, were a satire upon the writings of the Rev. William Gilpin.

Egyptian black: hard stoneware body heavily stained with manganese.

Easter eggs: 'nest' eggs decorated, inscribed with the name of the recipient, and given as Easter and birthday gifts.

Feeding-bottle: flattish oviform article with a small circular aperture at the top and a small nozzle.

'Female archer': subject of 'Pratt' type jugs and earthenware figures intended as satire upon the smart archery parties popular in 'high' society, 1800–50. Sometimes known as the FAIR TOSCOPHOLITE or TOXOPHILITE.

Ferruginous: containing iron rust and, therefore, reddish brown in appearance.

Flasks: in form of fish, mermaid, constable's baton, horse-pistol, boot, potato, cucumber, barrel, or a figure of some royal or political celebrity, commonly made in brown stoneware or 'Rockingham'-glazed earthenware, early nineteenth century. Chief centres: Denby, Chesterfield, Brampton, Lambeth. (*See* Reform Flasks.)

Fuddling-cups: cups of three, five, or more conjoined compartments communicating internally, made at Donyatt and Crock Street, Somerset, seventeenth and eighteenth century. (Fig. 5.)

Gotch: East Anglian word for a large stoneware jug.

Gretna Green: popular black-print showing a runaway couple being married by the Gretna blacksmith, accompanied by the verse, 'Oh! Mr. Blacksmith, ease our pains:/ and tie us fast in Wedlock's Chains'. Known alternatively as 'The Red Hot Marriage'.

Greybeard: a Bellarmine.

Grey hen: stoneware liquor bottle.

'Greyhound' jugs: jugs with greyhound handles and relief decorations of sporting subjects.

Hearty good fellow: Toby jug in form of a swaggering standing figure clasping a jug.

Hen dish: oval, basket-shaped egg-dish with cover in the form of a sitting hen. (Fig. 6.)

FIG. 6. HEN DISH

FIG. 7. HEN AND CHICKENS

Hen and chickens: emblems of Providence, hence frequent use as adornments of money-boxes. (Fig. 7.)

Image toys: mid-eighteenth-century description of small pottery figures.

Inlaid decoration: process used by medieval potters for decorating paving tiles (Cleeve Abbey, Westminster Abbey) and by Sussex potters, *c.* 1790–1850, for useful and ornamental wares. The decoration was formed by impressing the body with punches or with printers' types, and filling in with clay of a contrasting colour, usually white on red.

Joney or joney grig: a dialect term for a chimney ornament in the form of a dog. A well-known Burslem pottery in the nineteenth century was known as a 'doll and jona' (figure and dog) works.

'Keep within compass': a popular 'morality' used as decoration for earthenware by John Aynsley (1752–1829), showing the rewards of virtue and the punishments of sin.

Leeds horse: large model of horse on a rectangular plinth made specially at Leeds, and probably used as the sign of a horse leech.

Lustre: thin deposit of metal on pottery giving it an iridescent or metallic sheen.

Martha Gunn: female Toby jug modelled in the likeness of Martha Gunn (1727–1815), the Brighton bathing-woman.

Mocha: ware decorated with coloured bands into which tree, moss, or fern-like effects have been introduced by means of a diffusing medium, described by William Evans (1846) as 'a saturated infusion of tobacco in stale urine and turpentine', made from about 1780 until 1914. Named from mocha quartz.

Moco, Moko: buff or redware mottled by spattering various coloured slips over the surface before glazing. A cheap nineteenth-century substitute for mocha.

Money-boxes: made at most country pot-works from medieval times. Usual forms comprise houses, chest of drawers, globes, fir-cones, pigs, and hens and chickens. Associated with the custom of the 'Christmas box'. (Fig. 8.)

FIG. 8. MONEY-BOXES

'Mr and Mrs Caudle': relief decoration on brown stoneware spirit flasks, made about 1846 by Doulton of Lambeth, and based upon Douglas Jerrold's *Punch* papers ('Mrs Caudle's Curtain Lectures'). One side shows 'Mr and Mrs Caudle in Bed', the other 'Miss Prettyman'.

On-glaze: decoration applied after the ware has been glazed and fired.

'Orange-jumper': local subject on Yorkshire cream-coloured earthenware made at the Don pottery, *c.* 1808, depicting a coarse-featured local horse-breaker who acted as messenger for Lord Milton in the 1807 election. He is clothed in orange, the 'colour' of Lord Milton. Orange-tawny was considered the colour appropriate to the lower classes.

Owl jug: jug with a separate head forming a cup, made in slipware, *c.* 1700, and white salt-glazed stoneware, *c.* 1720–75. The proverb 'Like an owl in an ivy bush', used of a vague person with a sapient look, may explain its convivial associations. (Fig. 9.)

FIG. 9. OWL JUG

Pancheon: large shallow earthenware bowl with sloping sides used for settling milk.

Pap-dish: a shallow boat with a tubular spout for feeding infants.

'Parson and clerk': figure group showing a drunken parson being led home by the faithful Moses, first made by Enoch Wood (1759–1840) as a sequel to the 'Vicar and

(A) Spirit flask. Brown salt-glazed stoneware. Mr and Mrs Caudle and Miss Prettyman. Doulton, Lambeth, *c.* 1846. *Doulton & Company Ltd.*

(B) Hen money-box. Green-glazed earthenware. Height, 5¼ in. Yorkshire, eighteenth century. *Captain and Mrs E. Bruce George.*

(C) Cradle. Brown earthenware with white trailed slip. ¼ in. long. Staffordshire, *c.* 1720. *Hanley Museum and Art Gallery.*

(D) Tobacco pipes. 'Boney.' Height, 5½ in. North Country, *c.* 1810. Bird and bird's nest. Whieldon colouring. 6¾ in. long. Staffordshire, *c.* 1760. *Mrs Frank Nagington.*

PLATE 63

To face page 112

(A) Blue dash charger. Tin-glazed earthenware decorated with colours. Bristol, *c.* 1700. *Hanley Museum and Art Gallery.*

(B) Equestrian figure. White earthenware sparingly picked out in red clay. Height, 9 in. Astbury, Staffordshire, *c.* 1730–40. *J. R. Cookson Ltd.*

(C) Heenan and Sayers. Earthenware, sparingly coloured and gilded. Sampson Smith, Longton, Staffordshire, *c.* 1860. *Brighton Museum and Art Gallery.*

PLATE 64

Moses'. A satire on the drinking, hunting squarson type of incumbent. (Fig. 10.)

Pastille burners: box-like containers, often in the form of cottages, churches, or summer-houses, with detachable perforated lids for burning cassolette perfumes. These consisted of finely-powdered willow-wood charcoal, benzoin, fragrant oils, and gum arabic. Extremely popular, 1820–50. (Fig. 11.)

FIG. 10. PARSON AND CLERK

'Paul Pry': model for pottery figures and Toby jugs based upon the meddlesome hero of John Poole's comedy of that name, 1825.

Peasant style: ornament derived from peasant art: specifically earthenware painted in the 'resist' lustre style with a restricted palette of colours.

FIG. 11
PASTILLE BURNER

Peever: a piece of slate or stone used in the game of hopscotch, also a disc of pottery, so used, coloured and lettered with the name of the owner. Made at Alloa and elsewhere in Scotland, nineteenth century.

'Peggy Plumper': crude decoration showing Peggy Plumper sparring with Sammy Spar for mastership of bed and board, accompanied by a long rhyme 'about wearing the breeches'.

'Pelican in her piety': a Christian emblem representing the old popular fallacy that the pelican feeds her young with her own blood. Used on Staffordshire slipware.

Penny bank: earthenware money-box in the form of a house or chest of drawers.

'Pew' group: figure group representing a man and woman sitting upon a high-backed settle, made in white salt-glazed stoneware, *c.* 1730–40.

Piggin: a small milk pail. A PIG-WIFE is a woman who sells crockery.

Pilchard pots: made in North Devon, South Wales, and Cornwall for the West Country fishermen, and known by size as 'gallons', 'bussas', and 'great crocks', etc.

Pipkin: earthenware cooking vessel.

Pirlie-pig: earthenware money-box. 'Pig' is a North Country word for an earthen jar: 'pirlie' is a diminutive indicating something of slight value.

Pitcher mould: mould made of clay and fired.

Pope and Devil: reversible bell-shaped cup showing the Pope in his triple tiara when held one way up, and the Devil when reversed. Sometimes inscribed 'When Pope absolves, the Devil smiles'. Late eighteenth century.

Porringer: child's basin for broth, or porridge.

'Portobello' ware: made at Tunstall, Staffordshire, *c.* 1830, in imitation of banded and 'Pratt' type wares made at Portobello in Scotland.

Posset: beverage comprising hot ale, milk, sugar, spices, and small pieces of bread, toast, or oatcake, said to have been a common supper beverage in Staffordshire and Derbyshire on Christmas Eve. Enjoyed widespread popularity.

Posset-pot: straight- or curve-sided vessel with loop handles and spouts, generally covered with a slanting or dome-shaped lid, and occasionally crowned with an elaborate knob, used for posset, and made in delftware and slipware, seventeenth and eighteenth century. (Fig. 12.)

FIG. 12. POSSET-POT

Pottle-pot: quart pot.

'Pratt' type: wares made at the end of the eighteenth and the beginning of the nineteenth century, decorated in a distinctive palette of colours, consisting of drab blue, dirty brown, ochre, orange, yellow, and dull green. Made in Staffordshire by Pratt and others; also in South Wales, Liverpool, Sunderland, and Prestonpans.

Punch: beverage consisting of spirits blended with hot milk or water, sugar, and flavoured with lemon and spice.

Punch-bowl: large basin for serving hot punch, sometimes called a 'jorum'.

Puzzle jug: vessel made in earthenware, delftware, or stoneware with a hollow tube round the lip opening into three or more spouts, and connected with the inside by the hollow handle. Sometimes there is a hole under the top of the handle. The neck is pierced with ornamental motifs, and usually inscribed with a challenge to the drinker. To empty the vessel without spilling the contents it is necessary to stop all the apertures except one, and to drain it by suction.

FIG. 13. PUZZLE JUGS

Reform flasks: brown salt-glazed stoneware spirit flasks made by Doulton (Lambeth), Stephen Green (Lambeth), Oldfield (Chesterfield), and Joseph Thompson (Wooden Box Pottery, Hartshorne), in the form of prominent politicians and royalty, at the time of the Reform Bill, 1832. Personalities portrayed included William IV, Queen Adelaide, Lord Grey, O'Connell, Brougham, Richard Cobden, and Lord John Russell. (Fig. 14.)

FIG. 14
REFORM FLASK

'Resist' lustre: on-glaze decorative process used generally with silver lustre, giving an effect of a light or coloured decoration against a metallic background. The ornament is painted on the ware with a 'resist', covered with the metallic solution, and fired; the infusible 'resist' being removed by polishing with whiting afterwards.

Salt-glazed stoneware: stoneware in which the glaze is formed by throwing common salt into the kiln when it reaches the maximum temperature. The salt decomposes, forming sodium oxide and hydrochloric acid, the former combining with the alumina and silica of the surface of the wares to form a thin coating of glass.

Salt kit: dome-topped ovoid jar surmounted by a knob and loop-handle with a wide circular aperture at one side; used for storing salt, etc.

'Scratch blue': decoration characteristic of white salt-glazed stoneware comprising incised floral arabesques and inscriptions into which clay stained with cobalt was rubbed. Examples dated from 1724 to 1776 recorded.

Sgraffiato: cutting away, incising, or scratching through a coating of slip to expose the colour of the underlying body. Popular technique in South Wales, Devonshire, Somerset, and Staffordshire.

Siamese twins: the 'monstrous' birth in Somerset, 19 May 1680, recorded on a *sgraffiato* dish and Bristol delft platter. The Kentish Siamese twins, Eliza and Mary Chulkhurst (d. 1734, aged 34) occur on redware copies of the 'Biddenden' cake.

Skillet: earthen saucepan with three legs.

Slip: clay reduced to a liquid batter.

Slipware: earthenware decorated with white or coloured slip. (*See also* COMBED SLIP, SGRAFFIATO, TRAILED SLIP, and INLAID DECORATION.)

Snufftaker: standing Toby jug in the form of an ugly man taking a pinch of snuff, usually with a deep purple-brown lustrous 'Rockingham' glaze.

Spinario: figure of boy extracting a thorn from his foot, copied from statue in the Capitoline Museum, Rome.

'Sponged' ware: a crude, easily-recognized peasant style originally made by Adams of Tunstall, and, because of its 'bright fancy character' (Jewitt), extensively exported.

Steen: originally an earthen vessel with two ears to hold liquids, later used for bread, meat or fish.

Stoneware: opaque, dense, intensely hard and completely vitrified pottery.

Sussex pig: pottery jug with a loose head used as a cup, enabling the user to drink a hogshead of liquor without disquieting after effects. Peculiar to the Sussex factory of Cadborough, Rye, nineteenth century. (Fig 15.)

FIG. 15. SUSSEX PIG

Taws: marbles or small balls made in earthenware.

Teapoy: an incorrect name for a tea caddy.

Texts: wall plaques with lustre 'frames' and cottage mantelpiece ornaments in the shape of pedimented façades enclosing a clock, sun, and moon, and boldly-lettered scripture verses ('PREPARE TO MEET THY GOD'), nineteenth century.

Tin glaze: lead glaze made opaque by the addition of tin ashes.

'Tithe pig': figure subject in porcelain and earthenware, also used as decoration of mugs and jugs accompanied by such rhymes as 'In Country Village lives a Vicar/Fond as all are of Tithes and Liquor'. A well-known Toby jug is inscribed 'I will have no child tho the X pig'. The collection of tithe in kind was abolished by the Tithe Commutation Act, 1836.

Toad mug: surprise mug with a large toad inside, seen only as the vessel is emptied, and causing consternation because of popular superstitions connected with toad poison. Often inscribed 'Tho' malt and venom seem united, etc.' Made at Sunderland, late eighteenth to the end of nineteenth century.

Toby Fillpot: nickname of a noted toper, Harry Elwes, who, through contemporary engravings, served as model for the original Toby jug.

Toby jug: jug in the form of a man holding a foaming jug of ale and a clay pipe, made from about 1765 by Ralph Wood. Numerous variants made by the Woods and other potters (*see* article on page 117).

Tortoise-shell glaze: mottled glaze stained with manganese and cobalt used by Thomas Whieldon, of Fenton.

Trailed slip: slip applied by trailing it from a spouted or tubular vessel.

Transfer-printing: process of decorating pottery with transfers from engraved copper-plates.

Tyg: beaker-shaped drinking vessel with from two to twelve handles.

Underglaze decoration: decoration applied to bisquit pottery before the addition of glaze.

Venisons: bowls 'made to fit into one another . . . in capacity ranging from a pint to a peck' (George Bourne), made at Frimley, Cove, and Farnborough, *c.* 1800–50.

'Vicar and Moses': popular satire on the drinking parson, showing a clergyman asleep in the pulpit with the parish clerk conducting the service. First made by Ralph Wood of Burslem, *c.* 1775.

Wall pocket: flower or spill vase shaped as a mask, fish, or cornucopia, made in Staffordshire salt-glaze, and in Liverpool and Lambeth delft, eighteenth century.

Wassail bowl: two-handled loving cup passed clockwise around the company on convivial occasions.

'Wassailing': originally a rite to ensure fertility in cereals, fruit crops and cattle, but later a term of abuse to describe Christmas revels.

'Welsh' ware: shallow meat dishes with feathered slip decoration, in form like a gardener's trug, commonly made in Staffordshire, Sunderland (Scott's 'Superior Fireproof') and Isleworth, under this name.

'Whieldon' ware: ware made in cream-coloured earthenware under a glaze splashed with metallic oxides to give tortoise-shell or mottled effects, made by Thomas Whieldon (1719–95) at Fenton, and others.

'Willow' pattern: pseudo-Chinese underglaze blue transfer-print first engraved by Thomas Minton (1765–1836), and known in numerous variants.

BOOKS FOR FURTHER READING

GENERAL

GEOFFREY BEMROSE, *Nineteenth Century English Pottery and Porcelain* (1952).

REGINALD G. HAGGAR, *English Country Pottery* (1950).

HODGKIN, *Examples of Early English Pottery* (1891).

LLEWELLYN JEWITT, *Ceramic Art of Great Britain* (1878).

LOMAX, *Quaint Old English Pottery* (1909).

MARX and LAMBERT, *English Popular and Traditional Art* (1946).

RACKHAM and READ, *English Pottery* (1924).

SPECIAL

BAINES, *Sussex Pottery: (I) East Sussex* (Hastings Museum, 1948).

GEORGE BOURNE, *William Smith, Potter and Farmer* (1919).

BUCKLEY, 'Potteries on the Tyne', *Archaeologia Aeliana* (1927).

CHARBONNIER, 'Notes on North Devon Pottery', *Transactions, Devonshire Association* (1906).

COOPER, *Pottery of Thomas Toft* (Leeds Art Gallery, 1952).

CRAWLEY, *Potteries of Sunderland and District* (Sunderland Museum, 1951).

DAWSON, 'Sussex Ironwork and Pottery', *Sussex Archaeological Collections*, Vol. 46.

EVANS, 'Ewenny Wassailing Bowls and Puzzle Jugs', *Apollo* (1954).

FLEMING, *Scottish Pottery* (1923).

REGINALD G. HAGGAR, *Staffordshire Chimney Ornaments* (1955).

HEMMING, 'Sussex Pottery', *Connoisseur* (1909 and 1912).

MARSHALL, 'Potteries and Pots in North Herefordshire', *Woolhope Transactions* (1946).

MEAGER, *Swansea and Nantgarw Potteries* (Swansea Art Gallery, 1949).

PARKER, 'Nottingham Pottery', *Transactions, Thoroton Society* (1933).

PEATE, *Welsh Bygones* (National Museum of Wales, 1929).

ROBERT PLOT, *The Natural History of Staffordshire* (1686).

RACKHAM, *Early Staffordshire Pottery* (1951).

READ, *Staffordshire Pottery Figures* (1929).

G. W. and F. A. RHEAD, *Staffordshire Pots and Potters* (1906).

ROTH, *Yorkshire Coiners and Notes on Old Halifax* (1906).

SHAW, *History of the Staffordshire Potteries* (1829).

WALTON, 'Some Decadent Local Industries: (I) Pottery', *Transactions, Halifax Antiquarian Society* (1938).

TOBY JUGS

By LORD MACKINTOSH OF HALIFAX

THERE have been many speculations as to the sources which inspired the first Toby Jug. Some think it may have originated from 'Uncle Toby', the real hero of Laurence Sterne's *Tristram Shandy* (1760). Others ascribe it to an old print with some doggerel verses known as *The Brown Jug* and published in 1761. But more likely it owes its inspiration to some happy thought of the potter; and, if the truth were known, I should not be surprised to find that Aaron Wood was the man who modelled the first Toby Jug.

Strictly speaking, the earliest Toby Jugs are not Tobies at all but can be more properly described as Figure Jugs. Throughout the ages every nation has modelled some sort of drinking vessel in the human form. In England, perhaps, the first to be made were those rare jugs known as Fiddlers, or Midshipmen (*see* Plate 65 for group of five).

These jugs are crude in modelling, potting, and glazing, for they are the work of the potter trying his hand at a figure for the first time. From historical and technical evidence they must date from about 1730. They are six and a half to eight inches high and have a strong family likeness to the still earlier salt-glaze Pew Groups, and were probably by **Astbury** (1678–1743).

Astbury can be said to have been the father of the Staffordshire potters, as **Ralph Wood Senior** and **Whieldon** were his apprentices at the same time. **Josiah Wedgwood** was also a pupil. These craftsmen were of peasant stock, and each became famous in his own day and generation. Their craftsmanship has never been excelled and their works are highly prized by collectors today. But it is with the Wood family that we are concerned. Ralph Wood Senior (1716–72) was joined by his son, **Ralph Wood Junior** (1748–95), and the business was continued under their nephew, **Enoch Wood** (1769–1840). It is to the two Ralph Woods, however, that we are indebted for the Toby Jugs.

There is one other member of the family who must be mentioned: **Aaron Wood** (1717–85), brother of Ralph Wood Senior and father of Enoch. He was never a potter himself but a modeller and block-cutter for nearly all the Staffordshire potters. It is likely that he modelled what was probably the first genuine Toby Jug, and perhaps his brother, Ralph Wood Senior, was the potter, and the date was probably not later than 1750 (*see* Plate 67C, size 9½ inches high). This jug is sometimes called a 'Twyford' Jug and sometimes a 'Step Toby'. The potting and the glazing is more crude than in later models. The base is thinner than the 'Ordinary Model' and the glazing has almost the feel of salt-glaze.

One cannot be quite sure of the chronological developments, but I am inclined to think that the next step was the so-called 'Thin Man Toby' (*see* Plate 69). Here, again, both the modelling and the glaze had not yet reached perfection. They seem to have a close family and technical resemblance to the jugs just described. Some people think Whieldon was the potter concerned, and it is quite possible, although I am inclined to think that this Thin Man was also made by

Ralph Wood Senior, and a few years later than the 'Step' Tobies.

In about 1760 the Toby Jug reached its zenith in quality with the Ralph Wood Toby Jug in its translucent colour glazes. Ralph Wood's greatest achievement was undoubtedly the quality of his colour glazes.

The dictionary gives the word 'translucent' as 'shining through, transmitting light', and that is just what happens. The light does shine through Ralph Wood's coloured glazes. Lead glaze is clear and transparent – like looking through plain glass – whereas the coloured glazes of Ralph Wood are like stained glass. The light is reflected from the white or cream body beneath, through the coloured glazes, and the whole thing becomes as alive and beautiful as the best stained glass. For perfect beauty of glaze it has never been equalled in the whole history of English ceramics. It is akin to the glaze used by Palissy two centuries earlier in France, and compares favourably with the self-colour glazes of early Oriental porcelain.

As the lead glazes in the kiln had to stand a temperature of something around a thousand degrees, the only colour media that could be used were other metallic substances. The lead glazes, therefore, were mixed with oxide of copper to give green, iron for yellow, cobalt for blue, and manganese for a rich brown. Red was never obtained. This meant that the palette was limited to these colours, and had to be applied in broad planes. The colours were applied by brush in the form of a paste. One often comes across a small area which has received no glazes at all and the biscuit shows through. The bottom of the base was often slightly glazed or left unglazed. This is not an infallible test of a Ralph Wood Toby Jug, but is one of the indications. The colours, when applied, would be more or less the same in appearance, grey and pinkish pastes, and only under the fierce heat of the kiln, when the glaze fused to the biscuit and cooled, would the colours appear.

The colour materials used by the old potters were not always pure, nor were the kilns scientifically controlled as in a modern pottery, and the slight impurities in the colouring matter or slight differences in the temperature of the firing produced varying grades of colour, so that one scarcely ever sees two Ralph Wood Toby Jugs alike. Not infrequently one finds that a fault in the firing has caused one glaze to run into the next – a not unpleasant feature.

The two Ralph Woods manufactured a great variety of figures, of which the Toby Jug was only one. For more details the reader might like to refer to my *Early English Figure Pottery* (1938). The technique of potting and glazing was identical in all that they made during this period between, say, 1750 and 1780 or so. These men owed their success to the fact that they knew not only the possibilities but the limitations of their craft.

The great majority of the jugs were what is now known as the 'Ordinary Model' (*see* Plate 67D. It is ten inches high on a square base). But there are slight variations even in the 'Ordinary Model' which add to the interest of the collector. For instance, some are about an inch taller than the usual model and have a long face, while others are slightly thinner. Some have rather bigger heads, while the noses vary from the snub to the aquiline, and even when the features are identical the application of the flesh-tinted glazes make each one an original character.

A genuine Ralph Wood Jug is on the light side in weight, and the very finest jugs are often the lightest. For instance, the 'Shield Toby' (Plate 69), so called because a shield is found at the left-hand side with the words impressed 'It's all out then fill him again'. There are perhaps not more than a dozen of these models known. They are always exceptionally well potted with fine, though thin, glazing and invariably have a Roman nose.

The base of a Toby Jug, although it looks solid, is in fact hollow, and part and parcel of the mould of the figure itself. Several moulds were used in the production of one jug, and the mark can be seen down the side of the jug at the junction of the two main portions, the back and the front. The limbs, jug, handle and hat, etc., were made from separate moulds and all assembled while the clay was in a plastic state. A little hand-tooling would then be added here and there.

The jug was then fired, and when it came out of the kiln it was matt, white or cream in colour, known as biscuit. The glazes were then applied before the final firing, as already described. Originally all Toby Jugs had a crown to the top of the hat which formed a lid to the jug, but usually these have long been missing. People often ask whether Toby Jugs were intended for drinking purposes. It is difficult to be sure, but I should doubt it. I think they were meant as simple ornaments to grace the chimney corner of farm, cottage, or the village inn.

It was not usual until later for the potter to mark his pieces with any identification mark. Perhaps Ralph Wood was the first to do this, but he can only have done it very rarely, as so few have survived, especially on Toby Jugs. Very occasionally one comes across the impressed mark: {'Ra Wood. Burslem' 'R. Wood Burslem'} is supposed to be the work of the father and 'Ra' of the son. One occasionally comes across the mould No. 51 on Toby Jugs.

So far I have been describing the 'Ordinary Model', and this far outnumbers all other designs taken together. But some of Ralph Wood's best work was put into his Special Models: and the finest of all is the very rare 'Prince Hal Jug' (*see* Plate 67A and B, two views). We can trace in this model the influence not of Aaron Wood but of the French modeller **Voyez**, which would bring this fairly late in the Ralph Wood era; or about 1775, as Voyez did not leave Wedgwood to join Ralph Wood until the early 1770s.

As the British Navy was very much in everyone's minds at this period, it is not surprising that two jugs were connected with the sea. The 'Sailor Jug' (Plate 70A), sometimes called the 'Planter', is a most attractive jug and depicts Jack Tar of the period seated on his sea-chest with the usual jug, glass, and pipe, and on some models an anchor at his feet. This model is slightly taller than the Ordinary and is almost invariably well potted and beautifully glazed. Occasionally it is found with the impressed No. 65. The other jug associated with the sea is one known as 'Admiral Lord Howe' and sometimes 'Admiral Vernon' (*see* Plate 70A). This model sometimes bears the impressed No. 63 and is somewhat smaller than the usual jug.

Reference to the sea recalls another rare model known as 'Martha Gunn' (*see* Plate 70B). This is the only Ralph Wood example of a woman figuring as a Toby Jug. Martha Gunn was a Brighton character, a bathing woman, who was reputed to have taught George III to swim when he was a child. At any rate, she wears the Prince of Wales's feathers in her hat. There are only three or four models known in Ralph Wood glazes.

The 'Squire' Jug is another favourite with collectors (*see* Plate 69). It shows a comfortable country squire seated cornerwise in an armchair. This jug usually has a green or blue coat with rich brown hat and breeches.

An even rarer model is known as the 'Welshman' (*see* Plates 70B), of which only two other examples are known to the writer. He is seated on a chair with the Welsh goat between his legs. Perhaps the rarest jug of all is that shown in Plate 68A. This jug is slightly larger than the 'Ordinary Model' (nearly eleven inches high). The back has a lovely sweeping line and a distinctive feature is that the chair on which the figure is seated has four chair legs instead of resting on a flat base. The 'Miniature Tobies' (Plate 69) are small replicas of the full-size jug (about six and a half inches high), but in every other feature are identical with the Ordinary Ralph Wood model.

Before leaving Ralph Wood jugs to mention jugs from other potters, it might be interesting to consider their original cost. We have no actual evidence of the sale price of his Toby Jugs, but there exists an invoice of 1783 from Ralph Wood to Joseph Wedgwood for a consignment of nearly three hundred figures, the total cost of which was £9 6*s* 4*d* and the individual models varied from 2*s* to a few pence. From this evidence it would appear that the wholesale price for a Toby Jug would not be more than 2*s*. It is interesting to speculate what these three hundred figures would fetch today – certainly over £20,000.

The various periods of Staffordshire pottery

are largely determined by the methods of colouring and glazing. The translucent-coloured glazes of Ralph Wood have already been described. This was followed by what is sometimes known as the underglaze colours. That is, the metallic oxides, instead of being mixed with the clear glaze, were painted on the biscuit before the lead glaze was applied. The piece was then fired and the result is that one sees the colours under the glaze rather than part of the glaze itself. Some potters obtained almost identical results by applying the colour agents over the glaze and then firing both together. This period was a short one, towards the end of the eighteenth century, and some very attractive jugs were made. They cannot, however, compare with the lovely translucent glazes. There are, naturally, many pieces where the two techniques overlap, and in these borderline cases the collector must decide for himself.

Perhaps the best-known potters of this second period were **Neale**, **Walton** and **Pratt**, all of Staffordshire and the Leeds pottery. But no doubt most of the Staffordshire and other potters of the time tried their hand at this type of Toby Jug. It is quite possible that the Wedgwood potteries also made Toby Jugs, but I have never seen one I could identify; and, as a matter of fact, we do know that Ralph Wood frequently manufactured figures for Wedgwood. During this period very few new models were fashioned, but all the Ralph Wood designs were repeated with but slight variations.

There is only one other period of Toby Jug production which the collector need take into account, and that is by far the largest and most varied. It is what is known as the Enamelled Decoration. This was a new technique developed towards the end of the eighteenth century. It was discovered by the porcelain factories that if a piece were first fired with a clear glaze, enamel colours could then be applied. The figure was then subjected to a separate firing in a muffle kiln at a low temperature. This resulted in the multitude of porcelain and pottery figures of the period. Now a great range of colour from the artist's palette was at the disposal of the potter, and the most elaborate detail of decoration could be applied exactly like painting a picture. Accordingly, flowered waistcoats, rosy cheeks, striped trousers, and other elaborate decoration, were obtained at the expense of the charm of the translucent glaze. Nevertheless, it was a great period of pottery decoration and one which has lasted until today. Enamel colours, unlike the earlier glazes, did not run. The uncertainties and vagaries of the colour glazes were gone: every piece came out perfect and each one like its neighbour.

Enoch Wood, the third generation of the famous family, lived far into this new era, and became one of the greatest potters in Staffordshire; and his figures as well as Toby Jugs, using as he did the original models but in the new technique, are eagerly sought after by collectors. Plate 66A shows the three periods of glazing: Ralph Wood translucent glaze; underglaze colour; and enamel colour. Unfortunately, the camera does not do justice to the difference.

All the potters I have mentioned previously, and many others, now took up the manufacture of the Toby Jug. Many new and intriguing models appeared, all the old ones being, nevertheless, continued. Amongst the new ones were the jugs known as 'The Hearty Good Fellow', 'The Night Watchman', 'The Bargeman' (a very rare one), 'The Drunken Parson', and many others (*see* Plate 66B). At first the modelling of these enamel jugs was as good as the earlier ones, but gradually the modelling became less careful until, eventually, at the beginning of the Victorian era, they became a mere travesty of what had once been a work of art, or at least an example of fine craftsmanship. For instance, Plate 68C shows a 'Darkie' which some people think is by Davenport, but it is certainly much later than any other illustrated here – probably about 1860, at the time of 'Uncle Tom's Cabin', when the coloured people of the Southern States were much in everyone's minds. The point to notice in this model is that instead of the figure being made up of a number of moulds for body, arms, legs, etc., all separate, all are combined in two moulds, one for the back and one for the front. Perhaps this was the beginning of simplification and mass

A group of Astbury figure jugs, known as Fiddlers and Midshipmen.

PLATE 65

To face page 120

(A) These pieces illustrate the three periods of glazing: Ralph Wood translucent glaze, underglaze colour, enamel colour.

(B) The Night Watchman — The Hearty Good Fellow — The Drunken Parson

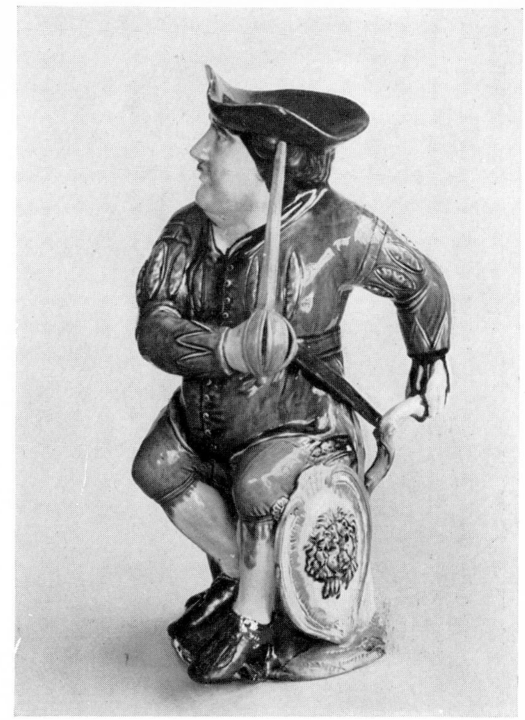

(A) and (B) Prince Hal Jug, by Ralph Wood. Two views.

(C) The 'Twyford' Toby Jug, sometimes known as the 'Step Toby'.

(D) Ordinary Model. Note superb glaze.

PLATE 67

(A) A unique jug by Ralph Wood, *c.* 1783; 11 in. high.

(B) A Toby jug of 'Sir Winston Churchill'; 7 in. high; made by Leonard Jarvis.

(C) 'Black Man' Toby Jug.

(D) Pink lustre jug.

PLATE 68

Thin Man
Miniature

Squire

Welshman
Shield

(A) Two jugs connected with the British Navy: 'The Sailor Jug', sometimes called 'The Planter', and the 'Admiral Lord Howe'.

(B) 'Martha Gunn', the only Ralph Wood piece featuring a woman as a Toby Jug, and the rare 'Welshman'.

A

The Bristol City Art Gallery

B *E. C. Rouse, Esq., M.B.E., F.S.A.*

C

D *British Museum*

For descriptions see page 122

A

B

C

D

(A) PLATE, *c.* 1730, Yung Cheng, decorated in *famille rose* with yellow diaper border and inset panels.

The arms are those of Mathew. There is a tea service of the same date finely enamelled in blue diaper pattern and bearing the same arms.

(C) PLATE, *c.* 1740, Ch'ien Lung, a 'journey' service, the ports of arrival and departure on the rim and destination in the centre.

The arms are those of Sir George Cooke, Chief Protonotary of Common Pleas, knighted in 1715, with, in pretence, those of his wife Catherine, daughter and heir of Sir Thomas Twysden, 4th Baronet, of East Peckham. Sir George also had a tea service, decorated with small flower sprays and a gold spearhead pattern on the rim.

(B) PLATE, *c.* 1730, Yung Cheng, with scenes in sepia on the rim of Canton Harbour and Old London Bridge, the spires of twenty-nine City churches in the background.

The arms are those of Edward Lancelot Lee of Coton, co. Salop, who also possessed a tea service, of the same date, decorated in a pattern of pink diaper. His great-great-grandfather, John Lee, was the ancestor of the Lees of Virginia, from whom came General Robert E. Lee of the American Civil War. His eldest daughter, Isabella, married George Hurst, and an armorial service painted with their arms was made about 1750.

(D) DISH, *c.* 1750, Ch'ien Lung, with a border of gold scrollwork and scallop shells.

The arms are those of Thomas Howard, 2nd Earl of Effingham, who married a daughter of Peter Beckford of Jamaica.

A

B

C *Victoria & Albert Museum*

D *H. R. Marshall, Esq.*

For descriptions see page 122

B

D

A

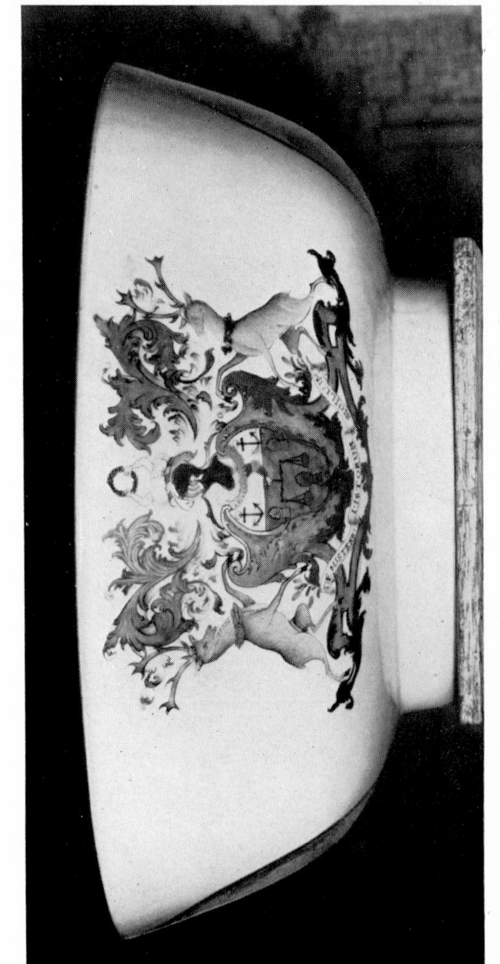

C

For descriptions see page 122

(A) Goblet, *c.* 1762, by Beilby of Newcastle, enamelled in colours with the arms of George III and on the reverse with the Prince of Wales' feathers. *Messrs Sotheby & Co.*

(B) Goblet, *c.* 1765, made in Norway by Keith, an Englishman, the Newcastle tradition is very evident—to commemorate the marriage of Christian VII of Denmark to Matilda, daughter of George II, with the arms of Denmark and England engraved by Köhler. *Messrs Sotheby & Co.*

(A) Bowl, *c.* 1700, engraved with the arms of Arundel.

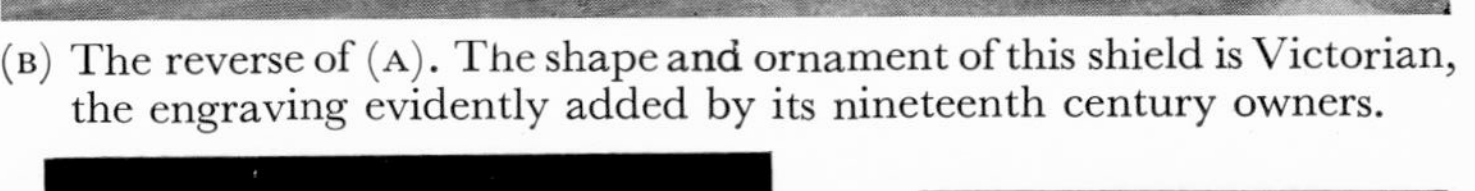

(B) The reverse of (A). The shape and ornament of this shield is Victorian, the engraving evidently added by its nineteenth century owners.

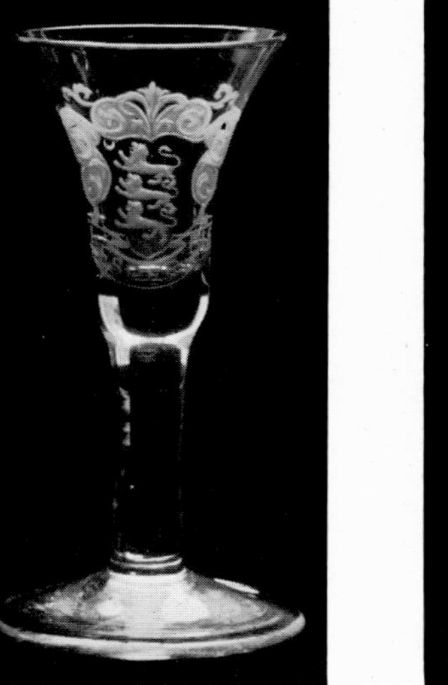

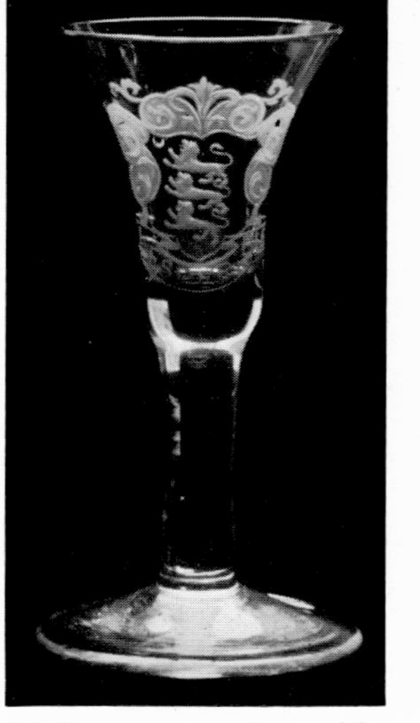

(C) Rummer, *c.* 1810, with the arms, bare of any ornament, of the Blacksmiths Company of London.

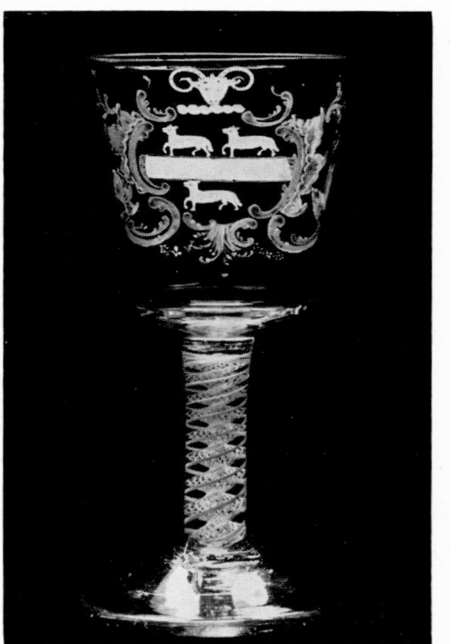

(D) Goblet, *c.* 1765, by Beilby of Newcastle, enamelled with the arms of Lambton, Co. Durham, with monogram on the reverse.

(E) Rummer, *c.* 1795, engraved with the arms of Yarmouth in a shield with wreath and ribbon ornament, and flanked by a crown and mitre.

(F) Wine Glass, *c.* 1730, engraved with the arms of Carey.

All pieces from
Messrs Arthur Churchill Ltd

PLATE 76

To face page 121

production in the potteries. Of course, these later jugs are much easier to acquire than the earlier Ralph Wood type. They are not without charm and considerable interest to the collector and, of course, have the advantage of being very much more reasonable in price. During the early part of the nineteenth century lustre-ware became popular, but it is rather surprising that a lustre Toby Jug is very rare indeed. Plate 68D shows a pink lustre jug, probably Sunderland ware.

It is sometimes difficult for a collector to be sure whether a piece is a genuine effort of a pioneer, struggling for the first time with a new technique, or the work of a later potter who was simply not master of his craft. This is one of the problems which make collecting fascinating. It will, however, be seen that Toby Jugs of interest to the serious collector cover the period from about 1750 at the earliest (with the exception of the few early Astbury Jugs, Plate 65) to, say, 1830 or thereabouts – a matter of eighty years. The Toby Jug has, of course, been manufactured right down to the present day, with a few outstanding examples in recent years, but these do not strictly come within the province of the collector's interest. An exception, perhaps, are those made of politicians and generals, made shortly after the 1914–18 war. But none that I know of has ever attempted the Ralph Wood translucent glazes until the last year or two, and then only one potter. Plate 68B represents a Toby Jug of Sir Winston Churchill made by **Leonard Jarvis**, the well-known Restorer. He has taken the early Astbury Jugs as his model for this Churchill Jug. It stands seven inches high and the potter has reproduced the old translucent glazes with great success, at the same time creating an original work of art.

It is a hundred and fifty years at least since Ralph Wood made his first Toby Jug, but they continue to give pleasure and satisfaction to succeeding generations. There is an Heirloom Jug which was at one time in the possession of a descendant of Ralph Wood. It bears the following inscription together with the initials R.W. and is dated 1770:

> 'No art with Potters can compare
> We make our pots of what we potters are'.

That is true of all of us, whatever our vocation in life, but it was particularly true of these old peasant potters, for they lived on the site of their kilns, where they dug the clay and mined the coal. They spent their lives giving of their best to their native art.

ARMORIAL CHINA AND GLASS

DESCRIPTION OF PLATES (Preceding page 121)

PLATE 71

(A) JARDINIÈRE, *c.* 1692–7, K'ang Hsi, decorated in underglaze blue.

The arms are those of Sir Henry Johnson, an opulent shipbuilder of Blackwall, and of Aldborough, co. Suffolk, knighted in March, 1684/5. He married, in March 1692/3, Martha, only child and heir of John, 3rd Lord Lovelace, who succeeded her grandmother as Baroness Wentworth in her own right in 1697. The shield shows the arms of Lovelace impaled with Johnson and cannot therefore date before 1692 or after 1697, when Martha succeeded as Baroness Wentworth. This is the earliest known piece of armorial china to which a positive date can be given, and provides a good example of the way in which a coat of arms can establish proof of date.

(B) BOWL AND COVER, *c.* 1715, K'ang Hsi, decorated in Chinese Imari.

This early tea service, with a dinner service to match, bears the arms of the Rt. Honourable James Craggs, Secretary of State to George I in 1718 until his death in 1721. He was one of the directors of the South Sea Company, several of whom possessed armorial services: Sir John Lambert, George Edwards of Henlow, Robert Chester and Samuel Salt among them. It is curious that Sir Joseph Jekyll, Master of the Rolls 1717–38, who was prominent in exposing the South Sea directors, and Lord Somers, Lord Chancellor in 1697, whose daughter and heir, Jane, he married, should both have owned armorial services. The Somers service, decorated in the Chinese Imari, was evidently copied from another made about the same date (1710) for a Dr Walker of Lancaster, for although the Somers crest surmounts his shield, that of the rising sun of Walker remains in the decoration of the rim.

(C) DISH AND PLATE, *c.* 1720, K'ang Hsi, decorated wholly in underglaze blue.

The arms on the plate are those of the Rt. Reverend William Talbot, Bishop of Durham in 1721. On the dish are the arms of his daughter Catherine, impaled with those of her husband, Exton Sayer, M.P. for Tottenham, who died in 1731.

(D) PLATE, *c.* 1725, Yung Cheng, decorated in *famille rose* with diaper and inset panels and green diapered rim.

This lovely service was made for Mary Izod, the daughter of Henry Izod of Tuddington and Stanton, co. Gloucester.

PLATE 72

(Descriptions on plate)

PLATE 73

(A) BOWL, *c.* 1780, Ch'ien Lung, with small flower sprays and a festoon pattern draping a scalloped shield.

The arms are those of Washington of Sulgrave.

(B) BOWL, *c.* 1790, Ch'ien Lung, the rim in deep blue and powdered with gold stars.

The arms are those of James Graham, 3rd Duke of Montrose.

(C) TEA-POT, *c.* 1765-70, Worcester, decorated with flower sprays and formal border pattern in gold.

The arms are those of Joseph Edmondson and were granted to him in March 1765, a year after his appointment as Mowbray Herald Extraordinary.

(D) TEN PIECES OF WORCESTER, 1755–80, as follows:

(i) Cocks, *c.* 1760.
(ii) The Plumbers Company, *c.* 1770.
(iii) Kaye, crest only, *c.* 1770.
(iv) Gavin impaling Hearsey, *c.* 1765.
(v) Tracy impaling Bathurst (*vide* page 124), *c.* 1755.
(vi) Boscawen impaling Glanville, *c.* 1760.
(vii) Case quartering Jesson and impaling Weston, *c.* 1760.
(viii) Grand Lodge of England, *c.* 1765.
(ix) Snell impaling Bathurst, *c.* 1755–60.
Susan Bathurst, who married Powell Snell of Guiting Grange, co. Gloucester, was a first cousin of Harriet Bathurst, the wife of Thomas Tracy (*vide* (v) above).
(x) Mackenzie quartering Sulyard, *c.* 1780.
(*Courtesy of H. R. Marshall, Esq.*)

PLATE 74

(A) TEA-POT, *c.* 1750, Ch'ien Lung, spearhead border in gold and small flower sprays.

A tea service made for Anthony Askew of Storrs Hall, co. Lancaster, who married, firstly, Margaret, daughter of Cuthbert Swinburne, and, secondly, Elizabeth, daughter of Robert Halford. The shield shows his coat of arms of nine quarterings impaling the quarterly coats of each of his two wives, one above the other.

(B) OCTAGONAL PLATE, *c.* 1755, Ch'ien Lung, border finely diapered in red, blue and gold with spearhead edging.

This service, an example of the exception of the diaper pattern at this date, bears the arms of Samuel Chase of Luton, co. Bedford, who died in 1803, aged eighty-two.

(C) BOWL, *c.* 1760, Ch'ien Lung, with flower sprays and gold spearhead pattern edging the inside rim.

The arms are those of the Bakers Company. Among other City Company services are those of the Poulters (*c.* 1745), Butchers (*c.* 1750) and Fishmongers (*c.* 1775).

(D) PLATE, *c.* 1760, Ch'ien Lung, a scene in sepia of Aurora pursuing the fleeting night.

This service illustrates the use of a purely European pattern, the arms of Humberstone in a typical 'Chippendale' shield being relegated to the rim.

PLATES 75 AND 76

(Descriptions on plates)

ARMORIAL CHINA AND GLASS

By JAMES TUDOR-CRAIG, F.S.A.

(*A*) CHINA

SERVICES of china painted with coats of arms were fashionable throughout the eighteenth century. All, until about 1755, and the great majority thereafter, were made in China, at Ching-te-chen, and were ordered through the agent of the East India Company or the resident merchants at Canton, and there painted with a coat of arms, of which a sketch or bookplate had been sent out from England. The period of decoration thus covered the blue-and-white and *famille verte* of **K'ang-hsi** (1661–1722), the *famille rose* of **Yung Cheng** (1723–1735), and the gradual decline in quality and design during the reign of the Emperor **Ch'ien Lung** (1736–95).

It is the special interest of armorial china that the coat of arms can reveal not only the identity of the original possessor but, particularly where the arms show a marriage, the date when the service was made.

The heraldry is frequently confusing. The sketches from which the arms were to be copied were not always clearly drawn nor, often, were colours plainly shown; and the Chinese painter, who had no idea what the charges in the shields were supposed to represent and who was unacquainted with European birds, carefully copied what he saw. The arms on some 2,500 services, English and Scottish, have nevertheless been identified. On the evidence of date so provided it is possible to group the changes in border patterns and subsidiary motifs so that these fall into clearly-defined periods, irrespective of that of the coat of arms, and to trace the influence of European taste, which, by the end of the century, had eliminated the Chinese designs.

The primary clue to the date of a service is found in the shape and ornamentation of the shield; for in these were reflected the changes in design and decoration over the century. The plain shields of the late seventeenth century became curved and surrounded with scrollwork which, gradually elaborated, developed by about 1750 into the rococo ornament familiar in the designs of Chippendale. By 1770 this ornate treatment had begun to disappear: shields became spade-shaped, scalloped on the top edge, and wreathed in designs of ribbon or flower festooning made fashionable by Robert Adam. About 1790 the shield is sometimes set upon a draped mantle, but the free treatment of the shield as the central object of decoration had virtually ceased some years before that date.

Borders in the services of the **K'ang-hsi** period may be decorated in the blue, red and gold of 'Chinese Imari' (a pattern copied from the Japanese), entirely in underglaze blue, when the arms are treated likewise, or painted in *rouge de fer* and *famille verte*, with patterns, as in underglaze blue, of utensils, emblems, flowers and birds, or diapered with inset panels containing the same motifs or miniature scenes. This diaper decoration continued during the years of Yung Cheng, but in more open trellis-like form, often in sepia, and was accompanied by finely-enamelled flower sprays in *famille rose*. Patterns remained, in fact, in the pure Chinese taste. Early in the **Ch'ien Lung** period, however, European influence is apparent. Services are decorated with pastoral scenes and mythological subjects, the arms being relegated to the rim; the diaper, with one or two marked exceptions, becomes a shadow of its former self, and a gold spearhead or chain pattern, with small flower sprays in the Meissen style, is common to most services until about 1760. Between 1750 and 1770 a design of gold scallop shells joined by thin gold scrolls, evidently a stock pattern, is found on many services. Within these dates, also, falls the 'journey china' painted on the rim with panels of shipping scenes illustrating the ports of despatch and arrival, and in the centre with a building representing the destination of the service in the home of its owner, his arms appearing on the base and his crest on the top of the rim.

After 1770 little of the Oriental remains. Borders vary from swags or festoons of flowers and ribbon or dotted lines wreathed with flowers to a wavy diaper in dull underglaze blue or a double banding of deeper blue edged in the spearhead pattern. By 1790 had appeared the stock pattern of a narrow blue-banded rim powdered with gold stars and painted over the glaze, which persisted over the next ten years, and was followed, about 1800, by a wide spearhead border, in blue, green or rust red, with four peonies set to surround the shield in the centre, a pattern known in America as 'Fitzhugh'. This is a corruption of Foochow, whence large consignments of china carrying this design were shipped to Salem in Massachusetts.

The earlier services of armorial china were dinner services. These might vary considerably in size. In the British Museum is the invoice, dated Canton, 10th December, 1731, for a dinner service shipped to Charles Peers consisting of 524 pieces, of which 312 were plates, 56 were dishes, and the balance tankards, sauce-boats, bowls, and ewers and lavers. A similar invoice, dated from Canton in 1743, details a service of 4 large dishes and 50 plates consigned to Leake Okeover. Specimens of both services are in the British Museum collection. Other services, such as those made for George Verney, 12th Lord Willoughby de Broke, and James Brydges, Duke of Chandos, both made about 1715, and the latter decorated in Chinese Imari, were very large and included everything from candlesticks to chamber-pots. The usual dinner service, however, seems to have comprised soup tureens and vegetable dishes with sauce-boats, soup and meat plates, and to have run to between 400 and 800 pieces.

Few tea services are found before 1730, by which time tea-drinking was becoming a fashionable habit, when they are of fine-quality porcelain, often of 'eggshell' thinness. They comprised such pieces as spoon-trays and teapot-stands and tea-caddies, besides a generous complement of tea-bowls (no handles) and saucers, milk-jugs, sugar-bowls and covers, and two or more tea-pots. Their decoration, together with that of coffee and chocolate services, mostly dating after 1740, conforms to that of the dinner services. Often tea, dinner and coffee services were ordered together, the same arms appearing on all three, though the services themselves may be of different patterns.

On 10th February, 1755, Thomas Charles Tracy, son of Thomas Charles, 5th Viscount Tracy, married Harriet, daughter of Peter Bathurst, of Clarendon Park in Wiltshire, and in 1756 succeeded his father as the sixth viscount. A tankard made at Worcester and bearing his arms with those of his wife, no doubt one from a service given as a wedding present, provides the earliest instance of the manufacture of armorial china in England. Of the services made at **Worcester** during the **Dr Wall** period (1751–83), some two hundred are known and the arms on them identified, with the result that it has been possible to date the decorative patterns in the same way as those of Chinese services.

Worcester seems to have given a lead followed by other English factories; for **Joshua** and **John Green** produced, at their pottery at Leeds, about 1760, a service made for Sir John Smyth, Baronet, of Hill Hall, in Essex, bearing his arms with those of his wife, Elizabeth Burges. **Richard Champion**, of Bristol, made a service, probably about 1775, with the arms of Rebow, an interesting copy of a Yung Cheng service made for Isaac Rebow, Member of Parliament for Colchester, who died in 1734. And from Champion, too, came the service presented to Mrs Burke on the election of Edmund Burke as Member for Bristol in 1774. Several services were produced by **Josiah** and **Thomas Wedgwood**, decorated in purplish brown, between 1785 and 1790, one, for example, with the arms and crest of Thompson. There are also many instances of replacements by the English factories to Chinese services – Spode, Derby and Chelsea among them – notably by Chelsea to the service made about 1735 for Henry Talbot of Dorking, whose wife Catherine Clopton was the direct descendant of Sir Hugh Clopton, from whom Shakespeare, in 1597, purchased New Place at Stratford-on-Avon.

The English factories continued to produce armorial services during the first quarter of the nineteenth century. Chamberlain, at Worcester, being responsible for forty or more, and their increasing general production, together with the high protective duty, made the import of Chinese wares unnecessary in practice and prohibitive in price. Few Chinese armorial services are known after 1800, and none after 1825.

The armorial services made in China were not confined to the English market. Most of the European countries had substantial interests in the East Indian trade, with factories and agents in Canton, and many services were made for Dutch, French, Portuguese and Swedish families. Apart from those bearing Dutch coats of arms, these services for the most part date after the K'ang Hsi period, and their Continental heraldry lacks the decorative quality of the English coats. Their border patterns, however, broadly correspond to those of the English services. A border of coloured scallop shells, for example, decorates the service made about 1760 for Jeanne Antoinette Poisson, Madame de Pompadour, while a rococo shield carries the fish of her punning coat of arms. But the identification of the arms, the primary interest of armorial china, is an obstinate problem with European heraldry, and the English or American collector may be more profitably concerned with those armorial pieces carrying English or Scottish coats.

(*B*) GLASS

English glass bearing an engraved or painted coat of arms is rare. Its period is broadly spanned by the hundred years of the eighteenth century. The softness of English lead glass was unsuited to the technique of engraving, and the decoration of glass in England by engraving or painting did not develop as standard manufacture until after 1745. The invention of wheel-engraving was German: the harder glass of Germany, which flooded Western Europe after the restoration of peace with the Treaty of Utrecht in 1713, allowed just that precision and freedom which the process required. Of the English armorial glass of the first quarter of the century, while some was diamond cut by English gem engravers, the bulk was engraved by Dutch or German craftsmen working in England. But both then and later glass was sent to Germany and Holland for the decoration to be done there. Glass made, for example, at Newcastle, where families of glassmakers had been settled since the early seventeenth century, and where a considerable export trade existed with the Netherlands, was sent to Holland to be engraved with coats of arms by Dutch engravers.

In 1745 an Excise Act imposed a duty on the 'materials and metals' used in making all 'Crown Plate and Flint glass', with the result that the proportion of lead used, hitherto so important a determinant in the size and design of English glass, declined. The glass thereby lost some of its brilliance; it also became harder – deficiencies in quality which glassmakers familiar with German glass promptly sought to make up by the application of engraved or painted ornament that was not of any personal relevance, such as an inscription, portrait or coat of arms, but did in fact decorate the glasses. After that date, therefore, glass which had formerly borne heraldic engraving might be decorated with a variety of patterns, formal, natural, or designs of subjects or scenes.

Just as these patterns, and the design and shape of the foot and stem, define the period of manufacture of the glass, so can the coat of arms, as distinct from the ornamentation of the shield, establish within precise limits the date of the glass. This factor is of particular importance in the early heraldic engraving, where, for example, a goblet bearing the arms of Queen Anne before the Union with Scotland gives proof of date between 1702 and 1707. Such armorial glasses as this were special orders and were to remain rare until about 1735, when Benjamin Payne of London advertised 'the arms of all the Royal Family finely engraved on glasses'. By that date the plain shield of the early engraving had begun to develop, in its curved shape and cartouche, the rococo ornament which prevailed from 1750 to 1765, but was thereafter to be discarded with the change of taste during the last quarter of the century. After 1775 shields became spade-shaped, scalloped at the top edge and set in festoon patterns of wreath and ribbon or dotted lines. At the turn of the century these patterns disappeared; shields for the most part were bare of surrounding ornament.

The change in the quality of English glass which had fostered the engraving of ornament also permitted the process, borrowed from Germany and, to a lesser degree, from the Netherlands, of enamel painting. Glasses and decanters, painted in colours with coats of arms were produced between about 1760 and 1775, notably by the Beilby family of Newcastle, whose signature – *Beilby Ncastle invt & pinxt* – appears on a glass enamelled with the arms of George III and the feathers of the Prince of Wales, probably commemorating the birth of George III's eldest son, George Augustus Frederick, in 1762. While, however, engraved armorial glasses covered every type and size, these Beilby glasses were mostly wine-glasses or goblets, either with slender Newcastle stems and straight-sided bowls – and usually fictitious heraldry – or goblets with bucket bowls carrying elaborately decorated shields and supporting motifs. A decanter, in the Wilfred Buckley bequest, enamelled with the arms of Newcastle, is signed *Beilby Junr*, and must have been made while his father, Ralph Beilby, was alive, i.e. before 1765.

The increasing debility of decoration after 1775 was accompanied by an expanding interest in the chemistry of glass. Materials and methods began to be of more importance than the objects produced from them: glass-making was turning from a craft into an industry. By 1800 the loss of virility of line and ornament was complete, and with it the interest of the collector ceases.

BOOKS FOR FURTHER READING

Francis Buckley, *Old English Glass* (1925).
Wilfred Buckley, *European Glass* (1926).
F. A. Crisp, *Armorial China* (1907).
R. L. Hobson, *The Later Ceramic Wares of China* (1925).
J. A. Lloyd Hyde, *Oriental Lowestoft* (New York, 1936).
H. R. Marshall, *English Ceramic Circle Transactions*, No. 9, Vol. II (1946).
W. A. Thorpe, *History of English and Irish Glass* (1929).
Sir A. Tudor-Craig, *Armorial Porcelain of the Eighteenth Century* (1925).

WEDGWOOD

By GEOFFREY WILLS

JOSIAH WEDGWOOD, F.R.S., F.S.A., came into the world of ceramics at a time when the laborious manual methods were being replaced by mechanical processes; when pottery was threatened by the rivalry of porcelain; and when the demand for both decorative and useful articles was growing so fast as to stimulate and well-nigh outstrip production. Wedgwood was born in Burslem, Staffordshire, in August 1730, the thirteenth child of Thomas Wedgwood, who owned the Churchyard Pottery in that town. The Wedgwoods were members of a family long resident in the district, and related by birth and by marriage to other families whose names were, and still are, well known in the Potteries, by which name the district of Staffordshire centring on Stoke-on-Trent has been known for centuries.

On the death of his father in 1739 Josiah went to work in the family pottery. He became apprenticed for a period of five years in 1744 to the new owner, his eldest brother, also named Thomas. At the end of his apprenticeship he became a partner in a pottery at Stoke, and helped in the manufacture of the salt-glazed and colour-glazed wares that were the normal productions of the district.

After a few years, in which it is presumed he was gaining much practical experience, he formed a fresh partnership with Thomas Whieldon of Fenton Low (near Stoke-on-Trent), and spent his time in attempting to improve the quality of the pottery made there. He experimented with success in producing glazes of deeper and purer colours, and applied them to a body of a better quality than had been made hitherto. He recorded the results of his different experiments. After stating that trade in the Potteries was decreasing, complaints being general, and that the public was tired of the salt-glazed and other wares that were then being made, he wrote: '. . . something new was wanted to give a little spirit to the business . . . some more solid improvement, as well in the body as in the glazes, the colours, and the forms of the articles of our manufacture. I saw the field was spacious and the soil so good as to promise ample recompense to anyone who should labour diligently in its cultivation.'

The business arrangement with Thomas Whieldon, who was one of the most respected potters of his day and whose name is still associated with some of the best eighteenth-century work in that medium, endured from 1754 to 1759. By this last date Josiah Wedgwood, aged twenty-nine years, had accumulated sufficient knowledge, capital and initiative to commence making pottery on his own account. This was at Ivy House, in the town of his birth, Burslem; where the site of the building is now occupied by the Wedgwood Institute.

He married a distant cousin, Sarah Wedgwood, in 1764. By about this same date he had extended his business premises and was busily engaged in making his own improved versions of the usual wares of the district, both salt- and colour-glazed. His greatest and most enduring success in this direction was with cream-coloured pottery. For this he secured the patronage of Queen Charlotte and named it *Queen's Ware* in recognition of the honour.

He earned also the distinction of being styled 'Potter to the Queen', although he does not seem to have been granted a formal patent to this effect. Within a short time of its first introduction, Wedgwood produced this fine-quality earthenware in large quantities, and by so doing brought a good-looking and practical domestic china within the reach of thousands of families. In the first half of the eighteenth century the majority of households used tin-glazed pottery (English or foreign delftware), pewter or wooden articles, which were being ousted with success by the wholesale importation of Chinese and Japanese porcelain and, after 1750 or thereabouts, by home-produced porcelain. The Queen's Ware competed with all these and found its way quickly into many homes.

In 1765 Josiah wrote to his brother John at Cateaton Street in the City of London, who acted as agent for him: 'I have just had the honour of the Duke of Marlborough, Lord Gower, Lord Spencer, and others at my works. They have bought some things and seemed much entertained and pleased. The gentlemen above mentioned wonder I have not a warehouse in London where patterns of all the sorts I make may be seen.' This advice was accepted, and in due course was acted upon. At the same time, in spite of his preoccupation with fulfilling the numerous and growing orders of royalty, the nobility and others, Josiah Wedgwood was steadily widening his range of friends. Before long he numbered among them Joseph Priestley, the chemist and theologian; Erasmus Darwin, the physician and poet; Matthew Boulton, the Soho, Birmingham, manufacturer; and many others who were eminent in their respective spheres. By reason of his active interest in the newly-proposed Trent and Mersey Canal, of which the engineer, James Brindley, was another of his friends, he was well acquainted with the local landowners, and was appointed Treasurer to the Canal Company. As a result of his wide interests and business acumen it can be seen that, when just over thirty years old, Wedgwood had already become widely known to an influential circle of people.

It was shortly after 1760 that Wedgwood formed what was to endure as a lengthy friendship, to be broken only by death. The potter had travelled on business to Liverpool, became ill there, and the doctor who was called to attend him later introduced him to a friend of his, Thomas Bentley (1730–80), a local resident. Bentley had a thriving business as a general merchant in the city, but as a result of his growing acquaintance with Wedgwood it was not long before it resolved principally into that of an earthenware dealer, and large quantities of ware from the Burslem factory were sent to Liverpool to be exported to America, the West Indies, and elsewhere. In return Bentley was instrumental in the importation of china clays sent from Dorset, Devon and Cornwall in the south-west of England by coastal boats to Liverpool in the north-west, and then overland to the potteries. The two men had interests that allied them, in addition to business, and it is agreed that it was Bentley's influence that led Josiah Wedgwood to take an interest in antique Greek and Roman art.

Not long after their first meeting it would seem that Wedgwood mooted the idea of a partnership between Bentley and himself. In the spring of 1767 Wedgwood wrote to him: 'Your most acceptable letter of the 15th gave me the highest pleasure in setting before me a nearer prospect than I had yet had of a union that I have long coveted, and which I do not doubt will be lasting, delightful and beneficial to us both, and as to the time and manner of leaving Liverpool, make it most agreeable to yourself in every respect, and it will be perfectly so to me.' At the time of writing this letter Wedgwood was engaged in purchasing land for the purpose of building a bigger and a better manufactory. Writing, again to Bentley, he said: 'I am going on with my experiments upon various earths, clays, etc., for different bodies, and shall next go upon glazes. Many of my experiments turn out to my wishes and convince me more and more of the extensive *capability* of our manufacture for further improvements. It is at present comparatively in a rude, uncultivated state and may readily be polished and brought to much greater perfection. Such a revolution, I believe, is at hand, and you must assist in profit by it.' Matters progressed, and,

Hercules and
the Cretan Bull.
Unmarked.

Hercules and
the Nemean Lion.
Unmarked.

(*Above*) Red stoneware tea-pot. Marked 'WEDGWOOD'. Height $3\frac{1}{4}$ in. *Victoria & Albert Museum.*

(*Left*) Tea-caddy with green and brown glazes. Marked 'WEDGWOOD'. Height $4\frac{3}{4}$ in. *D. M. & P. Manheim.*

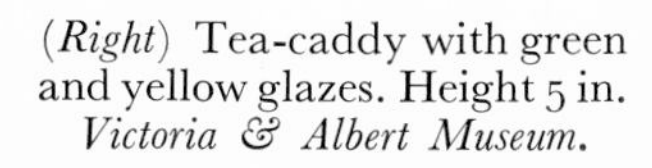

(*Right*) Tea-caddy with green and yellow glazes. Height 5 in. *Victoria & Albert Museum.*

George Washington

William Shakespeare

Tea-pot with green and yellow glazes. *Victoria & Albert Museum.*

PLATE 77

(A) Supper-set of cream-ware painted in brown and yellow. Marked 'WEDGWOOD'. Diameter $13\frac{5}{8}$ in.
Victoria & Albert Museum.

(B) Cream-ware butter or jam dish and cover. Marked 'WEDGWOOD'. Diameter $5\frac{3}{4}$ in. *Victoria & Albert Museum.*

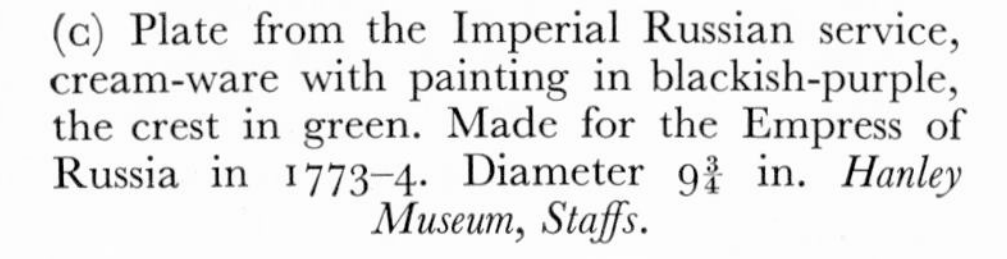

(C) Plate from the Imperial Russian service, cream-ware with painting in blackish-purple, the crest in green. Made for the Empress of Russia in 1773–4. Diameter $9\frac{3}{4}$ in. *Hanley Museum, Staffs.*

PLATE 78

following a visit to Liverpool, Wedgwood again wrote: 'I am always so much better satisfied in my own mind, and pleased with everything about me after spending a few days with you, that I long more and more for the time of your settlement at Hetruria'. This is the first recorded mention of the now-famous name for the new factory. The out-of-date spelling was dropped shortly afterwards, and the more recognizable form, 'Etruria', was adopted. It was not until 1768 that the plan for a partnership came to fruition, and in March of that year Wedgwood leased a large showroom in Newport Street, near Leicester Square, London. This was opened, complete with the Royal Arms over the door, five months later.

The partnership between Josiah Wedgwood and Thomas Bentley related only to vases and ornamental articles. What were termed 'useful' wares continued to be made at Burslem, where the Brick House works (later known as the Bell House works) replaced the earlier Ivy House, which had proved too small. The Burslem factory was managed by Thomas Wedgwood, Josiah's cousin, who was also a partner, but only with regard to the 'useful' wares. The Etruria works opened in 1769, but it was not until 1773 that all branches of the manufacture, with the exception of the enamelling establishment in London, were concentrated there finally. In that latter year Wedgwood received an order for a creamware service which captured people's imagination, no less at the time it was made than it has continued to do to this day. The service, which greatly enhanced Wedgwood's growing reputation, was to the order of the Empress Catherine of Russia, and was for one of her palaces known as 'La Grenouillière' (The Frog Palace) (*see* Plate 78C).

It is assumed generally that it was through the influence of his partner Thomas Bentley that Wedgwood was led to take an interest in ancient Greek and Roman art, and to adapt it skilfully and with success for a more modern market. The researches of the antiquarians of the mid-eighteenth century were followed as eagerly by the educated public as they were by the two potters. Wedgwood and Bentley found, from trial and error, or they realized intuitively, that the public would like their neat adaptations of Mediterranean forms, and they were not slow to take advantage of the fact and to exploit it to the utmost. Both of them clever men, they were also astute at business, as examination of their letters reveals.

Greek pottery vases were the models for the first productions from Etruria: such pieces were supposed at that date to have been of Etruscan origin, hence the name of the factory. Josiah Wedgwood, not having been entirely satisfied in the making of classical shapes in cream-ware or with pseudo-marble glazes, engaged himself actively in the task of improving the body already used in the locality for the making of black stoneware, known as 'Black Egyptian'. The first successful pair of vases in the new medium was sent to a relative of a Liverpool Member of Parliament in August 1768 for the purpose, it is alleged, of gaining the politician's interest in a local project. The vases were sent by way of Bentley, and a covering letter added: 'There are three other imperfect ones to shew you a little into the *light of our imperfections* in the manufacturing of these delicate compositions, and the disappointments you must expect to meet with when you become a Potter; so that if you can be picking up a little patience, and storing it against a time of need, there may be no sort of harm in it. Every vase in the last kiln were spoiled, and that only by such a degree of variation in the fire as scarcely affected our cream-colour biscuit at all.'

Sufficient progress was made in the development of the improved black stoneware – named 'basaltes' – that it is said that the opening of the Etruria works was celebrated by Josiah Wedgwood himself throwing several Etruscan vases, with Thomas Bentley turning the wheel for him. These pieces were duly inscribed: 'JUNE XIII, MDCCLXIX. One of the first Days Production at Etruria in Staffordshire by Wedgwood and Bentley.' Before long the basaltes body was used widely for the making of all sorts of wares, from medallions to vases, candlesticks, baskets, flower-pots and, not least, a fine range of bust portraits of ancient and modern celebrities (*see* Plate 80B).

The general interest in the remains of the classical world was not confined to Greek or Etruscan vases but extended to other objects, which in the originals had been executed in different materials from pottery. This led Wedgwood to develop further stoneware bodies, and the result was one of great fineness made by him and called 'jasper'. With this he was able to reproduce gems that had been carved originally in stone, and to make the many articles in the classical style that have made him famous. The cameo medallions were made in very great numbers, and by 1780 over 1,700 different subjects had been produced. At the same time beads, buttons, bell-pull handles, snuff-box tops, plaques for inlaying in furniture and for setting into mantelpieces, bases for candlesticks and mounts for opera-glasses were among the great variety of articles in which the ware was employed. Etruria was conveniently close to Birmingham, where Matthew Boulton had his metal-ware manufactory, and it was mounted there in gilt-bronze or in cut-steel. The most famous use to which the jasper body was put was in the making of copies of the Portland vase (Plate 80C), an undertaking that occupied no less than three years.

Of Wedgwood's other innovations mention may be made of his pearl-ware, cane-ware, bamboo-ware, rosso antico and the use of 'lustre' glazes. All of these enjoyed success in varying degrees and helped to extend his fame. During all the time that his basaltes, jasper and other bodies were being produced the Queen's Ware was being made. In 1769 Wedgwood opened an establishment in Chelsea for the enamelling of it. It was under the supervision of Bentley, who, on his marriage in 1772, lived in nearby Cheyne Row. The Russian service, mentioned earlier, was enamelled there, the ware being sent from Burslem for the purpose.

Thomas Bentley died in 1780, Josiah Wedgwood lived for a further fifteen years. In 1790 he took his three sons, Josiah, John and Thomas, and his nephew, Thomas Byerley, into partnership, and the first-named remained in charge of the factory until 1841. Most of the wares introduced by Josiah Wedgwood Senior continued to be produced and, in addition, some bone porcelain of the type made at other factories was made for a few years following 1812. The firm flourishes today, still under the control of the descendants of the man who founded it and made its name a household word throughout the civilized world.

It is not always remembered that Josiah Wedgwood was not the most robust of men. In the 1740s, when about ten years of age, he had caught the dreaded smallpox, and this had left him, according to report, with an affection of the right knee. This weakness greatly troubled him over the years, and there can be no doubt that the inability to stand for long hours at a potter's wheel, or at any other task, may have forced him to take a deeper interest in the administrative side of the business. Before he was forty he had his right leg amputated, but in spite of the handicap he suffered because of this he was a ceaseless worker.

Josiah Wedgwood was a man of the times in which he lived: a man who knew how to please prospective buyers, but who was strong-minded enough to maintain at a high level the wares he sold. He did not hesitate to employ reputable artists to assist him, was never lacking in original ideas and the zest for experiment, and he did his utmost to make each new venture a success. He was possessed of his full share of the innate good taste of the period, together with a regard for detail and a remarkable capacity for organization. A modern writer has described him aptly as an 'artist-manufacturer'. Josiah Wedgwood and his friend Matthew Boulton were certainly the precursors of the nineteenth-century industrial magnates.

GLOSSARY

Agate: wares made in imitation of this stone. They were made either of differently-coloured clays, mixed, and with the colours going right through the body of the piece, or the effect was achieved by means of coloured clays on the surface of plain pottery.

Bamboo-ware: a variety of stoneware, of a darker tint of brown than the cane-ware, introduced by Josiah Wedgwood in 1770.

Basaltes: the name given by Josiah Wedgwood to his fine-quality black stoneware introduced in 1766.

Blake, William: the artist, poet and visionary, was employed to draw and engrave a catalogue of Wedgwood cream-coloured wares in the years 1815 and 1816. The engravings run to eighteen in number and illustrate 185 pieces of domestic china. Eight of the actual copper-plates are still in existence, but have been altered since they left Blake's hand. Some correspondence between the artist and Josiah Wedgwood is printed by Geoffrey Keynes in *Blake Studies* (1949). Sixteen of the engravings are reproduced in W. Mankowitz's *Wedgwood*. Keynes gives two, one of which is not in the latter volume.

Boulton, Matthew (1728–1809): in partnership with John Fothergill (to 1781), and with John Watt, was a manufacturer of metalwork at Soho, Birmingham. He mounted Wedgwood cameos, etc., in cut-steel and in gilt-bronze. Writing to Bentley in 1768, Wedgwood said: 'We have an order from Mr Boulton for some bodys of vases for mounting, which I must either comply with or affront him, and set him a-trying to get them elsewhere . . .' One of a pair of jasper-ware vases, with gilt metal mounting, is shown in Plate 81C.

Cane-ware: a cane-coloured (buff) stoneware introduced by Josiah Wedgwood in 1770.

Chelsea: it was to this riverside village, then a rural retreat outside London, that Josiah Wedgwood removed his enamelling workshop from where it had been for a short while in Newport Street, Leicester Square. The premises were taken at the end of 1769. They were not far from Thomas Bentley's house in Cheyne Row, and he was able to supervise operations there. The Imperial Russian service was decorated at Chelsea between 1773 and 1774. In the latter year the establishment was closed and the enamellers were housed in a part of the new premises in Greek Street, Soho, London.

Encaustic painting: Josiah Wedgwood was granted a patent in 1769 for: 'The purpose of ornamenting earthen and porcelaine ware with an encaustic gold bronze, together with a peculiar species of encaustic painting in various colours in imitation of the antient Etruscan and Roman earthenware'. He prepared a number of substances by which were produced the following colours: red, orange, white, green, blue, yellow and both a matt and a 'shineing' black. The principal use for these colours was in the decoration of the basaltes body, which was modelled and painted in imitation of ancient Greek ware.

Etruria: the name given to the Staffordshire works opened by Josiah Wedgwood and Thomas Bentley in the year 1769. At first only the ornamental wares were made there, but within four years the entire output of the firm, including the 'useful wares', was produced from this single factory (apart from some of the enamelling which was being done in London). It is said that the name 'Etruria' was suggested by Wedgwood's friend Dr Erasmus Darwin, who was known for his classical leanings.

Flaxman, John, R.A.: a well-known sculptor who was employed by Josiah Wedgwood from 1775 to 1787. Much of his work has been identified; it includes a number of plaques in relief, some portraits, and a set of chessmen (*see* Plate 79E). His father, also named John, supplied plaster casts of antique busts to Wedgwood, and some confusion has resulted in the classification of the work of father and son.

Hackwood, William (d. 1839): Wedgwood's principal modeller from 1769 to 1832. Hackwood spent much of his time in adapting the antique, but is known also to have done some original work. Occasionally he signed his work with his name in full, or with initials.

Imitations: Wedgwood's success was so phenomenal that from the start of his career as an independent potter he was plagued by imitators. Each of his innovations was copied as soon as it came on to the market, but few of the copyists reached the standard of quality in both the body and the modelling of it that was set at Etruria. The cream-coloured wares were copied in quantity at Leeds and at many other factories nearer to Burslem. The principal imitator of the jasper wares was William Adams, of Greengates, Tunstall, who had been one of Wedgwood's pupils. He made very good copies in the style of his former master, and many of his original pieces have merit. Adam did not hesitate to mark them clearly with his own name: not only an action that showed his honesty but a considerable aid to collectors at the present day. On the Continent the Sèvres manufactory made jasper-ware plaques in imitation of those from Etruria, and they are found sometimes mounted on pieces of furniture of the Louis XVI and Empire periods. The basaltes, jasper, agate and cream wares were imitated also by Humphrey Palmer of Hanley. Wedgwood wrote to Bentley in 1769 respecting Palmer's piracies: 'I saw one of P.'s black vases yesterday. The body is very good, the shape and composition very well . . . upon the whole it was better than I expected.'

Imperial Russian Service: known also as the 'Frog' service. Josiah Wedgwood received the order to make this enormous service of cream-coloured earthenware in March 1773. It was for the Empress Catherine of Russia, and was to be placed in her palace near St Petersburg (Leningrad), known as 'La Grenouillière'. The device of a green frog was painted in a shield in the border of each piece. The service numbered more than nine hundred pieces, each of which bore at least one painting of an English view, the obtaining of which caused a great deal of difficulty. The cost of the actual ware came to £51. 8*s* 4*d*, but the decoration and other charges raised the final total to nearly £2,500. The Empress is believed to have paid £3,000 for it, and Wedgwood wrote: '. . . there will not be near the proffit upon this service that we have upon our commonest painted goods'.

The painting of the service was done at Chelsea, where Wedgwood had an enamelling establishment under the supervision of Thomas Bentley. It was commenced in April 1773, and when the newly-acquired showrooms at Portland House, Greek Street, were ready for opening in June of the year following, it was found that a sufficient number of pieces of the service had been completed for an exhibition to be made of it. The service was shown there with success, and was seen by many famous people, including Queen Charlotte. It is at present in the Winter Palace at Leningrad.

Jasper-ware: a fine-quality stoneware perfected by Josiah Wedgwood by 1774. It contained an ingredient that was new to ceramics in the form of a Derbyshire mineral known as 'cawk' (sulphate of barium). Normally a pure white, the jasper body could be coloured evenly throughout and was made eventually in the following tints: pale blue ('Wedgwood blue'), dark blue, sage-green, olive-green, lilac, yellow and black. After a short while the colours were applied in the form of a surface wash, and the ware was then referred to as 'jasper dip'. The edges of pieces made by this process often reveal the outer layers of colour with a central core of white. The copies of the Portland vase were made with a body of a specially composed jasper-ware, coloured an intense black in an attempt to simulate accurately the dark blue glass of the original. Wedgwood named his discovery 'jasper' because of its density and smoothness and because it could be polished on the lathe or grindstone to the same degree as the natural stone of that name.

Lustre: this decoration, which consists of a metallic coating over the pottery body of the article, was used by Josiah Wedgwood Junior from the end of the eighteenth century. Pieces were made which were coated either entirely with lustre, or showed the pottery body through a pattern traced in the lustre. This latter type is known as 'resist-lustre', and was made at many of the Staffordshire factories just before and after 1800.

Marks: considering the enormous quantity of wares of different types that emanated from the manufactories of Josiah Wedgwood, remarkably few marks are to be noted. Without exception, they incorporate the name of the founder of the works but are also to be seen with the addition of the name of his partner, Thomas Bentley.

The early productions from the Ivy House works bear no marks, nor do many of the early pieces from Etruria. Notable exceptions in the case of the latter are the few vases thrown on the first day and inscribed to record the event (*see* p. 129). The circular mark shown at 1 was used between 1769 and 1780; as was the mark shown at 2. In both

Fig. 1

Fig. 2

these the letters are *raised*. Variants of the latter (3) were used on smaller pieces. Following the death of Thomas Bentley in 1780, his

WEDGWOOD
&BENTLEY

Wedgwood
& Bentley

Fig. 3

name was dropped and the single word 'Wedgwood' was used both in different sizes and with the type composed wholly of capital letters (4), or with capitals for the initial only (5). These marks (3 to 5) were impressed

WEDGWOOD

Fig. 4

Wedgwood

Fig. 5

clearly into the wet clay before it was baked. Porcelain was printed over the glaze with the word 'WEDGWOOD', either in red, blue, black or gold.

Josiah Wedgwood is said not to have approved of his artists and workmen adding their names to their productions, and the evidence would seem to favour this assumption. Rarely a piece is to be found with the signature or the initials of the modeller, William Hackwood. The identification of other initials has been attempted, but in general with few satisfactory results. It may be remarked that Hackwood's initials, when they are there, are to be found on the front of cameos. Other letters are normally on the backs. Numerals usually refer to catalogue numbers.

Some pieces in the form of a tripod incense-burner, both in black basalte and with a lustre glaze, are known with a mark beneath the base which reads: 'JOSIAH WEDGWOOD Feb 2nd. 1805' (*see* Plate 82A). No acceptable reason for the recording of this particular date has been advanced.

Many of the imitators of Wedgwood's wares had no scruples about forging his mark as well. The most notorious was a firm of potters at Stockton-on-Tees, who marked their productions 'Wedgewood', and against whom an injunction was obtained eventually. Forgeries of the Wedgwood mark were also used abroad. A quantity of pottery has been recorded that bears genuine Wedgwood marks but is not of varieties known to have been manufactured by Josiah Wedgwood. It has been suggested that these pieces may have been made elsewhere in Staffordshire to fulfil orders received by Wedgwood that he could not carry out at his own works, and that they were so marked on his instructions.

The early copies of the Portland vase are unmarked, except for a numeral written in pencil inside the vase. The one illustrated in Plate 80C bears the number '29'. Later reproductions bear the usual impressed mark.

Modellers: Josiah Wedgwood employed a number of well-known artists from time to time. Much of the ware he made was in imitation of, and adapted closely from, the antique, and this did not call generally for a display of originality on the part of sculptors and draughtsmen. James Tassie, known for his casts in glass of antique gems, was employed in connection with the production of jasper-ware cameos. The wax-modellers Matthew and Isaac Gosset worked on the production of heads of their contemporaries for the making of cameo portraits. Similarly employed were Lochee, Pesez and Joachim Smith. Amateurs who designed reliefs for Wedgwood included Lady Templetown and Lady Diana Beauclerk. The most renowned of all the modellers, and one who is recorded as having done a considerable amount of work for Wedgwood, was the sculptor John Flaxman. His connection with the potter lasted for some twelve years, from 1775. After leaving England for Rome, Flaxman corresponded with Josiah Wedgwood and with

Henry Webber supervised a number of artists who were engaged in copying the antique for use at Etruria. These men included Davaere, Dalmazzoni, Pacetti, Angelini and Mangianotti. Their work was not signed, it was usually adapted when it reached the works, and only a proportion of it has been identified at present. John Voyez, John Bacon and Pierre Stephan are known to have worked for Wedgwood at one time or another but, again, little of the work they executed has been recognized with certainty. Henry Webber was employed both at Etruria and at Rome and, while at the former place, was entrusted with the task of making a model of the Portland vase, the original being considered too delicate to withstand the operation of taking a cast. Finally, while many of the artists at Etruria are unknown now (and others have been omitted from this brief survey), a place must be found for William Hackwood, who served there from 1769 to 1832. He alone of all the employees occasionally signed his finished work, either with his name in full or with initials. But even that was a rare occurrence and, like those of his fellow-workers, the productions of Hackwood can in the main only be guessed.

Pearl-ware: a white variety of the cream-coloured pottery ('Queen's Ware') introduced by Josiah Wedgwood about 1779. It had a nacreous glaze, hence the name given to it.

Porcelain: in 1812 Josiah Wedgwood Junior commenced the manufacture of bone china, a china of which one of the constituents is the calcined bones of animals. The manufacture is supposed to have ceased after four years, but evidence has been brought to light that orders for it were sent to the firm as late as 1822. These, however, may well have been supplied from existing stocks, and do not indicate necessarily that the porcelain was being made at that date.

Portland House: Wedgwood and Bentley's showroom in Greek Street (No. 12) was given this name. It was opened in June 1774, and the cream-ware service made for the Empress of Russia was placed on exhibition. In 1791 one of the best copies of the Portland vase, after having been shown to Queen Charlotte, was placed on view there.

Portland Vase: this vase, which is in the British Museum, London, is in the form of an *amphora* about ten inches in height. It is made of glass of a deep blue colour, over which is a layer of white glass. The body of the vase is cut in relief with scenes from the story of Peleus and Thetis. It dates from the first century A.D. The base, which does not belong to the vase, is of the same materials, and is carved with the bust of a youth wearing a Phrygian cap.

The vase was said to have been found in a marble sarcophagus in a tomb near Rome in the year 1582. The statement that it was from this source was published first in 1697, but a contemporary description of the discovery of the tomb makes no mention of the vase, and it is presumed that the latter has no connection with it.

From the mid-sixteenth century the vase was in the Barberini Palace in Rome (it is frequently referred to as the 'Barberini Vase'), where it was seen, described and engraved by many visiting artists and antiquarians. It remained there for some 150 years, when it was purchased by James Byres, a Scotsman who resided for some forty years in Rome and who acted as a guide and art-dealer to Englishmen who were on the 'Grand Tour'. Byres, in turn, sold it for £1,000 to Sir William Hamilton, who, in 1784, parted with it to Margaret, Duchess of Portland, for 1,800 guineas. It remained in the family and, in 1810, the fourth Duke of Portland placed it on loan in the British Museum, where, except for brief intervals, it has remained on view to this day.

Since it has been in England the vase has been frequently before the public eye. In 1785, the year after she had purchased it, the Duchess of Portland died. Her great collections, catalogued as *The Portland Museum*, were sold by auction in a sale that lasted for thirty-eight days, commencing on 24th April 1786. Lot 4155, the last item of the final day, was the now-famous vase, which was bought by the late owner's son, the third Duke of Portland, for the sum of £1,029.

In 1845, when it was on view in the British Museum, a drunken or insane scene-painter, William Lloyd, seized a lump of basalt from a nearby shelf, hurled it at the fragile vase and broke it to fragments. The greatest legal punishment that could be visited upon the criminal, who was contrite when he stood in the dock, was a fine of £3 or two months' hard labour as an alternative. The recovered pieces of the vase were restored in due course.

In more recent days, on 2nd May 1929, the vase appeared once more at auction, and again was repurchased by a member of the family: this time at the figure of 29,000 guineas. At a later date it became the property of the British nation.

The story of Josiah Wedgwood's connection with the Portland vase, a connection that brought added fame to the already famous potter, is given in Miss Meteyard's *Life of Wedgwood*. Within a short while of the 1786 auction sale the vase, which Wedgwood had considered purchasing himself, was loaned to him by the Duke of Portland. Over three years later the first successful copy was produced, after the intervening period had been spent in continual experiment.

It is believed that fewer than fifty copies of the vase were made by Josiah Wedgwood at this date, of which less than a score have survived. After the smashing of the original, many more copies were made by the firm of Wedgwood. These latter bear the Wedgwood mark, and lack the design of the bust of a youth beneath the base.

On seeing one of the original copies, Sir Joshua Reynolds gave Wedgwood a certificate worded as follows:

> 'I have compared and examined the copy of the Portland vase with the original with great care, and I can declare it to be a correct and faithful imitation, both in regard to the general effect and the most minute detail of the parts.
>
> J. REYNOLDS.
>
> Leicester Fields, 15th June, 1790.

It is a judgment with which few persons have disagreed subsequently.

Printing: the process of printing, or transfer-printing, on pottery and porcelain is carried out by means of an engraved impression on paper, which is then applied to the article to be decorated. The engraving being printed with a special ink, and used while it is still wet, is thus transferred. This is done on a piece that has been glazed already, and when it is fired the printing sinks into the glaze and a smooth surface results.

The invention is an English one, and its use was practised in the first place at the Battersea enamel works, near London, in 1753. Shortly afterwards it was in use at Worcester and at Liverpool. John Sadler and Guy Green, of the latter town, claimed credit for the original invention, stating that they had made it in 1749. No evidence in favour of this claim has come to light.

The invention proved a workable and economical one, Sadler and Green stating that they had within the space of six hours 'printed upwards of twelve hundred tiles of different colours and patterns, which, upon a moderate computation, was more than one hundred good workmen could have done of the same patterns in the same space of time by the usual way of painting with the pencil'.

By the year 1764 Wedgwood is known to have been sending plain cream-coloured pottery to Liverpool to be decorated by Sadler and Green by the transfer process. A typical example, a tankard dating from about 1775, is shown in Plate 79D.

Printing in blue, which was done by a similar process but prior to the application of glaze to the article, was developed at Worcester soon after the invention of the first process, and outstripped the latter in popularity. It was employed extensively at Caughley and by Spode, but an example bearing the Wedgwood mark, dating from about 1840, is shown in Plate 82C.

Queen's Ware: cream-coloured earthenware improved and marketed by Josiah Wedgwood. He named it 'Queen's Ware' in honour of Queen Charlotte, the wife of George III.

Rosso antico: the name given by Wedgwood to his red stoneware, which was a successor to imitations of the 'Boccaro' ware imported from China in the seventeenth century. It was decorated by being polished on a grindstone and by means of 'engine-turning' applied on a lathe.

Sprigging: the term used to describe the method of ornamenting wares by means of applied reliefs. The 'sprigs' are moulded separately and attached to the plaque, vase or other object by means of water or thinned clay. Wedgwood used sprigging for the decoration of his jasper-ware.

Stubbs, George, R.A.: the painter who excelled in the delineation of the horse was an acquaintance of Josiah Wedgwood. In 1777–8 the latter was attempting to assist the painter, who wished to attempt enamel-painting by using large plaques of china for the purpose. Three of these made of cream-ware, one of which is a panel thirty-six inches in height, painted with a portrait of the potter by Stubbs, are in the Lady Lever Art Gallery, Port Sunlight. Stubbs also designed some cameos with equestrian subjects, and painted on canvas a characteristic 'conversation' portrait of Mr and Mrs Josiah Wedgwood and their family. This was exhibited at the Royal Academy in 1780.

Supper-set: a supper-set is shown in Plate 78A. For this style of article there is a contemporary notice from which its introduction can be dated with reasonable accuracy. Mrs Philip Lybbe Powys, who carefully recorded the events in her daily life in a series of Diaries covering the years from 1755 to 1809, entered under the year 1797:

> 'August 31st.—In the morning we went to London a-shopping, and at Wedgwood's, as usual, were highly entertain'd, as I think no shop affords so great a variety. I there, among other things, purchas'd one of the newly-invented *petit soupee* trays, which I think equally clever, elegant, and convenient when alone or a small party, as so much less trouble to ourselves and servants.'

Webber, Henry: a modeller employed by Josiah Wedgwood between the years 1782 and 1794 both at Etruria and at Rome with John Flaxman. He was engaged in the copying of the Portland vase.

Webber received a gold medal from the Royal Academy in 1779. On that occasion he gave his address as 'Etruria', and his association with Wedgwood may be ante-dated perhaps from the accepted period given above.

CHRONOLOGICAL TABLE

1730	July	Birth of Josiah Wedgwood, at Burslem.
	July	Birth of Thomas Bentley, at Scropton, Derbyshire.
1739		Death of Thomas Wedgwood, father of Josiah
1744		Josiah apprenticed to his brother Thomas.
1749		Partnership with Alders and Harrison.
1754		Partnership with Thomas Whieldon.
		Thomas Bentley married.
1759		Ivy House works taken by Josiah Wedgwood.
1762		Meeting at Liverpool with Thomas Bentley.
1762 ?		Cream-coloured pottery perfected.
1764	Jan.	Josiah married to his seventh cousin, Sarah Wedgwood.
		Brick House (Bell House) works taken.
		Birth of first child, Susanna (baptised Jan. 1765).
1765 ?		Cream-ware first named 'Queen's Ware'.
1766		Birth of John, second child.
		Thomas Wedgwood, cousin, made a partner.
1767		Death of John (of Cateaton Street), brother of Josiah.
		Birth of Richard (d. 1768), third child and second son.
1768	July	Showroom opened in Newport Street, London. Partnership with Thomas Bentley.
		Basaltes-ware introduced.
1769	June	Opening of Etruria works.
	Aug.	Birth of Josiah, third son and successor.
	Nov.	Encaustic painting patented.
1770		Cane-ware introduced.
1771	April	Birth of Thomas (d. 1805), fourth son.
1772		Thomas Bentley's second marriage.
1773	March	Order received for Imperial Russian service.

(A) Cream-ware vase with marbled glaze. Marked 'WEDGWOOD AND BENTLEY'. *The Castle Museum, Nottingham.*

(B) Tea-pot of basaltes-ware with encaustic decoration in red and white. Marked 'WEDGWOOD'. Height $4\frac{3}{4}$ in. *D. M. & P. Manheim.*

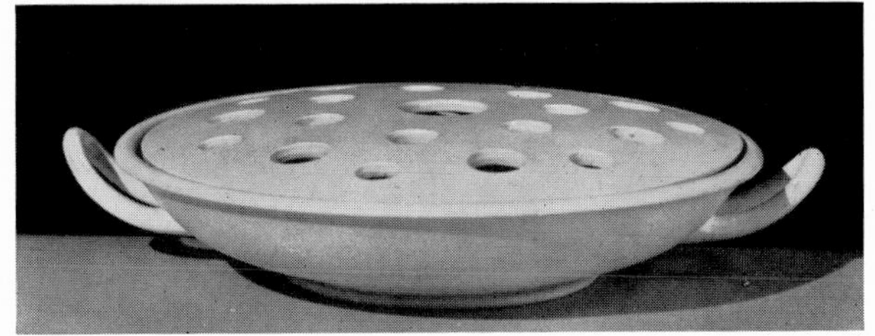

(C) Flower-bowl in cane-ware. Marked 'WEDGWOOD'. Width $10\frac{1}{4}$ in. *Private Collection.*

(D) Tankard of cream-ware with printed decoration. Marked 'WEDGWOOD'. Height 6 in. *Victoria & Albert Museum.*

(E) Thomas Bentley, modelled by John Flaxman and initialled on the truncation.

(F) Henry IV, King of France, 1555–1610.

(G) Benjamin Franklin, 1706–90.

(F) and (G) are stamped 'WEDGWOOD & BENTLEY'.

PLATE 79

To face page 136

(A) Hilt of a sword set with jasper-ware cameos in cut-steel. Probably the work of Matthew Boulton, Soho, Birmingham. Reputed to have belonged to Beau Brummell. *The Castle Museum, Nottingham.*

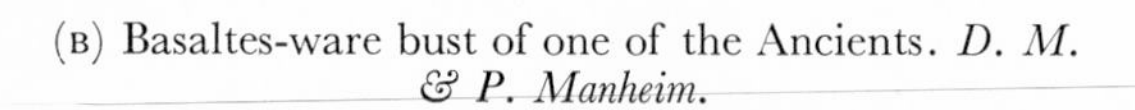

(B) Basaltes-ware bust of one of the Ancients. *D. M. & P. Manheim.*

(C) The Portland Vase. This specimen is No. 29 of Josiah Wedgwood's original copies. Height 10 in. *The Castle Museum, Nottingham.*

(D) Lamp of basaltes-ware. The figures from a design for Pope Julius II's tomb by Michelangelo; whose original wax models of these are at the Victoria & Albert Museum. *The Castle Museum, Nottingham.*

(A) Plaque in blue jasper-ware with relief in white of 'The Sacrifice of Iphigenia', modelled by Pacetti from a Roman original. This plaque also exists with the figures undraped. *The Castle Museum, Nottingham.*

(B) Tea-pot of jasper-ware; the body white, the festoons green and the medallions lilac. Marked 'WEDGWOOD'. Height 3½ in. *D. M. & P. Manheim.*

(C) One of a pair of vases and covers of blue jasper-ware with reliefs in white. Marked 'WEDGWOOD'. Height 13 in. *D. M. & P. Manheim*

(D) One of a pair of vases and covers of blue jasper-ware with reliefs in white. The gilt bronze mounts made by Matthew Boulton at Soho, Birmingham. Marked 'WEDGWOOD'. Height 11¾ in. *D. M. & P. Manheim.*

(A) Jar and cover on tripod support, lustre glaze. Marked 'JOSIAH WEDGWOOD FEB 2nd. 1805'. Height $5\frac{3}{4}$ in. *Victoria & Albert Museum.*

(B) Figure of a triton, forming a candlestick. Designed by John Flaxman. Height $11\frac{1}{8}$ in. *The Castle Museum, Nottingham.*

(C) Meat dish with printed decoration in blue. Marked 'WEDGWOOD'. Width $20\frac{5}{8}$ in. *Victoria & Albert Museum.*

1774	June	Opening of showroom in Greek Street, Soho, London.
	Nov.	Birth of Catherine, second daughter.
		Jasper-ware perfected.
1776	Sept.	Birth of Sarah, third daughter.
1778	Aug.	Birth of Mary Ann, fourth daughter and eighth child.
1779		Pearl-ware introduced.
1780	Nov.	Death of Thomas Bentley.
1782		Josiah elected Fellow of Royal Society.
1786		Portland Vase lent to Josiah Wedgwood.
		Josiah elected Fellow of Society of Antiquaries.
1788	Oct.	Death of Thomas Wedgwood, partner in 'useful' wares.
1790	Jan.	Josiah's three surviving sons and T. Byerley partners.
		Copies of Portland Vase completed and issued.
1795	Jan.	Death of Josiah Wedgwood.

BOOKS FOR FURTHER READING

W. B. Honey, *Wedgwood Ware* (London, 1948).

W. Mankowitz, *Wedgwood* (London, 1953).

W. Mankowitz, *The Portland Vase and the Wedgwood Copies* (London, 1952).

Eliza Meteyard, *The Life of Josiah Wedgwood*, 2 vols. (London, Hurst & Blackett, 1865–6), is a source of much detailed and reliable information on Josiah Wedgwood, but it is confusingly arranged and not very well indexed. Most books dealing with English eighteenth-century pottery give a proportionate amount of space to the achievements of Wedgwood, and contain illustrations of his productions.

SHEFFIELD PLATE

By G. BERNARD HUGHES

GEORGIAN Sheffield plate is beautiful and distinguished, its range of design rivalling that of eighteenth-century hand-wrought silver. Shortcomings in the processes involved, however, made it difficult to follow the florid cast silver patterns introduced by the silversmiths from 1797 after the Goldsmiths' Company had complained to Parliament that 'plated manufacturers have produced articles of the highest elegance and fashion, many of which are now made with solid silver – borders, shields, ornaments, finished in exact resemblance of real plate – and which do material injury to the sale of wrought plate'.

Beautiful table accessories were no longer the prerogative of the rich. Families of moderate means were now dining from Wedgwood's creamware or Spode's bone china, graced with elegant accessories in radiant Sheffield plate. The effect of this was so devastating upon the silversmith's craft that for the next half-century little wrought plate was made in England.

The fact that Sheffield plate reacted like a single piece of metal when shaped by silversmiths' tools, raised it to an important position during the reign of George III (1760–1820). Skill and time expended upon it by the craftsmen were no less than for solid silver, however. The tax of sixpence an ounce levied upon manufactured silver plate from 1782 had the effect of enabling Sheffield plate to be sold at one-third the price of silver: in 1815 the silver tax was increased to eighteen pence an ounce.

Many enthusiastic collectors prefer the peculiar lustre radiating from plate made by fusing silver over copper, to the brilliance of silver plate. Similar patterns were made over such long periods that only a detailed knowledge of the processes involved in Sheffield plating will enable a collector to place examples within closely-defined periods.

Sheffield plating is one of the many industries entirely English in origin. The discovery that silver and copper could be united by fusion was made in 1743 by Thomas Bolsover (1704–88), a Sheffield cutler. It is uncertain how Bolsover's achievement came about: the story of the broken silver knife handle and the copper penny bears no investigation, for such a coin was not included in the English coinage until 1797.

Aware that silver and copper would fuse together, he experimented with rolled copper plates and sheets of silver foil. These he fused together as a single entity. With borrowed capital of £170 and Joseph Wilson as partner, Bolsover began to manufacture silver-plated buttons. The venture prospered, and within a year the loan had been repaid with interest. During the following twelve months he experimented further, fusing a plate of silver to an ingot of copper and reducing them to plate thickness by passing between heavy spring rollers. The relative proportions of silver and copper remained unaltered and the copper was silvered on one side only. Bolsover named his production Copper Rolled Plate, and although he did not patent the process, it appears to have remained under his sole control until 1758. During this period he manufactured small circular and oval boxes with pull-off lids hand-embossed in low relief.

Joseph Hancock, a former apprentice of Bolsover's, discovered the single-lapped edge and, aware of its potential value, had established himself as a competitor by 1758. His vision carried him further, and by installing horse- and water-power he rolled heavier ingots into plates large enough for him to enter the field formerly the prerogative of silversmiths. He issued a wide range of domestic ware, including tea- and coffee-pots, hot-water jugs, saucepans, all tin-lined, as well as candlesticks. Bolsover, already a rich man, made an unsuccessful effort to follow suit, and eventually sold his business to Hancock.

It was probably to Hancock's workshops that Matthew Boulton (1728–1809) was sent in 1760 by his father, a Birmingham toymaker, who appreciated the potentialities of the silver-plated ware. After mastering the technique, Matthew Boulton returned to Birmingham, and by 1762 was producing plated ware at Soho, two miles to the north. Three years later he founded the Matthew Boulton & Plate Company in Birmingham to organize the sale of silver and plated ware, issuing an ever-increasing stream from his factory.

The wide variety of ware issued by the Sheffield platers is shown by illustrated pattern books dating from about 1790. In the Victoria and Albert Museum are several such books, the earliest a folio of 84 plates issued by John Green, Sheffield. On the first page is written his name and the year 1792, with a note to the effect that a discount of 30 per cent was allowed. Unfortunately, however, the articles are not priced. The objects illustrated are tea- and coffee-sets, cake-baskets, hot-water jugs, tea-caddies, tankards and beakers, teapots, wine-bottle corks, bottle labels, waiters and trays, cruet frames with glass accessories, toasters, breakfast dishes and covers, soup tureens, chamber candlesticks, wax-taper holders, snuffers and snuffer trays, toast-racks, standishes, wine funnels, sand boxes, salt-cellars, candelabra, spoons and forks, fish servers, sauce-boats and sauce tureens, tumbler stands, egg-cups, mustards, sugar-basins, table-heaters and stands, ladles, oil-bottle stands.

Another catalogue, issued in 1797 by John Cadman, Sheffield, is a folio of 70 plates illustrating similar objects in different patterns but showing, in addition, tea-urns, candlesticks in perspective and half section, and this firm's well-known telescopic candlestick marked 'patent'. Prices have been written in with pen and ink.

A further catalogue, undated but with pages watermarked 1811, illustrates a widening range of ware with the addition of cigar-cases, oil lamps to fit candle-sockets, combined egg-cup holders and muffineers, tea-bells, spirit-frames and bottles, knife-rests, wine-coolers, beefsteak dishes, saucepans, cream-buckets, cream-ewers, argyles, strainers and plate-covers.

These pieces continued in production throughout the traditional period to the establishment of Elkington's electroplate, during which German silver gradually superseded copper as the foundation for Sheffield plate. The decline was slow, for in 1865 there were nine platers operating in Birmingham using between them about ten tons of plate annually.

GLOSSARY

Argyles: gravy-warmers evolved during the early 1770s by John, Fourth Duke of Argyle. They resembled long-spouted teapots and were so designed that the gravy container was surrounded with hot water. This was inserted through a socket position at the rim near the handle terminal, and provided with a screwed stopper. It is doubtful if they were made in Sheffield plate until the late 1790s, with vertical-sided, round or oval bodies. The spout passed through the hot water into the gravy-container. From about 1815 a hinged cover was substituted for a screwed cap on the hot-water socket. At about the same time variations in design were made. Interiors of some argyles were now divided horizontally, the upper section for gravy, the lower for hot water, and a nose was substituted for the tubular spout. Double-jacketed sauce-boats were also made.

Bat's-wing fluting: graduated gadrooning curved to resemble the outline of a bat's wing and encircling hollow-ware.

FIG. 1. BAT'S WING FLUTING.

Beefsteak-dish: similar to an entrée dish, and described in the 1797 catalogue as fitted with 'the handle to screw off to make a pair of dishes occasionally'.

Bright cutting: recognized by its delicate facet effect, was most popular in the 1790s and early nineteenth century, but continued on encircling bands of silver sweated on to hollow-ware until the 1820s. This style of engraving was carried out on heavily-plated metal, 24 ounces of silver to each 8 pounds of copper. The tools were gouges of various sizes, sharpened chisel-wise, bevelled from corner to adjacent corner and with two cutting points. Edge and point produced what was really a kind of chip carving, outlining patterns of flowers, ribbons, and so on, by cutting narrow channels with variously slanting sides.

Britannia metal, Plating on: introduced in the early 1820s by Kirkby, Smith & Company, Sheffield. A sheet of pure silver was laid on a flat surface and well heated. Molten Britannia metal was poured over this. When cold it was found to have picked up the silver. The two were then rolled into sheets as for plated copper. Owing to difficulties in assembling the method was soon abandoned, but examples are to be found from time to time.

FIG. 2.
BRIGHT CUTTING.

Burnishing: gave a highly-polished surface and at the same time assisted in the concealment of joins. The plate was cleaned and the part to be burnished rubbed with soap. A light steel tool was pressed backwards and forwards on the metal, being dipped frequently in soap-suds the while. This process closed the pores of the silver and resulted in a bright but not brilliant surface, as the coarse texture of Georgian steel caused dragging. Finishing with a bloodstone produced a brilliant surface, difficult to tarnish.

Butt joint: a joint made by soldering two ends of plated copper on the flat without fold or overlap.

Candlesticks: articles associated with domestic illumination were in great demand throughout the Sheffield plate period.

Pillar candlesticks: among the first objects made by Joseph Hancock from 1758, at a time when interest in ancient Grecian and Roman ornament was finding expression in England. Early examples were, generally speaking, simple in design, but after 1820 they became overburdened with ornament and might have as many as twenty invisible seams. Pillars were always filled with a mixture of resin and sand to give stability.

The majority of candlesticks in Sheffield plate were designed with circular stems, tapering towards a circular foot. At first surfaces were smooth, without ornament, edges being lapped, or joins might be concealed beneath reeded moulding cast in solid silver. During the 1780s foot, stem, and nozzle might be ornamented with gadrooning and the lower stem plain or fluted. The downward taper was less acute than in earlier examples. Stems might be fluted throughout their length, with foot and sockets fluted to match. By about 1820 the stem might end in a spherical knop, with elaborate ornament encircling shoulder, foot and socket. The shouldered stem was also made four-sided, rising from a rectangular or square foot and with a socket shaped as a classic urn.

FIG. 3. PILLAR CANDLESTICK, 1790s.

Ornament followed that of the round-stemmed candlestick. One early series was made hexagonal in the style of Queen Anne candlesticks. From about 1820 such stems might be reversed, the shoulder rising from the foot and tapering upwards.

Candlesticks with stems in the form of architectural columns are comparatively rare owing to the time occupied in their production. There were plain Tuscan and Doric stems and plain Corinthian columns with decorative capitals supporting loose nozzles. Their columns might be fluted in Ionic or Roman styles: the plain square feet were usually splayed.

Less costly were cylindrical-stemmed candlesticks. At first they rose from trumpet-shaped feet, later ornamented with silver stamped mounts. Square feet appeared in the 1790s, and in 1797 such candlesticks were catalogued at 20*s* a pair. The same catalogue illustrates the well-known sliding or telescopic candlestick, patented by Roberts, Cadman & Company in 1795. These followed the prevailing styles in mounts and are priced: 12 inches in height, 48*s* a pair; 10 inches in height, 37*s* a pair.

The variety of candlestick designs in Sheffield plate are beyond computation, but they follow definite fashion styles. Bradbury refers to a firm in Sheffield which, during twenty-eight years, issued candlesticks in 1,190 patterns.

Candelabra: branches were fitted to Sheffield plate candlesticks in the 1760s, but in greater numbers from 1780, when it was customary for them to twist around a central finial

FIG. 4. THREE-LIGHT CANDELABRUM BRANCH.

rising from the supporting column. This was often a candle-socket fitted with an ornamental cover which could be removed, enabling the piece to be used for three lights. Stems, feet and sockets replaced the shapes and ornament found on candlesticks. Many silver candlesticks were accompanied by branches in Sheffield plate. To strengthen and assist stability their arms were filled with soft solder.

Chamber candlesticks: consisted of a round or rectangular flat dish with a centrally-placed socket raised upon a short stem slotted immediately above the tray, into which are fitted a pair of candle-snuffers. Hooked into a socket on the curve of the bow or ring handle was a cone-shaped extinguisher with a finial on its apex. Silver-mounted, such candlesticks were catalogued at about 40*s* a pair.

FIG. 5. CHAMBER CANDLESTICK.

Canoe shape: a piece oval on plan with the two ends, seen in elevation, higher than the centre, such as in some standishes and cruet frames.

FIG. 6. CANOE-SHAPED CRUET-STAND.

Dish crosses: sometimes known as 'spiders', were intended to keep food warm in entrée and other serving dishes. They consisted of a spirit lamp forming the central point from which hinged four diagonal stays fitted with sliding brackets. These could be so manipulated that either round or oval dishes of various sizes could be accommodated.

Edgings: *see* Mounts.

English plate: a term used by Sheffield platers to distinguish ware in which the silver was plated on copper, from that plated on white alloy such as German silver.

Engraving: it was customary for Sheffield plate to be engraved with the coat of arms or crest of its owner the more nearly to complete its semblance to silver plate. From about 1815 tea and coffee services, kettles, trays and waiters, and other articles of the tea equipage, might be engraved all over with complicated patterns surrounding the heraldic device. To prevent the copper from showing when the silver was cut with a graving tool the whole surface was coated more thickly than usual.

Where only coats of arms and the like were to be engraved it was at first customary to cut a suitable area of metal clean out of the article and insert a thickly-silvered section of metal. The scarcely perceptible join was masked by wavy borders, but examination of the reverse of a coat of arms will show if insertion has been effected.

This method was discarded between 1810 and 1815 in favour of 'sweating-on' or 'rubbing-in' a circle or shield of four-gauge pure silver of suitable size. The plate to receive the extra silver was heated over a clear charcoal fire, then placed in position and rubbed vigorously with a steel tool until it adhered to the plated copper. After burnishing it was impossible to detect the join except by warming the piece, when a difference in the colour of the silver is noted, the sweated-on piece then showing lighter in hue than the surrounding metal. A small dot was always made in the centre of such shields so that the engraver was sure of his mark. (*See* Bright cutting.)

Fakes: in England it is an offence to describe as Sheffield plate any ware which has not been manufactured by actually laying silver upon copper. Among the subterfuges adapted to keep within the law is to add the letter 'd' and thus label pieces electrically plated in Sheffield as 'Sheffield Plated'. Some of the original tools are still in use for making Sheffield plate by the original methods.

Bradbury devotes a chapter in his book to detailing methods by which fakes and reproductions may be recognized. (*See* Replating and Tests for Sheffield Plate.)

Fish-slices: these usually have fish-shaped blades with convex edges of solid silver. Blades are pierced and engraved in many intricate designs. The handles, usually of ivory, were ferruled in silver.

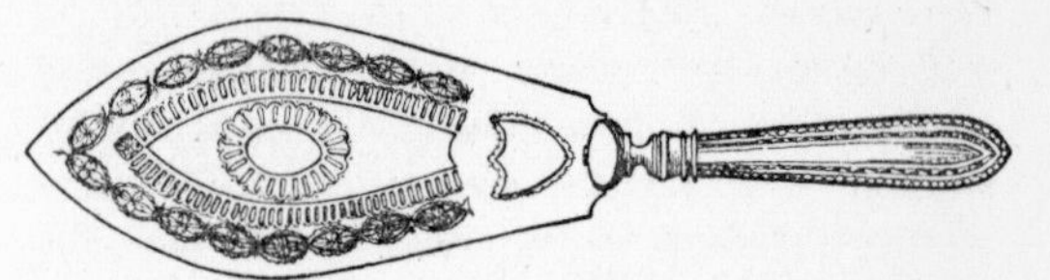

FIG. 7. FISH SLICE.

German silver: introduced to the plating trade by Samuel Roberts, who was granted a patent in 1830 by which 'a layer of German silver or other white or light-coloured metal was introduced between the silver and copper'. A coating of silver could thus be applied with the knowledge that if it wore thin the defect would be far less perceptible than if applied direct to the copper. This method was superseded in 1836 by Anthony Merry's patent by which the copper was omitted, plating the silver direct to a foundation metal of German silver. Stronger and more durable than copper, German silver consisted of nickel, copper, and zinc in varying proportions. Workers in this medium described themselves as 'platers on white metal'.

Gilding: the exterior of Sheffield plate was rarely, if ever, gilded. Sugar-basins, cream-jugs, mustard-pots, and salt-cellars were gilded inside as protection against the foods concerned, which tended to corrode silver and produce black spots difficult to remove. In tea services the teapots were also gilded to match.

Handles, Bale: a hoop or semicircle hinged on a pair of pivots or looped ears on hollow-ware, such as a basket or cream-pail.

FIG. 8. BALE-HANDLE.

Hinges, Book: found on lids of coffee-pots, jugs, and so on. They have a round back resembling a book spine, and the pin-joints, where the base metal is left bare, are concealed beneath slightly ornamented silver caps.

Knife-rests: were of two types and sold by the dozen: (*a*) cross-ends joined from their centres by a short rod: in 1797 priced 20*s* a dozen and with ball centres 24*s* a dozen; (*b*) solid or pierced triangular ends joined from each angle by short rods.

Marks: it was illegal until 1784 to strike a name or mark upon Sheffield plate. In that year the law was amended so that reputable platers 'working within one hundred miles of the town of Sheffield' might be enabled to distinguish their work by name and emblem. These marks, required to be registered at the Sheffield Assay Office, displayed the plater's name or initials, together with a personal device or trade mark. Such registration continued until 1836, Sheffield recording 55 marks and Birmingham 77. The majority of firms appear to have issued their ware unmarked, although some of this was of excellent quality and design.

A crown might be struck on fine quality Sheffield plate after 1820. This was exclusive to the Sheffield Assay Office, its purpose being to distinguish Sheffield products from the tawdry imitations then being imported from France and Austria. At the same time some platers began to impress their ware with a stamp indicating the proportions of silver and copper used, such as BEST SHEFFIELD HEAVY SILVER PLATING 80 DWTS TO 8 LBS, or SHEFFIELD LIGHT SILVER PLATING 50 DWTS TO 8 LBS.

Registration of marks was no longer required after 1836, but the right for platers to strike marks was not withdrawn. Some manufacturers then began to mark their plate, most of it on a German silver base, with devices so closely resembling hall-marks on silver that only the knowledgeable could distinguish between them. A row of five marks was usual and were issued unflawed. Examples are found, however, with four marks in excellent condition and one so mutilated that the uninitiated might accept it as the lion passant of sterling silver. Even today such pieces are passed off as sterling silver.

Mounts and edging: a basic problem facing the early Sheffield platers was that of concealing the dark reddish streak of copper visible when the silvered plate was sheared. This problem was never satisfactorily solved by Bolsover, and his ranges of productions were drastically limited.

(a) *Single-lapped edge* (1758–1780s): Joseph Hancock introduced the single-lapped edge in 1758. This required a thicker coating of silver to be applied to the copper than had been customary. The edges of the plated copper were cut with a blunt tool so manipulated that the layer of silver was extended sufficiently beyond the edge of the silvered copper to lap over and effectively conceal the raw edge.

(b) *Double-lapped copper mount* (1768–early nineteenth century): this followed as a direct result of George Whateley's patent of 1768, by which he 'plated silver upon mettal wire and drew the same into small gauge wires'. A thick cylindrical ingot of copper-brass alloy was plated with rolled silver and passed through a series of holes in a draw-plate until reduced to the required gauge: the thicknesses of the copper and silver remained in their original proportions. This wire was then passed between polished steel pressure rollers, thus forming a thin flat ribbon of plated metal silvered on both surfaces and the edges. This was the immediate forerunner of plating on both sides of the sheet.

This paper-thin ribbon was soldered to the silvered edge of the plate, so that it protruded sufficiently over the edge to permit it to lap over the raw edge and be flat against the underside. So skilfully was lapping carried out, that upon the plated surface it was difficult to detect the joins.

(c) *Silver-lapped mount* (1775–1815): this followed the introduction of double-plated copper in the early 1770s. A narrow ribbon of paper-thin silver, which might measure as little as one-sixteenth of an inch wide, was passed through a small round hole in a draw-plate, thus making a fine-bore tube. The seam was then opened throughout its length to the same width as the gauge of the plate upon which it was to be mounted. This was accomplished by fixing into a vice a steel plate of the same gauge as the plated copper. The seam of the tube was inserted into this and opened by drawing the silver along. The resulting U-shaped silver wire was then fitted to the plated edge and soldered into position on both surfaces. These were vigorously burnished until the joins were invisible.

(d) *Solid silver mounts* (*c.* 1780–*c.* 1830): these ornaments for fine Sheffield plate were cast and hand-chased by silversmiths. They were hard-soldered into position. These hand-chased mounts are sometimes difficult to distinguish from blurred stamped work finished by chasing.

(e) *Drawn silver wire mounts* (1785–*c.* 1820): Valentine Rawle in 1785 patented a method by which the joints of articles made from Sheffield plate could be strengthened 'by covering the mitres, angles and joints with drawn silver wire, the invention being likewise applicable to wares made round and oval'. Silver wires were drawn in a range of decorative cross-sections – flat, half-round, hollow U, sharp L, angles, and curves. These were filled with a mixture of lead and tin, and could be easily shaped by the hand to fit the piece they decorated. Before such mounts were applied to edges, silver wire measuring one thirty-second of an inch in thickness was soldered beneath the rim. Rawle licensed his patent to other platers.

(f) *Silver stamped mounts* (from early 1790s): these first appeared on Sheffield plate during the early 1790s, following the introduction of a hard steel capable of making profitable runs on the press when cut in deep, sharp relief. As in drawn silver-wire mounts, the silver was either pure metal or alloyed with brass, but better than sterling. Sterling silver produced finer work both as to colour and durability, but unfortunately wear on the tools was much harder, considerably reducing their useful life. Pure silver mounts were used on common ware, as it could be rolled much thinner for stamping without danger of splitting in the tools.

The first mounts to be stamped in silver included bead, thread, and a variety of gadroon patterns. Early in the nineteenth century technical improvements permitted the stamping of mounts composed of festoon and bead, leaf and scroll, laurel leaf, egg and dart, scallop shell and scroll, and others. The under seam was made invisible by vigorous burnishing.

Wide, deeply-struck mounts in elaborate rococo designs seldom date earlier than about 1815. Earlier mounts had been struck from silver so thick that the sections could be hard- or silver-soldered into position after filling back hollows with soft solder. From about 1815 thinner silver and soft solder were used.

These mounts were applied to edges in which the copper was already concealed by a silver-lapped mount. The division between the two mounts is unmistakable.

(g) *Improved silver stamped mounts* (from 1824): this method of applying elaborate rococo mounts to Sheffield plate in such a way that the junction between body and mount was rendered invisible, was patented in 1824 by Samuel Roberts of Sheffield, who licensed the process to other platers of repute. After shaping the edge of the ware to be ornamented to follow the indentations of the mounting, drawn silver wire was hard-soldered over the bare copper edge. This was flattened with a hammer until it extended a little beyond the ornamental silver edge. The projecting part of the soldered silver edge was then filed off. Burnishing made the join invisible, even to the enquiring fingernail.

Night light: a square, oval, or circular tray having a central cylindrical candle-socket enclosed within a gallery pierced with a double circuit of crosses towards the lower edge. This was fitted with a

Fig. 9. Night-light.

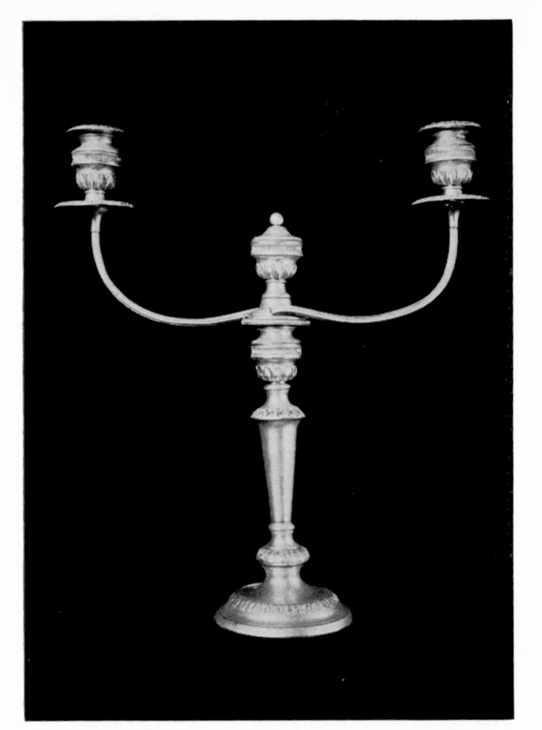

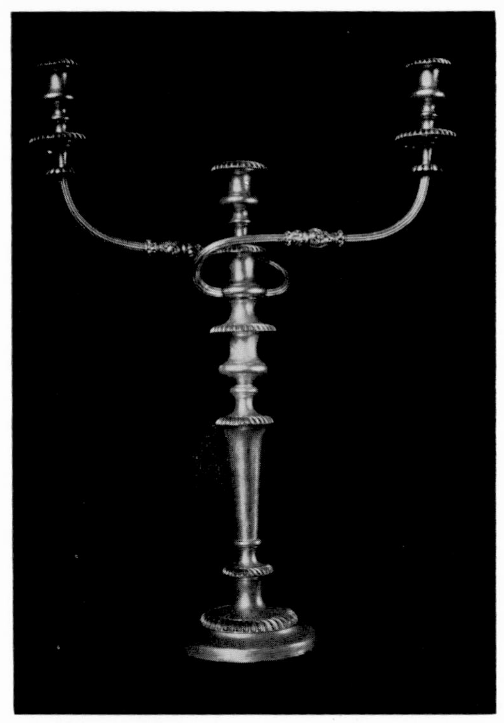

(A) Candelabra by Roberts Cadman & Company; (*Left*) Two-light with urn centre, *c.* 1810; (*Right*) Three-light, *c.* 1820. *John Bell, Esq.*

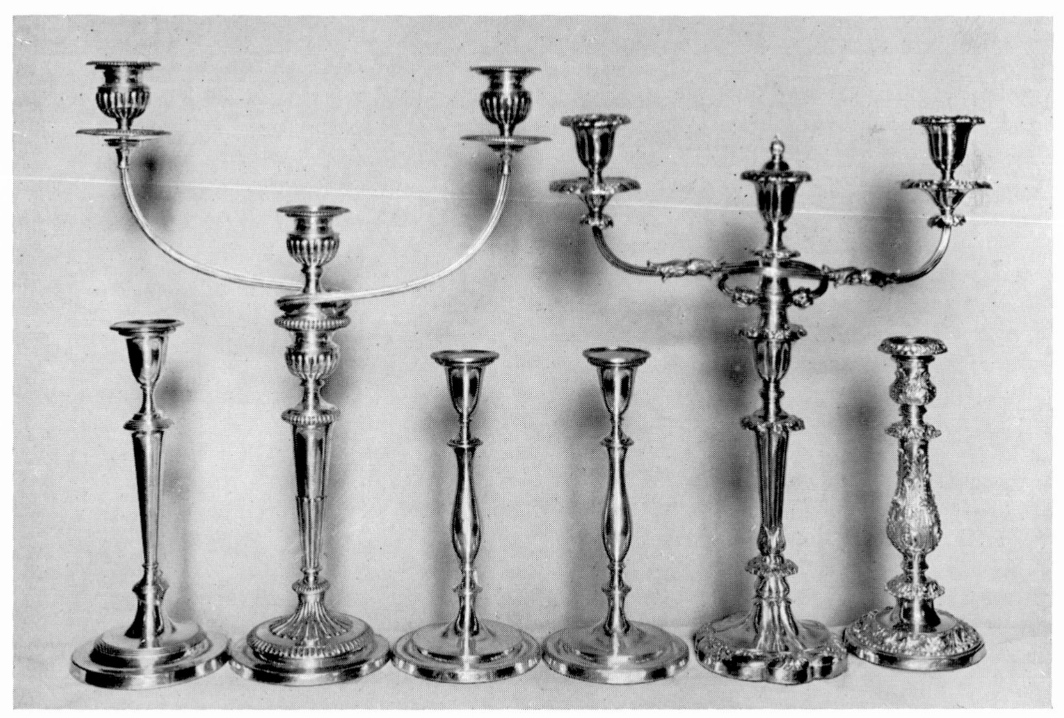

Round-based candlesticks and candelabra with spiral branches: (*Left to right*) Candlestick with shouldered stem tapering towards the base and ornamented with reeding; three-light candelabrum with fluting and gadrooned ornament; (*Centre*) Pair of slender baluster stem candlesticks; candelabrum with three candle-sockets, the baluster stem, with fluted mushroom shoulder; floridly-decorated baluster candlestick.

To face page 144

(A) (*Left to right*) A two-bottle standish with taper-stick, by Matthew Boulton & Company; decanter wagon with plain sides, gadrooned rims and solid wheels; a wax taper-jack with open-frame stand, by Roberts, Cadman & Company.

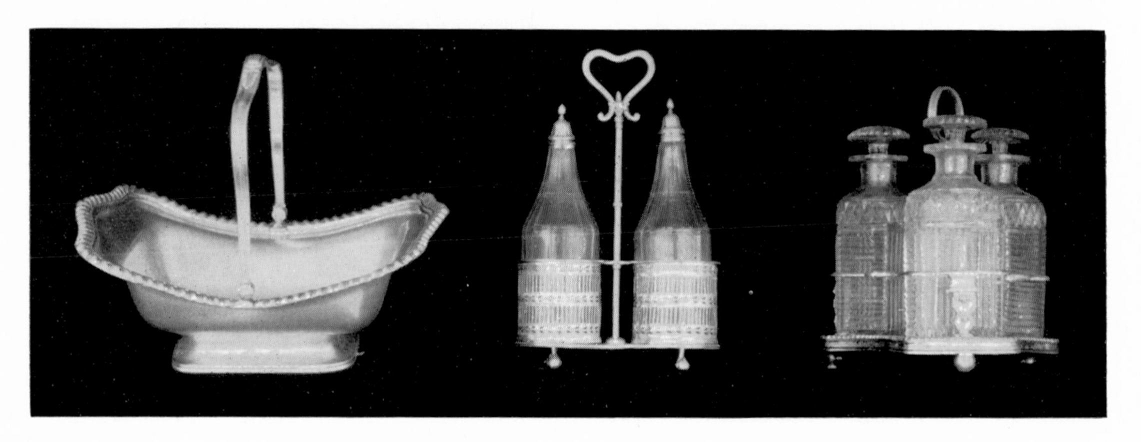

(B) (*Left to right*) Oblong cake-basket with gadrooned rim and plain foot; two-bottle soy frame, galleries pierced with vertical pales, late eighteenth century; four-bottle spirit frame with shell ornament on supports, *c.* 1820.

(C) (*Left to right*) Coffee-pot with German silver base, 1830s; covered pitcher with stained boxwood handle, 1770s; pitcher with fluted body, quart capacity, *c.* 1820.

Set of four decanter stands with silver stamped mounts and plain bars. 7 inches diameter overall.
Messrs Charles Woollett & Son.

Kettle on stand with spirit lamp. 1820s.
John Bell, Esq.

Egg-frame, with egg-cups, spoons and central salt. 1790s.
John Bell, Esq.

Tea-urns bearing the mark of Roberts, Cadman & Company; (*Left*) With hemispherical body, heated by spirit lamp, 1790s; (*Right*) Urn-shaped body with box-iron heater, *c.* 1820.

Epérgne with central boat-shaped dish and four matching branches rising from a revolving stand fitted with wirework frames containing cut glass oil and cruet bottles with plated accessories, *c.* 1800.
Messrs Birch & Gaydon Ltd.

(A) (*Left*) Cream-jug, chased and pounced, with improved stamped silver mounts and stamped and filled handle and feet, 1820s; (*Right*) Cylindrical taper-holder with slip-on cover and cone extinguisher. *Messrs Asprey & Co. Ltd.*

(B) One of a pair of entrée dishes and warmers, with stamped silver mounts, feet and handles, *c.* 1820. *Josephine Grahame-Ballin.*

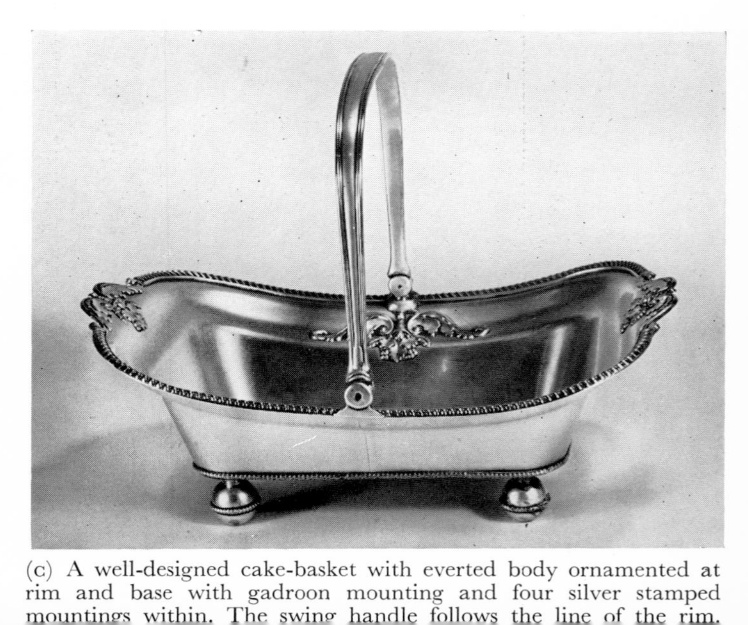

(C) A well-designed cake-basket with everted body ornamented at rim and base with gadroon mounting and four silver stamped mountings within. The swing handle follows the line of the rim.

(D) An oval cake-basket, a magnificent example of piercing. The border and swags are embossed in the plate and the base encircled with gadrooned wrought and filled centre motif.

(A) George III oval tray with scalloped border stamped and filled D-handles, engraved border and coat of arms.

(B) Large scalloped salver with silver shell and flowered border on three claw feet.
Messrs Charles Woollett & Son.

(C) Rectangular tray with gadroon and shell border to rim and stamped and filled D-handles (*c.* 1810). *John Bell, Esq.*

(D) Elaborately-chased tray with improved silver-stamped mounts and four claw feet. Struck with the mark of Roberts, Cadman & Company. Made between 1824 and 1828. *John Bell, Esq.*

(A) Stemmed wine-cooler with applied decoration in silver, 1820s

(B) Wine-cooler, entered as an ice-pail in old pattern books: fluted, with silver masks and gadrooning, *c.* 1800. *Asprey & Co. Ltd.*

(C) A group of late eighteenth-century tankards. The example lower left resembles a drawing illustrated in a pattern book of the 1790s, where it is described: 'Wine measure, 38*s* each; Winchester Measure, 40*s* each; if without cover, 10 per cent less'. *Messrs Birch & Gaydon Ltd.*

(A) Regency three-piece tea-set. Tea-pot, sugar-basin, cream-jug, encircled with oval fluted ornament on ball feet. *John Bell, Esq.*

(B) Group showing (*left to right*) wirework sugar-basket with glass liner; pair of second-course dishes with warmers; argyle; (*centre*) loving-cup; centre dish with warmer; wirework cake-basket; entrée dish with warmer. *John Bell, Esq.*

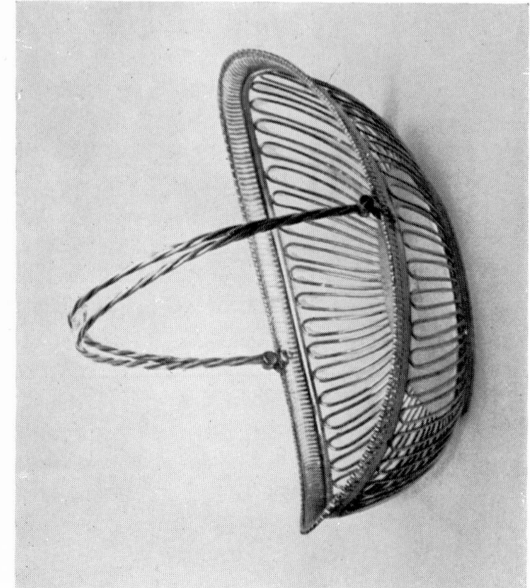

(A) Oval wirework cake-basket bordered with pierced pales, twisted wire handles. Late eighteenth century. *Josephine Grahame-Ballin.*

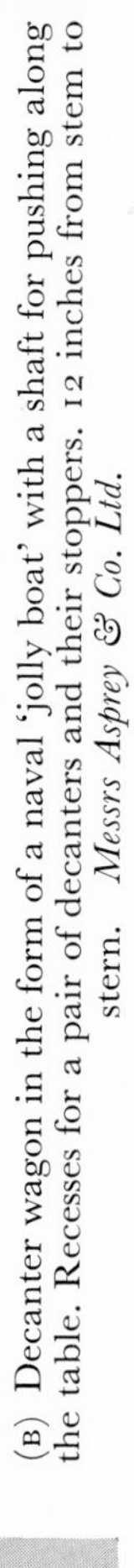

(B) Decanter wagon in the form of a naval 'jolly boat' with a shaft for pushing along the table. Recesses for a pair of decanters and their stoppers. 12 inches from stem to stern. *Messrs Asprey & Co. Ltd.*

PLATE 92

glass chimney. By burning a fine wax night light, no snuffing was required. An extinguisher was hooked to the handle, a rod extending from its apex enabled it to be inserted down the chimney without lifting it off.

Piercing: the application of ornamental piercing to Sheffield plate was governed by the development of hard-steel tools. The fret-saw was useless because such cutting exposed the central core of copper in such a way that it could not be concealed. Shortly after the introduction of double plating in the early 1770s, fly presses were used with hardened punches so designed that a layer of silver protruded very slightly beyond the copper, enabling it to be lapped over and thus conceal the tell-tale line. With adequate burnishing the laps were virtually invisible. At first each pierced motif was pressed singly: by the mid-1790s they were produced in small groups, and the collector will easily detect this work. After about 1820 piercing machines with hard-steel tools did this work much more quickly.

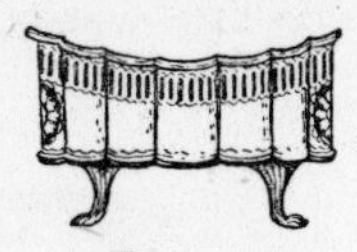

FIG. 10. PIERCED SALT.

Plating: until the 1790s copper was silver-plated in the actual factories in which the ware was fabricated. Afterwards plating became a specialist trade, being made and stocked in three standard qualities, according to the thickness of the silver. This was sold to the plate workers.

An eight-pound copper ingot alloyed with about one-fifth its weight in brass, and measuring eight to ten inches long by about three inches wide and two inches thick, was smoothed and cleaned on the upper and lower surfaces. At first this was done by hand-filing; from about 1820 by steam-driven planing machines.

An ingot of silver was rolled to the required thickness, as needed for varying qualities of metal, the lowest weighing sixteen pennyweights, to cover one face of the copper. This was increased to as much as eight ounces for the very rich plating used before the introduction of silver mountings and for the lavishly engraved work from 1820. The coating of silver required to be more than a mere film, otherwise it discoloured when heated by the soldering iron. A rectangle of silver plate, flawless in texture and unpitted, measuring about one-eighth of an inch less each way than the surface of the copper ingot, was cleaned on one side. The two bright surfaces were then placed together and bedded by placing a heavy iron upon the silver and striking it with a sledge-hammer until every part of the two surfaces was in close contact.

A heavily whitewashed piece of thick sheet copper was placed over the silver and firmly bound to the ingot with iron wires, burnt borax and water being applied to the edges of the silver to act as a flux. The ingot was now placed in an oven containing a charcoal fire and its door pierced with a small hole through which the plater could observe its progress. A bright line encircling the edges of the silver told him when fusion had taken place. He immediately removed the ingot and plunged it into diluted spirits of salt. After cutting the wires the ingot was compressed in a rolling machine, repeated annealing being required as it was gradually converted into sheets of specified width and gauge. These sheets, in which silver and copper were perfectly united, were not silvered on both sides until the early 1770s.

Replating: the problem of detecting Sheffield plate replated during mid-Victorian days is difficult to solve. Advertisements were consistently inserted in newspapers and elsewhere from 1849 offering to replate at one-third of the original cost. Such pieces have toned down with a century of cleaning and now closely resemble genuine plating. Fused plate is much harder than electroplate, the effect of introducing alloy into the silver, this being plus rolling and hammering. Electroplating tends to soften the foundation metal. Electroplated silver is always white; Sheffield plate has a faintly bluish hue owing to the presence of alloy.

Salts: were sold in pairs and catalogued in three qualities, the first two fitted with blue-glass liners: (*a*) tinned inside; (*b*) plated inside with silver edges; (*c*) gilt inside with silver edges. Until

FIG. 11. SALT.

1820 they were made with three or four feet.

Shaping: the silvered copper could be shaped by any of the hand-raising processes customary in silversmithing, by stamping, or by spinning.

Hand-raising: was carried out by the braziers, who constituted the largest single group of craftsmen employed in the Sheffield plate trade, raising hollow-ware from the flat plate or a soldered cylinder. With wooden mallets the sides of the metal were gradually contracted by repeated blows on steel heads. The full parts, if at all intricate, were shaped by striking the metal inside with a long-ended hammer upon a leather bag filled with sand, which prevented the metal from stretching too far under a single blow. The copper was annealed two or three times during the process. After reaching the basic form, bright steel hammers were used for final shaping. Ornamental fluting and other simple embossed designs were less expensively raised by fitting the body of the work with pitch and then tracing the design with steel punches.

In silver work every blow of the hammer was visible as a distinctive mark. Plated ware was always smooth, to prevent wear and cleaning wearing off the silver on high spots, thus revealing the copper beneath. To achieve a fine even surface the platers tied a cloth over the steel head and wired a piece of thin sheet steel to the face of the hammer, thus completely obliterating all signs of blows.

Stamping: during the 1780s lids and spouts – termed noses by the platers – were stamped by drop hammer. By the 1790s flat and plain work such as trays and waiters were stamped, and from about 1815 complete body parts might be shaped in this way. The later stamping dies were of cast iron which had undergone a process of chilling, which gave them a very close fine texture. A pair of dies might be used to stamp parts for more than one article: a snuffer dish stamping, for instance, might equally well be utilized in a standish.

Spinning: used in the production of hollow-ware from the 1820s, replacing stamping where the number of pieces required did not warrant the cutting of costly dies for stamping. The copper was of a finer, softer quality than that normally used. The form of the article to be spun was first turned in wood and fixed in a lathe. The plated metal was held against this by a short rod extending to the back centre of the lathe. The spinner then greased the centre of the metal and with a long shaft of hardwood pressed the metal as it revolved in the lathe, forcing it closely to the wooden form. Puckering was prevented by manipulation of a wooden block held in the spinner's

FIG. 12. SPUN TUREEN SAUCE-BOAT.

left hand. Compression made the metal hard, so that it required occasional annealing during the spinning process. When finally brought to the shape of the form, the spinner lapped over the rim.

Collectors of Sheffield plate should be aware that during the 1820s and 1830s large quantities of cheap, thin-gauge, poorly-plated ware was imported from France. The copper, which was quick to spin and required no annealing, contained less alloy than its English counterpart, and consequently was of a redder tinge, which imparted a faintly pinkish hue to the thin film of silver.

Sheffield plate: originally known as Copper Rolled Plate. The term Sheffield plate has been noted as early as 1771, when an advertisement in Felix Farley's Journal, Bristol, referred to Sheffield plate candlesticks.

Splayed: a candlestick or other foot is termed splayed when the top and bottom diameters are different.

Taper-holders: contained coiled sealing-wax tapers and were evolved in response to the vastly increased letter traffic.

Boxes: cylindrical containers measuring about three inches in diameter with flat-topped slip-on covers fitted with a central nozzle through which the end of the coiled taper was drawn by hand. The majority of boxes were undecorated and fitted with a loop or scroll handle, a cone-shaped extinguisher pegged to a loop on the body and attached to a chain extending to a small eye fixed below the rim. Many taper-box containers were ornamented with piercing between about 1790 and the 1820s: first a single band of piercing encircled the body, followed by the addition of vertical pales above and below. From 1815 both cover and sides might be pierced. Rims of nozzles were plain at first, then from the late 1790s might be beaded and fitted with a grease-pan. Vase-shaped nozzles date from about 1820.

Jacks: open-frame stands so arranged that the end of a long coil of wax paper wound on a vertical or horizontal spindle can be pushed through the nozzle whilst it is burning. The frame was supported by a tray foot or a circular, stemmed foot with a scroll- or ring-handle.

Teapots: were made in shapes following those of the silversmiths, with handles of ivory, ebony, horn or hardwood. The catalogues of the 1790s illustrate forms that had been in use for quite twenty years, for the most part severely straight-sided with straight, tapering spouts rising from the lower part of the body. Lids were flush with the body rim and might be either flat or domed. None have the ball or moulded feet such as were used in the early nineteenth century.

FIG. 13. TEA-POT.

Bodies were straight-sided and might be oval in plan in sizes of one and a half pints or one quart. Bodies might also be vertically fluted or serpentine on plan composed of a variety of concave convex curves. Others had urn-shaped bodies tapering to a narrow stem rising from a round spreading foot. During the next twenty years the cape teapot was fashionable – a rim or gallery encircling its opening and overhanging the body. Patterns were now so diverse that full description is impossible.

Tests for Sheffield plate: period examples plated on copper were constructed from separate units. Seams or other joins normally invisible can be detected by close examination with a magnifying glass. If none can be found, it may be assumed that the piece has been electroplated, thus concealing joints beneath a film of electrically-deposited silver.

Texture and colour are important points in enabling collectors to distinguish rolled plated ware from the electroplated imitation. In electroplating, minute particles of silver are deposited on the copper, producing a crystalline coating of pure silver, to which a high polish could only be given by power-driven machinery. Close inspection will show the silver to have undergone transmutation, colour and surface texture being entirely different from the fused metal.

Tinned: coated with pure tin, deposited on the copper surface by first sprinkling it with sal ammoniac, and then washing with molten tin. Early hollow-ware was tinned inside: after the introduction of double-faced plate the backs of large trays and waiters were usually tinned, and the interiors of tea-urns, dish-covers, coffee-pots, and hot-water jugs. Even in the 1820s catalogues describe trays, snuffer-dishes, and so on, as having either 'tinned' or 'plated' backs.

Trays and waiters: these followed the shapes customarily used by silversmiths. Early examples might consist of two sheets of single-sided silver plate soldered back to back. More usually the plate was finished with zinc beneath until the 1770s, when they were tinned, a feature that continued until 1830. From about 1800 they might be plated beneath, and fine-quality work might be gilded. Until early in the nineteenth century they were oval or round, and might have a pair of loop handles and a thread of narrow silver stamped mount edge. At first rims were hand-raised, but from early in the nineteenth century they were shaped by means of drop hammers by those platers in a large way of business who also sold the blanks to the small men.

With the introduction of wider mounts trays might be rectangular with D-shaped handles. From about 1815 wide rims with florid ornamental silver mounts were usual, and from about 1820 shapes might be of irregular outline based on a rectangle. Vine-leaf, grape, shell, and acanthus-leaf ornament were included in a wide range of patterns applied to the deeply concave raised rim. The D-shaped handle became weighty with scroll-work and other relief ornament.

From about 1820 the tray surface might be all-over engraved with complicated scroll designs, laden with flowers and foliage, requiring the application of an extra thick coating of silver.

Wine-coolers and ice-pails: these successors of the wine cistern contained single bottles of wine on ice. They were for table use and usually sold in pairs. Early examples consisted of a cylindrical vessel with a pair of D-handles and a ring foot, and might be gadrooned or otherwise ornamented around the lower body. This was fitted with a cylindrical bottle-container, from the rim of which extended a cover to conceal the ice in the outer chamber. By 1806 wine-coolers might be raised upon three or four short feet. The concealed surfaces might be tinned.

From about 1815 the body was urn- or vase-shaped, raised on a low-stemmed foot. The lining was dispensed with, the bottle resting directly upon ice placed inside the vessel.

Wire work: among the rarest pieces of Sheffield plate are those constructed from plated wires, dating chiefly between 1785 and 1815. They were a direct result of George Whateley's patented invention of 1768, by which copper rods, round, flat, square, and triangular, could be silver-plated. Not until after the expiry of the patent in 1782 was this work carried out on a considerable scale, the demand being chiefly for a wide range of inexpensive table baskets, toast-racks, and épergnes. The wires at first were cut into short lengths, fitted into holes drilled into rim and base, and soldered into position. Early in the nineteenth century less expensive wire ware was made by bending lengths of wire into continuous curves forming patterns. These were soldered to rim and base, thus saving the cost of drilling. Ball handles might consist of flat wire curved and spaced with balls or other ornament, or of twisted wire of various sections.

Collectors should realize that dessert, cake, and sweetmeat baskets in many period styles have been made by the twentieth-century copyists. Wires in sections other than round are not found in this series, in which the soldering lacks the experience of the old workers.

BOOKS FOR FURTHER READING

FREDERICK BRADBURY, *History of Old Sheffield Plate* (1902).
J. W. CALDICOTT, *The Values of Old English and Sheffield Plate* (1906).
ARTHUR HAYDEN, *Chats on Old Sheffield Plate* (1920).
H. N. VEITCH, *Sheffield Plate*, London, Bell (1908).
BERTIE WYLLIE, *Sheffield Plate* (n.d.).
W. A. YOUNG, *The Silver and Sheffield Plate Collector* (1928).

AMERICAN SILVER

By HELEN COMSTOCK

AMERICAN silver which claims the interest of student and collector falls within the approximate dates of 1650 and 1810. It is rarely possible to date an American piece exactly, due to the absence of assay offices and a definite system of marking, as in the case of English silver, but occasionally there are commemorative pieces with recorded date which offer a guide to progress of design.

American silver naturally shows close connection with English, but there are other influences which came into play. Dutch styles prevailed in New York, which had been founded as New Amsterdam in 1625 and did not come under English rule until 1664. The majority of early New York silversmiths were Dutch (when they were not French Huguenots), and Dutch influence is seen in the applied foliated borders on beakers, and in a novel application of these leaf bands on late Stuart and William III flat-topped ale tankards, producing a distinctive New York form (Plate 93C). The corkscrew thumbpiece on the New York tankard is also of Dutch origin.

French influence was felt through the presence of Huguenot silversmiths such as RENÉ GRIGNON in Boston, BARTHOLOMEW LE ROUX, founder of the Le Roux family in New York, CESAR GHISELIN in Philadelphia, all before 1700. At least one New York maker produced something like the French *écuelle* in a porringer with a two-handed cover, while the Huguenots, remembering the *réchaud*, may have contributed to the development of the American chafing-dish, of which some two dozen are known from Boston and occasional examples elsewhere. The chafing-dish was only occasionally made in England. There was at least one English chafing-dish here, an example of 1734, illustrated in Francis Hill Bigelow's *Historic Silver of the Colonies*, which might have suggested imitation, but so general a preference for the form as was evident in America was much more apt to have been the result of French, and also of Dutch, influence.

A Scandinavian style accounts for the inset coins in some New York tankard lids, also the rich embossing (Plate 94D). The heavy ornament of flowers and fruit on the handles of certain American tankards is Scandinavian in origin.

Portuguese influence, while rare, was logically felt in Boston, which carried on a lively trade with the merchants of Lisbon and Oporto. The wide fluting characteristic of Portuguese silver has an adaptation in the boldly-fluted rim of a punch-bowl by Jeremiah Dummer of Boston, made before 1700.

PIECES DISTINCTIVE OF AMERICA

Certain pieces have no exact European prototype, such as New York's pumpkin-shaped bowl with panelled sides enclosing floral motifs (*see* Plate 96C); although there is in Danish silver a panelled floral bowl, but standing on ball feet and having a cover.

A plain two-handled, bell-shaped cup with strap handles (*see* Plate 99B), first made by John Dixwell, son of the regicide who fled to America, was frequently made for ecclesiastical use. This cup has no English prototype, although a lower cup, frequently with gadrooned and fluted base, was made both in England and America.

While the Boston 'Sugar Box' (*see* Glossary) resembled the Charles II sweetmeat-box in the work of John Coney, Edward Winslow's elaborate boxes of casket shape are apparently without European prototype, although Copenhagen's gadrooned-covered bowls with similar ring handles show kinship. With their richly-embossed sides alternated gadrooning and fluting, and embossed medallions of St George and the dragon, who makes here a solitary appearance in American silver, their covers with ring handles and embossed foliage suggesting Renaissance ornament, these boxes by Winslow seem possibly to have been decorated after engraved illustrations from publications reaching Boston in the early eighteenth century.

Distinctively American is the use of cast cherubs' heads on tankard handles and on handle tips (*see* Glossary, Cherub's Head). In Dutch silver the embossed cherub's head is a frequent border motif on dishes, accompanying fruit designs, a combination occasionally seen in English border designs, but taken over for handle decoration in American work.

STYLE PERIODS

While the style periods have English names, the dates are later, since fashions crossed the Atlantic slowly, and had the tendency to linger.

Early Stuart and Commonwealth (*c.* 1650–1700). The earliest American silver may have been made before 1650, but existing examples are generally of the third quarter of the seventeenth century. The Puritan influence which dominated Boston was in accord with Cromwellian taste, and thus one sees early Stuart styles in a simplified form, evident in the first beakers, caudle-cups and tankards. A handsome standing cup of 1674 by Hull & Sanderson of Boston (*see* Cup, Standing) recalls a Charles I form, with bell-shaped body on baluster stem, severely plain, as becomes Puritan taste.

Late Stuart, and William and Mary (1700–15). The lavish use of gadrooning and fluting, often in juxtaposition with the addition of embossed ornament and chasing, and elaborate baroque mantlings for coats of arms, distinguish early eighteenth-century silver. Characteristic is the gadrooning on the surface of the bell-shaped covered cup (*see* Cup, with Cover); a gadrooned step on the tops of tankards (*see* Plate 94D); gadrooned bands added to a reel-shaped salt (*see* Plate 94B), which otherwise is like an English plain octagonal example of 1683 belonging to the Saddlers' Company. Winslow's elaborate sugar boxes belong to this period, as well as Coney's fluted monteith with chased foliage and chiselled heads of amorini (*see* Plate 96B) made for John Colman, a wealthy Boston merchant. The baluster candlestick, which appeared in England in the work of Pierre Harache in 1683, was adopted.

Queen Anne (1715–50). The plainer surfaces of Queen Anne silver were not the fashion in America until the reign of George I but lasted until shortly before 1750, when the rococo styles were adopted. The typical Queen Anne teapot, with flaring sides, appeared in Boston and New York, in the latter city well represented by the work of Pieter Van Dyck (1684–1750). Gadrooning and applied strap work were continued, but with a lighter touch. Domed covers were given to tankards; beakers, which were plain and bell-shaped, standing on a moulded foot, display a beautifully functional form which lasted past mid-century in church silver. Coney, working first in the baroque style, adopted the plainer Queen Anne forms with great success, and followed his fluted monteith for Colman with one with severely plain sides for Robert Livingston of New York. Some fine two-handled covered loving-cups belong to this period (*see* Plate 96D). Typical is a slightly curved pear-shape for the bodies of canns and a globular form for teapots (*see* Plate 99A).

Rococo (1750–85). Actually the final ten years of this period produced almost no silver, due to the Revolution, but the succeeding classical period did not begin until after 1785. During the period following mid-century, contact with the Mother Country was especially close, due to the participation of the Colonies in the French and Indian war, ending in 1763. The result in regard to silver was that American pieces show closer resemblance to the English, the chief difference being that there are not nearly so many forms, as discussed hereafter under 'American Silver Types'. The inverted pear form was used for tea-pots, and the elongated, inverted pear shape for coffee-pots. One of the rococo masterpieces is a tea-kettle on stand by Joseph Richardson, senior, of Philadelphia (*see* Plate 99D). Cast ornament reached its finest expression, as in the Myer Myers snuffer and tray (*see* Plate 100A). Typical is the use of a double-scroll handle on tea- and coffee-pots and cream-pitchers.

Classical Period (1785–1800). A return to simplicity, marked by straight lines, fluted surfaces sparingly engraved, and urn-shaped forms of classical inspiration marks the silver made in the early days of the new republic. Ornament usually consisted of beading and bright-cut engraving, the latter in floral festoons and drapery swags suggesting the inlay on Adam and Hepplewhite furniture. Tea-pots were oval or drum-shaped; sugar-bowls were like urns, creamers like helmets. A classically inspired sauce-tureen is seen in Baltimore work (*see* Sauce-boat). The use of a pierced gallery was liked in Philadephia (*see* Plate 95B). Fluted sides were given to oval, straight-sided tea-pots (*see* Plate 97B), and small-footed trays accompanied tea-pots (*see* Plate 95A).

TYPES OF AMERICAN SILVER

There are fewer types of American silver than English. One looks in vain for epergnes, and dinner and dessert services. A large soup tureen by a Baltimore maker is considered unique, although there are small sauce tureens as successors to the sauce-boat. There are no toilet services, argyles, biggins, stirrup-cups, vinaigrettes, and flatware does not show the great variety of forms found in English work. Popular forms include beakers, tankards, caudle-cups, two-handled covered cups, punch-bowls, porringers, mugs, canns (a mug with curving sides), porringers (called in England cupping-bowl), spout-cups, salvers and waiters, candlesticks, inkstands, sauce-boats, tea-caddies, trencher and circular salts, mustard-pots, casters.

Rare are reel-shaped salts, snuffers, the dish-ring and dish-cross, the cake-basket (until the late classic period), rapier hilts and sconces. Wine-coolers have never been exhibited, but a unique pair is understood by the writer to exist.

On the other hand, the chafing-dish, so seldom made in England, was frequently made in Boston, and a low tumbler for use as a wine-cup, rare in England, was frequently made in New York.

Small objects include snuff-boxes, tobacco-boxes, knee and shoe buckles, buttons, thimbles and rings.

CENTRES OF AMERICAN SILVERSMITHING

Boston, New York and Philadelphia were the chief centres, but silver was made in Newport, Rhode Island, New Haven, Connecticut, Baltimore and Annapolis, Maryland, and Charleston, South Carolina and elsewhere.

Boston. The earliest American silver was made in Boston by JOHN HULL (1624–83) and ROBERT SANDERSON (1608–93). Hull is thought to have been trained by his half-brother, RICHARD STORER, who was apprenticed to a London goldsmith, JAMES FEARNE. No piece by Storer is known, and he probably returned to England. Sanderson learned his trade in London, where he was apprenticed to William Rawlins in 1623. By the end of the century JEREMIAH DUMMER (1645–1718), JOHN CONEY (1656–1722) and EDWARD WINSLOW (1669–1753) offer the student some of the finest Boston silver in existence. They were followed by JACOB HURD (1702–58), representing the second quarter of the eighteenth century with distinction, a prolific silversmith whose work is of uniform excellence. In PAUL REVERE (1735–1818) the rococo and classic styles found noteworthy expression in the second half of the eighteenth century.

Other important Boston makers: John Allen (1671–1760), John Edwards (1671–1746, partner of above), Zachariah Brigden (1734–87), John Burt (1692–1745), Benjamin Burt (1729–1805), John Coburn (1725–1803), William Cowell (1682–1736), Timothy Dwight (1654–91), Daniel Henchman (1730–75),

Samuel Minott (1732–1803), John Potwine (1698–1792, removed to Connecticut 1737), Edward Webb (d. 1718).

New York. New York retained a strong Dutch influence in social and economic life. The conviviality and hospitality of New Yorkers were mentioned by Madam Sarah Knight in her *Journal* of a trip by horseback from Boston to New York in 1704 and by Dr Alexander Hamilton in his *Itinerarium* in 1744. The New York tea-pot was more capacious than that of Boston, and the typical piece in New York silver is the ale tankard. Fine examples appear in the work of HENRICUS BOELEN (1697–1755), CORNELIUS KIERSTEDE (1675–1757), GERRIT ONKELBAG (1670–1732), BARTHOLOMEW SCHAATS (1670–1758), JACOBUS VANDERSPIEGEL (1668–1708), BENJAMIN WYNKOOP (1675–1728) and PIETER VAN DYCK (1684–1750). The last was probably the leading New York silversmith. Along with these makers of Dutch descent were the Huguenot BARTHOLOMEW LE ROUX (d. 1713), first of a family of silversmiths, of whom there were three others, BARTHOLOMEW, CHARLES and JOHN. SIMEON SOUMAIN (1685–*c.* 1750), JAN NIEWKERK (working 1708), JOHN MOULINAR (freeman 1744), JOHN HASTIER (working 1725), ELIAS PELLETREAU (1726–1810), OTTO PARISIAN (working 1763), PETER QUINTARD (1699–1762) are among those representing French influence.

In the second half of the eighteenth century MYER MYERS was an outstanding maker, a master of the rococo style which he used with distinction in such pieces as the snuffers and tray (*see* Plate 100A), and the only known American dish-ring, now in the Garvan Collection. He was president of the New York Gold and Silversmiths' Society in 1776.

Other important New York makers: Thauvet Besley (freeman 1727, d. 1757), Jacob Boelen (1654–1729), John Brevoort (1715–75), Peter de Riemer (1738–1814), Daniel Christian Fueter (fl. 1756), Thomas Hamersly (b. 1727), George Ridout (freeman 1745), Nicholas Roosevelt (1715–69), Tobias Stoutenburgh (freeman 1731), Jacob Ten Eyck (b. 1704), Koenraet Ten Eyck (1678–1753), Cornelius Vanderbergh (fl. 1685–95), Peter Vergereau (freeman 1720).

Philadelphia. William Penn's desire to attract craftsmen to the province of Pennsylvania was early answered among silversmiths by the French CÉSAR GHISELIN and the Dutch JOHANNIS NYS, both of whom were working before the year 1700 in Philadelphia, which had been founded only twelve years before. There is little to represent the first decade of Philadelphia silver among examples now in existence, but a porringer by César Ghiselin, made for Anthony Morris and his wife Mary Coddington (d. 1699), has recently turned up in the family of the original owners.

Other early makers were WILLIAM PASCHALL and CHARLES PICKERING, both before 1700, PHILIP SYNG I, who came to Philadelphia about 1720, WILLIAM VILANT (fl. 1725), and possibly a dozen or so more. But the most important name in Philadelphia silver was that of the family of Richardson, which supplied five working silversmiths to the city. The senior FRANCIS RICHARDSON is mentioned in William Penn's account book and is represented by a fine George I tankard with low, domed lid, flaring sides and moulded midband, now in the Philadelphia Museum of Art. He died in 1729, leaving his tools and his business to his sons, FRANCIS and JOSEPH, who soon maintained separate shops. The genius of the family was Joseph, Senior (1711–84), who became a master of the rococo style (*see* Plate 99D).

Among the more important Philadelphia makers are: Joseph Anthony Junior (fl. 1783–1809), Elias Boudinot (fl. 1747), Abraham du Bois (fl. 1777–1802) (*see* Plate 95B), Daniel Dupuy (fl. 1746–1805); César Ghiselin (fl. *c.* 1693; removed to Annapolis 1715; d. 1733); William Hollingshead (fl. 1757–85); Richard Humphreys (1771–96); John Letelier (fl. 1770–93); Joseph Lownes (fl. 1780–1816); Edmund Milne (fl. 1753–73); Johannis Nys (fl. *c.* 1700–*c.* 1723), Francis Richardson (1681–1729; fl. *c.* 1700), Francis Richardson II (fl. 1729), Joseph Richardson, Senior (1711–84) (*see* Plate 99D), Joseph Richardson, Junior (1752–1831), Joseph and Nathaniel

Richardson (fl. 1785–91), Philip Syng I (1676–1739; fl. 1720), Philip Syng II (fl. 1738–*c.* 1772), Daniel Van Voorhis (fl. 1779–82, when he moved to New York), William Vilant (fl. 1725), Christian Wiltberger (fl. 1793–1817).

Connecticut. Some good silver was made in the colony of Connecticut although there were no large cities, and the wealthy families generally patronized Boston or New York makers. However, a number of silversmiths from those two cities worked in Connecticut at various times, as indicated in the following list of makers, and their work, in addition to that of such local makers as PYGAN ADAMS, EBENEZER CHITTENDEN, ABEL BUELL and AMOS DOOLITTLE (the last two being engravers as well), has attracted considerable interest on the part of students. For the loan exhibition held in Hartford on the occasion of Connecticut tercentenary in 1935 the catalogue prepared by the late John Marshall Phillips has become a permanent record of Connecticut work.

Pygan Adams, New London (1712–76); Abel Buell, New Haven, Hartford (1742–1825); Timothy Bontecou, Senior, Stratford, New Haven (1693–1784); Ebenezer Chittenden, New Haven (1726–1812); Daniel Deshon, New London (1698–1781); John Gardiner, New London (1734–76); René Grignon, removed from Boston to Norwich about 1708 (d. 1715); Cornelius Kierstede, removed from New York to New Haven, 1722 (d. 1757); Myer Myers, removed from New York to Norwalk about 1776–82; John Potwine, removed from Boston to Hartford, 1737 (d. East Windsor 1792); Peter Quintard, removed from New York to South Norwalk, 1737 (d. 1762).

Maryland makers: George Aiken, Baltimore (1787–1823); Standish Barry, Baltimore (1784–1810); Charles L. Boehme, Baltimore (fl. 1799–1812); James Chalmers Senior, Annapolis (fl. 1749–80); John Chalmers, Annapolis (fl. 1770–91); William Faris, Annapolis (fl. 1756–1804); César Ghiselin, removed from Philadelphia to Annapolis 1715 (fl. 1728), returned to Philadelphia, where he died 1733; Christopher Hughes, Baltimore (fl. 1771–90); Peter Leret, Baltimore (1787–1802); Philip Syng Senior, removed from Philadelphia to Annapolis 1730 (fl. 1739); Samuel Soumaien, Annapolis (fl. 1740–54), removed to Philadelphia.

Newport, Rhode Island, makers: Isaac Anthony, 1690–1773); Thomas Arnold (1739–1828); Benjamin Brenton (1686–1740); Jonathan Clarke (1705–70); John Coddington (1690–1743); Arnold Collins (d. 1735); Jonathan Otis (1723–91); Daniel Rogers (d. 1792); Daniel Russell (*c.* 1698–*c.* 1771); John Tanner (1713–85); Samuel Vernon (1683–1737).

GLOSSARY

[This Glossary has been compiled with the object of drawing attention to the special distinctions of, and terms which apply particularly to, American silver. General silver definitions were given more completely in the first volume to this Encyclopædia.]

Alms-dish: ecclesiastical plate for the receiving of donations. John Coburn, of Boston, made one of the finest American examples, engraved with the Hancock arms, given to the Brattle Street Church in Boston in 1764. This is now in the Boston Museum.

Annealing: process of softening the silver by heating over coals, as it became brittle under hammering during the process of raising from a flat sheet.

Applied: a term used in connection with ornament; certain parts, such as spouts, handles, covers, were made separately and applied with solder.

Baptismal basin: while many baptismal basins were made specifically for the purpose, there are instances of the bequest of rose-water basins to churches to serve in this capacity, such as the one now belonging to the First Parish Church, Cambridge, which was made by Jeremiah Dummer of Boston. Earliest baptismal basins are of the seventeenth century.

FIG. 1. BAPTISMAL BASIN, 1716.

Beading: contiguous half-spheres used as border ornament, generally cast and applied. Beading was especially popular in the classic period, 1785–1810.

A line of beading on a tankard handle appears on early eighteenth-century examples, as in the work of Dummer in Boston, and a flattened bead used by Charles Le Roux in New York.

Beaker: cylindrical drinking vessel for domestic use which was also dedicated to ecclesiastical use in New York and New England; early ones, straight-sided with flaring rim, were followed by a Queen Anne bell-shape on low moulded foot; the body became ovoid in Federal period, *c.* 1800.

Bright cut: a form of engraving produced with a bevelled gouge having two cutting points, thus producing greater light reflection; in use in America at same time as in England, *c.* 1785–1800.

FIG. 2.
BEAKER, 1665.

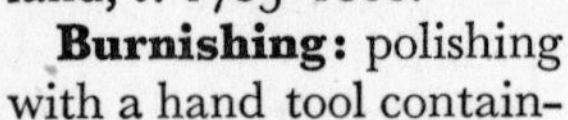

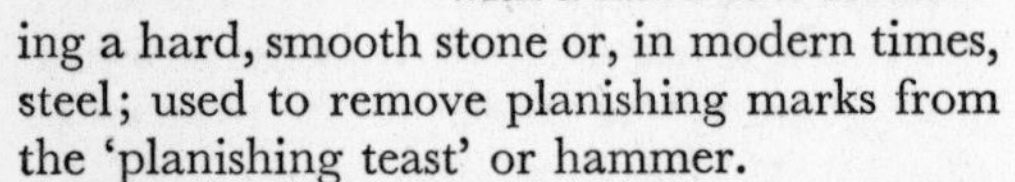

Burnishing: polishing with a hand tool containing a hard, smooth stone or, in modern times, steel; used to remove planishing marks from the 'planishing teast' or hammer.

Cake basket: very rare. Simon A. Bayley of New York, *c.* 1789–96, made one, and a recent acquisition of the Museum of Fine Arts, Boston, is the work of Daniel Christian Fueter, *c.* 1765, also representing New York (*see* Plate 100B).

Candlestick: the earliest, 1686, by Jeremiah Dummer, Boston (*see* Fig. 3), shows architectural influence, continued in a different form in baluster stems of the early eighteenth century, used by Coney in Boston and George Rideout in New York; fluted columns on square or octagonal bases are seen in work of Boelen and Kierstede. After about 1715 candlesticks were cast in moulds, being raised from a flat piece of silver in the earlier period. Baluster forms continued to be most popular throughout the eighteenth century.

Cann: drinking vessel, usually of one-pint capacity, like a mug, but always having rounded sides, and standing on a moulded base. The term 'cann', not used in English silver, appears in old inventories.

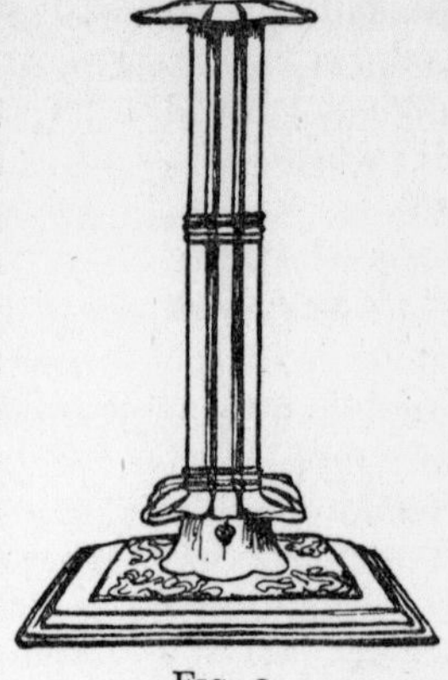

FIG. 3.
CANDLESTICK, 1686.

Caryatid: the cast thumb-grips on the handles of caudle-cups generally take this form, derived from the classic draped female figure used as a support for an entablature.

Cast: to shape in a mould, which was generally of brass. Certain small parts, thumb-pieces, finials for covers, hinge-plates, handles for cups, etc., were given their form in the molten state. These were finished by filing and chasing after removal from the mould.

Casters: generally made in sets of three with pierced covers, for sugar and spices. The early cylindrical form was followed by pear-shape and vase-shape; frequently polygonal. The pepper caster was a small cylinder or octagonal form with low, rounded, pierced cover; it sometimes stood on feet.

Caudle-cup: a two-handled cup, with or without cover, generally of gourd-shape; used for caudle, a thin gruel mixed with spiced wine or ale; also used for other drinks, as posset and syllabub; frequently left to churches, they became communion-cups.

Chafing-dish: a familiar form in Boston work, at least two dozen being known, also made in simpler form in New York; possibly their popularity was result of Huguenot and Dutch influence. The American chafing-dish

FIG. 4. CHAFING DISH.

is made for the use of coals, and the dish supports are continued downward to form the foot.

Chalice: a bowl on a high stem, made with paten cover, similar to late seventeenth-century English work, was made in Boston, New York and Philadelphia for communion plate in early eighteenth century; based on presentation plate from William and Mary, and Queen Anne.

Chasing: working on the surface by hammering and thus producing a design in relief. The interior was filled with pitch, which provided resistance to the hammer blows; the result was a design in low relief. The tools were chasing punches, hammers and gravers.

Cherub's head: a cast cherub mask appears on the curve and at the tip of the handle of New York tankards, at tip in Boston work. The European source of design was identified by Marshall Davidson (*Antiques*, April 1940) in cast ornament of sprandrels of Dutch and English clocks of the late seventeenth century. The cherub mask with pendant leafage on handles duplicates a French seventeenth-century *applique de cabinet* (*see* 'Le Bronze', second part of a catalogue of metalwork, Musée des Arts Decoratifs, Plate 26, Fig. 256). Masks and pendants as used by different silversmiths are so similar as to suggest the moulds were imported.

Chinoiserie: Chinese motifs have an unusually early example in a salver by Timothy Dwight of Boston, made before 1700 (Plate 96A) but the style did not take hold in America. Kierstede used chinoiserie ornament on a rare pair of columnar candlesticks in New York, with an exceptional standing snuffer-stand, similarly decorated, now in the Metropolitan.

Chocolate-pot: the earliest were made in Boston at the end of the seventeenth century by Coney (ogee-shaped body) and Winslow (tapering, 'lighthouse'-shape, domed cover, the handles at right angles to the spout). Chocolate did not gain in popularity and pots became still more rare, although some are known in the work of Coney, Burt and Hurd of Boston, Le Roux and Van Dyck in New York, and of the elder Richardson in Philadelphia. In shape they were like the coffee-pots, a tall pear-shape, but had a removable finial for the insertion of a swizzle-stick.

FIG. 5. CHOCOLATE POT, 1701.

Coat of arms: arms on earliest pieces were engraved in a flat-topped shield (on a lozenge for widows or spinsters), surrounded with a plumed mantling. A baroque form with broad, curling acanthus leaves was favoured in New York in early eighteenth century. About 1740 a new style was adopted with imbrication in the framework surrounding the arms; then followed the Chippendale rococo, well exemplified by Revere and Nathaniel Hurd; Guillim's *Display of Heraldry* was largely used by American silversmiths. In the classic period, 1785–1810, the shield showing the arms has floral garlands suspended on either side.

Coffee-pot: the earliest coffee-pots, *c.* 1700, were of severe tapering form like the earliest English type, followed about twenty years later by a modification of the tapering form, being rounded at the base, and standing on a narrow moulded foot. The rococo coffee-pot was, like the English, pear-shaped and tall, stood on a spreading foot, and had a domed cover. In the Federal period (late eighteenth and early nineteenth century) the coffee-pot was an inverted pear with a simple scroll handle of wood; some were made in classical urn shape.

FIG. 6. COFFEE POTS, 1720 and 1770.

Coin: inlaid in lid of tankards; Scandinavian practice, followed in New York.

Coin silver: the stamp, *coin*, after 1850, signified pieces made from silver coin, 900 parts pure silver, 100 alloy, or less than sterling.

Corkscrew: a thumb-piece of twisted shape derived from the Dutch form, used especially on New York tankards.

Creamer: earliest cream-pitchers are of second quarter of the eighteenth century and are pear-shaped with collared foot and domed cover. Next came a higher form with larger lip, three cabriole legs, double-scroll handle. This was followed by the inverted pear-shape; then the classic helmet.

C-scroll: a term applied usually to the shape of a handle in form like the letter C; also called 'single scroll'.

FIG. 7. TWO-HANDLED CUPS, 1701 and 1720.

Cup, Two-handled, with Cover: a bell-shape with footed cover is known in three examples from late seventeenth-century New York (*see* Plate 96D). In Boston the earliest, 1718, by Coney, also has bell-shaped body on moulded foot; by mid-century had domed cover, spreading base; two by Le Roux in New York have applied strapwork on body like Huguenot work in London.

Cup, Standing: wine vessel on baluster stem. The oldest is Charles I style by Hull and Sanderson, Boston, 1684, followed by examples with gadrooned bowls by J. Dummer of Boston in William and Mary style, 1700.

Cup, Wine-: a wine-cup of tumbler form was popular in New York.

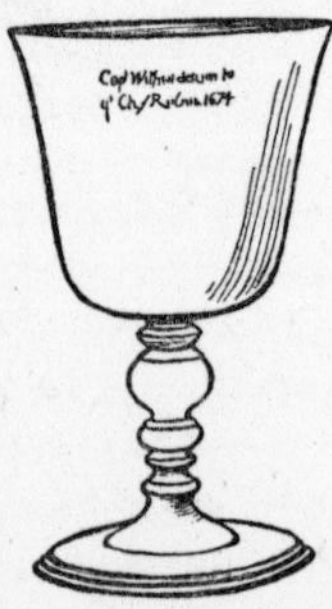

FIG. 8. STANDING CUP.

Cut-card: applied decoration cut from a flat piece of silver and soldered to the body of the vessel. Introduced through Huguenot silversmiths.

Cypher: double monogram, especially popular on New York tankards. Sympson's *Book of Cyphers*, published in London about 1726, was widely used in America.

Date letter: there are no date letters on American silver.

Dish-cross: a support for a dish, with spirit lamp for warming food. Very rare: one by Myer Myers of New York, recently exhibited from a private collection at the Museum of Fine Arts, Boston, may be the only eighteenth-century example; one by Gerardus Boyce, working in New York, 1814, is also known.

Dish-ring: a circular stand to support a dish; the only surviving American example is by Myer Myers of New York, now in the Garvan Collection.

Dolphin: a thumb-piece design, generally on Boston tankards, showing addorsed dolphins with a mask.

Domed: spheroid form of cover, used on tankards, tea-pots, coffee-pots beginning about 1715.

Double-scroll: a sinuous line of S-shape, or composed of reverse curves, employed especially in design of handles.

Embossing: raising ornament by hammering from within (repoussé).

Engraving: incised lines made with gravers, for ornament, initials, inscriptions, and heraldic devices.

Feather edge: decoration of edge of spoon-handle with chased, slanting lines.

Finial: the small cast ornament at the top of a cover; sometimes acorn-shape in early eighteenth century; flame-shape in rococo period, urn-shape in classic period. Pineapple used also in rococo period, and pine-cone, beginning *c.* 1782.

Flagon: tall cylindrical form introduced first quarter eighteenth century for

FIG. 9. FLAGON, 1710.

ecclesiastical use in episcopal churches following presentation of English flagons by William and Mary, and Queen Anne.

Flat chasing: a form of low relief chasing, popular in England in early eighteenth century, but widely used in America, 1750–1785.

Fork: extremely rare in American silver but mentioned in old inventories.

Freedom box: small boxes, generally of gold, engraved with arms of a city, were given as a municipal present, with a document conveying the freedom of the city in recognition for distinguished public service.

Gadroon: convex channelling for ornamentation produced by hammering from within, or by casting.

Geometric: pierced handle of early eighteenth-century porringer; in Boston and Philadelphia, crescent, heart and tulip; in New York, cross, heart and diamond.

Goldwork: rare, but appears in New York. Garvan Collection at Yale has eight gold teaspoons and strainer by Soumain, child's spoon with bells by Vanderspiegel, rattle by Fueter, necklace by Van Dyck, freedom box by Samuel Johnson; all of New York.

Granulated band: a form of decoration, generally on beakers, derived from Scandinavian and German work.

Graver: tool used to engrave silver with initials, coats of arms, etc., or to sharpen the chased ornament.

Hall-mark: there are no hall-marks on American silver. In 1814 Maryland established an assay office at Baltimore, but other assay offices were non-existent, although in Pennsylvania, beginning in 1753, many attempts were made to have the Assembly enact legislation (*see* Pseudo hall-marks).

Ink-stand: not common. Examples by Coney of Boston (*see* Plate 100C) and by Philip Syng of Philadelphia are known.

Keyhole: the name given to the pierced handle of a porringer which has a central pierced design similar to a keyhole, surrounded by interlacing scrolls; introduced first half of eighteenth century and continued in more delicate form to about 1810.

Ladle: for punch: the first had hollow handles of silver, followed by turned wooden handle. Bowls became double-lipped about 1725.

Lion passant: the lion walking with dexter paw raised appears in relief on seventeenth-century tankard handles by New York makers (*see* Plate 94C). This is not an English style and probably comes from a Continental source.

Mace: official insignia; rare examples by American makers include the silver oar of the Vice-Admiralty Courts of Massachusetts and New York by Jacob Hurd and Charles Le Roux respectively.

Maker's marks: the early marks are composed of the first letters of the maker's given name and surname, generally in a shaped shield, and frequently with some device, such as a fleur-de-lys. In the eighteenth century the full name, or the surname and initial were used.

Matted ground: a dull surface made by light punchwork, to secure contrast with a burnished surface.

Midband: a moulded band slightly below centre of a tankard to strengthen as well as ornament; introduced in Boston in first quarter of eighteenth century. Also used on large two-handled covered cups about 1740.

Monteith: bowl with notched edge for cooling wine-glasses, based on English form (*see* Plate 96B). Another by Coney known and a much later one (1773) by Daniel Henchman, Boston, showing the survival of the form for a long period, although never common.

Moulded: an edge formed of convex and concave members; of classic origin; formed by hammering or casting.

Muffineer: tall caster with high pierced dome, for sugar and cinnamon, a quite different use of the term from the English. Caster is the more common term for all types and sizes in American silver.

Mug: a drinking vessel in pint or quart size, with flaring sides; no cover. When having rounded sides is called a 'cann', as commonly named in eighteenth-century inventories.

Fig. 10.
Mug, 1715.

Mustard-pot: no seventeenth-century mustard-pots are known, but the form appears in the eighteenth century.

Onslow pattern: design for flatware copied from English design in which the handle is shaped as an Ionic volute.

Peace medal: late eighteenth-century medals were engraved for presentation to Indian chiefs on occasion of ceremonial visits to the national capital, then in Philadelphia. They are dated between 1792 and 1795, and were the work of Joseph Richardson, Junior, of Philadelphia, who was assayer of the United States Mint.

Pegged tankard: a tankard which has on the interior a vertical row of small pegs to indicate measurement in gills. The pegged tankard has only recently turned up in American work in a hitherto unpublished tankard by Cornelius Kierstede of New York, probably before 1700 (*see* Plate 94C). As it was discovered in England, it was probably originally owned by a Loyalist at the time of the Revolution. The presence of the impaled Pemberton and Stapylton arms (commemorating a marriage of 1854) may provide a clue to its origin. Among the Loyalists was the Reverend Ebenezer Pemberton (1704–77), whose wife, Catherine Smith, inherited silver plate which had belonged to Colonel William Peartree, 1642–1714, mayor of New York, 1703–7. His will left silver plate to Mrs Pemberton's father. The period of Mayor Peartree would be correct for the style of tankard, which shows the late seventeenth-century lion passant on the handle.

Pine-tree shillings: made by John Hull and Robert Sanderson of Boston, 1652; first silver currency in Massachusetts. Hull was appointed mint-master of Colony in that year.

Pipkin: small vessel, like saucepan with spout and turned wooden handle, for warming brandy.

Planishing: making flat by hammering with an oval-faced punch, called in the old days a planishing teast.

Porringer: low bowl with pierced flat handle, called in England a bleeding-bowl or cupping-bowl. The term porringer is never used in America for caudle-cup or posset-pot. Made in Boston, Newport, Philadelphia, New York. Earliest had handle of geometric type (q.v.). 'Keyhole' design (q.v.) introduced about 1725; two pierced arches in handle near body of vessel on first 'keyholes' disappear about 1740.

FIG. 11. PORRINGER, 1709.

Posset-pot: same as caudle-cup (q.v.).

Pricking: earliest pieces show pricked initials of owners, but after 1680 engraved letters began to be used.

Pseudo hall-marks: devices were occasionally adopted by individual makers to suggest English hall-marks.

Punch-bowl: the earliest is one of 1692 by Jeremiah Dummer of Boston in the Garvan Collection, and shows Portuguese influence. New York punch-bowls had panelled sides enclosing embossed and chased floral ornament for which no European prototype is known. A rare Boston armorial punch-bowl is illustrated (*see* Plate 98A). Punch-bowls are not common in American work.

Punchwork: ornament by indentation made by a blow with a chasing punch or small hammer while the vessel was filled with pitch.

Raising: working up an object in silver from a flat piece of metal, with different hammers, on an anvil. The term 'raising' is used whether there is elevation in form or not. Raising involves creasing, or fluting, in which indentations are hammered into the silver while it is held against the anvil, or 'stake'. After each step it must be annealed, or heated, to overcome brittleness, and the process repeated until the desired form is reached. The flutings are then removed with a special hammer, which in the eighteenth century was called a 'planishing teast'.

Ram's-horn: thumb-piece of twisted form seen on early Boston tankards. It differs from the New York corkscrew.

Reeding: a series of convex, parallel bands, opposite of fluting, which consisted of concave grooves.

Rococo: the rococo style, characterized

by asymmetrical forms and rocaille ornament, did not appear in America until about 1750 and ended about 1785.

Rosewater dish: a rare form, but two Boston examples, bequeathed to churches in Boston and Cambridge, became baptismal basins.

Salt, Standing: No seventeenth-century example has survived. Three reel-shaped salts by Boston makers in the early eighteenth century are by Edward Winslow, Jeremiah Dummer and Allen & Edwards, in partnership.

Salt-trencher: salts of oval or octagonal form with splayed, moulded sides were made to about 1730; after that, circular and footed; made especially in New York and Boston.

Salver: a form of small tray with central foot to be grasped by the servant in offering wine. The form appears about 1720 and was popular with Boston, New York and Philadelphia makers. Another form of salver, generally called a waiter in English silver, had low feet supporting the rim and was used in the serving of tea and coffee. These first appeared in America in the second quarter of the eighteenth century.

Sand-box: also called pounce-box; one of the three receptacles requisite to the ink-stand, or standish, the others being the ink-pot and wafer-box.

Sauce-boat: introduced about 1715; earliest are double-lipped, followed by lengthened single lip, and high-standing scrolled handle; stood on three hoof feet. The classic period used an urn-shape sauce tureen.

FIG. 12.
SAUCE-BOAT, 1770.

Sconce: wall lighting fixtures almost unknown in American silver. A pair by Knight Leverett (1703–53), Boston, is in the Winterthur Museum.

Serrated: knotched, said especially of the shaped edge of the rim of tankard lid.

Shield: the handle frequently terminated in a shield on Boston tankards.

Snuff-box: among small objects in silver was the snuff-box, generally oval in form. Most popular about the middle of the eighteenth century.

Snuffer: a scissor-like instrument for trimming wick of a candle; not common in American silver.

Spoons: the Dutch seventeenth-century spoon had cast caryatid handles. Slip-end spoons may be dated about 1650; trifid about 1690; wavy end about 1700; mid-rib about 1715. The rat-tail continues on back of bowl until about 1730–40, after which it was replaced by a double-drop or shell. The feather-edge spoon appeared about 1770; bright-cut engraved ornament about 1785. The 'coffin-end' was introduced about 1800. The principal types were table, porringer, tea and basting. Marrow spoons very rare, but one by John Burt Lyng of New York is known.

Spout-cup: popular in the early eighteenth century and later; a feeding-cup, generally with bulbous body and domed cover; handle generally at right angle to spout, and spout of duck-neck shape, close to body; for feeding children and invalids (Plate 93B).

Stake: an iron tongue or anvil, on which the silver object is formed. Many kinds of stakes are used, shaped for certain purposes, such as to give an inward curve, a flat surface, etc.

Standish: early name for ink-stand (q.v.).

Stepped: a term indicating the elevations on a lid, as 'single-stepped' or 'double-stepped'.

Sterling: this word appears on Baltimore silver, 1800–1814, and, after 1860, elsewhere. However, eighteenth-century silversmiths used the same standard as English sterling, and so advertised their wares.

Stoning: polishing with an emery-stone.

Strainer: spoon with pierced bowl for removing tea-leaves or seeds from punch; introduced about 1725; strainers had pierced bowl and two handles; finely-pierced designs are seen in Boston work.

Strapwork: interlaced bands, sometimes enclosing foliage; a survival from early seventeenth-century design, which is seen only occasionally on American silver but is found on the dish-ring (*c.* 1785) by Myer Myers of New York, in the Garvan Collection.

Sucket-fork: two-pronged fork with flat handle, a spoon at other end, used for eating fruit. A rare example by William Rouse, Boston, was made before 1689.

Sugar-bowl: earliest were about 1725, covered bowls based on Oriental tea-bowl, made in New York, Boston, Philadelphia; later they follow the changing forms of the tea-pot.

Sugar-box: like English Charles II sweet-meat-box; term adopted in America because of its use in old inventories, with 'sugar chest' or 'sugar trunke'. Seven Boston examples known (*see* Plate 98B).

Sugar-tongs: tongs appear about mid-eighteenth century in a scissor-form ending in cast shell grips; after 1760, bow-shaped 'spring tongs', in which a spring joins the arms.

Tankard: drinking vessel usually of one-quart capacity, but larger are known. Used for ale or cider; in Nonconformist New England tankards were used rather than flagons in communion service. In New York the tankard was larger and heavier than in New England. Early forms were tapering and cylindrical; the flat-top cover (like English Stuart form) persisted in New York, but Boston adopted a domed cover about 1715 and used a midband on the body. The New York tankard is distinguished by an applied foliated band at the bottom. New York silversmiths frequently used a cork-screw thumb-piece, Boston a dolphin, and many American makers used for ornament on handle a cast cherub's head (q.v.). Tankards of pear-shape body and domed cover were made in the rococo period, 1750–85, but the flat-top, Stuart tankard was continued in New York past mid-eighteenth century. The tankard went out of fashion in the late eighteenth century.

Tea-caddy: the caddy was first made in America about 1720; early New York makers were Thauvet Besley and Simeon Soumain; later examples followed rococo and classic forms.

Tea-kettle: earliest tea-kettle is by Cornelius Kierstede, New York, in Metropolitan Museum. A rococo example (*c.* 1755) is the only one to survive with stand (*see* Plate 99D). One was made in Boston by Jacob Hurd. Tea kettles remained a great rarity in America.

Tea-pot: earliest general form was Queen Anne pear-shaped (*c.* 1715), succeeded by globular or bullet shape (*c.* 1725); next came

FIG. 13. TEA-POT.

the inverted pear (*c.* 1750); cylindrical drum-shape, frequently with beading (*c.* 1782); urn-shape (*c.* 1790); boat-shape (*c.* 1810).

Tea-tray: trays are among the rarities in American silver but nine were made by

FIG. 14. TEA-POTS.

(A) Sugar caster with the Schuyler arms, by Pieter Van Dyck, 1684–1750. Height 7¾ in. *Garvan Collection.*

(B) Early eighteenth century spout-cup with cover, by Jacob Boelen, New York, 1654–1729. *Metropolitan Museum.*

(C) The William III tankard persisted in New York well into the eighteenth century. Adrian Bancker made this in 1735 for the marriage of John and Anne (Jacobs) Gillingham of Philadelphia. It shows a typical New York decoration, a cypher of imposing proportions. Height 6½ in. *Ginsburg & Levy.*

Loving cup, by Jacob Hurd, Boston, 1744. Presented to Edward Tyng for a naval victory in King George's War. Height 15½ in. *Garvan Collection.*

PLATE 93

(A) John Coney's covered caudle cup with the Addington arms, 1679, is earliest American covered cup. Height $6\frac{7}{8}$ in. *Garvan Collection.*

(B) Standing reel-shaped salt, by Jeremiah Dummer, Boston; early eighteenth century. Height $5\frac{1}{2}$ in. *Museum of Fine Arts, Boston*

(C) Late seventeenth century New York tankard, by Cornelius Kierstede. *Robert Ensko, Inc.*

(D) Early eighteenth century New York tankard, by Pieter Van Dyck. *Garvan Collection.*

(A) Tea-set by Paul Revere, Boston, presented 1799 to Edmund Hartt, builder of the frigate *Constitution*. *Museum of Fine Arts, Boston.*

(B) Tea-set by Abraham du Bois, Philadelphia, *c.* 1790, showing the ovoid forms and pierced gallery favoured in Philadelphia in the classic period. *Garvan Collection.*

(A) Boston salver with chinoiserie decoration in late Stuart style; made by Timothy Dwight who died 1691–2. Diameter 11 5/16 in. *Museum of Fine Arts, Boston.*

(B) John Coney's monteith was made for John Colman, a Boston merchant, in the early eighteenth century. The rim is not detachable as on English monteiths. Diameter 11 in. *Garvan Collection.*

(C) New York punch-bowl of pumpkin shape and panelled sides with repoussé and chased floral ornament. By Cornelius Kierstede, *c.* 1698. Diameter 9¾ in. *Metropolitan Museum.*

(D) New York cup and footed cover showing English and Dutch influence. Made by Gerrit Onckelbag for the christening of Judith Bayard, December 13, 1696. Height 5¾ in. *Garvan Collection.*

(A) Transition, rococo to classic; sugar-bowl, by William Gilbert, New York, *c.* 1785. *Museum of the City of New York.*

(B) Fluted oval teapot with accompanying stand; ornament in bright cut engraving. By Ebenezer Moulton of Boston and Newburyport, Massachusetts, 1768–1824. *Minneapolis Institute of Arts.*

(C) One of a pair of salvers, by Myer Myers of New York, showing the Phillipse arms *c.* 1770. Diameter 8 in. Spoons from set of six, made for same family by Simeon Soumain, New York. *Ginsburg & Levy.*

(A) Rare heraldic punch-bowl, showing six coats of arms of Boston merchants; probably second quarter of the eighteenth century. By John Burt, 1692–1745. Diameter 7 in. *Collection of Walter M. Jeffords.*

(B) Edward Winslow's sugar-box, made for himself, is one of four of this design, *c.*1700–15. Length 7½ in. *Garvan Collection*

PLATE 98

A

D

B

C

(A) Exceptional example of the globular teapot in the work of John Potwine, Boston, *c.* 1730; shows arms of Samuel Welles, 1660–1731; cover has a rare bayonet fastening. *Robert Ensko, Inc.*

(B) Two-handled cup by John Dixwell, Boston, 1722. Height $5\frac{1}{4}$ in. *Spalding Collection, Museum of Fine Arts, Boston.*

(C) Typical New York teapot, by Adrian Bancker, *c.* 1740. Height 8 in. *Tiffany & Co.*

(D) A masterpiece of the rococo is this Philadelphia tea-kettle on stand with spirit lamp, by Joseph Richardson, Sr., before 1760. Height $14\frac{1}{2}$ in. *Garvan Collection.*

Photograph courtesy of Philadelphia Museum of Art

A

(A) The use of cast ornament of the rococo period has an outstanding example in this rare set of snuffers and tray, by Myer Myers of New York, 1723–1795. Length $7\frac{3}{8}$ in. *Garvan Collection*

B

(B) Cake basket by Daniel Christian Fueter, New York, *c.* 1765, with the Harrison arms; a great rarity in American silver. *Museum of Fine Arts, Boston.*

C

(C) Triangular inkstand on cast recumbent lions, by John Coney, made for Governor Belcher of Massachusetts. Height $4\frac{1}{4}$ in. *Metropolitan Museum.*

PLATE 100

To face page

Jacob Hurd, Boston, while Paul Revere's large oval tray made for Elias Hasket Derby in the Garvan Collection is one of the masterpieces of American silver.

Tobacco-boxes: these were generally oval in form and were popular in the mid-eighteenth century.

Touch: maker's mark, impressed with a punch.

Toys: rare in America, but a set made for Bethea Shrimpton by an unidentified silversmith is in the Garvan Collection at Yale.

Tulip design: floral decoration in form of a tulip is found in Boston and New York silver, known through both Dutch and English precedent.

Tureen: small tureens succeeded sauce-boats in the period of classical influence but were by no means common. Larger tureens were almost unknown, a soup tureen by Boehme of Baltimore in the Metropolitan Museum being considered unique.

FIG. 15. TUREEN.

Urn: spouted urns for the tea and coffee equipage were introduced at the end of the eighteenth century. Three by Paul Revere of Boston are known.

'Whistles': the hole at end of a tankard handle, mistakenly called a whistle, was actually a vent for intake of cold air during construction.

BOOKS FOR FURTHER READING

C. LOUISE AVERY, *Early American Silver*, Metropolitan Museum of Art, New York (1920).

FRANCIS H. BIGELOW, *Historic Silver of the Colonies*, Macmillan (London, 1914).

KATHRYN C. BUHLER, *American Silver* (Cleveland, Ohio, 1950).

STEPHEN G. C. ENSKO, *American Silversmiths and their Marks* (III), privately printed (New York, 1948).

E. ALFRED JONES, *Old Silver of Europe and America* (London, 1922).

JOHN MARSHALL PHILLIPS, *American Silver* (London and New York, 1949).

MUSICAL INSTRUMENTS

By ERIC HALFPENNY

COLLECTING old musical instruments is a specialized activity about which it is difficult to offer general guidance for the beginner. No doubt few people would interest themselves in the subject without some previous practical acquaintance with music-making. Indeed, without some such background musical instruments are likely to remain very much of a closed book. Early instruments, however, call in more than one way for attention and interest, and the motive for collecting them is prompted by individual taste.

Instruments exist in the first place because they generate pleasing sounds, and because many people want to play them. They are the 'tools' which make musical performance of any kind possible. Like other tools, they have to be fashioned to fit both their function and the limitations of the human frame. Somebody, somewhere, and at some time has had to design and make them; somebody has had to discover the best way of playing them; and somebody has had to invent suitable music for them to play. We may study them as musical vehicles or media; as objects of craftsmanship; as social documents; or as interesting curiosities of the past. Some instruments have assumed major roles in the development of musical art, others have performed only minor or subsidiary functions; some are attractive in appearance but musically insignificant, and vice versa; some have long, unbroken histories which can be traced, others have appeared and disappeared with changing fashions in musical taste.

What criteria, then, must one apply? Perhaps the best answer that can be given here is to outline a few out of the thousands of possible types which are attractive and 'collectable' and which are likely to come the way of the beginner in this field. Any such selection is bound to be an arbitrary one based on personal experience. Much more could be said about any one of the instruments mentioned. But the present limited object is to stimulate interest and give a few suggestions on the more obvious and immediate objectives of the beginner-collector. I have not emphasized any one aspect, such as musical importance or curiosity value. It is a starting point only, from which it is hoped that individuals will be encouraged to develop their own expertise. Fortunately, there exists an extensive literature on musical instruments in all their aspects.

BOWED STRINGED INSTRUMENTS

Violins: the instruments of the violin family (violins, violas, 'cellos and double basses) are so familiar that they scarcely need any description. There are literally thousands of these instruments in existence – good, bad, indifferent, old, bogus-old and new. The collection of really fine violins requires a lifetime of experience and no inconsiderable fortune. It is perhaps unnecessary to say that violin connoisseurship is an expert's job. The literature of violin lore is enormous, and that in itself limits the usefulness of any brief remarks that can be made here. But a beginner choosing violins is at least fortunate that reliable advice is fairly easily accessible. The opinion of a good maker or repairer can usually be depended upon. He develops an eye for the look of a fiddle and, although he may not be able to say definitely who made it (the label inside it can, on occasion, be the least reliable guide in this matter), he will probably give a very good guess at its nationality and age, if nothing more.

As everyone knows, old Italian instruments are, not without reason, the most highly-prized and sought-after, and the finest of these are liable to fetch prices running into four figures. Not all old instruments are good, nor is every good instrument necessarily an old one. As a modest suggestion for the collector who would like to have one or two interesting but not-too-valuable examples, the eighteenth-century English school of makers is recommended. They have nothing like the *éclat* of the Italians, and the models used are not particularly popular with present-day players. But their very plainness and matter-of-fact workmanship give them an individuality not always achieved by flamed sycamore and a superb patina (*see* Plate 104E).

A few of the better-known of these English makers may be mentioned: Benjamin Banks (of Salisbury), 1727–95; John Betts, 1755–1823; Nathaniel Cross, *c.* 1700–51; Richard Duke, *c.* 1750–80; William Forster, 1739–1808; Henry Jay, *c.* 1746–68; Alexander Kennedy, 1695–1785; Barak Norman, 1688–1740; Thomas Smith, 1740–90; Robert Thompson, *c.* 1749–64; Peter Walmsley, *c.* 1715–51.

Most of these makers were founders of family businesses which carried on for several generations. Many made instruments of several qualities to suit the pockets of different clients. Some supplied the embryonic music 'trade' of the late eighteenth century. For example, any violin or 'cello branded on the top of the back 'Longman & Broderip' was probably made by Banks or Jay. This branding is reliable evidence of genuineness in such cases, and the instruments are worth possessing. Duke was perhaps the only English maker to achieve the dubious honour of having cheap forgeries of his work uttered. The above list is by no means even approximately complete.

Viols: these instruments are currently very popular after nearly two centuries of comparative neglect, owing to their revival for the playing of certain types of old string music. Though similar in general appearance to the violin family, they show the following differences of detail:

Viols	*Violins*
Six strings	Four strings
Sloping shoulders	Rounded shoulders
Blunt corners	Pointed corners
Flat back	Modelled back
Long flat neck	Short rounded neck
Short fingerboard	Long fingerboard
C-shaped soundholes	F-shaped soundholes
Edges of table and back flush with ribs	Edges of table and back overhang ribs
Carved head or open scroll to pegbox	Solid scroll to pegbox

The viols were made in five or six sizes from a small treble (*pardessus*) to a great bass (*violone*). Some of the larger instruments have seven strings. When these instruments are played the necks are 'fretted' by tying on gut loops to form semitone stops for the fingers.

Modern players usually have to make do with modern replicas. Not very many genuine old specimens have survived. Unlike the violins, where the treble is the dominating instrument, the most characteristic member of the viol family is the *viola da gamba* (Plate 104A), approximating in size and pitch to the 'cello, though rather smaller in the body. A fair number of English gambas are known, many of them made by, or attributed to, Barak Norman. Viols are sometimes found which have been converted for modern use as violas or 'cellos by being renecked and having the shoulders cut down, an unwarrantable and often useless vandalism.

In view of the practical interest taken in these instruments at the present day (there is in England an active and flourishing Viola da Gamba Society), and the fact that genuine specimens are generally rather early in date, and therefore scarce, the collector may count himself fortunate if he succeeds in finding one.

Viola d'Amore: this instrument stands on its own between the viols and violins, and is chiefly notable for its system of 'sympathetic strings', a duplicate set of wires passing under the fingerboard and through the bridge. Although out of reach of the bow and fingers, these strings vibrate freely 'in sympathy' with the notes played and produce a peculiarly ethereal effect. There are seven bowed (gut) strings and seven (steel) sympathetic strings, and since all terminate on separate tuning pegs in the head, this is of extraordinary length. A fair number of these instruments was made in Italy, France, and Germany during the eighteenth and nineteenth centuries. They are occasionally met with, and are well worth having. The instrument usually has a viol-type body, the top is traditionally decorated with a carved head of a blindfold cupid, and the soundholes are of an unusual 'flame' pattern. The broad neck is not fretted (Plate 104D).

PLUCKED-STRINGED INSTRUMENTS

Instruments whose strings are plucked with the fingers, or with a horn or quill 'plectrum' held in the fingers, are found in every region of the world and at all stages in the history of civilization. The varieties peculiar to Europe alone are so numerous that only a few of the better-known can be dealt with. Most of these instruments, being small, portable and capable of playing chords, have had a wide domestic use, and are often finely decorated.

Harps: the largest and most familiar of these is the double-action harp used in modern orchestras, usually known as the 'Gothic' harp, on account of its elaborate appliqué gilt decoration in high relief. These instruments may have forty-seven strings or more, tuned diatonically, and seven pedals working in notched slots, each of which gives three positions. By means of a complicated mechanism in the fore pillar and 'comb' (the curved top member of the frame) the pedals reset the tuning of the strings. In the middle notch a pedal raises the strings it controls by a half-tone, and in the lower by a whole tone. The invention was due to Sébastien Erard in 1810. Numbers of smaller double-action harps, usually about five feet six inches high, known as 'Grecian' harps, were made after this date by several makers in England and elsewhere, and are occasionally found. Before that date single-action harps, with only one notch for the pedals, will be found. There is sometimes an eighth pedal working a crescendo shutter in the body of the instrument.

A number of smaller harps and harp-like instruments also appeared in the early nineteenth century. Among these may be mentioned the Royal Portable Irish Harp of Egan and the various inventions of Edward Light, of which the most commonly encountered is the Harp Lute (Plate 104B), virtually a small harp with additional strings on a fingerboard like a guitar. These instruments, though attractive in appearance, were practically domestic toys for the strumming of drawing-room ballads, and they died a natural death with the growing popularity of the pianoforte.

Lutes: only very rarely will a specimen of the true lute be found, since few were made after the beginning of the eighteenth century. The heyday of the instrument was the late sixteenth and early seventeenth centuries. Nevertheless, it must be considered because of the growing attention it is receiving at the present day. The lute proper has a large pear-shaped body of the form now familiar in the mandoline, a wide, flat neck and a head or peg-box turned back almost at right angles. It may have anything from twelve to twenty-two strings arranged and tuned in pairs, and is intended to be played with gut frets on the neck, like the viols. The soundboard or table is ornamented with a 'rose' of open fretwork which, in the earliest examples, is carved from the thin pinewood table itself (Plate 108). Instruments of approximately this form, but with only six single strings, were made in Germany during the nineteenth century in considerable numbers. They are *not* lutes as we understand the term, and are neither very old nor very valuable.

Guitars: the Spanish guitar is too well known to need much description. It is without doubt the finest of the plucked-string instruments. In its own country it has an unbroken record of continuous use for several hundreds of years, and its vogue elsewhere from about 1800 onwards has produced some superb instruments. The guitar lends itself to decoration, and makers took full advantage of the fact without detracting in the least from the musical quality of their work. Choice woods and inlays of mother-of-pearl and ivory were used with considerable delicacy and care. No two guitars seem to be alike in decoration, a fact which makes them particularly attractive to the collector. Many fine instruments are obtainable. The long neck of the instrument has fixed frets of metal or ivory, and there are six single strings. The head is either flat to take violin-type pegs pushed through from the back, or is slotted for the strings and has the familiar worm-and-wheel 'machine' pegs. Two of the most celebrated makers of their time were Lacote of Paris and Louis Panormo of London, both of whom were active in the 1830s (Plate 104C). Many of Panormo's instruments had machine heads of superb workmanship by Baker, with chased and pierced fretted brass plates and fretted mother-of-pearl fingerpieces.

Mandolines of several types: the Milanese, with six single gut strings; the Paduan, with five pairs of strings; the Genoese, with five or six wire strings; and the Neapolitan, the most common in England, with four pairs of wire strings. All are played with a plectrum. The *Portuguese guitar* has a flat, pear-shaped body, six double strings and a peculiar radial arrangement of screw pegs. The Spanish *Bandurria* is a short, stubby guitar-like instrument with six double gut strings. In the eighteenth century the *English guitar* was popular, a small pear-shaped instrument with flat back and six pairs of wire strings played with the fingers and not with a plectrum. Many of these have a peculiar tuning device of small screw-nuts which are turned with a watch-key. The English guitar was an adaptation of the sixteenth- and seventeenth-century *Cittern* of similar form, but with four double strings on ordinary violin-type pegs, a longer neck and a flat body which, however, tapered in thickness towards the lower end.

KEYBOARD INSTRUMENTS

Unlike most other instruments, stringed keyboard instruments are also items of furniture. Their large wooden cases have always been decorated in the prevailing style of domestic cabinet work. They fall naturally into two great classes: those instruments whose keys work a plucking device and those with a hammer action. The former embraces such instruments as the Virginals, Spinet, and Harpsichord, and the latter the Clavichord and the Pianoforte. The difference between these instruments is not always made clear, and there has always been a good deal of confusion which has arisen through describing them by the wrong names.

Virginals, Spinet: the virginals and spinet are both small domestic instruments with only one string to each note and one row of jacks or plectra, one for each string. The virginals proper is a rectangular instrument (sometimes with the rear corners cut away) the whole interior of which is covered by the soundboard. Through this the jacks protrude to reach the strings. These pass diagonally over the soundboard on two bridges. The form belongs peculiarly to the sixteenth and seventeenth centuries and not many examples are known. They are usually finely decorated within and without (Plate 101B). Such instruments are valuable and rare and do not often come on the market. The Spinet is a little more common, as its manufacture spread till a later date, though, once again, specimens are sought after and rare. The shape is that of a harp on its side, with the keyboard along the shorter of the straight sides which converge on the left of the player. They are united on the right by the curved side of the 'harp'. These instruments sometimes date from the seventeenth century and reflect Jacobean tastes, with their oak casework and stands. Later instruments in walnut or mahogany with bandings of other woods are more numerous.

Harpsichords have been known since the fifteenth century, but the name suggests to most people the fine eighteenth-century English instruments of Shudi, Kirkman, and their contemporaries. A few English and Netherlands instruments are known of the seventeenth century and before, but they are so excessively rare and valuable that the possibility of discovering an example is hardly worth considering.

The large English harpsichords from about 1730 onwards have two keyboards or 'manuals', usually five hand-stops on the front board above the upper keyboard, and two pedals. There are three strings to each note, two 'unisons' and one tuned to the octave, which can be used separately or together by means of the stops. On Shudi's instruments the right pedal works the 'Venetian Swell', a louvred inner lid over the strings which can be opened by degrees to produce a crescendo. The invention was patented in 1769. The left pedal on most instruments operates the 'machine' when a bolt in the left keyboard cheek is moved, and alters the arrangement of hand-stops in use, producing registration effects similar to that of an organ (Plate 102). A few single keyboard harpsichords are known, but most probably the demand was not great for anything less than the most elaborate type, which contained all the effects for performing the finest keyboard compositions of the period. The wide outer surfaces of the harpsichord case lent themselves to fine veneer work in walnut or mahogany, with banded and inlaid panels of exquisite figure. Many of the stands – when the originals survive – are on short cabriole legs. The hinges of the lid are usually of the strap type in finely-fretted brass. Another handsome detail is the hanging S-hooks which secure the lid when closed. The original music desks are marvels of joinery, with sliding candle-sconces and the music rack adjustable for height and angle.

Clavichords, Pianofortes: the small rectangular instrument called the clavichord, in which the strings are set vibrating by small blades fixed directly into the ends of the keys, survives in England in only a handful of known examples. The present vogue for the instrument has had to be met by modern replicas. From the collector's point of view the clavichord is practically non-existent. But while clavichords and, to a lesser degree, the plucked instruments are excessively rare and costly, it is still possible to obtain early pianos at reasonable prices and without much difficulty. They have in the past been unjustly neglected, but are gradually becoming recognized as instruments in their own right, which in their time have left their mark on the development of keyboard music. Unlike the plucked instruments, whose mechanism has remained unchanged for many centuries, the hammer action has had to be evolved and modified, and the problems were not solved easily or immediately by makers. Consequently, early pianos are full of interesting quirks of mechanism and form which are a happy hunting ground for the enquiring mind.

The history of the instrument in England commenced about 1760, when pianos first began to be made there, not in the usual 'grand' form of the harpsichord but of the small rectangular type known always as the 'square' piano. These are the instruments which every dealer insisted on calling spinets until a comparatively short while ago. Even now they are often reported as 'harpsichords' by owners who are ignorant of their nature but suspect them to be very valuable. The popularity of the square was at its greatest about 1780–1800 as the ideal domestic keyboard instrument. After that it gradually declined in favour of the 'upright' piano, until by 1850 hardly any were being made. Instruments before about 1810 are usually dated on the name-board above the keys. The earliest specimens have a compass of five octaves or less, bicord – that is, two strings per note – throughout the compass. Pre-1780 instruments are rare, but between then and the end of the century many were made. They are usually about five feet long by twenty inches wide, with a depth of less than six inches to the bottom board, later increased to over seven inches in instruments with more elaborate actions. The plainest cases are solid mahogany with inlaid stringing, associated with a short trestle stand of mahogany quartering. The better-class instruments show the same fine casework as the contemporary harpsichord, with satinwood bandings, marquetry name-boards, and full-length stands on square taper legs in Sheraton style (Plate 101A). Such stands were known as 'French stands'. Some of the finest square cases are seen on pianos by Christopher Ganer, a German maker from Leipzig who settled in England some time in the second half of the century. The early square had no pedals, but was usually fitted with from one to four hand-stops, housed in the left-hand front corner of the case beside the keyboard. These lifted the dampers (as in the modern 'loud pedal') and applied a mute to the strings for soft effects. Many different actions and other devices were first tried out on the square, and one frequently finds pasted inside them instructions for the management and adjustment of these new mechanisms. A detail which is often missing is the inner dust cover, a thin board completely enclosing the interior beneath the lid. Before 1800 the compass was being extended to five and a half octaves. These instruments were usually associated with a new type of overdamper introduced by William Southwell in 1794, which was raised by a pedal. Before long the square began to assume Regency characteristics, with turned and fluted screw-in legs, generally six in number, four in front and two behind, fretted nameboards and boule-work garnishes. These instruments are about five and a half feet long by two feet wide and are extremely elegant in appearance.

With the growing use of metal structures in the piano after 1820, the opportunity was taken to extend the compass of the square first to six and afterwards to six and a half octaves. These larger squares, though technically interesting, are heavy and ungainly in appearance, and it is clear that they defeat the chief object of the square piano as a compact domestic instrument.

Grand pianofortes: since the grand is a continuing form which has passed through many phases, it only seems necessary to consider the light-toned all-wooden instrument which preceded the use of metal frames. In England the grand was developed in the 1770s, a fairly late and apparently independent start compared with what had been done on the Continent. These English instruments are still coming to light (Plate 103). In appearance they are exactly like the contemporary harpsichord and seem to have been modelled on it. They are tricord throughout the five and a half octave compass (some early examples are five octaves only). They have two pedals, the damper lifter (loud, or sustaining, pedal) and the 'soft' pedal, which slides the keyboard from left to right to engage only two of the three strings per note. When a small bolt on the right keyboard cheek is raised this pedal may be further depressed, to give the *una corda* (one string per note) *pianissimo*, which is marked in some of Beethoven's music. In restored condition these instruments have a fine distinctive tone quality, which is ideal for contemporary piano music, and is a welcome foil to both the harpsichord and the modern piano, neither of which can exactly supplant it.

BRASSWIND INSTRUMENTS

Under this head it is necessary to consider all those instruments which the layman classes as 'trumpets' and which we associate most naturally with outdoor music of various sorts. Not many very old brass instruments survive. They are, of course, easily crushed and dented, and the metal frequently perishes with age. It will be a very fortunate discovery to find a 17th-century sackbut (trombone) or an 18th-century herald's trumpet.

Attractive though the brass undoubtedly are, most collectors will find that a few specimens go a long way. Such instruments are always cumbersome and difficult to display because of their bells and of the length of tubing involved in their anatomies. They need regular periodic cleaning if they are to look at all well; and some of the later types, though no doubt extremely interesting, are fussy in appearance by reason of the valve and other mechanisms attached to them.

In this section it is useless to try to confine attention to instruments made before 1830, as so few are likely to be found. The brass instruments that look best are the simplest types, which have never gone out of date and are still to be found performing their traditional functions in ceremonial parades and in the hunting field.

Coach and post horns: these are traditionally made in a single straight tube in England, the coach horn being more conical

(*continued on page 169*)

MUSICAL INSTRUMENTS

DESCRIPTION OF PLATES

PLATE 101

(A) Square Pianoforte, by John Broadwood, London, 1792. Compass five octaves, bicord. Brass under-dampers (Broadwood patent, 1783). No stops or pedals. Mahogany case and 'French' stand, with undershelf; banded in harewood, with inlays. In fine original playing condition. A printed label inside gives instructions in English and French for the care of the dampers and hammers. Length 5 ft. 2 in., width 1 ft. 9 in. *Author's Collection.*
(Photo: Henry Ramage)

(B) Virginal, English, signed 'Stephanus Keene Londini fecit, 1668'. The keyboard compass of four octaves and a sixth, FF–d^3, and the dimensions, 6 ft. by 1 ft. 10 in., makes this the largest recorded English virginal. The case is of oak, the inside of the lid and the front board are painted in tempera, as is the sound-board, which is pierced by four carved sound holes, or 'roses'. The front of the instrument and the inside of the case are covered with gilt paper embossed with the Stuart arms. *Property of Raymond Russell.*
(Photo: The Galpin Society)

PLATES 102 AND 103

Descriptions on Plates

PLATE 104

(A) An English Viola da Gamba, by Henry Jay, 'in Southwarke, 1619'. A fine example of a 'consort bass', the largest of the gambas much used in concerted music for the viols. Smaller instruments of the same pitch and tuning, used in solo work, were known as 'division viols'. The body of this instrument is completely covered with a fine network of inlaid 'purfling' in geometric and floral designs. In addition to the carved head, the sides of the pegbox have a floral pattern in light relief. *Hill Collection* (*Messrs W. E. Hill & Sons*).

(B) A Harp-lute by Wheatstone, *c.* 1815. With eight diatonic 'harp' strings and six additional strings arranged on two fingerboards.
(Photo: Henry Ramage)

(C) A Spanish Guitar, by Louis Panormo, London, 1833. Body of inlaid rosewood. Table inlaid ebony, sycamore and mother-of-pearl. Hickory neck and sycamore head. Ivory pegs. Machine head by Baker, with fretted mother-of-pearl fingerpieces. *Author's Collection.*
(Photo: Henry Ramage)

(D) A Viola d'Amore, German, *c.* 1700. Head not original. A typical specimen, with fourteen strings, seven of which pass through the neck and bridge at a low level and vibrate 'in sympathy', being untouched by the bow or fingers. *Hill Collection* (*Messrs W. E. Hill & Sons*).

(E) An Old English Violin, by James and Henry Banks, 1798, in fine preservation. Reddish varnish, Amati model. James and Henry were the fourth and sixth sons of Benjamin Banks of Salisbury, and succeeded to his business in 1795, later moving to Liverpool in 1811. James was the violin-maker, and he closely followed his father's work in quality and appearance. The label reads 'James and Henry Banks: Musical Instrument Makers: and: Music Sellers: Salisbury'. The date is added by hand. *Messrs W. E. Hill & Sons.* *(Photo: Henry Ramage)*

PLATE 105

(A) French Horn, with crooks, by Courtois, Paris, *c.* 1870. Although the valved horn was by this time well established, it continued to be used with crooks, putting it into the key of the music. A complete set of eight crooks and two intermediate 'couplers' is shown, with an additional tuning slide and mouthpieces. This example is unusual in being built 'the wrong way round' for a left-handed player. *Author's Collection.*

(B) Cornopean, by Charles Pace, London, *c.* 1830. This is an early example of a 'valved' instrument, the forerunner of the cornet, two crooks are also shown. Note the protecting caps for the valves when not in use, also the 'shake' key on the rear curve of the instrument. *Author's Collection.*

PLATE 106

(A) A pair of silver-plated fanfare or herald's trumpets, made by Keat of London in 1891 for the High Sheriff of Gloucester. *(Photo: Henry Ramage)*

(B) An orchestral slide-trumpet by Köhler of London, *c.* 1880, with crooks for F, E natural, E flat, D and C. The slide is in the upper part, and is kept closed by a piece of elastic in the centre tube. Note the traditional 'bosses' and 'garnishes' with which these instruments are decorated. *Author's Collection.* *(Photo: Henry Ramage)*

(C) Serpent, by T. Key, London, *c.* 1830. Although the serpent was invented at the end of the sixteenth century, it was not until just before 1800 that it came into general use as a wind bass for military bands and orchestras. It is built up from segments of chestnut wood, carved to shape and covered with leather. The fine example shown has seven brass keys and ivory-bushed finger-holes. *Author's Collection.*
(Photo: Lancelot Vining)

PLATE 107 AND 108

Descriptions on Plates

A

B

For a description of these plates see page 168

PLATE 101

To face page 168

Harpsichord, by Burkat Shudi, London, 1766. A superb specimen of this maker's work, with two manuals, five stops, 'machine' and 'Venetian swell' pedals. Three of the stops and the hand bolt engaging the 'machine' are visible to the left of the keyboards. The swell shutters of the inner lid may also be seen. Keyboard surrounds are in burr walnut. Four-panel case of mahogany with banding and inlays. Stand is on cabriole legs. Length 7 ft. 1 in, width 3 ft. 1 in. *Property of William R. Thomas.*

Grand Pianoforte, by John Broadwood, London, 1798. Compass five and a half octaves, tricord. Two pedals working through the front legs of the stand, on which the instrument rests in locating sockets. The pedals are as on the modern piano, left, 'soft' and right, 'loud'. The left pedal slides the keyboard and action sideways in two shifts, to strike, respectively, two and one of the tricord. Case mahogany veneer on oak, with three-section banded and inlaid panels. Length 7 ft. 5 in, width 3 ft. 6 in. *Author's Collection.*

(*Photo: Henry Ramage*)

PLATE 103

A B C

D E

For a description of these plates see page 168

PLATE 104

A

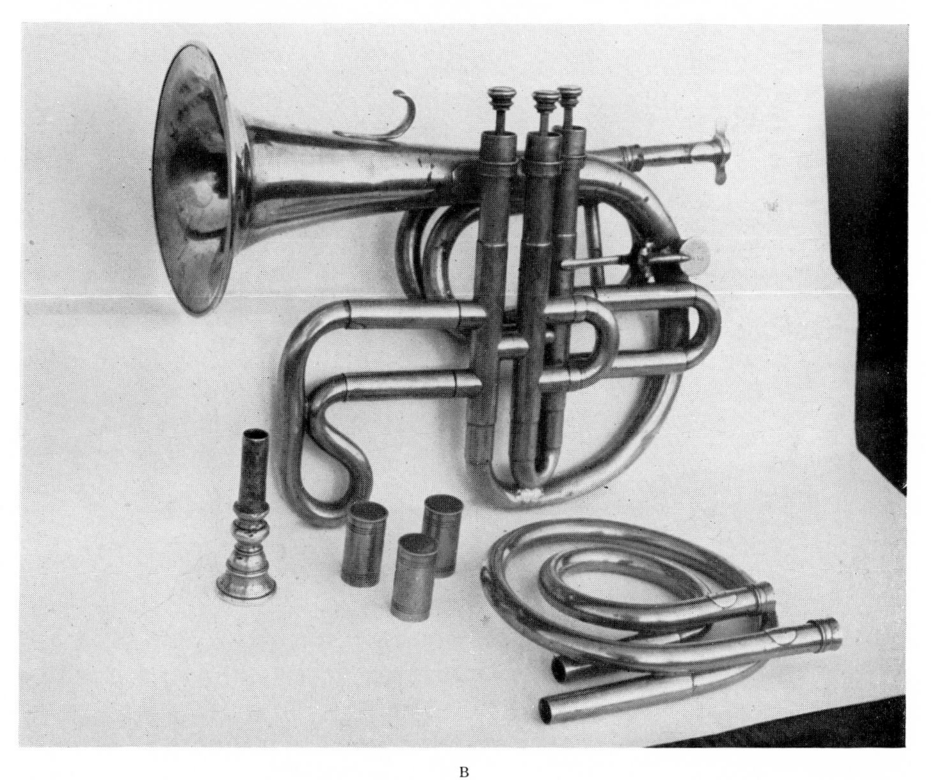

B

For a description of these plates see page 168

PLATE 105

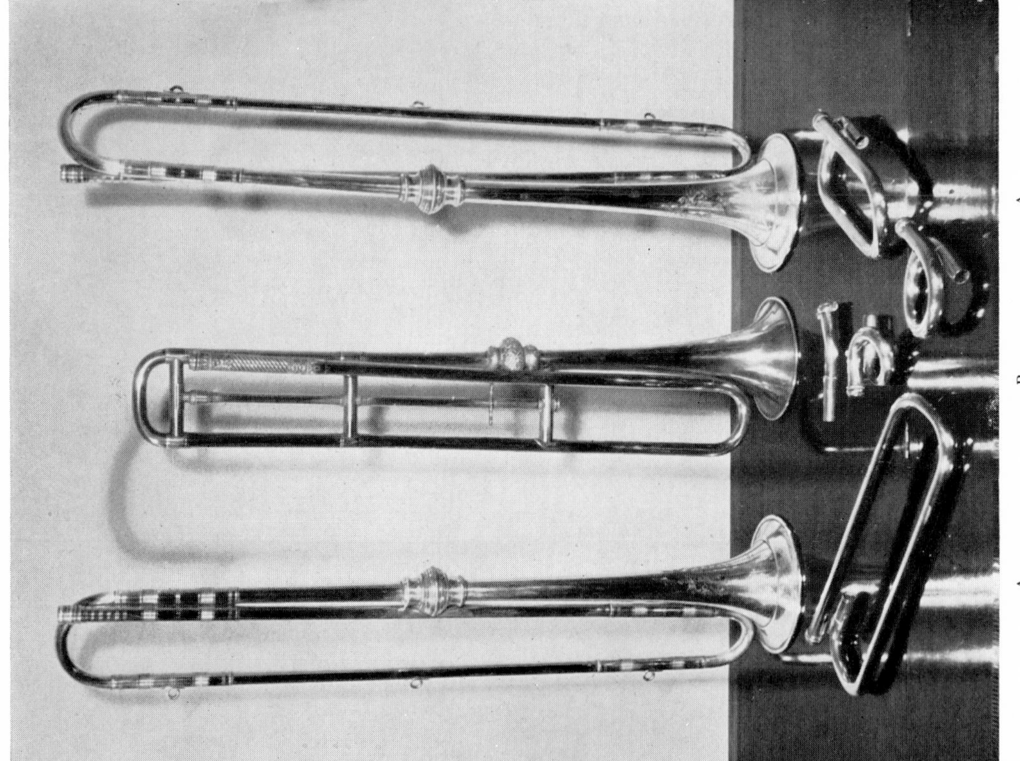

For a description of these plates see page 168

PLATE 106

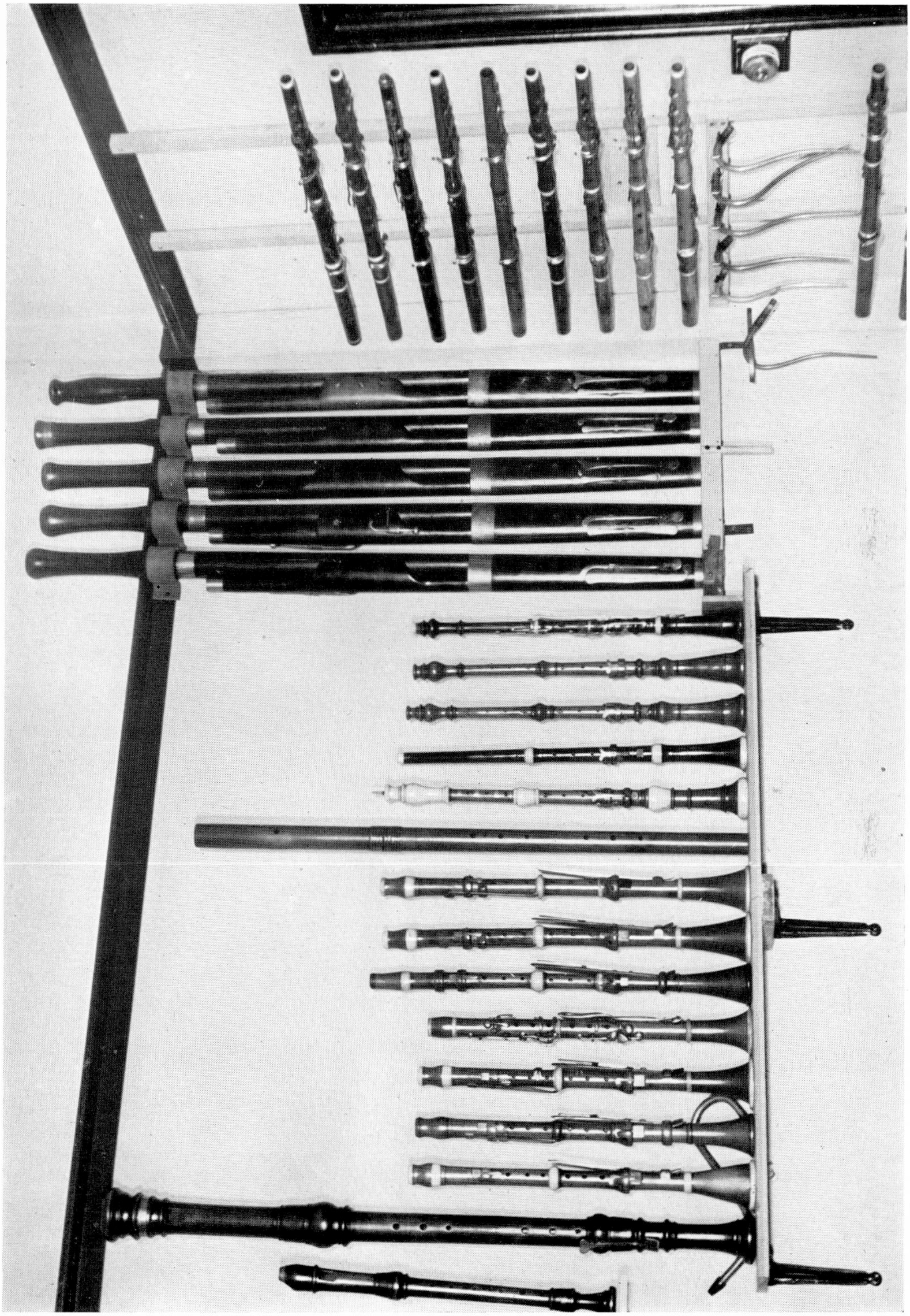

A Group of Woodwind Instruments, sixteenth to nineteenth centuries. *Left to right*: treble and bass recorders (*c.* 1700), four clarinets in C and three in B flat (*c.* 1770–1830), a rare bass flute (late sixteenth century), five oboes (*c.* 1690–1820), five bassoons (*c.* 1760—1820), and eleven flutes of the early nineteenth century. Most of these are by English makers. *Author's Collection.*

(*Photo: Henry Ramage*)

A Rare Sixteenth-century Lute by Hans Frei of Bologna (*c.* 1550). Bologna lutes continued to be prized long after they were made. Evelyn, the diarist, mentions, in 1645, Frei as one of the celebrated 'old masters' of that city. This instrument has ten 'courses' (nine paired and one single string). The body is of figured sycamore in eleven sections or ribs. The soundboard 'rose', of arabesque pattern, is delicately carved in the thin wood thereof. The inlay on the fingerboard is repeated on the back of the neck, black on white. *Inset*: The label inside the instrument.

Author's Collection.

(Photo: Henry Ramage)

PLATE 108

To face page 169

and funnel-shaped, the post horn having a narrower tube and a more marked 'flare' or trumpet bell at the wide end. They are frequently made of copper and possibly look best when made only of that metal. Usually a short section near the mouthpiece is of brass, German silver, or silver, and sometimes the bell is also mounted to match. The mouthpiece should be a fixture (i.e. not detachable as in band instruments). Coach horns may vary from thirty inches to fifty-four inches in length, but possibly the finest are those of about four feet, beautiful alike in sound and appearance when in good condition. Apart from the mouthpiece section, they should be in one piece. Two-piece instruments have either been broken at some time and joined together or are common modern replicas made for the 'antique' market.

Post or tandem horns are more frequently of brass and may vary between twenty-four inches and forty-eight inches, the most favoured being about midway, known as the 'yard of tin'. They may be recognized by the narrow tube and wide bell. It is impossible to date either of these instruments closely, for they were still in regular use on the roads before the First World War, and are still made for coaching enthusiasts by Köhler's of Piccadilly.

Hunting horns: the English hunting horn must surely be the smallest brass instrument ever to be made, a diminutive straight ten-inch affair with a funnel bell and a built-in mouthpiece, which is usually of silver or silver-rimmed. Again it is difficult to date specimens of an instrument which is still being made, unless they happen to come from hunting families who know their history; and, again, bogus replicas are abundant in the curiosity shops.

English hunting horns were not always so small. In the eighteenth century copper horns were made bent into a half-circle, in imitation of the animal horns they replaced. The latter are rare, but sometimes appear in the sale-room, as also the seventeenth-century wooden French *huchet*. A characteristic of the early animal horns is that the mouthpiece cavity is hollowed from the solid end of the horn itself and is not a separate metal accessory. More readily available, again because they are still being made, are the beautiful wide-hooped French *trompes de chasse*, the prototype of all orchestral horns, and surely the most graceful brass instrument ever made. The slender, conical fourteen-foot tube is coiled three times to form a circular hoop about sixteen inches across, terminating in a ten-inch bell.

Bugles may have some slight interest. They are usually of copper with brass mounts and a wide, expanding tube folded twice in an oblong coil.

Trumpets: all the above instruments are broadly classed as horns because their tubes expand gradually from the mouthpiece to the bell. The trumpet differs in this respect, that two-thirds of its tube length is cylindrical, a fact which has a marked effect on its tone. The true trumpet has an unbroken line of association with pomp in high places. The herald's trumpet is not the straight instrument of popular belief but is folded once in a long slender oblong loop the front bend of which fits into the curve of the bell. These instruments are sometimes made of solid silver, when, of course, they become important as 'plate' and may be dated by their markings. A few seventeenth- and eighteenth-century trumpets have survived, but the traditional form continues to be used for state occasions. The High Sheriffs frequently kept their own trumpets, for use during their appearances at the Quarter Sessions. Nowadays, if and when these ceremonies are retained, they usually devolve upon the local military, playing their own duty trumpets. So sometimes these relics of more spacious days find their way on to the market, and are always worth having both for their associations and their appearance (Plate 106A). Many made as late as fifty years ago retain the traditional 'garnishes' of the trumpet, the ornamental sleeves joining the straight sections of the tube to the curves, the boss, or ball holding the bell and mouthpipes together, and the wide, turned-back rim to the bell.

The slide-trumpet may be mentioned, since it preserved many of these features of the classic trumpet. This was an orchestral instrument, with a short trombone-like slide at the upper end, near the player. It was much used in England during the nineteenth century, and specimens are still fairly plentiful (Plate 106B).

MISCELLANEOUS

Besides these simple instruments, there are the innumerable progeny of the wind band and orchestra. These are too numerous to mention in detail, and only a few of the most interesting may briefly be touched upon.

'Crooked' instruments: before the days of valves, which automatically alter the active tube-length of the instrument to obtain chromatic notes, the limited scale of horns and trumpets could only be varied by having separate detachable loops of tubing of different lengths, which the player could change at will. These are the 'crooks'. Their use survived the change-over to valves and many later instruments – cornopeans (Plate 105B), cornets, slide- and valved-trumpets and horns – are found with complete sets of crooks (Plates 105A, 106B).

Side-hole instruments: the most curious 'brass' instruments for the general collector are perhaps those with side finger-holes to obtain the scale. This very old device is found at its most typical, perhaps, in the **serpent**, an eight-foot-long wooden instrument wrapped into the peculiar shape that gives it its name. No collection is complete without its serpent. Quantities of these instruments were made in England in the early nineteenth century, and specimens are fairly easily obtainable. Many, however, are in very poor condition. The serpent is a vulnerable beast, for all its sinister appearance. The English instruments usually have brass mounts at each end, six ivory-bushed finger-holes, and from three to thirteen keys. There should also be a brass right-angled 'crook' and an ivory mouthpiece (Plate 106C). Serpents are often cracked beneath the leather covering, and the various fittings are often missing or broken. These points should be looked for before settling on a price. A really sound specimen is something of a rarity.

Other instruments on this principle, which had a vogue in the first half of the nineteenth century, are the keyed bugle and the ophicleide. The first of these was a treble instrument made of copper, with from five to ten brass keys. The ophicleide is a bass instrument, usually of brass but sometimes partly of wood, with from nine to eleven keys.

WOODWIND INSTRUMENTS

Not very much useful guidance can be given under this heading without going into a highly technical and detailed account of each instrument at various stages of its history. Very briefly, the flutes, oboes, clarinets, and bassoons of the modern orchestra have, in most cases, direct ancestors reaching back to about 1650. But woodwind instruments have changed a great deal during three centuries – more so than any other group of instruments.

Up to about 1830 the smaller woodwind were made almost always of box, pear, and other fruit woods, turned in sections in the lathe. The sections fit together with tenon-and-socket joints, and at these points the tube was usually strengthened with ivory rings or ferrules. Keys, which varied in number, shape and appearance with the period of the instrument, were sometimes of silver, more often of hard brass. Fashions in external lathework changed from time to time; so also did the style of staining and polishing of the tube. Some instruments were made of solid ivory.

Not many instruments have survived from before about 1775. From after that date there are still to be found innumerable flutes – for it was an amateur's instrument in great vogue – and occasionally oboes, clarinets, and bassoons. All are worth having if they can be found. Dating these instruments is an intricate business. Small details changed fairly rapidly and their recognition needs considerable experience. Makers were many, but fortunately they usually put their stamp and mark on their work. In most cases an approximate working period is known. But to delve further into this matter one needs to have an eye for turnery and 'treen' comparable with that of the violin expert in his own sphere (Plate 107).

BOOKS FOR FURTHER READING

The beginner's primary needs are plenty of illustrations and information about makers and descriptions of instruments and how they work. Reference books are often costly and many are out of print. These may, however, usually be consulted in any good reference library. Not every instrument has been exhaustively treated by any writer, but hints for further reading may often be gleaned from the bibliographies printed in most good textbooks.

GENERAL

F. W. GALPIN, *Old English Instruments of Music*, Methuen, 3rd Edn. (1932) (the classic handbook of the collector).

F. W. GALPIN, *A Textbook of European Instruments*, Williams & Norgate (1937).

KARL GEIRINGER, *Musical Instruments*, George Allen & Unwin (1943).

GALPIN SOCIETY, *British Musical Instruments*, Galpin Society (1951) (contains tabloid information on over three hundred instruments of all classes).

ROBERT DONINGTON, *The Instruments of Music*, Methuen, 2nd Edn. (1953).

STRINGED INSTRUMENTS

C. STAINER, *A Dictionary of Violin Makers*, Novello (1896) (an excellent concise handbook, the smallest of many such works).

W. MEREDITH MORRIS, *British Violin Makers*, Robert Scott, 2nd Edn. (1920).

R. B. ARMSTRONG, *English and Irish Instruments*, Edinburgh (1908) (for descriptions of harp-lutes, English guitars, and kindred instruments).

A. P. SHARPE, *The Story of the Spanish Guitar*, Clifford Essex (1954).

NOTE—*The Strad*, published monthly, issues a description, with photographs, of a fine violin in every number.

KEYBOARD INSTRUMENTS

PHILIP JAMES, *Early Keyboard Instruments*, London (1930) (finely illustrated; lists of makers).

ROSAMOND HARDING, *The Piano-forte, its History to 1851* (Heffer, 1933) (much information on mechanisms and patents; lists of makers).

WIND INSTRUMENTS

ADAM CARSE, *Musical Wind Instruments*, Macmillan (1939) (the standard work; many illustrations of wood and brasswind instruments).

ADAM CARSE, *Catalogue of the Adam Carse Collection*, London County Council Publication No. 3712 (1951) (descriptions of all the wind instruments presented to the Horniman Museum, 1947, with historical introductions).

GEOFFREY RENDALL, *The Clarinet*, Williams & Norgate (1954) (an exhaustive treatise with, however, much of general interest on woodwind history; lists of makers).

COINS AND MEDALS

By R. A. G. CARSON

The collecting of coins has almost as long a history as coins themselves, for we are told by Suetonius that the Roman emperor Augustus, if not actually a collector, did at least assemble some ancient pieces, presumably Greek, which he gave as gifts to his friends. The princes of the Renaissance were the first collectors proper of coins, and ever since then collections have been formed by all sorts and conditions of men.

The attractions of coin-collecting are manifold. There is, initially, the fascination of handling objects that have passed through the hands of men in all the civilizations from the seventh century B.C. onwards. Coins form, moreover, the most complete series of artistic objects that can be assembled from the pristine vigour of classical Greek art, through the formalism of Byzantinism and the strivings of the Middle Ages to the heights of the Renaissance and on to our own day. Again, in the great sweep of centuries before the invention of printing, coins provide a great, continuous series of historical documents, giving contemporary comment on events and recording the likenesses of history's great men, the details of ancient architecture and the accompaniments of the world's religions. Unlike many other antiquities, where each piece is unique, the special work of a craftsman or artist never exactly repeated, many of the most beautiful coins of all ages were produced in their thousands and exist, even today, in their hundreds; for once the artist had engraved his dies, or made the model for his mould, the limit to the number of pieces which could be produced was the physical limitation of these instruments.

To form a collection of coins is not, even in this present age, the privilege of wealth: but since the field is so vast, complete coverage can be contemplated by, say, only a national collection, formed over centuries, and the private collector will be counselled to select an artistic or historical period which appeals to him. Even within the major periods which are described below, a selected portion – one century or one state – will provide great variety and range.

GLOSSARY OF GENERAL TERMS

Cast: a piece produced by pouring molten metal into a previously modelled mould. The early Roman *aes grave*, many coins of the Greek 'imperial' period and medals of the fifteenth and sixteenth centuries were cast. In most other series the minute roughness of a cast surface is indicative of a forgery.

Die: the metal punch in which the design for a coin or medal is engraved in intaglio. From the die, placed on a piece of metal and struck, a coin is produced.

Edge: on medals of all periods, usually smooth. On coins up to the introduction of mechanical striking in the sixteenth to seventeenth centuries, also smooth; thereafter, milled or ribbed to prevent clipping. Some large coins have an inscription engraved on the edge.

Exergue: the portion of a coin or medal below the ground line of the design. Often contains specific information, such as mint-mark or date.

Fabric: the metal from which a coin is made, including the characteristic surface and appearance imparted by production.

Field: the flat portion of either side of a coin not occupied by the design.

Incuse: a design or mark sunk into a coin; the opposite of relief (q.v.).

Inscription: the words which often accompany a coin design. These usually run circularly round the coin but can occupy any position.

Legend: another term for inscription (q.v.).

Mint-mark: the mark, in the form of a small symbol, letter or series of letters, placed on a coin to indicate the place where it was struck.

Obverse: the principal side of a coin ('heads') on which the more important design appears. From Hellenistic times the obverse has usually been reserved for the ruler portrait.

Relief: the protrusion from the field of the design of a coin.

Reverse: the less important side of a coin ('tails').

Struck: the term applied to coins produced from dies (q.v.). The surface of a struck coin is characteristically smooth.

Type: the design, whether in relief or incuse, on either side of a coin or medal.

(*A*) GREEK COINS

The term Greek coins is loosely used to cover not only the coinage of Greece proper but of all the places in the Mediterranean basin to which Greek civilization spread, including with Egypt, the Near East and the Black Sea. Greek coinage is the earliest coinage of Western civilization, and its development from the seventh century B.C. till the extinction of its last remaining forms in the third century A.D. provides a continuous illustration of that civilization and art from which most subsequent European forms spring.

ARCHAIC (700–480 B.C.). The earliest coins in the seventh century in Asia Minor were simply pellets of electrum with, on one side, the badge of the city, guaranteeing the piece (Plate 109B). Croesus, king of Lydia, struck similar pieces in the sixth century, but in gold and silver, an example followed by the Persian kings with their silver shekels and gold darics (Plate 109A). In Greece proper the earliest coins, also with a badge on one side and a rough incuse square on the other, were struck at Aegina (Plate 109C). Other states, such as Corinth and Athens, quickly adopted the idea. Probably the earliest coinage with devices on both sides was developed at Athens in the sixth century (Plate 109E). The early coins of Magna Graecia were round and flat, and some cities, such as Metapontum, have a curious fabric with the same device on both sides, in relief on the obverse and incuse on the reverse (Plate 109D). The coinage of this period is somewhat angular and stiff in style, and the human eye, even when shown in profile, is drawn as if seen from the front.

CLASSICAL (480–336 B.C.). The features of this coinage are the delicate and detailed rendering of the subjects, particularly the human body and the high relief of the experiments in portraiture, including facing heads. In the Asian cities the incuse of the Archaic period remained popular, though later two-sided types appeared. In the fifth and fourth centuries in Greece proper the coinage of Corinth (Plate 109F), with its obverse type of Pegasus, rivalled that of Athens in its circulation. Mid-fourth century, however, saw in Greece the rise of Macedonia under Philip II to political hegemony, of which the symptom and instrument was the rich series of gold staters with head of Apollo and *biga* reverse (Plate 109I). This popular coinage was copied extensively in Europe, successively in the Danube basin, Gaul and Ancient Britain. In the West a magnificent series of coins issued from the cities of southern Italy and Sicily, particularly from Syracuse after the Athenian defeat (Plate 109G). Of equal quality are the coins of the Phœnician merchant city Carthage (Plate 109H).

HELLENISTIC (336–1 B.C.). The extension of Macedonian hegemony over most of the Greek world in the East by the conquests of Alexander the Great brought a reduction in independent coinages and the establishment of the first 'world' coinage with his series of gold staters and silver tetradrachms

(Plate 109J) issued at mints throughout his Empire. The kingdoms into which Alexander's empire split on his death lasted till the establishment of the Roman Empire in the last century of the era. The features of the coinage of these kingdoms is the development of true and expressive portraiture as in Bactria in North West India (Plate 109K) and the Seleucid kingdom (Plate 109L) and in Egypt under the Ptolemies though on much copper coinage the gods retained their place (Plate 109M). The silver *cistophoros* with its Bacchic *cista* and snakes types, beginning in the second century B.C., was the standard coinage of western Asia Minor into Roman times (Plate 109N).

IMPERIAL (A.D. 1–296). Under the Roman Empire, almost the only autonomous coinages of the Greek cities were in bronze. These and the 'imperial' issues with emperor portrait from Greek cities and colonies, though of comparatively poor workmanship, provide an interesting record of local cults, ancient works of art and architecture (Plate 110B). A continuous series of tetradrachms with an imperial portrait was issued from Alexandria in Egypt, but by the close of the third century A.D. the tetradrachm, shrunk and debased, is scarcely recognizable as the ultimate descendant of the great Greek series (Plate 110A).

GLOSSARY

Cistophoros: large silver coin, issued from *c.* 200 B.C. under the kings of Pergamum and in other cities of western Asia Minor and continuing under Roman proconsuls and emperors. Types, mystic Bacchic *cista* and entwined snakes.

Daric: gold coin of the Persian kings, with type of king shooting with bow – incuse reverse. Name derived from Persian king Darius.

Drachm: small silver coin struck by many cities and states. The didrachm, the double, is the commoner. Multiple of four, the tetradrachm, was the standard large silver coin, while the ten piece, the decadrachm, was issued only occasionally.

Electrum: natural mixture of gold and silver found locally in Asia Minor; the metal of the earliest coins.

Obol: generally small silver coin, one-sixth of a drachm. Various multiples also issued.

Stater: generically a piece of a given weight. Sometimes applied to the principal silver coin of each city but more commonly denotes a gold or electrum coin.

(*B*) ROMAN COINS

Roman coinage, beginning only in the third century B.C., combines a native Italian bronze coinage with a coinage of silver didrachms in the Greek style. This latter was replaced in the second century by the silver denarius, which, with a modified bronze series and an occasional issue in gold, provided the staple coinage throughout the Republic. The features of early Roman coinage are the absence of portraiture and the prolific variety of types alluding to events in Rome's history and legends and to the family history of the moneying magistrates. The Imperial coinage, instituted by Augustus at the end of the first century B.C., added a consistent gold coinage and a new series of bronzes. Portraiture, begun during the civil wars preceding the establishment of empire, is the prime feature throughout all Imperial coinage, while the reverses provide a commentary on events, actions and policies. Currency reforms in the third and fourth centuries A.D., though changing denominations, did not alter greatly the shape of the Roman coinage.

GLOSSARY

Aes: the term used for coinages in copper and bronze.

Aes Grave: the heavy cast bronze coinage of the Republic in the third century B.C. The unit was the As with its fractional parts.

Aes Signatum: the earliest Roman coinage. Large rectangular blocks of bronze, stamped with a design on either side.

Antoninianus: the double denarius, instituted by the emperor Caracalla in A.D. 215. The obverse bears an Imperial portrait wearing a radiate crown. The piece was originally issued in silver, but through successive debasements it became by mid-third century a copper piece with a surface wash of silver, and disappeared in Diocletian's reform of A.D. 296 (Plate 110J).

Argenteus: the larger silver coins issued from the reform of 296 throughout the fourth century.

As: the unit of the early Republican bronze coinage with, obverse, head of Janus and, reverse, the prow of a galley and sign of value (Plate 110D). After the reorganization of the coinage by the emperor Augustus in 27 B.C. the *as* was struck as a quarter of the large bronze sestertius. On the Imperial *as*, which continued to be struck till the late third century A.D., the types are, on obverse, the Imperial portrait and titles and, on reverse, a personification or scene (Plate 110K).

Aureus: the chief Roman gold coin. Little issued in the Republic except by the contenders for power in the civil wars at the end of the first century B.C. Under the emperors the aureus became a regular issue and was struck at varying standards till its replacement by a new piece in A.D. 312 (Plate 110H).

Contorniate: bronze pieces with a distinctive flattened edge issued in the fourth century A.D. Types are heroes of mythology, former great emperors and scenes alluding to sports. These were not coins but a kind of token used in connection with the public games.

Countermark: a symbol, letter or group of letters punched into the face of a coin to extend the validity of the coin in time or space. Commonly found on bronze coins of the early Empire.

Denarius: the standard silver coin of the Republic and early Empire, first introduced in 187 B.C. Types under the Republic: first, the helmeted head of Roma on obverse with mark of value X (ten asses) and Dioscuri on reverse; later, scenes alluding to the family history of the moneying magistrates appeared on the reverse (Plate 110E). In the first century B.C. both obverse and reverse have personal allusions (Plate 110F), but portraiture of living persons is not found till the issue of Julius Caesar in 44 B.C. Throughout the Empire the denarius had on obverse the portrait and title of the Emperor or one of his family and on reverse a personification with well-marked attributes as a pictorial shorthand for various qualities and acts of the Emperor (Plate 110G). The denarius was ousted by the antoninianus in mid-third century.

Didrachm: silver coin copying the standard and style of Greek silver coins. The earliest Roman silver coins, with their parts and occasional token bronzes, were issued from 269 to 187 B.C.

Dupondius: two as piece in *aes*. In the Empire it was in size and types similar to the *as* but was distinguished from it by the radiate crown worn by the emperor.

Follis: the large *aes* coin introduced by the reform of Diocletian in A.D. 296 (Plate 110M).

Medallion: large pieces of medallic type (in all three metals) issued by the emperors on special occasions. Many issues in gold and silver were, from their weight, intended to be multiples of the standard coins. The larger flan – a disc of metal before stamping – provided opportunity for more elaborate portraiture and types (Plate 110L).

Miliarense: silver coin equal to one-thousandth of the gold pound; introduced by Constantine the Great in the early fourth century.

Quadrans: quarter of the *as*. In the Republican *aes grave* types are head of Hercules on obverse and prow on reverse with mark of value • • • . The quadrans is found only occasionally as a small bronze coin in the early Empire.

Quadrigatus: the commonest of the Republican silver didrachms with types, young Janus head on obverse and, on reverse, Jupiter in a four-horse chariot (Plate 110C).

Quinarius: the half-denarius, a rare issue, both in the Republic and Empire. Types usually identical with the denarius. Early quinarii have mark of value V.

Semis: the half *as* piece of the Republican *aes grave* with prow reverse and obverse, laureate head of Saturn with mark of value S. In the late Empire the semis was the half solidus and of similar types.

Sestertius: in early Republic a small silver coin, the quarter of the denarius with identical types. In the Imperial coinage the sestertius was the major bronze piece, equal to four *asses*. The types after the first two emperors are, consistently, an Imperial portrait and titles on the obverse and a personification or scene on the reverse with the letters SC (Plate 110 I).

Siliqua: small silver coin of the fourth and early fifth centuries. Types, diademed imperial head on obverse and reverse commonly a seated figure of Roma.

Solidus: the lighter gold piece introduced by Constantine the Great about 312 A.D. Obverse type a diademed Imperial portrait. Reverse types limited to Victory types and a few personifications of Imperial qualities (Plate 110N).

Tremissis: small gold coin, equal to a third of the solidus and of similar types.

Triens: third of the Republican *as*. Obverse type, head of Minerva in crested helmet and mark of value • • • • .

Victoriate: early Republican silver coin, normally with head of Jupiter on obverse and Victory crowning a trophy on the reverse.

(*C*) BRITISH COINS

The Ancient Britons struck a coinage of gold staters, imitating the types of the stater of Philip II of Macedon, and later, in the first century A.D., produced some silver imitating Roman types. The first Anglo-Saxon coinage was of small silver sceattas with designs elaborated from late Roman coins, but in the eighth century the silver penny, parallel to the Continental denier, began to be struck. This denomination, acquiring in time a royal portrait type, persisted, with variations of design, as the standard coin till the fourteenth century, when the fourpenny piece, or groat, was added, together with a coinage in gold. With the Renaissance and prosperity under the Tudors, larger denominations of greater intricacy of design made their appearance in both gold and silver. The introduction of mechanical means of coin production after the Restoration brought a standardization of coin types and the discarding of unusual denominations, leaving the coinage in much the form which it retains today.

GLOSSARY

Angel: gold coin of value 6*s* 8*d*, introduced by Edward IV in 1465 with types of St Michael slaying dragon and ship bearing shield with cross above. The angel was struck up to the reign of Charles I (Plate 111 I).

Bawbee: billon coin issued in sixteenth and seventeenth centuries in Scotland with types of thistle and cross. Later, royal portrait on obverse (Plate 111J and L).

Bonnet-piece: Scottish gold coin of James V with profile portrait of king wearing bonnet and Scottish arms on reverse (Plate 111H).

Crown: (a) gold coin of value 5*s* struck in the reigns of Henry VIII and Edward VI with Tudor rose types, and in reigns of Edward VI, James I and Charles I with various portrait types; (b) large silver coin of same value first struck by Edward VI with equestrian portrait (Plate 111K). Continued in all subsequent reigns, usually with profile portrait.

Farthing: struck in silver commonly from time of Edward III in England and Alexander III in Scotland, with types similar to those of the penny. Farthing tokens in copper issued by James I and Charles I. Types with obverse portrait and Britannia reverse first struck in 1672.

Florin: gold coin of value 6*s* struck briefly in 1344 by Edward III with obverse type of king enthroned.

Groat: silver coin of value 4*d*. Issued commonly from Edward III to William IV with types similar to penny and, later, royal portrait and shield (Plate 111G). Scottish groat from time of David II.

Guinea: gold coin of varying value, finally settling at 21*s*. Issued from 1670 to 1813. Types, royal portrait obverse and heraldic design on reverse (Plate 111N). Multiples of five and two guineas and fractions also issued.

Halfpenny: silver coin with same types as penny, struck occasionally in the Saxon coinage and commonly in later Middle Ages. Copper halfpenny with royal portrait and Britannia reverse first issued in 1672 by Charles II.

Laurel: gold coin of 20*s*, issued by James I. So called from obverse portrait crowned, in the Roman manner, with a laurel wreath.

Lion (or St Andrew): Scottish gold coin issued from Robert III to Mary. Types, arms of Scotland and St Andrew on cross.

Maundy money: silver coins of 4*d*, 3*d*, 2*d* and 1*d* given by the sovereign as alms on Maundy Thursday. In the earlier reigns these were the ordinary current coins, but from George II were special issues with royal portrait obverse and plain figure giving value on reverse.

Noble: large gold coin first issued by Edward III in 1344 of value 6*s* 8*d* with obverse, king standing in ship and reverse an ornate cross (Plate IIIF). A Scottish noble appeared under David II.

Penny: the standard silver coin from eighth to fourteenth century. In the early Saxon kingdoms the obverse bore the king's name and the reverse that of the moneyer; types, usually, cross motif. An occasional portrait type was used for obverse and became common after the unification of the kingdom when the place of minting also appeared on the reverse (Plate IIIC). Types with variations of cross reverse continued under the Normans and Plantagenets (Plate IIID). Similar pennies were struck in Scotland and Ireland (Plate IIIE). The familiar types of copper penny were first issued in 1797 (Plate IIIM).

Rose-noble (or Ryal): large gold coin of value 10*s* issued by Edward IV in 1465 to replace the noble. Designs similar to those of noble but with rose on ship's side. This coin with variations in design was struck by the Tudor and Stuart monarchs.

Sceatta: small silver coin issued in seventh and eighth centuries with developments of types and designs copied from late Roman coins (Plate IIIB).

Shilling: silver coin first issued by Edward VI with types of profile portrait and shield on cross. With minor variations in design this remained a standard denomination.

Sovereign: large gold coin of value 20*s* introduced by Henry VII in 1489 with types of king enthroned and Tudor rose on shield. Continued under the Tudors with variations of portrait. The modern sovereign with reverse type of St George and the dragon was introduced in 1820.

Stater: gold coin of the Ancient Britons of first century B.C. imitating the stater of Philip II of Macedon. Of original types of laureate head of Apollo and horse-drawn chariot, little survived after successive copying across Europe except the wreath on obverse and disjointed horse on reverse (Plate IIIA).

Thrymsa: small gold coin struck in seventh and eighth centuries with types imitating the tremissis of the late Roman Empire, usually obverse portrait and cross motif reverse.

Unite: gold coin of value of 20*s* first struck by James I. So named from the allusion of the inscription to the Union of the Crowns. Types, a profile portrait and an heraldic design. Charles I also issued this denomination together with some triple unites struck at provincial mints during the Civil War.

(*D*) MEDIEVAL COINS
(Sixth—Fifteenth centuries)

Following the break-up of the western Roman Empire in the late fifth century, the Visigoths in Spain and the Merovingians in France produced a coinage of small gold, imitating the tremissis of the late Empire. Under the Carolingian Empire, covering a great part of Western Europe, a new coinage of silver deniers, rated at 240 to the pound, was established in the eighth century. This denier, under various names and with varying types, remained the standard coinage throughout Western Europe under the German Empire and in the great number of independent states and kingdoms which emerged through the centuries. In the early fourteenth century larger silver pieces, roughly equivalent to the groat in England, were added, while about the same time increasing trade and prosperity re-introduced coinages in gold.

The eastern Roman Empire which held precariously together till mid-fifteenth century continued the Roman coinage of gold *solidi* and bronze coins but little silver.

A new series of bronze coins was introduced in 492 and the dumpy *solidus* became thin and scyphate and from the eleventh century this, the *nomisma*, became the sole gold coinage. This Byzantine coinage influenced the shape of coinage in the Balkans and Eastern Europe and, till the eighth century, North Africa and much of Italy.

GLOSSARY

Ambrosino: (1) gold coin of Milan of thirteenth century with type of St Ambrosius; (2) silver coin of thirteenth to fifteenth centuries with types, cross and St Ambrosius.

Ange d'or: gold coin instituted by Philip IV of France in 1341 with types of St Michael and the dragon and an elaborate cross with four crowns. Imitated with variations in the Low Countries.

Aquilino: silver coin of *gros* class, struck in Tyrol and North Italy in thirteenth century with types of eagle and double cross.

Augustalis: gold coin of Frederick II of Sicily (*c.* 1231), with profile portrait type in Roman manner on obverse and eagle reverse (Plate 112 I).

Bezant: general name given to gold coins of the Byzantine Empire and their imitations (*see* Nomisma and Solidus).

Bolognino: silver coin originally issued by Bologna from twelfth century with types, Imperial title and word BONONI. Widely copied throughout Italy.

Botdrager: silver coin of double *gros* class in fourteenth century in Brabant and Flanders. Name derived from obverse type of helmeted lion, colloquially termed the 'pot-carrier' (Plate 112N).

Bracteate: thin silver coins with type in relief on one side and incuse on other, widely issued in Germany and Switzerland from twelfth to fourteenth centuries. Types, facing portraits, buildings, and heraldic devices (Plate 112D and F).

Carlino: gold and silver coins introduced by Charles II of Naples in 1287 with types of angel greeting the Virgin and shield reverse.

Chaise d'or: large gold coins issued in France in fourteenth century with type of king enthroned.

Denga: Russian silver coin issued from fourteenth century by Dukes of Moscow and Kiev. Often of irregular shape. Common type, figure on horseback.

Denier (denar, denaro, etc.): silver coin similar to English penny issued from time of Charlemagne (768–814) and copied all over Western Europe. Variety of types including the inscription type with monogram of Charlemagne (Plate 112A), ecclesiastical buildings, portraits, mint names (Plate 112C).

Ducat: the gold *zecchino* of Venice, struck from late thirteenth century with types of Christ in oval frame and kneeling Doge receiving standard from St Mark. Name derived from part of the Latin inscription (Plate 112K).

Florin: the *fiorino d'oro* struck in Florence from 1252, with types of St John the Baptist and reverse the lily, the arms of Florence (Plate 112J). The *fiorino d'argento* of same types also issued.

Genovino: gold coin issued in Genoa from thirteenth century with types of gateway and cross.

Gros (groot, groschen, grosso): silver multiples of the denier. Issued commonly throughout Western Europe from twelfth century onwards, with great variety of types. An example is the *gros tournois* of France, with representation of Tours and cross reverse (Plate 112G).

Guiennois: large gold coin of Edward III and the Black Prince, issued in their French possessions in Guienne. Types, prince in armour and elaborate cross reverse.

Hardi: gold coin of the Black Prince struck in the French possessions with types, half-length figure of prince and elaborate cross.

Matapan: silver coin of Venice issued from late twelfth century onwards with types similar to the ducat (q.v.).

Mouton: gold coin of France of fourteenth and fifteenth centuries with types of Lamb of God with cross and standard, and floreate cross reverse. Widely copied with variations of design in the Low Countries.

Nomisma: the gold coin of the later Byzantine Empire. Usually scyphate in form with types of the Emperor, Christ, the Virgin and saints (Plate 112L).

Nummus: generic term for coin but commonly applied to the multiple bronze coins of the Byzantine Empire with emperor's portrait and Greek numeral of value (Plate 112B).

Pavillon: gold coin issued by Philip VI of France (1328–50) with obverse type of king seated under canopy. Imitated by the Black Prince in his possessions in France (Plate 112M).

Real: silver coin of *gros* class, issued in Spain from fourteenth century onward, with types the crowned royal initial and arms of Castille and Leon (Plate 112H).

Rider (or rijder): gold coin also called the Phillipus, struck by Philip le Bon for Brabant in 1435 with obverse type of prince on horseback and reverse elaborate cross (Plate 112O).

Salute: gold coin of Charles VI of France (1380–1422) and Henry V and VI in the English possessions in France. Types as *carlino* (q.v.).

Solidus: gold coin of the Byzantine Empire with obverse type, usually the Imperial portrait (*see also* Nomisma).

Toison: gold coin of Philip le Beau (1496–1505), issued in Brabant with obverse type crowned shield with, below, insignia of Order of the Golden Fleece. Also a silver piece of similar types.

Tremissis: small gold coin, the third of the solidus. Widely copied throughout Western Europe from sixth to eighth centuries, particularly by the Merovingians in France. Favourite types, obverse portrait and cross reverse (Plate 112E).

Zecchino: *see* Ducat.

(*E*) MODERN COINS

The later fifteenth century, when the spread of the Renaissance in art and technique began to make its effect felt, marks the beginning of modern coinage. Increasing prosperity arising from the unification of petty states into sovereign powers and the growth of commerce, making necessary a wider range of coinage, coincided with the discovery of supplies of precious metals in the New World. Larger silver pieces, such as the franc in France, the teston in Italy and the Papal giulio were introduced, while Spain, with its control of American silver, issued her large 'pieces of eight'. In Bohemia the silver from the Joachimstal was issued as thalers, a denomination copied in many German states and the antecedent of the American dollar. Coinage in gold in a variety of denominations became more abundant, particularly in mercantile Western Europe. Demand for small change produced a coinage in copper or bronze somewhat later, while in Northern and Eastern Europe readily available supplies produced for a time a full value copper coinage, not merely tokens. By the seventeenth century mechanical production of coins had effected a standardization of design and denomination, and with the adoption of the decimal system in most of Europe and America in the late eighteenth and early nineteenth centuries, coinage settled down into its modern shape.

GLOSSARY

Albertin: gold coin named after its issuer, Albert, Archduke of Austria, governor of Spanish Netherlands (1598–1621). Types, busts of Albert and wife Elizabeth with reverse cross and date.

Baiocco: Papal copper coin of eighteenth and early nineteenth centuries. Usual types, Papal arms with reverse, word Baiocco.

Cent: copper coin of U.S.A., one hundredth part of a dollar. Various types of which the most famous is the Indian head.

Daalder: silver coin of the thaler class in the Low Countries. Most common type is a standing mailed figure holding shield and provincial arms.

Dobra: gold coin of Portugal of two, four and eight escudos struck by John V (1706–50). Types, royal portrait and Portuguese arms.

Dollar: large silver coin of U.S.A. issued from 1785. Name probably derived from thaler. Types, the head of Liberty and American eagle (Plate 113J).

Doubloon: more properly dublone, Spanish gold coin of two escudos. Introduced in later Middle Ages but struck in quantity from gold of the New World. Types, Spanish arms with value and arms of Leon and Castille. Multiples of four and eight escudos (Plate 113B).

Ducat: Venetian gold coin continued from Middle Ages. Name applied to many other similar gold coins throughout Western Europe with varying types. One of the most important was that of the Netherlands with types, mailed figure and inscription reverse (Plate 113D).

Escudo: Spanish gold coin originally with types of Spanish arms and cross; latterly from Charles III, royal portrait and Spanish arms. Multiples of two, four and eight.

Franc: French silver coin in sixteenth and early seventeenth centuries of testoon class with types, royal portrait and floreate cross. In 1795 established as the unit of the decimal system, and issued in one-, two- and five-franc pieces. Types, head of Liberty or royal portrait and reverse, value in laurel wreath.

Giulio: Papal silver coin of *gros* class, originally issued by Julius II (1503–13) but continued into later centuries. Types, portrait of Pope and reverse figure of saint (Plate 113C).

Guilder: silver coin of the United Provinces of the Netherlands in seventeenth and eighteenth centuries, with types, provincial arms and personification of the Netherlands with hat on spear. Multiples of one and a half, two and three.

Heller: from seventeenth to nineteenth centuries a copper coin of many German states, especially Cologne and Aachen. Multiples of two, four, eight and twelve, with variety of types (Plate 113G).

Kopek: in sixteenth century Russian silver coin with type of Tsar on horseback. In eighteenth century a value, not token, copper coin with types Imperial arms and monogram of ruler within wreath. Variety of multiples and divisions (Plate 113H).

Kreuzer: billon coin of sixteenth and seventeenth centuries and copper in eighteenth century in many German states. Name derived from its cross design. Multiples in silver in later eighteenth century in Austria, Hungary and German states.

Louis: French gold coin introduced by Louis XIV in 1640 with types, royal portrait and elaborate cross with *lis* in angles. Continued, with variations of type, up to the Republic (Plate 113A).

Onza: Spanish gold coin of eight escudos (q.v.) (Plate 113B).

Peso: Spanish silver coin of four or eight reales (piece of eight) struck from late fifteenth century. Types, originally Spanish arms with value VIII and arms of Castille and Leon. From Charles III royal portrait on one side. Pillars of Hercules type on peso struck in Latin American mints (Plate 113F).

Piece of eight: *see* Peso.

Pistole: Spanish gold coin, a double escudo (q.v.), introduced by Philip II. Type and standard copied in most West European states.

Plate money: large flat squares of copper with mark of value in each corner and centre, issued in Sweden in seventeenth and eighteenth centuries.

Rappen: small Swiss copper coin of late eighteenth and early nineteenth centuries with types of shield in wreath and value and date (Plate 113E).

Rouble: large Russian silver coin of thaler or crown class, issued from time of Peter the Great with types, Imperial portrait and Russian double-headed eagle.

Scudo: large silver coin in Italy, particularly in Papal states from sixteenth century onwards with types of ruler's portrait and various reverses – eagle on globe, shield, etc. Scudo d'oro with similar types.

Tari: silver coin, principally of Knights of St John in Malta. Multiples of eight, twelve, sixteen and thirty. Types, bust of Master of the Order with reverse, shield or St John's cross.

Thaler: large silver coin of crown class. Name derived from original coins struck from silver from Joachimstal in Bohemia in 1518. This quickly became the pattern for large silver coins throughout Western Europe and was struck in most countries under variety of names and with many types, latterly with rulers portrait obverse and armorial shield reverse (Plate 113 I).

(*F*) ORIENTAL COINS

In the Near and Middle East some series of Oriental coins preserve the characteristics of the Greek and Roman coinages with which they are contemporary. The Jewish coinage, under the Jewish rulers in the last two centuries B.C., under the procurators of the Roman Empire and during the two revolts against the Romans, normally eschewed portraiture but had types in Greek fashion with inscriptions in Hebrew. The coinage of the Parthians from third century B.C. to third century A.D. was a portrait coinage in the Hellenistic manner but with a distinctive Assyrian flavour. The features of the Sassanian coinage from third to seventh century A.D. are the portrait types with Pehlevi inscription and an invariable fire-altar reverse.

The rise of Islam in the seventh century and the subsequent extension of its power produced in the Near and Middle East, across North Africa and into Spain and into West and South-west Asia a coinage mainly of gold dinars and silver dirhems, uniform but for the titles of rulers, names of mints and religious formulae. Portraiture on Mohammedan coinage is rare and artistic effect lies in the calligraphic designs.

In India, on the other hand, the types of coinage are as numerous as the constituent states. An outstanding medieval series was that of the Gupta kings, a rich succession of gold coins with figure types, showing still some connection with the Graeco-Bactrian coins of the north-west. In the extensive series of the Mogul emperors, as well as the calligraphic patterns, common to all Mohammedan coins, there was a rich variety of representations on some of the gold coins. In medieval Ceylon, the designs on the coinage were a uniquely formal art style, of its own culture (Plate 114 I).

Coinage in China is said, traditionally, to date from the second millenium B.C. Early types were small scale reproductions in bronze of objects exchanged in barter – knives, spades, etc. From about the middle of the first millenium B.C. these pieces were inscribed. Although this type of coinage lasted down to the beginning of the Christian era, round money in bronze, with a square hole in the centre, and inscribed with characters, was in circulation several centuries before this. Apart from varying characters, Chinese coinage retained this form till comparatively recent times. The Japanese coinage is a derivative of the Chinese which it closely resembles apart from its distinctive characters. In the sixteenth century gold coins in the form of thin oval plates began to be issued and there were also small rectangular silver blocks.

GLOSSARY

Akce: Turkish silver coin issued between fourteenth and seventeenth centuries with inscription types on both sides.

Altun: Turkish gold coin introduced by Muhamad II in 1454. Obverse type, Sultan's name with mint and date; reverse, titles.

Anna: copper sub-division of the silver rupee in India. Types, badge of East India Company and balance.

Cash: generic term for many small Oriental copper coins, particularly Chinese (*see* Ch'ien).

Ch'ien: Chinese round copper coin, first introduced in twelfth century B.C. Earlier type up to sixth century B.C. has round hole in centre and characters indicating weight and source. Later types up to nineteenth century have square centre hole. Still later, characters indicating value were added (Plate 114K).

Dinar: Islamic gold coin. The earliest dinars in later seventh century were imitations of Byzantine solidi. From beginning of eighth century the dinar has Arabic inscription types on both sides giving mint, date and religious formulae. Later, ruler's name was added (Plate 114D).

Dinara: gold coin of the Kushan kings in North West India and later in fourth and fifth centuries of the Gupta kings in India. Types, commonly standing figure of the king and reverse, a seated god with inscriptions in Sanscrit (Plate 114F).

Dirhem: Islamic silver coins with types generally similar to those of dinar (Plate 114E).

Drachm: silver coin of the Parthian and Sassanian kings. Parthian types, bust of king with, reverse, seated figure and inscription in

Greek (Plate 114C). Sassanian types, bust of king with head-dress and, reverse, fire-altar (Plate 114B).

Fanam: small gold coin of southern India, Ceylon and Malabar coast, struck with great variety of types from tenth to eighteenth centuries. Silver fanams also issued from sixteenth century.

Fels: Islamic copper coin. Earliest were imitations of Byzantine pieces but from beginning of eighth century have types similar to those of dinar and dirhem.

Fuh: another name for early Chinese copper cash (q.v.)

Koban: thin, flat, oval gold coin of Japan issued from late sixteenth to early nineteenth centuries. Plain surfaces except for stamps indicating value, etc. (Plate 114N).

Larin: thin silver bars in shape of fish-hook, sometimes with stamp. Current in coastal districts from Persian Gulf to Ceylon in sixteenth and seventeenth centuries.

Mohur: gold coin of the Mogul emperors in India, introduced by Akbar in 1563 and issued into nineteenth century. Early examples were square but remainder round. Types, names of early Caliphs and, reverse, Emperor's name and titles with date and mint. Jehangir (1605–28) struck some portrait types and designs illustrating the signs of the Zodiac (Plate 114G).

Oban: multiple of ten of the Koban (q.v.) with similar types.

Pagoda: small gold coin issued in great number of states in South India from seventh to eighteenth centuries. Great variety of types, often representation of a god.

Pu: early Chinese bronze coin of the type imitating, in miniature, original objects of barter such as knives and spades. In circulation in last half of the first millenium B.C. (Plate 114M).

Punch-marked: flat, square silver coins of India of the last few centuries B.C. Surfaces covered with small punch marks of natural objects, animals and symbols, probably the marks of merchants and states guaranteeing the pieces.

Rupee: Indian silver coin, first commonly issued by Mogul emperor, Akbar (1556–1605) and continued to nineteenth century. Types as for Mohue (q.v.). Often square in shape (Plate 114H).

Sen: cast copper coin of Japan from eighth to tenth centuries, similar to Chinese cash. Issue resumed in sixteenth century.

Sequin: popular name, derived from Venetian zecchino (q.v.), for Turkish gold altun (Plate 114J).

Shekel: Jewish silver coin issued in the two revolts against the Romans in 132 B.C.–A.D. 5 and A.D. 66–70. Types, chalice, screen of Tabernacle, etc. (Plate 114A).

Shu: rectangular silver coin of Japan, issued from seventeenth to early nineteenth centuries. Types, normally Japanese characters indicating value (Plate 114L).

Tical: silver coin of Siam. Small silver bars bent inwards in bullet shape. Plain, except for punch-mark, usually on inside and outside of bend. Issued from fourteenth to nineteenth centuries.

(*G*) MEDALS

The art of the medal is patently related to that of coins but it is a special and comparatively modern development of certain features of coin art; for the medal is no older than the Renaissance of the fifteenth century. It is true that certain large Greek coins and, to an even greater extent, the Roman Imperial medallions have a medallic character but these pieces were primarily monetary whereas the medal is essentially an artistic commemoration in metal of persons and events.

FIFTEENTH CENTURY. In Italy, in the growing interest in the civilization and art of the ancient world, one feature in ancient coinage which obviously fascinated was the great series of Roman Imperial portraits, particularly those on the large bronze sesterii. From this and similar inspirations developed the school of Italian Renaissance medallists of whom the earliest, and possibly the greatest, was Pisanello (fl. 1452) (Plate 115A). The qualities of the art of this century are realism of portraiture and naturalism of design, a striking antithesis to medieval art. Of the very numerous artists of this period, mention can be made of only a few such as Matteo de Pasti, Sperandio and Niccolo Fiorentino.

SIXTEENTH CENTURY. Although by the end of the fifteenth century medallic art had spread to most countries in Western Europe, examples are rare outside Italy, but the sixteenth century saw the medal firmly established with a great variety of practitioners and styles. Already far removed from the style of Pisanello is the richly ornate English medal by Nicholas Hilliard on the defeat of the Armada in 1588 (Plate 115C). In Italy there was a more continuous development by such artists as Benvenuto Cellini (1500–71), Leone Leoni (1509–90) (Plate 115D) and Jacopo da Trezzo (fl. 1589). In France, where the qualities of sculptural art were being blended into the medal, two of the great masters were Germain Pilon (1539–90) and Guillaume Dupré (1574–1647) (Plate 116A). The peculiar quality of the German medal of this century, a certain rough strength, is due to the fact that the original models were carved in wood or stone, not modelled in wax as elsewhere. Prominent artists were Hans Schwarz (1493–1530), Hans Reinhardt (fl. 1535–49) and Cristopher Weiditz (1523–37), and a number of medals are regarded as being at least from the designs of Albert Dürer (Plate 115B).

SEVENTEENTH CENTURY. Much of the pristine freshness and vigour of medallic art disappears in this century with the establishment of a more formal 'classical' style. The exponents of this style were principally French, medallists such as Jean Varin (1604–42), Jean Mauger (1648–1722), and his pupil Jean Dassier (1676–1763), the last of whom produced numerous series of medals of famous characters in history. This style became international and varied only according to the quality of the individual artist. A particularly successful portrait modeller was Thomas Simon in England (Plate 115E), though only one of quite a school in this country. An unusual treatment of the portrait is that of the Dutch artist Jerian Pool (fl. 1653–67) in his three-quarter facing portrait of Admiral Tromp (Plate 116B). Typical of the long series of Papal medals is that of Urban VIII by Gaspare Mola (1580–1642) (Plate 115F).

EIGHTEENTH AND NINETEENTH CENTURIES. Medallic art in this period underwent a continuous decline in standard, although medals continued to enjoy a great vogue and to be produced by artists in all countries. The best of the medals, however, seldom achieve more than a high level of technical accomplishment, and the decline in standard was possibly hastened by the introduction of the reducing machine, so that the artist no longer worked his original model on the scale of the finished product. It may suffice for this period to cite a few typical medals, such as the extremely popular series struck in England in 1739 in honour of Admiral Vernon by a variety of artists (Plate 116C) or the Nelson medal of 1805 by Conrad Kuchler (Plate 116E). In France towards the end of the eighteenth century the Revolution injected some fresh life into the art, producing pieces such as those by Benjamin du Vivier (Plate 116D).

BOOKS FOR FURTHER READING

GREEK COINS

BARCLAY V. HEAD, *Historia Numorum: A Handbook of Greek Numismatics*, Oxford (1911).
CHARLES SELTMAN, *Greek Coins*, London (1933).

ROMAN COINS

HAROLD MATTINGLY, *Roman Coins*, London (1928).
HAROLD MATTINGLY, E. A. SYDENHAM, C. H. V. SUTHERLAND and R. A. G. CARSON (Editors), *Roman Imperial Coinage*, Vols. I–V and IX, London (1923–51).
E. A. SYDENHAM, *Coinage of the Roman Republic*, London (1952).

BRITISH COINS

G. C. BROOKE, *English Coins*, London (1950).
I. H. STEWART, *The Scottish Coinage*, London (1954).

MEDIEVAL AND MODERN COINS

A. ENGEL and R. SERRURE, *Traité de numismatique du moyen âge*, Paris (1891–1905).
A. ENGEL and R. SERRURE, *Traité de numismatique moderne et contemporaine*, Paris (1897–9).
W. C. HAZLITT, *The Coinage of the European Continent*, London (1893).

MEDALS

L. FORRER, *Biographical Dictionary of Medallists*, London (1902–30).

(The long series of British Museum Catalogues of Coins cover the following series: Greek, Roman, English, Byzantine and Oriental Coins; English Medals and Italian Renaissance Medals.)

DESCRIPTION OF PLATES

PLATE 109

GREEK COINS

(A) Persian daric, fifth century B.C.
(B) Electrum stater, Phocaea, *c.* 600 B.C.
(C) Didrachm, Aegina, sixth century B.C.
(D) Didrachm, Metapontum, *c.* 520 B.C.
(E) Tetradrachm, Athens, *c.* 510 B.C.
(F) Didrachm, Corinth, *c.* 430 B.C.
(G) Decadrachm, Syracuse, *c.* 400 B.C.
(H) Tetradrachm, Carthage, *c.* 380 B.C.
(I) Stater, Philip II of Macedon, 340 B.C.
(J) Tetradrachm, Alexander the Great, third century B.C.
(K) Tetradrachm, Eucratides, 160 B.C.
(L) Tetradrachm, Antiochus VII, 138 B.C.
(M) Bronze, Ptolemy X, 117–81 B.C.
(N) Cistophoros, Pergamon, 49 B.C.

PLATE 110

ROMAN COINS

(A) Alexandrain tetradrachm, Diocletian, A.D. 295.
(B) Bronze of Berytus, Elagabalus, A.D. 218–22.
(C) Quadrigatus didrachm, *c.* 200 B.C.
(D) As, *c.* 187 B.C.
(E) Denarius, moneyer Fostlus, 133–126 B.C.
(F) Denarius, Julius Caesar, *c.* 48 B.C.
(G) Denarius ('tribute penny'), Tiberius, A.D. 14–37.
(H) Aureus, Hadrian, A.D. 117–38.
(I) Sestertius, Nero, A.D. 54–68.
(J) Antoninianus, Elagabalus, A.D. 218–22.
(K) As, Severus Alexander, A.D. 222–35.
(L) Medallion, Probus, A.D. 276–82.
(M) Follis, Diocletian, A.D. 294–305.
(N) Solidus, Valentinian I, A.D. 364–75.

PLATE 111

BRITISH COINS

(A) Ancient British stater, first century B.C.
(B) Anglo-Saxon sceatta, seventh century.
(C) Penny, Aethelred II, 979–1016.
(D) Penny, Edward III, 1351–77.
(E) Irish penny, John, 1199–1216.
(F) Noble, Richard II, 1377–99.
(G) Groat, Henry VI, 1422–61.
(H) Bonnet-piece, James V, 1514–42.
(I) Angel, Edward IV, 1461–83.
(J & L) Bawbee, Charles II, 1678.
(K) Crown, Edward VI, 1547–53.
(M) Penny, George III, 1797.
(N) Spade guinea, George III, 1795.

PLATE 112

MEDIEVAL COINS

(A) Denier, Charlemagne, 768–814.
(B) Byzantine 40 nummi, Justinian I, 538.
(C) Denar, Otto III, 983–1002.
(D & F) German bracteate, twelfth century.
(E) Merovingian tremissis, seventh century.
(G) French gros tournois, Philip IV, 1285–1314.
(H) Spanish real, Pedro I, 1330–69.
(I) Augustalis, Frederick II, 1197–1220.
(J) Florentine florin, Pietro Adati, 1314.
(K) Venetian ducat, Doge Francesco Dandalo, 1328–39.
(L) Byzantine nomisma, Alexius I, 1081–1118.
(M) Anglo-Gallic pavillon d'or, Edward the Black Prince, 1362–72.
(N) Flemish botdrager, Louis de Male, 1346–84.
(O) Burgundian rider, Philip le Bon, 1419–67.

PLATE 113

MODERN COINS

(A) French louis d'or, Louis XIV, 1672.
(B) Spanish onza, Philip V, 1710.
(C) Papal giulio, Urban VIII, 1623–44.
(D) Netherlands ducat, 1726.
(E) Lucerne rappen, 1804.
(F) Spanish piece of eight, Philip III, 1620.
(G) Aachen 12-heller, 1765.
(H) Russian 5-kopeks, Catherine II, 1781.
(I) Austrian thaler, Ferdinand III, 1652.
(J) U.S.A. dollar, 1801.

PLATE 114

ORIENTAL COINS

(A) Jewish shekel, First Revolt, A.D. 66–70.
(B) Sassanian didrachm, Chusrau I, A.D. 531–79.
(C) Parthian drachm, Phraates IV, 38 B.C.–A.D. 3.
(D) Abbasid dinar, Haroun-al-Rashid, 786–809.
(E) Dirhem, Salah-ad-Din, 1171–93.
(F) Gupta dinara, Samadragupta I, A.D. 335–80.
(G) Mogul mohur, Jehangir, 1605–28.
(H) Mogul rupee, Akbar, 1536–1605.
(I) Singalese Bronze, Queen Lilavati, *c.* 1200
(J) Turkish sequin, Mahmud II, 1808–38.
(K) Chinese ch'ien, fourteenth century.
(L) Japanese, 2-shu, early nineteenth century.
(M) Chinese pu, *c.* 300 B.C.
(N) Japanese koban, early nineteenth century.

PLATE 115

MEDALS

(A) Leonelli d'Este, Pisanello, fl. 1452.
(B) Charles V, Albert Dürer (?), 1520.
(C) Armada medal, Nicholas Hilliard, 1588.
(D) Charles V and Philip II of Spain, Leone Leoni, 1509–90.
(E) Oliver Cromwell, Thomas Simon, 1623–35.
(F) Pope Urban VIII, Gaspare Mola, 1580–1642.

PLATE 116

MEDALS

(A) Henry IV of France, Guillaume Dupré, 1574–1647.
(B) Admiral Tromp, Jerian Pool, *c.* 1653.
(C) Admiral Vernon, Anon., 1739.
(D) Louis XVI, Benjamin du Vivier, 1789.
(E) Nelson, Conrad Kuchler, 1805.

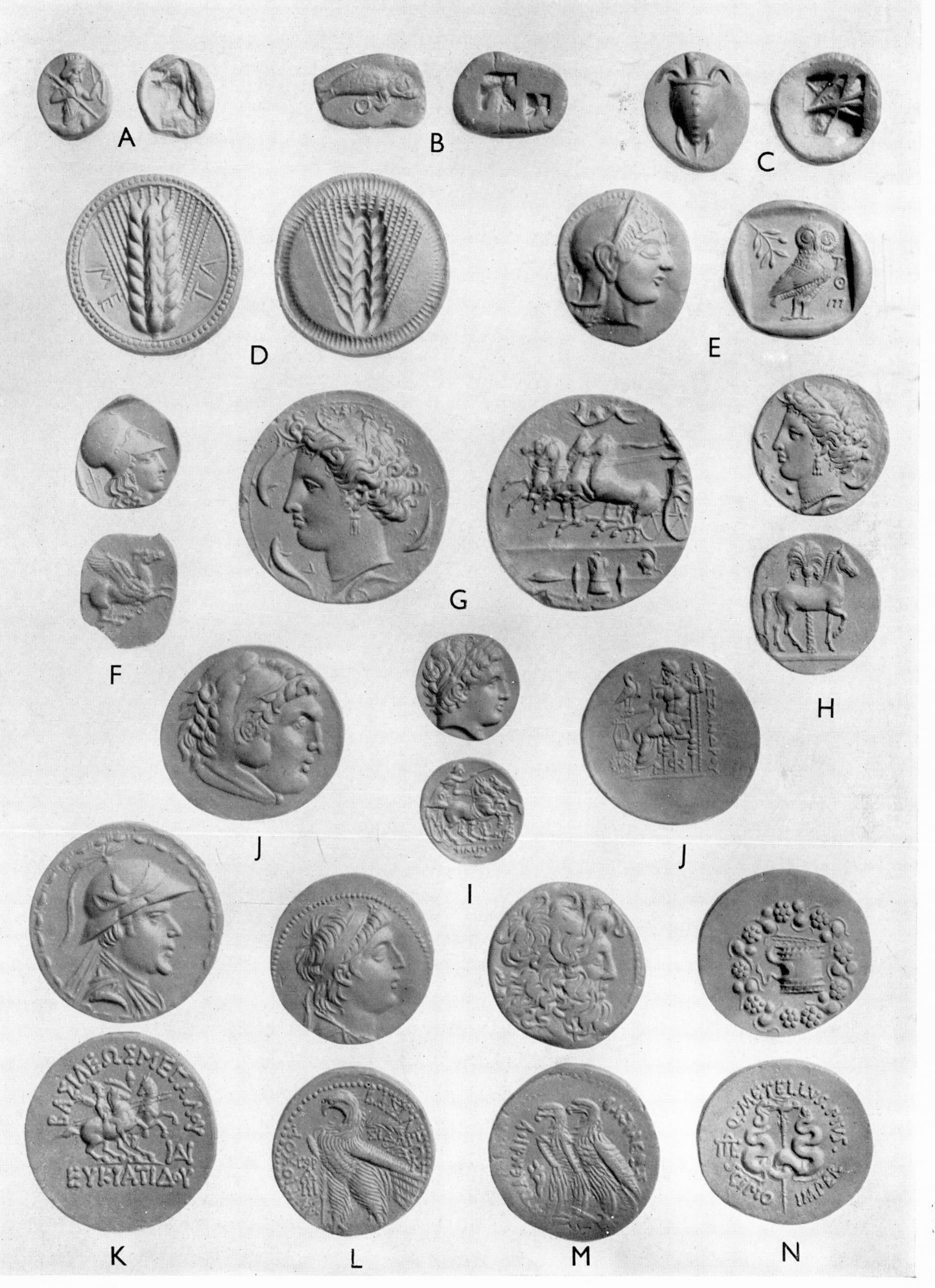

For a description of this plate, see page 184

PLATE 109

'ace page 184

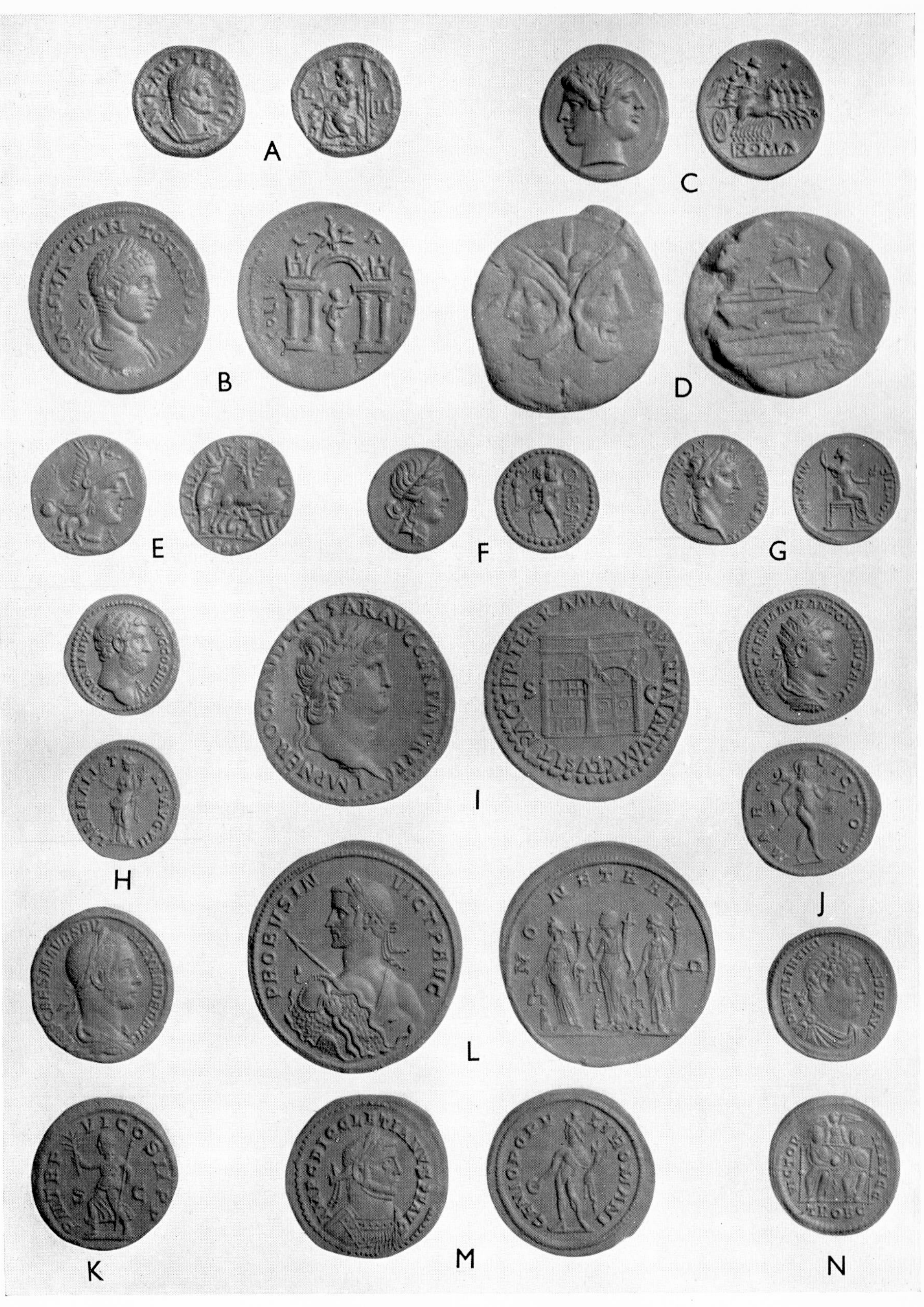

For a description of this plate, see page 184

PLATE 110

For a description of this plate, see page 184

PLATE III

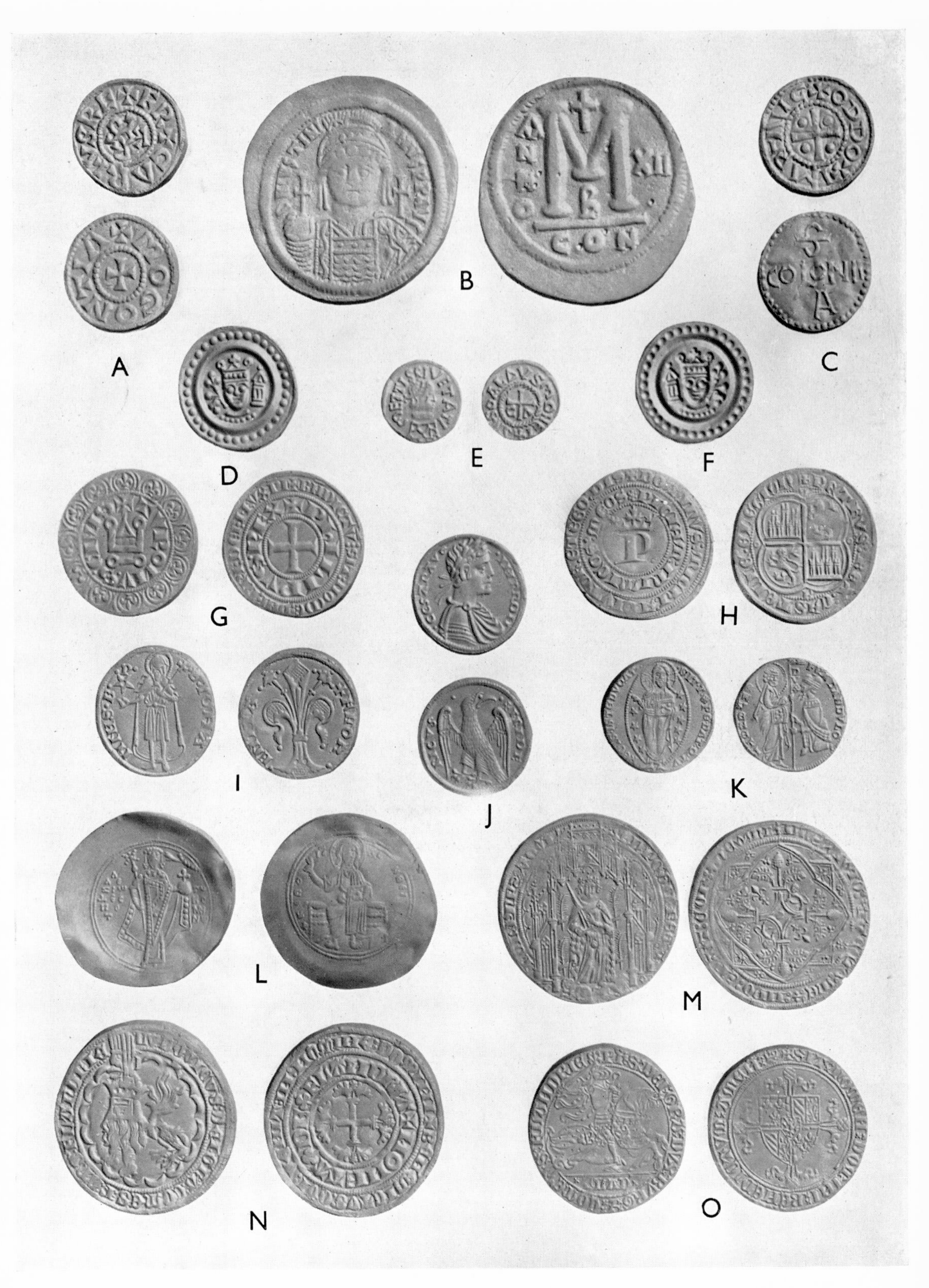

For a description of this plate, see page 184

PLATE 112

For a description of this plate, see page 184

PLATE 113

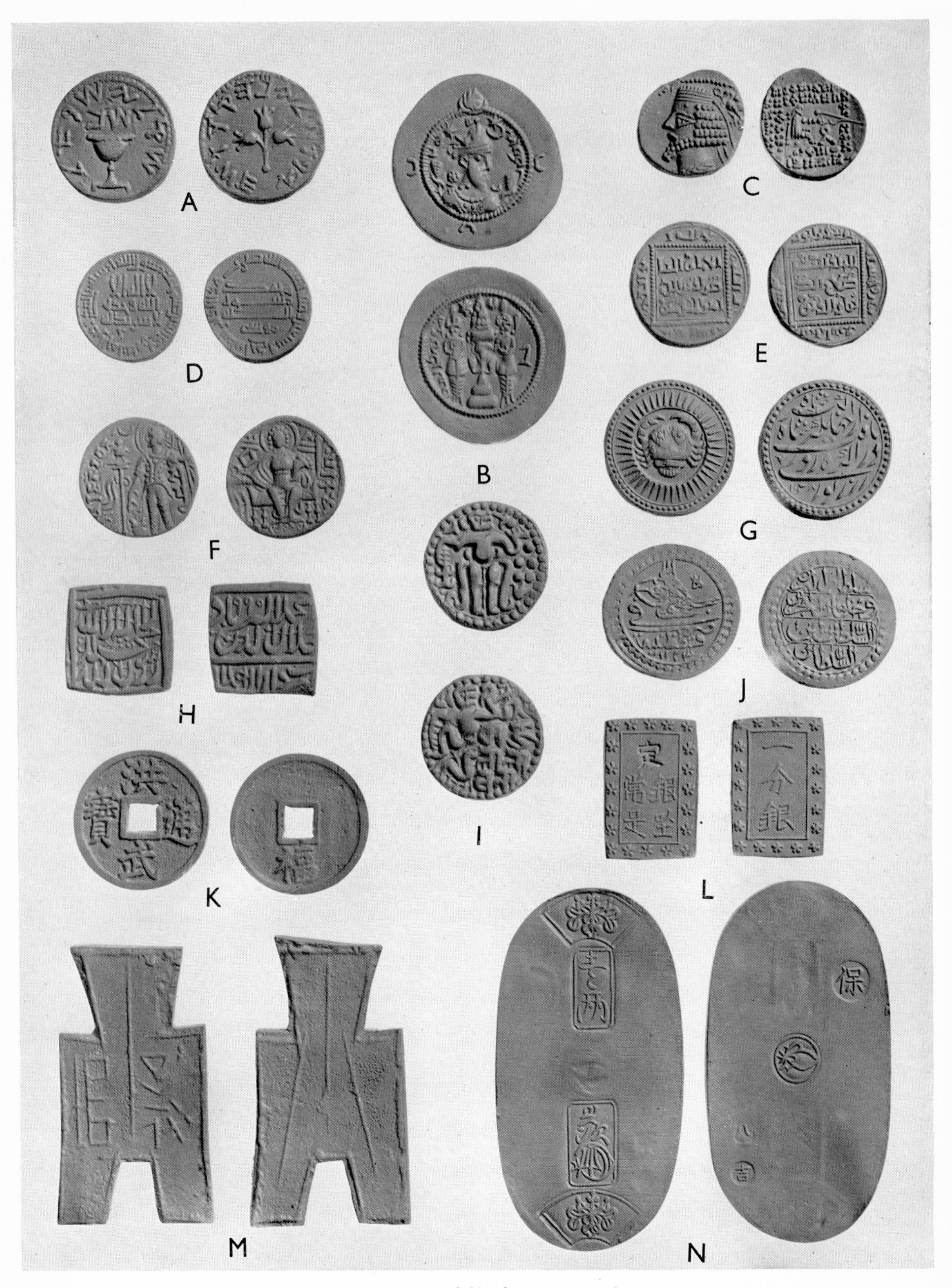

For a description of this plate, see page 184

PLATE 114

For a description of this plate, see page 184

PLATE 115

For a description of this plate, see page 184

PLATE 116

To face page

STAMPS AND THEIR FORGERIES

By ROBSON LOWE

THE forger and faker, and even the manufacturer, of bogus stamps has been in evidence ever since the earliest days of philately. Indeed, the faker came into being soon after the issue of the first adhesive postage stamp in 1840, his purpose being to defraud the Post Office Authorities. Sir Rowland Hill was considerably exercised as to the possibility of removing cancellations from stamps which had already performed their allotted function, and many experiments were made with the object of finding suitable inks of indelible quality, as well as safe methods of obliterating the labels, as they were officially termed. In addition, very careful research was carried out designed to defeat forgery – that is to say, the illegal reproduction of postage stamps for the purpose of fraud.

The collecting of stamps as a hobby certainly developed during the 'fifties' of the last century. The late W. S. Lincoln retained his earliest album, and in it was inscribed 'Collection of stamps made by W. Lincoln 1854'. By 1860 we have evidence of the spread of a more scientific style of collecting. In that year Dr. Viner took up the pursuit, and an active exchange of stamps used to take place in Birchin Lane, London, and in the gardens of the Tuileries in Paris. The formation of the Philatelic Society (now The Royal Philatelic Society) dates from 1869. It emerged from the meetings held at the Rectory of All Hallows, Staining, where the Rev. F. J. Stainforth gathered round him a number of serious collectors such as the late Judge Philbrick and Sir Daniel Cooper, Bt. It will be seen, therefore, that by the year 1860, if not even before then, there was an excellent potential market for the wares of the forger and the faker, and we find evidence of their activities in a book by the late E. L. Pemberton, *Forged Stamps and How to Detect Them*, published in 1863. He refers to a forger in Zürich who seems to have had an excellent business, since he possessed an agent in Basle. There was another in Brussels, and a third in Brunswick. Two years later J. M. Stourton listed and described 'nearly seven hundred forgeries, exclusive of essays and chemically changed stamps', and gave evidence of others engaged in the nefarious trade in Glasgow, Manchester, Newcastle and London, in Hamburg and New York. But the attitude of the collector in these early times towards forgeries, or, as some of their producers euphemistically termed them, 'facsimiles', was not that of the present-day philatelist.

It was argued then (and the same contention was used as late as 1913) that there was no harm in putting into a collection an imitation of a rare stamp the original of which, by reason of its high price, was unattainable. Many collectors frequently accepted that as a reasonable proposition, which accounts for the comparatively high proportion of forgeries, some quite obvious even to the inexperienced eye, which are to be found in old collections.

THE FORGER BEGINS

One of the earliest European firms manufacturing these 'facsimiles' was that of the Spiro brothers of Hamburg, who not only advertised their wares as genuine in a German philatelic paper of 1864 but the same year issued a wholesale list, being the second edition, for circulation amongst stamp-dealers.

In the *Stamp Collectors' Magazine* for October 1864 there is the statement 'they are made (and sold) by the thousands as facsimiles, and may be purchased as such from some few dealers, but usually as genuine, at the small charge of one penny; a guarantee, two pence extra'.

Another manufacturer of imitations was Samuel Allan Taylor, born in America in 1837 of Scottish parents. By the time he was twenty-eight he had settled in Boston, Mass., as a stamp-dealer. In 1864 he started publishing the *Stamp Collectors' Record*, the first stamp journal in America, and continued it until 1876, a very respectable life for a highly disreputable periodical. He received the nickname of 'Just-as-Good Taylor', by which he became known internationally from his regularly expressed dictum that for the purposes of the majority of collectors his forgeries were 'just as good' as the genuine stamp. He was quite open about his chosen profession, and in a letter quoted by the late Fred J. Melville in his *Lives of the Forgers*, Taylor says: 'In the early days all dealers sold imitations; some of them have changed their methods; I have not.'

The Stock Exchange Forgery

With the rapid increase in knowledge both of collectors and dealers, the producers of imitations had to improve their methods, and by the 'seventies' of the last century some really dangerous examples of their work were in circulation. What is known as the 'Stock Exchange Forgery' dates from 1872–3. In this case the forger made use of the fact that, for the convenience of members, it was possible to obtain at the Stock Exchange Telegraph Office a telegram form already stamped with a 1*s* adhesive. It was not until 1898, when the late Charles Nissen purchased a large number of the used forms, which had been stored and finally sent for destruction, that the fraud came to light. The design had been cleverly reproduced but, when the stamps had been soaked off the forms it became apparent that they had been printed on paper without the characteristic watermark which appeared on every genuine specimen. Who the perpetrator was of this fraud has never been ascertained, but it is certain that during the time in which it was being carried on (undoubtedly over twelve months) the Post Office was being defrauded of an average of about £50 a day.

Classification of Forgeries

It is clear, then, that forgeries fall into two groups: (*a*) those intended to defraud the Government, and (*b*) those designed to lighten the pocket of the unwary collector. The second variety may again be subdivided into: (i) those in which the whole stamp is forged; (ii) cases in which the stamp itself is genuine but some addition, such as an alteration in value or a change of purpose (e.g. the making of a stamp normally only used for revenue purposes into one valid for postal use) has been forged; (iii) genuine stamps which have been reperforated so as to produce a rare variety from a common one; (iv) forged cancellations, including the production of envelopes purporting to have been genuinely passed through the post; (v) the cleaning of used specimens by the removal of the cancellation and their sale as 'unused', in reality 'faking'; (vi) another product of the faker – the repairing of damaged stamps, including the mending of tears, the addition of margins and the filling up of holes or thin spots.

There is, in fact, no part of a stamp – paper, watermark, perforation, printed surface and cancellation – which has not received the attention of one or more of the practitioners in the art of producing objects which are not what they seem.

Detection of Forgeries

Strange as it may appear, it was owing to the forgers and fakers that modern philately developed out of the simple collection of stamps. As Sir John Wilson has pointed out in the introduction to his monumental Catalogue of the Royal Collection, in order to detect their forgeries it became necessary to study very closely all the minor differences to be found in the early and, in some cases, rather primitive labels which were issued by governments for the prepayment of postage. Thus arose what in modern parlance is called 'plating', a comparatively simple matter in the case of some of the cruder products of the engraver's art, as, for instance, the New South Wales 'Sydney Views', but requiring infinite patience, good eyesight and intimate knowledge of the technicalities involved when dealing with the skilfully produced work of such firms as Perkins, Bacon & Co., whose records have recently been published by the Royal Philatelic Society, London.

Plating consists of determining and recording all the minor and, in some cases, minute variations between the stamps in a complete sheet and their positions in relation to one another. If, for example, a stamp is printed from a plate containing a hundred 'subjects' then in theory, and usually in practice, it is possible to detect the small variations in the resultant sheet of one hundred specimens. Once these are recorded and available for the expert, the forger's productions lose a great part of their sting. A comparison between a doubtful stamp and the known details of a genuine example will speedily reveal whether or no the subject being examined is in fact the real Simon Pure.

A simple example will suffice to illustrate this point. The first issue of the Sudan consisted of current values of the stamps of Egypt overprinted with the name of the country in French and Arabic. The type from which the printing was done was set up in vertical strips of six, duplicated in sufficient numbers to cover the whole sheet. Each of these six 'types', as they are called, has been identified, and if a stamp under examination does not conform to one of them, then it is at once condemned as a forgery.

In order, then, to be able to detect forgeries and fakes the expert must in the first place be conversant with the appearance of the genuine stamp under examination. He must know the kind of paper employed in its manufacture, the watermark, the method of production, the means of separation, which may be rouletting (*see under* Colour Helps), or a variation of that process, or one of the many kinds of perforation, line, comb or harrow, to mention only three. He should also have some knowledge of the postal markings employed in the particular country at the time of issue of the specimen. For instance, if a stamp is presented cancelled with a type of obliteration which was not brought into use until many years after the issue had been discontinued, suspicions are immediately aroused. It may also be of assistance, in the case of a stamp used on an envelope, if the rates of postage are known and the usual routeing of a letter from, say, South America to England. This is particularly the case when the expertizing of a cover of the last half of the nineteenth century is required.

Generally speaking, there are three methods of production employed by the forgers. These are lithography, engraving and photography. Considering each in turn, the majority of the cruder reproductions have been lithographed. A few, notably those of the 1 rupee slate of the 1882–3 issue of India, were made by means of wood engraving.

The lithographic process produces a 'flat' effect. The lines of colour are neither indented into the paper, as so often happens in typography or engraving *en épargne*, nor are they raised so as to form tiny ridges, as in the case of recess-printing. If, then, a stamp which is known to have been produced by one of the methods of engraving has a flat, lifeless appearance, it is most probably a forgery.

A large proportion of the early album weeds were produced by this method. Many are so crude, that they announce their falseness at first glance. Such, for example, are the imitations of the first issue of Chile. The originals were printed by the firm of Perkins, Bacon & Co. Ltd., in London, experts in the production of delicate and brilliant work from steel plates engraved in recess. The lithographed forgeries resemble the genuine only in the general details of the design. Such, in the main, was the work of the Spiro brothers already mentioned. (*See* Plate 117.)

An English Rogue (*see* Plate 118)

With the 'eighties' of the last century there arose a much more dangerous type of forger and faker, unscrupulous rogues whose only desire was to filch money from the pockets of collectors. One of these, George Kirke

Jeffryes by name, started his career at the age of fifteen at his home in the East End of London. He had some skill as a printer and developed a talent for engraving. He also mastered to a considerable extent the intricacies of lithography. In the early days he devoted his attention mainly to the production of surcharges, that is to say, additions made to a genuine stamp with the object of altering the face value. His first efforts were directed to the South American Republics, for which he provided entirely non-existent varieties, such as a genuine ten centavos stamp of Colombia on which he printed DOS Y MEDIO in black.

In conjunction with this kind of business he also took to cleaning ink-marks off stamps which had been used for revenue purposes and providing them with imitation postal cancellations. Now the majority of collectors have little use for the fiscally or pen-cancelled specimen and, accordingly, they may be acquired very cheaply. The addition of a postal mark in many instances converts them into comparatively valuable additions to a collection. Jeffryes was a faker, and he still has many imitators. With the scientific equipment now available, such as the quartz lamp, it is always possible to detect such practices, even if very skilfully carried out; and the cruder attempts can usually be distinguished by examination under a magnifying glass.

Jeffryes joined forces with Alfred Benjamin and Julian Hippolite Sarpy, and together they formed a triumvirate which lasted until an appearance at the Old Bailey in 1892 put a temporary stop to their activities. But Jeffryes meanwhile was improving his technique as an engraver, and he produced some imitations of two of the early stamps of New South Wales, the so-called 'Sydney Views'. He and his colleagues did so well out of them that when Benjamin acquired a home in Kennington, he called it 'Sydney View Villa'.

A French Forger

The detection of engraved forgeries may involve a minute examination of a known original beside the doubtful copy, and a careful comparison of the two almost line for line. Some of the album weeds are extremely difficult to condemn, as, for example, many of those produced by an unscrupulous Frenchman of the name of François Fournier. He bought the business of a Swiss, Henri Goegg, trading as Louis Henri Mercier, who had already built up a substantial trade in forged stamps of Switzerland, and he extended it, issuing his own magazine, *Le Facsimile*, and his price-lists in large numbers. At his death it was found, to quote the late Fred J. Melville, that 'the Fournier Shop in Geneva was supporting a printing works that printed his price-lists and journals in large editions (the editions of *Le Facsimile* are given as 25,000), but the printery was equipped with almost every device for counterfeiting stamps'. These included presses for lithographic, copperplate, typographic and embossing processes, grilles for use on United States stamps, and tools for every style of perforation and roulette. These are now in the Geneva Museum of History and Art. (*See* Plate 117.)

One of the reasons why Fournier forgeries are so dangerous is that he was able to acquire some of the genuine watermarked paper used in the production of the genuine article. Thus he obtained a supply of the paper used for printing the 1860 issue of Tuscany. The watermark, which covered the sheet, consisted of interlaced lines and the inscription II E RR POSTE TOSCANE in outline capitals, diagonally from left to right, and Fournier produced his facsimile of the 3 lire, a £1,500 rarity in unused condition, on this paper.

Another skilful forger who calls for mention is Panelli. His work is particularly dangerous in the case of the more coarsely-engraved stamps, such as the 6*d* New South Wales issued for Registration purposes. He had a strong leaning towards the reproduction of the early issues of the Australian States, and, besides New South Wales, Queensland, Victoria, Western Australia and Tasmania all received attention from him. Canada, with its component parts of Nova Scotia, New Brunswick and Prince Edward Island, were also quite cleverly imitated by him, the last being an example of his lithographic work. As a rule he only employed engraving for making his reproductions, but some few specimens of his work are lithographed. (*See* Plate 118.)

An Expert in Imitation (*See* Plate 119)

Mention must be made of Jean de Sperati, now living in retirement in France. The whole of his stock of reproductions, together with his printing 'plates' and records, has recently been acquired by the British Philatelic Association, an organization designed to protect both dealer and collector.

Sperati was an artist in his craft. His early training and business connections enabled him to obtain supplies of paper, identical with, or closely similar to, that of the genuine stamps, and he perfected a method of reproducing, by means of photography, any of the rarities which he felt would repay his attention. Usually his reproductions were signed 'Jean de Sperati' on the reverse in soft pencil, but this could easily be removed by unscrupulous persons, and his imitations are so close to the authentic article, that they are dangerous to anyone who is not on his guard.

It is a remarkable fact that however carefully a reproduction is made it always falls short of the original in some respect. Even the photographic method adopted by Sperati, which might have been expected to yield an exact imitation, fails to do so, and for this reason, it is not humanly possible to imitate any engraving by a method other than that used in its original production. As soon as the distinctive characteristics of the various types of printing are known, careful comparison reveals the reproduction immediately, even though the actual lines are identical with those of the genuine print. To copy a stamp printed by the line-engraved, or 'recess', process by the same method is an impossibility. No human hand, or machine for that matter, can imitate exactly every minute dot and line of any large-size picture, let alone such a small one as a stamp.

In 1930, in order to commemorate the Europe–Pan-America flight of the Graf Zeppelin, the United States of America issued three Air Mail stamps. The highest value of the set, the $2.60 blue, has received the attention of the forger. Some of these counterfeits were sent from the Continent, where they were produced, to America, and there promptly confiscated by the U.S. Secret Service. The colour of the forgeries closely resembled that of the genuine stamp, but examination of the detail of the design reveals many points of difference.

Recourse must be had, therefore, to some other method of printing. And here again the would-be reproductionist fails. In order to understand the reason it is necessary to know something of the technicalities connected with the three main methods of printing already mentioned.

Printing Processes

In recess-printing, or line-engraving, the portions which are to be coloured in the print are cut into a copper, or more usually steel, plate. In printing from these the ink is forced into the lines and the surface cleaned. As a result, when a sheet of paper is laid on the plate and both are passed through the press, the ink is transferred to the paper in minute ridges. If the engraving is deep, these are perceptible to the eye under a magnifying-glass and often to the touch.

In surface printing, or typography, the uncoloured portions are cut away and the resultant plate shows all those parts, which will be coloured in the finished article, standing up from the metal. Prints from a plate of this variety frequently show some indentation of the paper, which may be discerned on the back. Furthermore, every genuine typographed stamp shows a small 'wave' of ink on one or more sides of the design because the pressure of the plate on the paper forces the ink towards the edges of every line.

Lithography is a process in which the sketch to be reproduced is drawn on a flat surface, usually stone or zinc, in greasy ink. The stone is then damped, and if an ink-roller is run over the surface the ink adheres to the greasy portions only, and consequently these alone are transferred to the paper during printing. It will be appreciated that this is the least difficult for the forger to imitate. The impression is 'flat', quite distinct from either of the other methods just described. But even here the nefarious artist has a difficulty to face.

In the building up of a lithographic printing plate it is usual to make a secondary stone by taking impressions from a single original, and arranging them side by side. From this secondary stone impressions are taken on suitable paper and transferred as often as necessary to build up the printing plate. Now every one of these secondary impressions differs in some respect from the original, and these details can be recorded. This is another form of 'plating' and, carried to its logical conclusion, it is possible to detect the variations in every stamp in the sheet. If a doubtful specimen does not show any of the characteristics known to exist in the sheet, or if it shows other variants, it is reasonably safe to condemn it as a forgery.

Other Clues

It is not practicable in the scope of this section to give details of the manufacture of paper. So many different varieties have been used in stamp production that this is a study in itself. But it may be said that those most commonly found are either 'wove' or 'laid'.

The former shows, on close examination under a strong magnifying-glass and by transmitted light, a fine mesh corresponding with that of the wire gauze used in its manufacture, and the fibres of the material employed in making it, be it silk or cotton rags or esparto or wood pulp, can be distinguished.

Now, unless the reproductionist has been able to secure a supply of the genuine paper used in the printing of the originals, which is not usually the case, it follows that a close examination of the paper on which the doubtful example is printed will generally give it away.

If the original is on paper watermarked with some device, this is another of the difficulties which the forger has to overcome. Watermarks, as a rule, are impressed into the paper during its manufacture while it is still in a soft state, with the result that there is a definite thinning at the point of impression. The finished sheet, if held up to a strong light, will show more or less distinctly the outline of the watermarked device.

Clearly a stamp which should show a watermark and which does not do so, is immediately suspect.

To overcome this difficulty, the maker of forgeries has adopted several expedients.

He may secure a common stamp with the desired watermark and chemically discharge the colour. He is then left with a tiny piece of genuine paper on which he impresses his reproduction. But the drastic treatment to which the paper has been submitted inevitably leaves traces behind, and the expert can distinguish such doctored examples.

Not all inks employed in stamp manufacture are capable of being removed, and it is therefore necessary for the forger to devise other means of solving the problem.

Attempts have been made to impress the watermark on the finished paper, but this does not give the same result as that made during manufacture. Another expedient is illustrated by the counterfeit of the New South Wales Registration stamp made by Panelli, and already mentioned. Both the original and its imitation were printed by the same process, namely, line-engraving; in the reproduction the correct watermark showed up very clearly when the stamp was laid face downwards on a dark surface. But, strangely enough, it did not show when examined by transmitted light. The reason was that the 'watermark' was not, in fact, any such thing. It was a 'paint' mark applied to the back of the stamp in a very faint tint. This method of producing the appearance of a watermark has been resorted to on a number of occasions. A very recent example is the St Lucia 4c. grey issued in 1949. The whole of the stamp, design, perforation and watermark is forged, but it was the unusually clear appearance of this last which led to the suspicion that something was wrong. Doubts being established, further examination showed the design had not the sharp definition of the original, and appeared to have been reproduced by some photographic process. The perforation, too, did not bear comparison with a genuine example.

Colour Helps

It is a well-known fact that it is very difficult to copy the precise shade and tone of a given mixture of ink, even though the exact proportions of each component colour are known. The forger then has to face an almost insoluble problem when he tries to produce the perfect imitation. But a variation in shade is not an infallible method of detecting a 'weed', since genuine stamps vary considerably, and allowance must be made for differences due to exposure to a strong light or climate influences. But, taken in conjunction with other tests, the colour of a doubtful specimen may be a deciding factor in determining whether or no it is a genuine original.

Mention has been made of methods of separation of one stamp from another. Within a few years of their introduction experiments were being made with the object of doing away with the scissors as a means of breaking up a sheet. Records show many ingenious inventions, but in general only two were found to be of practical application. These were rouletting and perforating. The former consists of a succession of short cuts in the gutter between the designs. These weaken the paper and so enable a single stamp to be removed as required. A better discovery was perforation. In this a number of pins are arranged with a bed-plate into which the pins fit exactly. These pins consequently punch out tiny bits of the paper, and thus provide the necessary means of separation. Philatelists have laid down as a standard the space of 2 cm., and they describe a given perforation according to the number of holes punched in this compass. If a specimen examined has not the same number of holes per 2 cm. as the original, it at once falls under suspicion.

There is a further guide. Perforations are divided into 'single line' and 'comb'. The machine in the first case perforates only a single row of stamps, either vertically or horizontally. It follows that it is extremely improbable that, at the point of intersection of two lines of perforation, the holes will exactly coincide.

The 'comb' machine, on the other hand, perforates the top and two sides of every stamp in a row. The sheet is moved and the next row is punched, and so on. In this case there is no point of intersection and, accordingly, the holes at the corners of the stamp are true.

A specimen which is known to have been perforated by a comb machine must be regarded as suspect if on examination it is clearly perforated 'single line'. (*See* Plate 122.)

There is a third type of machine known as the 'harrow', which perforates a whole sheet of stamps at one time. It has rarely been used in stamp production.

Cancellations

The type of cancellation in use at the time that a stamp was current must be known, also any others which were in use prior to its issue, in case a strange marking is due to the casual reintroduction of an old-type hand stamp. Cancellations themselves have been extensively forged, particularly in the case of those which indicate some special use. Thus, for example, certain of the South and Central American Republics had considerable correspondence with England prior to the introduction of their own stamps. Accordingly, the British Consulates in the principal towns were supplied with quantities of the current British stamps, and these were affixed to letters in the ordinary way, being cancelled with a distinctive mark. Many of these special marks are very rare and command high prices. Therefore, the forger has turned his attention to their reproduction, and by removing a pen cancellation (which is usually an indication of fiscal use and therefore renders the stamp of little value) and applying a fraudulent imitation of a genuine obliteration, he can enhance the value of his wares for the unsuspecting collector. (*See* Plate 122.)

The step from the forging of a single cancellation to the production of a completely forged cover or envelope is a short one and, as may be imagined, has been practised widely.

For a very brief period in March 1923 there was a shortage of 1*d* stamps in South Georgia, a dependency of the Falkland Islands. The Acting Magistrate there authorized the bisecting of the 2½*d* stamp, a single half having the franking power of 1*d*. As this provisional use was only authorized for a few days, it will be appreciated that examples of the half stamp genuinely used on original envelope with the 'South Georgia' cancellation, are extremely rare. This has offered the forger an excellent opportunity for lining his pockets, and he has provided some very dangerous imitations. However, as is always the case, he has been unable exactly to reproduce all the characteristics of the genuine cover, and expert examination can determine whether a given example has really emanated from Antarctic regions or has been no nearer its supposed place of origin than, say, London.

As another example of the care which must be taken in connection with rare covers, there is a very good imitation which came from the workshop of Jean de Sperati. The envelope carries two copies of the 1 franc of France, issued in 1849, in the rare orange-vermilion shade. Needless to say, they are imitations. The addressee resided in Erlengen, Bavaria, and the letter was apparently despatched from Orleans. All the postal markings which would normally be expected to appear on an envelope of this nature are there, the place of origin, the Receiving Office, a mark in manuscript and two hand-stamps. Each impression is in a different ink, as would naturally be the case. But there is one mistake which immediately draws attention to the fact that the cover is an imitation – namely, that the three impressions of the circular date-stamp of the place from which the letter is supposed to have originated, Orleans, are all identical, which is an impossible coincidence in real life. (*See* Plate 120.)

Surcharges and Overprints

One other type of forgery may be considered. To meet a sudden emergency stamps have had their face value altered by means of a surcharge, that is to say, by printing or writing a new value on the face.

In 1885 one of the innumerable shortages occurred in Ceylon, and several values, no longer required for use, were surcharged to reduce their value to five cents, so as to meet the local needs. More than one of these is valuable, and has received the attention of the imitator.

Now the obvious way of producing a forgery of this nature is to take an unsurcharged stamp and impress on it a reproduction of the genuine surcharge. The unfortunate thing is that, just as in the case of stamps printed by lithography, the type from which the genuine provisionals were made was set up in a certain way, and there are small variations in the letters which make it possible to assign any given specimen to one position or another in the setting. The forger overlooked this fact, and it is therefore comparatively easy to distinguish his wares from the original. He has even in some instances applied the surcharge to a used copy, and it is not difficult to see, on examination, that the cancellation is under the new value instead of being over it, as it should be. (*See* Plate 121.)

A far more dangerous imitation is known, however. In this the surcharge is perfectly genuine. It is the stamp itself that is not original. A comparatively common variety has been taken and the colour discharged by some means, leaving a blank piece of paper with the correct watermark and a genuine surcharge. On this paper has been printed, very ingeniously, a stamp of another value, so cleverly done that the result has every appearance of the surcharge being uppermost. It is a masterly production, but as the original stamp was printed by typography, it fails to answer the test given above.

An overprint is distinct from a surcharge; the latter alters the face value of a stamp, but the former makes it available for some purpose other than that originally intended. Thus, a stamp designed to collect revenue only can be made available for franking letters by the addition of the word 'Postage', or an issue of one country can be overprinted to make it available in another. (*See* Plate 121.)

Many British stamps have been so treated and used in Zululand, Niger Coast (at that time known as British Protectorate Oil Rivers), and at the present time Morocco Agencies, Tangier, Bahrain among others. In the case of Gibraltar, special printings were made of the stamps of Bermuda in different colours from those employed in the West Indian island, and the name of the Mediterranean Colony was overprinted in black. Dangerous imitations have been made of these. They all fail to answer the tests.

THE FAKER

The gentle art of faking is closely allied to that of forger. But instead of producing a whole stamp, the faker turns his attention to

SPIRO BROTHERS' FORGERIES

FOURNIER'S FORGERIES

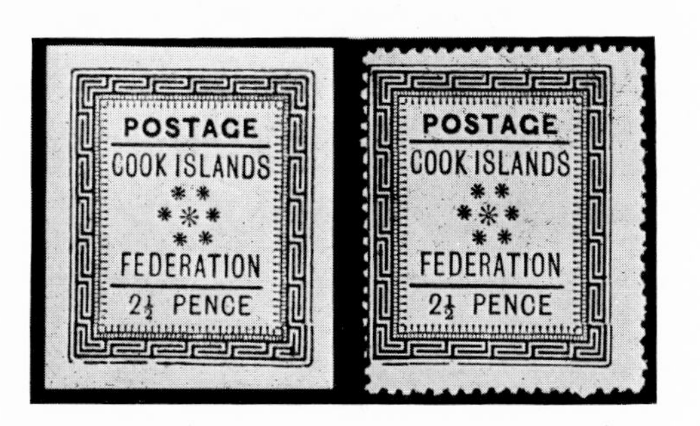

The genuine stamp is on the right and the forgery on the left, except in the case of the British Solomon Islands, where only the centre stamp is genuine.

PLATE 117

PANELLI'S FORGERIES

The three stamps at the top and the St Vincent 1*s* 0*d* on the left are forgeries; those below and on the right are genuine.

JEFFRYES' FORGERIES

The stamps on the left are forgeries; those on the right are genuine

SPERATI'S FORGERIES

All but the three Newfoundland are printed on genuine paper from which Sperati removed the impression of a genuine but common stamp and preserved the genuine cancellation.

Examples of Sperati's forgeries of the classic issues of European stamps of which he made many clever reproductions.

SPERATI'S FORGED COVERS

Everything about this letter sheet has been reproduced by Sperati. The stamps are the Swiss 1850 10 rappen with the cross framed. The value would be nearly £2,000 if genuine—Sperati's price was 18,000 French francs each.

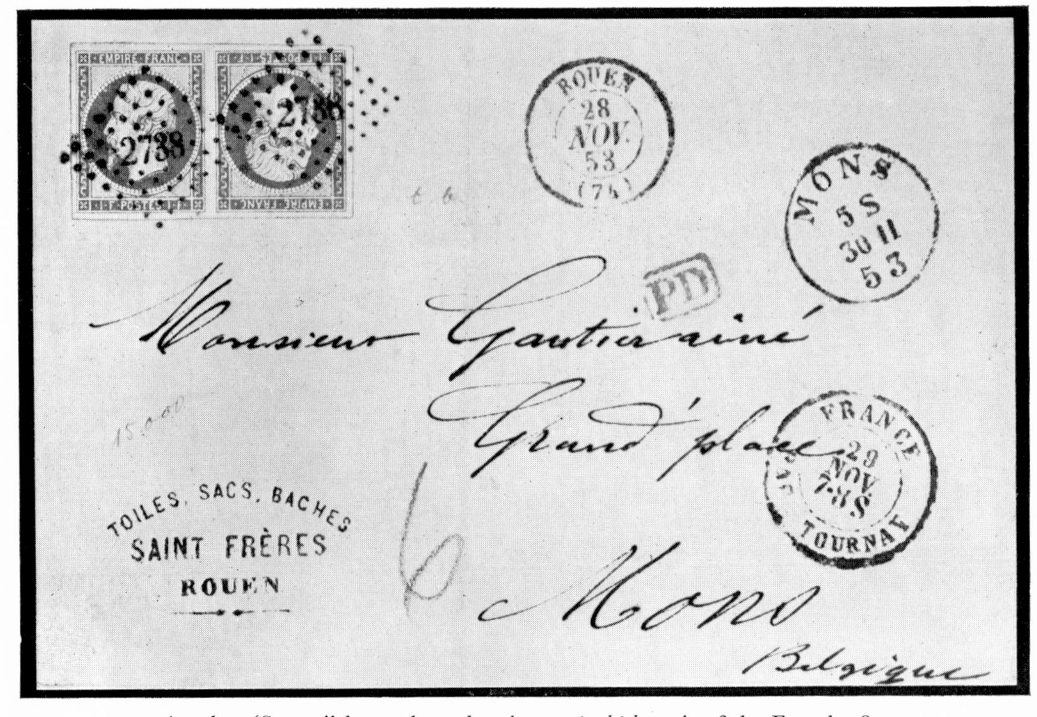

Another 'Sperati' letter sheet, bearing a *tête-bêche* pair of the French 1853 one franc. The wrong stamp is upside down. A £1,000 cover if genuine, Sperati's price was 15,000 French francs.

FORGED SURCHARGES

FORGED OVERPRINTS

In each pair, the stamp on the left is a forgery.

FORGED CANCELLATIONS

All the above have had manuscript cancellations removed and forged postal cancellations added.

FORGED PERFORATIONS

The Canadian and New Zealand stamps have all the perforations forged—the Rhodesian 4*d* has forged vertical perforations.

The Barbados 1*d* pair is common when imperforate, but rare when imperforate between the stamps. The U.S.A. 90 cents are comparatively common as imperforate proofs but rare when unused as issued.

PLATE 122

To face page 1

dealing with one or more parts of it. For instance, a genuine specimen may be torn, dirty, and have one or more thin spots due to the paper having been damaged. The problem is to restore this battered relic to something like its former self. The accumulated grime of years is first removed, possibly by the simple application of soap and water; then the tears are cleverly mended, pulp is spread carefully over the thin spots, and in due course there emerges what to the casual eye is a pleasant-looking example of a highly-priced rarity.

Or it may be that a specimen of the locally produced triangular Cape of Good Hope stamps, the so-called 'wood blocks', has been trimmed so close to the design that there is no margin left. The faker gets to work, and before long produces an immaculate example which would easily beguile a substantial sum from the pocket of the unwary collector.

A genuine example of a very rare stamp was sold in London at auction during 1954. This was the octagonal stamp of India, issued in 1854, with the peculiarity that the head of Queen Victoria, which occupies the centre, was upside down.

This and similar varieties naturally attract the attention of the fakers, who take a genuine normal stamp, carefully remove the centre panel, and replace it the wrong way up, covering the traces of their manipulations by various ingenious methods.

Yet another clever fake must be mentioned. The 1889 issue of Gibraltar shows a portrait of Queen Victoria with the name of the Colony in a tablet above and the value, also in a tablet, below. The value was inserted at a second operation, and by one of those mischances which occur from time to time sixty stamps in one sheet of 120 of the 10c. carmine were sent out to the colony with the bottom tablet blank. The error is a rarity and the faker has turned his attention to it. By taking a normal stamp and erasing the value by chemical means, very passable imitations have been produced. But the method used has its effect on the substance of the paper, and an expert can detect the fraud immediately.

Of recent years the quartz lamp has been extensively used in the detection of these fakes. Thus variation in the composition of the pulp and papers used to effect repairs, or to add margins to an otherwise worthless stamp, are immediately discovered.

Another variety which has received the attention of these manipulators is that known as *tête-bêche*. Good examples occur in the early issues of France which were produced from a plate made up of a number of loose *clichés* clamped together. If one of these is inadvertently inserted into its position upside down, the resulting print exhibits a pair of stamps inverted in relation to each other. This constitutes what is known as a '*tête-bêche* pair'.

Such varieties are mostly expensive additions to the collection, and naturally the faker has turned his attention to their production. By careful manipulation and the use of a very powerful adhesive and great pressure, he has been able to produce examples which have been known to deceive even experts for a time. However, the quartz lamp assists in the weeding out of such undesirables.

Yet a further form of faking results from an error on the part of the printers. A good example is the first twopence-halfpenny stamp of Great Britain. Issued in 1875, it bore in the corners a pair of letters, those in the bottom being the same as the upper pair but in reverse order. This lettering was introduced with our first adhesive as an additional means of checking attempts to defraud the Post Office. It so happened that in one of the printing plates of this 2½*d* value the twelfth and last stamp in the eighth horizontal row, which should have been lettered L-H, H-L, actually bore the letters L-H, F-L. Here was a heaven-sent opportunity for the faker, and he immediately produced the desired rarity from a specimen lettered L-F, F-L by the simple expedient of altering the F in the top right-hand corner.

The faker is ready to turn his hand, more or less successfully, to any trick. One of the easiest, from his point of view, is the tinting of paper. Certain British stamps were at one time printed on a bluish 'safety' paper, and some specimens of these command high prices; so they attract the attention of the nefarious brotherhood. A judicious application of the blue-bag produces a passable example of one of these rarities – passable, that is to say, to the inexperienced eye.

There is a very common stamp of France, a 1 centime, which was printed in black on blue paper of varying shade. One of these is, however, really rare, the paper being tinted Prussian blue. A surface wash of this colour can alter the value of a stamp from one penny to forty-five pounds, a not unremunerative morning's work. This fake is calculated to deceive the unwary collector.

Cleaning

The removal of pen or pencil cancellations from fiscally used specimens has already been mentioned in connection with the forging of postal cancellations, but the faker carries out the same operation, and after applying a wash of gum to the back, disposes of the result as an unused copy.

Collectors are ready to pay more for an unused stamp with gum, which is termed a 'mint' specimen, than for one which has had its adhesive properties negatived at some period of its existence. The faker is always ready to remedy the deficiency, but unfortunately, not being in possession of the original formula for the manufacture of the genuine gum, he is unable to reproduce it exactly, and his fraud can be detected by an expert.

In fact, the crooked manipulator is ready, and indeed eager, to turn his hand to anything which will lead to dishonest profit. He has been known to produce entirely fictitious stamps purporting to come from a real country, and even on occasion to invent a hitherto non-existent state and provide it with suitable postal labels. During the last few years a number of these have been put on the market, supposedly issued by the Government of 'Free Croatia' and other imaginary states. But the subject of 'Phantom Philately', as it is called, is outside the scope of this section.

It has been suggested that the attentions of the forger and faker must have had a bad reaction on philately in general. But this is far from being the case. On the contrary, the knowledge that he must be on his guard stimulates the collector, who looks upon forgery as a challenge, inducing careful study of known originals, so that he may be better equipped to counter attempts to foist on him imitations which, though clever, are comparatively worthless. It is true to say that the modern scientific study of stamps is largely the result of the attentions of the Panellis and Fourniers.

BOOKS FOR FURTHER READING

R. B. Earee, *Album Weeds*, 3rd ed., 2 vols. 1906 (a monumental record).

Fred J. Melville, *Phantom Philately*.

Fred J. Melville, *Chats on Postage Stamps*.

L. R. Ray and B. Rogers Tillstone, R.N. (Rtd.), *Background to Philately*.

J. L. Grumbridge, *Introduction to Stamps*.

Grateful acknowledgment is made to the British Philatelic Association for use of their reference material.

VICTORIANA

By HANDASYDE BUCHANAN and G. HEYWOOD HILL

VICTORIANA is one of a series of rather ugly words formed from another word with the suffix 'ana' – e.g. Americana, Londiniana, etc. – and is applied to the large body of interesting and collectable material about the Victorian Age: in particular, to anything peculiar to this age and no other. It is impossible to draw a hard and fast line about this, as all ages of taste overlap. But, broadly speaking, Dickens' books are hardly Victoriana, since Dickens was timeless, but a painting by Frith or the Albert Memorial are, since both could not have been created at any other time.

It is important to remember that the division in taste between what is Georgian and Regency and what is Victorian is not an arbitrary one. A fundamental change was taking place as Victoria came to the throne, and this change continued during a large part of her reign. The Industrial Revolution had created an immense amount of fresh wealth and an immense new class into whose pockets most of this wealth went. The industrial and manufacturing middle classes had more spending power than the old landed aristocracy. In addition to this, mass production by machinery was largely ousting the old craftsmanship by hand.

These two factors are vitally important when we look at Victorian taste as a whole; for, generally speaking, the country gentleman's mansion could accommodate large objects, books or otherwise. The urban or suburban business man's house could not. The former had a background fashioned by centuries. The latter had none. Hence, to take an example from books, Thornton's magnificent *Temple of Flora* and Repton's *Observations on Landscape Gardening* gave way to the more modest *Mrs Loudon's Annuals and Perennials* and Shirley Hibberd's *Rustic Adornments for Homes of Taste* (Plate 128); the reticent yet splendid bindings of Staggemeier and his colleagues to the more florid Gothic patterns of Wickwar, Hayday and others. And, perhaps, in every way embellishment and elaboration had become the criterion of the, by now, largely untrained taste; a taste which, however, as the Victorian Age went on, built itself up into a formidable and homogeneous unit and one, moreover, to which we are now increasingly inclined to pay respect.

Mr James Laver starts the introduction to his new book *Victorian Vista* (Hulton Press, 1954) as follows: 'Thirty years ago the Albert Memorial was only admired by the extremely naive and old-fashioned; today it is only admired by the extremely sophisticated and up to date. Thirty years ago the late Arnold Bennett was thought eccentric, and even a little perverse, to take an interest in papier mâché with scenes of Balmoral by moonlight in inlaid mother-of-pearl. Today tables and chairs of this kind command high prices in the sale-rooms, and are the prize pieces in cultivated living-rooms. It is, in a word, once more "done" to admire Victoriana. The slur of the old-fashioned is merging into the prestige of the antique.'

This judgment exactly hits the nail on the head. To us the Georgian and Regency periods have never been old-fashioned. Hence the emergence of the Victorian age has somewhat of the interest to the collector that the discovery of the prehistoric has to the archaeologist. Every schoolboy knows the antiques of the earlier time, but unearthing Victoriana still, especially in some of its lesser and fascinating sidelines, needs detective skill. For, despite the sale-room popularity to which Mr Laver so rightly refers, it is still possible to collect a very great deal of Victoriana very cheaply, so that collectors of moderate means can agreeably take part. Further, if the present trend of values continues, and it is highly likely that the fashion has only just started, it is almost certain that the intelligent collector will be able to see in a few years some considerable percentage of tax-free profit.

In the glossary which follows there has been an almost entire concentration on objects which are in some way printed, and therefore most of the individual articles will refer to Illustrated Books of all sorts, Fine Bindings, Prints and Lithographs, Children's Books, Panoramas, Peepshows, Games, Model Theatres, Christmas Cards and Valentines. It must be remembered, however, that the term Victoriana covers a very wide area, including bell-pulls, book-markers, needlework and bead pictures, musical-boxes, sand-toys, and many other items.

For further study of the Victorian outlook on the arts in general see John Steegmann: *Consort of Taste*, 1830–70 (Sidgwick & Jackson, 1950); also the reprint in *The Listener*, 11th September 1952, of a radio talk by Peter Floud on 'The Decorative Arts under Queen Victoria'. Mr Floud dislikes the taste of 1830–60, but praises that of 1860–80. He thinks that the *Illustrated Great Exhibition Catalogue*, which portrayed so many great designs, did much to obscure the work of the finer Victorian designers, and singles out Dr Charles Eastlake, author of *Hints on Household Taste*, and especially Owen Jones (whom see later), as powerful and beneficient influences.

GLOSSARY

Adhesive bindings: many illustrated books and, in particular, illuminated books of the 40's, 50's and 60's were composed of leaves of thick cardboard. These were very difficult to bind, since the weight of the cardboard tended to tear the stitches out. Hancock patented a process first used in 1839 for sticking the leaves to the spine of the binding case by a solution of caoutchouc. This solution was temporarily very popular, and many illustrated books, even when ordinary paper was used, were so secured. But the solution was perishable, and so a very large number of the books, and particularly the larger books of this period, fall to pieces when they are opened. The remedies are: (1) to have the leaves stuck in again, when, after another period, the process will repeat itself; (2) to have the rear edges of the leaves shaved and mounted on guards, since if this were not done the stitches would burst the binding, and then sew them in in the usual way. This is expensive. For books of no great value, therefore, the only practicable course is to allow the leaves to remain loose.

Annuals, Drawing-room scrapbooks, Keepsakes, etc. Annuals of all kinds are timeless, but the particular type of annual which developed into a book to leave on the drawing-room table has its origin in the period just before Victoria. In 1825 the first annual in this sense appeared in England, a volume bound in watered silk with contributions by well-known authors and illustrated by leading artists. Charles Heath produced, in 1832, as an Annual *The Drawing Room Scrap Book* and the *Book of Beauty* a year later. With Lady Blessington as editress until 1849, the *Book of Beauty* was a great success, and she also edited the *Keepsake* from 1841 till 1850 and contributed to other similar works. Many other books, though not annuals, made their appearance with a view to being glanced at in the drawing-room, such as Andrews's *Flower Book Gems for the Drawing Room*, Paul Jerrard's books, e.g. *The Floral Offering*, and Miss Giraud's *Flowers of Shakespeare*, *of Milton*, *and of Scott*. They represent a particular side of Victorian taste, and are not to be found at any other time (*see* Plate 129).

Aquatint: aquatint is the name of a process by which the plates, from which many coloured prints were produced, came into being. It is an indirect method in that, unlike the etching, where the engraving tool scratches the lines directly on to the plate, an upper surface formed of resin or other substance is placed over the plate, and this is worked on, leaving room for acid to come down on to the plate and eat its way in, thus producing the desired effect. Aquatint is therefore not a line process but one which produces a more general effect on the plate, and is softer than a line engraving. The aquatint flourished before the Victorian age, e.g. Ackermann's *Microcosm of London*, Dr Thornton's *Temple of Flora 1867*, and thousands of other examples, both as separate prints and in books. None the less, a number of aquatints appeared after 1837, notably the sporting prints of Herring and Dean Wolstenholme Junior (*see* Sporting prints), and therefore the definition must appear in this glossary. (*See* S. Prideaux, *Aquatint Engraving*, 1909.)

Baxter licensees: George Baxter (*see* Baxter Process below) granted licences to work his process of colour printing to a number of firms between 1849 and 1854, when the patent expired. The firms were all known as Baxter Licensees, and this name seems to have clung to them even after the expiry of the patent. The licensees were Le Blond & Co., J. M. Kronheim, Bradshaw and Blacklock, William Dickens, Joseph Mansell, Myers & Co. The work of all these firms, both in the form of individual prints and in books, has been collected by many. The best-known series, at one time eagerly sought after, were the Le Blond ovals, country scenes, whose shape, of course, gives them the name.

See Courtney Lewis, *The Story of Picture Printing in England during the Nineteenth Century* (Sampson Low, n.d. 1900), where a complete account is given of all the Baxter Licensees.

Baxter process: a process of printing in colours patented by George Baxter (1804–67) in 1835 and used by him with considerable success for a number of years. The method is very simply as follows: an uncoloured impression was taken from a key block and the colour was added by successive impressions from wood blocks, one block for each colour, using oil inks. The process was known as Oil Colour Picture Printing, but the oil is a reference to the inks and does not imply that Baxter prints are like paintings in oils. Many hundreds of Baxter prints appeared up to 1860, in particular in the early fifties. The first use of Baxter's work was in Mudie's *Feathered Tribes of the British Isles 1834*; the first complete book of Baxter's was *The Pictorial Album or Cabinet of Paintings 1837*. Baxter prints cover almost every possible subject, including some interesting illustrations of the Great Exhibition. They are of all sizes, from folio down to that of a postage stamp. No prints have been more collected; although the heyday of Baxter collecting has, at present, been passed.

For a full description of the Baxter process and the prints see Courtney Lewis (above); also R. M. Burch, *Colour Printing and Colour Printers* (Pitman, 1910); and Basil Gray, *The English Print* (Black, 1937) (*see also* Baxter licensees above) (*see* Plate 137A).

Binder's ticket: it is always more interesting to know who bound a fine binding, and most binders who were real craftsmen liked to proclaim their work. This was done in two ways: either by sticking a gummed ticket made of paper, though occasionally of leather, with the name and address or, at least, the home town of the binder in a suitable position, usually at the top of the front inside cover or at the bottom of the back inside cover, though sometimes in other places; or else by printing this information in small letters somewhere on the actual binding, at the bottom of the spine (though this is more a French than an English custom), but more often either on the small strip of leather at the top or bottom of front or back inside cover. The former is called a binder's ticket, the latter a signed binding. In Victorian times a binder's ticket is quite often to be found inside cloth as well as leather bindings, and since there were many more individual binders then than now, an interesting collection covering the most unlikely towns as well as better-known places can be formed; and for, at present, a very small outlay. The signed binding is always leather. Note that many booksellers also put their tickets inside books. These have no significance for the collector (*see* Plate 125).

Bindings: book bindings have always been a field for the collector, and Victorian bindings present him with a very wide choice. Books were bound in all forms of leather, calf, roan, morocco and the like, many with very intricate tooling, since floridness was perhaps a Victorian vice; also fine bindings of a Gothic type, enclosing perhaps a book by Pugin. Some books were bound in papier mâché, some in watered silk or other fabrics, some in wood, many in cloth with elaborate ornament (*see* Plates 125 and 135).

Birdbooks: books illustrated with coloured plates of birds are a most important feature of the Victorian Age, since, unlike flower books, they in many ways reached their peak during this time. This was partially due to scientific expeditions to hitherto out-of-the-way parts of the world, which discovered thousands of unknown birds to be illustrated; due also to the possibilities of reproducing them easily and not too expensively in lithography or chromolithography; but most of all to one man, John Gould (1804–81), who produced between 1832 and 1880 the largest body of pictures of birds of all sorts, from British to Australian, ever done, even up till now. Magnificently lithographed and printed, his plates remain as perhaps the greatest of all achievements in the way of illustrated books. Collectors of his works should remember, however, that Gould, like Dickens, was immensely popular in his lifetime, and that, therefore, his books, though valuable, are not, and especially in the case of his British birds, rare. A few copies coming on the market at once will sharply lower prices. On the other hand, since they are regularly torn to pieces for their individual pictures, the books are bound in the end to appreciate. Edward Lear (q.v.) helped Gould in some of his books. See *Fine Bird Books* by S. Sitwell, H. Buchanan and J. Fisher (Collins, 1953).

Bookcloth: before 1825 ordinary books were issued bound in boards, with often a paper label on the spine. In this year, however, Archibald Leighton of London introduced bookcloth, a cotton material to which gum or paste could be applied without harming it. And by 1837 the majority of books published appeared in cloth with the title and embellishments blocked in gold or other colour on to the cloth instead of being printed on to paper labels as before. The changes in publishers' binding styles with elaboration of design forms a fascinating subject for the collector of Victoriana. See Michael Sadleir, *The Evolution of Publishers' Binding Styles 1770–1900* (pub. 1930), and John Carter, *Binding Variants 1820–1900* (pub. 1932).

Children's books: a short account of children's books, even when limited to those published between 1837 and 1901, is almost impossible. The only solution is to indicate to the collector the scope of the field, to try to divide it so that he is not overwhelmed, and to give lists which will assist him as a framework. Best of all is to tell him where to look for fuller help: so we begin with two or three invaluable publications about Children's Books. First, *Children's Books in England*, by J. F. Harvey Darton (Cambridge, 1932). This book makes fascinating reading, but it is rather diffuse, and hence it is very difficult to find the facts that a collector will want most of all to know. So from his point of view there is a much more desirable book, a treasure-house of information very easily gleaned: *English Children's Books 1600 to 1900*, by Percy Muir (Batsford, 1954). No work of this kind can be absolutely complete, but it will be very difficult for the next historian of Children's Books to outdo Mr Muir. Finally, there is a very useful little book which covers only a section of the Victorian field: *Tellers of Tales*, by R. Lancelyn Green (Ward, 1946). This, in addition to other information, gives valuable lists of all published works of the authors treated, e.g. Mrs Molesworth.

Victorian Children's Books can be divided very roughly into two classes: the children's novel, whose immediate ancestors were the books written by Miss Edgeworth and Mrs Sherwood, and whose successors are the works of Arthur Ransome, of Violet Needham, and many many others. This type of book certainly burst right into flower during the period and produced a very fine blooming, both in quality and quantity, as the short list which follows will show. The second class consists of books whose importance lies in the illustrations and, while the picture-book had flourished in enormous numbers before, the Victorian book, by reason of the immense changes in methods of reproduction, can once again be considered independently. Also, looking at the connection between them and later illustrated books, the Victorians have the advantage that they possessed a greater degree of individuality, since the modern processes tend perhaps to standardize the picture-book.

Before giving general lists, mention must be made of the two outstanding figures as regards the Victorian children's book, Edward Lear and Lewis Carroll. Lear is a very considerable Victorian figure, and his works are so varied that they can form a collection on their own (*see* Lear, Edward, below). But the *Book of Nonsense* is perhaps the most famous of all children's books, with *Alice* as its only rival. Lear did not invent the limerick but his approach to Nonsense in general is unequalled. His children's books are: *A Book of Nonsense* (1846, enlarged editions 1861 and 1863); *Nonsense Songs, Botany and Alphabets* (1871); *More Nonsense Pictures, Rhymes, etc.* (1872); *Laughable Lyrics* (1877).

Lewis Carroll (real name Charles Lutwidge Dodgson) also wrote a number of books not for children. But they are all highly specialized, since he was a mathematics don at Oxford. *Alice in Wonderland*, his first important child's book, is also, in its true first edition, one of the most valuable of all books, since Carroll objected to the quality of the printing of the illustrations, and only a minute number of copies exist. Both *Alice in Wonderland* and the sequel, *Through the Looking Glass*, owe much to Tenniel's pictures. Carroll's most important children's books are: *Alice's Adventures in Wonderland* (1865–6); *Through the Looking Glass* (1872); *The Hunting of the Snark* (1876); *Sylvie and Bruno* (1889); *Sylvie and Bruno Concluded* (1893).

The first two only were illustrated by Tenniel. Holliday did the pictures for the *Snark* and Harry Furniss those for the *Sylvie and Bruno* books.

Children's books are, perhaps more than any other collectors' items, inclined to be in very bad condition. It must be pointed out that if a collection is being made with any thought of financial appreciation, only fine copies should be bought, however cheap inferior specimens appear to be.

Selected List of Authors of Victorian Children's Fiction, with representative book by each and the date of its publication.

Catherine Sinclair, *Holiday House* (1839); Harriet Martineau, *The Playfellow* (1841) (contains *Feats on the Fiord*); Captain Marryat, *Children of the New Forest* (1847) (most of Marryat's work was written for adults, e.g. *Peter Simple* or *Midshipman Easy*, but is enjoyed by many children); John Ruskin, *The King of the Golden River* (1851); W. H. Kingston, *The Three Midshipmen* (1862); Charlotte M. Yonge, *The Heir of Redcliffe* (1853). (Most of Miss Yonge's books were not written for children. It is not generally known that she wrote the text for *The Instructive Picture Book*, published in Edinburgh 1857, with charming coloured lithographs of flowers, fruit and vegetables, etc.); A.L.O.E. (short for 'A Lady of England', real name Charlotte Maria Tucker), *The Crown of Success*; W. M. Thackeray, *The Rose and the Ring* (1855); Charles Kingsley, *The Water Babies* (1863); Frances Browne, *Granny's Wonderful Chair* (1856); Mrs Craik (D. M. Mulock), *John Halifax Gentleman* (1856); Thomas Hughes, *Tom Brown's Schooldays* (1857); R. M. Ballantyne, *Coral Island* (1858); F. W. Farrar, *Eric or Little by Little* (1858); Charles Reade, *The Cloister and the Hearth* (1861); Juliana Horatia Ewing, *A Flat Iron for a Farthing* (1872); George Macdonald, *The Princess and the Goblin* (1872); G. A. Henty, *With Clive in India* (1884); Florence Montgomery, *Misunderstood* (1869); R. D. Blackmore, *Lorna Doone* (1875); Mrs Molesworth (Ennis Graham), *The Cuckoo Clock* (1878); Anna Sewell, *Black Beauty* (1877); Talbot Baines Reed, *The Cock House at Fellsgarth* (1891); F. Anstey, *Vice Versa* (1882); R. L. Stevenson, *Treasure Island* (1883); Richard Jefferies, *Bevis* (1882); Sir Henry Rider Haggard, *King Solomon's Mines* (1885); Frances Hodgson Burnett, *Little Lord Fauntleroy* (1886); Oscar Wilde, *The Happy Prince* (1888); Sir Arthur

Conan Doyle, *Rodney Stone* (1896); Stanley Weyman, *A Gentleman of France* (1893); Rudyard Kipling, *The Jungle Book* (1894); G. E. Farrow, *The Wallypug of Why* (1895); E. Nesbit, *The Story of the Treasure Seekers* (1899).

The Andrew Lang *Fairy Tales*, of which the first, the *Blue Fairy Book*, was published in 1886, do not quite fit into the above list, since they were not strictly original work, and were mainly translations. And yet, to many collectors of Victorian Children's Books, they have a very special place, and must therefore be mentioned.

Illustrators of Victorian Children's Books, with a typical example of their work.

When we come to the illustrators of Victorian Children's Books three names inevitably spring to mind: Kate Greenaway, Randolph Caldecott and Walter Crane. This is because each was a fine artist. But there were two contributory reasons. Firstly, each did a very large quantity of work, and secondly, and most important, because each was lucky enough to have a large body of their work finely reproduced in colour printing by Edmund Evans.

Edward Lear, *A Book of Nonsense* (1846); C. H. Bennett, *Aesop's Fables* (1858); Arthur Hughes, George Macdonald, *At the Back of the North Wind* (1871); George Cruikshank, Mrs Ewing, *Lob Lie by the Fire* (1874); Sir John Tenniel, *Alice's Adventures in Wonderland* (1866); George Du Maurier, Florence Montgomery, *Misunderstood* (1874) (not the 1st edition); Walter Crane, *Sing a Song of Sixpence*, n.d. (*c.* 1865); Randolph Caldecott, *John Gilpin*, n.d. (*c.* 1878); Richard (Dicky) Doyle, William Allingham, *In Fairyland* (1871); Kate Greenaway, *Under the Window*, n.d. (1878). Miss Greenaway, as well as illustrating books, made drawings for Valentines and Christmas cards, and was represented by pictures in many children's magazines, e.g. *The Girls' Own Paper*. Collectors of her work should see Spielmann and Layard, *Kate Greenaway* (Black, 1905). Gordon Brown, Crockett, *Sir Toady Lion* (1897); Henry Furniss, L. Carroll, *Sylvie and Bruno* (1889); Edmund J. Sullivan, T. Hughes, *Tom Brown's Schooldays* (1896) (not 1st edition).

The 'Aunt Louisa' books are another series with very enjoyable, if somewhat crude, coloured illustrations. Particularly pleasant are the pictures of dogs' and cats' dinner parties. These books were published by Frederick Warne & Co. and printed by Kronheim, the Dalziels, Butterfield, and others, in the 1870's and 80's. It is not often known that *Diamonds and Toads*, a rare title in the series, contains six full-paged unsigned illustrations which are early work by Kate Greenaway. The books were issued separately or several together in cloth, with titles such as: *Aunt Louisa's Keepsake*, *Aunt Louisa's Birthday Gift* and *Aunt Louisa's Choice Present* (*see* Plates 134B and 136).

Christmas Cards: the Christmas Card is a truly English and a truly Victorian invention, although it has affinities with the much earlier Valentine (q.v.). In 1846 Mr (afterwards Sir) Harry Cole, who was later so largely concerned with the Great Exhibition, wanted a specially designed greeting to send to his friends at Christmas. J. C. Horsley, R.A., produced a design, a rustic trellis in three panels, with a scene inside each panel. Jobbins, of Warwick Place, Holborn, produced one thousand copies of this design coloured by hand. This was reprinted by De la Rue in chromolithography in 1881.

This pioneer effort did not produce any immediate children, and it was not until the early sixties that the Christmas Card as we know it made its appearance commercially, and was sold in shops. Goodall's, Leighton, Maxwell, Dean and Thierry were all early manufacturers. The craze for Christmas cards caught on with amazing rapidity, and it was estimated in the *Studio* special number for 1894 that over 200,000 different Christmas cards had been produced by that date. It is therefore a large field for collectors, but it is possible to be selective and to collect cards put out by the better publishers, such as Marcus Ward, or drawn by better artists, such as Kate Greenaway, C. H. Bennett, Thomas or Walter Crane. Many Christmas cards were, even more perhaps than now, very un-Christmaslike, the most extraordinary

CHROMOLITHOGRAPH, finished by hand, from Dickinson's *Comprehensive Pictures of The Great Exhibition.* 1853–4.

PLATE 123

To face page 200

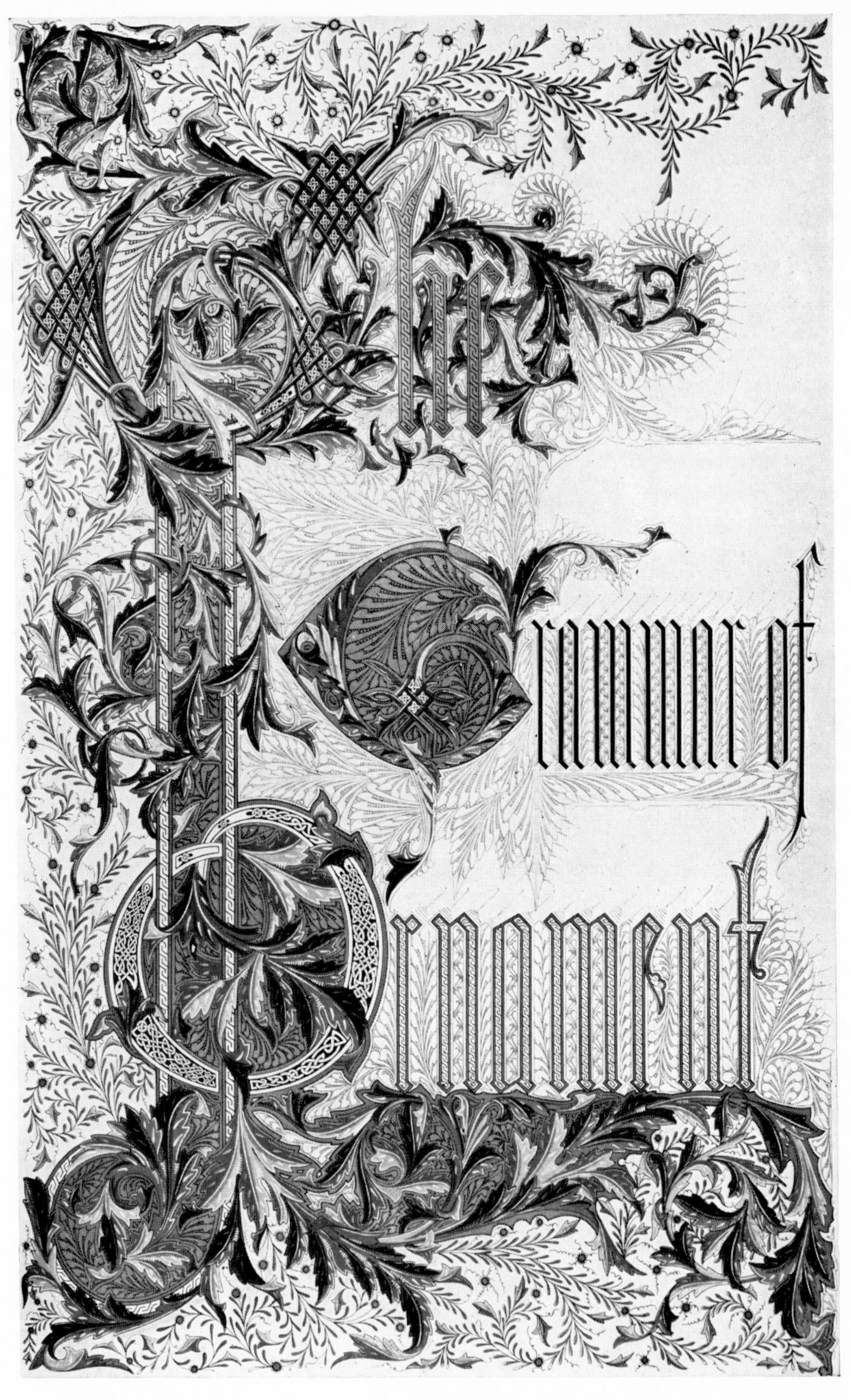

Title page to Owen Jones, *Grammar of Ornament*, 1856. Chromolithograph, finished by hand.

PLATE 124

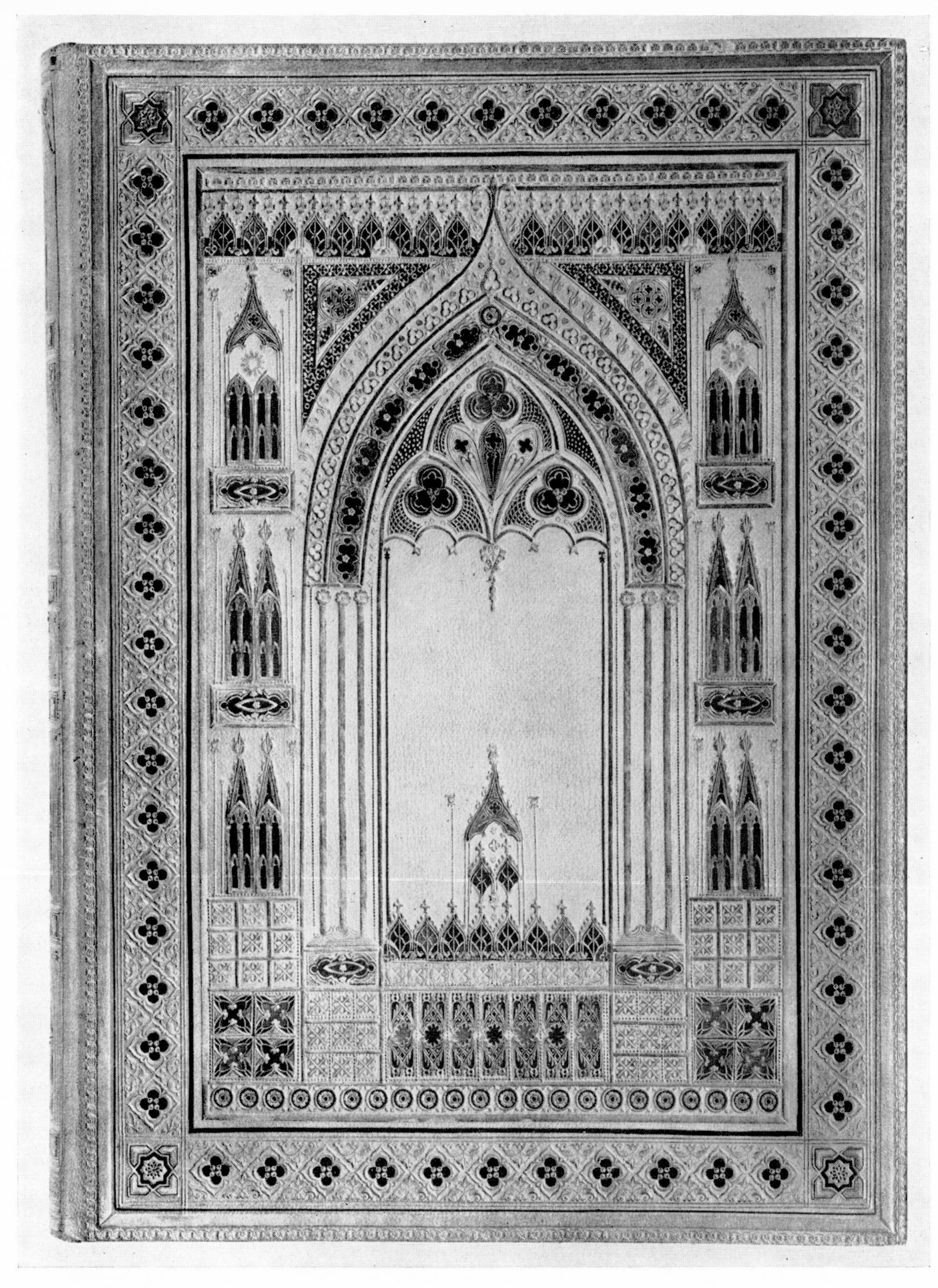

SIGNED BINDING by Wickwar in contemporary white morocco, back and sides profusely gilt tooled, and painted inlays of red, green, blue, brown and black morocco in the Cathedral Style of H. Shaw's *Specimens of Ancient Furniture*, 1836. The binding, put on the book shortly after its publication, just qualifies as a piece of 'Victoriana'. One of the most remarkable of all bindings of the period. The binder's name is printed at the bottom of the front inside cover. Reproduced by permission of J. R. Abbey.

PLATE 125

Title page to Edward Lear's *Views in the Seven Ionian Islands*, lithotint with vignette view hand-coloured, 1863.

PLATE 126

being a series of nudes of adolescent girls by W. S. Coleman published by De la Rue in the 80's. Kate Greenaway equally, though differently, depicted subjects unconnected with Christmas.

Frosting was used on Christmas cards as early as the sixties by putting on fine glass blown into thin bubbles and then burst. Jewelling, too, was applied by a thin film of copper faced with various chemicals and heated. In addition, real grass, seaweed and dried flowers, chenille, velvet and gelatine were some of the subjects used for decorating the cards.

Many Royal Academicians designed Christmas cards in the eighties, and among other publishers were Eyre & Spottiswoode and Raphael Tuck, the latter being then, as now, the biggest manufacturers of all. The *Studio* special number for Christmas, 1894, has a very complete account of the Victorian Christmas Card. There is also a shorter article in *Compliments of the Season* by L. D. Ettlinger and R. G. Holloway (Penguin Books, 1947), and just published is a considerable book, *The History of the Christmas Card* by George Boday (Rockliff, 1954) (*see* Plate 133).

Chromolithograph (*see also* Lithograph). The lithograph only requires one stone for printing, but the chromolithograph needs as many stones as colours are to be used on the finished print. A different colour is applied to each stone, and the various stones are applied in succession to the same paper until the complete picture is achieved.

The Victorian Chromolithograph, therefore, if produced untouched by hand, was an expensive affair and, moreover, one whose production took up an immense amount of space. Printing in ten colours for, say, a book with 200 illustrations, would require 2,000 stones, and if the book was a folio, these would be large stones. Hence, chromolithography was a very serious undertaking.

Charles Joseph Hullmandel (1789–1850) was not only one of the first English lithographers but probably produced the first book in chromolithography, namely, Thomas Shotter Boys's *Picturesque Architecture in Paris, Ghent, Antwerp, Rouen* (1839). Much of the colouring in Owen Jones's *Alhambra* (1842–5) was produced in chromolithographs by Day and Haghe, but the whole book is not printed in colour. Digby Wyatt's *Industrial Arts of the Nineteenth Century* at the Great Exhibition was probably the finest of all chromolithographic books: published in 1853 with 160 plates, 1,069 stones, weighing in all around 25 tons, were needed to produce it. Other famous examples of chromolithography were: Dickinson, *Comprehensive Pictures of the Great Exhibition*, 55 coloured plates, large folio, 2 vols. (1853–4); Waring, *Masterpieces of Industrial Art and Sculpture at the International Exhibition of 1862*, 301 plates (3,000 stones, weighing 40 tons, needed); Adveno Brooke, *The Gardens of England*, with 24 coloured plates, folio (1857); Joseph Nash, *Windsor Castle*, with 25 coloured plates, folio (1848) (*see* Plates 123, 134C and 138B).

Colour-plate books: colour-plate books are, naturally, all books illustrated by coloured pictures. A bookseller, however, will exclude by long but quite arbitrary practice all books about natural history: these are flower books, bird books, or the like. Not to know this can cause confusion when a catalogue is being perused. Although the great days of the colour-plate book were before the Victorian era, yet it developed a certain life of its own later, particularly until about 1870. Nayler, *The Coronation of His Most Sacred Majesty George IV*, with 45 coloured plates, folio (1839) and McIan, *The Clans of the Scottish Highlands*, 2 vols., with 72 coloured plates, folio (1845–7) are both cases in point, and other books are mentioned elsewhere in this glossary (*see under* Great Exhibition, Chromolithography, etc.). The finest catalogues of the Colour-plate Book in aquatint or lithography are: *The Scenery of Great Britain and Ireland 1770–1860* and *Life in England in Aquatint and Lithography, 1770–1860*, both from the library of J. R. Abbey, 2 vols., folio (Curwen Press, 1952–3). See also Tooley, *English Books with Coloured Plates, 1790–1860*, new, revised and enlarged edition (Batsford, 1954).

Colour printing: colour printing sounds complicated, but it is really quite simple. It consists basically in the colouring of the plate from which the impression or print is taken instead of the application of the colour directly on to the otherwise finished print. Hand-colouring was almost universal in 1837, while by the end of the Victorian era everything was in one way or another printed in colours. The principal methods of colour printing until late on in this period were by wood engravings or by stone (lithography and chromolithography, qq.v.). In either case a separate block or stone was prepared for each colour and was applied in turn to the print, usually starting with a key block in black or grey giving the principal outlines. A great many prints were, however, printed in colours, and touched up by hand, and most early chromolithographs were to some extent hand-coloured. Chromolithography was, to start with, more expensive than hand-colouring, and hence the cheaper books between 1840 and 1865 tended to be entirely hand-coloured.

The great exponents of colour printing from wood blocks, other than Baxter and his Licensees (q.v.) were Charles Knight (*Old England*, 2 vols., 1844–5, is a good example of his work); Leighton Brothers, who produced the plates for George Barnard's *Landscape and Water Colour Painting* (1858) (Barnard was drawing master at Rugby) and *Gems of English Art of This Century* (1869); and Henry Vizetelly, who assisted both Owen Jones and H. Noel Humphreys to produce 'Illuminated' Books, though only parts of these were illustrated with wood engravings, much being lithographed.

Engraved writing-paper: engraved writing-paper is headed with an engraving, usually of the owner's house or grounds, or of some feature of the town in which it was to be sold. Mostly reproduced by steel engraving, these letter-headings were often very charming indeed. They are essentially a Victorian product; although people now still sometimes have writing-paper which copies the Victorian style. An immense quantity of engraved writing-paper was produced, but for obvious reasons comparatively little survives.

Flower books: the great period of the flower book illustrated with coloured plates had ended before 1837. None the less, a number of interesting Victorian flower books can be collected, almost all containing hand-coloured lithographs or chromolithographs.

Some important books are: Elizabeth Twining, *Illustrations of the Natural Orders of Plants*, 2 vols., folio (1849–55); Sir J. Hooker, *The Rhododendrons of Sikkim, Himalaya*, folio (1849–51) and *Illustrations of Himalayan Plants*, folio (1855); H. J. Elwes, *Monography of the Genus Lilium*, folio (1877–80); and Mrs Loudon, *British Wild Flowers* (1849), *Ornamental Annuals* (1840), *Ornamental Perennials*, 2 vols. (1843–4), *Ornamental Bulbous Plants* (1841), *Ornamental Greenhouse Plants* (1848), all quarto. A second edition of these books published in the fifties has highly inferior plates.

See Wilfred Blunt, *The Art of Botanical Illustration* (Collins, 1951).

Games: Victorian table games were played with dice or tee-to-tums, a spinning top with numbered sides, and with counters, on the same system as our horse or motor-racing games of today. The boards were coloured lithographic pictorial sheets mounted on canvas, which folded into a cloth or card-board cover, earlier into a slip case. The great variety of these games, some of which are very rare, make them legitimate objects for the collector. The rules were sometimes printed separately, and hence are usually missing, but more occasionally were printed on the sheet itself.

Originating towards the end of the eighteenth century, when the sheets were hand-coloured copper engravings, these games were largely intended to be educational, so that there were historical, geographical, instructional or otherwise morally improving games. Typical titles of Victorian games are: *Ancient History*, *Peter Parley's Victoria Game of the British Sovereigns*, *Produce and Manufactures of the Counties of England and Wales*, *Eccentric Excursion to the Chinese Empire*, *The Railway Game*, *Pirates and Traders of the West Indies*, and the *Illustrative Game of the Great Exhibition*.

Prominent publishers were Darton & Clark, E. Wallis, J. Harris, J. Meyers & Co., William Spooner, J. Passmore and John Betts.

Jigsaw puzzles in wooden boxes with coloured pictorial lids were also published in large numbers, again with an educational bias. And wooden blocks or bricks in square boxes with printed pictorial sides, which, when put together, made various pictures, were also a peculiarly Victorian game.

For a list of games see F. R. B. Whitehouse, *Tables Games of Georgian and Victorian Days* (Peter Garnett, 1951). (*See* Plate 137B.)

Gauffred edges: many books, of course, have the edges of the leaves gilded. The gauffred edge is a pattern blocked or stamped on to the edges, so that a diamond or lozenge or some other decorative effect is produced. Some gauffred edges are very elaborate. This freak flourished in particular during the early and middle Victorian period, and although a good deal of searching would be needed, it would be possible to form quite a good collection of examples. (*See* Plate 134D.)

Great Exhibition: the Great Exhibition was held in Hyde Park in 1851. Conceived by Prince Albert and Mr (later Sir) Harry Cole, a civil servant, the Exhibition was housed in a gigantic glass structure, designed by Joseph (later Sir Joseph) Paxton, gardener to the Duke of Devonshire. The Exhibition was divided into four sections, of which two, Fine Arts and Manufactures, and especially the former, typified Victorian taste, and had a lasting influence because of the number of people who saw them. Hence, the Great Exhibition must be by far the most important single event for the lover of Victoriana. Quite apart from books, the Exhibition was portrayed in countless ways. There were contemporary medallions with the Exhibition on one side and the Prince on the other. There were pictures woven in silk, glass pictures, views on talc, papier mâché tables with a view of the Exhibition executed in mother-of-pearl inlay, panoramas and peepshows galore, sets of Baxter and many other prints. There was even the Crystal Palace Polka with a pictorial cover.

The literature of the Great Exhibition is colossal and ranges from humble guide-books to magnificent folios. There are such oddments as *1851, or the Adventures of Mr and Mrs Sandboys at the Great Exhibition*, by Henry Mayhew and George Cruikshank, or *Mrs Brown at the Crystal Palace*, an early yellow-back (q.v.) and *An Account of the Proceeding at the Dinner Given by Mr George Peabody to the American Connected with the Great Exhibition at the London Coffee House, Ludgate Hill.* But a few books are of outstanding importance. First, the *Official Descriptive and Illustrated Catalogue*, issued in four large octavo volumes together with a volume of *The Reports by the Juries*, 1851–2. The catalogue gives an account of everything exhibited with a great many uncoloured illustrations. The *Report* shows how the exhibits in each section were classified according to merit and which exhibits won medals.

Next comes Dickinson's *Comprehensive Pictures of the Great Exhibition*, two massive folio volumes, published in 1857, giving in all a nearly complete picture of the various sections. The prints were coloured lithographs from watercolours painted for the Prince Consort by Joseph Nash and others. This was one of the finest of Victorian colour-plate books, though it had a rival in *Recollections of the Great Exhibition 1851*, published by Day, with 25 plates, a much rarer book.

And, finally, M. Digby Wyatt's *Industrial Arts of the Nineteenth Century, A Series of Illustrations of the Choicest Specimens Produced by Every Nation at the Great Exhibition of Works of Industry 1851.* Published originally in forty parts, between 1851 and 1853, this illustrates 158 of the individual exhibits. The prints are chromolithographs (*see also under* Chromolithograph). It is possible that this book, with its rich elaborate leather bindings, is the most enjoyable of all pieces of Victoriana.

The actual exhibits in the Fine Art Section of the Exhibition had to represent arts which were connected with mechanical processes or mechanical processes which could be applied to arts. This meant, for instance, that paintings and even ordinary engravings were not permitted, though lithographs and chromolithographs were. Fine bindings were present, also wood-carving and sculpture.

For a more detailed account of the Great Exhibition, apart from the contemporary works mentioned above, see C. Hobhouse, *1851 and the Crystal Palace*, reissued by John Murray, 1950; also *The Great Exhibition: A Commemorative Album* (Victoria and Albert Museum); J. Steegmann, *Consort of Taste*,

1830–1870 (Sidgwick & Jackson, 1950); Yvonne ffrench, *The Great Exhibition*, 1851 (Harvill Press, 1950); and P. Howarth, *The Year is 1851* (Collins, 1951). Hobhouse's book in particular is of great interest. (*See* Plates 123, 127A and C, 134C and 137A.)

Illuminated books: books in which the plates, and often part of the text, notably the initial letters of chapters, are not only coloured but gilded in imitation of the illuminated manuscripts of the Middle Ages. The principal exponents of the style were Owen Jones (*The Victoria Psalter* (1861), *The Grammar of Ornament* (1856, 2nd ed. 1865) and Gray's *Elegy* (1846) are among his works); H. Noel Humphreys, *Illuminated Books of the Middle Ages* (1844) and *The Illuminations of Froissart*, 2 vols. (1846); and Henry Shaw, *Dresses and Decorations of the Middle Ages* (1843).

But there are many other examples, both of the work of these four and of others, and a large and interesting collection can be built up by confining oneself to this subject alone. Illluminated books were often published in outlandish bindings carved in papier mâché or covered with some unusual fabric, or specially bound in a signed binding. Owen Jones's *The Psalter* appeared in grotesquely-carved wood. The illuminated book is one of the most typical pieces of all Victoriana, since although it is, on the face of it, a pastiche of its medieval parent, anything more than a glance will show that it embodies the soul of the Victorian Age. No other subject could be more enjoyable to the student or the collector of Victoriana. Nothing like it has existed before or since. (*See* Plates 124, 138A.)

Illustrators of the sixties: this may be a slightly arbitrary definition, but since the appearance of one of the most important books of its kind on such a subject called *Illustrators of the Sixties*, by Forest Reid (Faber & Gwyer, 1928) there has always been a cult for this limited period, although most collectors would stretch a few years in either direction. The term naturally implies that the artists are considered by the collector as book illustrators only. But since the group includes Birket Foster, Tenniel, Rossetti, Holman Hunt, Burne-Jones, Millais, Arthur Hughes, Charles Keene, George Du Maurier and Walter Crane, to name only a few, it will be seen that it is of the highest importance, because these illustrators gave, as a body, a very fine picture of mid-Victorian life. Charles Keene, Du Maurier and Tenniel appeared mostly in *Punch*, but the latter illustrated *Alice in Wonderland* and *Through the Looking Glass*. Millais did the pictures for many of Trollope's novels, including *Phineas Finn* and *Orley Farm*.

A very large proportion of these artists' drawings were engraved by the Dalziel brothers, who started as a firm in 1843. Their work was always distinguished by fine craftsmanship (*see* Plate 134A).

Jones, Owen: Owen Jones (1809–74) had an enormous influence on Victorian taste and therefore deserves a few words to himself. Travelling abroad as a young man, especially in the Middle East, he was much influenced by Arabic ornament. He published a folio two-volume work on the Alhambra (in Granada) in 1845–7, and his *Grammar of Ornament*, folio (1856), had a great influence on designs for Victorian wallpaper, carpets and furniture. He was superintendent of the works for the Great Exhibition and, when it was moved, was made joint director of its decoration at the Crystal Palace, as it now became. He was particularly interested in colour, as used in decoration and ornament, and produced many illuminated publications (*see* Illuminated books above) and other works, including *Designs for Mosaic and Tessellated Pavements*, quarto (1842), *One Thousand and One Initial Letters*, folio (1864), and *Examples of Chinese Ornament*, folio (1867). It is possible to regard him as the greatest single influence on Victorian taste in Ornament and Design. (*See* Plate 124.)

Language of flowers: books appeared during the whole Victorian period which described either by a glossary or in other ways what the verbal meaning of a particular flower was, e.g. Ice Plant: 'Your looks freeze me'; Ranunculus: 'You are radiant with charms'.

Sometimes these would be illustrated with pictures and sometimes there would be a picture showing a letter written in Floral Language; Captain Marryat even produced a *Floral Telegraph* (published posthumously in 1840) or *Affection's Signals*, a kind of Floral Code. Most of these books were less elaborate in concept. They derived originally from France, where *Langages des Fleurs* appeared early in the nineteenth century. But they were in the main a Victorian development. R. Tyas, *The Sentiment of Flowers* (1842), with 29 coloured plates, and T. Miller, *The Poetical Language of Flowers* (1847), with 12 coloured plates, are typical examples.

Lear, Edward: Edward Lear (1812–88) deserves mention by himself, since he is, one might say, such a Victorian all-rounder. At the age of twenty he published a work on parrots from his own drawings. This is still the finest of all parrot books. He assisted Gould in some of his great bird books and worked for the Earl of Derby at Knowsley, publishing a folio volume illustrating the birds, etc., at the menagerie there. It was for Lord Derby's grandchildren that he invented the famous *Book of Nonsense*, the first of a number of world-famed 'Nonsense' books. In addition to this, he was devoted to landscape painting, and spent much of the last part of his life sketching mostly in Italy, Greece and the Mediterranean, but also in Palestine and India. Much of his work was published and is now greatly sought after. He gave drawing lessons to the young Queen Victoria. His principal works are: *Illustrations of the Family of Psittacidae* (1832); Gray's *Tortoises, Terrapins and Turtles*, drawn from life by Sowerby and Lear; *Views in Rome and its Environs* (1841); *Gleanings from the Menagerie at Knowsley Hall* (1846); *Illustrated Excursions in Italy* (1846); *Book of Nonsense* (1846) (2nd ed. 1862); *Journals of a Landscape Painter in Southern Calabria, Etc.* (8vo. 1852); *Nonsense Songs and Stories* (1871); *More Nonsense Songs, Pictures, Etc.* (1872); *Laughable Lyrics* (1877); *Nonsense Botany and Nonsense Alphabets*; *Journal of a Landscape Painter in Southern Albania* (1852); *Views in the Seven Ionian Islands* (1863); *Journal of a Landscape Painter in Corsica* (1870); *Tennyson's Poems*, illustrated by Lear, 4to (1889). See Angus Davidson, *Edward Lear* (1938). (*See* Plate 126.)

Lithograph: the lithograph was invented by J. A. Senefelder, of Munich, in 1796. It was patented in England in 1800. Briefly, it works as follows: stone will receive on its surface both grease and water, but these two are antipathetic. A drawing is made on a stone, level and polished, with a greasy crayon or other medium. The stone is then wetted, when only the non-greasy part that is not drawn on will receive the moisture. Next, by roller or otherwise, a greasy ink (of any colour) is passed over the stone. Only the unwet part of the stone, that already drawn on, will accept the ink. Then a piece of paper is pressed down on the stone and receives the drawing, giving, as in all forms of reproductions from plates, a reverse facsimile of the original. This process can be repeated again and again. Early lithographers employed only the one stone, and if the finished print needed to be coloured it was coloured by hand, as was the case with most earlier methods of reproduction. A very large number of coloured prints during the Victorian period were lithographs hand coloured, and a large number of book illustrations were the same. For lithographs printed in colour, i.e. chromolithography, see the separate heading above. For most of the illustrations in Gould's series of Birds of All Countries, perhaps the most considerable single body of coloured prints issued during our period, lithography was the method used. A lithographic print, since it is taken directly off the stone, does not have the surrounding plate-mark that all forms of relief processes – aquatint, etching, mezzotint, etc.– possess, as the paper is placed on the surface and not forced into the engraved plate. Lithographs are therefore easily distinguished from all other kinds of engraved prints by this absence of a plate-mark. The collector will, however, find little difficulty in differentiating them otherwise, since the effect produced is softer. Lines or stipple effects give way to an unbroken whole. At its earliest the lithograph and its brother, the chromolithograph, were usually works of art in the direct descent from their predecessors, but machinery and mass production had by the end of the Victorian age much degraded them. Prints of all kinds need individual craftsmanship, and this seems often to be lacking towards the end of the nineteenth century.

Lithotint: this was a development of the lithograph (*see* above) using the stone, by coating it with a resinous substance, as its predecessor used the aquatint. The resulting print was tinted and ranged in tones from brown to black. Charles Hullmandel was responsible for this new process, which he patented in 1840. A half-way house between the lithograph and the chromolithograph, the lithotint, was used in a number of books between 1840 and 1860, notably Hall's *Baronial Halls and Picturesque Edifices of England* (1848). Many lithotints were partially coloured by hand, producing a very drab effect. See Basil Gray, *The English Print* (1937) and Courtney Lewis, *Picture Printing in England during the Nineteenth Century*. (*See* Plate 126.)

Movable books: these are books for children in which, by moving small flaps or or ribbons which project below the level of the page, a transformation of some kind is effected. At its simplest a dog will wave its tail, a parrot its beak; at its most elaborate, by a series of slats, a whole picture will transform itself, e.g. Indolence will become Industry. These started in the forties and continued through Queen Victoria's reign. By their nature these books were fragile, and it is hard to find any in perfect condition. See Percy Muir, *English Children's Books* (Batsford, 1954).

Music-cover: the Music-cover for sheet music, with a picture, in some way representing the song inside, came into its own with the invention of chromolithography (q.v.). During the entire Victorian period many thousands appeared, some very poorly, others well executed. Almost all were interesting or amusing. They appear to have been drawn, as are modern vulgar postcards, by a very small body of men who were otherwise practically unknown. Baxter allowed twenty-three of his prints to be reproduced after the ordinary publication as music-covers, but with this exception none of the names of the artists now mean anything to us. Music-covers, however, are a legitimate object for the collector. They express perfectly the many sides of the Victorian spirit; and in a minor key, but on a much larger scale, do for the period what the famous Currier and Ives lithographs did for the United States. (*See* Plate 130.)

The authority on Music-covers is Mr A. Hyatt King. An article written by him for the *Penrose Annual*, 1952, has been reproduced in pamphlet form with eight coloured reproductions in photolithography.

Panoramas: these are sheets which either roll up round some central drum or fold up, and which in either case can be extended to their full length, when they display a picture more or less complete of some historical event or of some extended scene, e.g. *Queen Victoria's Grand Tour of the Thames from Source to Mouth*. They are coloured or uncoloured. The Victorian Age was the age of panoramas; although they existed much earlier and much later. Until comparatively recently street vendors used to sell panoramas of *The Lord Mayor's Show* which rolled up inside a brass case. *The Coronation*, *and The Wedding of Queen Victoria* and the *Duke of Wellington's Funeral* were the subjects of fine panoramas. The *The Position on the Alma* and a *Bengal Infantry Regiment on the March* are other subjects. The Great Exhibition produced a heavy crop. Some are: *The House that Paxton Built* (7 ft. 8 in. long), by George Augustus Sala; *The Great Exhibition 'Wot is to Be'*, a 'comic' also by Sala; *The Great Exhibition of Doings in London for 1851* (published by Ackermann & Co.); *The Overland Journey to the Great Exhibition*, by Richard (Dicky) Doyle. See also *Life in England in Aquatint and Lithography* 1770–1860, from the library of J. R. Abbey (Curwen Press, 1953). (*See* Plate 127A.)

Papier mâché: papier mâché or, more simply, paper mash made from waste paper, was an invention of the late eighteenth century. Its particular application in Victorian times was to trays, table-tops and boxes, with paintings of all kinds superimposed from engraved plates. George Goodman patented a process for doing this in 1852, so that reproductions of oil paintings could be made. By another process compressed papier mâché was made into intricate carved designs for use as book-covers, and many illuminated books, in particular, were bound in this way. For a good account of Papier Mâché see

Viva King, *Papier Mâché* (Apollo, 1949). (*See* Plate 135C.)

Peepshows: a peepshow derives from a cabinet carried round in the seventeenth and eighteenth centuries by peepshow men, into which the spectator could peer for a small sum, seeing something like a more modern stereoscopic view where the scene was made up of various pieces cut out and graduated at different lengths from the viewer. The Victorian peepshow folded up, then pulled out again with two eye-pieces through which the perspective view could be seen. Almost always coloured, it stretched to a convenient length between eyes and outspread hand. The *Thames Tunnel* was for some years the favourite of all peepshows, possibly because it was almost stereoscopic, a peepshow if one looked into the tunnel itself. The Great Exhibition, too, was the subject of Peepshows, of which Lane's *Telescopic View of the Interior and of the Exterior* are perhaps the most representative. Lane's also did *Telescopic View of London and The Thames from the Duke of York's Column.* Another typical peepshow is *Her Majesty's Royal Visitors and Staff at the Camp at Chatham.* Peepshows have always captured the imagination, and are therefore comparatively more expensive than most other forms of Victoriana. See *Life in England in Aquatint and Lithography* from the library of J. R. Abbey (Curwen Press, 1953). (*See* Plate 127C.)

Press books: these are books printed and published from a special press, where some attempt has been made to produce an individual outlook. There have been press books all through the ages. The Aldine Press (*c.* 1500), the Elzevir Press (*c.* 1600), the Strawberry Hill Press of Horace Walpole (*c.* 1800) were all earlier examples of this highly personal trend in printing. In the Victorian age this trend was at first submerged by mass production and more generally mass taste. However, later on in Queen Victoria's reign this peculiar form of individuality began to show itself once more. The Kelmscott Press, started by William Morris in 1891, and the Ashendene Press, 1894, are examples of presses which tied up with earlier productions. Yet from the point of view of the collector of Victoriana, press books scarcely exist. They are descendants of earlier days, drawing little or nothing from their Victorian background, and, although they have to some extent influenced their successors, it has been only in that they have passed on the earlier culture. The collecting of Press Books does not, strictly speaking, tie up with the collecting of Victoriana.

Prints: a print is an individual impression taken from any form of plate or block which has been worked on either by hand or by mechanical means or by a combination, so that the final impression will produce some design. Mr Basil Gray, in *The English Print* (Faber, 1937), says: 'The art of the print may be justly defined as the art of multiplying a design in such a way that each impression is, at least approximately, as good as any other'. He adds that mezzotint is a very poor medium, since the surface of the plate deteriorates so quickly and the aquatint equally fails because so much work, such as hand-colouring, had to be applied to the individual impression after it had been taken from the plate. If this rather questionable judgment is accepted, then the prints of the Victorian period, lithographs, chromo-lithographs and wood-engravings in the main come into the very highest class, since it was possible by all these processes to produce many impressions without touching up the plate. Further remarks on the print are to be found in other sections of this glossary, viz. Aquatint, Lithograph, etc.

Publisher's binding: a term used to differentiate the binding of a book, as it was issued by the publishers, whether in boards, cloth or leather, from a binding commissioned later by the purchaser or any other binding put on after publication. Many elaborate leather bindings were issued by the publishers on fine books during the Victorian period. Examples are: McIan, *Clans of the Scottish Highlands*, 2 vols. (1845–7); Wyatt, *Industrial Arts of the Nineteenth Century at the Great Exhibition*, 2 vols. (1853); Waring, *Art Treasures of the United Kingdom* (1858); Heath, *Beauties of the Opera and Ballet* (1841). (*See* Plates 135A and D.)

Sporting prints: the sporting print is of little or no interest to the collector of Victoriana. The great day of the sporting print was from the end of the eighteenth century to, perhaps, 1850. But all the best-known artists were at work well before 1837, and most of their best work had been done by that date. The principal artists, some of whose work comes within the period, are: Henry Alken (1784–1851), who produced an immense body of work, including the illustrations for R. S. Surtees's *Jorrocks' Jaunts and Jollities* (1837) (2nd edition 1843), and for Surtees's *Analysis of the Hunting Field* (1846) (2nd edition 1847); Charles Hancock (1795–1868); Charles Cooper Henderson (1803–77); John F. Herring (1795–1865), whose aquatints of race-horses are perhaps the best known of all sporting prints. Of these, only a very small number were published after 1837; James Pollard (1797–1867); and Dean Wolstenholme Junior (1798–1882). John Leech (1817–64) can be added to this, since he illustrated the best known of Surtees's works, *Handley Cross*, *Mr Sponge's Sporting Tour*, etc. But he is better known as a humorous illustrator in *Punch*. Many of his large drawings were reproduced as hand-coloured lithographs, but although some portray hunting and riding, they are basically comic pictures. For further information: F. Siltzer, *The Story of British Sporting Prints* (1925) (2nd enlarged edition 1929).

Steel engraving: a process of engraving, starting soon after 1800, upon steel rather than on copper plates. More impressions could be taken from a steel than from a copper plate. This was, however, such a mechanical process, where the actual engravers were treated merely as hands, that it quickly fell into disfavour, not before it had produced some fine books, such as Turner's *Rivers of England* (1833–1836). But it continued through the early Victorian years, though never as a serious force.

Collectors of steel engravings should note that it is highly unlikely that any book illustrated by this method was issued coloured. Many, however, seem to have undergone a transformation since. (*See* B. Gray, *The English Print*, 1937.)

Three-decker: the popular term for the novel issued in three volumes, an almost universal practice until the very end of the Victorian age. Collecting three-deckers can be a fascinating, and not necessarily an expensive, business, though it will naturally not suit the occupant of a small flat. (*See* Michael Sadleir, *Nineteenth Century Fiction*, 2 vols., 1951.)

Toy theatres: the Toy Theatre or Juvenile Drama started before the Victorian period, but achieved its greatest popularity, as well as having its best-known publishers, after 1837. It developed from individual portraits of famous actors and actresses in their well-known parts, which began to be sold at a penny plain and twopence coloured at the beginning of the nineteenth century. These portraits had a flavour of their own about them, showing the performers in a highly histrionic manner and being crude but not unpleasant; a flavour which was never lost as these portraits developed into the Juvenile Drama. This development took the form of a series of sheets which showed popular plays, giving not only the whole cast but the scenery, and with a book of words included. The figures on these sheets could be cut out and pasted on to cardboard, so that the juvenile producer could make them perform while reading aloud their various parts. During the thirties a further refinement was added, in that ready-cut tinsel made from coloured metal sheets could be bought to put on the figures.

By the fifties publishers of these sheets had ready-made wooden stages for the performers. There was a proscenium mounted on cardboard with wooden uprights on the platform. The lighting was at first done by candles, but later by tin footlights with oil wicks. The characters fitted into slides which moved through grooves across the stage, and later there were, instead, tin stands with wires attached. Coloured lights made from chemical powders were burnt in tin pans to give dramatic effect.

Getting ready a toy theatre was a long business, and so pleased both the young stage managers and their parents. By the seventies the real craze for the toy theatre was over, since the plays had not kept up with the contemporary theatre. The prices were now often reduced to a halfpenny plain and a penny

(A) PANORAMA. The Great Exhibition 'Wot Is To Be', by George Augustus Sala, 1850. (First two sections shown above. It unfolds to twenty-three sections altogether.)

(B) TRANSFORMATION, with pun title. C. Tilt, *c.* 1840.

(C) PEEPSHOW, 1851. Front cover, with eye-hole for viewing.

PLATE 127

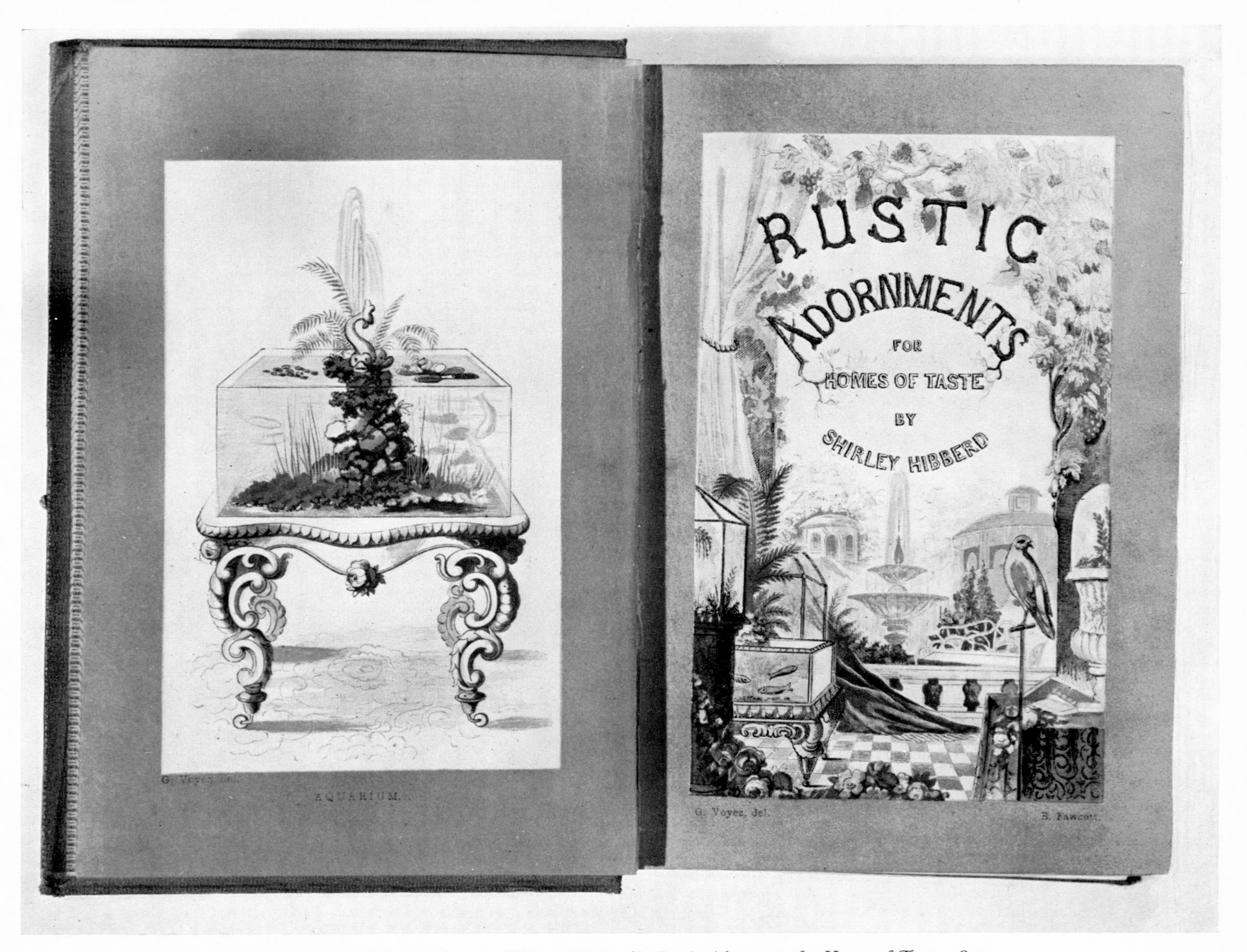

Title page and frontispiece to Shirley Hibberd's *Rustic Adornments for Homes of Taste*, 1857.

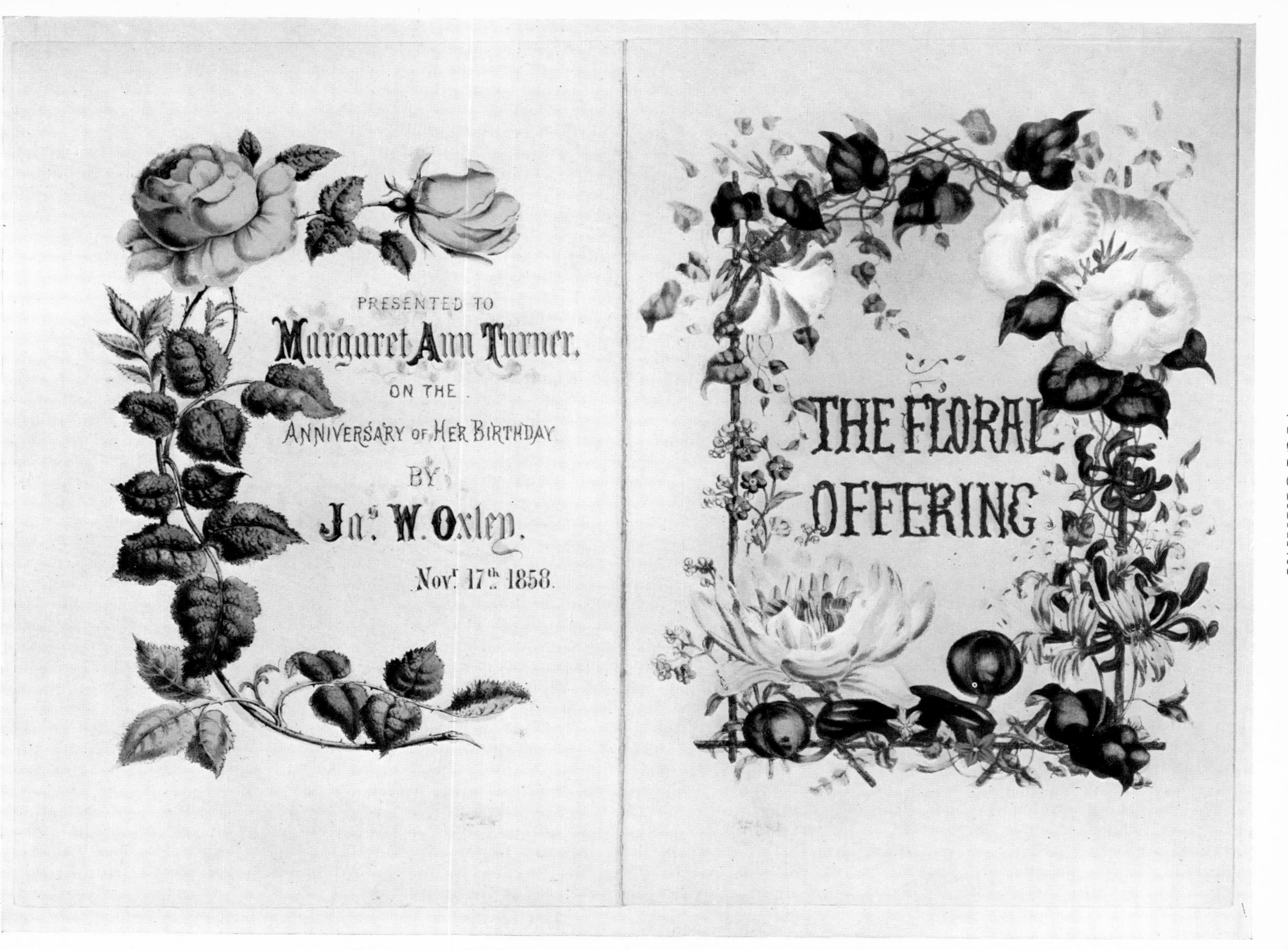

Title page and frontispiece to Paul Jerrard's *The Floral Offering*, 1858.

Music Covers, *c.* 1865.

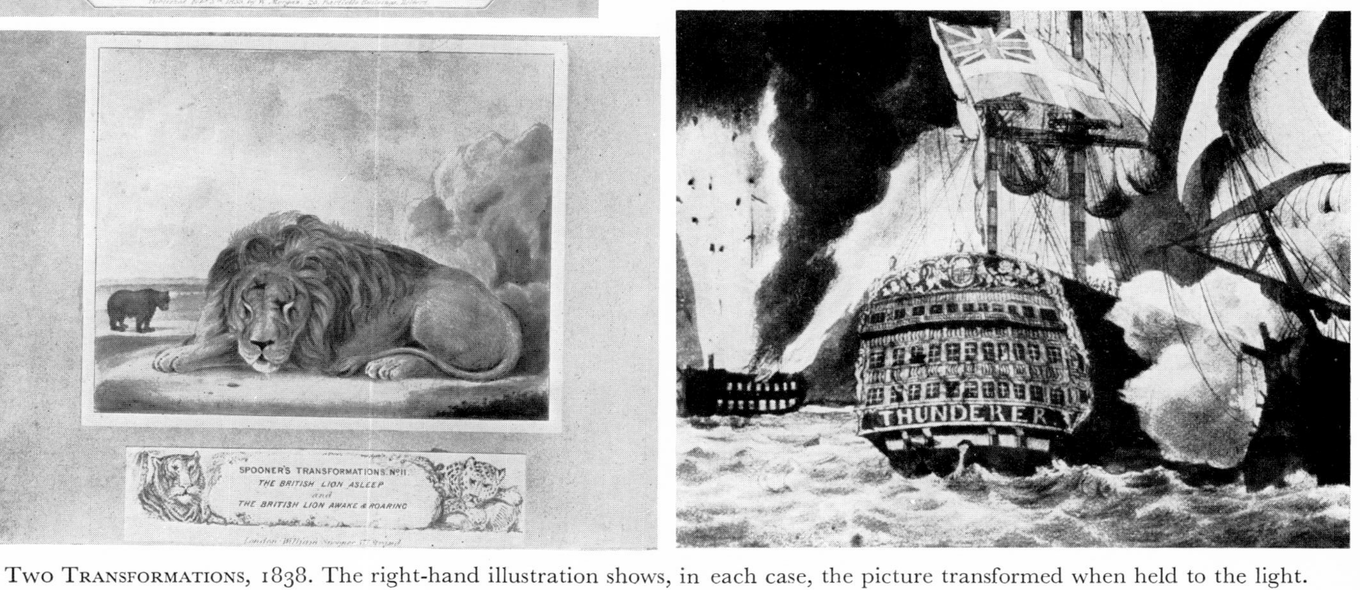

Two Transformations, 1838. The right-hand illustration shows, in each case, the picture transformed when held to the light.

(A) Valentine with gilded perforated surround, *c.* 1855
Percy Muir Collection.

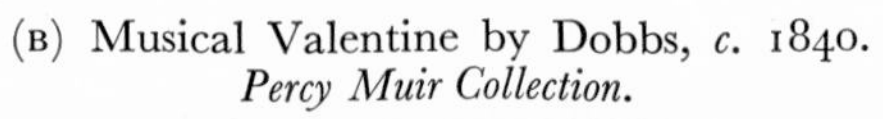

(B) Musical Valentine by Dobbs, *c.* 1840.
Percy Muir Collection.

(C) Comical Valentine, *c.* 1865.
Cara Lancaster Collection.

(D) Valentine, with applied stuff flowers, ivy and fern, *c.* 1875. *Cara Lancaster Collection.*

CHRISTMAS CARDS

The three lower cards are Kate Greenaway designs, published by Marcus Ward 1880.

(A) Illustration to *Tennyson's Poems*, 1864. Wood engraving by the Dalziel Brothers from the original of Holman Hunt. (B) Cover to *Nursery Songs*, one of the series of *Aunt Louisa's London Toy Books*, printed in colours by Kronheim, *c.* 1875.

(C) CHROMOLITHOGRAPH (Group of enamelled objects, by Morel of London) drawn by Dalziel and entirely printed in colours by Day and Son, from *The Industrial Arts of The Nineteenth Century at the Great Exhibition*, by Digby Wyatt, 1853. (D) Examples of GAUFFRED EDGES on Victorian books.

PLATE 134

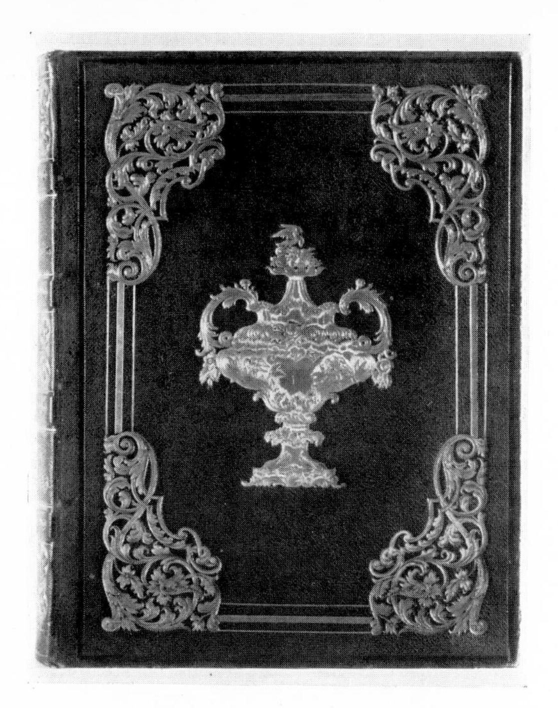

(A) PUBLISHERS BINDING in morocco gilt to Beattie's *The Waldenses*, 1838.

(B) IMITATION WOODEN BINDING. Hall's *Book of Gems*, 1877.

(C) PAPIER MACHE BINDING to H. Noel Humphrey's *Record of the Black Prince*, 1849.

(D) PUBLISHERS BINDING in morocco gilt to Heath's *Beauties of the Opera and Ballet*, 1841

CHILDREN'S BOOKS

(A) In Fairyland. A Poem by William Allingham, with coloured illustrations by Richard Doyle. 1870.

(B) The Fables of Æsop and Others translated into Human Nature, with coloured illustrations designed and drawn on wood by Charles H. Bennett. 1857.

(A) BAXTER PRINT. The Gems of the Great Exhibition, No. 2. (A set of prints, not issued as a book.) 1851.

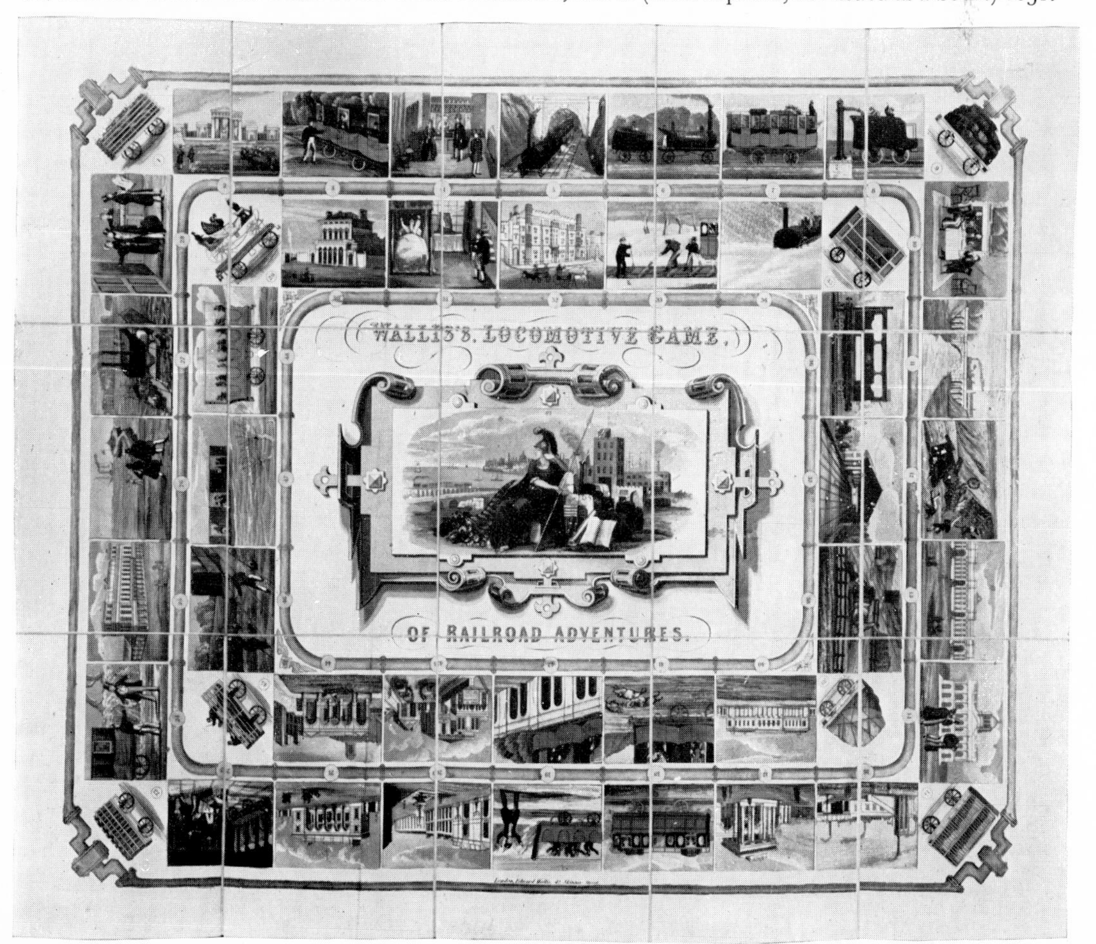

(B) GAME. Rail-Road Adventures. A New Round Game. Edward Wallis, *c.* 1840. Hand-coloured lithograph sheet, mounted on canvas, folding into cloth covers.

(A) Title page to A. Welby Pugin's *Glossary of Ecclesiastical Ornament*, 1844.

(B) Title page to Adveno Brooke's *Gardens of England*, 1857. Chromolithograph.

PLATE 138

coloured, since so many sheets, sometimes twenty or thirty, of cut-outs were needed for the production of one play, and with this the printing and colouring of the sheets became cruder.

Three basic colours alone were used for the sheets (carmine, gamboge and light blue), and a model sheet was coloured and sent out to copyists, though later stencils were used. Robert and George Cruikshank and William and Henry Heath did designs for the theatres, but a great many are by unknown artists.

The pioneer publishers of the toy theatre are William West (died 1854) and J. K. Greenwood (1790-1860). The latter announced himself as the 'Original Inventor and publisher of Juvenile Theatrical prints, established 1808' and continued publishing until 1857. After Greenwood's death, J. Redington (1819–76) took over his business. His daughter married Benjamin Pollock (1856–1937), who continued after his father-in-law died, while his daughter carried on until 1944, when the shop was finally closed. Pollock has somehow, and probably because of the chain of continuity, become the best known of the publishers of the Juvenile Drama. The collector is, however, inclined to seek the sheets of the earlier and more obscure publishers.

Pollock's contemporary rival was W. Webb (1820–90), who drew, engraved and printed his own plays and maintained a higher standard in his twenty-three publications than any of his contemporaries. It is said that Robert Louis Stevenson quarrelled with him and so did not mention him in his article 'A Penny Plain and Twopence Coloured' (*Magazine of Art*, 1884), and hence Pollock remained better known. Especially popular plays for the Toy Theatre were *The Miller and His Men*, *The Flying Dutchman*, *Der Freischutz*, *The Maid and the Magpie*, *The Old Oak Chest*, *The Woodman's Hut*, *The Forest of Bondy*. See also, for an excellent account, George Speaight's *Juvenile Drama, the History of the English Toy Theatre* (Macdonald, 1946).

Transparencies, Pinprick pictures, etc.: a Transparency is a coloured print mounted on a board and pasted over a transformation scene which will show through when the print is held before a strong light. The best-known Victorian series of Transparencies are Spooner's *Transformations* and Morgan's *Improved Protean Scenery*, both of which appeared in the late thirties and the forties. Two typical subjects are: the *Duke of Wellington*, changing when held before the light to the *Battle of Waterloo*, and the *British Lion Asleep* and the *British Lion Awake and Roaring*. A sleeping lion changes into the Battle of Trafalgar.

Pinprick pictures were a more simple form of transformation, since a coloured print was perforated with a number of small holes and, hence, when held to the light the print would appear to be illuminated. Coloured paper would sometimes be fastened behind the print to change, for instance, sunlight into moonlight or to show a church in the daytime illuminated at night when held up to the light. An elaboration of this was the making of small transparent slides, which were placed in a box and viewed through peepholes. By raising lids in the box at the top or at the back, the print could be transformed.

Mention can also be made here of another kind of transformation, published by Charles Tilt. This consisted of a coloured print with a flap or flaps which revealed another quite different picture, together with some kind of pun written below. For instance, a print of a pear would open to reveal the Queen and the Prince Consort, and was captioned *The Nonpareil: A Much Admired PAIR to be introduced at the Royal Table*. Tilt also published a series of coloured prints of human figures composed of the objects of their trade or profession. The fruiterer was built up entirely from fruit. The entomologist from insects, and so on.

The Transparency is *not* a Victorian invention but, like so many other peculiarities, achieved its greatest popularity in Victorian times. The classic book on the subject is *An Essay on Transparent Prints* by Edward Orme (1807). This is illustrated and tells how to construct a transparency. (*See* Plates 127B and 131.)

Valentines: valentines take their name from St Valentine, who was martyred in Rome by the Emperor Claudius the Second on what is supposed to have been 14th February, A.D. 270, for helping the early Christians. Further, and more legendary still, on the night before his death he sent a last message to his gaoler's daughter, whose sight he had miraculously restored, signed 'Your Valentine'. Early valentines were just written messages. There is one in the British Museum dated 1415, written from the Tower by Charles Duke of Orleans.

The commercial valentine, or the valentine as we now know it, started in the early part of the nineteenth century, and was a hand-coloured engraving, varying much in quality, with a motto in verse. The drawings of quite well-known artists, such as George Heath or George Cruikshank, were used for valentines.

The real age of the Valentine was from 1840 until around the turn of the century, lithography and chromolithography replacing the earlier methods of production and a great elaboration of design being introduced. The best period was from 1840–60. After 1860 they became mass-produced and over-elaborate, though this is admired by some collectors.

Borders of embossed lace and later of perforated lace were often used, with, occasionally, embossed envelopes to match. Silk was sometimes used in the middle of the design. Valentines could also be mechanical, i.e. by moving a tab protruding from the bottom of the card a lady's skirts could be raised or a gentleman's whiskers moved. There were valentines of an elaborate cut-out pattern, which, when raised, disclosed a romantic scene. There were puzzles, acrostics and cryptograms, and there were valentines showing dolls with real material stuck on to make the clothes. Others had layers of cloth, wax, dried flowers, seaweed or shells. In addition, velvet, net, plush, looking-glass, cork, feathers and imitation jewellery were used. A rare form of valentine was the musical, where the front page lifts to show a musical quotation.

The names of the publishers, who were very often the individual dealers, since the valentine seemed to encourage the individual, often appeared embossed in the details of the design. Many valentines have the name of the firms who made them and others can be deduced from their style. But in a large number of examples the manufacturer is unknown. Watermarks assist in dating valentines, but are not a sure guide, since, as with all prints, the paper may have been bought earlier. A few well-known makers of valentines were H. Dobbs; Joseph Mansell, who published some Baxter print valentines; Joseph Addenbrooke; T. H. Burke; De la Rue & Co.; David Mossmann; George Kershaw; John Windsor; George Meek; and E. Rimmel. The last produced a valentine containing a sachet of scent. Marcus Ward, better known for their Christmas cards, made valentines from drawings by Kate Greenaway and Walter Crane.

Comic valentines are a class apart and have not been extensively collected. They are usually very crude in design, often from woodblock, while the sentiment is astonishingly cruel, being usually a horrible caricature with very wounding words written below. The only good book on valentines is *The History of Valentines* by Ruth Webb Lee, English ed. (Batsford, 1953). Though an American book, this is authoritative both on English and American valentines. (*See* Plate 132.)

Wax-flower modelling: groups of wax flowers and fruit in glass cases were a particular Victorian feature of decoration. At their best they are fascinating, although it is difficult to find specimens in perfect condition with the colours unfaded. Several Victorian books deal with the subject, notably Mrs Peachey's (artist to Her Majesty) *The Royal Guide to Wax Flower Modelling* (1851) (with four coloured groups of flowers to help the budding modeller).

Wood-engraving: a very large number of engravings and, in particular, of book illustrations of the Victorian era were from woodblocks, the artists and engravers (often one and the same person) following after the great tradition started by Thomas Bewick (1753–1828). The illustrators of the sixties (q.v.) were largely reproduced by wood-engravings. (*See* Plate 134.)

Yellowback: the term applied to a series of cheap reprints, mostly of fiction, because of the colour of the binding, which was basically yellow. Cloth was not used but boards with a pictorial design, sometimes of a very striking nature. Many very famous books have appeared as yellowbacks: most of Trollope, some of Thomas Hardy, even Jane Austen. Collecting yellowbacks is amusing and does not cost much money, but unless space is no object considerable selectivity should be employed. Most yellowbacks are in an atrocious condition, and it is as well in this, as in all other forms of collecting, to refuse all but fine copies.

The inventor of the yellowback was Edmund Evans, who prepared an illustrated coloured cover as a novelty for a series of 'railway' novels, to be read on train journeys. The basic colour was originally white, but this was found not to wear and yellow was substituted. (*See* Michael Sadleir, *Nineteenth Century Fiction*, 2 vols., 1951.)

ANTIQUE STATUARY AND WAX-MODELLING

By RUPERT GUNNIS

(*A*) ANTIQUE STATUARY

SCULPTURE, in some form or other, goes back to the very beginnings of history: and there is practically no civilization which has not attempted to carve, model, or cast in some material or other – whether it be marble, stone, clay, ivory, wax, wood, or bronze – the representation of the human form. Such attempts range from the crude clay figures of the early Cypriote Bronze Age to the superb art of Praxitiles, and from the wooden carvings of the untrained Bantu to the works of Henry Moore.

English sculpture has of late years become, save for contemporary work, neglected and forgotten. This oblivion can be traced to two chief reasons: the size of many pieces of sculpture, once intended for the large rooms of country houses, but today too overpowering for the modern home, and the fact that in the last years of the Victorian age a vast amount of extremely bad sculpture was produced both abroad and in England. Therefore many people are more apt to remember the grimy bronze statue of some provincial mayor, clutching his top-hat in one hand and badly-furled umbrella in the other, and to forget Le Sueur's magnificent statue of Charles I in Trafalgar Square. Equally, there are many who are inclined to recall with a sneer the marble bust of some once eminent benefactor in the entrance hall of a public building (a likeness showing the hair carefully parted in the centre, a drooping moustache and a high winged collar) and to ignore the lovely portrait busts by Roubiliac in the National Portrait Gallery. It might be said that the life-size marble or terra-cotta bust is too large for most homes, but, if it is, there are always the cabinet-size ones or the small portrait bronzes and wax portraits waiting to be found, which add charm and interest to any room.

Sculpture in all its forms, save for modern works, is neither difficult or expensive to collect, and a bust by Nollekens which, a hundred and fifty years ago, cost the sitter one hundred guineas can today, with luck, be purchased for as many shillings, while wax portraits and bronze busts are equally reasonable. The collector of sculpture will find he has advantages over his friends who search for the more popular forms of art, since he is far more likely to discover a bargain; and it is also true that no antique shop is too small, and no second-hand store too dusty and crowded, that it is not worth his while entering on the chance of discovering a work by a sculptor who, admired in his time, is now, by a passing whim of taste, temporarily forgotten.

Fortunately, the majority of British sculptors signed their names on the back or side of a bust, and it is therefore easy to discover the name of the artist. Bronze and wax busts in the round (the best of which date from 1790 to 1840) are frequently signed on the back, and the majority have the words 'Published by', showing that a number of copies of this work were made; though, owing to their fragile nature, probably only a single copy of the latter may have survived the years.

Foreign portrait busts of any merit, especially eighteenth-century French ones, are not often to be discovered in England. On the other hand, busts by nineteenth-century Italian artists are only too frequent. Most of them are either copies of classical works or imaginary portraits mass produced by firms in Pisa, Florence or Rome.

In England during the last half of the eighteenth century a number of firms produced plaster copies, usually coloured black, of busts of famous writers, statesmen, soldiers, etc., or copies of Greek and Roman poets, emperors, etc. They were intended to stand on top of bookcases in country house libraries, and were usually sold in sets, the 'moderns' consisting of Pope, Locke, Inigo Jones, Newton, etc., while the 'antique' set contained busts of Homer, Virgil, Horace, Socrates, etc. When these busts went out of fashion at the beginning of the Victorian age, a number of sculptors modelled for various firms, such as Copeland and Minton, busts and figures made in white china or 'Parian', which is the finest description of biscuit china made. It differs only from porcelain in the use of a more fusible felspar instead of Cornish stone, and Parian figures of Wellington, Nelson, Queen Victoria, Wilberforce and others are not infrequent.

It is not perhaps generally realized that all eighteenth-century sculptors, and most early nineteenth-century ones, produced, in addition to likenesses of their living clients, an even larger number of posthumous portraits. Indeed, the largest part of their business was carving commemorative busts or monuments to be placed in churches, the former being either based on portraits or death-masks. Nollekens's best-known bust, that of the younger Pitt, of which he carved nearly a hundred replicas, was made from a death-mask, which the sculptor waited outside the dying statesman's house to take. The student of English sculpture will be well advised not only to study the collections in public galleries and museums but also to visit Westminster Abbey (and provincial cathedrals and parish churches), if he wishes to understand and learn about this art. Nor should it be forgotten that no church is too obscure to visit in the hope of discovering an unrecorded bust. It is only by studying the signed and documented works of the great sculptors that the collector will be able to recognize the unsigned ones by the same artists. At the same time it must be remembered that some of the most popular busts were frequently reproduced by minor sculptors and copyists. Sir Francis Chantrey produced only three versions of his famous bust of Sir Walter Scott, yet there are a large number of copies of this work in both private and public collections, nearly all of them, however ill carved, masquerading as Chantrey's work.

No mention has yet been made of 'Ideal' works, those life-size statues and groups of either classical figures and subjects or, in the mid-Victorian period, of heroes and heroines from Scott, Shakespeare and Wordsworth, and groups with sentimental titles such as *Cherub with Primroses*, *The Dove's Last Refuge* or *The Mother's Kiss*. These are now too large for any modern home but, if well placed, can add charm to the grounds or gardens, though those made of soft marble are apt in time to be affected by frost.

The garden sculpture which best can stand the English climate unmoved and unchanged are the terra-cotta works of Mrs Coade, who turned out a vast number of figures, busts, reliefs, vases, urns, fountains and other pieces at her Lambeth factory between 1769–1830. Mrs Coade, a remarkable business woman, was shrewd enough to employ the best artists. The Royal Academicians, John Bacon, John Flaxman, Thomas Banks and J. C. Rossi, besides sculptors such as G. Bubb and John De Vaere, modelled and designed for her. The Coade artificial stone is easily distinguished by the sharpness of the detail and its yellow, or sometimes pinkish, colour. As Mrs Coade herself said, in one of her catalogues, her work had 'a property peculiar to itself of resisting the frost and consequently of retaining that sharpness in which it excels every kind of stone sculpture'. This was not an idle boast; for many of her works are nearly as brilliant and clear-cut as on the day they left the factory.

The products of the factory are almost invariably signed and generally dated, the earlier works having 'Coade' and then 'Coade and Sealy' (i.e. John Sealy, Mrs Coade's cousin and partner). After the death of Mrs Coade and her daughter the works were purchased by William Croggon, who had been for many years manager. At his death in 1836 the long history of the firm came to an end, and the moulds and models were purchased by various manufacturers of terra-cotta, who tried to continue the production. But either they were inferior workers or they had not the secret of the materials used by Mrs Coade (of which molten glass seems to have played a large part), as the results were poor and none of the works is up to the standard of the great days when the indomitable Mrs Coade directed her manufactory.

The list of British sculptors which follows is only a very brief selection; for, though it is not generally realized, England produced literally hundreds of artists in marble, stone, bronze and lead during the last three hundred years. The names and brief details of some of those sculptors, whose works are not infrequent in private collections and the saleroom, have therefore been given.

REPRESENTATIVE BRITISH SCULPTORS

Adams, George Gamon (1821–1898). Made a number of busts of the first Duke of Wellington, both in bronze and marble, some executed from life and others based on the death-mask. Copies of both these are not rare and the one from the death-mask was considered by the Iron Duke's family to be the best likeness of any of the numberless busts made of him.

Abbott, George (1803–1883). In 1850 he executed bronze cabinet busts of Peel and Wellington. A large number of replicas of both these works were made, those of Peel being manufactured by Messrs Hetley of Soho Square.

Bacon, John, R.A. (1740–1799). (*See* Plate 146A.)

Baily, Edward Hodges (1788–1867). Best known for his statue of Nelson in Trafalgar Square. He produced a large number of busts, many of which had great charm. He was for many years chief modeller to the famous silversmiths Rundell & Bridge, designing racing trophies, presentation plate, candelabra, etc.

Behnes, William (1795–1864). Probably the greatest of the early Victorian portrait sculptors, and at his best a very fine artist. Unfortunately his extravagance forced him into the hands of money-lenders, and some of his later works were not worthy of him, though even towards the end, when penniless, harried by bailiffs and seeking refuge in drink, he could still turn out work of great beauty and charm.

Broadie, William (1815–1881). A prolific Scottish sculptor, whose busts are competent but uninspired. He was at his best when he carved small portrait cabinet busts.

Butler, Timothy (b. 1806). Exhibited more than one hundred busts at the Royal Academy between 1828 and 1879. Few of his works have much merit, but he was frequently selected by committees who wished to have the likeness of their chairman perpetuated in marble.

Campbell, Thomas (1790–1858). Spent most of his life in Rome and was much influenced by the classical school. Though now a forgotten and neglected artist, he deserves a better fate. He was a careful worker and took an infinity of trouble to give a characteristic likeness to each of his sitters. (*See* Plate 144B.)

Chantrey, Sir Francis, R.A. (1781–1841). The most popular sculptor of the Late Georgian era and his energy must have been heroic. From his studio flowed an almost ceaseless flood of busts and monuments, the former, considering the rapidity with which they must have been modelled, extremely good, some almost inspired. His busts of men are better than those of women. In his lifetime nearly everybody of importance sat to him.

Francis, John (1780–1861). His small cabinet busts are admirable. Many were of politicians; for Francis was a keen Whig and was called the 'official sculptor' of that party. His sitters used to order a number of replicas of their busts to present to their friends. Francis's work is therefore not rare, but that does not make it any the less attractive. (*See* Plate 141D.)

Garrard, George, A.R.A. (1760–1826). Though he produced a number of skilfully carved busts, Garrard will be best remembered for his accurate small-scale models of animals, particularly of dogs and cattle, which he executed both in bronze and plaster.

Gott, Joseph (1786–1860). A Leeds sculptor who is slowly gaining the recognition he deserves. His work is nearly always good, and his models of animals are full of charm.

Macdonald, Laurence (1799–1878). A prolific artist who spent much of his life in Rome, where his work was sought by the fashionable English visitors, his studio being described as containing 'the peerage done into marble'. Macdonald flattered his sitters, making all the men appear noble and all the women beautiful, with the result that his busts are inclined to be tame and insipid.

Noble, Matthew (1818–1876). Like Macdonald a prolific and fashionable artist, but he did not flatter his sitters so slavishly, and some of his busts have force and character. His large output mitigated against masterpieces, and there is a certain dull sameness about Noble's work.

Nollekens, Joseph (1737–1823). The greatest portrait sculptor of his time. Doctor Johnson said, on hearing a rival sculptor praised, 'I think my friend Joe Nollekens can chop out a head with any of them'. Even Nollekens's acid biographer, J. T. Smith, wrote: 'His fame for bust-making will never be diminished'. His most popular busts were those of the younger Pitt and Fox, the former based on the death-mask, while of the latter there are two completely different versions. Of the bust of Pitt over 90 replicas were made by the sculptor, and practically as many of each of the busts of C. J. Fox. (*See* Plate 141A.)

Roubiliac, Louis François (1705?–1762). Probably the grandest sculptor to work in England during the eighteenth century. His busts are superb, since he had both the seeing eye as well as the skilled hand. Vertue said of him that 'his inventions were copious and free, picturesque – so light and easy – as painting', and those who have seen his terra-cotta busts in public or private collections cannot fail to agree with this criticism. (*See* Plates 140, 141C.)

Rysbrack, John Michael (1694–1770). Rysbrack, who came over from the Low Countries to England, was very nearly as grand a sculptor as his contemporary rival, L. F. Roubiliac (q.v.), and his output was certainly greater. The difference between the two masters perhaps lies in the fact that Rysbrack's busts are wonderful portraits but have a faint air of English frigidity, while Roubiliac's have the spontaneous easiness and charm of French eighteenth-century art. (*See* Plate 141B.)

Turnerelli, Peter (1774–1839). He was son of an Italian sculptor but was born in Dublin. His busts are careful likenesses and have considerable merit. He was the first British sculptor completely to break away from the convention of portraying his sitters in classical costume, and to show them instead in everyday dress. His best-known work is the bust of Daniel O'Connell (1828), of which it was said ten thousand plaster copies were sold.

Woolner, Thomas (1825–1892). One of the best of Victorian artists, he was the sculptor member of the pre-Raphaelite brotherhood, and his busts are carefully, even painstakingly, modelled. Though without doubt admirable likenesses, they seem to lack the spark of true genius. (*See* Plate 146B.)

(*B*) WAX-MODELLING

Beeswax is possessed of properties which make it the most convenient medium for making portraits either by modelling or by casting in moulds, for it melts easily, mixes with any colouring matter, and can be tinted. Figures of wax were used by the Ancient Egyptians at their funerals, while wax dolls were known to the Hellenistic world, and waxen masks in Ancient Rome.

Wax-modelling can be traced from the Middle Ages, when it was chiefly in use for votive offerings to churches, though it first became of artistic importance in the Italy of the Renaissance. Owing to their fragile nature and rarity, few wax portraits earlier than the eighteenth century have survived. Indeed, it was well after 1700 that the art reached its greatest popularity, both in England and on the Continent. The finest foreign wax-modeller of this period was undoubtedly the German, **B. C. Hardy** (1726–1819), whose superb portraits are modelled in so deep a relief as to be almost in the round. There are also a number of French artists of the same period, but it was in England that the art flourished most, and many foreigners came to England to practise. The popularity of the art can be explained by the fact that it was a cheap, quick and accurate method of having a likeness taken, and was therefore open to a wider circle than that which patronized portrait painters.

Wax portraits are not infrequently signed, often on the truncation, and it is sometimes possible also to find the artist's trade card in the back of the frame.

Among the most important artists working in the eighteenth century in England were **Samuel Percy** (1750–1820) and **Isaac Gosset** (1713–99), while the best in the nineteenth century were **Peter Rouw** (1770–1852) and **Richard Cockle Lucas** (1800–83). Percy was an extremely versatile artist. He could produce either a simple portrait or an animated group, consisting of a number of miniature figures. His portraits are frequently in white wax, though most of his groups are brightly coloured. Gosset's portraits are nearly always in a yellowish wax (invented by himself) and modelled in a low relief, which thins at the extremities of the profile, so that the nose, hair and other features appear almost to be painted on the background.

Peter Rouw, a versatile artist, for he was also a sculptor and a gem modeller, produced a large number of admirable portraits, mostly modelled in pink wax. He is also known on occasions to have used colour or painted wax. With R. C. Lucas we come to the last of the wax-modellers in the old tradition. His portraits (generally ivory-coloured) are mounted on chocolate-coloured wax, while the frames, which he designed himself, have an inside edging of a very unattractive brown plush. A large collection of his works can be seen at the Bethnal Green Museum, London.

Among other workers who must, however briefly, be noticed are **James Tassie, John Charles Lochee** and **Eley George Mountsteven.** Tassie was born in Scotland in 1735, and as a young man moved to Dublin and worked with the physician Henry Quin. Together they invented an enamel or vitreous paste, in which Tassie cast his wax medallion portraits. In 1766 Tassie came to London, where he was employed by Wedgwood and later by Catherine, Empress of Russia. Tassie modelled portrait medallions in wax from life and then cast them in his hard, white-enamel paste. A large collection of these can be seen in the Scottish National Portrait Gallery. They are admirable works, since Tassie took infinite pains to get accurate likenesses. He died in 1799.

Lochee, born in 1751, studied at the Royal Academy and was, like Tassie, and a number of other wax-modellers, employed by Wedgwood. His portraits are usually in pink wax painted with colours, and the details, hair, uniform, etc., in considerably higher relief than the face of the sitter. Unfortunately, he does not seem to have been a good man of business. He was declared a bankrupt in 1791, and after that trace of him is lost.

The third of these artists, Mountsteven, was born in Ireland and worked in England between 1781–91. He used a white wax, and his portraits are very fine – indeed, it was said of him that he brought wax-modelling to 'a higher degree of perfection than ever it had obtained before'. He left England in 1791 and died abroad.

Like almost everything else one can collect, wax portraits have been copied, while those which represent famous persons, such as Nelson, Washington, Wellington and others, have been at one time or another mass-produced in large numbers. But most of these works are so coarse and clumsy that the beginner-collector will soon learn to recognize and spurn them. If he is starting to acquire wax portraits, he would be well advised to study the large series of documented portraits in the Victoria and Albert Museum. Luckily for such a collector, wax portraits and busts are not in very great demand. This is curious, for they are small and decorative and grace almost any room. The following list, by no means complete, gives the names and dates of some of the best British artists in wax, and may also prove of use to established collectors.

Andras, Catherine (fl. 1795–1824).
Bally, William (fl. 1832–1846).
Bouquet, W. V. (fl. 1782–1798).
Burch, E., R.A. (b. 1730, d. 1814).
Cave, J. (fl. 1820–1830).
Coffin, Edmund (fl. 1783–1803).
Cornman, H. (fl. 1799–1821).
Cramphorn, William (fl. 1807–1819).
Cunningham, Patrick (d. 1774).
Dell, J. (fl. 1793–1797).
De Vaere, John (b. 1755, d. 1830).
De Veaux, John (fl. 1821–1836).
Engleheart, Thomas (b. 1745, d. 1786).
Flaxman, John, R.A. (b. 1755, d. 1826).
Giannelli, J. G. (fl. 1808–1829).
Hackwood, James (fl. 1770–1790).
Hagbolt, T. (b. 1773, d. 1849).
Henderson, J. (fl. 1782–1797).
Hepstinstall, J. (fl. 1818–1822).
Lyon, Edwin (d. 1837).
Morison, David (fl. 1821–1850).
Peart, Charles (b. 1759, d. 1798).
Pingo, Lewis (b. 1743, d. 1830).
Pistrucci, Benedetto (b. 1784, d. 1855).
Plura, Giuseppe (b. 1753).
Poole, T. R. (fl. 1791–1809).
Smith, Joachim (fl. 1758–1803).
Smith, Thomas (fl. 1830–1850).
Stothard, Alfred Joseph (b. 1793, d. 1864).
Webber, Henry (b. 1754, d. 1826).

BOOKS FOR FURTHER READING

SCULPTURE

KATHERINE ESDAILE, *Life and Works of Louis François Roubiliac*, 1928 (Oxford University Press).
RUPERT GUNNIS, *Dictionary of British Sculptors, 1660–1815*, 1953 (Odhams Press) (contains lives of wax modellers).
M. I. WEBB, *Michael Rysbrack, Sculptor* (Country Life).

WAX PORTRAITS

D. R. REILLY, *Portrait Waxes*, 1953 (B. T. Batsford, Ltd).

ANTIQUE BRONZES

By P. E. LASKO

BRONZE, an alloy of copper and tin, was the earliest metal to be used by man, and the ease with which it can be cast, chiselled, chased and engraved, and the fine patina it acquires with age, have assured its popularity ever since, both for utilitarian and artistic work. There are many aspects of this vast field open to collectors – from prehistoric axes to the great portrait busts of eighteenth-century France or from Greek lamps to fine decorative plaques made to decorate eighteenth-century furniture. It is, of course, not possible to deal here with all or even most of these different fields. It should also be said that much of this material is no longer within the reach of collectors today – the collecting of Greek and Roman or Medieval bronzes can only be attempted by the really wealthy connoisseur. In spite of this, much still remains to interest the collector of modest means: the small statuettes and figure groups of Italian and French, as well of rarer Flemish and German origin from the late fifteenth to the eighteenth centuries; the fine household articles of the same period, such as ink-stands, fire-dogs and door-knockers; the delicate bronze-gilt mounts made in the seventeenth and eighteenth centuries to decorate furniture or clock-cases; the fine mortars of the late medieval period and later centuries from Italy or Flanders and even England and France; the plaquettes made for the decoration of furniture or household articles, such as ink-stands, as well as for acquisition by connoisseurs and collectors since the late fifteenth century.

A difficulty which confronts the collector of bronzes is to discriminate between the work of, say, the sixteenth century, and later casts after the same model, varying from work of the master's followers or his workshop to copies made as late as the nineteenth century. Only the handling of many bronzes and the careful study of the best work in public collections, like those at the Victoria and Albert Museum and the Wallace Collection in London, the Ashmolean Museum, Oxford, the Fitzwilliam Museum, Cambridge, or the Metropolitan Museum, New York, as well as a number of fine collections in Italy, France or Germany, will enable the aspiring collector to recognize quality of casting, the type of finish achieved by individual chiselling and chasing or polishing of the figure and the correct patina appertaining to individual periods.

Small bronzes are rarely signed and are usually attributed to individual artists on style or, when possible, by the direct relation the small work may bear to documented major sculpture by known masters. The basis for all study of Italian bronzes is still the great work by Wilhelm Bode, a pioneer in this field. More recent work has been done by Leo Planiscig. The rarer German bronzes have been studied by E. F. Bange. French bronzes of the seventeenth and eighteenth centuries still await comprehensive treatment, and are as yet little represented in the major museum collections, with the exception only of the Wallace Collection in London.

Sculpture in bronze, of such importance to Antiquity, saw its great revival in Italy during the Renaissance of the fifteenth century. At first the medium was used solely for major works under the patronage of the Church, like the two pairs of bronze doors for the Baptistry of Florence. The open competition for the first pair of these doors, held in 1401 and won by Lorenzo Ghiberti, heralded the beginning of the Renaissance.

Donatello, the giant of Italian sculpture of the next generation, was responsible for the revival of the conception of a free-standing figure, released from the subservience to any architectural setting, not practised since antiquity. He was probably also responsible for the revival of the small statuettes so beloved in the guise of little gods or ornamental detail in the Greek and Roman period, which were henceforth to decorate the rooms of Italian humanists and wealthy patrons. While in Florence in the studios of Verrochio, A. Pollaiuolo, and especially Bertoldo, this new cult of an aspect of the antique was further developed, it was in the university city and centre of learning, Padua, under the influence of Donatello's stay from 1443 to 1453, that a school of bronze casters developed which first fully exploited the possibilities of small bronzes for decorative and utilitarian purposes. The production of statuettes, often directly inspired by the antique, ink-stands, hand-bells, salts, small caskets, fanciful and grotesque oil-lamps, candlesticks, mortars, animals of powerful and, at times, almost hideous realism, began in the last decades of the fifteenth century: and the prolific production was carried on well into the sixteenth century. Outstanding among the many artists who must have been employed in their manufacture was Andrea Briosco, called Riccio. Works attributed to him, especially examples of a great variety of male and female satyrs made by him and his school, may be seen in a number of private and in most public collections. In the snakes, toads and crabs, one of the popular products of the Paduan school which were probably cast from Nature herself, one can see the emphasis on naturalism in this school and their desire to re-create, rather than slavishly follow, the work of Antiquity. At the smaller courts of northern Italy, however, the fashion for the Antique was stronger. At Mantua, for example, under the patronage of Isabella d'Este, Pietro Ilario Bonacolsi, who went to the extreme of using the pseudonym 'l'Antico', produced finely-chiselled copies of the Antique almost exclusively for the Mantuan court. A number of artists from the late fifteenth century onwards were engaged in producing small-scale, straightforward copies of the Antique for collectors. Among the most popular models were the 'Youth removing a Thorn from his Foot', after the original in the Capitoline Museum in Rome, and 'Hercules resting on his Club', after the colossal statue in the Naples Museum. After other sculptors produced fragmentary casts – for example, the Venus by the Venetian Tullio Lombardi – the imitation of the Antique could go no further.

The creation of the High Renaissance in the early sixteenth century by Leonardo da Vinci, Michelangelo and Raphael had both a direct and an indirect influence on the production of small bronzes. The indirect influence was a negative one. The new search for the revival of the grandeur as well as the forms of Antiquity forced the intimate art of the statuette temporarily into the background. The direct influence was, of course, the tremendous impact of Michelangelo's sculptural genius on Italian art.

In Florence his influence was almost disastrous and resulted in merely superficial imitation. Less overpowering, though strong, was Michelangelo's influence on Jacopo Tatti, called Sansovino, after his master, Andrea Sansovino. When after the sack of Rome in 1527 he settled in Venice, he formed a school which dominated the second half of the sixteenth century as Riccio's had dominated the first half. On his arrival in northern Italy, Sansovino found that the naturalism and rather laboured appreciation of the Antique as exemplified in Riccio's school and the naive and somewhat dry antique-inspired art of the Lombardi had already been redirected in the work of the Paduan Francesco da Sant' Agata and the Brescian Maffeo Olivieri, who worked in Venice. Both had sought to infuse a new dramatic sense of movement into the dry bones of Antiquity, an intention parallel to the new mannerist tendency in Michelangelo. Francesco achieved this by an elongated and elegant figure style, resulting in highly-polished statuettes; Olivieri by a more thick-set and dramatic style, in which the original wax modelling is left more apparent, the unevenness of the surface being retained in the finished work and not chiselled and polished down as in most of the work of his contemporaries. With Sansovino a new phase begins in north Italian sculpture. The unmistakable influence of Michelangelo, which he was the first to translate into the medium of the statuette, can be seen in his work. The powerful modelling of the anatomy of his figures, now more directly inspired by Nature than by the Antique and the strong *contra-posto* movement, point to it. His own contribution may be seen in the more delicate rendering of surface, the thinner, richer treatment of drapery and the full acceptance of the elegance and elongated proportions characteristic of sixteenth-century Mannerism. These latter tendencies were developed to full Mannerism in his pupils, Danese Cattaneo and, especially, Alessandro Vittoria. Characteristic for the transition in Venice from Mannerism to Baroque is the work of Nicolo Roccatagliata, who was active from the late sixteenth into the seventeenth century. His many variations on the theme of small child-statuettes has given him the title 'Master of the Putto'.

In Florence the best exponent of the Mannerist style was Benvenuto Cellini. His famous golden salt-cellar, made for Francis I, and now in Vienna and a work of great elegance, shows the abilities of this sculptor in work on a small scale. Unfortunately, it has not been possible to attribute any small bronzes to him. The most important sculptor of the later sixteenth century in Florence, however, was to be the Flemish-born Giovanni Bologna. Under him, aided by the lavish patronage of the ruling Medici princes, Florence again became the most important centre for bronze sculpture in Europe, and developed from the Mannerist to the Baroque style. His work was continued by his school, if anything even more prolific than Riccio's had been, well into the seventeenth century. The mannered elegance of his famous Neptune, designed in 1563 to crown the fountain for the Piazza Maggiore in Bologna (now in the Museo Civico), gives way in his later work to the intricate, spiral-like composition of Baroque vigour, like the group of the 'Rape of the Sabines', the original marble of which was set up in the Loggia dei Lanzi at Florence in 1583. Many small bronzes, often with slight variations in composition, of these as well as most of Bologna's major works are known: the most famous among them, no doubt, the 'Flying Mercury' first cast in 1564. His most important pupil and follower was Antonio Susini, whose workshop was continued by his nephew, Francesco Susini. With the end of the sixteenth century the importance of the small, free-standing bronze statuette diminishes. In the baroque conception of decoration everything is subordinated to an all-enveloping theme of grand dimensions, and the intimacy and individuality of the Renaissance figurine is no longer at home.

As has already been pointed out, German Renaissance bronzes are rarer than Italian, and therefore a more difficult subject for systematic collection. The popularity of bronzes, never as great as it had been in Italy, began in the early sixteenth century under Italian influence, and their production was mainly undertaken in southern Germany, with Nuremberg as its centre. The first half of the century was dominated by the Vischer family workshop, under the direction of Peter Vischer the Elder. Their major work, the Sebaldus Tomb in Nuremberg, shows the new interest in small figures and groups in its details, but the making of free-standing figures was only attempted by his sons, Peter and Hans. Their small statuettes of antique subjects, often adapted as ink-stands, clearly betray Italian, especially Paduan, inspiration. But they never descend to mere imitation. The naturalism they employ is of a northern and a Germanic kind, often still reminiscent of Late Gothic rhythms, and it is always further removed from antique formulas than their Italian counterparts. After the Vischer workshop was dissolved in 1549, Pankratz Labenwolf's workshop takes over the leading position until his death in 1563. His most famous production is the 'Man with the Geese' fountain in Nuremberg. It is also typical of the period, and its interest in the naturalistic rendering of genre figures, especially peasants, with not even an echo of the interest in Antiquity portrayed by the Vischer school. Small bronzes identical with and closely related to the 'Gooseman' have survived in numbers. At much the same time as Labenwolf's naturalism we also find Wenzel Jamnitzer, active mainly as a goldsmith, working wholeheartedly in the elegant style of the Italian mannerists for aristocratic and wealthy families.

During the seventeenth century, while Italy, in the field of small bronzes, does little more than continue to exploit her late sixteenth-century traditions, France takes over the leadership. Since the direct influence of Italian art at the time of Francis I and the school of Fontainebleau, French art was closely connected with the royal court and the servant of the lavish tastes of succeeding monarchs, culminating in the 'Grand Siècle' of Louis XIV (1638–1715). The small, intimate bronze had no place in their tremendous decorative schemes. Only one or two functions remained for original work on a comparatively small scale, such as the magnificent fire-dogs needed for the decoration of fireplaces. A pair crowned by the figures of Jupiter and Juno, cast by M. Anguier, after his master A. Algardi, are in the Wallace Collection. The style of such work did not accept the full religious fervour of the Baroque, but retained a more disciplined and colder classicism favoured at the court of Louis XIV, under the direction of Lebrun and the King's close adviser, Colbert, and which, through the school of Versailles and the Gobelins, dominated all France. There also survive a large number of bronzes representing small workshop copies of major works by leading sculptors of the period: for example, the equestrian statue of Louis XIV by F. Girardon or the 'Chevaux de Marly' by G. Couston. The fine life-size bronze busts of the period are outside the present terms of reference.

In the eighteenth century the light-hearted quality and feminine elegance that is characteristic of Rococo art under Louis XV and Louis XVI resulted in a new fashion for the small, intimate decorations which were to be found in every well-to-do home. The small porcelain figurines of the eighteenth century are another aspect of this revival for intimate decoration, and small bronzes are often closely related to the productions of the Sèvres factory. In some cases we can see in these bronzes the models made for the porcelain factory. One such piece is L. S. Boizot's group of Pluto carrying off Proserpine, in the Wallace Collection. In the utilitarian field fine bronze candelabra, usually with elegant figures supporting bronze-gilt candle-holders of foliate form, and the fine bronze-gilt decorative mounts applied to furniture, are typical of the period. One sculptor, J. J. Caffieri, a member of the family famed for the production of the latter, has left us a signed and dated group of 'Cupid Vanquishing Pan' (Wallace Collection), showing the playful and delicate style of the Rococo.

First signs of the renewed classicism characteristic of the period during and after the French Revolution appear shortly before that event, but the new style was consciously developed first by the bourgeois republicanism of the revolutionary period and later under the new Empire. Characteristic bronzes were produced by A. Canova, the first sculptor to aim at the revival of the purer Greek values rather than those of Rome, and by Claude Michel, called Clodion, who designed decorative accessories as well as producing major sculpture, both before the Revolution, in a vivid and sensuous style, and after the Revolution, adapting himself to the new taste, in the severe style of the Greek revival.

GLOSSARY

Bronzes d'applique: *see* Ormolu.

Bronze disease: natural patina formed in the soil, often of a soft and porous nature, tends to retain some of saline constituents of the soil. These salts, together with the moisture in the atmosphere, may form bright-green spots, which are sometimes dry or moist, a condition called bronze disease. The disease, if not attended to, spreads quickly and has a destructive corrosive action. Its cure by chemical processes is perhaps too complicated to be attempted by collectors, but is easily accomplished by an expert restorer.

Chasing or chiselling: the *cire-perdue* process of casting leaves roughness and poor finish as well as often resulting in the loss of detail. It is therefore necessary to work over the rough-cast with steel chisels and gravers. The absence of such evidence of individual treatment of bronzes may be taken at best as a sign of a poor workshop production, at worst as a sign of modern after-casting.

Cire-perdue: the 'lost-wax' method of casting, used for all casting of work of any complication from ancient to modern times. Its processes are, briefly, this: the work is modelled on a clay core in wax of a thickness intended in the final bronze product. The finished wax model, to which vents and pouring channels are added, is then surrounded by an envelope of finely-ground clay mixed with sawdust, chopped straw or some such inflammable material, which will burn out when the mould is fired, giving the envelope the necessary porosity. In the firing process the wax melts and leaves the mould through the vents and pouring channels – and the metal may be poured in to take the place of the wax. The mould is then broken off the bronze and the core removed by breaking it up. It is, of course, obvious that only one bronze can be cast from each wax model by this method. For each of the workshop productions of the Renaissance there must therefore have been a wax model first, and this explains the infinite slight variations in each example made after the master model produced by the head of the workshop. Moulds which may be taken apart in small sections are called piece-moulds, and have perhaps been known since the sixteenth century. They were probably never used for bronze sculpture until the nineteenth century, and the presence of small ridges, that are the result of the tiny gaps between each section of the mould, may be taken as the surest evidence of modern manufacture.

Mortars: in Antiquity mortars were usually made of stone or heavy pottery, but during the Middle Ages they were normally cast in bronze. Their use was widespread, both in the apothecaries' laboratories for the grinding and pounding of chemicals and in the home for the pounding of condiments and spices. In the painter's studio it might also have found its use in the pulverization of pigments. From the fourteenth century onwards mortars survive in considerable numbers, especially from Flanders and England, and later from Germany and Italy. With the exception of Italy, where they were produced by such schools as Riccio's, they seem to be mainly the work of the bell foundries, and, because the alloy used is so often close to that employed by these foundries, they are normally said to be made of 'bell metal'. An inducement to the collecting of this class of objects, rarely of any great artistic merit, is the fact that they more often than not bear inscriptions in raised lettering, usually pious in intention or giving the owner's or maker's name as well as the date of its production. Among the earliest of such mortars is the fine Gothic example in the York Museum, dated 1308 and signed 'Frater William de Towthorpe'. Flemish signed and dated mortars are more common, especially from the sixteenth century. But collectors should beware of the many nineteenth-century aftercasts of these, usually of very crude quality and slurred definition. Mortars of the fourteenth and fifteenth centuries are rare, the bulk being of the sixteenth and seventeenth centuries. During the eighteenth century their manufacture ceases.

Plaquettes: plaquettes are found cast in lead and silver as well as in bronze, and were used to decorate household utensils and furniture from the fifteenth century onwards. They have also been collected for their own sakes by connoisseurs since the sixteenth century, and formed part of collector's cabinets, together with medals, intaglios and cameos. It is not always easy to distinguish between medals and plaquettes, but basically the medal has an obverse and a reverse and is circular, whereas the plaquette is one-sided and square, oblong or oval. More precisely, the medal is commemorative or historical in character, bearing on its obverse the portrait of a notable personage, usually surrounded by an inscription, while plaquettes are purely decorative in intention, with mythological, historical or religious subjects depicted. Plaquettes belong to the category of reproducible objects, and one may almost speak of different 'states', as in the case of prints. In each reproduction it tends to lose some of its definition, and poorer, often modern, copies show little of the sharpness and individual chasing that characterize the first few to leave the artist's workshop. Plaquettes are more closely connected with painting than with sculpture, and their compositions can be related to the various Renaissance schools of painting – and especially to the engravings which gained in popularity during the sixteenth century. They were mostly issued from the schools of bronze casters already discussed, beginning with Donatello's in the fifteenth century. In addition, one or two artists who are known only by their plaquettes should be mentioned. The first, probably a Paduan in close touch with Riccio's school, was active in the late fifteenth and early sixteenth centuries, and signed a number of plaquettes of the first quality with the pseudonym 'Moderno'. In the first half of the sixteenth century the work of Valerio Belli of Vincenza and Giovanni Bernardi is worthy of note. They, like a number of the sculptors who issued plaquettes, also produced some fine engraved gems. In the second half of the sixteenth century Leone Leoni worked in this field among the Mannerist followers of Michelangelo, although he is more famous for his medals. Plaquettes of religious subjects were made north of the Alps from the fifteenth century onwards, and in the early sixteenth century, under Italian influence, secular subjects began to be produced in southern Germany, especially Nuremberg, in the Vischer school and by Peter Flötner, who is not known to have worked in the round at all. Plaquettes never attained the popularity in the Netherlands and in France which they enjoyed in Italy and Germany.

Ormolu: ormolu is the French name, first used in the seventeenth century, for the applied decoration, always of bronze-gilt, found on clock cases and furniture from the seventeenth to the eighteenth centuries. (See also the section in this volume on 'Miscellaneous Metalwork'.)

Sculpture d'appartement: a term often applied to the pairs, or groups, of figures, usually rather larger than the small bronzes we have discussed and made for the decoration of the great *salons* and galleries of the time of Louis XIV. They were normally enriched by much gilding and the use of coloured marbles.

DATES OF ARTISTS MENTIONED IN THE TEXT AND ILLUSTRATIONS

Italian School

Ghiberti, Lorenzo, 1378–1455
Donatello, ?1386–1466
Bertoldo di Giovanni, ?1425–91
Pollaiuolo, Antonio, 1429–98
Verrochio, Andrea, 1436–88
Vinci, Leonardo da, 1452–1519
Lombardi, Tullio, *c.* 1455–1532
Bonacolsi, Pietro Ilario, called l'Antico, *c.* 1460–1528
Belli, Valerio, 1468–1546
Briosco, Andrea, called Riccio, 1470–1532 (*see* Plate 148A)
Michelangelo Buonarotti, 1475–1564
Raphael Santi, 1483–1520
Olivieri, Maffeo, 1484–after 1534
Tatti, Jacopo, called Sansovino, 1486–1570
Francesco da Sant'Agata, active *c.* 1520
Bernardi da Castelbolognese, Giovanni, 1496–1553
Cellini, Benvenuto, 1500–71
Cattaneo, Danese, 1509–73
Leoni, Leone, 1509–90
Bologna, Giovanni, 1524–1608 (*see* Plate 152A)
Vittoria, Alessandro, 1525–1608
Campagna, Girolamo, 1549–after 1626 (*see* Plate 148B)
Roccatagliata, Nicolo, active *c.* 1600
Duquesnoy, François, called Fiammingo, 1594–1644 (*see* Plate 149A)
Susini, Antonio, d. 1624
Susini, Francesco, d. 1646
Algardi, Alessandro, 1602–54
Canova, Antonio, 1757–1822

German School

Vischer, Peter the Elder, *c.* 1460–1529
Vischer, Peter, 1487–1528
Vischer, Hans, *c.* 1489–1550
Flötner, Peter, *c.* 1493–1546
Labenwolf, Pankratz, d. 1563
Jamnitzer, Wenzel, 1508–85

French School

Anguier, Michel, 1612–86 (*see* Plate 152B)
Lebrun, Charles, 1619–90
Girardon, François, 1628–1715
Coustou, Guillaume, 1677–1746
Falconet, Etienne Maurice, 1716–91 (*see* Plate 150)
Caffieri, Jean-Jacques, 1725–92 (*see* Plate 151)
Michel, Claude, called Clodion, 1738–1814
Boizot, Louis Simon, 1743–1809

BOOKS FOR FURTHER READING

E. F. Bange, *Die Italicnischen Bronzen der Renaissance und des Barock. Zweiter Teil: Reliefs und Plaketten*, 1922.
E. F. Bange, *Die Deutschen Bronzestatuetten des 16. Jahrhunderts*, 1949.
W. Bode, *Italian Bronze Statuettes*, 3 vols., 1907–8.
W. Bode, *J. Pierpont Morgan Collection of Bronzes*, 2 vols., 1910.
W. Bode, *Die Italienischen Bronzestatuetten*, 1922.
F. Goldschmidt, *Die Italienischen Bronzen der Renaissance und der Barock. Erster Teil: Büsten, Statuetten und Gebrauchsgegenstände*, 1914.
J. G. Mann, *Sculpture*. Wallace Collection Catalogue, 1931.
L. Planiscig, *Die Bronzeplastiken*, 1924.
L. Planiscig, *Andrea Riccio*, 1926.
L. Planiscig, *Piccoli Bronzi Italiana*, 1930.
S. De Ricci, *The Gustave Dreyfus Collection: Reliefs and Plaquettes*, 1931.

(A) Matthew Boulton (wax), signed and dated 1814, by Peter Rouw. Diameter $14\frac{1}{2}$ in. *Victoria & Albert Museum.*

(B) Oliver Cromwell (marble), dated 1762, by Joseph Wilton. *Victoria & Albert Museum.*

PLATE 139

To face page 224

Matthew Prior (lead), by Louis F. Roubiliac. *Victoria & Albert Museum.*

(A) William Pitt, 1807, by Joseph Nollekens. *Author's Collection.*

(B) Sir Isaac Newton, *c.* 1739, plaster copy after Michael Rysbrack. *Author's Collection.*

(C) Louis F. Roubiliac. Self-portrait. *National Portrait Gallery.*

(D) The First Duke of Wellington, by J. Francis. *National Portrait Gallery.*

(A) William III (marble), by Alexander van der Hagen, died *c.* 1775. *Author's Collection.*

(B) Portrait of the artist (wax), by Samuel Percy, *c.* 1809. *Victoria & Albert Museum.*

(C) Augusta of Saxe-Gotha, Princess of Wales (wax), by Isaac Gosset. Eighteenth century. *Victoria & Albert Museum.*

(D) John Henderson (wax), by Eley Mountstephen. Eighteenth century. *Victoria & Albert Museum.*

(A) Dog Setting a Hare (wax), 1846, by L. Brown. *Author's Collection.*

(B) Wellington, by Thomas Wyon (wax). *Author's Collection.*

(C) Unknown Man, by Peter Rouw (wax). *Author's Collection.*

(D) One of a series of small plaster copies of the Raphael cartoons, 1820, by John Henning the Elder. *Author's Collection.*

A

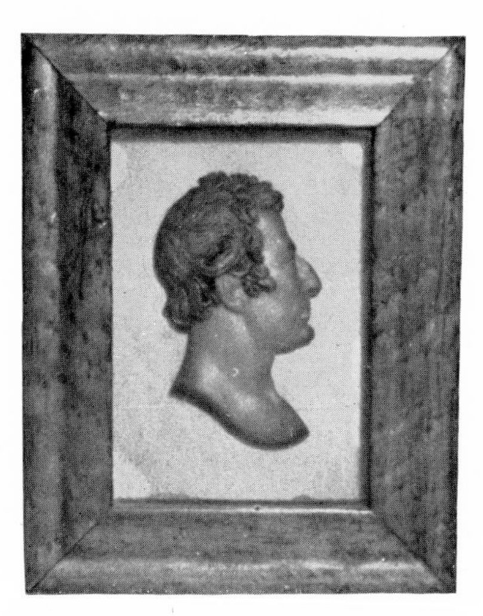

B

C

D

PLATE 143

(A) Princess Charlotte, by S. Percy. *National Portrait Gallery.*

(B) Sarah Siddons (marble), by T. Campbell. *National Portrait Gallery.*

PLATE 144

To face plate 145

(A) The Vegetable Woman (wax), by Caspar Hardy.
Collection the Hon. Mrs Ionides.

(B) The Sculptor at Work (wax), by Caspar Hardy.
Collection the Hon. Mrs Ionides.

PLATE 145

ce plate 144

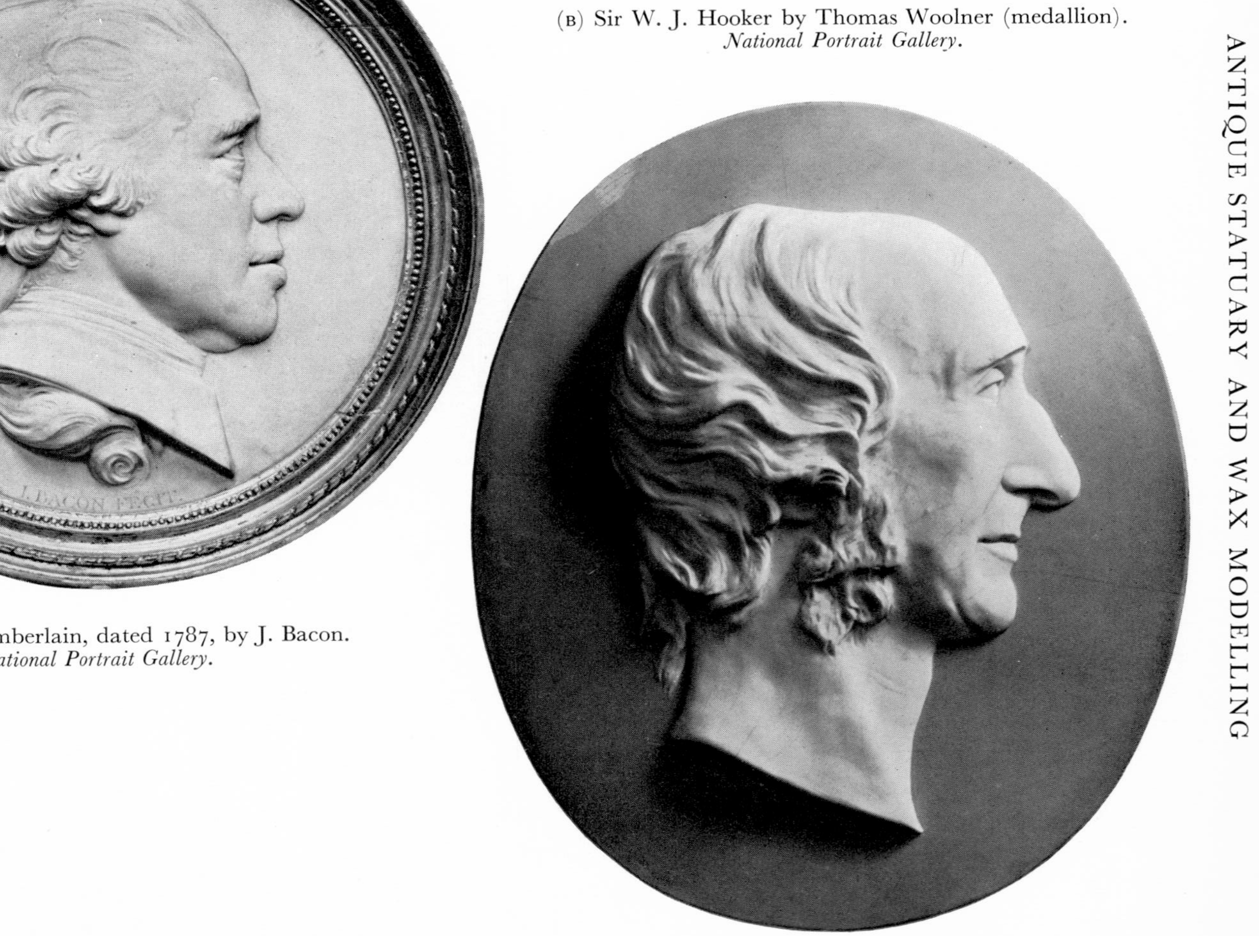

(A) Mason Chamberlain, dated 1787, by J. Bacon.
National Portrait Gallery.

(B) Sir W. J. Hooker by Thomas Woolner (medallion).
National Portrait Gallery.

A group of sixteenth-century Household Utensils. *Top row, left to right*: Handbell, Paduan; Double-burner Oil Lamp, Paduan (ex *Beit Collection*); Covered Inkwell, Paduan. *Bottom row*: Mortar bearing inscription 'ANNO SALVTIS NOSTRE 1584', Flemish; Oil Lamp in the antique style, Paduan; Handbell, bearing inscription 'MATER DEI MEMENTO MEI' and 'PETRVS GHEINEVS ME FECIT 1577', Flemish (Peetar van den Gheyn II of Mechelen, d. 1598); Oil Lamp, Workshop of Riccio, Paduan; Mortar, North Italian. *All pieces from Alfred Spero.*

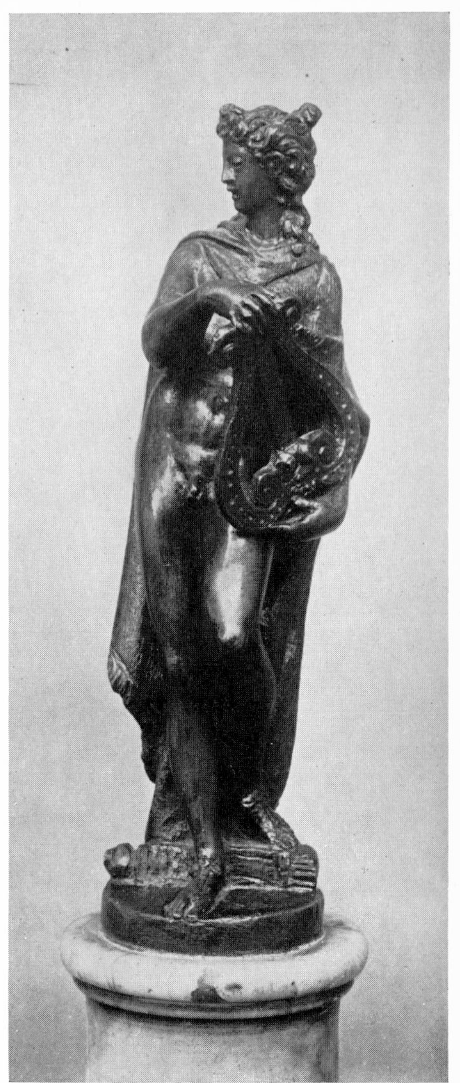

(B) Apollo, North Italian, probably by Girolamo Campagna, last quarter of the sixteenth century. *Collection of John Gere, Esq.*

(A) Seated Female Satyr, school of Riccio, late fifteenth century. *Alfred Spero.*

(A) Running Putto, by Fiammingo, Flemo-Italian, early seventeenth century. *Alfred Spero.*

(B) Apollo, French or Italian, late eighteenth century. *Alfred Spero.*

The Bather, companion to a Shepherd Paris, by E. M. Falconet, third quarter of the eighteenth century. *Wallace Collection.*

PLATE 150

Cupid Vanquishing Pan, signed and dated J. J. Caffieri, 1777. *Wallace Collection.*

(A) Rape of the Sabine Women, school of Giovanni Bologna, late sixteenth century
Wallace Collection.

(B) One of a Pair of Fire-dogs, showing Jupiter Victorious over the Titans, by M. Anguier after A. Algardi. French, mid-seventeenth century.
Wallace Collection.

(A) Autumn (*c.* 1767). Back painting of engraving after J. Williams by J. MacArdell. *Messrs John Beazor, Cambridge.* (B) Chinese mirror painting, *c.* 1780. 1 ft. 11 in. × 2 ft. 9 in. *Messrs H. Blairman & Sons Ltd.*

(C) Partridge shooting by J. B. Walker. Back painting published 1801. *Hilton Gallery, Cambridge.*

(B) Portrait of a gentleman by Mrs Isabella Beetham. Painted on the underside of a convex glass. $3\frac{3}{4}$ in. × $3\frac{1}{8}$ in. *Collection of W. F. Rollo, Esq., Lavenham.*

(C) Charles James Fox by Charles Rosenberg. Painted on the underside of a flat glass with verre églomisé edge. $6\frac{3}{4}$ in. × $4\frac{3}{4}$ in. *Private Collection.*

(A) Emma, daughter of George Engleheart, the miniature painter, by August Edouart. Cutwork. 9 in. × $6\frac{1}{2}$ in. *Author's Collection.*

(D) Life-size bust of George Washington cut by Eleanor ('Nelly') Parke Curtis. Traced by candlelight. *Courtesy of the Metropolitan Museum of Art.*

PLATE 154

(A) Portrait of a gentleman by A. Forberger. Verre églomisé. $2\frac{1}{8}$ in. × $2\frac{3}{4}$ in. *Author's Collection.*

(B) Silhouette portrait painted on a plaster slab by John Miers. Églomisé glass. 4 in. × 5 in. *Messrs C. H. Stockbridge, Cambridge.*

(C) Conversation by Francis Torond. Cut work. $12\frac{3}{4}$ in. × $10\frac{1}{4}$ in. *Private Collection.*

(A) Chamberlain Worcester vase with contemporary silhouette portrait of George III. Height 8½ in. *Messrs R. M. Waylett.*

(B) George III in Windsor uniform by William Hamlet of Bath, *c.* 1800. Painted on the underside of the flat glass and backed with card. 8½ in. × 7 in. *Collection of John Woodiwis, Esq.*

PLATE 156

To face page

SILHOUETTES AND GLASS PICTURES

By RAYMOND LISTER

(*A*) SILHOUETTES

ALTHOUGH its origins go back to classical antiquity, the silhouette as we recognize it today most likely originated at the end of the seventeenth century. Doubtless various influences contributed to its subsequent popularity, but probably the greatest stimulus it received came from the publication of Johann Kaspar Lavater's *Essays on Physiognomy* in the 1770's, in which, as well as claiming the silhouette to be the most faithful of all types of portrait, the author used many such portraits for illustrating his work.

At about this time silhouettes became fashionable and their popularity spread everywhere, finding admirers so diverse in character as Johann von Goethe, King George III of England, and the Empress Catherine the Great of Russia.

The earliest silhouettes were probably scissor-cuts. One was that of William and Mary, said to have been cut by Elizabeth Pyburg (fl. 1699). Indeed, these early cut silhouettes have great charm, and are much sought after by collectors. Some of them – especially those of Francis Torond (1743–1812) – are of great rarity.

But charming though these old cut silhouettes are, the art's highest peaks have undoubtedly been reached by artists producing painted work. It is generally agreed that one of the greatest silhouettists of all was John Miers (1758–1821), whose work is painted as finely as the most delicate miniature. Although not so prolific a worker as Miers, Isabella Beetham (fl. 1750), whose work was painted mostly on the reverse side of convex glass, is, so far as quality is concerned, at least his equal.

At the end of the eighteenth century the silhouette went into a period of decline, from which it was rescued mostly through the efforts of Augustin Amant Constant Fidèle Edouart (1789–1861), a French refugee who came to England in 1814. Edouart, a free-hand cutter, initiated the second and last great period of English silhouettes. His output was enormous (he cut something approaching a quarter of a million likenesses), and this fact, coupled with the publication of his (now excessively rare) *Treatise* on the subject, published in 1835, gave a great impetus to the numerous and often very able school of amateur silhouettists that arose at the time.

The Continent, too, produced a large number of good silhouettists during the eighteenth and nineteenth centuries. The art particularly flourished in Germany. Goethe himself was a cutter, and mention must also be made of the delicate and lacy cut-work of Christina Luise Duttenhofer (1776–1829) and that of Philipp Otto Runge (1776/7–1810). France produced A. Forberger (1762–1865) and E. P. Sideau (fl. 1782); and Austria H. Loeschenkohl (fl. 1780) and Leopold Gross (fl. 1790). In fact, most European countries can boast at least one or two silhouettists of some standing.

America produced a host of silhouettists, particularly cutters. Their works are, in fact, often the only form of portraiture available of American historical characters. It is difficult to know which ones to select to mention, but Charles Willson Peale (1741–1827), who was also miniaturist, silversmith, dentist, watchmaker, naturalist and harness-maker, cannot be ignored. Neither can William M. S. Doyle (d. 1828), who claimed to paint silhouettes 'in the manner of the celebrated Miers of London', Moses Chapman (1783–1821), who cut silhouettes both freehand and by machine, and Eleanor Parke Curtis (1779–1852). Although silhouette work continues to be used even today, its heyday as a form of portraiture ended with the invention of photography. It is one of the few fields still open in which the collector can obtain genuine rarities at reasonable prices.

GLOSSARY

Albums: silhouettes were often made by amateur artists and pasted in albums, particularly in the early years of the nineteenth century. Princess Elizabeth (1770–1840), daughter of George III, was among those who kept such albums. Professional artists, including A. Edouart, also kept albums of duplicates for record purposes.

Bronzing: the name of the metallic shading on some silhouettes. In some cases this was used with beautiful effect, particularly by John Miers, who used real gold. It was usually, though not exclusively, used on painted work.

Conversation: a silhouette representation of a group of people – usually a family – engaged together in some domestic pursuit. Some of its finest exponents were Francis Torond, a French refugee who worked in Bath and London, Johann Friedrich Anthing (1753–1823), a native of Gotha, who produced some outstanding conversations of the Russian Imperial Court, which he cut or painted at St Petersburg, August Edouart, William Wellings (late eighteenth century), Charles Rosenberg (1745–1844), and J. Dempsey (early nineteenth century).

Decorative borders: these were sometimes used as settings for silhouettes. They were of two kinds: (a) *Printed.* These were used in much the same way as the nineteenth-century photographers' cards, as cheap settings for the cut portraits which were pasted on them. They were particularly favoured by Continental silhouettists. (b) *Painted.* These were usually painted as an intrinsic part of the silhouette portrait, but sometimes were painted under frame-glass in *verre églomisé* (*see* Under-painting).

Engraved backgrounds: these were used by some cutters as settings on which to mount their portraits. A. Edouart used them widely and even used printed accessories such as newspapers, scrolls, etc., to place in the hands of his subjects.

Engraved silhouettes: books of printed silhouettes were popular in the eighteenth and nineteenth centuries, and the collector should be cautious of any such portraits framed up to look like genuine cut or painted examples. The books themselves are well worth collecting. On the other hand, it must be remembered that some silhouettes of celebrities were printed especially for framing.

Glass silhouettes (*see also under* Glass Pictures): silhouettes painted on to glass by one of the following methods: (a) *Verre églomisé* and *gold-glass engraving*. Silhouettes of this kind were produced by the Parisian artist A. Forberger (1762–1865), who backed his portraits with gold leaf or blue wax and often gave them floral borders, and W. A. Spornberg, a Swede, who worked at the end of the eighteenth century in Bath, and whose profiles are backed with red pigment and usually surrounded by a geometrical border. (b) *Painting on to the reverse side of flat or convex glass.* This was a common form of silhouette painting, and one capable of giving very effective results, particularly on those painted on convex glass, mounted over white backgrounds on to which their shadows could be thrown. Work of this kind was painted by Walter Jorden (late eighteenth century), Isabella Beetham, Charles Rosenberg (1745–1844), W. Rought (early nineteenth century), and many others.

Several silhouettists, among them John Miers, mounted their ordinary painted work beneath convex glass with *églomisé* borders and Mrs Beetham often combined *églomisé* mounts with portraits in plain black painted on the underside of the same glass. At least one silhouette in a glass millefleurs paper-weight is on record.

Ivory was sometimes used as a ground for silhouettes. It was particularly favoured for silhouettes intended for insertion in jewellery.

Jewellery and Trinkets: some of the art's most pleasing examples are set in jewellery and trinkets. Rings, brooches and snuff-boxes were particularly favourite repositories for shades. Some of John Miers's tiny shades, some less than half an inch high, are in such settings under coverings of rock crystal. Silhouette jewellery is of the greatest rarity.

Machine-cutting: silhouettes produced by a mechanical profile machine, of which there were many forms. Such work may usually be distinguished by a certain hardness and lack of freedom in its outlines. There were, however, a few machine-cutters who produced commendable work. One such was Mrs Sarah Harrington (fl. 1775), whose shades are full of vivacity. On the whole, however, machine-cutting is the art's most debased form.

Painted silhouettes: these were produced in a number of techniques on various materials, ranging from paper to glass. (*See also under* Bronzing, Decorative borders, Glass silhouettes, Ivory, Plaster, Porcelain.)

Plaster shades: shades painted on slabs of plaster, often with beer as the medium. This was at one time a common background, and it undoubtedly was effective, its snowy depth giving the greatest possible contrast and sharpness to the black of the shade. Probably the greatest master of this type of silhouette was John Miers. Another was W. Phelps (fl. 1788), although shades by the latter are excessively rare. Great care should be exercised in handling shades painted on plaster, as they are exceedingly fragile and will often crack at the smallest impact. Neither should any attempt be made to brush off dust that may have accumulated on them through the years, as they scratch very easily. If a plaster shade requires attention, it should be given to a specialist to do what is necessary.

Porcelain: porcelain was sometimes, particularly at the end of the eighteenth century, decorated with silhouette portraits, usually of royalty, though sometimes of other celebrities. The factories of Royal Worcester, Royal Copenhagen, Dresden, Meissen, Berlin and Sèvres all produced porcelain of this type. And objects so decorated include mugs, chocolate pots, jardinières, cups, saucers, plates, vases and simple plaques. No silhouette porcelain is common, and most of it is rare.

Profile: a silhouette portrait in which features other than the outline are drawn, sometimes in great detail. Silhouettes in which features and hair are drawn in gold paint on a black ground come into this category. Some profiles are merely miniatures painted in sharp outline. Edward Foster of Derby (1761–1865) painted many portraits of this type.

Scissor-work: silhouettes cut freehand from paper. Although this technique is not capable of giving such great refinements of finish as any of the painting methods employed, it is nevertheless capable of giving very striking effects of a different kind. Its most notable quality is the uncompromising sharpness it gives to the outlines of its subjects. It is possible for a cutter, by holding several thicknesses of paper together, to cut as many duplicates at the same time, thus giving several 'originals'. The most prolific cutter of all was A. Edouart. Other noteworthy cutters were Francis Torond, 'Master' William James Hubard (1807–62), who achieved notoriety as a protégé, and the ill-fated Major John André (1751–80), who was hanged by the Americans as a spy in the Civil War. One method of cutting was to cut out the portrait as a hollow from a piece of white paper and then mount it over a piece of black paper or material.

Shade: a silhouette portrait in which the face is painted in black. Ideally, the whole portrait should be in black, but sometimes clothes, nosegays or other details are inserted in colour, but the face itself must have no detail at all apart from that of its outline. J. Buncombe, who practised from *c.* 1745 to *c.* 1825 at Newport, Isle of Wight, painted fine shades of soldiers in which the uniforms are shown in colour and in great detail.

Edward Foster of Derby often painted faces in brown, blue or some other colour, and unless details are shown in the faces, such may also be termed shades. But this treatment is really a departure from the best practice. The most effective shades are those with faces painted in pure black on an unadulterated white ground.

Silhouette: the name usually given collectively to shades and profiles. It is derived from that of Étienne de Silhouette (1709–67), the parsimonious finance minister of Louis XV. He was an amateur cutter of shades. As such portraits were cheap, they were dubbed à la Silhouette, as indeed at the time were all cheap objects. He was not the originator of the art.

Trade labels: silhouettists, particularly in the eighteenth and early nineteenth centuries, often used trade labels which they fixed on the back of the frames containing their works. These labels in themselves form a fascinating subject for study. If still in place, covering the aperture at the back of a frame, a label can often be taken as at least a partial guarantee that the original contents of the frame have not been tampered with.

(*B*) GLASS PICTURES

Probably the earliest of all glass pictures were gold-glass engravings, used as early as Roman times for the decoration of glass vessels. The addition of colour to such decorations may have been suggested later by medieval stained-glass windows. Such a combination of ideas could certainly have given rise to the production of glass devotional pictures of the type that became common in the fourteenth century, a type itself which was later to develop into realistic pictures painted on the underside of glass.

In Switzerland from the sixteenth century onwards the art of glass-window painting in fired enamel colours developed a kind of glass picture in its own right. Such were the tiny windows (without lead lines), often measuring only a few inches each way, and painted with an almost unbelievable richness and elaboration, that are often seen in that country. The idea of the art of back-painting (described below) probably emanated from a desire to imitate under-glass painting, but so little is known of its origins that one can only guess.

Back-painting: the art of mounting prints on to the back of glass, making them transparent, and colouring them in from behind. This art, which probably originated in England, dates back to the second half of the seventeenth century. It is not known how it originated. There were several variants of the method used for making these prints, which was broadly as described in the next paragraph. This method is described in full in the chapter entitled *Process or Art of Making a Glass Picture* in the book *Polygraphice* (1700) by William Salmon.

The print itself was first soaked in water for four or five hours to remove the size from the paper. A sheet of fine Bristol glass was then covered with an adhesive (usually Venice turpentine) and the print, when dry, laid face down upon it. When it had set the back of the print was again damped, and the paper rubbed away with a sponge or the finger-tips, leaving only a thin tissue with the impression of the print adhering to the glass. After it had again dried out it was coloured in.

The earlier and more beautiful back-paintings owe their brilliant limpidity to the fact that only the smallest quantity of paper was allowed to remain on the print. Later examples made by amateurs or less skilled professionals have a much more opaque and stodgy appearance, owing to a greater thickness of paper being allowed to remain, the required transparency being partially produced by a white varnish. Back-painting was an anonymous art, although in its earliest days it is almost certain that the engraver of the print himself produced them.

Under-painting: this art is much older than that of back-painting. Examples are, in fact, known that belong to the fourth century A.D. In these older examples the technique by which they were produced consisted of engraving the picture on the back of a piece of glass (usually a goblet or some similar container) through a layer of gold leaf which had previously been attached to it. Sometimes colour was added from behind. Usually a second piece of glass was used to seal this engraving from behind, although this was more often omitted in later work intended purely as pictures, and not as incidental decorations for glass vessels. Many such pictures were made in Italy in the fourteenth century. The method is known as *gold-glass engraving*.

From this method was developed that known as *agglomizzato*, or *verre églomisé*, so called after Jean Baptiste Glomi (fl. 1760), an artist who used it, probably between two and three hundred years after its invention!

The technique of *verre églomisé* consisted of painting the picture in reverse directly on to the underside of a piece of glass and then backing the whole of the glass with either metal foil, wax or some other such coloured pigment. This method was used widely in Europe in the sixteenth century for painting devotional pictures, many of which were very crude.

From this to ordinary *under-glass painting* was but another step, and instead of the foil or pigment, realistic or decorative backgrounds could be painted in or, on the other hand, especially in the case of silhouettes produced by this method, the unpainted portion of the glass could be left perfectly clear. It was probably due to the silhouettist Isabella Beetham (*see above under* Silhouettes) and her husband, who, in Venice, rediscovered the art of under-painting, that it was reintroduced into England in the eighteenth century. Apart from silhouettes, really good work carried out in this technique is very rare indeed, most of it being crude in the extreme. The collector should beware of imitations made in the nineteenth century by cementing oil paintings on canvas to the underside of glass.

Another method of under-painting was *mirror-painting*. This was similar to the *gold-glass engraving* process, excepting that an amalgam of tin and mercury, to make it into a mirror, was first applied to the glass. The parts to be painted were then scraped away and painted in as required. Such paintings were often made in China, where the technique is thought to have been introduced from Europe by Jesuit missionaries. Vauxhall bevelled plate glass was actually exported to China for this purpose in the eighteenth century.

BOOKS FOR FURTHER READING

SILHOUETTES

MAX VON BOEHN, *Miniatures and Silhouettes* (Dent), 1928.

DESMOND COKE, *The Art of Silhouette* (Secker), 1913.

E. NEVILL JACKSON, *Silhouette Notes and Dictionary* (Methuen), 1938.

RAYMOND LISTER, *Silhouettes* (Pitman), 1953.

GLASS PICTURES

H. G. CLARKE, *The Story of Old English Glass Pictures, 1690–1810* (Courier Press), 1928.

L. LOEWENTHAL, *Pictures on Glass* (Privately published), 1928.

BAROMETERS

By H. ALAN LLOYD, F.S.A., F.B.H.I.

THE word Barometer derives from the Greek root *baros*, meaning weight. Thus, we have an instrument for the measuring of weight – of the atmosphere. In its earliest days the instrument was called a Barascope or referred to as the Torricellian Experiment.

That water could not be raised above about 33 feet with a single-stage suction pump had been noted by the scientists of the first half of the seventeenth century. The French philosopher Réné Descartes (1596–1650) had rejected the idea of the existence of a vacuum, and so had undermined the idea that Nature's abhorrence of a vacuum was the explanation of the action of water-pumps, thus leading the way to the correct explanation – that is, pressure resulting from the weight of the atmosphere. He claimed to have anticipated Torricelli, an Italian, who conceived the idea of experimenting with mercury, owing to its considerably greater density, and in 1643 found that the atmosphere would support a column of about 30 inches of mercury; but he did not appreciate that the height of the column varied with the state of the atmosphere. That the atmosphere has weight was shown by Galileo, who, in his book *Two New Sciences* (1638) estimated that the weight of the air was about one four-hundredth of that of the same volume of water. Torricelli was acquainted with Galileo and succeeded him as Grand Ducal mathematician on Galileo's death in 1642.[1]

Descartes also claimed that in 1647 he had suggested to Blaise Pascal (1623–62) to experiment with a mercury column at the bottom and top of a tower. This experiment Pascal carried out on the tower of the church of St Jacques in Paris, and established the fact that the height of the mercury column was greater at the bottom of the tower than at the top, thus demonstrating that the weight of the atmosphere varied with height. The church has disappeared, but the tower, enshrining a monument to Pascal, still stands.

On 19th September 1648, under Pascal's direction, his brother-in-law, Florin Perier, carried out the historic full-scale experiment on Puy-de-Dôme in Auvergne.[2]

It is very difficult to follow chronologically the various experiments made by scientists in the early days, since there is often many years' lag in publication. For instance, the Hon. Robert Boyle carried out experiments with his statical barometer in 1659 and 1660,[3] but the published account did not appear until publication of the first volume of the *Philosophical Transactions* in March, 1665–6. He describes how he made a large glass bubble to be counterpoised by a small solid glass ball. The changes in atmospheric pressure would be recorded by a very delicate balance and could be magnified by a long index at the fulcrum. This, he indicates in the published description, is similar to the index on Hooke's wheel barometer, which, as will be seen shortly, was not developed until 1664. It is evident that Boyle carried on with experiments and improvements in his statical barometer for some years. He says that his balance was capable of registering one-thirtieth of a grain and of indicating a pressure variation of an eighth of an inch, which might be bettered with a more delicate indicator.

At a meeting of the Royal Society on 6th December 1677, Dr Robert Hooke (1635–1703), that great seventeenth-century genius, affirmed that he had 'for these 15 or 16 years constantly observed the Barascope and that he had always found that in the said instrument the ☿ [☿ is the symbol for mercury] was always very exceeding low and fell to that stacion very suddenly whensoever any considerable Storme of Wind and Raine had happened in that time. . . .' And on 12th December 1695 Dr Hooke read 'an account of the several Barometers he had invented. That he was the first that had observed the changes of the height of the Mercury to answer the changes of the Weather.' From this we gather that Hooke was actively noting the connection between the barometer level and the weather since about 1661. Two entries from his Diary, which covers the years 1672–80, are given to illustrate his thoroughness: 'March 5th 1672/3—a cold morn. Some snow but fine for the most part. Wind N.W. Th. 2. ☿ 175 . . .' And 'March 9th, a fair cold morn. Th. 2. frost. ☿ 150. All the day dry but overcast. The wind changed to the South and the ☿ began gradually to fall all day and the air was warmer towards night, when ☿ 180. Th. 3½. Wind S. . . .'

In these comments it is not clear just what scale Hooke was using for the Mercury column: Th. standing for thermometer. At this date there was no recognized scale, and Hooke probably used a scale of his own contrivance. Fahrenheit was the first to devise a scale with fixed points. His first scale was divided between 90 and —90. An example of this is seen in Plate 158C, where the zero point occurs in the middle of the scale and is designated 'Temperate'. The earliest date for this scale, as we know it today, is given as 1717.[4]

In the Minutes of the Royal Society in 1663 we find recorded that 'it was proposed to make the Torricellian Experiment on the top and at the bottom of a mountain, checking the Temperature to demonstrate that the "stretching" of the Air does not altogether proceed from heat at the top of the mountain', thus extending the scope of the experiment made by Pascal.

Plate 157A shows a reproduction of the 'Torricellian Experiment' as demonstrated in the Science Museum, London. The tubes are inverted and filled with mercury. A finger is then placed over the open end and removed when this is below the level of the mercury in the cistern. That in the tube then runs out until the column remaining represents the height of mercury that the atmosphere can support at that moment. Torricelli thought that if there were any force due to the vacuum it would be greater in the larger vacuum. But as the two columns are of equal height, it shows the force to be wholly external and equal.

This simple device, by which changes of atmospheric pressure on the surface of the cistern are reflected in the height of the column in the tube, is that adopted by the earliest barometer makers. Later the siphon barometer was invented. In this type the tube for the mercury column turns up at the bottom to form a J, the short end being left open to the atmosphere (*see* Plate 157C and Plate 158C). Both systems were employed side by side for a hundred years or more, the cistern being more common in England and the siphon on the Continent.[5]

During the first thirty years of the life of the Royal Society, founded in 1660, we find many references to barometers of various kinds among their records. The prolific Dr Hooke figures in most of them. His first material contribution was his design for a wheel barometer. On 7th December 1663 he read a paper on his 'Weather Observations': 'For ascertaining . . . the moisture and dryness of the air with the degrees of it . . . this is to be observed with a good hygroscope, which may be had either with the beard of an Oate, a gut string or the like.' (On 27th June 1666 he recommends the 'Cod of a Vetch' as a substitute for a single beard of wild oat.) He continues: 'The greater or lesser pressure of ye aire, that in the differing heights of ye mercurial cylinder, and this to be observed wth an instrument that may show the least variation of that kind wch may be contrived in severall ways . . .'

One of the ways was, no doubt, the Wheel Barometer. For, on 30th December 1663 the Journal of the Royal Society records that Dr

Hooke produced 'a little engine to make the ascent and descent of Quicksilver in glasse-canes more discernible. It was ordered to prepare against the next Meeting a tube with Mercury and fit the Instrument to it.'

Hooke's original sketch, from the records of the Royal Society, is seen in Plate 157B. This sketch is not dated but appears among Hooke's papers about the middle of 1664, a description being published in Hooke's *Micrographia*, which appeared in November 1664. A small compensated weight floats on the surface of the mercury in the shorter arm, which is open to the air. To the weight is attached a silken thread carrying at the other end the compensating weight, the silken thread being wound round the arbor, or shaft, of the indicating hand. Thus, any movement of the surface of the mercury is transmitted to the arbor of the indicator and magnified to any desired extent by regulating the length of the indicating hand.

This remained one of the principal types of barometer until the coming of the aneroid barometer towards the middle of the nineteenth century, a period outside the scope of this section. Early wheel barometers with finely-designed cases were made in the latter years of the seventeenth century by Tompion, Quare and other leading clockmakers of that time. But since these are very rare, and nearly all are already held in royal or museum collections, none is illustrated here.

Plate 160B and C shows a pleasing wheel barometer of the mid-eighteenth century and its construction. At the top is a hygrometer. The small ivory setting knob for the barometer can be withdrawn and used to set the hygrometer, which now uses gut instead of the beard of a wild oat or the cod of a vetch, as recommended by Hooke in 1666. At the bottom is a spirit-level to check that the barometer hangs truly vertical, and, as is the case with most barometers, a thermometer is provided. For really accurate observations, allowance has to be made for the effects of temperature on the height of the mercury column.

One of the various ways of extending the reading scale of the barometer referred to by Hooke on 7th December 1663 may have been the diagonal barometer, sometimes known as the sign-post or yard-arm type. The maximum variation of the mercury at ground level is about three inches, and all the variations in the ordinary vertical tube have to be registered within these limits. We have seen that the wheel barometer magnified them, but by inclining the tube after the first, say, 27¾ inches of its length, the distance over which the reading can be extended is only controlled by the distance taken for the end of the tube to rise about three inches above the original point of inclination.

A very interesting and early example of the diagonal barometer is seen in Plate 157 (C and D). The printed back-paper gives John Boll as the maker and the year as 1666. Whether John Boll was in London is not stated. His name is not generally known. The construction is quite simple: three siphon barometers are used, each having a vertical tube about one inch longer than that preceding and having a rise of about one inch in about twenty inches of inclined arm. Thus, these three tubes of 28, 29 and 30 inches in length only start recording when the mercury reaches the height at which their respective bends are situated. The maximum anticipated variation of about three inches in this country is spread over sixty inches of tube, thus giving a spread of one inch for each twentieth part of an inch variation in the height of the mercury column.

The present outer casing is of mahogany but the back is of oak, and there is no reason to doubt that this portion is of the date shown, the mahogany facing having been fitted later in the eighteenth century, when this wood became fashionable.

The early barometers were not portable, and an early attempt to remedy this is recorded in the Royal Society's Journal (III, p. 214), 28th May 1668, when 'Mr Boyle brought in his Travelling or Portable Barascope, devised by himself to compare, by the help thereof the weight of the Atmosphere at the same time, not only in differing parts of the same country, but in differing Regions of the World: which is thus contrived, that the vessel containing both the sustained and stagnant Mercury is all of one piece of glasse of like bigness . . .'

Just what this means is not clear, but it would seem to be a siphon in which the return part is of the same diameter as the main tube. As will be seen later, other methods were adopted to render barometers portable.

Hooke's wheel barometer was not altogether successful. It is reported that it was liable to be jerky in movement and not easy to adjust. On 13th December 1664 he remarks that 'I have observed many circumstances in the heights of the mercurial cylinder which do very much cross my former observations'. In June 1668 it is reported that he 'thought of increasing the divisions by putting coloured Spirits of Wine or some other Liquor, not capable of freezing, on the Mercury, which Liquor was made to rise as the Mercury fell, and to fall as it rose, in a narrow cane, so as to make the utmost limits about two foot asunder . . .'; and many years later, on 3rd February 1685, he produced a tube in which a column of lighter spirits of wine was supported by a column of mercury. The length of the tube was unwieldy, but the idea developed into the double barometer which is seen in Plate 158A. The top of the left-hand tube being evacuated as the pressure falls, the mercury in this tube falls and the spirit in the right-hand tube rises over the extended scale for the oil. Low readings are therefore at the top. In this example, of *c.* 1750, it will be noticed that the thermometer carries the Fahrenheit scale.

As we have seen, Hooke had made a careful study of the relationship between atmospheric pressure and storms, and in Vol. II of the Royal Society's Journal on 6th December 1677 he reported that 'whenever the said ☿ was observed to fall suddenly very low, it had alwaies been a forerunner of a very great Storme to follow, sometimes within 12 houres and therefore he hoped that his Instrument might be of very good use at sea in order to the foreshowing of an ensuing Storme'. On 2nd January 1677–8 he pursues the idea, and, after dealing with the difficulties of using a wheel barometer at sea, he suggests 'as a better alternative, a Weather Glasse made with pure Air and Quicksilver, which latter is left open to the Pressure of the Air and so becomes agitated by a double principle of Motion, i.e. by Heat and Air Pressure . . .' To ascertain the changes due to heat, he provides a sealed thermometer with spirits of wine and graduates the two together in an oven. A table of differences is established, so that the resultant differences should be that due to air pressure.

This idea of Hooke, thrown out in 1667–8, seems, like so many of his ideas, to have lain dormant for many years. He returns to the question of a marine barometer in December 1694. At a meeting on the 5th of that month he was authorized to spend 40*s* on an example of his marine barometer. On 12th December he produced a sketch and description, and on 27th February 1694–5, 'Dr Hooke produced a second Contrivance of a Barometer for Sea use, made of two thermometers, the one, the common sealed Thermometer, the other made of Spirits of Wine also, but acted by the dilatation or contraction of Included Air; these Two being so Graduated, as suppose 30 inches, will by their difference show whether the weight of the Atmosphere be more or less than 30 inches and how much. It was ordered that Mr Hunt get one of these Instruments made.' At a meeting on 13th November 1695 this instrument was presented and was ordered to be hung in the Meeting Room. What is possibly this instrument is seen in Plate 158B. The thermometer with spirits of wine is on the right and that with mercury on the left. Missing is the scale, graduated 28 inches to 31 inches, on which was marked the barometer reading at the time of calibration of the thermometers and which slid up and down on a wire on the right of the mercury thermometer, to give the reading of the day.

In principle this idea is the air-thermoscope or weather-glass, invented towards the turn of the sixteenth to seventeenth centuries, later forming the basis of the Sympiesometer, patented by Adie in 1818. A more simple type of marine barometer was developed (*see* Definitions and Plate 161A).

In the meantime, in spite of Robert Boyle's idea in 1668, barometers were not portable. The Minute Book of the Royal Society for 16th January 1694–5, however, records: 'Mr Daniel Quare, Watchmaker, produced his Barometer so contrived as to be Portable, and even Inverted without spilling of the Quicksilver, or letting in any Air or excluding the pressure of the Atmosphere, which the Society were pleased to Declare, That it was the first of that sort they had seen. Mr Quare desired to be excused from Discovering the Secret thereof.' A fortnight later, 31st January, 'Dr Hooke mentioned that he had been told that a barometer made by Mr Tompion about a year since, which did the same thing with that of Mr Quare, and Doctor Sloane say'd That he had discoursed Mr Tompion about it, who say'd It was to be done by help of a Bladder, without further explaining himself'.

Quare's secret was the use of a plug at the end of a screwed thread, which could be used to seal off the bottom of the tube under the mercury. An example of such a Quare barometer and its sealing screw is seen in Plate 157E and F. Tompion's idea was probably that still used today, of retaining the cistern mercury in a leather bag within the wooden case, the bottom of the bag being adjusted to raise the level of the mercury sufficiently to fill the upright tube and then secured in that position.

Another point, taken for granted today, was the systematic recording of barometer readings. On 31st October 1683 'Mr Lister showed the way he had made for the keeping of his Account of the Barometer, which was approved of as very convenient. He showed also the Book containing 3 or 4 years account, every Table containing a Months Account, was printed off upon a Copper Plate. The upper line contained inches divided by lines into 10 parts, the lines by the side showed the days of the month. . . .'

The first self-recording barograph was made in 1765 for King George III by Alexander Cumming and is now in Buckingham Palace. A second, made by Cumming for his own use in 1766, is now in the possession of Mr Geoffrey Howard, with whose permission it is shown (Plate 162A). A pointer is carried by a ring floating on the surface of the mercury and, rising and falling with this, traces a continuous line on the outer dial, which is fitted with a graduated vellum disc and revolves once a year.

By the end of the seventeenth century practically all the problems had been solved. These now seem very simple, but so will, no doubt, Rutherford's early nuclear experiments to the scientists of two or three centuries hence. These detailed accounts have been quoted so that the reader may appreciate the time and thought given to the development of a new discovery and the earnest desire to utilize it promptly for the benefit of mankind.

Once established, the barometer was of easy construction. After the early years of the eighteenth century, with the possible exception of Patrick, there are no great names of barometer makers. One finds good and bad examples in both London and provincial productions.

GLOSSARY

Banjo: the type in which the case resembles the instrument named.

Barograph: a self-recording barometer actuated by clockwork.

Capacity error: that introduced by the alteration in the level of the cistern or siphon reservoir by the inflow or outflow of mercury from the vertical tube.

Cistern: the type in which the lower open end of the vertical tube is placed below the level of the mercury in open reservoir. The earliest type.

Diagonal: a type in which the recording part of the tube is at an obtuse angle with the lower upright part, so that the possible variation of the mercury height of about three inches may be spread over the inclined length of the tube.

Double: a type in which the mercury column is divided into approximately two equal halves fixed vertically side by side and connected by a tube filled with a lighter fluid substance, such as oil or air.

Fortin: a type in which the level of the cistern is adjusted to a fixed pointer before a reading by difference is taken, thus eliminating capacity error.

Marine: a type in which part of the bore in the vertical tube is constricted in order to minimize a movement of level in the vertical tube by reason of the ship's motion. This type must also be capable of plugging when not in use.

Meniscus: the surface of a liquid in a tube. It is usually curved, owing to surface tension effects.

Portable: a type in which the cistern or siphon can be entirely enclosed, and in which the mercury can be plugged in the vertical tube.

Sign-post: *see* Diagonal.

Siphon: a type in which the reservoir is situated in the return portion of a J-shaped tube.

Wheel: a siphon-type in which the variation of the mercury level is magnified and registered on a circular dial.

Yard-arm: *see* Diagonal.

REFERENCES

[1] *Canadian Royal Astronomical Society's Journal*, Dec. 1943, p. 407.

[2] *Encl. Britannica*, 14th Ed., Vol. 17, p. 351.

[3] *Philosophical Transactions No.* 9, p. 153.

[4] H. Dingle, *Philosophical Magazine 150*, Commemorative number, 1948.

[5] Science Museum, Meteorology Catalogue, 1922, p. 18.

The sketch of Hooke's Wheel Barometer and the quotations from the Royal Society's Journal and Minute Books are given by permission of that Society.

BOOK FOR FURTHER READING

Old English Barometers by G. H. and E. F. Bell (The Wykenham Press, 1952).

MUSICAL-BOXES

By ARTHUR HARDING

THE origins of the simple musical-box go back a surprisingly long way in history. Its direct ancestor was the carillon in the church tower that automatically played a tune when required; a performance that dates from at least the fifteenth century in England.

On the death of Henry VIII in the year 1547 a contemporary list of the musical instruments belonging to the late king included *a Virginal that goeth with a whele without playing uppon*. The principle of operation has remained the same over the centuries: in Henry's time it was a wooden barrel with projecting pins to strike the strings of a virginal. Ultimately, it was a brass barrel with pins that hit the teeth of a steel comb.

The musical-box that employed a steel comb for producing the sound is supposed to have been invented by a Swiss, Louis Favre of Geneva, some time in the second half of the eighteenth century. He is said to have applied the idea in the first instance to a watch, and before long this compact form of automatic music-making had been adapted to fit almost anything.

It was not until the nineteenth century, when the larger boxes were made in quantity, that barrel-and-comb mechanical music became divorced at all from snuff-boxes, umbrella-handles, etc., and began to be a source of entertainment instead of just a novelty. Not at any time since its first introduction, however, has it ceased to challenge the ingenuity of the craftsman, and while the output of large table-sized musical-boxes was increasing rapidly no less effort was put into the creation of fresh miniature novelties.

The century from 1800 onwards was the heyday of the musical-box, and its distinctive sound was as much a part of the home as the radio or television is today. It is not remarkable that so many people have collected, or have begun to collect, musical-boxes of all types. Not only can their fascinating melody be appreciated but the craftsmanship that has made the enjoyment possible is no less admirable.

GLOSSARY

Apollonicon: a very large mechanical organ that was exhibited in London between 1817 and 1840. It was either operated by three barrels or played by six performers, each of whom was seated at a console.

Barrel: the barrel of a musical-box is the device by which the notes are struck. It comprises a cylinder with projecting pins that are placed to hit the teeth of a steel comb, to trip hammers to hit bells, or to operate some other arrangement. The barrel was of wood or of brass. Metal lent itself to work on the small scale required for movements in snuff-boxes, watches, etc. Wood was used in the larger mechanical organs and carillons.

The circumference of the cylinder governs the length of the tune to be played, and much musical ingenuity used to be displayed in the shortening or protracting of the chosen melody in order that it should occupy the full space, and no more.

The setting of the pins on the barrel is a skilled task, and is known as *pricking*. Marks are made where each pin is to be placed and holes are drilled on the marks, the pins are inserted so that they stand out to an even height, and, if it is of metal, the cylinder is sealed up. (*See* M.-D.-J. Engramelle.)

Barrel-organ: the barrel-and-pin technique applied to the operation of an organ. Many such instruments were supplied for use in churches during the last years of the eighteenth century and in the early part of the century following. A few still remain in their original situations.

Bird: snuff-boxes containing singing and moving birds are dealt with in the section devoted to Automata (page 241).

Bird-organ: also known as a *Serinette* (French: canary). A small mechanical instrument, with both barrel and bellows, for teaching a bird to sing. Larger and louder was the *Merline*: for teaching a blackbird. There was also a *Turlutaine* (Turlu: curlew), probably used as a lure.

Clocks: the first mechanical music was performed upon cymbals or bells, and was a part of the display of some of the elaborate clocks made on the Continent of Europe from the fourteenth century and onwards. By the time of Queen Elizabeth I the mechanical principle had been extended to the operation of organs. There exists a description of a most complicated clock that was sent as a gift from the English sovereign to the Sultan of Turkey in 1593. This clock incorporated both carillon and organ, either of which could be played by hand or be set to operate when the clock struck the hour.

In the eighteenth century and later, large bracket-clocks and grandfather clocks were made with music on bells to be played each hour. They usually gave a choice of tunes, which could be changed by moving a pointer on a dial on the face. A musical movement was constructed also that operated a small bellows and worked a miniature organ. With the introduction of the comb this, too, was adapted to become part of a clock.

Among the more prominent English makers of musical clocks were: **Charles Clay,** who exhibited a bell and organ clock to Queen Caroline in 1736; *Markwick Markham*; *Christopher Pinchbeck*, inventor of the gilt metal which bears his name and a famed clock-maker; and **James Cox,** who exhibited to the public musical clocks and watches, along with other mechanical *objets d'art*, in the last half of the eighteenth century. The list of Continental makers should not omit **Father Primitivus Niemecz,** who made three famous clocks for the Hungarian Prince Esterhazy. These had music especially composed or arranged for them by Joseph Haydn (*see* Tunes).

Comb: the steel comb, first used some time in the eighteenth century, was arranged fanwise in its earliest form. Each tooth was screwed separately to the base. The succeeding development was the laminated comb, built up of sections. Each comprised three or four teeth. About 1820 the combs began to be made of a single length of metal. At about this same date *resonators* (small pieces of lead or brass) were affixed to the undersides of the bass notes, and *dampers* (tiny feather quills) were also attached beneath the teeth. Both these devices improved the tone of the instrument and helped greatly to increase its popularity (*see* Louis Favre).

Cylinder: *see* Barrel.

Engramelle, M.-D.-J. (1727–81): an Augustinian monk who wrote and published *La Tonotechnie, ou l'art de noter les cylindres* (*Tonotechnique, or the art of placing the notes on cylinders*), Paris, 1775 (*see* Barrel).

Favre, Louis: a native of Geneva, Switzerland, who is credited in some quarters with the invention of the steel comb for producing the sound in a spring-driven musical-box. Formerly this had been achieved principally upon bells. This greatly limited the size of the instrument and the variety of sounds it could make, as well as the repertoire it could perform. The introduction of the comb took place some time in the eighteenth century, but the exact date is no more certain than is the name of the inventor.

Maelzel, J. N. (1772–1838): a friend of Beethoven, who is remembered chiefly as the inventor of the Metronome, and who constructed the *Panharmonicon*, for which Beethoven wrote an overture, *The Battle of Vittoria*, in 1813. The *Panharmonicon* was a mechanical orchestra that reproduced the sound of many instruments. Some years later, in Boston,

Mass., Maelzel made a forty-two-piece mechanical orchestra. This excited much comment, and it is related that a price of $500,000 was asked for it.

Nicole Frères: Raymond and François Nicole each made musical-box movements on their own account from 1815. Fourteen years later they amalgamated and formed the firm of *Nicole Frères*. From their workshop in Geneva came large numbers of good quality musical-box movements. They had a world-wide business and had warehouses in London from 1860. By 1903 the competition of the gramophone began to be felt, and the firm gave up. The London branch was taken over by their agents and continued, one way or another, until the death at the age of eighty of the firm's chief mechanic in 1933.

Nicole Frères movements always bear the name of the firm stamped on them, as well as a serial number which indicates the year in which each was made. A key to these serial numbers is given by J. E. T. Clark in his book *Musical Boxes*.

Novelties: musical movements have been fitted, at one time or another, to almost everything. Tankards, jugs, fruit-dishes, and other objects play on being picked up from where they are resting innocently. Fob-seals, watch-keys, rings and scent-bottles surprise the hearer by the emission of sound from such small articles and at the same time challenge the craftsman to make ever minuter miniatures. Even the handle of a decorative and useful fan, or of an umbrella or a walking-stick, might conceal a musical-box. Gold cases for sealing-wax are also known. One of these rarities contained a movement only an inch and three-quarters in length and little more than half an inch in width and height. It played a tune on five tiny bells. Albums of photographs render *Auld Lang Syne* on being opened; cigar- and cigarette-boxes play selections from comic operas and nearly forgotten musical comedies; and apparently normal chairs startle the weary who sit on them.

Perhaps the most novel of novelties was a bustle presented to Queen Victoria by an ardent patriot on the occasion of her Jubilee. This device emitted the strains of *God Save the Queen* whenever the wearer seated herself. It is not known that it was ever worn by the recipient, but had it been used the effect it caused must surely have been worthy of record.

Serinette: *see* Bird-organ.

Snuff-boxes: these were in the past, and are still, immensely popular when fitted as musical-boxes, and were made in great numbers. At first they were costly and elaborately cased in gold, silver-gilt or silver. Movements were of small size and light in weight. After the first decade of the nineteenth century horn, tortoiseshell and composition, as well as painted tin, were used for making the boxes, which were decorated with embossed designs, prints and other ornament. Gradually the movement became heavier and larger in size, and the space that remained in the box for containing snuff became smaller in relation to the size of the whole box. It would seem that the majority of the boxes made in the early part of the nineteenth century, and later, were bought, as they are today, more as novelties than for any practical purpose.

Many of the snuff-boxes were made in Paris, and some of the horn and composition specimens have views of Paris landmarks in relief on their lids. London and provincial-made boxes are found with Swiss-made movements fitted in them.

Tunes: several great composers have not disdained to compose music especially for musical-boxes. Haydn wrote a series of pieces to be played by three clocks that had been made to the order of his patron, Prince Esterhazy. Mozart wrote his *Fantasias in F minor* for an automatic flute. It is related that Beethoven was fond of hearing Cherubini's overture to *Medea*, as played on a musical-box in one of the cafés in Vienna.

The more ordinary boxes played a wide variety of tunes ranging from traditional airs to operatic arias. Frequently it will be found that the tune gives a clue to the date of manufacture. Unless ordered specially, the barrels were always set with the most popular tunes of the day.

Watches: the addition of the playing of music to the normal performance of a pocket time-keeper grew from the repeater mechanism, which was a necessity for telling the time in the dark before the use of luminous composition or the invention of electric light. The hour was repeated on one or more tiny bells upon pressing a button, and very little adaptation of the basic mechanism was needed. With more bells, and more pins to hit the hammers, more notes could be played to form a simple melody.

With the advent of the steel comb a much greater compass of notes could be achieved with no increase in the size of the apparatus.

BOOKS FOR FURTHER READING

F. J. Britten, *Old Clocks and Watches and their Makers* (London).
John E. T. Clark, *Musical Boxes* (London, 1952).
Percy A. Scholes, *Oxford Companion to Music* (London). Under heading: Mechanical Reproduction.

AUTOMATA

By ARTHUR HARDING

PYGMALION, in ancient times the King of Cyprus and a sculptor of merit, is said to have created a statue so beautiful that he adored it, and requested to Aphrodite that it might be given life. The makers of automata have been perhaps a step ahead of the King of Cyprus in that they do their best themselves to imbue their models with life, and do not depend on the whims of Olympian goddesses to breathe movement into their *Galateas*.

The development of the automaton is bound up with the development of clocks and watches. With the invention of devices for the control of a falling weight, man had a source of power with which to animate a model. With the further invention of the tempered steel spring, not only a more adaptable power, but a portable one, was to hand.

Jacks: the first public time-keepers had no dials: they took the place of the men who had for centuries sounded the hours, and the clocks performed the same task by striking a bell at regular intervals. It was not long before the clockmakers made models of the old watchmen and, by connecting them to the mechanism of the clock, caused them to strike the bells. These figures were called jacks. A further logical advance was the animation of figures in a religious tableau placed within, or outside of, a church or other public building. In this way the attention of the passer-by was attracted by the bell, and at the same time was reminded of his religious duties by witnessing a brief mechanical performance of a Biblical scene. The great clock in Strasbourg Cathedral is one of the most noted of this type.

Smaller clocks: as the clock shrank in size the makers (especially in Germany, and elsewhere on the Continent) retained the jacks to perform inside a house the same task that they had previously carried out elsewhere and on a larger scale. Such clocks, the jacks supplemented by figures of dancers and by artificial waterfalls and moving clouds and aided by carillons and automatic organs, attained their apotheosis in the work of James Cox, pre-eminent among other eighteenth-century makers of similar costly show-pieces.

Automata: the first maker of actual automata as distinct from jacks, and of whom there is a full record, was Jacques de Vaucanson, who exhibited his three mechanical figures before the *Académie des Sciences* in Paris, in 1738. The success that greeted their appearance when they were later shown in London, St Petersburg and in Germany encouraged the making of more automata. The displaying of them became a common feature of the scene in any big city, and the fame of Spring Gardens in London, where Cox showed his pieces, was duplicated in other capitals.

Miniatures: not content with models a foot or so in height, craftsmen, principally Swiss, set to work to make miniature automata. They made snuff-boxes and watches with disappearing singing birds; boxes with magicians who held up inscribed plaques with answers to questions that were put to them; and other boxes in which landscape and other scenes surprisingly came to life on pressing a button. Watches were made with miniature jacks that struck miniature bells; others showed moving figures that danced to

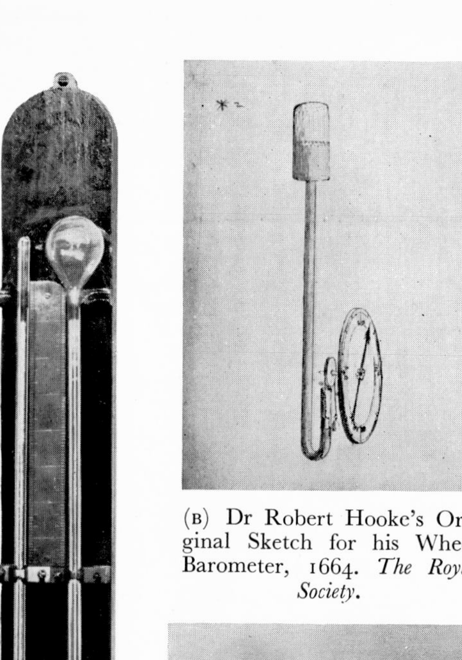

(B) Dr Robert Hooke's Original Sketch for his Wheel Barometer, 1664. *The Royal Society.*

(C) Triple Diagonal Barometer, by John Boll. On oak back with later mahogany front, 1666. *Messrs John Bell of Aberdeen.*

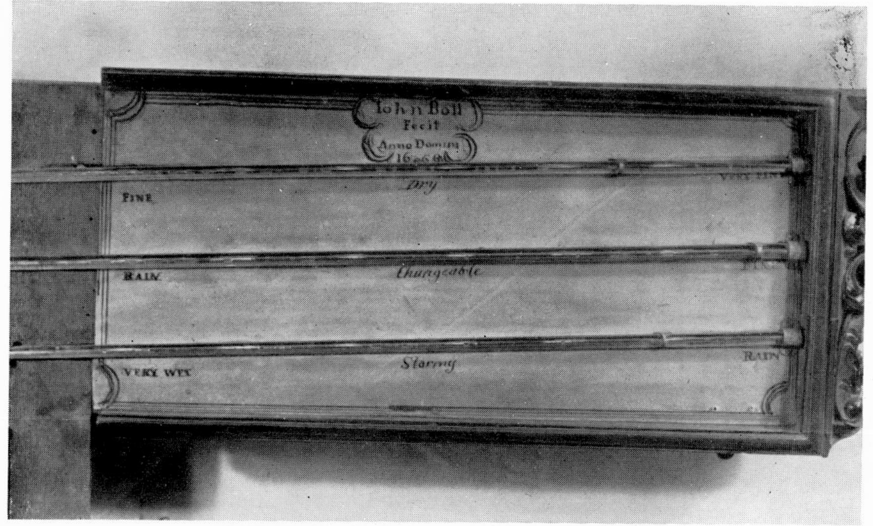

(D) John Boll, 1666.

) The Torricel-
an Experiment,
43. *The Science Museum.*

(E) Portable Barometer, by Daniel Quare, *c.* 1700. Walnut. Height 41 in. *Messrs G. Jetley.*

(F) Base of Quare's Barometer showing his Patent Screw-plug.

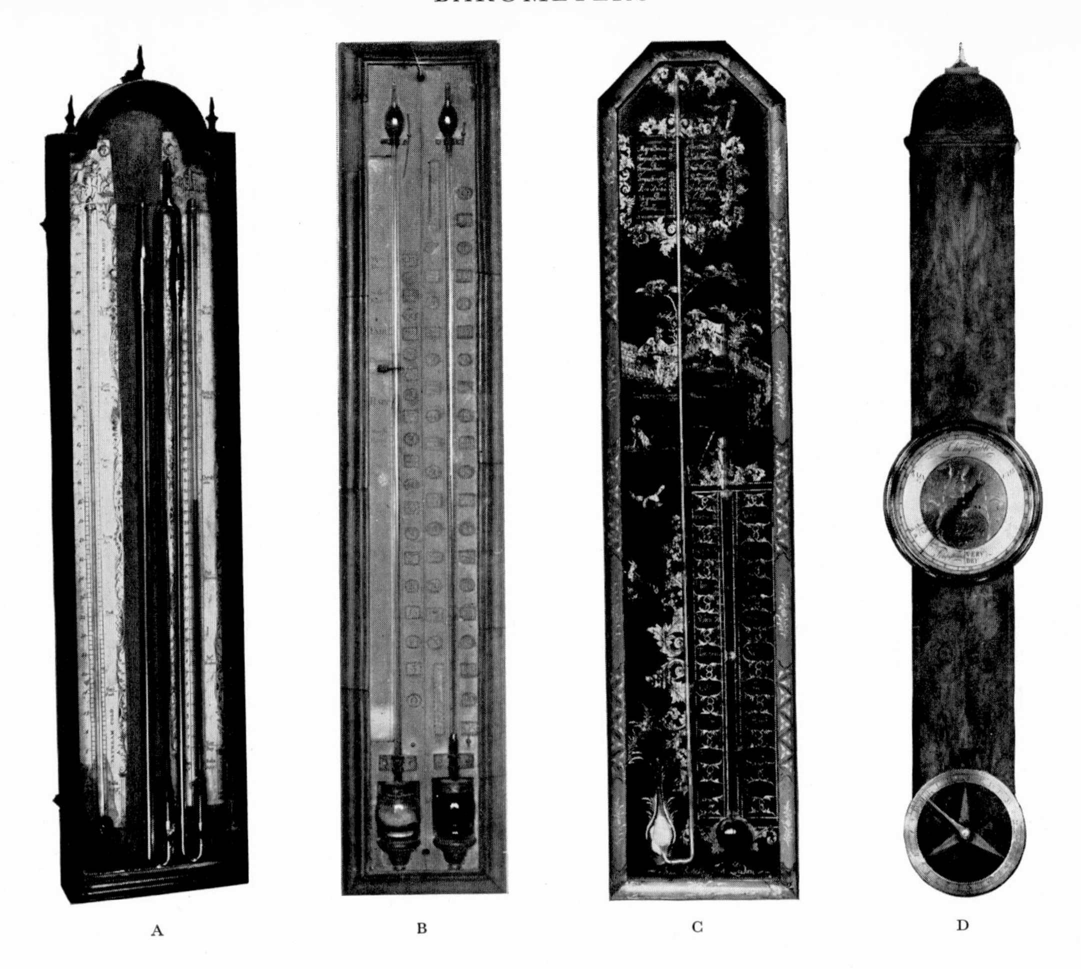

A B C D

(A) Double Barometer by Dom Sala, London, with Fahrenheit's Standard Scale, *c.* 1750. *Messrs Pratt & Sons Ltd.*

(B) Hooke's Marine Barometer, *c.* 1697. *Museum for the History of Science, Oxford.*

(C) Syphon Barometer, by Robelau, with Fahrenheit's early Thermometer Scale, 1719. *Science Museum, London.*

(D) Walnut Wheel Barometer, by George Hallifax of Doncaster. The days of the month inscribed on the dial (indicating hand for this missing). Comparison Dial at bottom, *c.* 1730. *Messrs Phillips of Hitchin.*

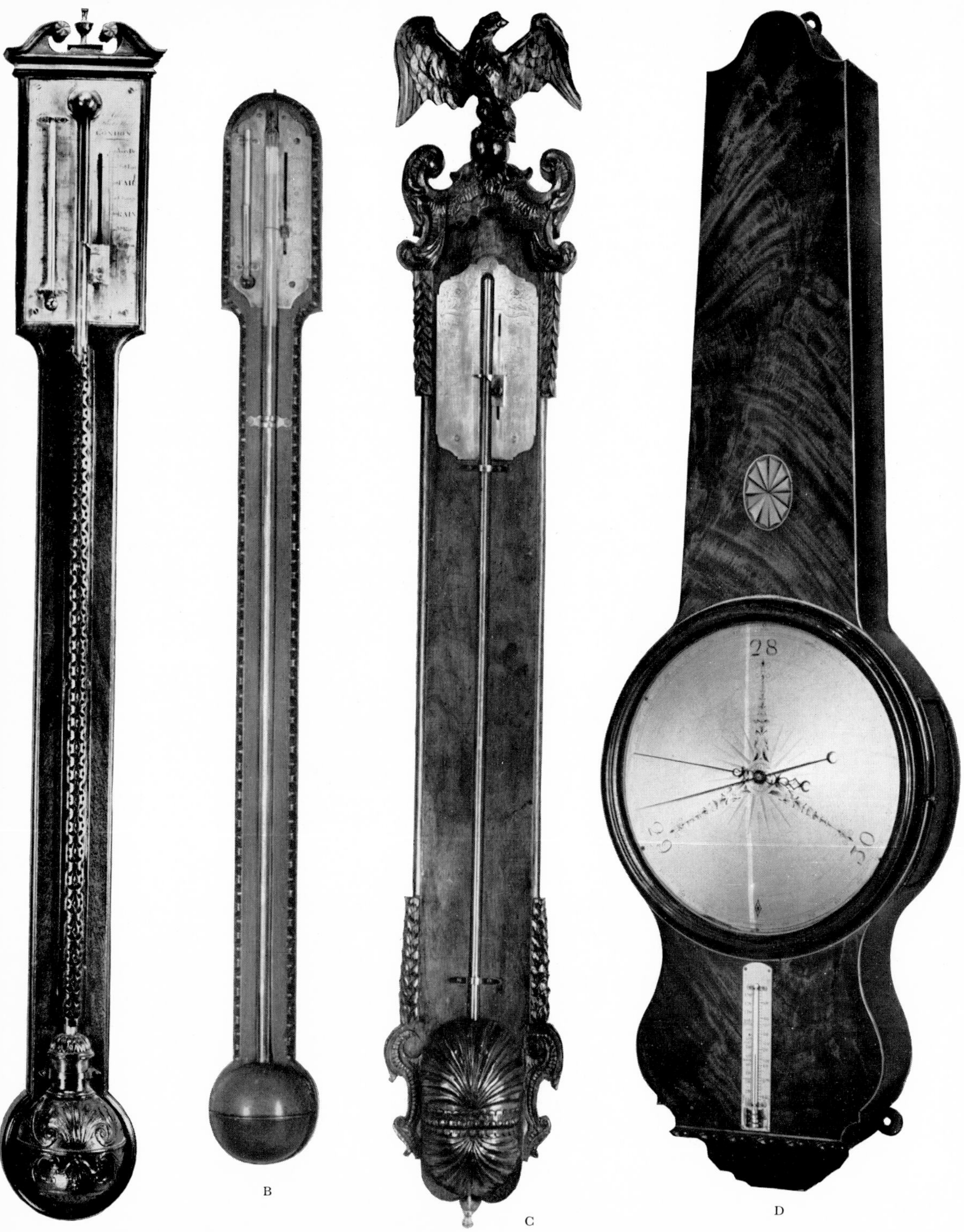

A

(A) A Mahogany Barometer, mid-eighteenth century. *Messrs Phillips of Hitchin.*

(B) Mahogany Barometer with 'Egg & Tongue' beading, *c.* 1750–60. *Messrs Moss Harris & Sons.*

(C) Chippendale Mahogany Barometer, *c.* 1760. *Messrs Frank Partridge & Sons Ltd.*

(D) Honduras Mahogany Wheel Barometer with dial graduated to 1/100th of an inch, *c.* 1780. *Messrs Moss Harris & Sons.*

PLATE 159

(A) Mahogany Diagonal Barometer with Hygrometer and Thermometer, 38 in. × 26 in., by Watkins & Smith, London. Mid-eighteenth century. Perpetual Calendar for the New Style, 1753. *Stanley Marling, Esq.*

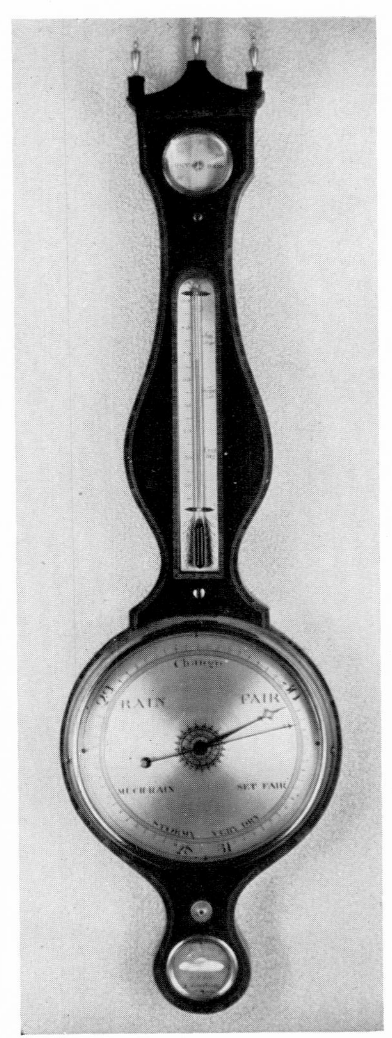

(B) Burr Walnut Wheel Barometer, by James Gatley, High Holborn, London. No. 130, with gut hygrometer, *c.* 1770. *Messrs Frank Sherrard, London.*

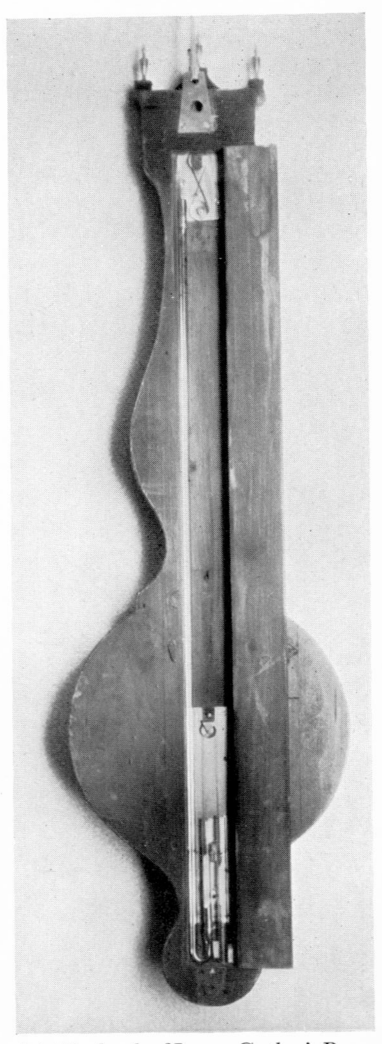

(C) The back of James Gatley's Barometer.

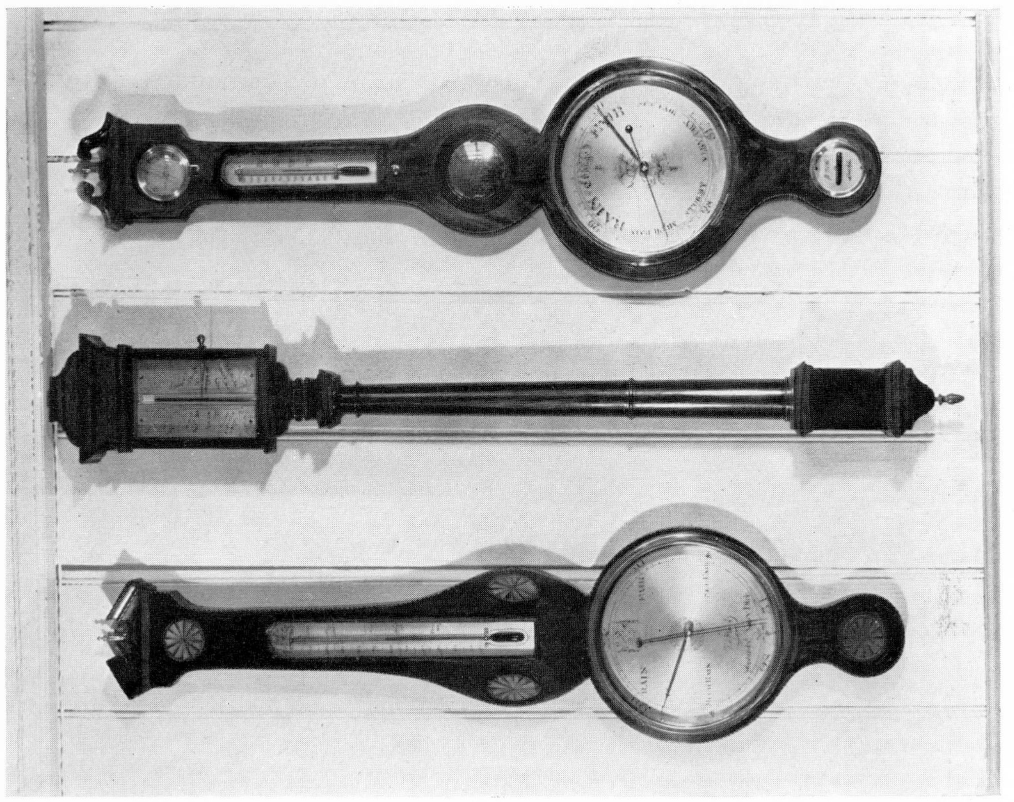

(B) *Left*: Sheraton Wheel Barometer, by J. Tarone, Holborn, London, *c.* 1780. *Centre*: Walnut Cistern Pediment Barometer, after the style of Patrick, *c.* 1725. *Right*: Sheraton Mirror Barometer, with hygrometer, by E. Cetti, London, *c.* 1800. *Messrs Frank Marson, London.*

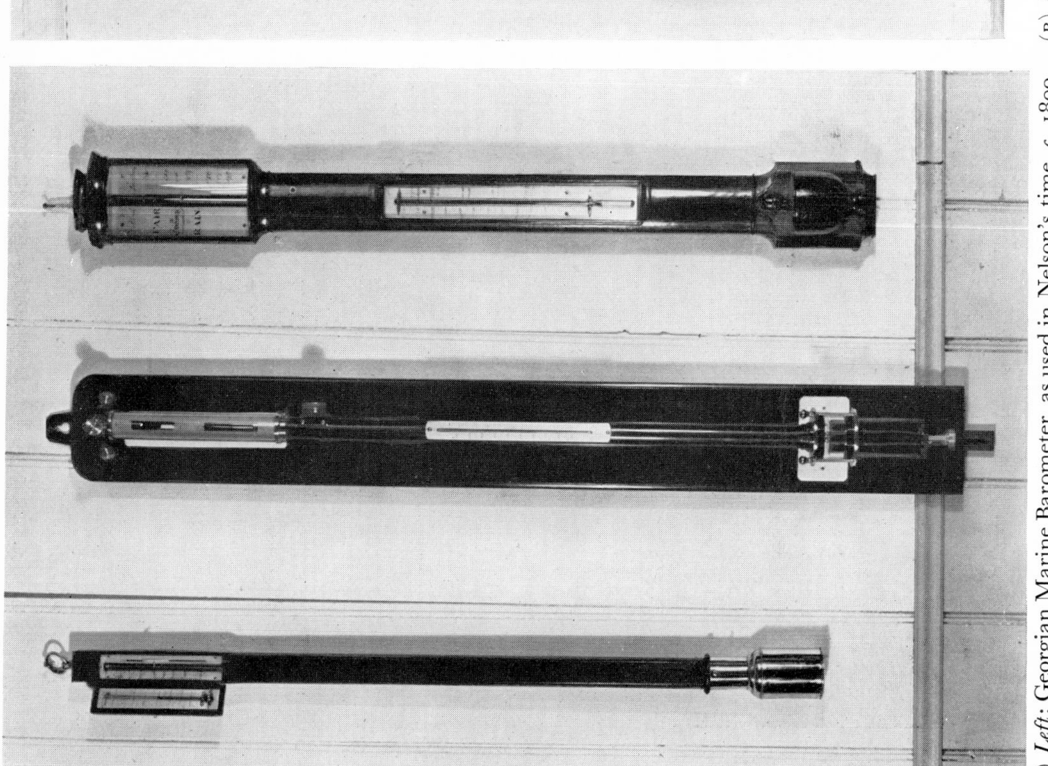

(A) *Left*: Georgian Marine Barometer, as used in Nelson's time, *c.* 1800. *Centre*: Fortin Barometer by Spencer Browning. Invented 1815. Note the ivory tooth seen impinging on the mercury level in the cistern. *Right*: Georgian Bow-fronted Pediment Barometer, by Dolland, *c.* 1810. *Messrs Frank Marson, London.*

(A) Self-recording Barograph by Alexander Cumming, 1766. *Geoffrey Howard Esq.*

(B) Wheel Barometer with Clock and Hygrometer in Rosewood with tulipwood banding by Cacanti, Town Malling, Kent. Height 5 ft., *c.* 1820. *Messrs Moss Harris & Sons, London.*

Clock, of gold set with agate plaques, by James Cox, signed and dated 1766. The lower dial shows the phases of the moon and in the base is a carillon that plays four tunes. Height $14\frac{1}{2}$ in. *Wartski Ltd, London.*

(A) Enamelled gold snuff-box, the lid painted with a scene of the Abduction of Helen by Paris and encircled by pearls. The interior divided: the upper part for snuff and the lower with a musical-box. Width $3\frac{1}{2}$ in. *M. Hakim, London.*

(B) Interior of (A). At the upper right is seen the toothed barrel. It plays a tune on the bells on the left-hand side.

(C) Silver snuff-box, with chased and engine-turned decoration, fitted with a musical-box. The silver box is hall-marked 1818–1819. Length $3\frac{1}{8}$ in. *Victoria & Albert Museum.*

(D) Fruit-knife, of enamelled gold inset with pearls, the handle containing a musical-box. Length 6 in. *Victoria & Albert Museum.*

(E) Gold musical-box in the form of a crown. Given to Princess Victoria in 1833, the future Queen noted: '. . . from the Duchess of Gordon, a lovely little crown of precious stones which plays "God Save the King" . . .' *Collection of the late Queen Mary.* Reproduced by gracious permission of Her Majesty The Queen.

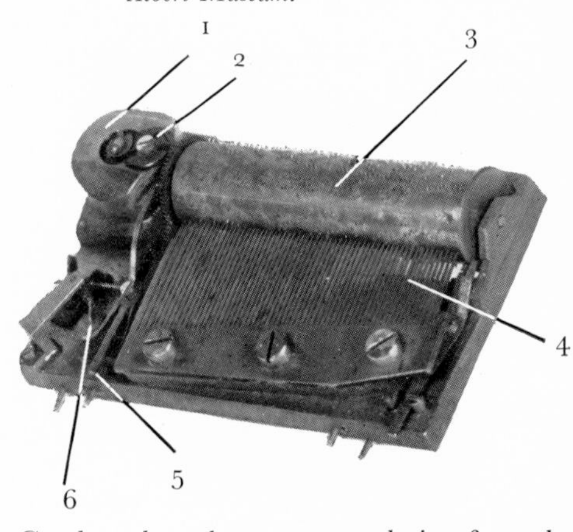

(F) Comb and tooth movement, dating from the early nineteenth century. (1) Mainspring; (2) Stop work – to prevent overwinding; (3) Barrel, with teeth; (4) Steel comb; (5) Starting lever; (6) Governor – to control speed.

Sixteenth-century bronze and gilt-bronze figure of a merman (?) seated astride a tortoise. Height $6\frac{3}{10}$ in. *Victoria & Albert Museum.*

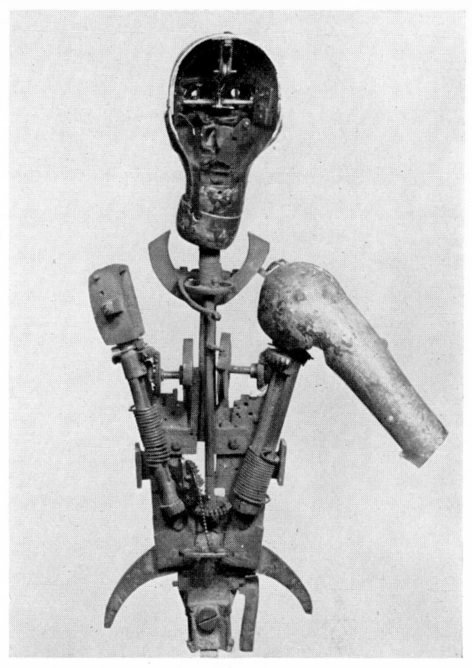

Skeleton of the figure of a lady from an eighteenth-century Swiss automata, showing the working parts. A fine operating chain is seen at lower centre, others are missing. *Private Collection.*

Mid-nineteenth-century figure of a mandolin-player. *Gordon Hand, London.*

English seventeenth/eighteenth-century carved oak jaquemart in the form of Hercules. Height 46 in. *Private Collection.*

A B C

French gold snuff-box set with pearls and a watch. The hinged cover conceals a singing bird, which rises and moves realistically when the button is pressed. *In the Collection of the late Queen Mary.* (Reproduced by gracious permission of Her Majesty the Queen.)

Early nineteenth-century Swiss watches with automata. (A) With jaquemart figures; (B) when the button is pressed two mounted knights in armour tilt at each other. Below, a third knight raises his trumpet to announce the victor; (C) with Cupid jaquemarts. In the centre a girl is seated on a swing which is pushed by a boy. To the left a fountain is playing. All three of these watches have repeater movements, and were at one time in the collection of Prince Farouk. *Wartski Ltd, London.*

Eighteenth-century model in silver by Weekes, London. To the accompaniment of music the water (in the form of barley-twist glass rods) appears to flow and the swan reaches its head down in an attempt to catch some of the fish seen swimming in front of it. Length 67 in. *Bowes Museum, Barnard Castle, Co. Durham.*

English dolls' house—about 1760. Height 5 ft., width 4 ft., depth 3 ft. With contemporary furniture, *c.* 1790. From the Bethnal Green Museum. *Victoria & Albert Museum.*

Gilt brass table, 1870. Silvered glass pieces, 1880. Dutch silver chair. Silver-plated tea-tray, 1850. Lead tea-urn, lead tray with goblets and sauce-boat. Lead aspidistra stand, lead fire-irons, 1880. Bristol glass-green glass decanters in stand, glass carafe. Staffordshire tureen, blue-and-white willow pattern. K'ang-hsi miniature cup and saucer, 1720. Prattware chicken on dish, 1820. Wooden spice rack and salt box, 1880. Doulton ginger-beer bottle. Terra-cotta jug. *Messrs Gordon Hand, London.*

(A) Two dolls dating from 1880, attired in sumptuous lace-trimmed Victorian ball-dresses with long trains. *Collection of Mrs Trounsell and Miss Foxhunter.*

(B) English male peddlar doll with tray of haberdashery. *c.* 1780. *Bethnal Green Museum.*

(C) 'Letitia Penn', earliest known play-doll in the United States of America, taken there from Europe by William Penn in 1699. *Collection of Mrs Imogen Anderson.*

(D) English wooden doll. Period Queen Anne. Height 1 ft. 10 in. *Victoria & Albert Museum.*

the music of a minute musical-box within the case. One can only marvel at the ingenuity and skill of the men who designed and made them – and, at the same time, envy those who are fortunate enough to possess these extreme rarities.

An examination of any of the larger automata cannot fail to excite an admiration for the craftsmen who laboured to make these nearly human figures, masterpieces that evoke so keenly the dust of the past. At the same time, one can well imagine that a sight of one of these rather *macabre* curiosities might have inspired Mary Wollstonecraft Shelley to create on paper the classic man-made monster – *Frankenstein.*

GLOSSARY

NOTE. The automata marked with an asterisk (*) are described fully and illustrated by A. Chapuis and E. Droz in *Les Automates*, Neuchâtel, 1949.

Birds: among the most popular of all automata were birds, from the duck of Vaucanson onwards. Marie-Antoinette, Queen of France, possessed a life-sized canary that was contained in a cage, the underneath of which showed the dial of a clock. The bird sang realistically. Catherine II, Empress of Russia, was presented in 1780 with a large caged mechanical peacock* made by James Cox. This is still in Moscow.

On the smallest scale were the singing birds fitted into snuff-boxes. These were quite invisible until, on the pressure of a button, they sprang up, moved their heads, wings and tails and sang. They were, understandably, highly popular and expensive. Many were mounted in gold boxes set with precious stones and contained a musical-box movement as well. The Jaquet-Droz and the Rochat brothers are among the best-known makers of these remarkable *tours-de-force*, which date from the late eighteenth and early nineteenth centuries. Even more remarkable are watches with singing birds and incredible gold pistols from the mouths of which tiny birds emerge and sing when the triggers are pressed.

Chess-players(*): there has always been much scepticism displayed on the subject of mechanical chess-players, of which several were made about 1800. It is agreed generally that they were hoaxes.

Clocks: clocks with automata marked the first appearance of mechanical figures. The figures (jacks) were designed to hold hammers, or other objects that had the same effect, to strike the hour upon a bell. Later came automata that performed their evolutions for purely decorative or educational reasons but that were still part of the clock and were brought into action by the time-keeping mechanism. The famous clock at Strasbourg in eastern France and others in the big cities of the late Middle Ages were designed to exploit the growing skill of clockmakers and to attract the interest of the public.

In the late sixteenth century began the practice of sending magnificent gifts to Eastern potentates in order to impress upon them the advanced craftsmanship and high standards of Western culture, to lull their natural suspicions and obtain trading concessions from them. Many of these gifts took the form of clocks, complete with organ, bells, cymbals and automata. They were set in costly cases and doubtless succeeded in the intention to delight both eye and ear. Turkey and China were notably recipients of these extravagances, which, in England, were made by several makers, of whom James Cox is the best known.

From the very large examples that were made during the sixteenth century and earlier the clocks shrank in size until many were little larger than a normal bracket-clock. At the same time, tall-case (grandfather) clocks, with musical chimes, tune-playing carillons and mechanically-operated scenes above the face, were made in both Holland and England.

Cox, James: an eighteenth-century London clockmaker and jeweller. He opened an exhibition of clocks, singing-birds and automata at Spring Gardens. According to one writer: 'The charge was half a guinea each person; a regulation providing for the presence of but few visitors at a time was, needless to say, quite unnecessary'. Cox made many elaborate and costly clocks for export to the Far East.

Conjurers: *see* Magicians.

Draughtsmen(*)**:** several automata that wrote words and sentences, or drew pictures, were constructed from 1750 onwards, notably by Friedrich von Knauss of Vienna (1724–89), Jaquet-Droz and Leschot, and Maillardet.

Jack: a mechanically-operated figure that strikes a bell on the outside of a clock. In the first instance jacks were of carved wood, a well-known example, dating probably from the fifteenth century, being *Jack the Smiter* at Southwold, Suffolk. Jacks of a later date, on smaller portable clocks and on wall clocks, were made of metal.

In the nineteenth century a French writer carefully traced the origin of the word to its being a corruption of *Jacquemart*: the name of a fifteenth-century clockmaker of Lille, France. Others have contended that it is an abbreviation of *Jaccomarchiadus*: a man in armour. In spite of this academic dispute, it seems hardly necessary to look farther than the still current and expressive name *Jack* for any man whose actual patrynomic is unknown. These lifelike and nearly life-size figures were doubtless the recipients of this commonly-used name, as they had none of their own.

Jaquet-Droz, Henri (1752–91): son of Pierre J-D, and also a famed maker of automata. His father's apprentice, J. F. Leschot (1746–1827), joined with him and formed the Geneva firm of *Jaquet-Droz et Leschot*, who made all types of automata, from figures to bird-boxes and watches (*see* Henry Maillardet).

Jaquet-Droz, Pierre (1721–90): maker of the famous automata *The Young Writer*, *The Designer*, and the six-foot-tall *The Musician*. They were made in collaboration with his son, Henri J-D, and all three (*) are now in the Museum at Neuchâtel, Switzerland.

Magicians: the world of magic intrigued the public not less in the eighteenth century than it does today. Many mechanical figures of magicians were made. A large clock in the Horological Museum at La Chaux-de-Fonds, Switzerland, is surmounted by a steeple-hatted soothsayer. It is typical of many others which were made both with and without the the time-piece. It operates by the insertion in a drawer of one of a dozen discs, each with a question written on it. The magician then rises up, rolls his eyes, makes *magic* passes, and indicates a window behind him where the answer to the question duly appears (*).

Other magicians effectively operate within the confines of snuff-boxes, many of which were most sumptuously made.

Maillardet, Henri (1745– ?): London agent for Jaquet-Droz and Leschot of Geneva, and himself a maker of automata, which he exhibited in England. His figure of a Draughtsman was a great success (*).

Maillardet, Jean-David (1748–1834): maker of clocks and automata. Noted for his figures of magicians (*) and conjurers.

Musicians: many figures of musicians were made that performed with varying success on their chosen instrument. Several complete orchestras were also made.

Pictures: framed pictures (landscapes, seascapes, etc.) were made. Figures, animals, windmills and water were all operated mechanically.

Rochat, Ami-Napoleon and Louis: well known for their automata, particularly singing-birds for snuff-boxes. They were active during the first part of the nineteenth century.

Strasbourg: the interior of the cathedral in this city of eastern France contains a famous clock, the third to be kept there. The first was completed in 1354, the second between 1547 and 1570, and the third, which is a rebuilt version of the second, occupied the years from 1838 to 1842 for its completion. This last clock has bells with jacks, automata and, surmounting the entire edifice, a cock that crows.

Vaucanson, Jacques de (1709–82): one of the earliest inventors and makers of automata of which records have survived. Three of his figures were exhibited in Paris in 1738, and later in London, St Petersburg, and in Germany. On the occasion of the London *début* a booklet was published, of which the title-page reads:

'An account of the Mechanism of an Automaton or Image playing on the German Flute; As it was presented in a Memoire to the Gentlemen of the Royal Academy of Sciences at Paris. By M. Vaucanson,

Inventor and Maker of the said Machine: Together with a Description of an artificial Duck, eating, drinking, macerating the Food, and voiding Excrements; pluming her wings, picking her feathers, and performing several operations in Imitation of a living Duck: Contrived by the same Person. As also that of another Image, no less wonderful than the first, playing on the Tabor and Pipe; as he has given an account of them since the Memoire was written. Translated out of the French Original by J. T. Desaguliers, LL.D., F.R.S., Chaplain to His Royal Highness the Prince of Wales.'

The three figures caused sensations wherever they were shown, and were the commencement of a long series of exhibition pieces.

Watches: not content with following the hours and sounding them, adding a repeater and, perhaps, music, the Swiss craftsmen found space for automata: from a dog that barked quietly, but with realism, at each hour to jousting knights complete with trumpeter; and see-sawing children enjoying themselves before a playing (glass) fountain. Mostly they were cased in gold, and the tiny figures and landscapes made of the same precious metal in different colours (*see* Birds).

BOOKS FOR FURTHER READING

A. Chapuis and Edouard Gelis, *Le Monde des Automates* (Paris, 1928).

R. Mosoriak, *The Curious History of Music Boxes* (New York, 1943).

A. Chapuis and Edmond Droz, *Les Automates* (Neuchâtel, 1949).

John E. T. Clark, *Musical Boxes* (London, 1952).

DOLLS AND DOLLS' HOUSES

By LESLIE DAIKEN

(*A*) DOLLS

DOLL, a term used generically, is often misused to describe all kinds of specimens quite unconnected with the play of children. Instances of this wide connotation are: fashion dolls; souvenirs dressed in pseudo-national costume; miniature replicas in silver or precious materials; marionettes; pagan figurines; musical automata; in addition to those models representing the story of the Nativity which were displayed in Christian churches during the Middle Ages. Collectors, therefore, who wish to concern themselves with what were used essentially as toys, are advised to employ the distinguishing term of *play-doll*. In a majority of instances research is confirming the view that play-dolls have come down to us in shapes which once were those of semi-religious, entirely religious objects, or totems.

The examples of ancient Greek and Roman dolls which survive are to be seen mainly in museums; though very occasionally in Paris and in some Mediterranean centres a specimen in terra-cotta, with articulated limbs, can be purchased through the trade. Egyptian prototypes offered as so-called 'dolls' are usually not playthings but votive objects. The argument that they were often buried with small children and that they were originally intended to be toys has little evidence to support it. Sometimes at national festivities one is confronted by the earlier and more primordial significance of dolls in ceremonial. An apt illustration is in present-day Japan, where the traditional *Tango-no-Sekku* of May 5th (The Boys' Festival), which is dedicated to valour and soldier-play, has also its girls' equivalent Festival of *China Matsuri* on March 3rd, an occasion when every year the virtues of truly womanly character are portrayed through children's loving care of dolls. Mythological dolls are quite easily obtained and represent but a sector of a widely-extended collectors' field.

During the past five hundred years play-dolls have undergone so many local changes in appearance, design, and process of manufacture, that their variety seems endless. These variations reflect the cultures and the climates in relation to which play-dolls were produced. Yet more is known about prehistoric or primitive examples relatively than is known about the origins and details of manufacture of, say, play-dolls made in Europe between 1750 and 1850. There are far many more persons urged by acquisitiveness than by any thirst for scientific and factual data: so that while many superb play-dolls have been preserved and cherished, the records and catalogues relating to their producers have been seldom sought and preserved.

Collectors in the United States are much more seriously concerned with checking and counter-checking makers' data, with idiosyncrasies of design, and with deductive analyses. From such preoccupation much valuable specialist information has come to light. It should be set on record, however, that the Herculean achievement in assembling facts, realized by Esther Singleton in her work *Dolls* (New York, 1927), seems to have been slavishly, and not always generously, reiterated by subsequent writers on this subject. Mrs Imogene Anderson, one of the leading American collectors and authorities, is at present combining with others to create and have ratified a dictionary of doll terminology. It is from her private collection that the illustration of the 1699 American play-doll 'Letitia Penn' is reproduced (Plate 168c).

The oldest examples extant of doll-figures known to historians have, no doubt, remained intact because they were made from substances more durable than cloth: beads, terra-cotta, glazed clay, or well-seasoned woods. There now remain very few traces of early dolls that could have been made from hair, straw, papyrus, linen, wool or other fabrics, all of which were more liable to decomposition.

The range of raw materials from which play-dolls have been constructed during ten centuries provides a key to their many-sided story. These, in style, comprise crude effigies fashioned in a single piece (often striking the European eye as being ungainly) as well as the more naturalistic kinds with articulated limbs. As manufacturers became more sophisticated, so their play-dolls became more like adults, juveniles, or babies. Their faces became more lifelike. Limbs and bodies were more cleverly animated with devices ranging from eyes that closed and noise-making apparatus to automatic movements powered by clockwork or friction.

Except for specimens of figures made from baked clay unearthed from pre-Mesopotamian civilizations (e.g. the excavations at Mohenjo-daro in North-West India), those which collectors prize most among the 1860 to 1880 range are the china and parian-headed dolls made by the Jumeau factory in France. Many of these were conceived more as fashion dolls than as play-dolls; pierced ear-lobes are one of the clues to quick recognition. Similar characteristics in respect of play-dolls that bear the names of famous German, Italian, Swiss, American, or English craftsmen are made known in the apposite literature.

In Europe, where the 'modern' conception of play-doll enjoyed remarkable development, the following are some of the materials utilized since 1800 for making doll-heads and bodies, each having had a varying duration of popularity: fabric, wood, wax, papier mâché, china, *bisqué*, composition, celluloid, rubber, leather, dressed hide, paper, metal, plastics.

The discovery of rubber as a new material from which to make toys practically revolutionized toy-making in Europe and in America. It put on the market inexpensive mass-produced play-dolls which, until then, had been made mainly from soft woods from the Thuringian Forest in Germany. Collectors should note that the eminent authority on all wooden dolls is Mrs Ruth Campbell Williams, of Chagrin Falls, Ohio. She is addressed professionally by the name of *Darcy the Wooden Doll Lady*.

Doll-collecting as a private hobby has become enormously popular during the past fifty years, and is continuing so. Intelligence is exchanged through doll societies and clubs. The pastime is pursued more eagerly perhaps in the United States and Canada. There, clubs publish their own magazines – e.g. *Doll Talk*, Kimport Dolls, Independence, Mo. ($1.00 for two years), *The Dollmakers' Guild*, 2112 Middlefield Street, Middletown, Conn. (20 c. per single copy), and many others, and *Doll News*, magazine of the United Federation of Doll Clubs Inc., 2507, 76th Street, Kenosha, Wisconsin, are but three typical publications.

These clubs number among their members doll historians, technical experts, and owners of remarkable collections. Of the latter, perhaps the most important and worthy of a visit is the Wenham Museum, Clafin-Richards House, Wenham, Massachusetts.

The haphazard collecting of antique dolls both in Europe and, more particularly, in the United States, has led to considerable confusion in the use of nomenclature. To establish a standard reference vocabulary acceptable to English-speaking peoples, a few methodically-minded collectors in the United States have formulated principles for identification. It is desirable and inevitable that these terms should be introduced into the United Kingdom, where the need for a common terminology is everywhere felt. An example of the four basic classifications universally cited by members of the International Doll Collectors' Club Inc. of America is: (i) *China*, (ii) *Pink Lustre*, (iii) *Parian*, and (iv) *Bisqué*. The Club's President is Edna Glenn Jones; its international offices are at No. 1004, East Tenth Avenue, Denver, Colorado. Its official magazine is published at the same address, and the Club issues to members its own stationery and pin bearing the Club emblem.

First British Doll Club was formed in July 1953. Among its aims are: (*a*) to ensure the preservation of old and interesting dolls; (*b*) to encourage the production of good modern dolls, dolls' houses, and accessories. It publishes a news-sheet, *Plangon*, from the address of its Hon. Secretary and Treasurer, Mrs de Clifford, 3 Holland Park Avenue, London, W.11. The annual subscription is five shillings for a full member.

The growing demand for historical dolls in Britain and abroad has rendered it less likely that the more unusual dolls can be picked up unnoticed in random places. At the same time, in order to safeguard collectors' interests and to stabilize supply and demand, many British dealers have tended to specialize. Among the specialists upon whose status in the trade would-be collectors can rely are: Gordon Hand, 170 Kensington Church Street, W.8 (all kinds of antique dolls, toys, miniatures); Roger Warner, Burford, Oxfordshire (dolls, toys, miniatures); Bracher & Partner, 1057 London Road, Thornton Heath, Surrey (play-dolls, automata, mechanical dolls, etc.); Baily's Gallery, Princes Arcade, Piccadilly, W.1. (doll's house accessories and miniatures); Alexandre Raghinsky, 77 Blandford Street, W.1 (curiosa, unusual models, toys, and working models); Beauchamp Bookshop, 15A Harrington Road, London, S.W.7 (ephemera, doll cut-outs, papiers de fantaisie, books about dolls, etc.); Bric-à-Brac, 200 Kensington Church Street, London, W.8 (period dolls, dolls' garments, old lace, miniatures); Miss J. B. Hickman, 15 Moscow Road, London, W.8 (period dolls, dolls' house furniture, accessories, clothes, repairs, etc.); Miller & Co., 65 Chancery Lane, London, E.C.4 (silver miniatures.

DOLLS' HOUSES

The doll's house, unlike the doll, has little recorded history in Britain before the seventeenth century. Examples dating from before 1700 are rare. After that date the *houses* were not toys so much as elaborate pieces of cabinet-making, resembling household furniture. These were used to display the pretty treasures of adults who, more notably on the Continent, liked to collect and to arrange behind glass a variety of clever figurines – effigies of their admired companions or respected acquaintances. Many pieces of carved and turned 'doll's furniture', sometimes known now as 'apprentice pieces', are thought simply to have been replicas of full-scale travellers' samples carried by merchants representing their Dutch or German workshops, who brought them to show to English customers. Similarly, the superbly wrought 'silver toys' are replicas of seventeenth-, eighteenth- and nineteenth-century household effects never intended for dolls' house usage. (*See* 'Apollo Miscellany 1950', *English Silver Toys*, by Charles Oman.)

Doll accessories, clothes, furniture, utensils, vehicles, and even miniature picture books, reached a height of popularity and production during the reign of Queen Victoria, of whose doll-dressing talents examples are on view in the Royal Room of the London

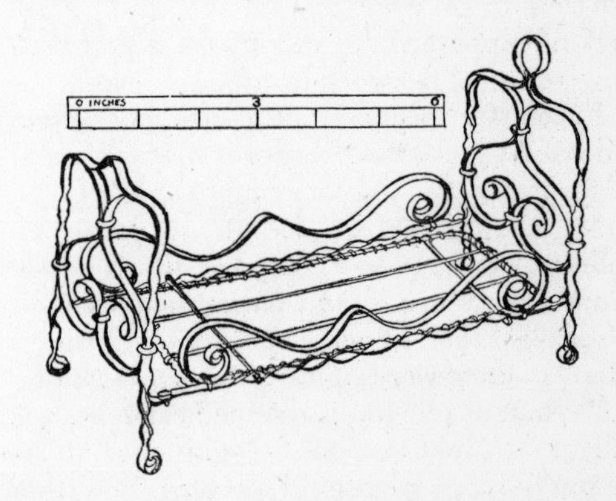

Museum. It was in that era that German-inspired ideas suggesting that small daughters should learn housecraft and mothercraft from doll's house play became the accepted English practice. Doll-play led naturally to a demand for all kinds of play-material

dramatizing the grown-ups' world, which was met in turn by ingenious tiny objects. Every child who could was encouraged to play at bathing baby, shops, baking, entertaining guests, mothers and fathers, doctors,

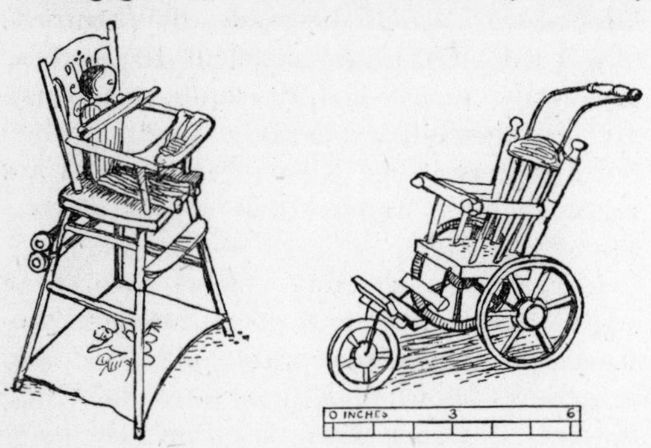

schools, etc. The most commonplace need about the 1850s was for dolls' houses in quantity. It is from this period that the majority of items now offered in stores and auction rooms derive. A fashion made popular by ladies skilled in needlework and embroidery during the 1820's and 1830's now was continued by governesses and nannies. This took the form of dressing Pedlar Dolls, sometimes of wax but more generally Pennywoods. The figures, in traditional bonnet and shawl, were equipped with trays, counters or entire booths, filled with haberdashery, articles of attire and of domestic use, and bric-à-brac great in variety, tiny in size and meticulous in workmanship (vide *Country Life Magazine*, Oct. 14, 1954, pp. 1273–4).

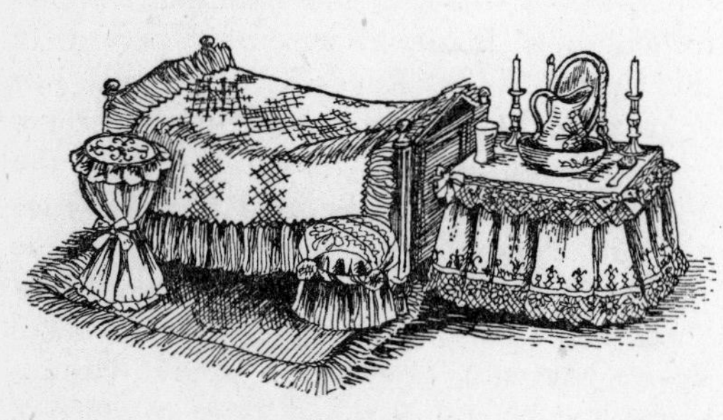

From Germany to Britain next came a doll's house of a more inexpensive kind. Known as a 'Nuremberg Kitchen', it consisted firstly of a single room, designed to encourage cookery games. The accessories consisted of a charcoal stove, ladles, spoons,

a set of pewter plates, tureens, dishes for joints, a grid-iron, pestle and mortar, poultry-spit, water vessel, fuel receptacle, vegetable squeezer, salt canister, and so forth. Later, to keep pace with these box-shaped, self-contained units, new and more elaborate equipment was added year by year. Very soon there came on the market realistic models of glassware, crockery, cutlery, silverware, vases, ornaments, period furniture, nursery items, baby carriages, bassinettes, and so on.

The craving to possess these miniature objects produced in blown glass, ceramic, porcelain, earthenware, lead, bone, horn, brass, tin alloys, wood, enamel-ware, etc., meant the creation of different rooms. Scale-model furniture made from bone-ivory, in filigree patterns like fan-sticks, are mainly of Far Eastern origin. Those looking more solid

and three-dimensional, sometimes having a centre design of a stag or a hound, are mid-European. Objects made from woven straw range from finely-meshed laundry baskets to cradles or shopping baskets of coarser weave. Italian straw-work has a sheen, whereas the miniscule baskets from Mexico are made from dyed hair.

Many of the finer articles made specially for houses were commissioned by their owners. Craftsmen and carpenters, and often silversmiths and coppersmiths, were approached individually, and each artisan faithfully copied the kind of things which at that moment he was producing for the normal market. Thus evolved the mass-produced modern dolls' house furniture as we know it.

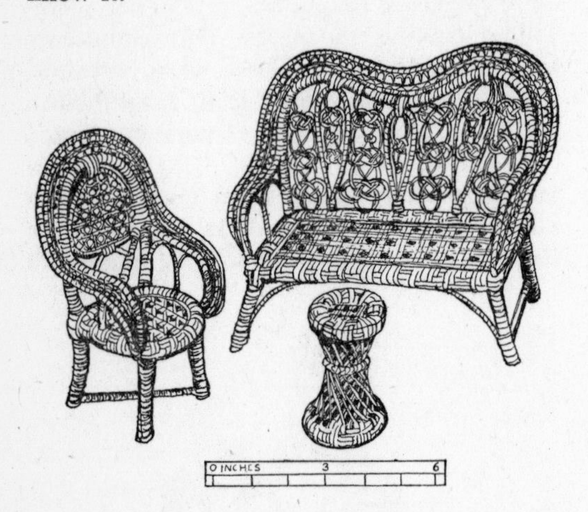

In the categories, for example, of crockery or cutlery, nothing is known to have been made in true doll's size until the mid-Victorian period. All the Georgian and Regency tea-sets and silver services were made in sizes too large for putting into houses, and clearly were intended for games. In the Alpine regions and in the Black Forest, where peasants during the winter were confined to their homes, small pieces of kitchen-ware would be made, hand-turned, of soft woods. With an excellent detail, these are mostly unvarnished. Examples exist which are exquisitely decorated with unrivalled floral patterns. The Russian equivalents are relatively larger and in idiom more characteristically Slavonic.

Curiosities, collectors' pieces, works of superlative artistry and good taste are preserved in some European and American museums. English dolls' houses are interesting for reasons other than that they are playthings. They reflect the diverse architectural styles in dwellings which are so often apt to change from economic causes and from building fashions or conventions. Widespread public interest was aroused by a doll's house designed by Sir Edwin Lutyens and presented in 1924 to the late Queen Mary (herself a devoted collector of miniature furniture), as a token of the nation's esteem. It is now on view at Windsor Castle, described as being 'so perfect as to seem incredible'. Another world-famous repository of remarkable replicas is Titania's Palace, which is at present on view to visitors to the home of the Countess of Wicklow at Ballynastragh, Gorey, Co. Wicklow, Ireland.

Less spectacular, but of strong appeal in one way or another, are examples of furnished dolls' houses representing periods of the Queen Anne, Regency, Victorian, Edwardian and Georgian reigns. Houses of these periods can be seen at museums such as the Victoria and Albert; Bethnal Green; Gunnersbury Park; the Toy Museum which tours Britain;* The Greg Collection, City of Manchester Art Gallery; Castle Museum, York; Bowes Museum, Durham; Uppark, Hampshire; and several National Trust properties. There are private collections in Britain, and the famous Westbrooke Baby House of 1705 is private owned.

* For details write to: Hon. Sec., Stephen Garrett, Esq., A.R.I.B.A., 21 Yeoman's Row, London, S.W.3.

BOOKS FOR FURTHER READING

DOLLS

W. Canning-Wright, *Peeps at the World's Dolls* (New York, 1953).
André Chapuis, *Les Automates, Histoire et Technique* (Geneva, 1952).
Leslie Daiken, *Children's Toys Throughout the Ages* (Batsford, 1952).
Doll Talk (magazine) (Kimport, U.S.A.).
K. Donderkery, *Journey through Toyland* (Indian Dolls), (Bombay, 1954).
Alice K. Early, *English Effigies, Dolls and Puppets* (Batsford, 1955).
Clara Hallard Fawcett, *Dolls: A Guide for Collectors* (Lindquist, 1947).
Ruth and Larry Freeman, *Cavalcade of Toys* (New York, 1942).
Eleanor St George, *Old Dolls* (M. Burrows, New York, 1950).
Lesley Gordon, *A Pageant of Dolls* (Edmund Ward, 1948).
Janet Pagter Johl, *The Fascinating Story of Dolls* (Lindquist, 1941).
Janet Pagter Johl, *More About Dolls* (Lindquist, 1946).
Janet Pagter Johl, *Still More About Dolls* (Lindquist, 1951).
Janet Pagter Johl, *Your Dolls and Mine* (Lindquist, 1952).
Frances H. Low, *Queen Victoria's Dolls* (London, 1894).
Lovett, *The Child's Doll: Its Origin, Legend, Folklore* (1915).
Eleanor St George, *The Dolls of Yesterday; Dolls of Three Centuries* (Scribners, New York, 1951).
Esther Singleton, *Dolls* (New York, 1927).
Notes on the Collection at the Wenham Museum (Wenham Historical Association, Mass., 1951).

DOLLS' HOUSES

A. C. Benson and Sir Lawrence Weaver, *Everybody's Book of the Queen's Doll's House* (Methuen, 1924).
J. Grant, *The Doll's House* (*Studio*, London, 1954).
Karl Grober, *Children's Toys of Bygone Days* (Batsford, 1932).
Karl Grober, *Das Puppenhaus* (Leipzig, 1954).
Flora Gill Jacob, *A History of Dolls' Houses* (Cassell, 1954).
E. Neville Jackson, *Toys of Other Days* (Newnes, 1907).
Children's Toys of Yesterday (*The Studio*, Supplement, London, 1932).
Dolls and Dolls' Houses, Small Picture Book No. 16 (H.M. Stationery Office, 1950).
Vivien Greene, *Some English Dolls and Dolls' Houses:* (B. T. Batsford).
The Greg Collection of Dolls and Dolls' Houses: Catalogue of; City Art Gallery, Moseley Street, Manchester.
German Kitchen of the XVIII Century at Room 19, The Bowes Museum, Barnard Castle, Co. Durham (Catalogue).

SHIP MODELS

By BASIL LAVIS

'It is upon the Navy under the Providence of God that the strength, safety, and prosperity of these islands do mainly depend.' These words form the preamble to the Articles of War which have been read in all British naval ships from the time of Cromwell to the present day. They indicate the importance of the sea and our ships to the people of the British Isles.

The love of the sea and ships is inherent in the average Englishman. As an island nation the British are dependent on the sea and on ships for their lives and their history. But the work, importance and influence of both their naval and mercantile fleets have been disregarded under the more popular episodes, such as the defeat of the Armada, the Last Fight of the *Revenge*, the Battle of Trafalgar, and other actions.

Since the seventeenth century the ship model has played an important part in British naval history. Moreover, there is something very personal in examining at close quarters the ship in miniature. The story of a voyage, the lives of the men who manned her, their hardships, endurance, their skill, are all brought within a compass that can be visualized without effort. Had more interest and knowledge been available to appreciate the value and importance of the genuine scale model a few years before the First World War, many of the finest models ever made would probably now be on view in an English museum instead of in museums in America. Some of them may have formed part of the Pett or Pepys collections of Navy Board models of the seventeenth century.

Ship modelling is as old as life itself, for it is natural for a man to shape a piece of wood and float it, stick a leaf or a tiny reed mat up for a sail until, with the progress of time and the acquisition of knowledge and skill born of experience, more elaborate work was produced. But model ships are fragile things: and all that are left of the earliest models are those which have been preserved in the protection of the tomb, the funerary boats of Ancient Egypt. These were placed therein for some religious rite, such as to enable the soul of the departed to be ferried across the River Styx. These are scarcely more than 'playthings' and do not represent any vessel in particular. They are of value only on account of their age and origin. Models of Egyptian trading vessels, Greek and Roman galleys, biremes, trieres, and the like, are unknown.

Then there are the church models, hung in churches in many parts of Europe, a custom persisting to the present time, and to be seen in English churches at Fordwich, Portsmouth, Southampton, and elsewhere. These models, usually commemorating the loss of a ship, or a blessing, are for the most part of crude construction and exaggerated proportions.

It is not until the Stuart era is reached that ship models are true-to-scale reproductions of the actual ship in all the details of appearance and construction. Considering how fragile even large-scale models are, subject to vibration in transit, the frailty of spars and rigging, the latter also very perishable, and loss through war damage, it is fortunate indeed that so many of these delightful examples of the shipwright's art remain intact.

It is noticeable how the appearance of the ship corresponds with the custom of the period. It is what one would expect. Nevertheless, it is a point to bear in mind. For instance, the King's Ships, and Ships of the Cinque Ports, seem leisurely to follow the appearance of the Viking ships with their pointed ends, a single pole mast set amidships with its large square sail. The introduction of 'castles' fore and aft, where the archers were stationed, also offered space upon which to display modest heraldic designs and pavesses (wooden shields). In the Tudor era the number of masts increased to three, and sometimes four, and enabled the ships to carry the symbols of the pomp and pageantry of the times to better advantage.

With the Stuarts the pinnacle of gorgeous extravagance is reached. Phineas Pett built the *Prince Royal*, which was launched at Woolwich in 1610. She is described as '. . . of the burthen of 1,400 tons. This royal ship is double built, and is most sumptuously adorned within and without, with all manner of curious carving, painting and rich gilding, being in all respects the greatest and goodliest ship that ever was builded in England.' Before building this ship Pett made a model of her 'most fairly garnished with carving and painting', which greatly delighted King James and his son, Prince Henry.

On March 7th, 1634, 'His Majesty [Charles I] gave an order for a great ship of 1,500 tons burthen besides tonnage, and Pett principally is appointed for building the same. He is to prepare a model for a ship of that burden and to bring the same to the Lords at Whitehall in Easter Week that they may give order for preparing the mould for the building the said ship' (Calendar of State Papers). This was to be the great *Sovereign of the Seas*, the 'pride and glory of the Ship Money Fleet', the most ornate and costly ship ever built. Though heartily criticized as being unfit for 'service in any part of the King's Dominions', she proved ultimately to be very seaworthy, a fine sailer, and soundly built, qualities which were recognized by those who chose her to be their flagship in each of the three Dutch wars. What a pleasant sensation there would be if one or both of these models should ever be discovered.

In the early days of the Commonwealth Cromwell issued an order removing all royal arms and decorations from ships. This was a period of austerity; and though some two hundred vessels were built, there do not appear to be any contemporary models of them in existence.

At the Restoration a return to the decorative was immediate. The royal arms and heraldic emblems were restored, and to the gilded work were added wreaths encircling all gun ports above those of the upper deck.

An entirely new type of vessel was introduced at this period. When the King left Holland to return to the throne, he was presented with a 'jaght'. Fast and handy, this type soon attracted attention, and the King's brother, the Duke of York, promptly had one built. Others followed, and so yachting and yacht-racing began in England. There are a few contemporary models of these vessels in the National Maritime Museum (Plate 170B).

The Navy Board models were really the forerunners of the modern shipbuilders' plans. The models were the work of the shipwright, made exactly as the real ship was constructed, with all the actual timbers, planking, wales, fittings and, occasionally, masts, yards, rigging and sails, all most accurately to scale. This was usually 1 : 48 – that is, forty-eight times smaller than the ship that put to sea. It will be noticed that the planking is omitted in most cases below the water-line. This is to permit of a view of the internal construction.

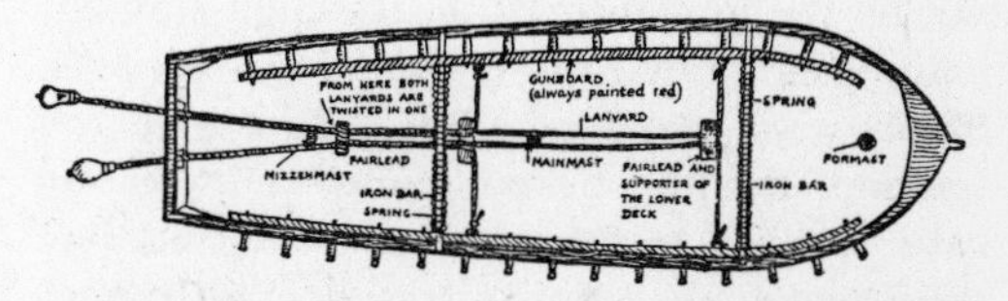

Mr Samuel Pepys had a special interest in these models, and he writes in his diary on 29th September, 1662: 'Home where I did find Mr Deane of Woolwich hath sent me the modell he had promised me, but it so far exceeds my expectation, that I am sorry almost he should make such a present to no greater person, but I am exceedingly glad of it, and shall study to do him a courtesy for it'. At his death Pepys had acquired a considerable number of these models, but their fate is hid in the mists of time. Some of them are very likely the ones to be seen and studied at Greenwich. Charles Sergison, who followed after Pepys to the Navy Office, also acquired a fine collection, which is certain to have included some of his predecessor's models, and had it specially housed at his estate, Cuckfield Park, Surrey, where it remained until as recently as 1922. It was then purchased by Colonel Henry H. Rogers, of New York, and he loaned it to the Metropolitan Museum of Art. At his death the collection was bequeathed to the United States Naval Academy, Annapolis, Maryland. A fully-illustrated catalogue of those models has been published by the Academy. It contains over a hundred photographs, which include enlarged details of heads, sterns and rigging.

Volumes could be written on these models, of their beauty, their accuracy, and the important part they have played in building up the British Navy, which, overcoming all opposition, has given to the world the freedom of the seas. Practically every decade witnessed some change, some improvement, in details of construction, arrangement and evolution of the sails, spars and rigging, and the changing phases of decoration.

It is a fascinating study to follow the evolution of the sailing-ship from the first three-masted, bluff-bowed, round-sided, transom-sterned vessel of the mid-fifteenth century, with their two square sails of the foremast, two on the main, and the triangular lateen sail on the mizzen-mast, to the high-sterned, gaudily-decorated and colourful vessels of the Stuart era, showing the evolution of the spritsail and the introduction of the exotic little spritsail topmast. Towards the end of the seventeenth century studding sails were introduced. One of the noticeable changes following the death of Queen Anne was the reduction in the amount of decorative work, and the disappearance particularly of the gilded port-wreath (Plate 169A). In the 1780s copper sheathing became the practice. Later again, we come to the ships of Trafalgar, with their black-painted gunport lids, forming the checkered pattern – 'the Nelson Fashion'. Finally, the peak of sailing-ship building is reached with the graceful, fine-lined, fast-sailing, multi-sailed clipper ship of a century ago, bending some forty or more sails, including such picturesque names as 'ringtails', 'moonrakers', 'skyscrapers' and 'stargazers'.

A class of ship model which calls for special mention is the bone model made by prisoners captured during the wars in the Napoleonic era and even a little before, when the high seas and the Narrow Seas were the scenes of naval engagements between British forces and the Dutch, the Danes, the Spanish, the French and, in 1812, the Americans. Prisoners taken from captured ships were incarcerated in prisons and hulks around England. For the most part these 'prisoner-of-war' models were constructed by the French. Some, however, were the work of Dutch sailors; and later, from 1812 to 1820, when the last prisoners were repatriated, the Americans. Conscription in the French Navy gathered in all kinds of craftsmen. Capture ending their sea-going career, they soon formed themselves into groups to occupy their time in some form of distraction and craftsmanship. Some groups employed themselves in making articles, trinket-boxes, toys and ship models. Materials used were straw for plaiting and covering boxes, scraps of metal and wood; and when any special piece was required for a small model, means were found of removing a suitable section from the hulk, and finally the bones from their meat rations were used.

These models are works of art (Plate 170C). In the majority the over-all appearance is satisfyingly seamanlike. The fittings are the work of skilled artisans. The rigging, the set of the yards, the rake of the masts, though sometimes a little out of proportion, are the work of practical seamen. But they invariably lack scale accuracy. The hulls are built of wood without any attempt to obtain anything but rough-guess measurements. When the wood was shaped, the ivory-carver would cover the hull with thin strips of bone. Then the head timbers, rails, knightheads, figure-head, and all the minute pieces which form the intricate forward section, would be carved and fitted (Plate 169D). Working along the sides, the gun-port lids, the entry port, the channels, the quarter galleries (Plate 169E), the stern galleries, all required painstaking care and skill. On deck there would be the bitts, the belfry, the galley funnel, pin racks, rails, ladders, etc. And after all the spars had been carved there would be the scores of dead-eyes and variously sized and shaped blocks. Guns, anchors, lanterns, and the ship's boats also had to be included.

A number of these models have two lanyards trailing out of the stern-chase ports. These, when pulled, released a spring which jerked the batteries of guns on either side into a position 'to engage the enemy'.

No attempt was made to regulate the size of these models. They varied from the minute little gems of a couple of inches, and in a few cases even an inch, in length, to the fairly large three-foot hull with another three feet for the flying jibboom and spanker-boom. In a very few cases is the name of the maker known. Sometimes the name of a ship is writ large across the stern, but sadly, more often than not, merely a chance, or perhaps a special request for a model of a particular ship. A few of these models are entirely of wood, mostly about twelve inches or less in length of hull. They are beautifully made, the fine detail of the carving, the fittings, and the rigging, being a great delight to the eye.

Nowadays one rarely comes across a Navy Board model for sale. They must all be safe in some museum or a greatly prized possession in a private collection. A bone model can, however, often be found at the Parker Gallery, 2 Albemarle Street, London, where such pieces are specialized in and are usually on view (Plate 170A).

The subject of the ship model had received little attention until about forty years ago. Even in museums the identity of a model had been either neglected or claimed without regard to historical details. A knowledge of naval architecture, heraldry and the evolution of sails and rigging, are needed for establishing the identity of a model (Plate 169B and C). Careful measurements multiplied to full-scale feet and inches may agree with the measurements given for a certain class of ship to be laid down under a specified establishment. The recognition of heraldic insignia may bring identification closer. The actual figurehead, stern or quarter decorations, rendered on canvas by the hand of an accurate and practical artist such as the Van de Veldes, may reveal the name of the actual ship. A knowledge of flags worn by ships, and occasionally found on a model, may further aid in the identification; likewise the shape and design of royal flags, the Union, ensigns, squadronal colours, and, in later times, House flags, have a bearing on the date and class of ship represented.

The whole subject can best be studied from the books available, together with a close examination of the models themselves at such museums as the National Maritime Museum, Greenwich; the Science Museum, South Kensington; the Royal United Service Museum, Whitehall; the Shipping Gallery, Liverpool Museum; and a number of others throughout the British Isles. A comprehensive list of these will be found in R. Morton Nance's book *Sailing Ship Models*. Part I of the catalogue 'Sailing Ships' in the Science Museum contains a valuable list of books which are essential for the study of this subject.

A word about the model-maker of today, who builds old-time ship models, may not be out of place because of the very high standard of workmanship now required and reached. There is a growing number of artists and craftsmen who, after painstaking research and close study of contemporary models, are able to build a model as perfectly and as artistically as the shipwright of three hundred years ago. The built-up hull, the beauty of the gilded and scroll work, the perfection of rigging, and all the minute details, are faultless. This can be seen in one model in particular, the *Naseby*, 80 to 86 guns, of 1655, in the National Maritime Museum (Plate 170D). Built by Mr Robert Spence to a scale of 1:48, she is an exact replica of a contemporary Navy Board model of the seventeenth century.

The Ship Model Section of the Model Engineer Exhibition held annually has done much to encourage the model-maker, and recent awards of the championship cup to models of old-time ships, such as H.M.S. *Victory*, now in the Victory Museum, Portsmouth, ensures a very high standard of perfection.

Repairs to contemporary models presents a problem not easy of solution. Not everyone can turn to and do it themselves. It requires the hand of the craftsman. Those repairers who can be relied upon to do the work accurately are now very scarce and are usually overburdened with work. Helpful advice on this matter can, however, be obtained from Captain Harry Parker.

JADE

By F. W. BARKER

THE WRITER wishes it to be understood that the following remarks about jade are for the general reader and not for the archaeological collector or specialist, who may consider some of them to be heterodox.

To those who have known jade for a long while in its broadest and most tolerant sense, it might be difficult to answer immediately if posed with the question 'What is jade?' The geologist assures us that, broadly speaking, it is divided into two groups: *nephrite* (a silicate of calcium and magnesium) and *jadeite* (a silicate of sodium and alumina). At the same time it is admitted that the difference between the two is not easily apparent to either touch or sight and can only definitely be settled by chemical analysis or specific gravity. It would also be admitted, probably, that the artistic appeal and the more sordid one of value is the same in both. One is tempted, therefore, to ask, 'Why trouble about it?'

The next question which quite reasonably occurs is 'From where did the Chinese get their jade?' Professor S. Howard Hansford in his erudite work *Chinese Jade Carving* (London, Lund Humphries, 1950) devotes a whole chapter of some twenty pages to a critical examination of the subject, and those who wish to study the proofs so skilfully marshalled will find much in these pages to interest them. He starts by saying: 'The rivers and mountains of Khotan and Yarkand, in Chinese Turkestan, have been famous for centuries as the main, if not the only, source of China's jade stone . . .' (the *nephritic* variety) and, at the same time, he adduces a considerable amount of information bearing on the *jadeite* question and its source in Burma at a much later date. It is unquestionably correct to say that no other stone than jade has had so long and unbroken a continuity with man and his social and, in a sense, his religious development. If we go back centuries before the Christian era we find it emerging as the visible and tangible – if somewhat arbitrary – symbols of his Heaven and Earth, and in one instance, at least, of a famous constellation. These arbitrary forms have been handed down through the ages to modern times, even when their original significance has become no more than a tradition: and this applies not only to objects of a strictly ritual character but also to those more intimately connected with everyday life.

Another point of great interest and significance in the study of jades is that as early as the seventh century B.C. jade was looked upon as containing in *itself* – that is, in its actual mineral structure – parallels to certain virtues. They were enumerated in a contemporary ritual as follows: 'If jade is highly valued, it is because, since very olden times, the wise have likened it to virtue. For them, the polish and the brilliancy of jade represent the whole of purity; its perfect compactness, and its extreme hardness represent the sureness of the intelligence; its angles – they do not cut although they seem sharp – represent justice; the pure and prolonged sound which it gives forth when one strikes it represents music. Its colour represents loyalty; its interior flaws, always showing themselves through the transparency, call to mind sincerity; its iridescent brightness represents Heaven; its admirable substance, born of mountain and of water, represents the Earth. The price which all the world attaches to it represents the truth.'

Among these parallels, the one which says that 'its interior flaws always showing themselves through the transparency call to mind sincerity' is worthy of being specially emphasized. So often one hears these interior flaws spoken of in a disparaging manner and evidently without the slightest knowledge that, to a cultured Chinese mind, they speak silently and permanently of that rarely-found virtue of sincerity. It must, however, be made clear that this does not apply to cracks caused by accident or by imperfections of the material.

The spirit and memory of these ideas evidently continued in the mind of some of China's poets, because in one of the 'Nineteen Pieces of Old Poetry', which were apparently composed at various dates round about the dawn of the Christian era, occur the lines:

> 'In Yen and Chao are many fair ladies,
> Beautiful people with faces like jade'

which, obviously, could only have reference to some implied qualities and not in any literal way to either the hardness or colour of jade. And from other angles jade provided the poet with unusual and charming similes. 'The sky', wrote Po Chii-i in the ninth century, 'is pillared on a column of green jade'; and, again, describing the trees in winter: 'At the year's end the time of great snow stamps their branches with a fret of glittering jade'. These, and many other references to jade as illustrating both the poetical and actual use of it in early times may be read – and, indeed, should be read – in the wonderful translations of Chinese poetry made by Mr Waley, to whom the world cannot be too grateful for opening to them the cultured Chinese mind.

The interest in jade is, in the great majority of cases, kept within the boundary of personal taste and inclination, and he to whom the early – often called 'tomb jades' – appeal, rarely seems to have an equal appreciation of the masterpieces of later centuries. The reason for this is undoubtedly the allure of age felt by some minds, amounting to a hypnotism, and the quite sincere conviction that the earliest Chinese jades have the most personality and therefore quite definitely close the mind to anything appreciably later than whatever dynasty they choose as the limit of their artistic appreciation. This attitude is one that the inexperienced collector should be very wary of adopting, and he should train himself to refrain from thinking that great age is *in itself* to be blindly accepted as a proof of artistic or aesthetic superiority.

'The preponderance', says Professor Hansford, 'among jades attributable to pre-Han periods of plaques designed for attachment to other materials, bears witness to their widespread use as jewels or embellishments.' These thin, flat plaques, whose outlines include formalized birds, animal masks, dragon motifs, etc., are of necessity of quite small size and could not be expected to be suitable for the vitrine but rather for the museum showcase or the student collector's cabinet. Their interest is archaeological. Even the larger examples of these pre-Han times cannot be claimed to have decorative appeal as a whole.

From time to time, however, there appeared carvings which were strikingly different, such as the standing courtier (11 inches high) and the fine green head and shoulders of a horse (7 inches high), both dating from the **Han Dynasty** (206 B.C.–A.D. 220). But the most impressive example in Great Britain of simplicity of treatment is unquestionably the magnificent reclining buffalo, which at one time was said to be 'possibly Han' but is now considered to be some centuries later. It has an unchallengeable pedigree in Chinese history since 1422, when it was then taken to Pekin by the Emperor, Yung-lo.

This bold simplicity of treatment seems to have continued down through the **T'ang Dynasty** (A.D. 618–906), and appeared intermittently through succeeding centuries, particularly those which covered the Sung, Yuan and perhaps the beginning of the Ming.

The evolution of a style – more naturalistic and more detailed – must have been a very gradual process: and the beginnings can only be suggested from the study of some well-known sculpture such as, for example, the unique black horse of the ninth century, whose mane and tail, and indeed the whole modelling, seem to suggest a breaking away

(A) Original Navy Board model of H.M.S. *Victory*, 100 guns. Proposed in 1758, the year of Horatio Nelson's birth, the ship was later considerably altered. *National Maritime Museum.*

B

C

(B) Contemporary dockyard model of the 70-gun ship *Ipswich*, of 1730. The rigging appears to be entirely contemporary. *National Maritime Museum.*

(C) The square-sided foretop of H.M.S. *Centurion*, 1745. This shape remained until the middle of the nineteenth century. *National Maritime Museum.*

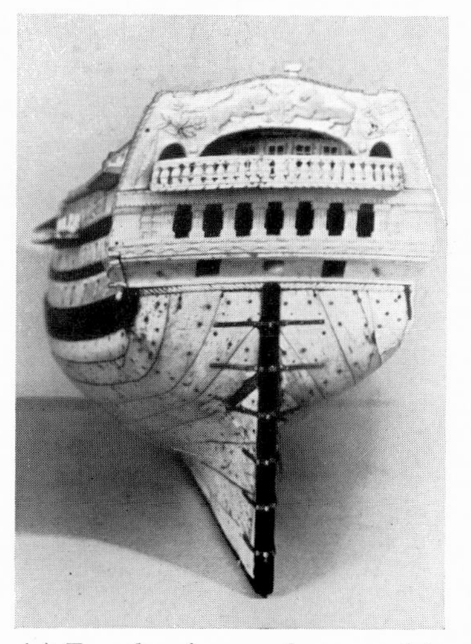

(D) French prisoner-of-war model. Note the delicate carving. *Collection O. Veil.*

(E) French prisoner-of-war model. Note the carving and scroll work. *Collection O. Veil.*

o face page 256

(A) Model of the French 80-gun ship *Victoire* made by French prisoners of war in Porchester Castle, *c.* 1800 (23 in. over all, hull 14 in., height 16 in.). Contemporary rigging. *Collection John C. Carras.*

(B) A Stuart royal yacht, *c.* 1675. This photograph is a model of 1675, but the sails and rigging are modern. *National Maritime Museum.*

(C) French prisoner-of-war model of a naval sloop-of-war of about 1815 rigged as a snow. Made of wood and bone. *Private Collection.*

(D) The *Naseby*, 80–86 guns, launched 1655 at Woolwich.

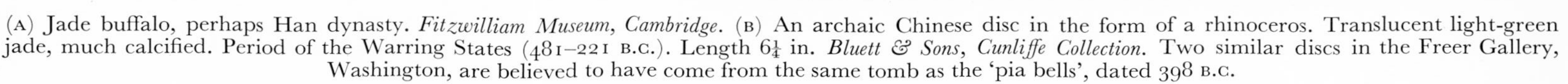

(A) Jade buffalo, perhaps Han dynasty. *Fitzwilliam Museum, Cambridge.* (B) An archaic Chinese disc in the form of a rhinoceros. Translucent light-green jade, much calcified. Period of the Warring States (481–221 B.C.). Length 6¼ in. *Bluett & Sons, Cunliffe Collection.* Two similar discs in the Freer Gallery, Washington, are believed to have come from the same tomb as the 'pia bells', dated 398 B.C.

(C) Jade dragon-headed horse. K'ang-hsi 1662–1722 A.D. *Fitzwilliam Museum, Cambridge.*

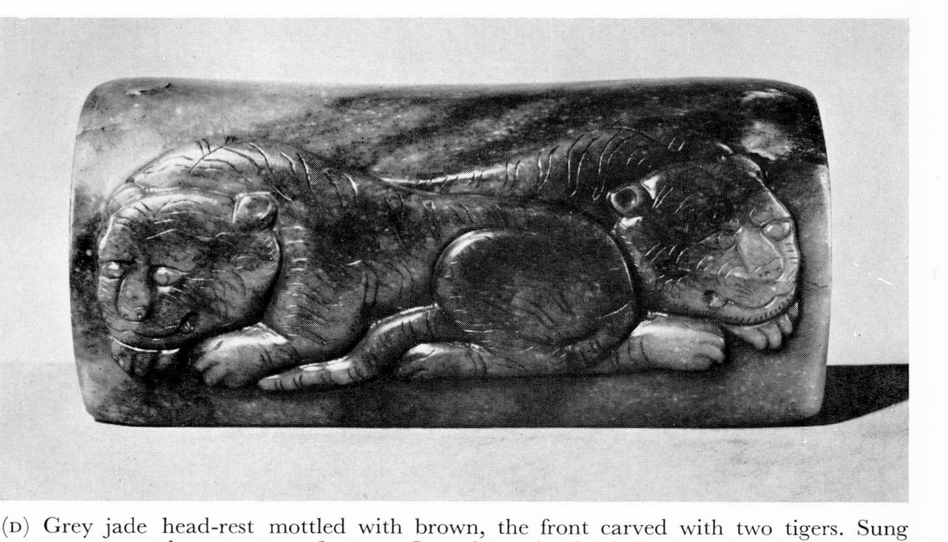

(D) Grey jade head-rest mottled with brown, the front carved with two tigers. Sung dynasty, A.D. 960–1279. Length 10½ in. *Spink & Son Ltd.*

(A) Chinese horse's head and neck about 12 in. in height. Han dynasty. 206 B.C.–A.D. 220 *Victoria & Albert Museum, London.*

(B) Celadon jade mountain with two poems by the Emperor Ch'ien Lung, 1736–95. Length 12½ in. *Spink & Son Ltd.*

(C) Jade Tsung. Early Chou dynasty *c.* 1122–249 B.C. *Eumopolos Collection, British Museum.*

(D) Pale grey jade incense burner and cover, copied from an early ritual bronze. Ch'ien Lung, 1736–95. Height 4½ in. *Spink & Son Ltd*

(E) An old Chinese plainly carved spinach green jade bowl. Ch'ien Lung period, 1736–95. Diameter 8½ in., height 3½ in. *John Spark Ltd.*

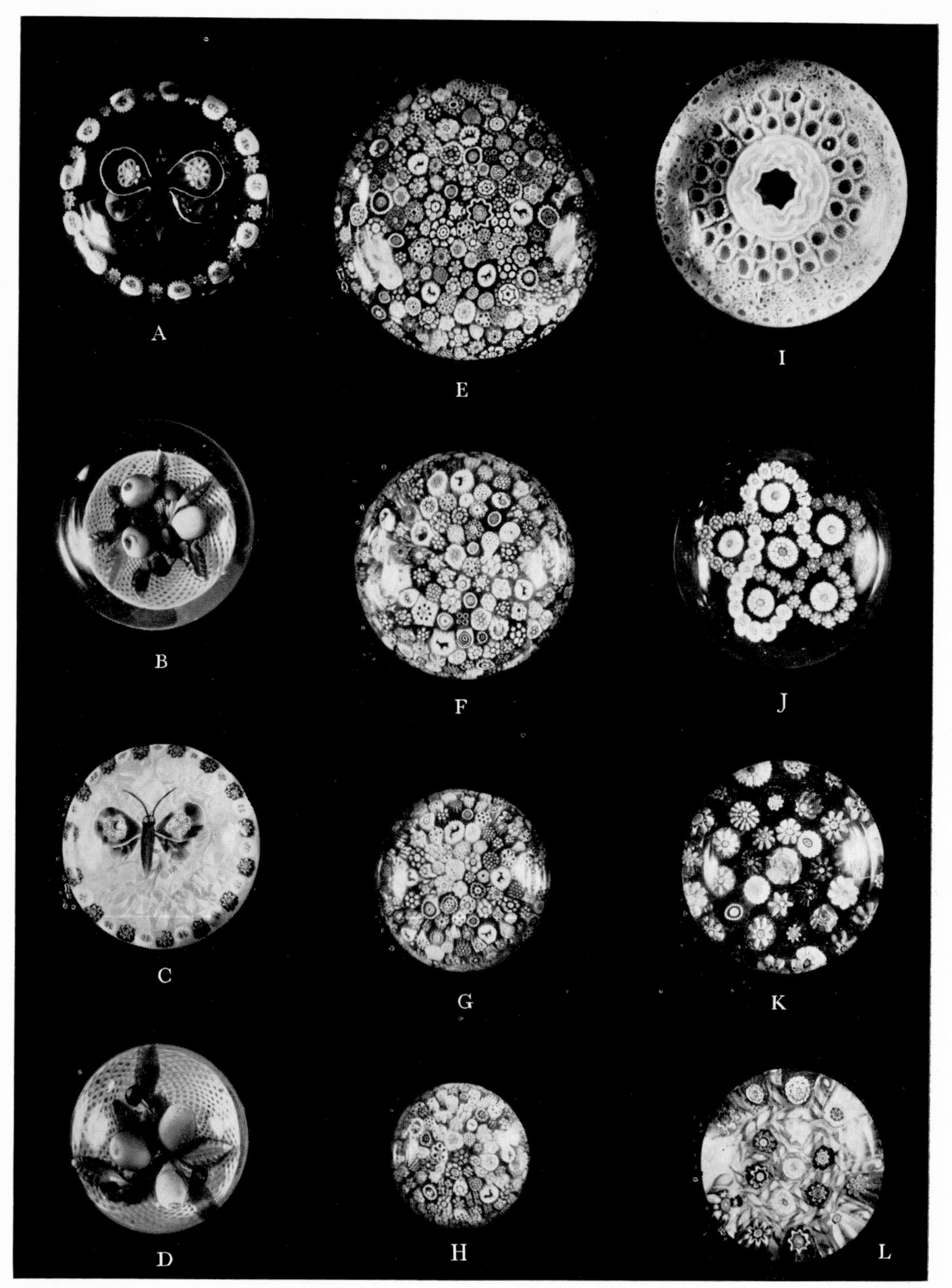

(A) Baccarat 'butterfly'. (B) Clichy 'fruit' on latticino ground. (C) Baccarat 'butterfly' on muslin ground. (D) Clichy 'fruit' on latticino ground. (E) to (H) A set of four Baccarat millefiore with animal silhouettes. Marked 'B' and dated 1848. (I) English, George Bacchus and Sons, Birmingham. (J) Clichy garlanded millefiore. (K) Clichy—note the centrally-placed typical rose. (L) Clichy. *Lories Ltd, London.*

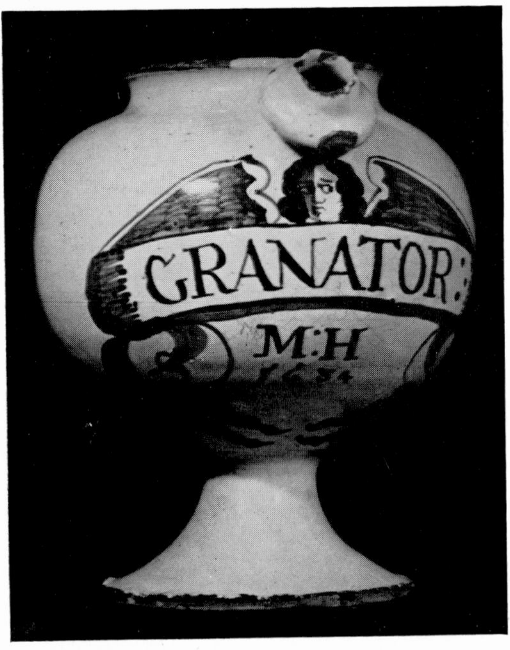

(A) Lambeth delft. Charles II period. 'Angel' jar dated 1684. Height 7½ in.

(B) Lambeth delft. Charles II period, *c.* 1680. Height 6½ in.

(C) Deruta, Italy, *c.* 1507. Height 8¾ in.
Victoria & Albert Museum.

(D) Nevers ware drug bottle. *Bleu persan.* Height 11½ in.
Collection: Dr C. H. Spiers

(A) Venetian *albarello* dated on the reverse 1578. Height 8½ in.

(B) Blue-and-white drug jar made at Bassano, near Venice, 1715. Height 5 in. *Pharmaceutical Society.*

(C) Massive Lambeth delft 'Bird' design jar, dated 1724. Height 13½ in. *Collection: Dr M. H. Caraco.*

(D) Reverse of (C), showing arms of the Apothecaries' Company painted in blue on white.

(A–F) Six labels with unusual names. *Paxaretta* was an Andalusian wine; *Montrachet* denoted wines from the Puligny-Montrachet vineyard; and *Cream of the Valley* was a polite reference to Gin.

(G) A Battersea enamel label engraved by S. F. Ravenet. It shows a cupid standing by a cyder-press; a yoke for a pony or an ass hanging at one end of the transverse beam.

(H–J) Three unusual labels. *Sarçeal* (Sercial) was a Madeira; *Morachee* is thought to be a mis-spelling of Montrachet (*see* above); and *Nig* is Gin spelt backwards – perhaps to fool the servants!

(K, L) Two pierced and engraved silver labels. *Mountain* was wine from Malaga; this particular label is engraved with a crest.

(M, N, O) Three labels of simple design; two with engraved borders, one having a shaped and engraved top.

All from The Hon. Mrs Ionides Collection and the Cropper Collection, both in the Victoria & Albert Museum.

PLATE 176

from formal conventions. Both this and the buffalo are now in the Fitzwilliam Museum, Cambridge.

Through the three centuries of the **Ming Dynasty**, stretching from 1368 till 1644, the process went on, and a magnificent illustration are the dragons on the huge jade basin in Pekin, one of the Chinese national treasures, which was carved not later than the middle of the fourteenth century and which is accepted as one of the largest specimens in the world. It measures twenty-six inches high by seventy inches long.

It is highly improbable that there were any fixed rules of treatment, and the colour and shape, whether it was a river pebble or a lump from the mountains of Turkestan or Burma, must have been studied by the carver, possibly for a considerable time, before he came to a final decision as to what would give the most attractive and artistic result and at the same time give full value to the quality of the material. One feels that the finished object must have been visible to him mentally from the very beginning. The reverence for the past was in no way forgotten or ignored, however, since if, shall we say, a copy of an archaic bronze vessel was demanded, this would be carried out with absolute fidelity to the original. The **Ch'ing Dynasty,** which assumed imperial power at the fall of the Mings, had as its second ruler the great Emperor K'ang-hsi, whose reign, which began in 1666 and continued until 1722, was a period of great prosperity and had a court of dignity and wealth under which the famous *famille-verte* and other sumptuous porcelains, probably the most colourful of Chinese ceramics, were made. Oddly enough, very little definite data seems available as to what jade carvings were produced during these sixty years. The one example about which there can be no doubt is the white jade dragon-headed horse (lungma) carrying the Books of Knowledge across the waves of the Yellow River. This was executed at the express command of the Emperor K'ang-hsi (*c.* A.D. 1670), to complete the animal trilogy of the large jade buffalo and black jade horse previously mentioned. With them this is also now at Cambridge.

It would be interesting and instructive if there could be brought together for *temporary* comparative purposes a group of jade animals which might date from the last quarter of the seventeenth century to the middle of the eighteenth, and see if there are any definite differences of technique which might lead to a more accurate dating. The general opinion seems to be that some of the numerous jades now classified as **Ch'ien-lung** (1736–1795) may belong to the two previous reigns: and against this view there is at present no way of definitely deciding. It seems justifiable to think that any carvings done during the short but artistically brilliant reign of **Yung Ching** (1722–1735) (the son of K'ang-hsi) would not have been at variance with the aesthetic quality of the delicate eggshell porcelains, probably the most sophisticated of Chinese ceramics.

It was, however, on the accession of his son, the Emperor Ch'ien-lung, that the golden age of decorative – as against archaeological – jade dawned, and during his long reign, which lasted from 1736 until 1795, many superb examples of outstanding quality and beauty issued from the jade-carvers *ateliers*, examples which not only won contemporary admiration but which the verdict of posterity, both Oriental and Occidental, has confirmed with an ever-increasing emphasis. The choice of subject was now so wide and free from the fetters of ritual compulsion, that it is not possible to marshal them in any particular order of merit; and apart from those done to imperial command, they would obviously illustrate the line of preference of wealthy and cultured patrons, who would be wise enough to commission artists according to the bent of their individual genius, and would not expect an incense-burner or a bowl from one whose skill was as a carver of animals or birds, or vice versa.

Let us briefly consider some of the many subjects of these great creative years. Among figures the favourite was *Kwanyin*, Goddess of Mercy, who is often shown with a vase in her hand from which she was supposed to pour the elixir of peace on the troubled waves of the world. In passing, it might be pointed out that the same goddess is often modelled in porcelain and carved in ivory with a child on her arm in her role as protectress of children, but this representation is very rare in jade, and for no ostensible reason. Others represented are *Shou-lao*, God of Longevity, with a stag and often holding a peach, sundry of the Taoist immortals, seated and holding their appropriate emblem, and *Putai* (the Japanese Hotei), with his well-known corpulency, his happy smile, his bag, and often one or two children, and fully justifying his title of 'god of contentment', the Chinese having accepted for centuries what is now widely admitted in the West, that most stout people are contented and good-tempered. Occasionally one meets with a figure of the Buddha, although he is generally sculptured in the Indian tradition with broad shoulders and constricted waist and closely-fitting garments. Domestic scenes are comparatively rare, and when found are almost invariably of a mother and children or children alone – two or three of them – climbing in or out of a large shallow bath. Occasionally a child is used as the body of a snuff-bottle.

As symbolism has been an integral part of Chinese mentality since its earliest days, it seems appropriate to indicate briefly such symbolism as is associated with some of the objects favoured by the jade-carver. Foremost among these are four mythical creatures, representations of which far exceed those which have the advantage of an actual existence.

Firstly, the dragon, which needs no introduction, as it has at all periods lent itself uniquely to representation in jade, since dragons among swirling waves and clouds recall their heavenly power as the bringers of beneficent rain as well as forming an artistic motif capable of a varied presentation. It was also the personal attribute of the Emperor in the same way that the Phoenix was of his consort. The kylen, that attractive and elegant product of imagination, with its slender, stag-like legs and bushy tail, was a creature of good omen, appearing only during the reign of a virtuous ruler, while the Buddhist lion, a fearsome beast but gentle, was the guardian of Buddhist temples and the prototype of the Pekinese dog.

And now to the natural creation. Longevity was characterized by the stag, the peach, the fir tree, the lotus and the tortoise. Conjugal felicity by the mandarin duck and also by two fish – usually carved with extreme formality at the bottom of a bowl – while the bat stood for happiness. The horse has often been carved, usually reclining, and sometimes is shown resting on waves and with the books of Buddhism on its back. The elephant is another animal fairly frequently carved in jade, sometimes richly caparisoned and bearing on his back a vase of auspicious emblems, or alternately free from all trappings, when it has a more sculptural effect.

Among other subjects with a less emphasized symbolism were the so-called 'longevity' mountains, with their rugged pine-clad sides and often inscribed with an Imperial poem and a somewhat similar type of decoration, e.g. views in the fabled Western Paradise, with sages seated by pavilions amid trees and waterfalls, which could be used to advantage for the cylindrical spill-vase and for table-screens. Bowls, of course, allowed a wide range of decoration, such as the Eight Emblems of Happy Augury, among scroll foliage on the exterior and a fine floral design in relief on the interior. The long, slender sceptre, or *ju-i*, which was supported to grant every wish, although they had a general similarity of outline, allowed for many variants of enrichment, from dragons and fruiting branches of peach or pomegranate to simple linear designs.

The one series which allowed of little or no latitude were the replicas of early bronze vases, incense-burners and other ritual objects which were reproduced with great fidelity and at times of imposing size. One might go on endlessly about the many *objets d'art* fashioned in this most fascinating medium, but it is hoped that this very brief survey may stimulate more interest among those who have considered jade solely as a decoration.

The question 'How was jade carved?' is one that cannot be answered simply and satisfactorily. In proof of this one cannot do better than quote Professor Hansford, who, in his standard work *Chinese Jade Carving*, says that it is a surprising fact that 'not the slightest reference is to be found in the classical writings, nor in those of the Han and T'ang dynasties' as to the way jade was ground and cut. Even in later days and right down to modern times, 'allusions are extremely scarce, and those that exist are often misleading'. The ensuing discussions as to what was really meant by certain expressions is far too erudite for any but the enthusiastic and serious student, and needs close and concentrated study. To any who are determined to follow the matter in a detailed way, the best advice is to secure a copy of the above work, in which the matter is fully gone into with illuminating photographs of modern jade-carvers at work.

FRENCH GLASS PAPERWEIGHTS

By JAMES MELTON

THE glass paperweight is a nineteenth-century production, a masterpiece of technical skill that achieved its greatest triumph just over one hundred years ago. In the very teeth of the Industrial Revolution, this individual expression of an anonymous inventor reminds us that, in spite of the ever-conquering machine, there will be found always some medium in which an artist and craftsman can differentiate himself from those around him, and thereby produce some new challenge to the advancing army of robots.

Originating in Venice, but perfected at the St Louis glassworks in France, the glass paperweight very soon found many imitators, both in that country and elsewhere. But it is conceded generally that few can vie with the French productions, whether from St Louis or from its contemporaries at Baccarat and Clichy. Not only in the past have these attractive objects suffered the close attention of copyists, but today they are equally carefully imitated. It is a part of the game of collecting that the enthusiast should learn to distinguish between genuine and spurious until he, or she, is able to tell one from the other without doubt or hesitation.

It is true to say that owing to the complexity involved in their manufacture each paperweight is slightly different from any other of the same type; and although we do not know the names of the men who made them, each weight bears some personal touch that distinguishes it from the next.

Glass paperweights are among the most difficult things to discuss on paper. This may be because they are so hard to photograph and reproduce on paper with success in order fully to illustrate their many details, and the touches that betray to the expert the factory whence they emanated. For that reason, as with other *objets d'art* great and small, they must be examined and handled over the years in order to acquire a real knowledge of their many 'points'.

GLOSSARY

America: the successful sale of French paperweights imported into the United States induced manufacturers there to imitate them with some success. Notably the factories of Deeming Jarves at Sandwich, Cape Cod, opened in 1825, and at East Cambridge and South Boston, in Massachusetts, opened in 1818 and in 1837. Not only were the French designs copied but original models were evolved.

Baccarat: this glassworks was one of the most eminent in France during the nineteenth century. All types of paperweights were made there, including encrusted (sulphide), millefiori, mushroom, flowers, fruit and butterfly. No dated weight from the Baccarat factory is known marked earlier than 1846 and, as elsewhere, none later than 1849. The numerals are in red, blue or green in white canes set in a line, and there is often a letter 'B', similarly coloured, above and between the figures '8' and '4'. The glassworks, which takes its name from the town in which it is situated, is still working.

Butterfly: a coloured butterfly occupies the centre of the paperweight. Sometimes the insect is poised over a flower, sometimes above a latticinio, or other filigree, ground.

Cameos: *see* Sulphides.

Cane: familiar name for the rods of coloured glass from which the patterns were formed in many types of paperweights (*see* Manufacture).

Clichy: Clichy, a suburb of Paris, was the home of a factory that made glass paperweights of most types. They were not dated but are found signed with an initial 'C'. The presence of a rose in the pattern is an indication that a paperweight was made there, and the colours are often noticeably vivid.

Crown: familiar name for a paperweight composed of coloured canes radiating in straight lines from the top.

Dates: dated paperweights from the Baccarat factory are known for the years 1846 to 1849. The St Louis weights start a year earlier, and also continue until 1849. The dates are often on millefiori weights, are not usually noticeable, and are never set centrally. Any paperweight in which the date is in the dead centre should be regarded with great suspicion.

England: French paperweights were copied widely in England, but it is doubtful whether any were made until quite a few years after the first appearance of the French ones. The glass-making centres of Stourbridge in Worcester and Bristol in Somerset both attempted to produce imitations of the imported article. The Whitefriars Glassworks in London and George Bacchus and Sons in Birmingham also made paperweights in the style of those from Baccarat and elsewhere.

The shapes of the English glass paperweights are usually different from the French ones, and the colour of the glass and of the canes embedded in it is seldom comparable.

The encrusted cameos (sulphides) made by Apsley Pellatt (1791–1863) are, however, a notable exception, and are difficult to distinguish in many cases from the French.

France: three glassworks in France were concerned in the production of glass paperweights. They were the *Compagnie des Cristalleries de Baccarat* and the *Compagnie des Verreries et Cristalleries de St Louis*, both situated in the Vosges to the south-east of Paris; and the Clichy glassworks, which stood in the suburb of Clichy in Paris itself.

All three manufactories produced similar work. But there is enough evidence from specimens presented by the manufacturers to the French museums on which to base identifications, in most cases, as to exactly which factory was responsible for certain noticeable differences.

Latticinio: familiar name for the filigree glass of Venetian origin, composed of crossing and interlacing strips of opaque and clear glass.

Manufacture: the processes involved in making glass paperweights call for great skill. The final correct placing of the pattern within the clear glass calls for a high degree of craftsmanship. This is even more apparent when it is realized that the operations are performed with the glass in a molten, or near molten, state. Only a general description of the complicated manufacturing processes is given here; details vary with the different types of paperweights, and no doubt each factory had its secrets.

The Canes to make the pattern are formed by several methods. In one, lengths of coloured glass are heated until they adhere together and form a solid mass. Alternatively, a rod of a chosen colour is dipped repeatedly in molten glass of other colours until a pattern is completed. In both cases, while still hot, the newly-made vari-coloured rod is drawn out until the section of it is of the required diameter.

The necessary canes are selected and sufficient thin slices cut from them and polished. The pattern is arranged on a piece of thin glass, a mould is placed over this, and molten glass is poured in. The half-formed paperweight is picked up on a pontil, dipped into molten glass, and shaped to the form of the finished article. Fruit and other subjects are made of coloured glass, but the process followed for making the paperweight is similar.

Great care is needed to maintain the temperature of the components throughout the manufacture, or cracking will result. The final operation is annealing: a slow cooling.

When it is cold the mark of the pontil is removed by grinding.

Millefiori: the first millefiori (Italian: thousand flowers) paperweights were made in Venice. St Louis made them in 1845. In the next year they were made at Baccarat, and before long they were produced at Clichy.

Mushroom: a paperweight in which the Canes are bunched together and raised in a sheaf from the bottom. Usually surrounded by a ring of lacework at the foot.

Overlay: the coating of the exposed surfaces of a paperweight with one or more layers of white or coloured glass. This finish is then cut to leave windows (*see* Punties), through which the interior of the paperweight is visible. Very rarely, after the above process, the weight is further encased in clear glass. Such a paperweight is known as an *enclosed overlay*.

Pontil: an iron rod held by the workman, and to which the glass adheres in the making of an article. When the finished work is removed it leaves a scar where it was broken off the rod – the pontil mark.

Punties: concave shaping cut on the surfaces of a paperweight. Overlay paperweights are often cut with punties.

St Louis: the St Louis glassworks was founded in the second half of the eighteenth century and became a close competitor of the Baccarat factory. The first dated paperweights were made at the St Louis works in 1845. They were of millefiori pattern. Paperweights are known with the letters 'SL'; sometimes with the 'S' reversed.

Sulphides: the earliest glass paperweights to achieve notice were the type known as sulphides, or encrusted cameos. In a few words, they comprise a plaque, made of unglazed white china with modelling in relief, embedded in glass. The process resulted in the china plaque appearing a bright silver colour. They were made at all three of the French paperweight factories and in England, with success, by Apsley Pellatt.

Swirl: familiar name for a paperweight composed of coloured canes radiating spirally from the top.

BOOKS FOR FURTHER READING

Evangeline H. Bergstrom, *Old Glass Paperweights* (New York, 1947).

E. M. Elville, *Paperweights and Other Curiosities* (London, 1954).

R. Imbert and Y. Amic, *French Crystal Paperweights* (Paris, 1948).

PHARMACY JARS

By AGNES LOTHIAN

ENGLAND

The 'green earthen pots'* of Shakespeare's time were probably the last of the green-glazed medieval pottery in use in the apothecaries' shops. By the beginning of the seventeenth century they were being gradually replaced by the tin-enamelled earthenware introduced into England in the reign of Queen Elizabeth I. (Fig. 1.) The early vessels were

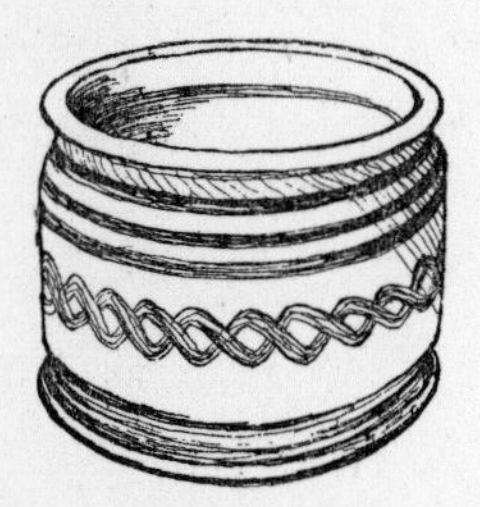

FIG. 1. ENGLISH DELFT JARS.
Seventeenth century. Height 3½ inches.

squat and cylindrical in shape; the stanniferous glaze either left plain or painted with simple designs or stripes in blue and sometimes manganese. By the middle of the century the apothecaries' shelves were lined with rows of blue-and-white jars inscribed with the name of the drug. These were specially made for them at the delft potteries on the south bank of the Thames.

One of these early **Lambeth** drug jars is shown in Fig. 2. This Commonwealth design (which also occurs on the posset-pots of the period) may be identified by the presence of a grotesque of a man smoking a pipe on either end of the cartouche enclosing the name of the drug. Below the centre there is

FIG. 2. MAN-SMOKING-PIPE DESIGN.
Lambeth, 1650–1660. Height 7½ inches.
Pharmaceutical Society

usually a mask. Only two dated examples are recorded: one is in the British Museum (1652), the other (1662) is in the collection of Dr M. H. Caraco, London.

The 'Angel' design found on 'Lambeth' drug jars from the Restoration until the end of the century is perhaps the most characteristic English seventeenth-century decoration (Plate 174A and B). The pomegranate syrup-pot, S. GRANATOR, is inscribed with the initials M.H. as well as the date 1684. The Howard collection includes a set of these jars originally made for Michael Hastings, a Dublin apothecary. The other jar, E. METHRID, once contained the famous electuary Mithridatium, believed to have been devised by King Mithridates VI of Pontus as an antidote

* 'I do remember an apothecary, –
and hereabouts he dwells, – . . . and about his shelves
A beggarly account of empty boxes,
Green earthen pots, bladders and musty seeds. . . .
Romeo and Juliet, v, i.

against poisons and venomous bites. The formula, which contained over fifty ingredients, included the bellies of scinks, a kind of lizard.

Drug jars decorated with swags and tassels underneath the cartouche first appear about 1670 and herald the naturalistic designs with birds, flowerlets and foliage. These were the forerunners of the popular 'bird and basket' pattern illustrated in Plate 175C, E. DIASCORDIUM (an anti-plague electuary). This massive jar, painted in clear cobalt-blue and dated 1724, has on the reverse the full arms of the Apothecaries' Company (Plate 175D), the design often seen on their pill tiles.

The **Cherub** motif is more frequently encountered than any other on English eighteenth-century drug jars. Instead of the songbird, a cherub holding a sprig of foliage or a trumpet sits on either end of a scrollwork cartouche. The Howard Collection includes two rare polychrome 'Cherub' jars – both dated 1723, and also a blue-and-white specimen dated 1738.

English delft drug jars were also made at Bristol and Liverpool during the eighteenth century.

The **armorial delft** of the Apothecaries' Company has always held great attraction for collectors, the pill tiles being especially sought after. These are usually decorated in blue and white with the arms and motto of the Company. Some have in addition the arms of the City of London. They are as a rule pierced with holes, in order that they may be hung up after use, and are oval, heart, shield or octagonal in shape. A rare heart-shaped polychrome example inscribed with the name THOMAS FAUTRART and the date 1670 is in the Museum of the Pharmaceutical Society. This Museum also possesses the earliest dated English drug jar. Made of 'Lambeth' delft, this magnificent specimen, which is almost sixteen inches in height, is decorated with the full arms of the Apothecaries' Company in dark blue and yellow, surmounted with the date 1647. Their motto, *Opifer que per orbem dicor*, is in blue. The rest of the decoration, painted in dark blue over a white background, consists of an all-over leaf design with a pomegranate and a bell-shaped flower amongst the foliage. Strongly-drawn gadroons ornament the top and base.

HOLLAND

The art of tin-enamelling earthenware was introduced into the Netherlands during the early part of the sixteenth century by potters from Italy who settled in Antwerp. From Antwerp the *maiolica* (or faience) industry spread to the North Netherlands. In Holland the centres were at Rotterdam, Haarlem and Middelburg. About the middle of the seventeenth century the town of Delft became celebrated for the manufacture of earthenware decorated in blue and white in imitation of the Chinese porcelain then imported by the Dutch East India Company. By the end of the century thirty potteries were flourishing in Delft.

In the traditional Dutch drug jar design a peacock stands on either end of a scrolled cartouche, which usually has a basket of fruit in the centre. Beneath is a cherub's head, which frequently has a pendant cross. A syrup jar with the peacock *motif* is shown here.

FIG. 3. DELFT SYRUP POT.
With peacock *motif*. P and V Duijn pottery marks.

The presence of a small compartment in the middle of the cartouche above the drug inscription, which often contains a letter (S for Syrupus, U for Unguentum, etc.), is almost certain evidence that the jar is of Dutch origin or produced in one of the Continental factories which copied Delft wares. An apothecary's syrup-pot was one of the objects which an apprentice had to turn on his wheel in a given time in order to be admitted to the Guild as a master potter.

The factories, all of which had picturesque

names such as the **Porcelain Claw** or **De Lampetkan** (the Jug or Ewer), used signs or the initials of their owners to mark their wares. The latter is easily identified, although this pottery used several marks on its drug jars – *L P K* or *lpkan* in script.

Figure 3 above is marked on the base with the letter P with a dot above signifying IP in monogram. This is the mark of **Johannes Pennis**, the proprietor of the 'Porcelain Dish' from 1723–63. Drug jars marked VDuijn are also from the same manufactory, this being the signature of J. van Duyn (1763–77), who registered this mark in 1764. AP in monogram was a mark registered by **Anthony Pennis** (1759–70) of 'De Twee Scheepjes'. HB signifies **Hugo Brouwer** of the 'Three Porcelain Bottles' (which ceased production in 1777) as well as the 'Porcelain Axe' (1775–88). The initials AK have been used by a number of Delft potters, which makes attribution uncertain without other evidence.

Fig. 4. Delft Confection Pot, HVH mark.
Messrs John Bell and Croyden

The confection pot C. FOL MALVAE (Fig. 4) has the letters HVH – the mark of **Hendrik van Hoorn**, who owned the pottery 'De Drie Astonnen' (The Three Cinder Tubs) from 1759–1803. His predecessor, **Zacharias Dextra** (1712–1762), used the mark Z.DEX sometimes with '3 astonne' underneath. **Jan Theunis Dextra**, the owner of the 'Greek A' pottery, used A D 22 and similar marks for his wares.

'De Drie Klokken', or Three Bells, pottery made polychrome as well as the more usual blue-and-white jars. The earlier mark – three bells in outline – is easily recognizable. Unfortunately, drug jars from the Three Bells have been reproduced in modern times, and collectors should always carefully examine specimens bearing this mark. Even the age-cracks have often been copied faithfully enough to deceive the unwary. Dutch drug jars are very rarely dated.

ITALY

The name maiolica is believed to have originated during the fifteenth century, when it was used to describe the Hispano-Moresque lustred pottery which reached Italy by way of Majorca. It is now used to describe Italian and other tin-enamelled earthenware. The earliest Italian maiolica drug jars were made at Orvieto, in Umbria, and Tuscany. From these developed the Florentine green and later the 'oak-leaf' jars of the fifteenth century. Drug jars decorated with strongly-scrolled leaves in green, orange and dark blue, known as 'Gothic foliage', were made at both Tuscany and Faenza in the last quarter of the century.

About 1500 a deep rich blue from cobalt was used by the potteries at Faenza, which had become an important centre for the manufacture of maiolica or faience. The wide, cylindrical jars of this period, 1500–20 (Fig. 5), have formal flowers and foliage with the shoulders and base ornamented with dashes or criss-cross patterns. Other early Renaissance wares include the magnificent polychrome set known as the Orsini Colonna pharmacy vases, with dragon-spout handles. The effective diaper pattern of peacock's feathers was later used also at Caffaggiolo (near Florence), another great centre celebrated for its beautiful maiolica during the early sixteenth century.

Fig. 5. Faenza, Italy. Early sixteenth century.

At Castel Durante, in the duchy of Urbino, the artist potters were responsible for the tall, slightly-waisted *albarellos** painted in blue,

* Cylindrical jars, often drawn in at the waist to facilitate grasping.

orange and copper on a greyish green background of cornucopias, drums and weapons. These jars, which are often decorated with the busts of warriors and portrait medallions, were much imitated by potteries in Palermo, Sicily. The latter may be identified by the SPQP (*Senatus populusque Panormitanus*) and by the recessed base. The drug jars made at the neighbouring city of Urbino, a centre famous for its beautiful maiolica, fall into two classes: (*a*) the colourful *istoriato* wares, where the whole surface is covered with a picture, and (*b*) designs with grotesques inspired by the frescoes of Raphael. The latter style, usually painted in orange or yellow, was introduced about 1560–70.

Perhaps the most beautiful drug jars of all were made at Deruta in Umbria between 1490 and 1550. The *albarello* (illustrated in Plate 174C), *c.* 1507, which is painted in yellow, brownish orange and copper-green, has on the front the typical Deruta wreath decoration. Above the drug inscription, DIA CHASSIA (cassia electuary), an apprentice in the dress of the period is working with a pestle and mortar. The provenance of a large family of drug wares, painted in an all-over leaf or scroll design in an insipid blue with brightly-edged drug cartouches in orange and green, is probably Montelupo, near Florence.

Two styles of late sixteenth-century Venetian drug jars are encountered. On the first the enamel, which is stained a light greyish blue, is covered with an all-over decoration of parti-coloured blue foliage. The *albarellos* of this type frequently have the waist almost encircled with the name of the drug, *see* Plate 175A, LOC DI PINO (pine linctus), dated 1578. The spouted jars often have handles with serpentine or relief decoration. This 'Venice foliage' pattern derived from Faenza, was also used on early Netherlands maiolica. The other important class of Venetian drug jars is painted with flowers and foliage in colours, on a background of deep blue with white scrolls. These jars often have portrait medallions. (The Sicilian imitations are more waisted and generally have a glazed *recessed* base.)

The later Venetian jars, especially those made at Bassano and Nove, are usually blue-and-white (but may be in polychrome) and on a short foot. The Bassano specimen illustrated is painted in blue on white. The lettering and date, 1715, is in manganese (Plate 175B).

Blue-and-white apothecary wares painted with motifs adapted from Chinese porcelain or Persian earthenware became fashionable during the seventeenth century. The preoccupation with Oriental themes can be seen on a class of wares made at Savona painted with birds among rocks, running animals, such as fawns and hares, in an all-over pattern of plants and foliage. Both the shield mark with the arms of Savona and the 'sunface' mark ascribed to Salamone are found on these drug jars. The Genoa beacon or lighthouse mark appears on both Savona and Genoese maiolica (Fig. 6). A landscape design of trees, houses and wandering persons is often used on

FIG. 6. GENOA BEACON MARK.

the lion-handled jars. A set of the latter shape, with a pictorial design of a cherub on a sea-horse, made in 1728 for the Ospedale Civici di Genova in this style, has the Savona shield-mark above the letter 'V'–the work of Guiseppe Valente of Savona. Ligurian jars which resemble the Bassano jar in Plate 175B in shape, but with dense leafy scrolls, are about 1750. Mock gadroons are another characteristic decoration on Savona pottery.

The artist potters at Castelli, in the Abruzzi, much favoured allegorical or mythological subjects as well as Biblical scenes. Many late seventeenth- and early eighteenth-century drug jars, painted in a characteristic dark brown associated with dull olive green, were probably made at or near Castelli. The drug inscription is often painted in a dull greyish blue at the foot of the jar.

FRANCE

In France the important sixteenth-century centres were Rouen, Lyons, Nîmes and Montpellier. According to records dated 15th May, 1543, Masseot Abasquesne, the Rouen maker of pavement tiles, made a very large number of drug pots for a local apothecary. The drug pots, which were painted in blue, yellow and green, were decorated in the Italian style with a portrait head in profile. Some of these bear the monogram of Masseot (MAB) or his son Laurent, who assisted him at the time. These and the other Italianate-French wares made at Lyons, Nîmes and Montpellier are dealt with exhaustively by Dr J. Chompret in his great book *Les Faiences françaises primitives*.

Polychrome as well as white faience were produced by the potteries at Nevers, the leading centre in the seventeenth century. The most distinctive wares for apothecaries were jars and bleeding-bowls ornamented in white over a deep cobalt blue glaze, as, for example, the drug bottle illustrated in Plate 174D, which is simply decorated with white spots. Other types of *bleu-persan* drug jars have Chinese designs painted in white or white, orange and yellow. Both belong to the second half of the seventeenth century.

During the eighteenth century the principal factories engaged in the manufacture of jars for pharmacies were at Moustiers, Rouen, St Jean du Désert (near Marseilles), Strasbourg and Niderwiller.

A characteristic feature of French drug jars is the serpentine handle, often twisted to leave the serpents' heads resting in relief on the front of the jar. On the later pots the serpent

FIG. 7. PARISIAN ELECTUARY JAR. Eighteenth century, with serpent *motif*. *Musée de la Pharmacie centrale, Paris.*

motif – symbolical of wisdom and the healing art – is rarely absent. The inscriptions, as often as not, are in French. The absence of marks and the tendency for the various factories to copy one another's designs makes identification difficult.

Scores of old hospital pharmacies still exist in France, where the antique drug jars may still be seen in their original wooden niches. Those of Besançon, Carpentras, Issouden, Louhans, Lyons, Nîmes and Troyes date from the sixteenth century. A large collection of eighteenth-century French pharmaceutical antiques is housed in the Pharmacie Centrale des Hôpitaux, near Notre Dame, in Paris, where all the drug jars and equipment from the old Parisian hospitals were taken after the laicization of the nuns in 1907.

SPAIN

Hispano-Moresque is the name given to the wares made by the Moorish potters in Spain during the fifteenth century. The lustred or 'golden pottery' made at Valencia is the best known. Various Arabic and leaf designs were employed on the *albarelos* and *cetrills* (oil jars), in which cobalt blue alternating with gold or

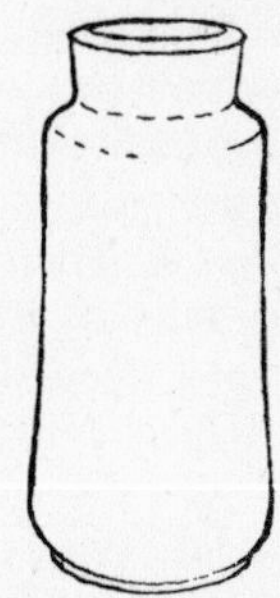

FIG. 8. VALENCIA (SPAIN). Fifteenth century.

copper lustre combine to make these beautiful drug vases masterpieces of ceramic art. Talavera de la Reina, in Castile, a leading centre from the sixteenth century onwards, made much domestic pottery as well as drug jars for pharmacies. These are ornamented in yellow, orange, green and brown, the designs varying from hunting scenes to stiff, scrolled foliage. The Talavera **albarelo** (Fitzwilliam Museum) illustrated in Fig. 9, which is of the seventeenth century, is decorated in blue and white with the arms of Castile, Leon and

Granada, surmounted by an abbot's hat and tassels. Talaveran ware was much imitated, especially by the Sevillian potteries.

FIG. 9. TALAVERA, SPAIN. Seventeenth century. *Fitzwilliam Museum*

Most characteristic feature of Spanish **albarelos** is their shape. They are usually tall jars with wide mouths; the earlier specimens have deep collars. The sides are slightly concave and drawn in at the base, making a short foot of about half an inch. The drug label, generally boldly lettered, is sometimes enclosed in a diamond or oval-shaped panel surrounded by floral decoration, more often on a diagonal or vertical scroll. Many specimens have heraldic devices of religious orders showing that they have been on the shelves of a monastic pharmacy. Other centres of production were Alcora, Aragon, Triana (a suburb of Seville) and Catalonia.

GERMANY

German drug jars other than wooden, pewter and stoneware containers are rarely met with in England. Early Nuremberg faience is painted in the Italian style. The Ulm Museum possesses an example with the portrait of a lady dated 1544. Eighteenth-century specimens, which often have a blue wreath looped at the bottom, may be identified by the potter's mark.

The Roche Collection, Basle, includes an interesting blue-and-white jar, *c.* 1700, formerly in the Schloss Apotheke, Berlin. This specimen, which is from the Berlin Fayencefabrik set up by the Elector Friedrich Wilhelm in 1678, is ornamented with a crown and his monogram. Factories at Berlin also turned out 'Peacock' jars similar to those made in Holland (mark B.L. for Berlin Lüdicke). A set of jars dated 1708, with a Moor holding a wreathed drug label formerly in the Mohren Apotheke (the Moor Pharmacy), Schmalkalden, is also attributed to a Berlin factory.

Potteries at Ansbach and Bayreuth also made jars for pharmacies. A rare Bayreuth jar (1767) in the Dörr Collection at Stuttgart depicts a horseman (Der Spornreither). Another, in the Roche Collection, with the drug label surmounted by a lion and crown, is signed B.P.F., the mark of Pfeiffer and Fränkel, the owners of the Bayreuth factory from 1747–60. Most important of all are the

FIG. 10. CREUSSEN, GERMANY. Seventeenth century.

Creussen faience drug jars painted in blue with an all-over spiral design. These were made at the workshop of Lorenz Speckner during the seventeenth century. A syrup-pot of this ware in the Folk Museum, Copenhagen, is dated 1668. Drug jars were also made at Fulda, Hanau and Frankfort, as well as other centres.

The Squibb Ancient Pharmacy now housed in the Smithsonian Institution, Washington, U.S.A., includes a representative selection of German drug ware formerly in the collection of Jo Mayer, Wiesbaden.

SWITZERLAND

Swiss faience is represented by the famous 'Apostle' drug jars, made at Winterthur by a

FIG. 11. WINTERTHUR APOSTLE JAR. St Simon leaning on his saw. *Roche Collection, Basle.*

family of potters named Pfau working throughout the seventeenth and eighteenth centuries. A complete set of these Apostle jars, which are painted in characteristic tones of blue, purple, yellow and copper-green, may be seen in the Kloster Allerheiligen in Schaffhausen, Switzerland.

BOOKS FOR FURTHER READING

D. ANDERSEN, *Gammelt dansk Apoteksinventar* (København, 1944).

P. BOUSSEL, *Histoire illustrée de la pharmacie* (Paris, 1949).

J. CHOMPRET, *Les Faiences françaises primitives* (Paris, 1946); *Répertoire de la majolique italienne*, Vols. 1 and 2 (Paris, 1949).

A. W. FROTHINGHAM, *Talavera Pottery* (N.Y. Hispanic Soc., 1944).

G. E. HOWARD, *Early English Drug Jars* (Medici Soc., 1931).

A. LOTHIAN, 'The armorial delft of the Worshipful Society of Apothecaries', *The Connoisseur* (March, 1951); 'Bird designs on English drug jars' (*Chemist and Druggist* (June 26th, 1954); 'Drug jars of Northern Italy (*Alchemist*, July 1953); 'Dutch drug jars and their marks' (*Alchemist*, August 1952); 'Saints and their emblems on drug jars' (*Chemist and Druggist*, June 6th, 1953); 'Vessels for apothecaries: English delft drug jars' (*The Connoisseur Year Book*, 1953).

B. RACKHAM, Catalogue of Italian Maiolica, Vols. 1 and 2, 1940 (*Victoria and Albert Museum*).

B. RACKHAM, *Italian Maiolica* (Faber, 1952).

E. R. SQUIBB & SONS, *The Ancient Pharmacy* (New York, 1940).

D. A. WITTOP KONING, *Delftse Apothekerspotten* (Amsterdam, 1954).

WINE, SPIRIT AND SAUCE LABELS

By J. K. MORRIS

To most people the term *Wine-label* means a small plaque that hangs by means of a chain unobtrusively round the neck of a decanter. It will be a surprise to many to learn that the number of different names on these plaques that has been recorded so far runs to no less than five hundred. A study of the names, and of the wine-labels themselves, of silver, Sheffield plate, mother-of-pearl, tiger's-claws, enamel and other materials, of which they are to be found, leads to a most engrossing research into the story of wines and spirits, of silver and other wares, and of the history of wining and dining down the ages. It can be said, with truth, that the wine-label epitomises all these things and is, at the same time, a work of art in miniature that displays frequently some of the best craftsmanship of the period in which it was made.

Broadly, the labels can be divided into two distinct types: those fitted with wires or chains, and those in the form of a ring. The latter are the rarest, but not always the most decorative.

Of those made during the eighteenth century, silver labels are the most common. Sheffield plate, mother-of-pearl and other materials are scarce, and enamelled copper is the most rare of any.

An array of these small articles, carrying with them their records of the long-forgotten wines and spirits and sauces of their titles, is among the most pleasant ways of evoking days gone by. Not least, it is also practical; the wine-label is small and extremely portable. It may be termed, without exaggeration, a twentieth-century man's brief guide to the past.

Battersea: the rarest and the most sought-after wine-labels are those that were made at the enamel works at York House, Battersea. This factory, which has achieved a fame far in excess of the length of its existence and the quantity of its productions, lasted only from 1753 to 1756. It was founded by Stephen Theodore Janssen, and the artists who engraved many of the plates used in the newly-introduced process of transfer-printing, which was initiated there with great success, included John Brooks, Robert Hancock and Simon-François Ravenet. To the latter has been ascribed the production of an important series of wine-labels.

The fact that such trivial articles as wine-labels were definitely made at the Battersea factory is known from advertisements that appeared on the bankruptcy of Janssen in 1756. The first notice related to the auction of the late proprietor's personal effects at his house in St Paul's Churchyard, and mentioned, among many other items *Bottle Tickets with Chains, for all sorts of Liquors, and of different Subjects*. The second auction sale was concerned with the disposal of the stock at York House itself, and included *Bottle Tickets*.

Bin-labels: large-sized labels, usually pierced with a hole for suspension from a hook or nail, for hanging beside a wine-bin. Some date from late in the seventeenth century, and it has been suggested that they were made at one of the Lambeth potteries. Later ones were made at some of the Staffordshire factories.

Bristol: this West-country port boasted many glassworks in the eighteenth century and later. The most characteristic productions were an opaque white glass, and pieces in a transparent dark blue, green and amethyst. Decanters and sauce-bottles are found in the latter three colours; often the name of their intended contents is drawn in gilt or white letters, together with other ornament, in simulation of a pendant label. The stoppers of these decanters and bottles sometimes bear an initial letter to correspond with the 'label' to ensure that the stopper is replaced where it belongs.

Decanter: as social life grew more polished the decanter took the place of the wine-bottle. The latter most probably bore a label of paper or parchment. The decanter itself was engraved or painted with the name of its contents. Fashion decreed that the decanter should be an example of the glass-cutter's art, and no surface of it remained uncut for the painting or engraving of a name. Hence, the universal call for a hanging ticket – the wine-label was born.

Designs: Dr N. M. Penzer, in his *Book of the Wine-label*, divides the designs he has encountered into twenty types. These, in turn, are sub-divided into many sections. They run from *Narrow Rectangular* (1) to *Miscellaneous* (20), and embrace, among numerous others, the *Crescent*, the *Cut-out Word*, and the *Architectural*. Some of these designs did not come into use until during the second quarter of the nineteenth century. Some are of even later introduction than that.

Enamel: elsewhere than at Battersea, enamel wine-labels were made at several factories. Quite a number, made in the last quarter of the eighteenth century, are thought to have emanated from South Staffordshire, from some of the many enamel works in the Wednesbury and Bilston area. The old enamel labels have been copied widely in modern times.

Lambeth: an indeterminate number of potteries was housed in this district of South London from the last quarter of the sixteenth century and onwards. To one of them is ascribed a number of small white-glazed jugs, with the names of wines on them in blue. These pieces bear dates running from 1637 to 1672, and some bear the names of their original owners. It has been suggested that bottle-labels and bin-labels of pottery may have been made at one of the Lambeth potteries.

Mother-of-pearl: this iridescent lining of a sea-shell is a delightful medium for use as a wine-label. The title and other ornament are engraved on it, and filled in with a black pigment. Sometimes the shaped plaque of mother-of-pearl is pierced with a bordering design to leave a central place for the name. Mother-of-pearl wine-labels exist both with chains for suspension and in the form of rings. They are not commonly met with.

Porcelain: wine-labels of porcelain exist, but they are not always as old as they appear to be. Considering that they are small, made of a thin and brittle material and suffer much handling, it is quite surprising that any should have been made at all.

Ravenet, Simon-François: engraver, of French origin. He worked at the short-lived enamel manufactory at York House, Battersea, and is credited with the production of some of the best wine-labels ever produced in any medium. These outstanding escutcheon-shaped *Bottle-tickets* are designed with figures of cupids, and most of the score or so that have come to light so far incorporate some element in their design that has a connexion with the history of the wine that they are intended to designate.

Sheffield Plate: the process of manufacturing what is known as *Sheffield Plate* came into use about the middle of the eighteenth century. By its adoption, in which the bulk of an article was made of copper instead of the more costly silver, a great deal of expense was saved. The finished article presented the appearance of one of solid silver but it was considerably cheaper. Wine-labels were made by the process, but from the small number that survive do not appear to have been produced in large quantities. They have received the keen attention of forgers, and the collector should be on his guard and duly suspicious of any he sees.

Silver: more old labels of silver have survived than those of any other material. No doubt this is because more were made of that metal, which lends itself so well to the purpose. It was not until the passing by Parliament of an Act in 1790 that the hall-marking of many small articles, including wine-labels, was made compulsory. Before that date there had been no necessity for the maker to have such objects stamped, and there is, for that reason, no record of when the first silver wine-label was made. In spite of the fact that it was enacted legally that a maker should have these small articles fully stamped at an Assay Office, it was not always done. They are most often found with the mark of the maker, but lacking any indication as to date.

Silversmiths in many towns throughout the British Isles are recorded as having made wine-labels. Not only is Hester Bateman listed, but among other well-known names may be found Paul Storr, Robert Garrard, Matthew Boulton, and Patrick Robertson.

Occasionally these eighteenth-century wine-labels may be seen engraved, embossed, and with their shining silver opulently gilded in that pale golden colour that it seems cannot be imitated.

Titles: the recorded names to be met with on wine-labels run, alphabetically, from *The Abbots Bottle* (silver, by Hester Batemen) to *Zantera*. Sauce-labels include such intriguingly outlandish names as *Cavice*, *Coratch* and *Zoobditty-Match*, and under the heading of *Miscellaneous* may be found *Acid*, *Eau de Rose* and the homely *Tooth Mixture*.

Dr Penzer has recorded nearly five hundred titles and, if variant spellings are included, the total comes to as many as eight hundred and seventy. These have been culled from about a dozen collections, public and private, and, in spite of its formidable size, the list is not exhaustive.

BOOKS FOR FURTHER READING

H. C. Dent, *Wine, Spirit and Sauce Labels* (Norwich, 1933).

N. M. Penzer, *The Book of the Wine-Label* (London, 1947).

INDEX

OF NAMES AND PLACES

T

INDEX

OF NAMES AND PLACES

INDEX